PAPERS IN
ECONOMICS AND SOCIOLOGY

CONTENTS

PREFACE TO THE POLISH EDITION

When it was decided to publish a collection of my papers, written over a period of thirty years, I had certain doubts about the interest my early work could arouse today, for writings in the social sciences quickly become out of date. Moreover, I am at present engaged upon setting out the results of my work, covering a long period of time, in a book entitled *Political Economy*, the first volume of which has recently appeared. Is there, then, any need to collect and publish my early works?

I have been convinced, however, by two arguments. One is that in *Political Economy*, on the remaining volumes of which I am working at present, I shall not be able to cover all the details of the problems with which I have been concerned in my research. This book will not, therefore, summarize the whole of my work. The second argument is to show the path I took which has led me to my present conclusions. This shows in a way the whole field of my research and what it covers, together with the gradual development of my conclusions.

It is these considerations which have determined the choice of papers in this collection. I have chosen papers directly connected with the general trend of my social and scientific interests and have left out those concerned with problems outside this general trend, namely those which are exclusively technical or political, and those which I consider as being of no interest whatsoever today. As a result, the collection consists of papers which I consider to be most characteristic of the development of my work and which, in spite of the time that has elapsed since they were written, are still of interest today.

To allow for the variety of topics with which these papers deal, the collection is divided into five parts. It seems to me, however, that from among these various topics the reader will perceive a single guiding idea, namely, an attempt to link a strictly scientific treatment of economic investigation with the needs of social practice, and in particular with the working-class movement and the question of socialism. This aim is served even by abstract, mathematical economic arguments, seemingly so remote from social practice.

vii

I think, moreover, that in these papers, written over a period of thirty years, the reader will detect a definite line of development. This line is not always a straight one, more than once breaking off and starting forward anew. This is brought about by the development both of scientific thought as such and of historical conditions, coupled with historical experience, which throws new light on a given problem.

For this reason, individual papers obviously do not always reflect my present views on a given problem; many of them show the path which led me to the views I hold today. In order to help the reader to see both this path and my present view on a given problem, some earlier papers are included next to more recent ones on the same subject. In this way, the reader can compare papers on the same problem written at different periods, and thus see which of my earlier views I still hold and which of those I have since abandoned.

Even papers published relatively recently do not always fully reflect my present views on a given problem. As an example I can quote certain proposals from the article *How I See the Polish Economic Model* (*Jak sobie wyobrażam polski model gospodarczy*) and in particular the proposal to establish a second Chamber in the Seym to represent the various branches of the socialist economy. The Polish Seym has worked out a different way of parliamentary control of the socialist economy with the help of a good number of permanent committees. This way has proved efficient and must be the basis for the further development of socialist democracy in Poland.

The papers contained in this collection have been reprinted without any major revision. In some cases the text has been condensed, and stylistic alterations have occasionally been made. On the other hand, the quotations contained in these papers are generally taken from the newest Polish edition of the given book. Thus, for example, in the paper published in 1931, the quotation by Lenin is taken from the present edition of the *Works* (*Dzieła*), published by Książka i Wiedza. In this paper, the quotation from Hilferding's book *Das Finanzkapital* is taken from the Polish translation published in 1958. This rule is observed throughout, thus making it easier for the reader to find the sources of the quotations.

Many of the papers were originally published in languages other than Polish.

At the end of the book a bibliography is given of the most important of my economic and sociological publications. This does not contain publications of lesser or only passing significance, nor those of a purely political nature.

OSKAR LANGE

Warsaw, September 1961.

FOREWORD

The table of contents of this volume points to the unusually wide interests of the author: they encompass not only all the economics, in the strict sense, but also related problems of sociology on the one hand and those of mathematics or mathematical statistics on the other.

However, in Lange's work three lines of thought seem to me most important: (a) the problem of functioning of the socialist system; (b) dynamics of capitalist and socialist economics; (c) historical materialism.

His essay on the *modus operandi* of a socialist economy, *Economic Theory of Socialism*, published first in 1937, was one of the most important of Lange's contributions. It played a crucial role in the discussion about the feasibility of rational management of a socialist economy which at that time was in full swing in the West. In reply to the point that such management would require a solution of an enormous number of equations, laboured by reactionary economists, Lange emphasized that the authorities of a socialist economy may always resort to a certain measure of market mechanism. This essay does not appear in the present volume since it was subsequently published in book form conjointly with a paper of Taylor. However, two items related directly to this subject are included: *How I See the Polish Economic Model* and *The Role of the Co-operative Movement in the Construction of Socialism*. It should be noted that the ideas expressed in these papers are not necessarily identical with those of *Economic Theory of Socialism*. This is, in fact, natural since they are not concerned with demonstrating the possibility of rational operation of the socialist system *in abstracto*, but with a specific analysis of the role of the market (or quasi-market) within the framework of a centrally planned economy. In addition, Lange's views on the subject are clearly influenced by his first-hand experience of the actual functioning of a socialist economy.

Lange's research in economic dynamics at the early stage of which he produced the well-known paper *The Rate of Interest and the Optimum Propensity to Consume* (1938) is represented in the present volume in particular by "Some Observations on Input–Output Analysis". This essay established the connexion between the Marxian schemes of reproduction and the input–output matrices. In the same category may be included two papers on planning economic development in the so-called mixed economies: *Observations on the Second Five-Year Plan in India* and *The Tasks of Economic Planning in Ceylon.*

Finally, a brilliant presentation of the gist of historical materialism is contained in an early paper (1936) included in this volume, *Ludwik Krzywicki—Theorist of Historical Materialism.* In another paper of the present volume, *Current Problems of Economic Science in Poland,* the applicability of the method of historical materialism to the evolution of socialist systems is developed.

All these lines of research as well as others were to converge in a great three-volume treaty on *Political Economy* which was to be in a sense the crowning stone of Lange's work. Unfortunately, only the most valuable first volume and a part of the second were published. The illness and the untimely death prevented bringing this great undertaking to an end. In the present volume Lange's ability of synthesis of the most important problems of economics is exemplified by the paper on *The Political Economy of Socialism* which was written initially for the Polish General Encyclopedia.

It follows from the above that the present book concerned with manifold subjects constitutes at the same time an essay on the subject *Oskar Lange — a Universal Economist.*

M. KALECKI

Part I

MARXIST AND SOCIALIST THEORY

THE ROLE OF THE STATE
IN MONOPOLY CAPITALISM

The most important problem facing the working-class movement today is the need to be clearly aware of the economic role which the State plays at the present stage of monopoly capitalism, and of the fundamental change taking place which is affecting its social function; for, the attitude the working-class movement adopts to all present-day economic and political problems may depend on just such awareness.

The transformation of freely competitive capitalism into monopoly capitalism begins with the concentration of production and capital. When a high level of concentration is reached, there must necessarily appear among the capitalist groups, controlling concentrated production plants, the desire to use their power to secure for themselves a monopolistic position and additional monopoly profits exceeding the level of profit resulting from free competition. This is achieved by agreements between the biggest capitalist magnates to form cartels, trusts or syndicates and to refrain from competing against each other. By this means they operate monopoly price and production policies and force the smaller producers of a given branch of production to follow these policies, threatening them with complete ruin should they fail to comply. Thus, the basis of capitalist monopoly is the economic power which results from the concentration of large amounts of capital in the hands of a small group of capitalist potentates. Concentration of capital is the basis upon which certain capitalist groups gain monopolistic positions, since by this means all the capitalists of a certain branch of production can be forced into a monopolistic agreement and all recalcitrant outsiders rendered harmless. This is the fundamental condition of the development of capitalist monopoly.

However, economic power resulting from concentration is not of itself enough to create a monopoly, for it meets with two serious obstacles. The most important obstacle is that as long as the agreement does not cover the capitalists of a given branch of production throughout the whole world, the fact that particular groups of capitalists have set up

3

cartels or trusts does not yet establish a monopoly, since the various groups of capitalists continue to compete among themselves. The only change which occurs is in the level at which the competitive struggle is carried out: competition between individual capitalists is replaced by competition between organized capitalist groups such as cartels, trusts, syndicates, large joint-stock banks, and so on. It is only the organizational form of competition which is changed; its economic content remains as before.

The second obstacle is the possibility that substitution goods may be brought into the market against the goods produced by monopolies, e.g. gas, electricity, oil, coal and so on. This would mean that a cartel would have to compete with the producers of substitution goods, and allow in its policy of prices and production for the possibility of a shift in consumption towards such goods. This difficulty can only be overcome by also drawing the producers of all these substitution goods into monopoly agreements, thus limiting the monopoly activities of rivalling cartels and trusts.[1]

It appears that the economic power of capitalist combinations, the concentration of control in the hands of a few groups with large amounts of capital, is in itself not enough to secure a monopoly position. Something more than economic power is needed for this: political power is also necessary—the need to exert appropriate influence on the State which alone can, by certain political acts, protect the monopoly combinations within its territory from competition of foreign capitalists. This protection must extend not only to goods produced within the monopolized sector, but also to all substitution goods. It is only State intervention that can create monopoly conditions for capitalist combinations, such as cartels, trusts and large joint-stock banks. Monopoly

---

[1] There is yet a third factor limiting monopoly control by capitalist combinations. Outsiders may appear for whom production is worth while even at higher costs than those prevailing in the cartel when the monopolists raise the price. The influence of this factor is usually over-estimated, for it cannot break up the monopoly since it is itself dependent on monopoly prices. On the break-up of the monopoly and the subsequent fall in prices, the outsider is eliminated since he is producing at higher than marginal costs. He can reduce the surplus profits of the monopolists, but he cannot earn them himself without being forced into liquidation. For this reason also, cartels and trusts tolerate such outsiders fairly willingly, especially during a boom, allowing them to meet part of the increased demand which the boom creates. However, it is on these outsiders that the whole weight of a crisis falls.

conditions are accomplished by a policy of tariffs and foreign trade regulations, a suitable system of trade agreements, a tariff policy for State railways, a colonial policy, and so on. Only such intervention by the State can transform the economic power of the capitalist combinations so that they occupy a monopoly position, assuring to certain groups of capitalist potentates monopoly profits exceeding profits which would result from free competition, due to the operation of the law of profit equalization.

Thus, the age of monopoly capitalism is increasingly characterized by the intervention of the State. With the end of the nineteenth and the beginning of the twentieth centuries, a fundamental change takes place in the function of the capitalist State. This change is connected in capitalist systems with growing trends towards the formation of monopolies. In the age of freely competitive capitalism, in the age of comparative liberalism, the bourgeois State followed the principle of non-intervention in economic life. It is true that this rule was quite frequently broken, but the State's general attitude to economic life was based on the principle of *laissez faire*, which was then the generally accepted ideal of the whole capitalist world. During the period of liberalism, the State confined itself to forming and supporting the general conditions of the capitalist economy, such as private ownership, maintenance of law and order, communications, the monetary system, legal security, and so on. However, with the appearance of capitalist combinations with clearly monopolistic tendencies, such as cartels, trusts, etc., the function of the capitalist State fundamentally changed. Henceforth the capitalist State does no longer confine itself to maintaining the general conditions of the capitalist economy, but actively intervenes in economic life. The principle of *laissez-faire* is left to the universities, and active intervention in economic life is considered by the State to be its highest duty. In this way, it contributes enthusiastically to "the favourable development of the national economy" and to the "protection of the nation's most vital interests", that is, to the creation of privileges for cartels, trusts and large joint-stock banks—privileges which give rise to high monopoly profits.

Thus, begins a great wave of protection by tariffs and control of foreign trade. In contrast to former "development" tariffs, which were designed to give less industrialized countries an equal start with highly industrialized England, and which were, therefore, of a temporary nature,[2] the State surrounds itself with a permanent, high tariff wall aiming at establishing monopolistic conditions for cartels and trusts. These new tariffs differ further from the previous "development" tariffs in that they also affect the main export industries, which are allowed to make use of their monopoly in the home market for dumping purposes, covering their export losses with monopoly profits obtained from the domestic market.[3]

Apart from the tariff policy, there are various other means of influencing trade, such as import and export controls; export subsidies and premiums, restrictions on goods in transit, a railways tariff policy, etc. Capitalist groups thus acquire monopolistic positions not only by virtue of their economic power, but also *by their political power, making of the State a pliant instrument of intervention in economic life for their benefit.*

Thus a change is brought about in the basic function of the capitalist State. From the ordinary guardian, guarding the security of private property and the other basic conditions of the capitalist system, the State becomes the active regulator of economic life. Liberalism is replaced by interventionism,[4] as a result of which high monopoly profits accrue to cartels, trusts and other groups of capitalist interests. The transition from freely competitive capitalism to monopoly capitalism is thus achieved.

The economic content of monopoly capitalism can be formulated as: monopoly in the home market and competition in the world market. However, even in the home market monopoly covers only certain

---

[2] The main theorist of development tariffs, Frederik List, was basically an advocate of free trade. He intended development tariffs to be only a temporary measure to secure an equal start with the more industrialized countries, after which the tariffs were to give way to free trade. See *Das nationale System der Politischen Oekonomie*, 5th edition, Chapter II, pp. 213–214, Jena, 1928.

[3] See R. Hilferding, *Das Finanzkapital*, pp. 613 ff, Vienna, 1910.

[4] Contemporary interventionism and the role of the State in Poland [1931] is of a somewhat different nature. Undoubtedly, the creation of monopoly conditions for various capitalist groups plays a large role here too. However, the true social nature of Polish interventionism and the role of the State can be understood only by seeing it as the economic policy of a military dictatorship. Added to this, there is the specific role played by the intelligentsia in the social structure of Poland, its decisive role in the independence movement and in its present influence on the State, which has found expression in the present regime. For the role of the intelligentsia see A. Krzyżanowski, *Bierny bilans handlowy* (The Unfavourable Balance of Trade) Cracow, 1928, Part I, *Etatyzm w Polsce* (State Ownership in Poland).

branches of production, leaving the rest to free competition. It is on these branches of production which are outside monopoly agreements that the whole burden of monopoly falls. This will be discussed below.

In the age of monopoly capitalism, the capitalist State assumes a new function, *namely, of creating monopoly positions for certain capitalist groups by its direct intervention in economic life.* In this new role, *the State becomes for these groups the creator of monopoly profits,* which accrue from its intervention in economic life. Since such intervention by the State is the source of monopoly profits for certain groups of capitalists, it is clear that these groups must seek to use the State apparatus in order to gain continually new monopolistic positions, as well as to extend those they already hold. The capitalist State now has a new function, namely, to extend the area over which the monopolies already created operate. This can be done, in particular, by extending the area of its own sovereignty. The greater the area subject to the sovereignty of the State, the greater the area over which monopoly can operate. In Europe, however, it is not easy to extend State sovereignty. Capitalist States, therefore, seek to control territories outside Europe, either as colonies, "areas of influence", or in some other form (e.g. League of Nations mandated territories). The area over which monopoly operates may also be extended by the existence of dependent weaker States, by forcing appropriate trade agreements on them, and by generally using political power as an instrument of international economic policy. These are the roots of capitalist imperialism.[5]

The pursuit of imperialist expansion in the age of monopoly capitalism becomes the essential feature of the capitalist State as the creator and defender of monopoly positions. This is accompanied by an enormous increase in armaments and by a whole series of imperialist wars. Competing with each other in the world market, the capitalist groups address consumers not in the language of low prices and good commodities, but in the language of political power backed up in the name of "national

---

[5] See R. Hilferding, *Das Finanzkapital*, chap. 22–25 (Kapitał finansowy), pp. 636 ff, Warsaw, 1958.

The pursuit of surplus monopoly profits suffices to explain completely the imperialistic nature of present-day capitalism. Consequently, special theories of imperialism which resort to artificial constructions, such as Rosa Luxemburg's theory (*Die Akkumulation des Kapitals*, Berlin, 1913, 2nd ed.) and Fritz Sternberg's (*Der Imperialismus*, Berlin, 1926), are quite unnecessary.

pride" by the rattle of arms. The transition from freely competitive capitalism to monopoly capitalism dispels illusions of sentimental bourgeois pacifism in face of the bloody reality of imperialism which is inherent in monopoly capitalism.[6]

By creating and extending monopoly situations, State intervention in economic life is the source of surplus monopoly profits for the capitalist combinations. But the creation of surplus profits for monopoly entails a simultaneous reduction in the level of profits in all those branches of production which do not enjoy monopoly *privileges*. Free competition tends to equalize the level of profit in all branches of economic life. This is effected by the flow of capital and labour to the most profitable branches. However, with the appearance of monopoly, equalization ceases and two profit levels are established: a higher one in the monopolized sectors of production, and a lower one in those branches which have not been monopolized. By preventing the flow of capital from branches which are not monopolized to those which are, an unequal level of profit is maintained at the expense of those branches outside the monopolized sector. Where there are several monopolized branches of production, there are several levels of profit, one for each monopolized branch and one for the remaining branches which have not been monopolized.[7] The

---

[6] Some (e.g. Kautsky) consider that the growth of international cartels and trusts leads to monopoly on an international scale and to an era of universal peace in world-wide monopoly capitalism. According to this view capitalism itself overcomes imperialism and enters a phase of what is known as "ultraimperialism". This is, of course, economically possible and certain tendencies in this direction undoubtedly exist. But in view of the unequal development of the various capitalist groups, such an arrangement would be very unstable and would continually break down, and the various groups would fight helped by political intervention of their States. (See V. I. Lenin, *Imperializm jako najwyższe stadium kapitalizmu*, (*Imperialism, the Highest Stage of Capitalism*), *Works* (*Dzieła*), Vol. 22, pp. 213 ff. Imperialism must therefore be considered as an inherent part of monopoly capitalism. International cartels only extend the basis of imperialism from individual States to groups of States. And even if it were at some time to lead to "ultraimperialism", this is a question of a future so remote that imperialism would meanwhile have time to destroy the whole modern civilization and culture. Thus, as regards a practical policy for the proletariat, this possibility does not arise.

[7] The existence of this unmonopolized sector is a necessary condition of monopoly capitalism. For the surplus profits of the monopolists are possible only when there are also unmonopolized branches of production which pay monopolists a levy in the form of a diminished level of profit. A monopoly covering all branches of production

greater the number of monopolies and the greater their surplus profits, the lower is the level of profit in the non-monopolized branches of production.[8]

In monopoly capitalism the State not only creates surplus monopoly profits for privileged capitalist groups, but it also assumes the role of general distributor of profits to individual groups. By its intervention in economic life, the State divides the capitalists into two groups. The first consists of privileged cartel and trust magnates together with financiers controlling the large joint-stock banks. By its intervention the State ensures for them considerable monopoly profits. The remainder consists of capitalists in "unprotected" branches of production. These, less fortunate, must content themselves with a lower level of profit, and they sigh for the good old days of non-interventionism and *laissez-faire*.

By the nature and extent of its intervention in economic life, the State determines the level of monopoly profits falling to cartels and trusts. Since the creation of a monopoly influences not only the profits of capitalists, but also the incomes of all social classes, and hence of workers, peasants, the *petite bourgeoisie*, the intelligentsia, and so on, the *State becomes the general distributor of social income*. Therefore, all economic conflicts in monopoly capitalism become *eo ipso* political conflicts.

Monopoly capitalism implies the involvement of politics in economic life, of which the State becomes the centre. By its activity of intervention the State creates monopoly profits for some, reduces the profits of others, and controls the distribution of the whole social income. This

---

would consequently destroy its own monopolistic activity. Hence monopoly capitalism always implies the control of certain branches of production by monopolists, preserving free competition in the remaining branches.

[8] This reduced level of profit outside the monopolized sector affects agriculture most of all. Generally carried on in conditions of free competition, it bears the whole burden of monopoly profits of industrial cartels. Tariffs on agricultural products do not help here, since the whole economic and social structure of agriculture renders it unsuitable for monopoly operation. Such tariffs can create monopoly conditions only for capitalist groups controlling trade in agricultural products; but for the producer they are useless. Of all the branches of production outside the monopolized sector, agriculture is the most defenceless, and it therefore feels most keenly the burden of capitalist monopolies. Chronic structural depression in agriculture is an unavoidable necessity in monopoly capitalism.

leads to a fundamental change in the capitalist State, *whose class character is revealed more and more clearly.*

The bourgeois State in the age of freely competitive capitalism was undoubtedly also a class State, but it differed in its class character. In the age of liberalism, when the State was confined to protecting the general conditions of the capitalist economy, such as security of property, the monetary system, communications, etc., its class character was not immediately apparent. It was visible only in relation to the working class, while in relation to all the bourgeois strata of society, and in relation to the landed gentry the State was serving the interests of all the capitalist classes and landed gentry to an equal extent. Indeed, the idea was simply that private property, communications, the monetary system, and all other general conditions of the capitalist system should be safeguarded, and that by its intervention in economic life, the State should not hinder the capitalists in their economic activities. Therefore, in conditions of *laissez-faire*, the capitalists willingly ceded administration of the State to the old aristocracy and to professional politicians, confining themselves to their economic activities.

In monopoly capitalism, however, the situation is different. Direct intervention by the State in economic life (tariffs, trade and colonial policies, etc.) is the basis of monopoly profits which accrue to big capital. By its intervention the State regulates the level of profits accruing to each particular group of capitalists. Consequently, the oligarchy which heads the capitalist monopoly combinations cannot be content to leave administration of the State in the hands of other social strata. Indeed, the level and range of monopoly profits, and even their very existence, depend upon the readiness of the State to submit to the will of the capitalist oligarchy. This oligarchy endeavours to subject the whole State apparatus to its direct and exclusive control, and to this end brings all its enormous power to bear upon the State. Capitalism then becomes political in nature. The capitalist potentates no longer leave administration of the State in the hands of landed aristocracy and professional politicians, but aim at direct control of the State. They themselves sit in parliament and hold positions in other State institutions or send their representatives there, and are active in politics.

The contemporary State becomes less and less the equal representative of all the bourgeois strata of society, and more and more the exclusive instrument of the capitalist monopolists. State policy is to an increasing extent determined by their interests. "It is no exaggeration to say that in America it is quite an open question whether the State will succeed in controlling the trusts or the trusts in controlling the State; while in Germany since the war there almost seems to have been a marriage of the two. In England, in spite of the wide democratic liberties, political decisions, both legislative and executive, have in recent years been increasingly influenced, directly or indirectly, by prominent financial and industrial interests—for instance, by such powerful bodies as the Federation of British Industries,[9] and the Conference of leading bankers of the City of London. One can scarcely fail to discern a certain parallel with the fourteenth century, when the municipal administration began to bow before the growing influence of *"probi homines"* and *"divites et potentiores".*[10]

The interests of other bourgeois strata of society are increasingly represented by the contemporary State only insofar as they do not oppose the interests of monopoly potentates. The State ceases to be the representative of all the bourgeois strata and becomes more and more the exclusive organ of certain capitalist groups, the organ of monopoly oligarchy and capital. In the period of monopoly capitalism the coercive apparatus of the State is directed not only against the working class, but more and more escapes the influence of the broad bourgeois strata, becoming the exclusive organ of the monopoly oligarchy. This transformation in the social nature of the State is as closely connected with monopoly capitalism as imperialism is. Economic intervention by the State in order to create monopolistic situations of benefit to capitalist combinations is possible only insofar as the given capitalist groups manage to acquire a decisive influence over the State apparatus and to paralyse the influence of other capitalist groups, against whom this intervention is directed. In its pursuit of direct and exclusive control of the State apparatus, however, the capitalist oligarchy is confronted with a considerable obstacle which makes such control increasingly difficult. This obstacle is political democracy.

It is true that, at the beginning of its development, monopoly capitalism is compatible with political democracy, and even manages to make good use of it for its own purposes. The economic power of the great capitalists enables them to seize control of all the means of influencing

---

[9] Now known as the Confederation of British Industries.

[10] M. Dobb, *Capitalist Enterprise and Social Progress*, pp. 336–337, London, 1926.

public opinion. Concealing its class interest under the guise of national interest and under the cover of high-sounding nationalistic phrases, the monopoly oligarchy wins the applause of large sections of the population. In the name of the nation's "economic independence", high tariffs are imposed; in the name of the "defence of the nation's dignity", preparations are made for imperialist intervention; in the name of "expansion of the State's power status", small nations are subjugated and monopolists acquire new areas of exploitation; in the name of the "historical mission of Christianity", new colonies are won; and so on. With the means of forming public opinion at its command the capitalist monopoly oligarchy can in time, democratically turn the State into its instrument. But this does not last long. The greater becomes the power of the monopoly, the more intensely is its weight felt by broad sections of the population. It is not only the working class that feels this, but also the peasantry, the lower and middle bourgeoisie, and the intelligentsia. The higher the development of monopoly in all the leading capitalist countries, the more difficult does imperialist expansion become, since it is met by greater resistance in other capitalist States. Imperialist expansion becomes increasingly expensive, and its cost falls upon the broad masses. Class oppositions become increasingly acute and increasingly dangerous. The opposition between the capitalist oligarchy and the working classes sharpens. But other strata of the population too—the peasantry, the *petite bourgeoisie*, and even part of the intelligentsia—are made aware of their opposition to the capitalist monopoly oligarchy. They rebel against the burden of monopoly prices forced upon them by capitalist monopolies, and they move closer to the working-class movement.

A great anti-monopoly bloc is formed which includes the working class, the peasantry, the *petite bourgeoisie*, and part of the intelligentsia— a bloc of all those who are working against the capitalist monopoly oligarchy. The greater the control wielded by the capitalist oligarchy over the State apparatus, and the more this apparatus is made into a docile instrument of monopolistic policy, the more glaringly is the class character of the contemporary State shown up, the more quickly do the broad masses escape from the ideological influence of capitalist propaganda, and the more do oppositions sharpen.

Leadership of this bloc falls naturally to the working-class movement as best understanding the mechanism of the capitalist economy, and as having the most clearly defined aims. Among the peasantry, the *petite bourgeoisie* and the intelligentsia, opposition mainly has the negative aim of abolishing monopoly and returning to free competition. However, rapidly progressing concentration and continual technical revolution make these dreams increasingly utopian and show the growing impossibility of destroying the capitalist monopolies without at the same time destroying the capitalist system. The peasantry, the *petite bourgeoisie* and the intelligentsia are faced more and more clearly with a choice between the yoke of monopoly oligarchy or socialism—a choice which must eventually bring them within the orbit of the ideological leadership of the working-class movement.

Social oppositions become increasingly polarized. On the one hand, there is the monopoly oligarchy of capitalists and, on the other, the working-class movement, supported by the peasantry, the *petite bourgeoisie* and part of the intelligentsia. In between, there remain only the helpless middle bourgeoisie and the landed gentry as owners of those branches of production which have not been monopolized. Fear of the working-class movement drives them under the yoke of the monopoly oligarchy. These two enemy camps face each other, preparing for the decisive battle. In these conditions, political democracy becomes a considerable obstacle to the monopoly oligarchy in its control of the State apparatus. Compelled to exercise complete control of the State apparatus in order to maintain its monopoly position, this oligarchy regards political democracy with increasing mistrust; for political democracy stands in the way of the further development of monopoly capitalism. The greater the masses' resistance to domination by the capitalist oligarchy, the clearer does it become that this oligarchy can maintain its influence over the State apparatus only by opposing democracy.

Thus, the monopoly oligarchy makes a general attack against political democracy. This attack, which may or may not be overt, depending on the circumstances, gains strength with the increasing resistance of the masses against monopoly domination. No longer can monopoly capitalism reconcile itself to the existence of political democracy, and a decisive conflict between the monopoly oligarchy and political democracy is inevitable. It is this conflict which opens the final chapter in the history of capitalism.

The approaching struggle between the capitalist oligarchy and political democracy inevitably brings the two hostile camps into conflict with each other—a conflict which is fought out in the name of the struggle for democracy. Monopoly capitalism seeks to destroy political democracy, but this is saved by the working-class movement under whose leadership are rallied all those sections of society which have been exploited by the capitalist monopolies. Saving political democracy, however, also transforms its social character. As the English Parliament was transformed from an institution of domination by the feudal nobility, and the French *Etats Généraux* from a constitutional organ of the feudal State, into instruments of bourgeois revolution, so political democracy is at present being transformed from a constitutional form of the bourgeois class State into an instrument of proletarian revolution, an instrument for the domination of the working-class and the abolition of capitalism. Political democracy is faced with two possible alternatives: either to perish under monopoly capitalism or to become the instrument of proletarian dictatorship.

JOHN STRACHEY ON CONTEMPORARY CAPITALISM

The task of following and examining the changes which are taking place in contemporary capitalism is a very important one. In this field, as in others, it is essential to know the facts and avoid superficial generalizations; for on this depends the effectiveness of our policy towards the capitalist world, as well as the true evaluation of the prospects of the working-class movement in capitalist countries.

John Strachey's article, together with the book which it summarizes, are an interesting contribution to discussion on the changes which are taking place in contemporary capitalism. It is especially interesting since it expresses a view which widely influenced Social Democratic circles in Western Europe.

After the Second World War, social democracy in Western Europe was considerably transformed. Before the war it had taken the reformist road of the gradual transformation of society from capitalism to socialism. Reformism was concerned with the road to socialism, although socialism was acknowledged (at least in official utterances) to be the ultimate aim of the policy of the Social Democratic parties. After the war, however, a considerable number of Social Democrats—probably the majority of them—gradually relinquished this idea of socialism as their final aim. Instead, the object of their activity was to reform capitalism in such a way as to ensure full employment, an increasing share of the national income for the working masses and the raising of their standard of living within the framework of the capitalist system. By discarding socialism as its ultimate aim, the character of social democracy has changed in post-war years. It is thus reformism of a new type, not concerned with the road towards socialism, but in fact rejecting socialism altogether.

Not all Social Democrats, however, have subscribed to this transformation. There is still a considerable number who remain faithful to the idea of socialism. Moreover, there is a whole range of intermediate views between those Social Democrats who only want to reform capitalism,

15

and those who really want to establish a socialist system. The working masses who support social democracy are all anti-capitalist, but the level of their socialist awareness varies, depending on the socio-economic conditions in which they live and the way in which the Social Democratic parties act towards them.

John Strachey belongs to those Social Democrats who are true socialists. "I believe", he says in his article, "that our problems can be finally solved only if we completely replace capitalism by gradually introducing new socialist relations of production." His views are therefore worthy of serious consideration.

The starting-point of Strachey's analysis is the Marxist idea of increasing concentration and centralization of capital and, following from this, increasing monopolization of the capitalist economy. In this he agrees completely with Marxist teaching and, in particular, also with Lenin's theses on monopoly capitalism and imperialism. Strachey considers, however, that in recent times there have been transformations in capitalism which call for a revision of Marxist theory on the consequences of monopoly capitalism, and which open new prospects of development different from those described by Marx.

There is indeed no doubt that capitalism has of late been profoundly transformed. No Marxist denies this; and if he did, he would be deserting the basic Marxist principle that an evaluation of social processes must be based on a precise analysis of facts. From this it follows that Marxist theory must examine new events and develop along with the transformations which take place within society. But are these transformations such as would force us to revise the basic principles of Marxism? Strachey here advances two facts. One is the rise in the standard of living of the working classes in countries of developed capitalism; the second is the gradual dissolution of the British Empire.

Strachey's assertion that the share of the working masses in national income is growing in capitalist countries arouses serious doubts. This is a matter which requires accurate statistical examination and I therefore cannot here go into details. It seems, however, that in the United States this share has not changed in recent times, and in France the share of the working class in the national income is clearly lower than before the war. As for Great Britain, the matter needs even more precise examination. There is no doubt that in the leading capitalist countries the standard of living of the working classes has risen, both in recent years and throughout the whole of the twentieth century. Bourgeois economists and revisionists see this as the automatic result of technical progress and increased labour productivity. They consider, too, that this contradicts Marx's thesis that capitalism results in the degradation and impoverishment of the working classes.

There is here, however, a certain misunderstanding due to an over-simplified interpretation of Marx's thesis. Even in 1891 Engels, evaluating the first proposals for the Erfurt programme of German social democracy, which referred to the increasing misery of the proletariat, said that the organization and growing resistance of the working class may "set up a dam" to oppose the increase of misery. Since then, the leading capitalist countries have seen an enormous rise in the organized strength of the working classes, which have thus gained wide democratic freedoms. In these conditions, the working classes have effectively managed to oppose the tendency of capitalism to degrade and impoverish them, and have secured for themselves a certain share in the growth of national income.

This has been the result of the class struggle of the proletariat, and its power to oppose the degrading tendencies of capitalism. Where, however, capitalism is faced with a weak, disorganized working class, deprived of political rights, its degrading and impoverishing effects are fully visible. This is evident in colonies and countries such as Spain and Latin America. The same British capitalism, within whose framework the British working class has managed to fight through to an improvement in living conditions, presents a different face in Singapore, Kenya or South Africa. American capitalism fully displays its degrading and impoverishing activity in Guatemala and in other Latin American countries. Moreover, Strachey himself emphasizes the fact that the achievements of the working class in raising the standard of living in the United States and Great Britain are the results of the effective struggle of the working class, using the democratic forms of the bourgeois State. Thus, we are not dealing here with a contradiction of Marx's theory nor with a transformation of capitalism which would eliminate its degrading and impoverishing tendencies in relation to the working class.

The concessions of capitalism in favour of the working class have been facilitated by the imperialist system, which each year transfers a certain part of the surplus value produced in the subjected countries to the imperialist metropolis. The proof of such a transfer is the continual negative trade balance of Western European countries. This negative balance is concealed by the profits of capital invested abroad and by those which accrue from various non-productive services (financial and trade) rendered to the less developed countries. Lenin, too, held that this enables monopoly capital to raise the standard of living of a certain section of the working class (the working-class aristocracy). Today monopoly capital can make concessions to considerably wider sections of the working class.

Strachey tries to minimize the role of the imperialist system with his assertion of the progressive dissolution of the British Empire. Political dissolution, however, is here considerably more rapid than economic dissolution. In former colonies, such as India, British capital still maintains its fundamental position. Strachey is, however, right when he talks of the dissolution of the imperialist system—such a dissolution is indeed taking place. However, it is not the result of the voluntary self-liquidation of imperialism, but of the successful national liberation struggle of subjected peoples against imperialism. The bitterness with which imperialism defends its position is shown if only by the past events in Algeria or by the armed intervention in Suez. Anglo-French aggression in Suez clearly shows that imperialism even endeavours to recover lost conquests. Where colonial countries gain independence by peaceful means, it is because the strength of the national liberation movement is so great that armed resistance appears hopeless. In such conditions it is better to grant the colony political independence and save one's economic position.

Thus, as far as imperialism is concerned, nothing has happened to make us revise the fundamental propositions of Marxism–Leninism. The internal stability of the capitalist system has not increased; on the contrary, it is now less stable than before the Second World War, although today the manifestation of this instability are different.

Between the wars, the chief contradiction of capitalism was the impossibility of fully employing the labour force, which expressed itself in crises, in massive unemployment. At present, in conditions of post-war reconstruction and the subsequent armaments boom, capitalism has in many countries managed to create conditions of full employment. However, this has not happened everywhere, for it does not include countries such as Italy and the less developed capitalist countries of Asia and Latin America. Moreover, imperialist export of capital is one of the ways of ensuring full employment in the imperialist metropolis, especially in the United States. Consequently, the internal contradictions of the capitalist system are today revealed above all in the relations between the capitalist metropolis and its periphery. These contradictions are expressed by the dissolution of the imperialist system and by the increasingly successful national liberation struggle in subjected countries against imperialism. The existence of the socialist bloc enables anti-imperialist forces to find support, both political and economic.

Strachey concludes his article with the assertion that "the chances for the peaceful and democratic evolution of our societies (i.e. capitalist societies) in the direction of socialism are now better than ever before". This is true, and was also asserted at the Twentieth Congress of the Communist Party of the Soviet Union. Marx and Engels, too, spoke of the possibility of a peaceful and democratic road to socialism, emphasizing that the condition of its success depends upon the strength of the working class which should be such as to render any opposition on the part of the ruling classes hopeless.

Therefore, in order to ensure peaceful social development for the nations of capitalist countries, there must be unity of the international working-class movement, co-operation between the working classes of socialist and capitalist countries, and co-operation among communists, socialists and all progressive groups.

FUNDAMENTAL PROBLEMS IN THE PERIOD OF SOCIALIST CONSTRUCTION

The transition from capitalism to socialism proceeds in a different way from that of feudalism to capitalism. Capitalism was born within the feudal structure. Towns arose, a bourgeoisie emerged and the production of goods began to contain the elements of capitalism. Capitalist relations of production were born within feudal society. Trade and usury provided the means for the development of the first enterprises of capitalist production which were mostly for manufactures. What is known as primitive capital accumulation—the mass appropriation by capital of small craftsmen-producers, the expulsion of the peasants and the plunder of colonial countries—provided the means for the development of capitalist production. All this took place within the framework of the old feudal society, when agriculture was still dominated by feudal relations, when a considerable part of production was under the restrictive rules of the town guilds of the middle ages, and when the political superstructure which had arisen from the feudal monarchy was transformed into an absolute monarchy.

The feudal relations in agriculture, the guild restrictions on urban production, and the whole superstructure of the feudal monarchy formed an obstacle to the further development of capitalist production. The result was the bourgeois revolutions which abolished feudal relations in agriculture, the guild restrictions in towns and, most important of all, the whole political superstructure of the feudal monarchy.

These bourgeois revolutions opened the way to the further development of capitalist production. They took place in the most important countries of Western Europe and in America—first in England, then in America (the War of American Independence) and subsequently in France. In other countries, however, the transition from feudalism to capitalism took place more gradually. In Germany, for example, the feudal superstructure of the State, and even the feudal agricultural system, were gradually adapted to capitalist conditions and linked to capitalist development. The elements of such gradual transition existed, indeed, in

England where the bourgeois revolution was not so radical as was the great French Revolution. Everywhere, however, the characteristic feature of the transitional period from feudalism to capitalism was that the capitalist relations of production arose first in industry. Afterwards, the feudal relations in agriculture were superseded and transformed and, finally, political revolution changed the political superstructure of the State, thereby eventually clearing the way for the full development of capitalism.

The transition from capitalism to socialism takes place in quite a different way. Socialist relations of production are not born within capitalist society. Only within a certain range of industry is private capitalist production transformed into State controlled capitalist production. We know, for example, the role nationalized industries play today in the leading capitalist countries, especially in England and France. This undoubtedly shows that the economy of these countries outgrows the possibilities of private capitalist organization and requires new organizational forms. In certain fields (for example, energy, coal and transport), it is the capitalist State which must create this new organization of production relations. The old type of capitalist production relations is already too constricting for the capitalist economy, which calls for wide State control by nationalization of certain sectors of the economy and by planned intervention of the State in the economic life of the country. In this sense it is a progressive process.

However, this is not at all the same as introducing socialist relations of production; for such nationalization and economic intervention is carried out by the capitalist State, in which the leading and decisive role is played by the capitalists. Moreover, the capitalist State, in the stage of imperialism, is under the pressure of monopoly capital which turns it into an instrument of its policies.

The working-class movement and Marxist theory have from the very beginning distinguished these elements of State capitalism from socialism. It is enough to read what Engels has to say on this subject in his *Socialism: Utopian and Scientific,* and the old school of Marxists from the period of the Second International which analysed the subject fully. At the end of the nineteenth century, however, there appeared within the working-class movement the trend known as revisionism, which saw the rise of new, socialist relations of production in the State capitalist forms of economic organization and in State intervention in economic life. This was an error resulting from the lack of perception as to the class nature of the power which creates State capitalist forms of economic life. For these transformations are not carried out in the interests of the working class, or of society as a whole, but for the purpose of preserving the capitalist economy and the narrow interests of certain monopoly financial groups which dominate society. These groups exert a decisive influence over State authority and use it in their own interests, and hence not even in the interests of the capitalist class as a whole, but only of narrow groups of monopoly capitalists.

Socialist relations of production, and the transformation of the capitalist economic structure into a socialist one, follow only after the success of the proletarian revolution, and hence after political power has been won by the working class.

The basic difference between bourgeois and proletarian revolutions is that the former is carried out on the basis of capitalist production relations which have to a certain degree already developed within the old feudal society. Such a revolution removes the obstacles to the further development of these relations, but does not create them. As already mentioned, they arise spontaneously, forming within the feudal society. Bourgeois revolution is to some extent the end of the process in the birth of capitalism, and at the same time it makes it possible for capitalism to develop fully—a possibility which did not exist in the feudal structure.

The proletarian revolution, however, precedes the establishment of socialist production relations. Only proletarian power abolishes capitalist production relations and makes possible the construction of socialist relations in production. This is the basic difference between the bourgeois and the proletarian revolution. One may say that the bourgeois revolution becomes the basis of a new social structure, or at least an important part of this basis, and causes a change in the political superstructure which in turn opens a direct way to the full development of the basis of a new society. The proletarian revolution, on the other hand, together with the political superstructure to which it has newly given rise, destroys the basis of the former capitalist society and creates the conditions for constructing the basis of a new society. It is clear that the rise of this new political superstructure, and of the power of the working class, does not come about of its own accord. It is the result of increasing class contradictions within the capitalist society—contradictions between the capitalist relations of production and the requirements for the further development of productive forces.

The basis for a new society arises only after a political revolution has been carried out. The new political power which acts as the driving force in the transformation of capitalist production relations into socialist relations is called the dictatorship of the proletariat. This term emphasizes the fact that it is the rule of the working class over the former ruling classes which removes the economic basis of the old society and constructs the basis for a new one.

Dictatorship of the proletariat may take various political forms. It may be a Soviet Republic, a People's Democracy or a republic in the form of a parliamentary democracy which, indeed, Engels considered as the typical Western European form of proletarian dictatorship. The particular form of this dictatorship depends on the whole complex of historical conditions of a given country. But the social function and content of this new State power is the same everywhere, namely, the elimination of capitalist production relations and the building up and organization of socialist production relations.

Already at the end of the nineteenth century, the revisionists repudiated the transition to socialism through dictatorship of the proletariat. They considered that socialist production relations could be created within the framework of a capitalist society. They identified the State capitalist form of society with socialism, and held that the political superstructure was gradually being adapted to this spontaneous process of economic development. They termed this "growing into socialism". This theory is today generally accepted in one form or another in Social Democratic programmes.[1]

---

[1] As far as the Social Democratic position on the question of the transitional period is concerned, two types of view must be distinguished. One, the old revisionist wing of the German Social Democrats, at the turn of the twentieth century, voiced the theory of growing into socialism; whereas the second wing, led by Bebel and Kautsky, took up a Marxist position. The views of this wing were expressed in literature available in Polish and other languages. In 1902 Kautsky published *Social Revolution*, in which he attempted for the first time to formulate his view on the transitional period.

Without entering here into a political evaluation of Social Democratic ideas, it may be said that their original views on the subject of the transitional period are basically similar to those which were later crystallized in one form or another in Marxist literature. This concerns above all Kautsky's first work of 1902, which also

Since the transition from capitalism to socialism takes place as a result of the political revolution which establishes the dictatorship of the proletariat and which, thanks to this dictatorship, rebuilds the production relations it follows that there must be a certain period of transition, or period of social construction.

The proletarian, as distinct from the bourgeois, revolution is not the end of the spontaneous process of development. It is only the beginning of the conscious process of social reconstruction, which may continue for a longer or shorter period of time, depending on circumstances. This reconstruction of the social structure, is not spontaneous, as in the case of the transition from feudalism to capitalism, but is the result of *the conscious and purposeful activity of the dictatorship of the proletariat,* or of the new State which organizes the construction of socialism.

The working class, which gains political power, which operates it, and which directs the process of socio-economic reconstruction—the process of the construction of socialism—is only able to do this as a class if it is organized, and if at least its leading elements are organized in a revolutionary party. The party leads the working masses by gaining control of the State. The party directs the process of managing the State and the construction of socialism.

The existence of a working-class party is not, however, enough in itself. To carry out its tasks, it must base its policy and its activity on the principles of a scientific understanding of the laws of social development. It must be based on the principles of Marxism–Leninism.

---

contains a discussion of the first stages of socialist construction, i.e., the expropriation of capital and the gradual transformation of agriculture by socialist co-operative combinations.

In later publications, some of which were also written by Kautsky (in the period of the German and Austrian revolutions), two basic elements were missing: (1) the political necessity of expropriating the former ruling classes, and (2) the need for a dictatorship of the proletariat. In these writings there is also no discussion of socialist industrialization, for the existence of a highly developed capitalist economy is assumed, which wanted gradually to be transformed into a socialist economy.

Since the Second World War, Social Democratic parties have largely abandoned their programmes for socialist transformation of the economy, confining themselves solely to ideas for the reform of capitalism. There is a fundamental difference between the classical Social Democratic programme and that of contemporary German, French, and to some extent even English, Social Democrats. The programmes of contemporary Social Democratic parties have lost their socialist content.

Let us consider the problems which, in the period of construction of socialism, face the working-class party and the State which it directs. There are problems which the party and State must solve immediately, and those which are solved gradually. One of the problems requiring immediate solution which goes back to the period of struggle for power before the socialist revolution is the problem of *the allies of the working class* in the struggle for, and exercise of, this power. The allies of the working class in the struggle for power are also, from the nature of things, allies in the exercise of power. This is true at least in the first stage of exercising this power.

The development of capitalism is distinguished by the fact that the disintegration of the capitalist structure occurs before all non-capitalist forms of production are eliminated. In different countries considerable elements of feudal relations still exist, to a greater or lesser degree, within the framework of the capitalist society. There are exceptions, such as France, where the radical bourgeois revolution rid itself completely of feudalism, or the United States, where there was no feudalism at all. On the other hand, capitalist society contains a well developed sector of small-scale peasant and handicraft production which comes into conflict with monopoly capital. As monopoly capitalism develops, part of the capitalist economy—small-scale capitalist production—also comes into conflict with the great monopoly capitalists. It is clear that the peasantry, the *petite bourgeoisie* and, in certain circumstances, part of the bourgeoisie too—namely, that part which comes into conflict with the monopoly capitalists—may, and usually do, become allies of the working class.

Before the First World War, the working-class movement showed tendencies of ignoring the problem of its allies. It was assumed that the socialist revolution would grow as capitalism destroyed the middle classes, and that the class struggle would ultimately be polarized into a struggle between the capitalists and the working class. We find a reflection of these tendencies in much of Marxist literature from the period of the Second International. They appear most clearly in the works of Rosa Luxemburg. Her theory, later known as "Luxemburgism", played in its time a dominating role in Social Democratic circles of Poland and Lithuania. Rosa Luxemburg held that capitalism would eliminate all the middle strata of society, turn them into proletarians, and force them into the ranks of the working class, and that it is the working class itself which would carry out the socialist revolution.

Capitalism undoubtedly contains tendencies of this kind. But on the other hand, the internal contradictions of capitalist society grow considerably faster than the rate at which these tendencies gain ground. In particular, the development of monopoly capitalism and imperialism creates a conflict between monopoly capitalists on the one hand, and the peasantry, the *petite bourgeoisie* and even part of the bourgeoisie on the other. This phenomenon differs from country to country. We know from historical experience that the conflicts of capitalism are greatest in underdeveloped countries, where capitalism has penetrated so deeply as to destroy the previous social structure with attendent overpopulation in the countryside and a poor standard of living of the *petite bourgeoisie*. Capitalism has not, however, managed to establish in these countries the conditions necessary for the full capitalist development of productive forces.

I shall not discuss here the causes of this phenomenon, for they are connected with the nature of contemporary capitalism, which has been able to remove certain contradictions and difficulties in the development of leading capitalist countries by shifting these difficulties to the less developed countries which are exploited by monopoly capitalists.

The first socialist revolutions matured and succeeded particularly in countries with wide non-capitalist strata of working peasants, craftsmen, *petite bourgeoisie,* and that section of the bourgeoisie which was in conflict with foreign imperialist capitalists (e.g. in China, where the national bourgeoisie had played a special role in the revolution).

The problem of allies for the working class is particularly acute in the less developed People's Democracies, but it appears in capitalist countries too; several elements of this problem exist in Italy and France, for instance. Moreover, the problem of allies for the working class also exists on an international scale. The anti-imperialist national liberation movements of the national bourgeoisie, the intelligentsia, the *petite bourgeoisie*, the peasantry, as well as the working class, of nations struggling against imperialism are movements which are allied to the working class in countries building socialism and in leading capitalist countries.

The main ally of the working class in countries of Eastern Europe and Asia has been the peasantry. This is associated on the one hand with the remnants of feudalism which survived in these countries until recently, and on the other hand, with the quite recent exploitation of the peasantry by both native and foreign monopoly capital. Thus, the main basis of the struggle to gain control of the State, and the main basis of the dictatorship of the proletariat, is here the alliance between workers and peasants.

Depending on the characteristic features of different countries, the circle of allies of the working class may be greater or smaller. As already mentioned, an important role among the allies of the working class in China was played by the national bourgeoisie, or that section of the bourgeoisie which came into conflict with foreign imperialist capitalists and with those domestic capitalists who were used by foreign capitalists or acted as their agents.

In the countries of Western Europe, the *petite bourgeoisie*, in addition to the peasantry, was of great importance as an ally of the working class. For example, the last Congress of the Italian Communist Party based the principles of the Italian road to socialism, which it was then formulating, on an alliance between the working class and the middle classes of the towns and countryside, and hence on an alliance with the *petite bourgeoisie* and the village peasantry.

The formulation of the question of allies varies not only according to the country concerned, but also according to the phase of capitalist development in a given country. It is, however, possible to generalize and say that in every country there appears in the struggle for power, and during the exercise of this power, a worker–peasant alliance and often, too, an even more far-reaching alliance with the *petite bourgeoisie* and possibly with a certain section of the upper bourgeoisie.

*

What further immediate tasks face a successful proletarian revolution? First of all, there is *the need to carry out those economic transformations which would remove the economic basis of the former ruling classes.* This is a task within the sphere of political economy, but it is of fundamental political significance. Let us remind ourselves that Social Democratic parties have often come to power in Europe and, when they did, have usually been faced with insurmountable difficulties. The accession to power of Social Democratic parties has not been associated with dispossessing the former ruling classes of their economic base. Sooner or later, however, they were faced with the alternative of resorting to revolutionary action dispossessing the great capitalists of the economic base of their domination, or of surrendering to them. In France not only Social Democratic governments, but even left-wing bourgeois governments, have always come to grief over this. Whenever a left-wing progressive government came to power, a flight of capital usually began, the franc fell and, after a few months, the government was forced to resign.

There are, then, two possible ways open to Social Democratic governments. One is that of a socialist government which opposes the bourgeoisie, depriving the capitalists of their economic base. So far, no Social Democratic government has chosen this solution. The second is to come to terms with the bourgeoisie, guaranteeing that there will be no fundamental changes in the social structure, that is, to abandon socialist aims. This simply means administering a capitalist society without disturbing its foundations, continuing a policy for social reforms which do not reach down to the foundations of the capitalist structure. This proved convenient for the bourgeoisie in times of crisis, for it could then throw responsibility for the country's economic state onto the government. This was the way chosen by the German Social Democrats, thereby contributing to Hitler's success; for Hitler made the Social Democrats responsible for the crisis and for all the internal contradictions of the German capitalist economy.

From the foregoing it is clear that the first step of every government which really wants to abolish the old structure and build a new one, must be to dispossess the former ruling classes of their economic base. This means that if feudal elements still exist within a given country, their economic base must be removed by agricultural reform. The revolutionary State must take over important capitalist property, banks, industry and transport, which will provide the framework for the further development of the national economy.

This is the first step essential for every effective revolution. A revolution which does not take this step is condemned to failure. Having dispossessed the former ruling classes of their economic base, the new State which has risen from the socialist revolution, must undertake a whole series of measures which fulfil the aspirations of the allies of the working class. At the same time, it must neutralize those sections of the middle classes which do not support the socialist revolution. This neutralization of the middle classes is of great significance since they are in a state of conflict with monopoly capitalists, and possibly also with feudal elements which the socialist revolution has eliminated. Such a policy may be useful for isolating the nucleus which directs the former ruling classes and for reducing the chances of a counter-revolution.

The most important of the allied classes is the peasantry. Thus we see that, apart from expropriating big business and banking, as well as industry and transport in which private capital is involved, the socialist revolution carries out agricultural reforms everywhere and pursues a policy of neutralizing the wealthy capitalist peasantry, thereby fulfilling the aspirations of the masses of the lower and middle peasantry.

It is undoubtedly true that agricultural reform fulfils the hopes of the lower and middle peasantry and may also neutralize the upper peasantry. The Chinese revolution gained the support of the lower and middle peasantry, neutralized the upper peasantry (of which, indeed, there is relatively little in China), and—not least important—neutralized the national bourgeoisie and even won it over to the revolution. Faced with a choice between two evils—a socialist revolution or the return of imperialism—the majority of the national bourgeoisie came to the conclusion that gradual transformation, carried out by the socialist revolution, was the lesser of the two evils, and submitted to neutralization. As far as the Russian revolution is concerned, the ally of the working class in this case was the lower and middle peasantry. The *kulaks* were neutral only at first, and the whole bourgeoisie joined the great landowners in opposition to the revolution.

From the examples above, it follows that the problem of allies of the working class is different in different countries. The working class is able to gain a particularly wide circle of allies when the social revolution is connected with national liberation. It can then win the support not only of the *petite bourgeoisie* and peasantry, but also of the intelligentsia and a section of the bourgeoisie, for it is guide and leader in the struggle for national liberation. This was undoubtedly partly the situation in 1944 and 1945 in Poland and the European People's Democracies. This was also the situation in China and other Asian People's Democracies.

The struggle for national liberation made possible the creation of a wide circle of allies of the working class—a relatively wider circle of social strata and classes nautralized in the revolutionary process than was the case during the Russian revolution, where there was no element of struggle for national liberation. The Russian revolution was carried out in conditions of national disaster suffered during the First World War, which limited the working class's circle of allies to the peasantry only.

The socialist revolution, which removes the economic base of the former ruling classes, thus fulfilling the aspirations of its allies and neutralizing certain social strata, must also consolidate the economic position of the working class. This process is achieved together with the nationalization of basic industries, banks, transport, etc. A new basis is thereby created for the working class and its State of directly influencing the national economy. It is also further implemented by satisfying working-class aspirations and allowing this class its rightful place even in the remaining capitalist sector.

Taking as an example the history of the Russian revolution, the Bolshevik Party in its programme at the beginning of the revolution called only for the nationalization of big industry and banks. It advanced, however, the issue of workers' control over the rest of capitalist production, and hence the strengthening of the role of the working class in the remaining capitalist sector. As it happened it was not possible to put this issue into practice, for civil war broke out in which the whole capitalist class and the majority of the bourgeois intelligentsia took the side of the counter-revolution. It then became necessary, not as a result of establishing the new Soviet rule of the original programme, but because of the civil war, to pursue immediate nationalization of all capitalist enterprises. In China, for example, which was developing more peacefully, there was an immediate strengthening of the working class's position in privately owned capitalist enterprises, where one of the aims of the trade unions was to gain jointly with the State control over them. This played a considerable role in the process of gradually transforming the capitalist sector into a socialist one. This process, although quite far advanced, has not yet been completed.

In Poland, immediately after the war, many of the industrial works were completely derelict, and in these a provisional management machinery was set up by the State. A large section of industry was in effect nationalized before being formally and legally so declared by an act of the National Home Council (*Krajowa Rada Narodowa*). Many enterprises were taken over by crews of workers, who, in unusually difficult conditions, undertook the task of rebuilding the works and putting them into operation again.

It is undoubtedly true that one of the essential aims in the first moves which the revolution and socialist government must make is to strengthen the economic position of the working class and to render it directly active. This is an essential condition for ensuring management by the working class of the social reconstruction process.

Although the dictatorship of the proletariat exercises its authority together with the allies of the working class by neutralizing certain social classes and strata, it is only the working class which manages to give a socialist direction to the processes of development. The reason for this is that, although the remaining classes and strata are in conflict with the monopoly capitalists, they nevertheless do not set themselves socialist aims, but only clear anti-feudal, anti-monopolistic and anti-imperialist aims. From the nature of things, management too must belong to the working class, which must be organized as a revolutionary party based on Marxist–Leninist principles. This is an essential condition if revolutionary transformations are to be pursued along socialist lines.

We have discussed the first steps in the field of economic policy which arise directly from the socialist revolution and from the political necessities of the new situation. These steps must be taken *immediately* after the revolution, with the aim of removing the economic base of the former ruling classes and of consolidating the new State authority. They do not yet in themselves, however, necessarily lead to socialism.

We have already mentioned the need to fulfil the aspirations of the allies of the working class and to neutralize the middle classes. Agricultural reform and the liberation of the *petite bourgeoisie* from exploitation by monopoly capitalists, as well as certain acts which neutralize other classes (e.g. the national bourgeoisie in China), do not yet in themselves have the character of socialist transformations. There is a socialist element only in those actions which consolidate and raise the economic position of the working class. Measures such as workers' control in enterprises during the period immediately after the October Revolution, or the reconstruction of enterprises taken over by crews of workers, such as occurred immediately after the liberation in Poland, undoubtedly bear a clear imprint of socialism. These measures often do not yet completely abolish the capitalist production relations, but they introduce some socialist elements by assigning a certain role to the working class in the supervision of productive processes, and by the control established by the new State which came into being with the victory of the working-class movement. New socialist production relations, in the true sense of the word, have yet to be established.

*

The creation of a socialist sector in the national economy is the first great positive task of the period of socialist construction. This task arises in practice immediately after the revolution, but crystallizes with complete distinctness only after the new political rule has been consolidated. This process of consolidation requires a whole series of measures to prepare the ground for socialist construction. Such preparation is carried out in particular by the expropriation of banks, big industry (expropriation included also medium-scale industry in Poland and, as a result of the civil war, the whole of industry in Russia), transport and energy, thus making available to the new State large stocks of basic means of production and giving it the possibility of organizing and financing the national economy.

The task to be first planned is, then, the organization of the utilization of these means. Also acquired by expropriation are the means inherited from the capitalist State; for there are already certain forms of State ownership of means of production in the capitalist structure, and the new government takes these means over. In Russia and Poland, for example, this was true of the railways; they did not have to be nationalized, since they were already State-owned.

The more developed is State monopoly capitalism, the greater are the means which the capitalist State owns and which the new socialist State inherits. Developing countries are in a similar situation. In these countries, the development of several areas of the national economy is possible only in some form of State capitalism. In such countries, the new authorities take over these areas, giving them a new social content and putting them at the service of the new socialist, rather than the capitalist, society. Thus, there are at the disposal of the new State whole stocks of means of production and transport and developed financial institutions, all of which must be organized as the socialist sector of the national economy. This is the task which must be planned first, since the socialist sector constitutes the basis for further development of the economy and for further social and economic transformations.

The socialist sector is organized by expropriation of great capitalist owners of finance, industry and transport, and the nationalization of their property. In addition to this, there is also the nationalized sector inherited from the capitalist system. It may be added that only the socialist State can achieve true nationalization; in the socialist system nationalization of the means of production is connected with the direct influence of employees on management. This is an essential component of the socialization of the means of production. It has become weaker as a result of certain bureaucratic distortions which have occurred in the past. It is worth remembering that in the October Revolution the question of the direct participation of workers in the control and management of enterprises was a matter of course. It is enough to read Lenin's works and the history of the revolution to become convinced of this. Only later was this principle disregarded, due largely to the weakness of the working class and the entry of a mass of peasant and *petit bourgeois* elements into its ranks. The State replaced direct working-class control with its own apparatus.[2]

The solution which we accept, and which may be found in Marxist literature preceding the First World War, is the socialization of basic means of production and their transformation into property belonging to the nation in general in such a way that it is the employees who manage them—not, however, as owners, but as trustees of the property which belongs to the society as a whole. Socialization of the means of production is a necessary condition for the full development of productive forces and for making possible the democratic guidance of this development by the working masses. Such is the significance of socialization under socialism. Without this condition—without socialization of the means of production—no social progress is possible in any field, including that of culture.

In certain conditions the municipal sector may be assigned a large role in the creation of a socialist sector. Such may be the case in countries where many public utilities have already in capitalist conditions become municipal property.

---

[2] There is, however, a difference between this approach to socialization and the anarchist–syndicalist approach. This problem has also arisen in the Soviet Union. What was known as the workers' opposition demanded that factories should be handed over to workers' collectives. The anarchist–syndicalist solution, which is directly opposed to the bureaucratic solution, means that the workers of a factory become its owners and are completely autonomous. In this case, however, the means of production cease to be general social property and become the property of a group. In such condition general planning and central direction of the national economy is no longer possible.

Thanks to the rise of a nationalized sector, the socialist State as a dictatorship of the proletariat gains key positions or—as it used to be said in the Soviet Union after the October Revolution—the chief positions of control in the national economy from which it is possible to influence the whole economy including that part which is outside the socialist sector.

The second move towards the construction of socialism is the subordination of the capitalist economy, and hence of the small- and medium-scale capitalist economy, to the socialist sector. The purpose of this move is to ensure for the new socialist State its role of domination over the capitalist sector, so that the capitalist sector cannot make use of its private ownership of means of production to oppose the policy of the new State. To this end there are various forms of State control over the capitalist sector, as well as of direct workers' control, and there is also the decisive importance of the newly built up socialist sector, which must be wide enough to control the whole economy, including the capitalist sector.

Although the first main tasks of the construction of socialism—the organization of the socialist sector—are generally carried out in individual countries in more or less the same way (disregarding particular organizational forms), the second task—control of the capitalist sector, its subsequent inclusion in the socialist economy and its socialist transformation—is carried out differently in different countries, depending on the political situation rather than on economic factors. During the Russian Revolution, an attempt was at first made to subject the capitalist sector to State control, reinforced by workers' control, the key positions and operation being the preserve of the socialist sector. Civil war, however, led to the complete elimination of the capitalist sector. All that Lenin wrote about State-capitalist forms of development, about integrating the capitalist sector within the socialist economy, thereby ensuring peaceful development of the process of socialist construction, was vitiated by the civil war. In the period of the NEP, the small-scale capitalist economy was reconstructed both in industry and trade. Socialist industrialization was associated not with integration and transformation of the capitalist sector, but with a policy of eliminating it. During the first five-year period it was assumed that socialist industry and the socialist State would eliminate the capitalist sector. It seems that the basis of these moves was political in nature. The whole capitalist sector was hostile to the new rule; co-operation with this sector and its gradual incorporation in the socialist economy were impossible.

In China the capitalist sector has followed a different path. At first, it was subject to State control, in that it was only the State which sold goods to this sector and bought from it. This was called State capitalism. The next stage was acceptance of the principle of the State's share in the profits of the capitalist sector, the basis of which was that the State granted credits for the development of the capitalist economy. A further stage was that the State's share in profits was replaced by fixed interest on capital in the capitalist sector. This is already a fundamental transformation. The former owner of an enterprise was changed from a capitalist taking part of the profits into a rentier generally engaged in managing the enterprise (a director or deputy-director), who simply earned interest on his capital. This is more or less the present position of the capitalist sector in China. In the future, the former owner will be transformed into the paid manager of a nationalized enterprise, who for a time will receive interest on his capital. Later, however, this interest will decrease and gradually disappear altogether. This process is known in China as the socialist transformation of the capitalist sector.

In the case of Poland and the other European People's Democracies, two periods should be distinguished. The first of these was based, indeed, on notions very similar to those which at present apply in China. These notions consisted in the subordination of the capitalist sector and its gradual transformation into socialist enterprises. This was the policy of neutralizing the bourgeois section and even of taking it over. This became possible thanks to the link between the power won by the working class and the act of national liberation, i.e. the expulsion of the German forces of occupation. On such a platform it was possible to make a nation-wide appeal for support of the new people's government. This policy was applied more or less until 1949. Afterwards there followed a radical change in favour of accepting the Soviet formula of eliminating the capitalist sector, which in Poland was to a large degree extended to even the small-scale handicrafts sector.

What determined this change? It was the result of increased tension in the international political situation, i.e., what is known as the "cold war", and the contemplation of the growing possibility of real war. This entailed all sorts of consequences, *inter alia*, a revision of the six-year plan and the building up of the armaments industry. This also had its effects on the capitalist sector. It was feared that, if the situation were to deteriorate further, this sector would become hostile, holding up the economic advance of the people's rule; and it was, after all, impossible to leave control of part of the national economy in the hands of elements opposed to socialism.

The second factor (which is connected with the first) was the mechanical imitation of the Soviet model. In Russia, however, the decision on the fate of the capitalist sector in favour of the policy of eliminating it, was made in completely different conditions. There, as we have already mentioned, the whole bourgeoisie during the civil war was on the opposing side, and there was, therefore, at that time no other possible alternative.

A further task for socialist rule is the integration of small-scale production—especially farmers and craftsmen—within the socialist economy, followed by its socialist transformation. Classical Marxists, and especially Engels, have already pointed to this course which was further developed by Lenin. It consists in nationalizing small-scale production by forming it into co-operatives. Engels wrote about this when discussing the peasant question in France and Germany. Lenin's great co-operative plan, which was later put into operation in the Soviet Union, was based on just this idea.

As regards small-scale production, it is clearly impossible to apply the principle of either expropriation or elimination, for it is production by allies of the working class. In small-scale production, the formation of co-operatives facilitates the transformation of private into socialist property. This is one form of such transformation. However, this has serious consequences, the full extent of which the classical Marxists did not realize, and which were fully revealed only in the Soviet Union. The fact is that, alongside nationalized socialist State ownership, there arises a second form of socialist ownership—co-operative, group ownership. This ownership of the means of production is of a socialist nature. It is not, however, ownership by the nation in general—it is narrower than this.

Thus, in the process of constructing socialism, co-operative ownership appears alongside socialist State ownership. This inherits the old co-operatives which formed under capitalism and which were then partly working-class co-operatives, protecting the working class within a limited area from capitalist exploitation, partly peasant and *petit bourgeois* co-operatives, and sometimes even small capitalist co-operatives. The old co-operatives are absorbed in the process of forming new, socialist co-operatives as a new mode of socialist ownership of the means of production.

As a result of all these transformations, it becomes possible to establish the planned economy which is an essential component of the socialist system. The basis of a planned economy is the socialist State sector, for it contains the key positions of the national economy, the whole of which can then be planned and influenced by various direct or indirect means. To this is added State control of the capitalist sector and the various means by which the State can exercise its power over the small-scale sector. The possibility of planning the economy strengthens the development of co-operatives, particularly in agricultural production, trade, and so on.

*

It so happened, and not by chance, that the first socialist rule, the first socialist revolution, occurred not in the most developed, but in underdeveloped, countries where capitalism had earlier shown itself incapable of further developing its productive forces; hence the additional problems which had to be solved, the additional tasks which arose in the underdeveloped countries after the working class had won political power. They resulted from the fact that the sector which was nationalized by the revolution, and which was the basis of the socialist sector, was relatively weak, since capitalism in these countries was also weak. The nationalization of large capital, of banks and even, as in Russia, of all industry, created only a small socialist island in the great sea of the peasantry, the *petite bourgeoisie* and, partly, the small capitalists, too. The newly created socialist sector was in a difficult position, and it was not easy for it to influence and control the whole economic life.

Moreover, the revolution was made in conditions of poorly developed productive forces for capitalism had not performed its historical task of expanding them. When Marx and Engels wrote about socialist revolution, when the working-class movement of the nineteenth and early twentieth centuries had such a revolution as its aim, it was assumed that it would come about first of all in those countries where capitalism was more advanced, and consequently that the task of developing the productive forces would have already been carried out by capitalism. It was, however, to be the task of the socialist revolution to carry out social transformations, to remove the capitalist restrictions which at a certain stage made it difficult to further develop the productive forces. But in Russia and in other countries where revolutions took place the situation was different. It laid upon the revolution the tasks which capitalism had not solved. There first had to be an anti-feudal agrarian revolution, as part of the proletarian revolution. This anti-feudal agrarian revolution was the result of the alliance between the working class and the peasantry, and satisfied the hopes of the peasant masses, but it was also an economic necessity. It was essential to abolish the restraints created by a system even older than capitalism, which even held up the development of capitalism itself.

*

This was the significance of the agrarian revolution which took place. After this revolution and the simultaneous creation of a socialist ·sector by expropriation of large and medium capital, two tasks arose: *socialist industrialization and modernization of agriculture.*

The old capitalist countries have been industrialized by capitalism, and hence, the task of industrialization would not arise, for example, in Germany, England, or France. In Russia, however, this became the main task of the new government. Thus, the first successful socialist revolution was confronted with a historical task which heretofore appeared to be the task of capitalism and not of socialism. Alongside this task there arose the problem of modernizing agriculture, which was exceptionally backward, and its modernization was a necessary condition of industrialization. It is impossible to industrialize if agriculture does not produce adequate surpluses of commodities to maintain the growing non-agricultural population as a result of industrialization. It is essential to raise productivity and output in agriculture. On the other hand, agricultural productivity and output can only be raised by industrialization, which provides agriculture with tools, machines, fertilizers, electricity, etc.

Industrialization and the building up of a modern agriculture are closely connected. These are the new specific tasks which confronted socialist rule in the Soviet Union and which arise in all developing countries, including Poland. The main difficulty in this sector is to find the necessary means, for industrialization and modernization of agriculture require capital accumulation.

There are three sources of accumulation: (1) profits from the socialist sector. The more this sector is expanded, the greater the means which are accumulated for further industrialization. The expropriation of large-scale capital, transport and banks, and the inheritance of the old State owned capitalist legacy, formed the first basis of the socialist sector, the profits of which could be used for accumulation. Every new socialist enterprise makes it easier to construct further ones. (2) Taxation of the peasantry, e.g. in the form of compulsory deliveries. The peasantry, having received land as a result of the agricultural reform, were to contribute to the process of socialist industrialization. (3) Various forms of direct levy on the population by means of taxes, loans, etc.

These are the three main sources of socialist accumulation which constitute the basis of socialist industrialization and modernization of agriculture by mechanization, electrification, etc.

In this connection there arose a whole series of new, special problems. For example, it appeared in the Soviet Union that the process of socialist industrialization required accelerated socialist reconstruction of agriculture. Speed in the process of industrialization requires a rapid expansion of agricultural production for the market. In these circumstances, it becomes more important to achieve greater market production than to increase agricultural production in general, for a large quantity of agricultural products must be provided for the maintenance of the working class. In the case of the Soviet Union, the rapid socialization of agriculture also made it easier for the latter to contribute to accumulation. The socialization of agriculture facilitated the collection of compulsory deliveries which in this vast country would otherwise have been impossible with scattered private agricultural holdings.

The role of accelerated socialization of agriculture in the process of socialist industrialization appears even more clearly in China, where people's communes have been created and are expanding. The smaller the economic role of industry in the initial period, the more must accumulation be based on agriculture and the greater the significance of socialization of agriculture for socialist industrialization. This significance is smaller, the greater the development of industry and the more industry is the principal source of socialist accumulation.

The policy of socialist construction in general, and in conditions of developing countries in particular, where there arise the additional tasks of socialist industrialization and rapid modernization of agriculture, requires a high degree of centralization in the direction and management of the national economy. Such centralization is required above all when revolutionary transformations are being pursued, such as the expropriation of large- and medium-scale capital, control over the remaining capitalist sector, and the struggle (which goes on everywhere) for control of the small-scale sector. Without central control it is impossible to ensure for the socialist sector a decisive, guiding role, and it is also impossible to ensure that the capitalist sector will not be a source of constant opposition, will not dominate the small-scale sector, and will not mobilize it against the socialist sector and the socialist State organs. Without central control it is impossible to carry out socialist industrialization, which requires concentrating all the means of production on decisive, chosen investments in fields which most contribute to the further development of the national economy.

Socialist countries have been or are passing to a greater or lesser extent through a phase of centralized control. Against this background, however, numerous deviations have since developed in many socialist countries, taking the form of bureaucracy and inflexibility in the administration of the national economy, accompanied by restrictions on the further development of productive forces. As a result of these deviations, a certain portion of the State and of the economic apparatus becomes a State within a State, carrying out its own policy. In Poland and in the Soviet Union, we are all familiar with these tendencies which have shown themselves, for example, in the setting up of a security apparatus over the Party and the State.

In these circumstances, new problems arose which made it necessary to retreat from excessive centralization, to ensure democratic control within the State, Party and economic apparatus, to set up direct workers' self-government in the form of national or other councils, to establish self-governing co-operatives and agricultural circles and to promote trade union activity in enterprises, as organs of social control. It became necessary to work out new, less centralized forms of directing and managing the national economy—forms which were to be based more on the initiative of workers or on local, professional initiative, in the enterprise and in industry as a whole. The course chosen varies from country to country, but in all of them there is a current of change in the forms of directing and managing the national economy and in making this a democratic process. It is happening not only in the Soviet Union, Poland, Czechoslovakia and in the other People's Democracies, but even in China.

New organizational forms of the national economy are beginning to take shape. The organizational form of a national economy is not something which is fixed once and for all. The social content of the socialist economy is fixed once and for all: the socialist ownership of the means of production and the socialist management of economic activity, so as to satisfy the needs of society, and not to ensure profits for some particular class or section of society. However, these organizational forms change. They are different at different stages of development of the socialist economy and they are different in different countries, depending on historical conditions. Briefly, one may say that, together with the development of the productive forces of the socialist society, the socialist production relations take on more and more these new organizational forms.

The superstructure of management of the socialist economy and the control of its development also change extensively. At a certain stage the inflexible, excessively centralized system of management begins to burst, due to the development of the productive forces. The departure from previous methods of management is then connected also with the development of these productive forces. The greater the development of a given economy, the more difficult it is to manage it by centralized methods. The more initiative is curbed, the greater are the disadvantages of centralism as compared with its advantages. Increased productive forces and the number and variety of enterprises are factors which compel reforms in the economic model. We do indeed have here the adaptation of organizational forms to the development of productive forces. Socialism as a living system continually develops, changes and adapts itself to new conditions. It adapts the organization of socialist relations in production and, even more, its economic base and the organization and forms of management, to the level of productive forces.

These changes point to the crystallization and maturing of socialism as a system. The forms of highly centralized direction and management belong to the transitional period and are the product of the requirements of this period. They are characterized by the use of non-economic means,

means of non-economic coercion and political persuasion and propaganda rather than by the normal functioning of economic laws. This is a typical feature which is characteristic of the transitional period, in which the new socialist economy does not grow spontaneously from capitalism, but is the conscious, planned creation of the socialist State.

Political revolution leads to the transformation of the social and economic structure into a socialist State; dictatorship of the proletariat is the motor whereby the socio-economic structure is transformed. This means that the transformation is achieved to a large extent by means of non-economic coercion, and above all by the expropriation of the capitalists, by agricultural reform, and so on. But at the same time the socialist State organizes, regulates, appeals to the consciousness of the working class and uses a whole range of non-economic, legal, administrative and propaganda means. These are, and must be, predominant in the transitional period. Moreover, these means gain particular significance in the conditions of a developing country, which is faced with the task of socialist industrialization and modernization of agriculture.

As the new socialist society matures, however, the role of these means diminishes. They can even become a brake on the rational economy. It is for this reason that are made the changes which we see today throughout the whole socialist world, as well as the search for new methods of directing and managing the socialist economy, for new "models" based on the internal forces of the socialist economy rather than on means of non-economic compulsion. From the nature of things, this process assumes different forms at different stages in different countries, but its direction is on the whole the same everywhere. The more mature the new socialist structure, the less it needs the help of non-economic coercion by the State, the more it stands on its own feet and is based on the operation of economic laws.

It may be said that, when non-economic coercion as a means of directing and managing the socialist economy is no longer necessary, when this economy is "prepared" and is based on the operation of its own economic laws which, through the direction of the national economy are skilfully used to realize consciously determined social aims—when these conditions are met, then the transitional period comes to an end. Thus, the end of the transitional period is the end of the period of the construction of

socialism, the end of the period in which the revolutionary State of proletarian dictatorship eliminates the old production relations by means of
non-economic coercion, forms socialist relations of production, and
organizes the economy on these new relations.

It is difficult to define precisely just when this occurs; it is a gradual
process and often lasts a long time. One can only say that it requires the
consolidation and generalization of socialist ownership of the means of
production, at least in so far as the economic laws resulting from socialist
production relations are fully operative, and the non-socialist relations
of production which still exist play only a peripheral role, their further
absorption by the socialist economy being carried out by purely economic
means.

This raises the question of the fate of the small-scale sector in the
process of forming the socialist economy. In the Soviet Union, the
socialist transformation of the small-scale sector was carried out particularly rapidly. The capitalist sector was liquidated during the civil war,
and rapid mass collectivization followed. The NEP was weak, and the
extrusion of capitalist elements did not present great difficulties.

This problem is considerably more difficult to solve in Poland where,
from the point of view of the construction of socialism, we have not
even solved to the present day the problem of agriculture. But this is
only one part of the problem. In the specific conditions of the Soviet
Union it was necessary to liquidate rapidly every non-socialist structure,
even the small-scale. This need arose on economic as well as political
grounds. In conditions different from those in the Soviet Union, there
is no need for such a rapid transformation of small-scale ownership into
socialist production. In conditions where the socialist sector constitutes
the greater force, where it dominates the national economy from the
very beginning, there is no need for such haste. The greater importance
which industry has in the economy from the very start means that it
provides the greater part of accumulation. Industrialization is from the
beginning based largely on internal accumulation of the rapidly growing
socialist industries, and with growing industrialization agriculture is
gradually drawn into the orbit of the socialist economy. The position
of the socialist sector in the national economy—a dominant position
from the outset—means that there is less danger that the small-scale
sector will become a point of support for hostile social and political
forces. In such conditions, the primary consideration is likely to be not

to hold up the normal process of production, and not to weaken the alliance with the peasantry and *petite bourgeoisie*. This is the basic difference between the situation of the Soviet Union in the period of revolution and Poland.

In other countries this question may be framed differently. At the last Congress of the Italian Communist Party, Comrade Togliatti said that it was difficult to foresee when the small-scale economy would cease to exist. For, if the Italian road to socialism depends upon an alliance with the middle strata of society in the towns and countryside, and if the people's rule is not going to carry out a policy of forcing them to change to socialist forms of production, it is an open question as to whether small-scale producers, small-scale craftsmen, and the remaining merchants, will want to form co-operatives or continue working privately.

It may be asked whether the small-scale structure will be a permanent component of the socialist economy as it was in the capitalist economy. This is not very likely. The small-scale structure lasted in capitalism because it was a safeguard against and a refuge from the proletariat. There will be no such motive under socialism. As the socialist economy develops, it will pay less and less to persist in inefficient small-scale production, and the advantages of being linked to the socialist economy, e.g., by co-operatives, will increase. The stronger the development of the productive forces, the sooner this will come about. The socialist State holds decisive means of directing the economy, and if small-scale production continues for some time, it will not impede the construction of socialism. The country's economic development is decided by the large socialist sector which dominates the national economy. Sooner or later the peasant and *petit bourgeois* elements will reach the conclusion that it is in their interests to join the socialist economy. Just when this will happen, however, is difficult to foresee.

In certain cases, as in the Soviet Union, it is possible to set definite dates to mass collectivization in agriculture, and to the results of socialist industrialization. In other cases, e.g. Italy, this transition will be gradual and very slow. It is essential that the socialist sector should, after a certain time, cover almost the whole national economy, and that what remains of the small-scale sector should be reduced to a role which socially, politically or economically is no more than that of a mere relic.

In this way, the socialist economy gradually matures. As it ceases to be based on non-economic coercion, and more and more on the operation of its true economic laws, with the disappearance of the remaining more important elements of non-socialist production relations, the transitional period of socialist construction gradually comes to an end.

LENIN'S THEORY OF REVOLUTION
AND THE ECONOMICALLY LESS DEVELOPED
COUNTRIES

Evaluating today Lenin's theory in historical perspective, it may be said that it reveals the greatness and originality, as well as the fundamental validity, of his theory.

Lenin substantially developed the work of Marx and Engels both in the field of theory and of revolutionary practice of the working-class movement. He has made the greatest contribution to the theory of this movement since the times of Marx and Engels.

This contribution has many aspects and is extremely wide and varied. Two main problems emerge: imperialism and world-wide socialist revolution. These two problems are closely connected with one another. It may be said that the analysis of imperialism provided Lenin with a starting-point for a new approach to the problem of socialist revolution.

The originators of scientific socialism considered it natural, in a sense, that socialism should succeed first of all in the leading capitalist countries, i.e. in the most highly developed capitalist countries. It is in these countries too, they asserted, that the contradictions of the capitalist system are most acute. Having succeeded in the leading, most highly developed capitalist countries, socialism was, according to Marx and Engels, to shed light from these to the economically and socially less developed parts of the world. In this way, the economically less developed countries were to develop further, under the influence of successful socialism of the most highly developed capitalist countries, which meant in practice the countries of Western Europe and the United States of America.

Engels most clearly expressed this idea of the order of development of social structures on a world-wide scale, in a letter to Karol Kautsky in 1882. It is worth quoting extracts from this letter:

"In my opinion, the colonies proper, i.e. the countries occupied by a European population—Canada, the Cape, Australia—will all become independent; on the other hand the countries inhabited by a native population, which are simply subjugated—India, Algeria, the Dutch, Portuguese and Spanish possessions—must be taken over for the time being by the proletariat and led as rapidly as possible towards independence. How this process will develop is difficult to say."

Engels continues: "Once Europe and North America are reorganized, they will form such a colossal power and furnish such an example that the semi-civilized countries will follow in our wake of their own accord. Economic needs alone will be responsible for this. But as to what social and political phases these countries will then have to pass through before they likewise arrive at socialist organization, we today can only advance rather idle hypotheses, I think. One thing alone is certain: the victorious proletariat can force no blessings of any kind upon any foreign nation without undermining its own victory by so doing".[1]

This was the view of Marx and Engels. As we know, history took a different course. Socialism was first victorious in Russia, an economically underdeveloped country, and subsequently in other countries, the majority of which also belong to the category of less developed countries. Lenin was the first to foresee such a course of history and on the basis of such a prognosis—a prognosis which history has wholly confirmed— he formulated the theory of the victory of socialism on a world-wide scale.

What happened between the time when Marx and Engels, and particularly the latter, made the prognosis quoted above, and the time of Lenin's appearance with a new conception of the process of transition from capitalism to socialism on a world-wide scale? One thing occurred: the transition of capitalism from the phase of free competition to that of monopoly and imperialism. This was a new development which Marx and Engels did not experience, though it was to a large extent foreseen by them. This was a new development which required further and thorough elaboration of the Marxist analysis of capitalism and of the transition from capitalism to socialism. Lenin formulated and elaborated these new concepts, and that is why we say today that the theoretical foundation of our movement and Party is the theory of Marxism–Leninism. Lenin's name was added to that of Marx to denote the whole theory of social development on which the contemporary revolutionary working-class movement is based.

---

[1] K. Marx and F. Engels, *Selected Works*, Vol. 2, Lawrence and Wishart, pp. 665–666, London, 1942.

The analysis of imperialism was the basis of Lenin's development of Marxist theory. Already before this, from the end of the nineteenth and beginning of the twentieth centuries, imperialism had begun to attract the attention of the working-class movement. If we trace the history of the Second International, we see that the problem of imperialism, and particularly the problem of the danger of an imperialist war, becomes increasingly clear. Finally, in 1912 at the Basle Congress, the International passed the famous resolution on the task of the working class in the event of an outbreak of war. This resolution stated that war must be averted by all possible means. If, however, war were to break out, the proletariat should use the resulting social and political crisis to shake the foundations of the capitalist system and to hasten its downfall. The Social Democrats, however, later betrayed this resolution. Even so, it became the foundation of the struggle against imperialist war, and made the revolutionary section of the working-class movement gravitate more and more around Lenin and the Bolshevik Party.

In theoretical Marxist literature, too, imperialism began to be a subject of analysis. In 1910 Hilferding published his work *Das Finanzkapital*, in which the last chapter is devoted to the question of imperialism. In 1913 Rosa Luxemburg published her famous book on capital accumulation with the subtitle *A Contribution to the Theory of Imperialism*. Without going here into an appraisal of these works, it should be noted that they show that the working-class movement had become aware of the problem of imperialism. Only Lenin, however, in his work *Imperialism, the Highest Stage of Capitalism*, written in 1916, analysed not only the socio-economic foundations, but also the political consequences of contemporary imperialism, as well as its influence on the revolutionary strategy and tactics of the working-class movement. Lenin's work on imperialism thus became the starting-point for a new evaluation of the political situation of world-wide capitalism, and for a new approach to the problem of the transition from capitalism to socialism. Lenin's analysis of imperialism leads to the Leninist theory of world-wide socialist revolution.

What are the basic ideas of Lenin's theory of the world-wide victory of socialism over capitalism? As a result of imperialism, by which the whole world was submitted to the economic domination of the leading capitalist monopolies and the political domination of the leading capitalist States, the problem of socialist revolution became a world-wide problem. This is no longer just a problem for each country on its own, nor even for just Europe or North America. The inter-connections of the whole world economy created by the imperialist system are so far-reaching, that the problem of revolution becomes a problem not of the end of capitalism in the abstract, but the concrete problem of abolishing the capitalist system and all its consequences both in the leading capitalist countries and in the subjugated countries, whether colonial, semi-colonial or otherwise dependent on the leading imperialist powers.

Lenin's analysis of imperialism led him to his conclusion on the marked increase in the uneven development of the capitalist world during this period. From this uneven development, expressed by Lenin in his analysis of imperialism, it follows that socialism can prevail at first in one or a few countries, but that it is unlikely to prevail throughout the whole world simultaneously. In 1915 Lenin wrote in his article The United States of Europe Slogan:

"Uneven economic and political development is an absolute law of capitalism. Hence, the victory of socialism is possible, first in a few or even in one single capitalist country."[2]

In which kind of capitalist country? Not necessarily in a highly developed one, according to Lenin. It may happen in a capitalist country in which the contradictions of the capitalist system reach the greatest tension; and Lenin maintained that this may be, and even probably will be, a less developed capitalist country, where the contradictions of the feudal system which has still not been abolished completely together with the possible contradictions arising from the given country's international position, may intensify the contradictions of capitalism. Russia was just such a country.

When the revolution broke out in Russia, many old Social Democrats, brought up in the spirit of bygone expectations—they formed the greater part of the Second International—asked, "How is socialism to begin in backward Russia?", Lenin answered them:

"Infinitely commonplace, for instance, is the argument they learned by rote during the development of West European Social Democracy, that we are not yet ripe for Socialism; that, as certain of the 'learned' gentlemen among them express it, we lack the objective economic premises for Socialism in our country."

---

[2] V. I. Lenin, *Selected Works*, Vol. 5, Lawrence and Wishart, p. 141, London, 1936.

He goes on: "But what if the peculiar situation drew Russia into the world imperialist war in which every more or less influential West European country was involved; what if the peculiar situation brought her development to the verge of the revolutions that were maturing, and had partly already begun in the East at a time when conditions enabled us to combine the 'peasant war' with the working-class movement, which no less a 'Marxist' than Marx himself, in 1856, suggested as a possible prospect for Prussia?"[3]

This was what Lenin wrote in 1923 in his paper *Our Revolution*. Developing this prospect—now already based on the concrete experience of the victory of the socialist revolution in Russia—Lenin comes to a further conclusion on the significance of two factors for the victory of the socialist revolution: first, the significance of the peasant masses as an ally of the revolutionary working class, and secondly, that of the anti-imperialist movements of national liberation.

It may be said that in the period of the Second International, social democracy lost sight of the question of allies for the working class—a question which played a large role in the thoughts of Marx and Engels. *The Communist Manifesto* raises the problem of an alliance between the working class and the progressive sections of the bourgeoisie, the problem of transforming the bourgeois-democratic revolution into a socialist one. And subsequently, various papers by Marx and Engels raise the question of an alliance between the working class and the peasantry, which Marx wrote about in 1956 as quoted here by Lenin. The industrialization of Germany, France and other countries, together with the increase in the numbers of the working classes in the leading capitalist countries, gradually led, as far as the Marxists of those days were concerned, to the disappearance of the problem of allies for the working class. Instead of this, the view was put forward that capitalism would eliminate the middle strata of society and the structure of class forces would be increasingly polarized around two classes only: the bourgeoisie and the proletariat. It was thought that the proletariat coming to form, in time the majority of the population, would itself, without allies, overthrow the domination of the bourgeoisie. This view, put forward by Kautsky in later years, was also held by Rosa Luxemburg and other leading Marxists of the period.

---

[3] V. I. Lenin, *Selected Works* (two-vol. ed.), vol. II, Lawrence and Wishart, pp. 837–838, London, 1947.

The new historical perspective presented by Lenin had necessarily to lead to a revision of this view. If the socialist revolution can succeed first of all in less developed countries, where the contradictions of capitalism are at work alongside those resulting from the remnants of the feudal system, then the peasant question arises—the question of an alliance between peasants and workers. The skill of the working class and its Party in leading the peasant masses becomes an essential in the strategy of social revolution. In this way, the question of a worker-peasant alliance was put forward as a practical problem, not only in the period of imperialist war, but earlier too.

We know the role which this problem plays in all Lenin's political papers. He held that the strategy of the revolution in Russia was one which was to a large extent based on the formation and revolutionary utilization of an alliance between the workers and the peasants. And alongside this alliance a second question was put forward—the national question, which plays a large role in the theory of Marx and Engels. It played a similar role in the period of bourgeois–democratic revolutions and national-liberation movements in Western Europe. Later, social democracy also partly lost sight of this problem, since it was no longer found at the centre of social development in the countries of Western Europe.

Under Lenin, on the basis first of the experiences of the Russian revolution or of its preparation, and subsequently as a result of the significance which he ascribed to the anti-imperialist struggles of nations subjugated by imperialism, the national question again assumed its full significance, becoming one of the fundamental problems of the strategy and tactics of the socialist revolution. And in this national question, the struggle of the subjugated nations against imperialism became particularly important. The nations struggling for liberation become, according to Lenin, a natural ally in the struggle between the working class and the bourgeoisie in countries of advanced capitalism. Lenin was the first to draw attention to the world-wide importance of anti-imperialist national movements, to the fact that these movements arise and grow in strength, and that their historical role will increase.

At the third Congress of the Communist International in 1921, Lenin said: "With the beginning of the twentieth century there have been considerable changes in this respect, namely, millions and hundreds of millions—in fact, the overwhelming majority of mankind—appear now in the role of independent, active, revolutionary forces. And it is clearest of all that in the forthcoming decisive battles of world-wide revolution, the movement of the majority of mankind, striving at first for national liberation, will turn against capitalism and imperialism and will perhaps play a considerably greater revolutionary role than we think".[4]

Elsewhere, namely, in an article written in the same year, on the occasion of the tenth anniversary of *Pravda*, Lenin says:

"And India and China are in a turmoil. There are more than 700 million people there. They together with the population of the neighbouring Asian countries, where the situation is exactly the same, constitute over half the population of the globe. The year 1905 is irresistably and with increasing speed overtaking these countries, but with the important and colossal difference that in 1905 the revolution in Russia could still have been (at least at first) an isolated revolution, i.e., one which does not immediately draw other countries in its wake. The revolutions which are growing in India and China, however, have today already become part of the revolutionary struggle, part of the international revolutionary movement".[5]

They give rise to anti-imperialist alliance between national revolutions and the proletarian revolution of the advanced capitalist countries. According to Lenin, this alliance is decisive for the fate of world capitalism. Even earlier, during the 1917 war, in his article *A Caricature of Marxism and Imperialist Economism*, Lenin wrote: "The social revolution cannot come about except in the form of an epoch of proletarian civil war against the bourgeoisie in the advanced countries, combined with a whole series of democratic and revolutionary movements, including movements for national liberation, in the underdeveloped, backward and oppressed nations".[6]

Lenin condenses his idea into a formula thus: "Proletarian uprising against the bourgeoisie of its country, national uprisings in colonial and dependent countries."[7]

Revolutions of national liberation in colonial and dependent coun-

---

4 V. I. Lenin, *Sochinenya*, 4th ed., Vol. 32, pp. 457–458.

5 *Ibid.*, 4th ed., Vol. 33, p. 313.

6 V. I. Lenin, *Selected Works*, Vol. 5, Lawrence and Wishart, London, 1936, p. 296.

7 V. I. Lenin, *Sochinenya*, 4th ed., Vol. 30, p. 82.

tries, together with a revolutionary movement in countries with a highly developed capitalist economy, undermine the capitalist system, since the basis of contemporary capitalism is imperialism. In breaking up the imperialist system, they remove the base which prolongs the life of capitalism in the advanced capitalist countries by reducing the internal economic contradictions, and even by winning over part of the working class.

Lenin maintains that the Russian revolution plays a special role in this field. Tsarist Russia was not a country conquered by imperialism, but one which began, or tried to embark upon imperialist expansion and to move along the road of imperialism. But Russia differed from the leading imperialist countries by being a less developed country with feudal elements which checked economic growth. Russian imperialism was beyond the country's economic conditions and possibilities, and, moreover, Russia had herself become infiltrated and influenced by foreign capital. These two elements, coupled with the fact that the first socialist revolution broke out in Russia, accounted, according to Lenin, for Russia's special role as a link between the proletarian revolution, carried out in the leading capitalist countries and the national-liberation revolutions in countries subjugated by imperialism.

According to Lenin, the decisive element in the course of history is the fact that revolutionary Russia and the countries struggling for national liberation from imperialist domination, constitute the majority of the world population. In 1923, in one of his last works, *Better Fewer, but Better*, Lenin surveyed the world situation and the structure of social forces in the world. In this survey he says:

"In the last analysis, the upshot of the struggle will be determined by the fact that Russia, India, China, etc., account for the overwhelming majority of the population of the globe. And it is precisely this majority that, during the past few years, has been drawn into the struggle for emancipation with extraordinary rapidity, so that in this respect there cannot be the slightest shadow of doubt what the final outcome of the world struggle will be. In this sense, the complete victory of Socialism is fully and absolutely assured".[8] This, briefly, is Lenin's theory of world revolution.

---

[8] V. I. Lenin, *Selected Works* (two-vol. ed.), Vol. II, Lawrence and Wishart, London, 1947, p. 854.

This theory entails two consequences, which Lenin himself perceived, although it did not fall upon him to lead the way to the process which he foresaw. One consequence is: since socialism prevails first of all only in certain countries and not in all, it follows that a period of coexistence is necessary between countries with a socialist system and those with a capitalist system. This means that there must be a period of coexistence between two socio-economic systems, and this period of coexistence is a period of competition between them.

Tracing Soviet foreign policy in Lenin's life-time, we see what great importance he attached to the fact that the struggle between socialism and capitalism on a world-wide scale, in the form of coexistence between socialist and capitalist countries, should be peaceful rather than war-like. Lenin is thus the father of the contemporary doctrine and policy of the peaceful coexistence of the two systems. In this competition the Soviet Union, and perhaps the other countries in which socialism prevails, are at first economically less developed countries in which the majority of the population consists of peasants. This presents a new problem, namely of developing these countries on a socialist basis, by socialist construction. Lenin formulates this problem thus: these countries are backward, the majority of the population are peasants. How can socialism be built in these countries? How can they manage to survive against a hostile capitalist world?

Speaking of Russia, Lenin says in the article mentioned above, *Better Fewer, but Better*:

"If we see to it that the working class retains its leadership in relation to the peasantry, we shall be able, by exercising the greatest possible economy in the economic life of our state to use everything we save to develop our large-scale machine industry to develop electrification, for the hydraulic extraction of peat, to finish the construction of Volkhov-stroi, etc."

"In this, and this alone, lies our hope. Only when we have done this will we, speaking figuratively, be able to change horses, to change from the peasant, *muzhik* horse of poverty, from the horse of economy fit for a ruined peasant country, to the horse which the proletariat is seeking and cannot but seek—the horse of a large-scale machine building industry, of electrification, of Volkhovstroi, etc."[9]

---

[9] V. I. Lenin, *Selected Works* (two-vol. ed.), Vol. II, pp. 854–855.

There is here a clearly defined programme of industrialization based on socialist accumulation. Socialist industrialization proceeds on the political platform of an alliance between workers and peasants. This is the way to raise the productive forces in less developed countries in which the socialist revolution has won through. Along with socialist industrialization, agriculture is expanded by the development of co-operatives. Finally, there arises the need to carry out a great cultural revolution.

In reply to the Western European Social Democrats and the Mensheviks, Lenin said: "You say that we are backward and uncultured, but what does it matter to us that we must begin with the process of civilizing our country, of raising its cultural level? Must we wait till others do it for us? Is the proletariat not in a position to do this itself?"

In this way, then, Lenin crystallizes his programme for the construction of socialism in an underdeveloped country. This programme—Lenin has already launched the slogan—is one of catching up with the leading capitalist countries in the development of productive forces as well as in the level of culture. It is a programme of catching up with the intention of later outstripping them. This is how Lenin outlines with full clarity the directions of historical development.

The genius and validity of this conception is today fully visible in the perspective of historical experience. This conception has been further developed and in places supplemented. New historical experience called for a more accurate formulation of its various aspects. However, the basic elements of this conception of the development of socialism on a world-wide scale—the role of the national-liberation movements in countries subjugated by imperialism, the significance of the worker–peasant alliance, of socialist industrialization, of the development of co-operative forms of agriculture, of the cultural revolution, of the coexistence of the two systems and the competition between them, of the desirability that this competition should be of a peaceful nature—all these already appear clearly in Lenin's writings.

The transformation of the Soviet Union from a backward country into a leading industrial power, the successful Chinese revolution, the bourgeois–democratic and other revolutions—I would call them national–popular—which occurred in Asia and which are today occurring in Africa—all these events confirm the validity of what Lenin foresaw. These events also show the need for further developing Lenin's ideas on the necessity of accounting for peculiar and varied roles of the national bourgeoisie at different periods and in different countries, for the alliance in certain conditions between the working class and not only the peasantry, but also the *petite bourgeoisie* and the national bourgeoisie. Such development is called for by the specific features of anti-imperialist revolutions in countries which are so underdeveloped that they as yet have scarcely any bourgeoisie. These problems require further illumination and thorough examination by Marxists, but based on Leninist assumptions.

I am not going to discuss any of these problems here, but I should like to draw attention to one point. Let us compare this historical development, and Lenin's prognosis which anticipated it, with the conception of Marx and Engels as expressed by Engels' letter quoted above. At first sight, these conceptions are very different and, indeed, they do differ. The leading theoreticians of Marxism from the period of the Second International, such as Kautsky, Plekhanov, Guedes and others, clung tightly to the old conception. This rendered them incapable of understanding the enormous significance of the October Revolution. Today, however, with the Soviet Union transformed into a leading industrial world power, with socialism successfully established in the European countries of the People's Democracies, with the construction of socialism, including the vast Chinese nation, and several other Asian countries, this first conception of Engels again assumes a certain topical interest. The crux of this conception is that the socialist countries lead the way and shed light for the less developed parts of the world. For some time, due to the advent of imperialism, all the results of which could not be foreseen by Marx and Engels, the historical situation has been changing. But the situation is again approaching the stage discussed by Engels in his letter.

The socialist countries, and especially the Soviet Union, are no longer backward, but count among the leading industrial countries of the world. In this new position, they and their social system have begun to lead the way for the less-developed parts of the world, as Engels foresaw. We see today the role played by the Soviet Union and other European socialist countries in the growth of the developing countries of Asia and Africa. And this role is both political and economic.

The existence of a socialist power, i.e. of the Soviet Union, and of the power of the socialist bloc constitutes a protective wall, sheltering the newly liberated countries from renewed subjugation by imperialism·

This facilitates the liberation process from imperialist domination in other countries. This is the political illumination shed by the Soviet Union and the whole socialist bloc. In addition, economic and technical illumination is growing in strength. The great role which Soviet economic and technical aid today plays in the industrialization of the countries of Asia and Africa is well known.

The notion of an economically highly developed country is not, therefore, today synonymous with the notion of a capitalist country, as it still was not so long ago. This creates a new situation in the world. The example of the development of socialist countries, together with the political, economic and technical aid which they give, strengthens the socialist forces, the progressive forces, and the anti-imperialist forces in general in the Asian and African countries of today. We are now near to the situation which Marx foresaw, namely, that socialism in these economically highly developed countries would shed light upon the rest of the world and would help the socially and economically less developed nations to find a progressive path of development. To this we are rapidly drawing near, and in this way the old conception of Engels will again come into its own.

Finally, as far as it is possible to extrapolate development into the future, the following remarks may be made. The socialist countries' importance in the world economy will grow more and more. It is forecast that in 1965 half of world output will be produced within the framework of socialist methods of production. Thus Engels' conception will become even nearer reality, that is, economic progress will for the developing countries clearly be synonymous with socialism. We shall then indeed be able to say that, as Engels foretold, the socialist countries are economically the most developed countries in the world. This makes it easier for the rest of the world to find progressive and, ultimately, socialist solutions to its problems.

Rapid economic and technical development will be significant not only for those countries which are at present economically less developed, but also, increasingly, for the countries which are at present in the van of capitalist economic development. Already today there are growing fears in these countries of being left behind as a result of the rapid economic development of the socialist countries, for they are faced by the threat of becoming economically less developed in comparison with the socialist countries, as a result of being run by an obsolete socio-economic system, which capitalism will increasingly appear to be. Just as Spain became backward in relation to the capitalist countries by holding on to an obsolete feudal structure, so those capitalist countries which are today in the lead may be left behind in relation to the socialist countries. This new situation will mobilize the progressive social forces in the capitalist countries, particularly the working class, to the struggle for a socialist path of development.

Thus Lenin's theory of the paths of transition from capitalism to socialism will become of increasing topical interest also for those countries which are today still at the summit of the capitalist world.

LUDWIK KRZYWICKI—THEORIST
OF HISTORICAL MATERIALISM

Historical materialism as a theory which explains social development in a uniform way, and which formulates the causal mechanism of this development in definite laws, has found many distinguished followers in Poland. Names such as Stanisław Krusiński, Edward Abramowski, Kazimierz Krauz and Stanisław Brzozowski are evidence of this. Prominent among them is Ludwik Krzywicki, editor of the first Polish translation of Marx's *Capital*, and the first scholar in Poland who began to apply systematically the Marxist method in his work. It was with this work that Krzywicki introduced historical materialism into Polish research.

Equipped with a wide knowledge of economics, history, ethnology and anthropology, he handled an enormous amount of factual material which, with the help of the theory of historical materialism, he arranged into a systematic whole, thereby showing the extreme fruitfulness of this method. There have been in Poland many instances of a brilliant and original approach to historical materialism. Krauz and Abramowski are among these, each in his own way enriching the theory with his achievements. But it is to Ludwik Krzywicki that historical materialism in Poland owes its synthetic approach, the confrontation of theory with extremely rich factual material, and extensive application to sociology, ethnology and the history of culture. Krzywicki is, however, not only the author of a systematic exposition of historical materialism and of the numerous applications of this theory to sociology, ethnology and the history of culture, he has enriched the theory by linking it to an analysis of the operation of the anthropological factors of social life and by a fine analysis of the "migration" of ideas. All this makes Krzywicki not only the most outstanding representative of historical materialism in Poland, but sets him on a par with the most distinguished of the European exponents of the theory who were his contemporaries. As a theorist of historical materialism, Krzywicki stands on a par with Kautsky, Plekhanov, Mehring, Cunow and Labriola.

Krzywicki gives a systematic exposition of historical materialism in his *Idea a życie* (Idea and Life). His first article on the subject was published in 1884 in the socialist journal *Walka klas* (The Class Struggle),[1] and in 1888 he developed the problem further in a monthly supplement to the *Przegląd Tygodniowy* (Weekly Review). In 1891 there appeared in *Pravda* a symposium in honour of Aleksander Świętochowski's twenty-five years of work; this was to some extent a continuation of the article called *Rodowód idei społecznych* (The Genealogy of Social Ideas). The *Wędrówka idei* (Migration of Ideas) appeared in *Pravda* in 1897, and in the same year, an article *Przeżytki* (Relics) in Warsaw Library. These papers provide an exposition of all Krzywicki's views on the causal mechanism of social development. All these articles, revised and slightly supplemented by the author, were reprinted in a book called *Studia socjologiczne* (Sociological Studies).[2] Apart from this, Krzywicki also wrote some lesser works on historical materialism.[3] Of these it is especially worth mentioning the concise presentation of the theory of social development which appeared in Social Development among Animals and Human Beings (Rozwój społeczny wśród zwierząt i u rodzaju ludzkiego), contained in the fourth volume of the publication *Świat i Człowiek* (The World and Man).[4] I do not mention works dealing with the application of historical materialism to particular problems since these applications form nearly the whole of Krzywicki's work.[5]

I

Examining the origins of the social bond, Krzywicki relates sociology to biology. Society as "an organization for mutual protection, giving each of its participants the prospect of a longer life and of a more favourable

---

[1] Materialistyczne pojmowanie dziejów ludzkości (A Materialistic Interpretation of the History of Mankind), *The Class Struggle*, No. 6, 1884, pp. 6–8, cf., *Dzieła* (Works), vol. V, pp. 169–174, Warsaw, 1958.

[2] *Studia socjologiczne* (Sociological Studies), pp. viii+344, Warsaw, 1923.

[3] A bibliography of these works is given in *Studia socjologiczne*, pp. 305–306.

[4] Rozwój społeczny wśród zwierząt i u rodzaju ludzkiego (Social Development among the Animals and the Mankind) (*Świat i Człowiek* (The World and Man), Book IV, Warsaw, 1913)—cited below as Rozwój społeczny (Social Development).

[5] Of these works there should, however, be mentioned the interesting study Rozwój moralności (The Development of Morality), included in the fourth issue of the publication *Świat i Człowiek* (The World and Man), *ed. cit.* In this study Krzywicki applies the theory of historical materialism to a problem as difficult as the development of morality.

endurance in the struggle for existence",[6] is characteristic not only of the human species, but is met also in the animal world. Human society and animal groups "are a continuation of this same line of development which at its lowest levels formed organic groups of units, and from these groups, organisms".[7] Recognizing this fact Krzywicki's theory is distinct from those sociological theories which treat society as an organism.[8] For these theories only lead to the fruitless use of biological terminology to denote sociological phenomena instead of leading to a concrete analysis of the nature of the social bond, which is an essential task of sociology. Now, according to Krzywicki, "human societies have emerged from the social bonds characteristic of the animal world, and the binding social links of the primitive human group are also derived in the same way".[9]

These binding social links are, says Krzywicki, maternal feelings, the sex instinct and, growing from this, paternal feelings, together with the herd instinct which is the quintessence of the brother–sister relationship. Beyond all this, however, the social bond among men is more particularly based on the consciousness of a certain social purpose.[10]

The existence of the *consciousness of a social purpose* is a characteristic feature of the social bond among men. In a more-developed society this consciousness is in the nature of a social *idea*. Consequently, the examination of the origins of the development and operation of social ideas is the fundamental problem of sociology. Human society is a collection of individuals whose behaviour is directed by certain ideas. Thus, the analysis of social phenomena amounts to the examination of three problems, namely: how these ideas arise and what determines their content; by what mechanism the ideas are spread; and finally, what is the predisposition of a particular individual to react to the given ideas. The first question is the subject of historical materialism as the theory of social development; the second is the subject of the psychology of communal life; and the third belongs to anthropology.[11]

---

[6] Rozwój społeczny (Social Development), p. 3. (In *Świat i Człowiek* (The World and Man), *ed. cit.*)

[7] *Ibid.*, p. 14.

[8] *Ibid.*, p. 14.

[9] *Ibid.*, p. 38.

[10] *Ibid.*, pp. 15–27.

[11] See the article Istota zdarzenia społecznego (The Essence of Social Events) in *Studia Socjologiczne* (Sociological Studies), *ed. cit.*

Apart from the consciousness of social purpose, human society also differs from animal groups by the existence of *binding links through objects*, which arise from man's use of tools and the division of labour associated with this. By the use of tools, man has become independent of the direct influence of the natural environment, and has created for himself an artificial environment which mediated between him and his natural one. Thus, whereas animal societies live under the direct influence of surrounding nature, the development of human society is influenced by the development of this artificial environment, of these binding links through objects which emerge between man and nature. These binding links through objects constitute the historical attainment of human societies, and their absence is the reason for the non-historical nature of animal groups. These binding links, however, begin to play a decisive role from the moment of the breakup of the clan system and the transition to the territorial organization of societies.

The breakup of the clan system was a result of the transition to a settled way of life. This slowly loosened the bonds of the clan and eventually created a new social organization: the *territorial system*. The transition from the clan to the territorial system was, in Krzywicki's opinion, one of the greatest breaksthrough made by human society in its historical development.[12] As a result of this breakthrough, the ties through objects became the foundation of the social bond. The immediacy of the bond among individuals is broken. Objects creep into relations among people, and these relations become the result of people's relations to the objects. Krzywicki illustrates this with several graphic examples. "If we consult the Land Registry in any town", he says, "what do we find? Enormous registers serially numbered, each of which represents a house. On examining the contents of these registers, we find that they record the mortgages and obligations of each house, i.e. they show its past and present condition. The names of the owners and creditors change, but the register remains as unchanged as the house. The people, insofar as their names appear in this mortgage register, are only living representatives of an inanimate object, namely, of the house and of the capital lent on it; they are, in a sense, something of a tag, such as we place round a bottle of wine".[13] Or another example. Let us take a railway

---

[12] See Rozwój kultury materialnej, więzi społecznej i poglądu na świat (The Development of Material Culture, of Social Bonds and of Views on the World) (*Świat i Człowiek*, No. III, p. 93, Warsaw, 1912).

station. "There must be someone in the booking office at the appropriate time, someone else must weigh the luggage or keep track of the train, there must be others to drive the engine, check the coaches, and operate the telegraph.... Each person is, as it were, a living adjunct of this or that inanimate object—the train, the booking office, the warehouse. This group of people, together with the entire railway line, form a single whole: their activities cannot be understood without bearing in mind the timetable, the way in which the trains operate, and the movement of goods".[14] This bond through objects, which is the basis of the organization of a territorial society, also influences the way in which people think. Krzywicki says: "We feel sympathy with the peasant who has gone off to some celebration or to the fair. Deep in his mind he has the vision of his cottage with its thatched roof, which he has left for a while, and he worries in case it is on fire, or his cow dies, or an approaching storm destroys his crops".[15] In a territorial society the interests and views of the individual are determined by the relation between him and some object. The shareholders of a railway company have different interests in and views of the railways from those of the workers employed by the company. Thus, a territorial system is "an organization of people through the medium of objects".[16] In this system the consciousness of social aims—that is, social ideas—is closely connected with the nature of the relations through objects, which form the basis of the social bond. The laws governing the development of social ideas—a development which depends on the transformations of the relations through objects (and hence on the way in which these relations are formed)—are formulated by the theory of historical materialism.

II

Krzywicki bases his theory of the genealogy of social ideas on an analysis of the social development of Western Europe. The rise of towns

---

[13] *Ibid.*, p. 86.

[14] Rozwój społeczny (Social Development), In *Świat i Człowiek* (The World and Man), *ed. cit.*, p. 39.

[15] Rozwój kultury materialnej, więzi społecznej i poglądu na świat (The Development of Material Culture, of Social Bonds and of Views of the World), in *Świat i Człowiek* (The World and Man), No. III, p. 86, 1912.

[16] *Ibid.*, p. 87.

in the Middle Ages, the development of their internal relations, the growth of crafts and trade, the evolution of the modern State, the Reformation and the great middle-class revolutions, the reform of electoral law in England in 1832, the development of modern capitalist production and its social, political and cultural effects—all this is the factual material on which Krzywicki bases his theory of social development. From an analysis of this historical material, he arrives at the following picture of the causal mechanism of the historical processes of development.

Every social transformation is a gradual change, a slow development of relations through objects, these relations forming the basis of the social bond in a territorial society. The transformation of this foundation of the social bond is the result of the gradual improvement in the methods and tools of production used by man, i.e., the result of the development of what is known as productive forces. Such development occurs spontaneously, with no idea or social purpose behind it. Its driving force is solely personal interest, people's personal aims. "To increase their earnings, people moved away from their old towns, which had seen better days, leaving them to decay. Some set up workshops or market stalls in Manchester, others became lawyers or doctors there".[17] The driving power behind the development of the productive forces is so great that it is augmented even by those who do not at all desire the social effects which this development produces. "Both those who desire the introduction of new relations, and those who oppose them most bitterly, contribute jointly to the progressive development of the productive forces.... We do not realize that, in acquiring common-place objects, we are daily and even hourly contributing to the centralization of industry and to the ruin of crafts, to the organizing of factory brigades, and, further, to the growth of urban elements, ... in a word, to the rise of a material foundation for social ideas and aspirations, to which some of us are bitterly opposed".[18] "When a shoemaker talks to a blacksmith, he complains against shoe factories, and the other against factories manufacturing nails. When, however, he needs nails for his shoes, he does not buy them from his friend the blacksmith, but goes to a shop and gets manufactured ones .... The feudal lord perhaps listened in horror to the

---

[17] Rozwój społeczny (Social Development), p. 45.

[18] Rodowód idei społecznych (The Genealogy of Social Ideas), *Studia Socjologiczne, ed. cit.*, p. 37.

arguments of townsmen, demanding that the monarch should disband the private armies of the lords and curtail the rights of the barons, but, in spite of his indignation, he bought his armour and weapons, silks and jewels from these merchants and craftsmen, thereby increasing their prosperity, and contributing to the rise of the towns".[19] Because the development of productive forces is based on purely personal aspirations, interests and ends, with no underlying social purpose, and is simply the product of individual aspirations and endeavours to achieve these same ends, there is a "necessary" connection between the trends of social development and the desires and will of the individual. The period of the gradual, spontaneous development of productive forces, which in the mind of the individual is unaccompanied by any awareness of the social effects of these transformations, is a period of organic labour preparing the rise of new social ideas.

The gradual development of productive forces changes the material base of the social bond. In this process of change the nature of the social bond also changes, giving rise to a new division of society into classes and strata. This change in the social bond is equally as spontaneous as the transformation of its material base. With the rise of a new social bond and its new material base new needs develop. However, this new type of social bond and the new needs which appear under the influence of the development of productive forces, are impeded by the existing political-legal system which has arisen on the basis of social bonds and needs corresponding to a different past level of productive forces. Against this background, dissatisfaction with the existing political–legal system grows among the classes or strata associated with the new nature of the productive forces. This growth of dissatisfaction among these classes or strata of society begins to crystallize into a conscious social purpose—the transformation of the political–legal framework. A new social idea forms. The rise of a social idea, formulating the needs of the classes or strata which are connected with the new nature of the productive forces, is the second stage in the process of social transformation.

With the appearance of the social idea begins the third and final stage in the process of social transformation. The new idea spreads. As already mentioned, the mechanism by which it spreads is a subject of the psychology of communal life, and the examination of the reaction

---

[19] *Rozwój społeczny* (Social Development), pp. 51–52.

of individuals to this process belongs to anthropology. The result is, however, that the new idea spreads mainly through those classes or strata of society whose prosperity is connected with the development of the productive forces and with the new shape of the political–legal system; whereas the class or stratum whose economic interest is connected with the past political–legal system, opposes and struggles against the new idea.[20] Thus social ideas become the expression of class interests, and the struggle of ideas is the class struggle. In this period the struggles between the old political–legal system and the new social development cease to be organic and gradual, and there is the possibility of revolutions and upheavals. There follows a period of social revolution which brings about a new political–legal system, within whose framework the new productive forces can freely develop. In this final period, during the active struggle for the realization of the new idea and during the period of its implementation, *"awareness becomes a factor of primary importance. A very wide field for conscious action is opened up, in which the solution depends not only on the enthusiasm of crowds, but also on the social initiative of individuals, their talents and their courage"*.[21]

III

The development of productive forces explains the origin and development of social ideas without, however, explaining entirely the result to which these ideas lead. For, this result depends not only on the content of the idea but also on the existing political–legal framework, the social bonds, and the psychological characteristics of people, all of which affect the idea. "Our customs and prejudices, our principles and beliefs, our feelings and temperament, our political and legal institutions, our moral and ethical views, and finally our philosophical systems—all in our historical development", says Krzywicki, "form a single coherent

---

[20] Of course, this does not mean that individuals taking part in the struggle for or against the new idea do so consciously from self-interest. On the contrary, on both sides of this struggle numerous examples may be found of sacrifice, devotion and heroism. However, for individuals, membership of a class constitutes, with few exceptions, a way of thought, their social and ethical ideals, and so on. On this, see Krzywicki's article Jednostka a klasa (The Individual and the Class) and Gromady klasowe (Class Groups), published in *Studia Socjologiczne, ed. cit.*

[21] *Rodowód idei społecznych* (The Genealogy of Social Ideas), p. 43.

concept of our *historical foundation*".[22] The historical foundation is the collection of institutions and psychological characteristics of the population prevailing at a given moment. These institutions and psychological characteristics often have their origin in the distant past. They are sometimes the direct counterpart of the productive forces existing at any given time. Frequently, however, they are merely the remains of productive relations which have long since disappeared, remains which owe their existence to human inertia and traditionalism. Thus, the historical foundation is composed of elements whose origin dates from very different times. Only a concrete analysis can identify these various elements. The historical foundation is, however, a very important factor in social development; for, a newly arisen social idea does not operate in a vacuum. It meets with a definite historical foundation, on which those who struggle for the realization of the new idea also act. Therefore, the result to which the social idea leads depends not only on the idea itself, but also on the historical foundation confronting it and against the background of which it is realized.

The final outcome of social development in a given set of conditions is a *resultant* of the ideas which have arisen under the influence of the development of productive forces, and the existing historical foundation. In this way, the same development of productive forces may lead in different countries to different results depending upon their different existing historical foundations. "The direction in which the social bond is transformed, that is, its laws and principles, depends on the transformation of material factors. However, when we examine the results to which the development of social life has finally led, i.e., the particular framework within which the idea has been brought to fruition, we must also take into account the effects of the historical foundation. Ways of solving a historical problem depend not only on the needs to which the present gives rise, but also on the organized bond which has survived from the past. The same productive powers in different countries can and must give rise to different results: the structure of the middle-class in England is different from that in America or France, since the foundation on which the liberation of the bourgeoisie took place was different in each case".[23]

---

[22] Przeszłość a teraźniejszość (The Past and the Present), (*Studia Socjologiczne, ed. cit.*, p. 83). In this article Krzywicki develops his theory of the significance which the historical foundation has for social development.

[23] *Ibid.*, pp. 89–90.

Historical development is the resultant, on the one hand, of the productive forces and social ideas produced by this development, and, on the other hand, of the historical foundation which exists at a given time and place. Allowing in this way for the role of the historical foundation, historical materialism does not overlook any factor in its formulation of the laws of social development. "In the number of factors of social development", says Krzywicki, "there is room even for Cleopatra's nose";[24] in its analysis of social development, historical materialism takes account of each factor. It ascribes different roles, however, to the individual factors, that is, it distinguishes between *active* and *passive* factors. The development of the productive forces and the revolutionary social ideas to which this development leads, are active factors; whereas the historical foundation, which includes the ideas corresponding to the existing social framework, is a passive factor. "The needs and ideas arising from the new material conditions of social existence are active forces; the sum of relations which characterizes the social system in which these ideas have arisen is passive".[25] The essence of the theory of historical materialism consists in the demonstration that, in the final analysis, the development of productive forces is an active factor in social development, that this development is a stimulus forcing society to transform itself, and that all other factors are passive. But saying that the remaining factors are passive does not at all belittle their role or significance; social development is in fact the resultant of all these factors. Those factors which Krzywicki defines as passive also help to determine this resultant.

Krzywicki's exposition of the role of the historical foundation in social development is a clear and original approach to the problem (rather obscurely and superficially presented by other theorists of historical materialism) of "the interaction between what is known as the ideological superstructure and the economic foundation".

Human psychological characteristics are one of the most essential component factors of the historical foundation. Foremost among the factors which shape these characteristics is the *anthropological structure* of the population.[26] This anthropological structure must be understood

---

[24] Rozwój społeczny (Social Development), p. 59.

[25] *Ibid.*, p. 59.

[26] Krzywicki analyses the role of the populations' anthropological structure in his book *Systematyczny kurs antropologii—Rasy psychiczne* (A Systematic Course of

as embodying three factors, namely: physical, psychological, and occupational. Physical differences among different groups of people are significant only in that they can be distinguished by different psychological features. Recognizing this fact, Krzywicki none the less rejects the view of those sociologists who see these differences as a means of social development.[27] He rejects this view for two reasons. First of all, while recognizing that the racial-physical composition of the population is significant as a factor of social development, he nevertheless considers it, together with the whole historical foundation, as a passive factor, and, while as a constituent force it does indeed contribute to the determination of the resultant of social development, nonetheless it is not a stimulus to social transformation. Secondly, it is very difficult to distinguish which psychological attributes are the result of the psychological characteristics of a group, and which are the result of social and cultural development, and therefore have nothing to do with the group's physical characteristics. And as long as this distinction cannot be made, it is difficult to construct a theory of the significance of physical types in historical development.

Although it is difficult to establish a correlation between physical types and psychological attributes, there is no doubt that individual nations, or even social groups, possess certain psychological characteristics which are peculiar to them and which are conditioned by their anthropological structure. Krzywicki defines these as *psychological types*. They are the result of the selective effect either of natural conditions, that is, of the natural environment, or of the social institutions in which the given human group lives. In the primitive state it is the selective effect of nature, by which man is surrounded, that predominates. The result of this is what is known as mezological types, such as highland types, steppe types, Pomeranian and insular types, riverine types, etc. Apart from this, however, there is also the selective effect of social institutions and, at the highest level of cultural development, this kind of

---

Anthropology—Psychological Types), Warsaw, 1902, and in several papers of which the more important are published in *Studia Socjologiczne* (Sociological Studies) under the collective title of Typy zawodowe (Occupational Types). A brief exposition of Krzywicki's views on this subject is contained in the article Rozwój człowieka (The Development of Man) in *Świat i Człowiek* (The World and Man), No. II, Warsaw, 1912. Cf. L. Krzywicki, *Dzieła* (Works), Vol. 3 pp. 225–230, Warsaw, 1959.

[27] Cf. Rasy psychiczne (Psychological Types), in *Studia Socjologiczne, ed. cit.*, pp. 261–281.

selection is of decisive significance. "Social institutions", says Krzywicki, "produce a continual selective effect upon the members of the society. Every institution, every custom, by affecting the psychological structure of the nation, transforms it in whichever direction it likes and destroys in society certain types together with their progeny. The daily way of life with its influences, forms of marriage bond and ownership, moral views, needs resulting from the conditions of production, emigration—all these are instruments transforming the psychological make up of a nation".[28] The selective mechanism of social institutions is the same as the mechanism by which natural selection operates. Just as natural selection eliminates individuals who are not adapted to the natural environment and prevents them from transmitting their hereditary characteristics, so social institutions stunt and reject those individuals not adapted to the given conditions of social life, making it difficult for them to transmit their hereditary characteristics. "Selection is the means of anthropological development of ethnic groups.... It operates by systematically rejecting certain characteristics and aptitudes from society, leaving others to be passed on from parents to children. Fortified by selection, these types spread more and more throughout the nation, and the proportion of courage, initiative, industry, of one temperament or another, rises or falls from one generation to the next".[29] Thus the selective effect of social institutions attunes the anthropological composition of the population to the needs of a given social system. The anthropological composition of the population in a civilized society is not, therefore, something "given by nature", but is a historical creation, the result of the selective effects of the social framework over a long period of time; it is part of the historical foundation encountered by the new social ideas brought into being by the development of productive forces.

A psychological type is not, however, a homogeneous creation. It is composed of anthropological elements of very different tendencies,

---

[28] Rozwój człowieka (The Development of Man), p. 284.

[29] Rasy psychiczne (Psychological Types), p. 82. It should be mentioned that according to Krzywicki, unfavourable selection predominates in contemporary civilization, eliminating the physical and moral vigour produced by selection in barbaric times in favour of types capable of routine work, submission and obedience. See Rasy psychiczne (Psychological Types), pp. 84–87, 289–309 and Rozwój człowieka (The Development of Man), p. 284.

characters and capabilities. Krzywicki defines these components as *occupational types* since, in a society with an advanced division of labour, these types aim at different "occupations";[30] and the choice of a proper occupation determines the success or failure of a given type, often forcing them in the last resort to crime. And although not all the population consists of distinct occupational types, the majority of it being rather a formless mass of different tendencies and aptitudes, defined with varying degrees of clarity, nevertheless the fact that it contains a certain number of clearly defined occupational types gives social development a specific imprint. For these types provide the historical processes with their guides and leaders, their ideologists and evangelists, their champions and finally their persecutors. An analysis of the role of occupational types in the historical foundation enables the theory of historical materialism to take full account of the role of human personality in the course of history.

Krzywicki's analysis of the role of anthropological factors in social development and their connection with the theory of historical materialism is an important and original achievement. With this analysis, the method of historical materialism acquires flexibility in Krzywicki's hands, enabling it to be applied to problems for which it would otherwise be unsuitable. In the light of this analysis, the development of productive forces becomes a powerful anthropological factor of selection, its result depending also on the selective effect of the social framework. "Developing spontaneously, relations through objects require definite temperaments in the nation so as to meet new commitments pushing aside those which predominated hitherto. It may happen that the nation will not contain a sufficient number of persons equal to the new social needs .... In this case, the influence of the historical foundation is felt in the legacy of the past, restraining the rate of progress because of the shortage of people capable of acting as instruments of progress".[31]

IV

In addition to his detailed exposition of the role of anthropological factors in social development, Krzywicki enriches the theory of historical

---

[30] The term "occupation" is used in a wide sense, e.g., being a tramp or a peddlar is also an occupation.

[31] Przeszłość a teraźniejszość (The Past and the Present), pp. 80–81.

materialism with an interesting analysis of the *migration of social ideas* in space and time. This phenomenon is, it is true, known to other theorists of historical materialism but, as far as I know, no one has studied it in such detail as Krzywicki; and a study of this phenomenon is of particular importance for an examination of the historical development of Poland.

As shown above, social ideas appear as the crystallization of new needs which result from the development of productive forces and the consequent transformation of the material base of the social bond. This causal mechanism of the rise of social ideas refers only to countries which develop independently, that is, under the influence of their own relations and patterns. Social development proceeded in such a way in Western Europe, particularly in France and England; but even there, with the possible exception of England, development has not solely been due to internal causes. Independence of development was broken by the adoption of Roman law. This adoption was undoubtedly conditioned by the development of productive forces which broke up the framework of medieval economic isolation and created extensive trade relations among towns. It seemed as though Roman law had been created for these new forms of economic life. But the fact that it existed as something ready-made changed the mechanism of social development. The new idea, instead of being conceived and crystallized with difficulty, appeared ready-made, equipped with the authority of a great past. "A whole system of laws which otherwise would need formulating step by step, was there already set out and systematized:... and this immediately saved the generation of that time from having to look for solutions to successive problems by their own independent efforts, and from obtaining the necessary sanctions for each of these solutions".[32] "Without the legacy of Roman law", says Krzywicki, "the development of Europe might have been delayed by a couple of centuries, in which case it may have turned out rather differently".[33]

An even greater role than that of the migration of ideas in time[34] is

_____

[32] Wędrówka idei (The Migration of Ideas) in *Studia Socjologiczne* (Sociological Studies), p. 46.

[33] *Ibid.*, p. 47.

[34] The question of the migration of ideas in time, and that of the rise of a social idea which overtakes the development of economic relations by reference to a past idea, were studied in particular by Kazimierz Krauz. On this basis he attempted to formulate a law known as the sociological law of retrospection. Cf. Kazimierz Krauz, *Materializm ekonomiczny* (Economic Materialism), Cracow, 1908.

played by the migration of ideas in space, which operates in a similar manner. Social ideas from more advanced countries penetrate into countries whose social development is retarded and, being the products of a higher culture and civilization, they influence the development of the less advanced countries. Poland's social and cultural development took place under the influence of social ideas which had originally developed in Western Europe. This influence began with the adoption of Christianity. The derivation of the words *szlachta* (nobility) and *herb* (heraldry) shows that foreign influences hastened the formation in Poland of a class of knights. The adoption of German municipal civil law, the influences of foreign humanism, the history of culture of the Sigismund period, the Jesuit reaction, the period of reform from the second half of the eighteenth century, the development of scientific, philosophical and social ideas in the nineteenth century—these are further stages in the influence of foreign ideas on Polish history.[35] Similarly, the development of Russia from the time of its "Europeanization" was influenced by foreign ideas, and so partly was the development of Germany.

The migration of ideas hastens the social development of less developed countries. Of course, an idea spreading from one country to another becomes a factor in the development of the latter country only when it falls on suitable ground, prepared by the development of productive forces. Otherwise, it will remain only a "fad", fashionable for a short time, but without any influence on historical development. However, when it does fall on ground prepared by the development of productive forces, it hastens social development by saving the class which is leading that development the arduous task of elaborating its social ideology; it provides it with a ready-made ideology, bearing the authority of a higher culture or foreign civilization. It may happen, however, that an idea arrives from outside when the social forces, whose exponent it may become, are only at an initial stage of development. The idea then *outstrips social maturity*. "It contributes to a more rapid consciousness of those who are still unconscious even though there exist elements receptive to it; it shows the undeveloped and inorganized social elements a course of action, so that in one way or another it changes the course of history which, without its intervention, might have taken a rather different direction".[36] One can best arrive at a clear picture of the histori-

---

[35] Cf. Rozwój społeczny (Social Development), pp. 54–55.
[36] Wędrówka idei (The Migration of Ideas), in *ed. cit.*, p. 47.

cal role of such a migrating idea if one thinks what the development of Russia would have been without the influence of Western European Marxism.

*

In countries where the idea outstrips the growth of productive forces, the social movements bear its specific influence. Around such an idea, groups of ideologists gather, "forming to some extent the general staff of a future social army which slowly builds up under its influence as the relations through objects (or consciousness of those already existing) mature".[37] There is, however, a certain difference between the social ideology of such a country, and the directions of social movements in a country developing exclusively under the influence of internal forces. In a country in which a social idea is born, the leaders of the social movement arise slowly from among that stratum which sees the given idea as the formulation of its own aspirations. By means of this idea, these leaders become conscious of the connection between their aims and the needs of life—they know what to struggle for and why. On the other hand, ideologists in a less developed country, whose social ideas come from outside, lack this direct feeling of the connection between the idea and the needs of life. For them the idea is an abstract concept, their arguments draw from the abstract principles of ethics or philosophy. "They tend to consider the idea, with which their minds are imbued, as a product roaming independently about the world; they look down upon the hard facts of life which, in their own environment, from time to time strip them unmercifully of various illusions. For them the idea loses its class character, ceases to be the formulation of people's tangible interests and needs and thus, stripped of historical substance, is changed into a fleshless creation, a work of critical thought, a declaration of the principles of a truth which is absolute for all eternity. This lasts so long as life does not destroy the appropriate material elements of the idea which give ideologists real and useful work, instead of the weaving of poetic dreams and metaphysical inferences".[38]

The spreading of ideas depends on the conditions of communication,

---

[37] Wędrówka idei (The Migration of Ideas), in *Studia Socjologiczne* (Sociological Studies).

[38] *Ibid.*, pp. 48–49.

which in turn depend on the development of trade relations. In the Middle Ages the range of influence of social ideas was very narrow; such influence often did not extend beyond the gates of a single town. With the development of trade relations, the migration of ideas acquires increasingly greater significance, and now, in the age of worldwide economic relations, ideas know no territorial boundaries. For, the more social relations are everywhere moulded according to a common principle, the more intensive becomes the migration of ideas, and the more far-reaching its effects.

V

For all its potency, historical materialism as a method of analysing the causal connections of social development has, of course, its *limits of application*. These arise from the fact that the causal connections, formulated by the theory of historical materialism, are concerned with the social processes of a group, and not with the behaviours of single individuals, and only then at a certain level of social development. Krzywicki himself formulates these limits.

The laws of social development, formulated by the theory of historical materialism, relate to social phenomena of the group. They tell us nothing of the behaviour of any particular individual. Consequently, the theory of the origin of social ideas, as presented above, relates only to those ideas which become the basis of the social movements of groups. All the great historical ideas which have turned the scales of history are of this kind. But, besides great historical ideas, human minds produce a multitude of the most disparate schemes and thoughts, but their followers hardly exceed a handful of individuals. "Someone may wish to reorganize society into monasteries, someone else to convert his little village into the capital of the country".[39] Such ideas have no immediate impact on the course of social development, either in their development or in their effects. As for the social effects of such ideas, they either exert no influence at all, or else their influence does not extend beyond a temporary handful of followers. They never attract great following and never affect the course of history. Such ideas are not founded on the real conditions of life. They may be interesting products of individual

---

[39] *Rozwój społeczny* (Social Development), p. 47.

psychology, but in their effects they are utopian. Utopias, as Krzywicki puts it, are the "idealistic shavings of the course of history".[40] Such utopias can sometimes be transformed into historical ideas. This happens when a certain idea is premature, i.e. it appears before the development of productive forces has created the conditions in which it can be understood. Such an idea is then initially utopian, but it loses this quality with the maturing of social relations.

It follows that historical materialism is not a theory of the development of ideas in individual minds, but one which explains the *selection* of ideas, turning some into instruments of historical development, and relegating others to a short and fruitless life of utopianism. "Therefore", says Krzywicki, by asserting that historical ideas are a declaration of real needs, "we have sought to explain, not so much their conception in the minds of outstanding individuals, as their influence on the masses".[41] It is clear that even the conception of an idea in the mind of an individual is not fortuitous, that here too social relations play a certain role; but this dependence tends to be loose, thwarted by a host of individual factors, and in any case it is no guarantee that the idea is marked by an understanding of social aims and needs.

Since historical materialism explains not the conception of ideas by individuals, but the *selection* of ideas, through which great historical ideas are shaped, it follows that the method of historical materialism can have only limited application in sciences which examine the products of the human mind as, for example, in the history of literature or the history of philosophy. Almost nowhere in his writings does Krzywicki state this *explicitly*, but such a conclusion follows from those of his views which have just been discussed. Consequently, I believe that Krzywicki would agree with the following thesis. Historical materialism can be applied to such fields as the history of art, the history of literature, or the history of philosophy, only where they concern an artistic, literary or philosophical enquiry into *mass currents of thought*; and then only in so far as the artistic, literary or philosophical ideas which express these currents are in the form of social ideas, that is, are in their content, or in their psychological aspect, in some way connected with the structure of the social bond. In these cases, the method of historical materialism

---

[40] Rodowód idei społecznych (The Genealogy of Social Ideas), p. 44.
[41] Rozwój społeczny (Social Development), p. 48.

is invaluable in explaining the process of selection which has enabled certain artistic, literary or philosophical ideas to gain the approval of a wide public, whereas others have always failed to secure more than a small handful of followers. Where, however, purely individual phenomena are concerned, such as the views of a particular philosopher, the genius of a great painter, or the inspired creation of a poet, historical materialism as a theory of *mass* social phenomena cannot, by its very nature, be applied.[42] Awareness of this limitation of historical materialism would save much wasted effort, which has more often than not discredited historical materialism rather than benefited its scientific reputation.

The second limitation of the theory of historical materialism, according to Krzywicki, lies in the fact that the laws of social development, formulated in it, cover only a certain level of social development, namely, societies with a *territorial* structure. For, only in such societies are ties through objects the basis of the social bond and only in such societies are social ideas, that is, the consciousness of social aims, closely connected with the nature of the relations through objects which are the basis of the social bond. Krzywicki clearly emphasizes[43] the fact that the theory of historical materialism relates only to societies with a territorial structure, but unfortunately he does not formulate clearly his view of the principles which govern social development in the period of the clan system. It seems, however, that for Krzywicki, the main instrument in the development of earlier societies, is not so much the development of productive forces, as demographic factors, particularly the growth of population. In any case, the transformation of man's relation to the tribal territory (that most important phenomenon in the history of primitive societies) was, according to Krzywicki, induced by the growing population.[44] Krzywicki's view is reminiscent of Engels'

---

[42] This is partly explained in Krzywicki's book *W otchłani* (In the Abyss), Warsaw, 1909.

[43] Cf. Rozwój społeczny (Social Development), pp. 46 and 50–51.

[44] Cf. *Ustroje społeczno-gospodarcze w okresie dzikości i barbarzyństwa* (Socioeconomic Systems in Savagery and Barbarism), pp. 525–529, Warsaw, 1914, and Rozwój stosunków gospodarczych (The Development of Economic Relations) in *Świat i Człowiek* (The World and Man), No. III, p. 259, Warsaw, 1912; *Społeczeństwo pierwotne: jego rozmiary i wzrost*, pp. 408–410 and 413–416, Warsaw, 1937, also published in English under the title *Primitive Society and its Vital Statistics*, pp. 293–295 and 298–301, Warsaw–London, 1934. Cf. also Krzywicki, *Dzieła* (Works), Vol. 2, pp. 564–579, Warsaw, 1958.

well-known theory, according to which it was not the productive forces, but "the reproduction of life itself" which in primitive society was the instrument of social development.[45] Engels held that in this primitive period of the history of human development (which was to end with the disintegration of primitive communism), social development was to be determined by the evolution of the family, which took place under the influence of natural selection; and only with the triumph of private property did the productive forces replace natural conditions as a stimulus to social development.[46] On the other hand, the principles of historical materialism will not, according to Krzywicki, obtain in a socialist society of the future; for, in a socialist system, the development of productive forces loses its spontaneous character, which at present makes transformations "necessary", and becomes a conscious and purposive act of the social will.[47] "These principles, leading to social development," says Krzywicki, referring to historical materialism, "do not represent, then, any 'iron law', binding in every period of history. They are characteristic of a territorial system, and were conceived and fully developed only when that system matured and destroyed in communal life the binding links of the clan. Finally, if a territorial system is for some time based on consciously organized production throughout the whole country, this spontaneity disappears, and with it the principles of development which we have identified."[48]

---

[45] Cf. F. Engels, *Pochodzenie rodziny, własności prywatnej i państwa* (The Origin of the Family, Private Property and the State); K. Marx and F. Engels, *Dzieła Wybrane* (Selected Works), Warsaw, 1949, Vol. II, p. 176.

[46] This view of Engels was opposed by certain advocates of historical materialism who saw in it a rejection of the monistic nature of the explanation of social development, which in their opinion historical materialism should give. Such a standpoint was taken, among others, by H. Cunow, *Die Marxsche Geschichts-Gesellschafts- und Staatstheorie*, Berlin, 1923, Vol. II, pp. 138–142, and Karol Kautsky, *Die materialistische Geschichtsauffassung*, Berlin, 1927, Vol. I, pp. 842ff. In Poland this standpoint was taken by Kazimierz Krauz, *Materializm ekonomiczny* (Economic Materialism), Cracow, 1908, pp. 71ff.

[47] The view that historical materialism is not applicable to social development in a socialist system is shared by many Marxists of today, and in particular by one of the most eminent—Sidney Hook. Cf. Sidney Hook, *Towards the Understanding of Karl Marx*, New York–London, 1933, p. 90.

[48] Rozwój Społeczny (Social Development), pp. 50–51.

VI

There is a fairly widespread view that historical materialism is a fatalistic doctrine, with no room for conscious and purposeful human behaviour. There is no need to show here that this is fundamentally wrong. Even a superficial acquaintance with the theory under discussion is enough to demonstrate that this view is groundless. It is the result of a certain type of criticism which, Krzywicki once said, contains more prejudice than good intent, and in particular more ignorance than understanding of the essence of the theory under consideration.[49] Krzywicki in his first article Idea a życie (Life and Idea) written in 1888 examines the question of whether, and to what extent, historical materialism leaves room for free social creative activity of the individual. He says, "Finally there arises one more problem, which may be called the alpha and omega of social policy, namely, whether it is within a man's power to mould social development to his will and, if he is able to influence it, in what area can this be done"?[50] He answers this question in a later article in the series. To retain the forcefulness of his answer, I quote it here in full:

"Man became aware that society is governed by laws which he must obey.... And realizing this, he became able to exert a conscious influence on social development. Against lightning, a primitive witch-doctor has a host of means: prayers, fasts, charms. If he were told that this natural phenomenon occurs according to immutable laws, he would consider such an approach as a limitation, and perhaps a negation, of human activity and that the influence of the rational individual is limited. Science, after investigating electricity, has discovered that, acting on the basis of the appropriate laws, lightning can be subjected to the human will and made harmless. The same may be said of society. A knowledge of the laws of development and understanding of present-day necessities only apparently limits the effectiveness of individual effort, for basically it frees the human individual from unnecessary and fruitless activity. It does not destroy the efficacy of his actions; it does not free him from social work; but it indicates in what circumstances, and what kind of

---

[49] Krzywicki's preface to K. Krauz, *Materialism ekonomiczny* (Economic Materialism), *ed. cit.*, p. XV.

[50] Parę słów wstępnych (A Few Introductory Words) in *Studia Socjologiczne* (Sociological Studies), *ed. cit.*, p. 2.

activity it is useful or not. In confining historical possibilities to a particular sphere and establishing only limited paths for human activity, the
realization that development is governed by laws does no more than
eliminate fruitless daydreaming in the social sphere.... Instead of para-
doxes and metaphysics, an evaluation of the facts is needed which,
though perhaps trivial, is nevertheless much more useful, and in which
there is no room for *dolce far niente*, a pretended fatalistic view of
development, nor for fantasies and idylls adjusted to one's own inclinations".[51]

In this way, social awareness becomes the basis of social practice.

Our exposition of Krzywicki's views on historical materialism is
drawing to a close. We have seen an approach to this theory which is
as clear as it is profound; and in many places it is extraordinarily original—in particular, the analysis of the role of the anthropological composition of the population and the migration of ideas in social development. Thus, Krzywicki's work on historical materialism is an important
stage in the development of this theory.

Today historical materialism is unfashionable. This is only to a small
extent due to reservations about the scientific value of the theory. It is
unpopular for reasons which the theory itself perfectly explains. In any
social system in decline, scientific analysis of social life based on rational
methods is unpopular. The declining system, finding no justification in
the rationality and social usefulness of its structure, seeks support in
mystical feelings and metaphysical speculation. These feelings pervade
social science too, or rather its exponents. Mystical and metaphysical
theories of the "social spirit", of "race and blood" play their pranks.
We are witnesses of a revival of all social metaphysics. Scientific method
withers away in an atmosphere of social irrationality.

However, where the spirit of scientific thought is alive, the theory of
historical materialism is alive too, even today. This theory is so far the
only attempt to find a consistent, homogeneous explanation of the causal
mechanism which governs social development, an attempt whose usefulness has been shown by countless applications. Undoubtedly, the
theory suffers from numerous shortcomings, both in the definition of
the concepts which it uses, and in the explanation of various facts within
its field. Science does not progress, however, by the wholesale rejection

---

[51] Wędrówka idei (The Migration of Ideas), in *ed. cit.*, p. 59.

of old theories and the devising of new ones, but by arduous work on enriching and improving existing scientific achievements. And as regards the investigation of social development, historical materialism seems to be the only theory which can serve as a basis for the further progress of knowledge. It is in this way that historical materialism is treated by Ludwik Krzywicki, one of the most outstanding of its exponents, who devoted his industrious life to deepening and developing the theory. As a result, he has greatly enriched our social knowledge and has helped to create a powerful instrument for its further progress.

Part II

POLITICAL ECONOMY
AND SOCIALISM

THE POLITICAL ECONOMY OF SOCIALISM

Socialism is a new economic system which is only in the making. Consequently, its economic theory is only beginning to be formulated. Some of us know how much time it took to understand the economic operation of the capitalist system, and I am not quite sure that we always fully understand it even today, because the capitalist system is continuously changing. Thus, there is nothing surprising in the fact that the problem of the economics of a socialist system is new and the scientific treatment of it is still provisional and tentative.

The founders of scientific socialism, Marx and Engels, devoted all their efforts to the analysis of the capitalist economy. They made some highly generalized observations on the socialist economy and refused, as a matter of principle, to enter into the problem in greater detail out of fear of becoming utopian rather than scientific. The great socialist movement of the nineteenth and the beginning of the twentieth centuries also devoted all its scientific efforts to the analysis of capitalism, though we have some attempts at projecting in perspective a socialist society in the writings of Bebel and Kautsky.

The situation changed after the First World War, when under the impact of the October Revolution the question of socialist construction became a practical problem. In Central European countries, such as Germany and Austria, the revolutions which took place there brought forward the question of transition from capitalism to socialism, and in this period we have a certain amount of literature dealing with economic problems of socialism. In the Soviet Union it was first of all Lenin who initiated the discussion on the problems of a socialist economy. Bukharin, Preobrazhenski, Strumilin and others continued this discussion in their writings. In the social democratic movement at that time, quite a substantial literature came out from the pen of people like Otto Bauer, Kautsky and others who dealt with the problems of a socialist economy, though in a very tentative way. During this period, there also emerged some non-Marxist literature on the problems of a socialist economy, trying to show the impossibility of establishing proper economic accounting under socialism. Max Weber, Mises, Hayek produced arguments which socialist circles tried to refute. I myself wrote on this subject, and there were also Lerner, Dickinson and Maurice Dobb in England.

In the meantime, in the Soviet Union, socialism became a practically operating system which provided new experience. This, for the time being, resulted in but few theoretical generalizations (though there were some as, for instance, the writings of Ostrovitianov). The first great attempt at a theoretical generalization of the experiences of the Soviet economy was given in Stalin's famous booklet *Economic Problems of Socialism in the U.S.S.R.*; and then in the text-book of political economy published by the Academy of Sciences of the U.S.S.R. These two publications tried to give a theoretical generalization of the experience of the socialist economy in the Soviet Union. In the meantime, other socialist experience was being accumulated. First in Yugoslavia, later in China, Poland and other People's Democracies. And it seems thus that the time is slowly maturing for a synthetic theoretical analysis of the underlying principles of a socialist economy.

Of course, such a synthesis can only be preliminary and provisional. Therefore, what I am going to say here represents only my personal views. Among Polish economists there were many discussions but also many divergencies of views on this subject. This is quite natural taking account of the yet very immature stage of the problem. Thus, the views expressed here will be my own personal views; and I should add, my provisional views. I would not be surprised if I should change my views on certain subjects both as a result of further study and also on the basis of further practical experience of socialist economics.

The basis for the scientific treatment of the political economy of socialism is the assumption that there exist in a socialist society objective economic laws. I shall start my exposition with the statement that a socialist society is subject first to the general laws of social development, which are formulated by the theory of historical materialism, and secondly, to special economic laws.

Concerning the operation of general laws of social development, it sometimes has been denied that a socialist society is subject to the operation of the laws of historical materialism. For instance, in Poland we had a great Marxist sociologist, Krzywicki, who maintained that the laws of historical materialism are not applicable to a socialist society. But besides this, so to speak, formal, explicit denial, there has been very frequently an implicit denial that a socialist society is subject to the laws of historical materialism. This was done by denying that the development of socialist society takes place through the operation of contradictions. It was frequently thought that all social contradictions, all contradictions of human life, somehow automatically disappeared in a socialist society. This is a view which is quite incompatible with Marxist theory. This view expresses, if I may say so, a Christian-eschatological and not a Marxist-scientific attitude. Socialism is not the realization of the religious ideal of the Kingdom of God, but a new stage in the development of human society which can and must be studied by the methods of Marxist analysis. It is the merit of Mao Tse Tung to have recalled with emphasis the fact that socialist society, too, develops through contradictions.

There are two basic contradictions which are the moving force of social development, according to the theory of historical materialism: first, the contradiction in the development of productive forces and the conservative character of production relations; and, second, the contradiction in production relations, or what is called the economic base of society, in the superstructure of organization and management of the economy, in the political organization, in moral and psychological attitudes, conservatism of habits, etc. These basic contradictions also take place in the course of development of socialist society. The essential difference, however, between socialist society and societies based on class domination is that in societies based on class domination these contradictions, particularly the contradictions between the development of productive forces and the conservative character of production relations, are connected with class interests and take the form of class struggle. This does not happen in a socialist society. Therefore, we usually speak of these contradictions under socialism as being non-antagonistic in character.

But this does not mean that social conflicts cannot develop in a socialist society, because, in addition to social classes, there exist social strata. The difference between social classes and social strata is that, whereas social classes are based on production relations, social strata have their economic base in the particular form of the superstructure of the society. To give an example: in a capitalist society, capitalists are a class, but bankers, merchants, lawyers, priests, government officials are social strata. The latter have their economic base in the organization of the superstructure and not in production relations. In terms of the sources of income they receive, I would say that whereas classes receive income in the process of primary distribution of income, such as wages, and surplus value, social strata derive their income from secondary distribution. For instance, government officials from taxes, priests from donations, merchants or bankers from part of the surplus value which is used to remunerate their non-productive (but in the capitalist framework necessary) activities.

In society there are not only social classes but also social strata. Consequently, the contradictions which may arise in the development of socialist society between the requirements of the economic base and antiquated superstructures, such as methods of management of the national economy, political superstructures and others, may also arouse opposition from vested interests of certain strata, which makes a change difficult. But these are not social classes—there are no class struggles. To overcome these obstacles there is not required a basic change in production relations, i.e., a social revolution, though it may lead to all kinds of friction in the superstructure during the period of transformation and of adaptation of the superstructure to new requirements of the economic base.

That much can be said about the operations of the laws of historical materialism in a socialist society. I do not want to dwell on the further perspective as regards the role of social strata in the transition to communism, for I think that everything that we could say at this stage would really have no scientific basis because of lack of knowledge of the relevant empirical facts.

The second problem is that of the operation of economic laws in socialist society. There have been many Marxist economists who held the view that in socialist society there are no economic laws operating and that political economy, as a science, loses its role with the end of capitalism. The most prominent Marxian to express this view was Rosa Luxemburg who actually coined the famous phrase that the proletarian revolution is the last act of political economy as a science. Others who took the same view, particularly in the early years of the Soviet Union, were probably under the influence of Rosa Luxemburg. Bucharin and his school essentially took the same view that political economy is a science of capitalism and ends together with the capitalist system. This was not the view of Marx, Engels or Lenin; however, this is not the most important aspect of it. The important thing is that the experience of a socialist economy has shown that economic laws do operate in it.

At a certain period in the Soviet Union, though the view was not always very clearly and openly put forward, there was a tendency which later came to be called by Soviet economists "voluntarism", i.e., the denial of the operation of economic laws under socialism and the belief that the leaders of economic policy in a socialist State can do whatever they wish.

The essential difference concerning the operation of economic laws in socialist society is that under socialism economic laws do not operate in an elemental way, but that organized society shapes in a conscious, purposive way the circumstances which determine the operation of economic laws. In consequence, the economic laws can be made to operate in accordance with the human will, just as man with the help of modern technology can utilize the laws of nature and make them operate in a way which conforms to his will. That was the famous idea which already was expressed by Engels, when he spoke of society being able to control consciously the laws of its own operation and called this "the leap from the kingdom of necessity into the kingdom of freedom".

Speaking of the economic laws operating in a socialist society, I think that we can distinguish four types of such laws, according to the way in which they are connected with the socialist mode of production.

First, there are economic laws which are general in the sense that they operate in every socio-economic system.

These are the laws of production and reproduction, namely, the laws which concern the general features of the organization of the labour process, co-operation and division of labour, the role of indirect labour crystallized in means of production and of direct (live) labour in the process of production. Then, the laws of reproduction for the replacement of means of production used up in the process of production, of division of the product between consumption and accumulation, the laws of balance in the process of reproduction in various branches of economic activity. All such laws apply to any mode of production whether socialist, capitalist, feudal, or any other. Obviously, these general economic laws also operate in a socialist economy. These laws establish certain technical balances between material objects. They show, for instance, that one cannot accumulate if one consumes the whole net product, that one cannot maintain reproduction if one does not replace the used-up means of production, that to produce a certain amount of steel, a certain quantity of coal is required for that purpose. These kinds of balances between material objects must be satisfied in any economy whatever the social system; they refer to the operation of productive forces.

The second type are the laws which are specific to the socialist mode of production. This means laws which are determined by socialist production relations, which in turn determine the incentives governing human economic activity. For the ownership of means of production determines for what purposes the means of production are going to be used. For instance, for purposes of profits of owners of means of production, as under capitalism, or for the satisfaction of the wants of society, as in a socialist economy. It really says nothing new, the thought is basically in Marx's writings. It says, when we study a social system we have to see the economic law which, so to speak, organizes the whole system and this law depends on production relations. Under capitalism, it determines that production is carried on for private profit; under socialism, it determines, that production is carried on for the satisfaction of human wants. Thus, there exists first this "fundamental law" for each mode of production, which determines the purpose of the use of means of production.

In addition to the purpose for which means of production are used and for which the whole production process is organized, production relations also determine the mode of social interaction of human activities; for instance, whether the interaction of human activities takes the form of competition, of monopoly or of planned direction. This is also a result of the mode of production, and here, socialist production relations do produce certain specific economic laws.

Thus, socialist production relations based on the social ownership of means of production have two consequences. One is that production and all economic activity are pursued for the satisfaction of the needs of society. The other is that the basic mode of social interaction in economic activity is planning, by which I mean a conscious guidance of economic processes by organized society. I do not enter here into the method of planning, whether centralized or decentralized, and so on. But I wish to emphasize that the very fact that means of production are social property carries the consequence that the whole productive and economic process is consciously and purposively guided by socialist society, and in this sense is planned. This is the reason why the economic laws in such a society are not elemental, but their operation is consciously directed by human aims.

Besides general economic laws, which operate in any social system, and laws specific to a particular mode of production, we also have laws which are of an intermediate nature. They are not general, but they are specific to more than one mode of production; they operate in several modes of production and express certain of their common features.

Such are the economic laws which are the result of commodity production, i.e., the law of value, and as commodity production in practice implies exchange for money, the elementary laws of monetary circulation must also be mentioned. In pure theory, we may distinguish the process of exchange of commodities and monetary circulation, but in practice the two are always connected. Developed commodity production is a production where exchange takes place with the aid of money. Thus, I would add here also the elementary laws of monetary circulation.

Commodity production takes place, and consequently the laws of value and monetary circulation operate, already in pre-capitalist societies, though in a restricted field. Under capitalism, all production takes on the form of commodity production and is subject to the law of value and the laws of monetary circulation. In a socialist economy, the law of value continues to operate because production continues to be commodity production. The reasons why production in a socialist economy is commodity production, and consequently subject to the law of value, is the existence of a multiplicity of owners of products in a socialist society. The multiplicity of owners of products in a socialist society results from two of its features. First, from the existence of various forms of social ownership of means of production which causes that there is not just one owner of means of production, but many owners; second, from the method of distribution of the product in a socialist society where the products produced in the socialist production process pass to private ownership by consumers.

The reason why there are various forms of social ownership of means of production is historical. As we know, in the existing socialist countries means of production may be owned socially, as property of the whole nation as well as property of co-operatives, municipalities, various societies and institutions, for instance, trade unions. Thus, we see that we have various types of property of socialist ownership. The various types of socialist ownership result from the historical conditions in which the transition from capitalism to socialism takes place. In this respect there are differences in various countries. In the nineteenth century and at the beginning of the twentieth century, many socialists thought that there will be only one form of social ownership, namely, national ownership, which in the long run, when national socialist states merge into one world, socialist federation would merge into international socialist ownership. Such was the picture which was prevailing in the socialist movement at the end of the nineteenth and the beginning of the twentieth centuries. It also was thought that the transition to socialism would take place purely by the expropriation of the capitalist class, which, by the way, already was highly concentrated, so that the social revolution would be rather a simple and easy act.

Historical experience has shown that the crisis of the capitalist system takes place earlier, namely, before capitalism has had the possibility of working out its tendency to destroy non-capitalist forms of production, particularly small commodity production. This fact is connected with the phenomenon of imperialism. Its consequence is that the breakdown of capitalism takes place first in the less developed countries. Socialism starts first to develop in these less developed countries which are prevented by imperialism from developing along capitalist lines. Thus, in addition to the expropriation of the capitalist class, which leads to one type of socialist ownership, i.e. national ownership, it is necessary to organize socialist ownership on the basis of small commodity production, which leads to the great significance of the co-operative form of socialist ownership.

In some countries the working class is able to establish control of municipal and local government before it is able to conquer State power. This may lead to the development of municipal forms of social ownership of means of production.

This does not exhaust all the possibilities. I just want to show that the particular historical conditions in which the capitalist system breaks down and the construction of socialist society begins, determine the variety of forms of socialist ownership of means of production. This fact, as well as the fact that distribution under socialism is such as to make the products of socialist production pass into individual private property of the consumers, causes production to be in the nature of commodity production, and the law of value therefore operates.

I might add that the second condition alone is a sufficient one. Even if there was only one form of socialist ownership of means of production, for instance, national ownership, the very fact that by distribution products pass into consumers individual ownership would be sufficient to give to socialist production the character of commodity production and to make the law of value operate. The multiplicity of types of socialist ownership of means of production is a further reason.

Products become commodities and are subject to the operation of the law of value when they change owners. This happens as we saw, in a socialist economy. The question might be asked, how should we consider products which are "exchanged"(let us put the word "exchanged" in quotation marks) between units of the nationalized socialist sector of economy. If they are exchanged between co-operatives then they, of course, pass from one owner to another. That is clear. But means of production which go from one unit of the national sector to another unit of the national sector do not change owners. I call such products quasi-commodities. The law of value operates here indirectly by means of imputation. As the final products are sold to consumers, co-operatives, municipalities or any other body, they are commodities. By imputation, this transfers a kind of commodity character on to the means of production which are used to produce the finished commodities. The value of the finished commodities is by an accounting process reflected (imputed) backwards to the means of production which are used to produce them.

Thus, the law of value also operates in a socialist society, though it is not specific to the socialist mode of production alone: it operates in the capitalist mode of production, too, and in a limited way it also operates in pre-capitalist societies. It expresses a certain common feature of several modes of production.

There is still a fourth type of economic laws in a socialist economy. These are laws which are not connected with the socialist mode of production, but result from the particular types of the superstructure of the management of a socialist economy, and which, therefore, change when the organizational and managerial superstructure changes. In a capitalist economy we also have laws which are specific not to capitalism as a whole, but to particular types of organizational and managerial superstructure. To give examples: there are general laws of monetary circulation, which by the way, are not specific to capitalism, but to commodity production. But when we have a gold standard, or paper money, specific laws operate which are peculiar to the particular type of monetary system. Another such law in the field of monetary circulation is Gresham's law which operates only if both types of metallic money have the same legal value.

Different methods of managing a socialist economy which change historically and also from country to country produce their own particular economic laws. They produce specific economic laws, because they produce specific incentives for action and opportunities of action.

There are here two points to be considered. One is the relative scope of administrative allocation of goods, and the other the law of value. In a socialist society the law of value operates; however, under certain forms of management of a socialist economy, use may also be made of various administrative allocations (which even sometimes happens under capitalism). Of course, the relative operation and interaction of administrative allocation and of the law of value produce their own economic consequences and regularities which have a character of economic laws operating under these circumstances (for instance, various types of "black market" phenomena).

The second point relates to the consequences of different types of labour remuneration—how we pay labour, how far and in what form the workers participate in the profit of the enterprise, and so on. This also produces certain economic consequences of quite a regular character, which are in the nature of economic laws. I shall give you an example of our Polish experience. The fact that premiums paid to managing personnel and to workers in the enterprises were connected with the extent to which the plan was overfulfilled, brought about two consequences which show the regularity of an economic law: first, that plans are too low, because there is an incentive to have a low plan which can easily be exceeded, second, the plans are only slightly overfulfilled in order not to have the plan raised too much next year. For this reason, we now abolish in Poland the connection between the payment of premiums and the overfulfilment of plans. The same thing is now being proposed in Czechoslovakia. We want to abolish this type of economic law. Instead, premiums will be based on the enterprise's improved results over those in the preceding period.

This brings me to the question of opportunities and incentives in a socialist economy. Social ownership of means of production implies new opportunities of economic development. These opportunities result from the absence of private vested interests hampering the rational use of means of production according to social needs. Social ownership of the means of production makes possible economic planning, i.e. planning of the rate of accumulation and of basic investments, determining the direction of development of the national economy, planning of the division of national income and planning of production to ensure co-ordination of the various branches of the national economy and harmonious economic development.

These opportunities, however, are no more than opportunities. They result from the abolition of obstacles to the rational use of means of production and the harmonious economic development inherent in capitalist society; they do not automatically guarantee the attainment of these objectives. For this purpose, incentives must exist in the organization and in the methods of management of a socialist economy. Such incentives partly result directly from the socialist relations in production, and partly depend on the organizational and managerial superstructure of the economy.

With regard to incentives resulting from socialist production relations, we have to observe that production and other economic activities are organized in the form of socialist enterprises, i.e., their organization of activities is designed to carry out certain specific social tasks. In order to carry out these tasks properly the persons participating in socialist enterprises must be interested economically and morally in the efficient performance of the tasks in the enterprise. The incentives, therefore, must be established in such a way that the personal and collective interests of the crew constituting the enterprise are identical with the social tasks the enterprise has to perform.

To conform to these requirements the socialist enterprise must satisfy two conditions. It must act as trustee of the general social interest and it must be a self-governing body. As there are two types of socialist ownership of means of production, namely, national ownership and group ownership (co-operative, municipal, etc.), there is a certain difference in the legal status of the corresponding type of socialist enterprises. In co-operative and other group forms of enterprises, the group owns the means of production and governs itself autonomously; in nationally owned enterprises, the enterprise acts as a trustee of the means of production which are national property. However, in both cases, the socialist enterprise is a trustee acting in the general interest of society. This holds also for co-operative and other enterprises based on group ownership which in socialist society must act in accordance with the general social interest. The very justification of co-operative and other group forms of socialist ownership is that in certain fields it allows better harmonization of the incentives for the crew of the enterprise with the general social interest. On the other hand, in nationally owned enterprises there must be substantial self-government of the workers of the enterprise, otherwise, the economic and moral incentives are inoperative, the enterprise becomes bureaucratized and does not fulfil its social task or does it very inadequately.

Thus, socialist enterprises must be bodies of self-governing workers, acting as trustees of the social interest. Two extremes may endanger the proper socialist character of the enterprise. One is the absence of trusteeship of the public interest. In this case, the ownership of the means of production, whatever its formally legal character, ceases to be socialist ownership and becomes pure group ownership devoid of any responsibility towards society. I shall call this anarchist-syndicalist degeneration.

The other extreme, which I shall call the bureaucratic degeneration, consists in the absence of effective workers' self-government at the enterprises. In such cases, the socialist character of the ownership of means of production becomes rather fictitious, because the workers have little direct influence on the practical use made of the means of production; whatever the influence, it is channelled through a centralistic bureaucratic machine. There is a danger of a new type of "alienation" (to use a well-known term of Marx) of the producer from his product, and thus of a deformation of the socialist character of production relations. Socialist ownership of means of production implies both the use of the means of production in the interest of society as a whole and effective democratic participation of the producers and other workers in the administration of the means of production.

These are the essential features of socialism. The particular forms in which they are embodied may vary from country to country and from one stage of development of socialist society to another. In the transition period, and in the first stages of socialist society, some deformations may take place of necessity. For instance, co-operative ownership may not act sufficiently in the general social interest, or the needs of centralized management may hamper the development of workers' self-government. The extent to which such deformations disappear is therefore a measure of the degree of maturity attained by socialist society.

Besides, under social ownership of means of production incentives are determined by the managerial superstructure of the economy, the methods of planning and of realization of the plan, the principles of economic accounting adopted, the methods of paying wages and salaries, the modes of participation in the profits of enterprises, the role of the market, etc. All these influence the incentives of the workers. Thus, proper organization of the managerial superstructure of the economy is essential to promote the operation of the incentives necessary to ensure that production is adjusted to the needs of society, and that the use of resources and the promotion of technical progress is rationally pursued.

Special consideration has to be given to the role of the state in the construction and guidance of a socialist economy. This role varies in the different stages of development of a socialist society. Unlike the bourgeois revolution which comes about when capitalist relations of production have already considerably developed within feudal society, the socialist revolution precedes the establishment of socialist relations in production. The revolutionary State, i.e., the dictatorship of the proletariat abolishes capitalist relations in production and establishes and organizes socialist production relations. This process may be sudden or more or less gradual. In any case, the political power of the State is the moving force in this process. In underdeveloped countries (in which most socialist revolutions so far have taken place) socialist production relations result also from the development of productive forces (industrialization, modernization of agriculture) which the new revolutionary State initiates.

Thus, in the first stages of the emergence and development of a socialist economy, the extra-economic force of the State plays a dominant role. It is the creative factor which brings about the changes from capitalist to socialist production relations and which, particularly in underdeveloped countries, fosters rapid development of productive forces. In this period, the economic laws specific to capitalism are being abolished and the economic laws of the new socialist society emerge and take shape. As the economic laws of a socialist society become more and more operative, the role of the extra-economic force of the State recedes. Extra-economic force is gradually replaced by the operation of economic laws, i.e., by the establishment of proper economic incentives which produce the results desired by the will of organized society.

The organizational expression of the replacement of extra-economic force by the utilization of economic laws must be a gradual separation of the management of the national economy from the extra-economic activities of the State, i.e., from the exercise of political power. Let me remind you of the distinction made by Engels between "Government of persons" and "Administration of things and direction of production processes". In the long-run perspective of communist society, the "government of persons" gradually disappears while the "administration of things and direction of production processes" remain the chief objectives of social organization. This is the substance of the process of "withering away" of the State.

While this certainly is a long-run perspective, the institutional preparation has to be undertaken at a much earlier stage. It is done by a gradual separation of the institutions of economic management from the institution of political government. As early as in 1918, Lenin said in his address to the first Congress of Councils of National Economy: "There is no doubt whatever that the further the achievements of the October Revolution penetrate, the more the changes initiated by this Revolution will be deepened, the more solid will become the foundations of the achievements of the socialist revolution and the consolidation of the socialist order, the greater will become the role of the councils of national economy which, of all the institutions of the State, alone will retain a permanent position. The more important this position the closer we shall be to introducing the socialist order, and the less necessary will become the purely administrative apparatus. This administrative apparatus, in the narrow sense of the word, i.e., the apparatus of the old State, is doomed to wither away after the final collapse of the resistance of the exploiters and after the working masses have learned to organize socialist production. Instead, the apparatus of the type of the supreme Council of National Economy will grow, develop and acquire strength in the most important field of activity of organized society".

The process of gradual separation of economic management from political government thus prepares the institutional conditions for the "withering-away" of the State. The gradual decline in political guidance of the economic process is an essential reflection of the process of maturation of socialist society. The farther socialist society has moved away from its capitalist heritage as well as from the heritage of the period of transition, in which extra-economic force plays a decisive role, the more the guidance of economic processes becomes separated from the exercise of political government. This process prepares the long-run perspective of the "withering-away" of the State.

THE ROLE OF PLANNING IN A SOCIALIST ECONOMY

Economic planning or, more precisely, the planning of economic development is an essential feature of socialism. It shows that a socialist economy does not develop in an elemental way, but that its development is guided and directed by the conscious will of organized society. Planning is the means of subjecting the operation of economic laws and the economic development of society to the direction of human will.

The experience of the construction of socialism in various countries indicates that the establishment of a planned economy is one of the first achievements of the socialist revolution. It precedes the full development of socialist relations in production, though it requires a certain minimum of such relations. In the transitional period, when non-socialist modes of production still play an important role, the economy is already subject to planned direction of its development. This is made possible by the existence in the economy of a large socialist sector which controls, as is frequently said, the "commanding outposts" of economic life. This is the minimum requirement for establishing a planned economy.

Economic planning starts with the direct intervention of the State in economic relations. This intervention has for its objectives the liquidation of capitalist relations in production and the control of the remaining non-socialist sectors of the economy. The control of the non-socialist sectors is made possible by the existence of a socialist sector, particularly that part of the socialist sector which is nationalized (i.e., state-owned), and which controls the commanding outposts of the economy.

In this first, transitional phase, the new revolutionary State is not neutral with regard to the various sectors of the economy. It consciously utilizes the nationalized socialist sector as a means in controlling the development of the whole economy. The policy pursued consists of economic measures which result from the existence of the nationalized sector comprising the decisive controlling part of the economy; and also of intervention by political force, i.e., non-economic force. In the first revolutionary period, intervention in economic processes by political force plays a decisive role.

In the first period of development of a socialist economy both the planning of economic development and the day-to-day management of the socialist sector is highly centralized.

There may be some doubts as to how far this represents a universal necessity. For instance, in Poland, we had discussions on whether such a period of highly centralized planning and management was a historical necessity or a great political mistake. Personally, I hold the view that it was a historical necessity.

It seems to me that, first, the very process of the social revolution which liquidates one social system and establishes another, requires centralized disposal of resources by the new revolutionary State, and consequently centralized management and planning. This holds, in my opinion, for any socialist revolution.

For underdeveloped countries, a further consideration must be added. Socialist industrialization and particularly very rapid industrialization, which was necessary in the first socialist countries, particularly in the Soviet Union, as a political requirement of national defence and in the solution of all kinds of political and social problems, due to backwardness, requires centralized disposal of resources. Thus, the very process of transformation of the social system and, in addition, in underdeveloped countries, the need for rapid industrialization, impose the necessity of higher centralized planning and management.

The process of rapid industrialization requires such centralized disposal of resources for two reasons. First, it is necessary to concentrate all resources on certain objectives and avoid dissipation of resources on other objectives which would divert resources from the purpose of rapid industrialization. This is one of the reasons which lead to highly centralized planning and management and also to the allocation of resources by administrative directives, according to priorities. The second reason why rapid industrialization demands centralized planning and management is the lack and weakness of industrial cadres. With the rapid growth of industry the cadres are new and inexperienced. Such old cadres which had some experience in management of industry and other economic activities are frequently politically alien to socialist objectives. In consequence, high centralization of managerial decisions becomes necessary.

Thus, the first period of planning and management in a socialist economy, at least according to our present experience, has always been characterized by administrative management and administrative allocation of resources on the basis of priorities centrally established. Economic incentives are in this period replaced by moral and political appeals to the workers, by appeals to their patriotism and socialist consciousness. This is, so to speak, a highly politicized economy, both as regards the means of planning and management and the incentives it utilizes.

I think that, essentially, it can be described as a *sui generis* war economy. Such methods of war economy are not peculiar to socialism because they are also used in capitalist countries in war time. They were developed in the First and the Second World Wars. In capitalist countries similar methods were used during the war, namely, concentration of all resources for one basic purpose, which is the production of war materials, and centralized disposal of resources in order to avoid leakage of resources to what was considered as non-essential uses (everything which was not connected with the prosecution of the war). Allocation of resources by administrative decision, according to administratively established priorities, and large-scale use of political incentives to maintain productivity and discipline of labour by patriotic appeals were characteristic of the war economy. This was the case in all capitalist countries during the war.

It shows clearly that such methods of centralized planning and management are not peculiar to socialism, that they are rather techniques of a war economy. The difficulty starts when these methods of war economy are identified with the essence of socialism and are considered essential to socialism.

One of the methods of war economy, which most of the socialist countries used at one stage or another, were compulsory deliveries by peasants of part of their produce. Many comrades in my country feel rather upset by our government's present programme, abolishing such deliveries. They fear that this implies giving up some socialist principle. I usually answer them by asking whether they remember who in Poland first introduced compulsory deliveries by peasants. Such deliveries were first introduced during the First World War by the occupation army of Kaiser Wilhelm the Second, whom I do not think anybody regards as a champion of socialism. These methods cannot be considered as an essential aspect of socialism, they are merely methods of war economy necessary in a revolutionary period of transition.

The fate and history of these methods is a classical example of the dialectical character of the development of socialist society. Methods, which are necessary and useful in the period of social revolution and of intensive industrialization, become an obstacle to further economic progress when they are perpetrated beyond their historic justification. They become obstacles because they are characterized by a lack of flexibility. They are rigid, and lead therefore to waste of resources resulting from this inflexibility; they require a wasteful bureaucratic apparatus and make it difficult to adjust production to the needs of the population. However, it seems that the greatest obstacle to further progress results from the lack of adequate economic incentives in this bureaucratic centralistic type of management. This hampers proper economic utilization of resources, encourages waste and also hinders technical progress.

Therefore, the moment, when socialist society starts to overcome these centralistic, bureaucratic methods of administrative planning and management, indicates that the new socialist society is beginning to mature. Previously we spoke in the discussion about the period of transition, when it ends and how it should be defined. I would not want to enter into this problem here, and make this the final definition of the period of transition. But I might say that the substitution for the methods of administrative and centralized management and development of new methods, based on the utilization of economic laws, indicates the end of the period of transition and the beginning of the functioning of an established socialist economy. I would not say that this is the only aspect of the problem of the period of transition, but it certainly is one of its important aspects.

The period of centralized planning and management, as I said, is the result partly of the necessities for the revolutionary transformation of society and, in underdeveloped countries, also of the needs for rapid industrialization. In studying this period, a certain important sociological factor has to be taken into account, namely, the weakness of the working class in an underdeveloped country. It seems to me that it is on the basis of this weakness of the working class, under conditions of under-development, that the bureaucratic state machine gains great importance, and phenomena such as the "cult of personality" develop. It in a way replaces the spontaneous activity of the working class.

But here again, the dialectics of the processes of construction of socialism become apparent. The centralistic methods are successful in achieving rapid industrialization and, as a consequence, cause a rapid growth of the working class. The working class grows in numbers as well as in consciousness and political maturity. Next to the growth of the working class another important sociological element appears. This is the growth of a new socialist intelligentsia coming largely from the ranks of the workers and peasants. When it becomes clear that highly centralized administrative and bureaucratic methods of management create obstacles to further progress, part of the political and state apparatus also becomes convinced that a change of methods in administration and management is needed. Thus, new social forces mature which require and also make possible a change in these methods.

This, precisely, is the basic difference between the development of socialist society and a society which is based on antagonistic class relations. There is no ruling class which may oppose these changes. There may be, as I previously said, certain strata or groups, which have a vested interest in the old methods and create obstacles, but these obstacles can never become of such importance as to render inoperative the changes required by new historical circumstances.

This was quite evident, for instance, in the experience of Poland, where the industrialization by means of centralized administrative planning and management has led to a substantial growth of the working class. Our working class is now more than three times the number it was before the war. The working class has gained experience in large industrial establishments. It was at first to a large extent of peasant origin and that, of course, weighed on its psychology. But that was only a transitional phase. Industrialization and the social revolution have created a new intelligentsia, largely coming from workers and peasants. All that led to a maturation of the forces in the new socialist society. In consequence, we arrived at such a phenomenon as the great movement of workers' councils demanding self-government of workers in industry, the general demand for a change in the methods of management of the national economy. The Party accepted these demands of the people and gave them organized expression.

Changes in the methods of planning and the management of the economy are taking place today practically in all socialist countries. Forms and contents are different; but all these changes entail a certain decentralization or deconcentration in the management of the economy.

I do not want to enter into a description of the process of change in various socialist countries. I shall rather present to you what I personally believe is the proper formulation of the role and methods of planning in a socialist economy.

First, it must be stated that in a socialist society planning of the economy is active planning. Some of the economists in Poland use the term "directive planning" but this term is ambiguous; therefore I shall rather use the term "active planning". By this I mean that planning does not only entail the co-ordination of the activities of various branches of the national economy. It is something more, namely, it is an active determination of the main lines of development of the national economy. Otherwise, if planning were mere co-ordination, the development of the socialist economy would be elemental, and would not really be directed by the will of organized society. If economic development is not to be elemental but is to be directed by organized society, then planning must be active economic planning.

Two problems arise with regard to active economic planning. First: what is its scope, what are the activities in the economy that have to be planned? And second: what are the methods of ensuring the realization of the plan?

The active character of planning does not require that the plan goes into each detail of economic life. We actually had a period in the socialist countries—may be with the exception of China, which already started at a later level and profited from the experience of other socialist countries—when the output of even the least important commodity was planned. There was the famous joke in Poland—it really was not a joke, it was true—that the production of pickled cucumbers is in the national economic plan. Another case which was not a joke either but was a fact was that the State Planning Commission provided in the plan for the number of hares to be shot in a hunting season. At the same time, buttons or hairpins for ladies, for instance, were unobtainable simply because they had been forgotten in the national economic plan.

Active planning and effective direction of the development of the national economy is quite possible without planning such details. Even more, planning such details hampers really effective direction of the national economy. I think it may be said that incorporating such details in the national economic plan had nothing to do with planning. It was part of the highly centralized day-to-day management of the economy by means of administrative measures. This is a different matter from planning.

However, the national economic plan which is to determine the development of the national economy must at least provide for two issues. First, the division of national income between accumulation and consumption. Second, the allocation of investments to the different branches of the economy. The first determines the general rate of economic growth, the second determines the direction of economic development.

Unless these two issues are suitably provided for in the plan, there is no active guidance in the development of the national economy. This is, therefore, the minimum requirement of the plan. In addition, the plan may or may not include targets for the production of certain basic commodities, such as basic raw materials, basic means of production, and so on. These are technical and not fundamental problems.

Such are the fundamental aspects of the plan which determine the pace and the direction of development of the economy. In addition to these, economic planning must be concerned with co-ordination of the activities of the various branches of the economy. First of all, it must co-ordinate the financial and the real aspects of the plan, in particular the total purchasing power at the disposal of the population and the amounts of consumer goods which are to be provided for individual consumption. The plan must also in some way and by some means provide for the co-ordination of the output in the various branches of the national economy. Otherwise, it may not be possible to realize the planned directions of development as provided for in the plan. If there is no proper co-ordination between the output of the various branches of the economy, it may not be possible to carry out investments, because the necessary investment goods would not be produced. All kinds of bottlenecks may appear and cause difficulties, which may make it impossible to carry out the investment plan. So much about the content of the plan.

The second problem is that of the methods of ensuring the realization of the plan. Here, we have basically two possible methods. One of administrative orders and administrative allocation of resources. The various units in the socialist economy are ordered to do certain things, for instance, to produce fixed quantities of certain items. The resources which are necessary for that purpose, both material and financial, are allocated in an administrative way. This was the traditional method of realizing the plan in the past. The second method consists in the use of what we call "economic means", namely of setting up a system of incentives which induces people to do exactly the things which are required by the plan. It seems to me, that in effective planning of a socialist economy, both methods have to be used, though in different proportions.

Preference should be given to the use of economic means. Administrative methods should be limited to such fields where, for some reason or other, economic means are ineffective. Such situations, where economic means are not effective, always do exist. They exist, of course, particularly in periods of very great changes, because economic means are rather subtle instruments responding to "normal" changes in the situation, and frequently breaking down when very fundamental or revolutionary changes are needed. In such cases the use of administrative means must be accepted. Even in a capitalist economy, in situations of profound changes, the State uses in its economic policy measures of administrative control, because the normal kinds of economic means are not sufficient to produce the responses which are necessary.

The fundamental decisions of the plan concerning the division of national income between accumulation and consumption, and concerning the basic directions of investments are really of a political character, while the means of implementation must partly be administrative. The decision of the plan concerning the rate of accumulation is basically realized by administrative measures. Part of the national income produced is not paid out in the form of individual incomes, part of the profits of the socialist enterprises are held back by the State and this is an administrative measure. So are also all forms of taxation of enterprises and individuals. The basic directions of investments, for instance, the decision to build an electric power plant, are usually not made in response to a market situation, but are made as basic decisions of economic policy. Though in the realization of such decisions uses may be made of all kinds of economic instruments.

We may ask in what sense the economic plans must take account of economic laws. Even when the realization of the plan is achieved by administrative measures, the plan must observe the general economic laws concerning the proportions necessary in the process of production and reproduction. For instance, if the plan provides for an increase in the production of steel, it must provide for a certain additional output of coal which is needed to produce the additional steel. Any kind of planning has to take care of such objective kinds of relationship.

There are also other economic laws which must be observed by the plan. These are the laws which result from the operation of economic incentives under the circumstances created by the plan. The process of realization of the plan sets into motion definite economic incentives to which the people react in a certain way which can be calculated. Even in the period of administrative planning certain economic incentives were operative and their consequences had to be taken into account. In this period, however, economic means were only subsidiary in relation to administrative means. I would say that now the situation has to change in the sense that the economic means are the rule and administrative means become subsidiary to the economic means. Thus, the plan has to observe the laws of production and reproduction; and in so far as the realization is based on the use of economic means, i.e. the operation of economic laws, it also has to consider these laws.

By utilizing economic means planning makes use of the automatic character of people's responses to given incentives. Thus, certain automatic processes in the economy are established. However, these automatic processes are not elemental (*stikhiiny*). These two aspects must be distinguished. The difference is that in a socialist society, where these automatic processes are part of the method of realization of the plan, the conditions determining incentives are set up by economic policy, whereas in a capitalist society these conditions develop in an elemental way. There is a basic difference: in one case (capitalism), the incentives develop in an elemental way and are not subject to conscious control of society; in the other case (socialism), they are consciously established by organized society in such a way as to produce the desired results. As Engels said: "the social causes set into motion will produce to an ever increasing extent the results desired by man".

I shall illustrate this by an analogy of the following type. The capitalist economy may be compared to an old-fashioned balloon which is moved by the currents of the air in the direction in which the wind pushes it. Man has no control whatever over the direction in which the balloon is moving. The socialist economy in the period of realization of the plan by administrative measures can be compared to an old-fashioned airplane, where the pilot with his hands moves the steering rod. By sitting always by the steering rod the pilot directs the plane in the direction he chooses, whenever the current of the air changes, he moves the rod in such a way as to keep his chosen direction.

Planning in which the realization is based on economic means I would compare to a modern plane which has an automatic steering mechanism. The pilot sets the mechanism in the direction in which he wants the plane to fly and the automatic mechanism keeps the plane in the desired direction. The pilot can read a book or a newspaper in the meantime, and the plane by itself flies in the desired direction. But it is not the direction in which the wind pushes the plane, but the direction which the pilot has consciously chosen. It is the pilot who determines the direction of the plane, if he wishes he can change the direction by setting the automatic mechanism in a different direction.

If I wished to carry the analogy to the end, I would say that the pilot must, of course, from time to time watch whether the automatic steering mechanism works. As a rule, experience shows that when the wind is very strong the automatic mechanism does not work and the pilot has to take the steering rod in his hand and steer himself. When the wind quietens down he can again let the automatic mechanism work. In sudden perturbed situations, administrative measures have to be used in managing the socialist economy.

The next problem is to what extent the decisions laid down in the plan—not their realization—can be centralized, or can, or even must be decentralized. The need for centralized decisions in the plan obviously results from the need for co-ordination. Similarly to the basic directions of investments, such decisions must be centrally planned since they too must be co-ordinated as the activities of various branches of the economy are co-ordinated. Each plan must have centralistic elements. I would say that the basic decisions of the plan must be made centrally. In addition, the plan may have as subsidiary parts certain decentralized subsidiary plans, in order to ensure adequate flexibility of the plan. There are two criteria which determine the degree of decentralization which economic planning can or must have. One determines the possibility of decentralization and the other the necessity for decentralization.

Economic planning can be decentralized, if it is feasible, and in so far as it is feasible, economic incentives should be so chosen that the decisions of the decentralized units are the same as those made centrally. Second, economic planning must be decentralized in all cases where the central decision responds to a situation too late. Because in such cases unless there is decentralization central planning becomes fictitious; what actually is obtained is an elemental development. It is important to notice that in all socialist countries in the period of highly centralized planning and management there was a great number of this type of elemental processes in the economy.

For instance, in Poland at a certain period, the amount of elemental processes became so great that you could ask whether there still exists a planned economy. On the one hand there was a plan, but on the other the economy produced results in a very elemental way. The elemental character of this process was the result of two facts. One was the over-centralization of the plan. Before the processes which were taking place in various branches of the economy came to the attention of the central authority, and before the central authority took action irreversible events had already happened. The result was purely elemental. The other fact was the existence of "wrong" economic incentives. When the old incentives of the moral and political appeal stopped working, because such incentives can only work for a certain period, it was discovered that all kinds of incentives were implicit in the plan of which the central authority was not aware, and which hampered the realization of the plan.

Thus, it is a practically important question how many of the decisions are made in the central economic plan, and how many decisions are delegated to lower economic units, e.g., enterprises or industries, etc. This is particularly important with regard to investment plans. In Poland, for instance, we are now developing a scheme which provides central planning for the so-called fundamental investments, such as building new plants or enlarging substantially existing plants. We shall give enterprises the right to undertake subsidiary investments autonomously without prior approval.

The latter has proved to be necessary in order to ensure greater flexibility of investment decisions; for instance, if the enterprise needs to put up funds for unforeseen repairs, or if it wants to buy machines to increase output quickly, or to make some technical improvement. Our experience was that before approval was obtained from the central authority for the carrying out of the necessary investments, the whole situation had already changed. Thus, the situation was utterly inflexible. The financial resources for such subsidiary investments would consist of part of the depreciation fund of the enterprise and of bank credits it could obtain for the purpose of such investments. Investments of small enterprises are to be entirely financed by bank credits, without appearing at all in the central economic plan.

Now, of course, one thing should be borne in mind. The fact that part of that investment is financed by bank credits does subject them in an indirect way to central planning, because obviously the bank can refuse to give the credit. The bank acts on the basis of a certain general economic policy. How much credit it is going to give, for what purpose it is going to give it, on what conditions it will give it, these are indirect ways of influencing subsidiary investments by the central authority.

A similar economic problem, and a more acute one, exists with regard to the planning of production. In the former period even the smallest product had to be in the central economic plan. Now, however, only the basic production of enterprises is in the central economic plan; the enterprise has the right to undertake what is called subsidiary production, which is not in the plan. There is much controversy among Polish economists as to whether production should be in the economic plan. There are a few economists who think that production should not be at all in the economic plan, but it should only respond to the economic incentives of the market. The practical solution which will probably be adopted in Poland will be to put in the central economic plan the output of certain basic commodities, such as coal, steel, raw materials, certain means of production, textiles of mass production, i.e., commodities of a particular significance for the national economy. As to the rest, the enterprises should have a plan of output in terms of total net value of output without prescribing detailed assortments. A shoe factory, for instance, would have a total value plan of output but would be free to produce any assortment, for instance men's shoes, ladies shoes, childrens' shoes, according to its own decision.

All these are already problems of techniques and not problems of principle. I think that the one essential issue in the socialist economy is that the plan has to be an active plan which determines the pace and the direction of development of the national economy. The other issues are really questions of techniques which may change under different conditions. There is, however, one more problem which I want to mention in this connection. This is an essential and not a technical problem, namely, that the plan must be based on correct economic accounting of economic costs and benefits, and consequently on a correct price system.

In a socialist economy prices serve a double purpose: one is as a means of distribution and the other as a means of economic accounting. Therefore, there are two principles which must be taken into account in the formation of prices. This requires a calculation, at least as we see it now in our work in Poland, of two kinds of prices, namely market prices and accounting prices.

Unless distribution of consumer goods is done by rationing, the market price must obviously be such as to establish equilibrium on the market, to equalize demand and supply. The same holds also for prices of means of production when administrative allocation is removed and enterprises freely buy and sell their products. Market conditions determine the equilibrium prices which equalize demand and supply. The principle in determining market prices is very simple. They simply must equalize demand and supply.

However, market prices are not sufficient. In addition, there must be calculated accounting prices which reflect the social cost of production of the various products. The accounting prices, of course, may strongly differ from the market prices. In Poland we propose now to calculate, what we call, the initial or normal prices representing the cost of production plus profit which are to cover accumulation and collective consumption of society. To these normal prices we propose to add a (positive or negative) mark-up in order to obtain the market prices which equalize demand and supply on the market. Then the (positive or negative) differences between the market prices and the normal prices would be an indicator for economic planning.

The indication would be to increase in the next plan the output (by making the necessary investments) of commodities, where the market price is high above the normal price, to stop expansion or even diminish output where the market price does not even realize the normal price.

The great controversy at this moment among Polish economists is what costs should be included in the normal prices. Whether it should be average costs of enterprises in a given industry or marginal costs. The majority of economists take the view that it should be marginal costs. The remainder are in favour of average costs. But those who are in favour of average costs really represent two groups: one, in principle, is in favour of average costs and the other of marginal costs; the latter group believes that this would in practice be a very difficult system of calculation and takes average cost simply because the other solution, though theoretically better, is very difficult to realize in practice.

The proponents of marginal cost, of course, propose to use a practical approximation to marginal cost. The cost on the basis of which the normal price is to be calculated is the average variable cost of the group of enterprises which have the highest cost in the industry. Classify the enterprises into several groups (not too many, because it has to be practically easy), and then take the group of enterprises which have the highest cost as the pilot group, which serves as the indicator, and take the average variable cost in this group. There is a reason for taking the average variable cost. Because if we take just one enterprise we may arrive at a very random result, and we do not want to have purely random fluctuations. We want to have something which represents the real cost structure of the industry. Therefore, we take the average variable cost of the enterprises in that last group.

The argument in favour of marginal cost and procedure of practical interpretation of marginal cost is this. We have, for instance, electric power plants. Each plant produces at a different cost. Suppose we can save electric power. What is the diminution of cost to society? Obviously, when we save electric power we still stop or diminish production not in the plants which have the lowest cost, but in the plants which have the highest cost. The cost in the latter plants represents the resources we save, it represents the saving of cost to society. If we have to expand output of electricity, the cost to society is the cost of operation of electric power plants which produce at the highest cost and which are necessary to cover the increased demand for electricity. Consequently, if changes in the use of electric power take place, the effect on cost to society of these changes is in the most costly plants, i.e., the marginal cost. We consider the average variable cost in the most expensively producing power plants, because the fixed cost is anyhow given and does not change in consequence of a change in consumption of electricity.

This is basically the system which the majority of Polish economists propose. To the marginal cost there must be added something to cover all the fixed costs in the industry. This may be zero, because the larger profits of the enterprise which produce at lower cost may be sufficient for this purpose. If not, we must add something to marginal cost. Such additions would have to be everywhere proportional to the marginal cost so that the normal prices would be proportional to the marginal costs of the various products to cover the fixed cost.

The indicator for the plan would be whether the market price is higher or lower than this normal price, i.e., whether it socially pays to expand or reduce the output of a product. I should add that this normal cost would also have to include a surcharge to cover capital accumulation and collective consumption, e.g., non-productive expenses of the State, etc. Such additions would have to be in the same proportion in all branches of the economy so as not to affect the proportions between the normal prices and marginal costs.

So much on this subject. Now, it is clear that good and effective economic planning requires a development of economic science, that it must be based on scientific economic analysis. This is one of the basic differences between a socialist and a capitalist economy. In a capitalist economy the economic processes are elemental, whereas under socialism they can be directed on the basis of scientific knowledge of the needs and possibilities of the whole national economy.

FROM ACCOUNTING TO MATHEMATICS

The application of mathematics to the management and planning of the national economy is steadily gaining in popularity. Amongst other reasons, this is due to the development of knowledge and to the elimination of prejudice and dogmatic belief that mathematics cannot be applied to economics since the latter is a humanistic discipline. The widening scope of application of mathematics in recent years, and particularly the development of its new branches, has shown that mathematics is today becoming more and more important in humanities, and that at least in some branches of humanistic disciplines its role is comparable to that in the natural sciences. The growing interest for the use of mathematics in the planning and management of the national economy is also a result of new needs which have been brought about by the development of the socialist economy.

The more the socialist economy grows and the more it matures, the more precise and refined are the methods required for planning its further growth and for managing its everyday activities.

Balancing Calculations

Looking back at the history of the development of planning under socialism, we can distinguish two fairly distinct stages. The first stage, during which the main problem was the co-ordination of particular branches of the economy, aimed at ensuring internal consistency in national economic plans. The national economy constitutes a closely knit entity, and its development plan must also constitute an integrated entity. If we plan to raise the output of steel, we also have to plan for appropriately increased supplies of iron ore, coal and many other factors. In the absence of such co-ordination, the plan will turn out to be lacking in internal consistency and its practical implementation will not be feasible.

This problem was solved by balancing calculations. The method of making out balance sheets, historically developed in capitalist enterprises,

115

subsequently has been extended to cover the national economy. The balancing and the co-ordination of particular branches of the national economy has become a basis for planning economic growth.

At first, simple bookkeeping arithmetic sufficed. But even at a fairly early stage it turned out that balance sheets are like equations in which certain magnitudes are given by objective conditions, others are postulated as the assumptions of the plan and others still must be calculated, being the unknowns in these equations. In this way, balancing calculations have led, in their further development, to a mathematical analysis of balance sheets which assumes the form of input–output analysis. This was the first step toward the introduction of mathematics in national economic planning. But this first step, if it is to become something more than a theoretical postulate and an interesting mathematical exercise, requires tools with which sets of many equations could be solved rapidly. This possibility is provided by electronic computers and, therefore, the development and the application of mathematical methods to balancing calculations is closely related to the development of electronic computers.

The role played by mathematical methods in balancing calculations is today generally known and recognized. However, we are now only at the very initial stage of their practical application. Studies in input–output analysis are, so far, of a rather retrospective nature and they are still concerned with past statistics. If these methods are to become an actual tool of economic planning, they have to be applied to prospective, hypothetical statistical data.

This requires, however, that certain quantities be determined. Even in traditional methods of planning we have introduced standard norms for the wear and tear of machinery and equipment, norms for material and labour input; these norms are calculated per unit product. They are technical norms and have been worked out in workshops and laboratories. Where such norms are lacking, statistical norms are used as temporary substitutes. These norms are basic coefficients used in input–output analysis. They are parameters appearing in sets of equations. In addition to these technical parameters there are others, such as the composition of labour resulting from demographic processes and the consumer demand for particular goods and services depending upon income and the price structure. All these parameters can be called econometric parameters. As we know, their determination and the forecasting of their development is the task of econometrics.

The Optimization of the Plan

These were the main characteristic features of the first stage in the development of socialist economic planning, and of the role of mathematical methods during this stage. The second stage, which has begun only recently, introduces into planning the concept of the optimization of the plan. Today we are not satisfied with ensuring internal consistency of the plan. There may be many such plans (theoretically their number may be infinite) and it is necessary to select the optimal plan (or plans). This, of course, has also been done before, albeit in an intuitive way, and lively discussions and arguments used to be held, concerning the content and the nature of the plan and of its possible alternatives. But these discussions were based on the criteria of common sense and intuition. Today, this approach does not suffice. Science with its newly developed theory of programming and the techniques of electronic computers are very helpful in achieving further progress in this field. These new techniques now make feasible and practicable numerical calculations of optimum plans with a large number of parameters and unknowns.

In practice the optimization of the plan is still at a rather embryonic stage; we have just managed to comprehend fully the importance and the ramifications of the problem. We have also attained the beginning stage of applying optimization calculus to particular problems, such as some transportation problems, combinations of factors at which the cost of production is minimized, etc. We still do not apply optimization calculus to the national economy as a whole. But sooner or later such a need will arise. With economic growth and with the resultant increasing complexity of the socialist economy simple common sense and intuitive criteria will not suffice any more. They are partly inadequate even today. The practical significance of the application of optimization calculus to the national economy as a whole is that a choice can be made between alternative plans.

Today, we do not avail ourselves of this chance as yet. We prepare our plans according to certain criteria of common sense and intuition, and then we balance them and are quite satisfied when the balanced plan does not display any major internal inconsistencies. Then, during further discussions within government authorities at different levels and in Parliament certain connections are introduced. Nobody raises the question of preparing an alternative plan, because this would not be feasible from the practical point of view. The preparation of the plan and the balancing calculations are a tremendous task requiring the co-operation of so many people that, quite naturally, once the draft of the plan is prepared, it carries a great deal of weight and becomes rigid and inflexible. The possibility of a broader approach to and greater precision in the solving of the problem of the optimization of the plan for the whole national economy is closely tied up with technical means of rapidly performing balancing calculations and of computing different variants of the plan already balanced.

Criteria of Appraisal

What is the best plan? What are its proper criteria? Even today heated discussions go on amongst economists concerning the question whether in a socialist economy one can talk of a single target expressed quantitatively, to which the whole economy could be subordinated, or whether there are many such targets, not comparable with each other; or, using the language of mathematics, whether the aim of a socialist economy can be conceived as a magnitude that can be expressed in terms of scale and, thus, in the form of a single numerical index, or whether it is a vector whose magnitude cannot be uniquely controlled, a set of different, not comparable indices. Personally, I think that the aim of a socialist economy can be assumed to be a magnitude of scale expressed in terms of national income. In this case, the task of the optimization of plans would be a programming problem in which, given the limiting conditions, the object is to maximize the national income within a defined period of time. It can be shown, that this is tantamount to the maximization of the rate of growth of national income within a given period of time. In this way, we have a uniquely defined magnitude to be maximized, that is to say, a target function, and national economic planning becomes simply an ordinary mathematical programming problem.

The problem of the target function for the national economy is a very important one. Depending upon the target set for the whole economy, the subordinate targets are automatically determined and thus also the target functions, in particular partial objectives of programming. For instance, for a long time now discussions have been going on concerning criteria of the effectiveness of investments in a socialist economy. These discussions were inconclusive because in the circumstances under which they were held they could not have been conclusive. The effectiveness of investments in the national economy depends upon the target set for the economy. If this target is not distinctly determined, then it cannot be determined which investment is better and which is worse. If, for instance, we determine the target of national economic planning as the maximization of national income, or, what amounts to the same, as the maximization of its increase within a definite period of time, then we automatically obtain certain criteria of the effectiveness of investments. The criterion of the effectiveness of investments is then the extent to which a given investment contributes to the increase in national income. When other targets are set for a socialist economy, other criteria of the effectiveness of investment will have to be used.

In this way, we are embarking upon the second stage in the development of national economic planning, the stage of searching not just for balanced plans, but for optimum plans of the development of the national economy. It can be said that, not only in Poland but also in other socialist countries, and particularly in the Soviet Union, discussions indicate clearly the transition to the second stage. The problem of optimum plans has now become the crux of economic discussions.

Mathematics and Management

There is also the problem of applying mathematical methods to management, to the day-to-day functioning of the socialist economy. Here too the problem of optimization arises with respect to the optimal organization of the national economy, the optimal methods of its functioning. Several years ago an extensive discussion has been going on in this country about these problems, treated as the problems of the "model" of the socialist economy. Today, the same subject is extensively discussed in the U.S.S.R. A very valuable contribution can be made in this field by econometric methods. They can help to determine how changes in prices and in the distribution of income affect demand, how changes in the wage structure affect the efficiency of labour, etc. This should increase the precision and logic of reasoning in solving problems involved in managing the national economy. The problem of planning and managing the national economy and the application of mathematical methods to these tasks are peculiar to a socialist economy; to a limited extent, these problems also exist in capitalist countries. We are now witnessing in those countries a growing interest in mathematical methods and their application to the management of the national economy. But in those countries such possibilities are very limited because a capitalist economy considered as an entity is not a consciously managed system, such as a socialist economy is. For this reason, in a socialist economy these methods can be applied on a national scale and can be used for seeking an optimum system for the organization and management of the national economy.

The problem now facing a socialist economy is not only the development of productive resources but also the development of the methods of managing the economy. In this respect mathematical methods will play an increasingly important part. Up to the present, we have been using the method of common sense and intuition, but mathematical methods do not contradict common sense or good intuition which plays an important part both in scientific research and in every day human activities. On the contrary, these methods are of great help and they provide common sense with precise criteria and tools for checking whether intuition is correct, for facilitating its precise formulation and very often they give rise to new intuition.

Economic Cybernetics

The importance of mathematical methods is not confined to their purely computational application or to the formulation of balancing and programming tasks and to solving them by mathematical methods. I think that of very great importance is the educational role of these methods as a school of precision in formulating these tasks. It is now possible to approach these problems in a more precise way owing to the development of a new discipline closely related to mathematics, a discipline called cybernetics. The problem of particularly great importance is the optimal ratio of centralization to decentralization in managing the national economy. This subject is often discussed, but, strictly speaking, there is not much sense in talking about an economy completely centralized or completely decentralized. The management of a socialist economy can be more or less centralized or more or less decentralized; the point is to arrive at optimal relations and scope. This gives rise to many important problems. One of them is the circulation of information in the national economy; another is the decision making capacity of particular centres of authority.

Let us consider, as a starting point, a system completely centralized in which all decisions are made by only one central authority. Such a system could hardly operate in practice, since the decision making capacity of one central authority is limited. It would turn out that problems awaiting decision pile up and are considerably delayed at the central authority. If to this we add the length of time required for the transmission of information to the authority, and for the channelling back of decisions, as new information, to lower authorities which are to implement them, it would turn out that most decisions would arrive too late. This would be the case, for instance, if all fire brigades in the whole country had to report each fire to the head office in Warsaw and wait for a decision as to what should be done. In most cases fire brigade intervention based on this system would be too late. On the other hand, however, we would not want to have, say, twenty independent fire brigade centres in one city. It would be too costly, it would require a great deal of equipment which would not be fully utilized and it would not leave any room for manoeuvre in shifting men and equipment from one point of the city to another. Thus, the problem is to arrive at some optimal organization, both sufficiently centralized and decentralized. There is a certain similarity here to the functioning of automatic industrial equipment. In this kind of equipment there appear the same problems: the length of time required for the flow of information and the reaction of particular elements of this equipment as well as the problem of the capacity of the steering mechanism in the equipment. All this indicates that cybernetics can help considerably in arriving at the optimal organization of the socialist economy.

Precision in Economic Thinking

When the problem of balancing in the input–output analysis of production is formulated precisely in mathematical terms, a certain degree of precision is also achieved in our economic thinking; we have to distinguish between objective actual data, postulates, plans and the unknowns which we want to determine; we have to recognize the existence of such problems as the number of the degrees of freedom given by the balance sheet and the proper role of particular parameters, e.g. technical norms in making up the balance sheet. The development of the theory of programming has enabled us also to formulate precisely a number of conceptual problems in national economic planning. In consequence, the application of mathematics improves the methods of planning and management also where no mathematical equations and computers are used. In cases when the circumstances of the problem, e.g., its simplicity, enable us to use the traditional methods of common sense and intuition, the knowledge of mathematical methods contributes to greater clarity and precision in thinking. Therefore, as last but not least, I rank the indirect importance of mathematical methods for developing common sense and enriching intuition which are both always indispensable in management and in national economic planning.

Part III

ECONOMIC THEORY

FORMS OF SUPPLY ADJUSTMENT
AND ECONOMIC EQUILIBRIUM

1. Since the classical economists it has been held as undisputed that the market economy, when its equilibrium is disturbed, attains by itself a new equilibrium, if no further variations in important factors take place and the entrepreneurs adapt production to the movement of the market-price. Then, if the market price is higher than the equilibrium price (i.e., than the "natural" price according to the classical authorities), additional capital flows into the appropriate branch of production and production increases until the market price again coincides with the equilibrium price. If the market price is lower than the equilibrium price, then an analogous process takes place in reverse. But now new authors, namely Ricci, Schultz, Tinbergen and Rosenstein-Rodan, have demonstrated that this automatic adjustment of the market price to the equilibrium price (and the quantity actually produced to the equilibrium quantity) is, in fact, not so natural as people have believed since the classical authorities. Supply adjustment to the change in price requires, as a rule, a certain period of time and, throughout this period, both the price and the produced quantities are subject to oscillations which can be illustrated by the well-known "cob-web theorem" (cf. Fig. 1).

These oscillations only converge to the equilibrium point when the supply elasticity in this sphere is smaller than the demand elasticity.

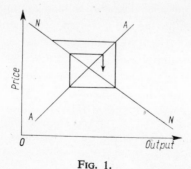

Fig. 1.

If both these elasticities are equal, one obtains an oscillation of a constant size. If the elasticity of supply is greater than that of demand, it grows in size and the oscillation becomes "explosive".[1] In consequence, the assumption of the traditional theory that, when entrepreneurs adapt their production to the market price, equilibrium is always established, seems to be disproved. An automatic change in economic equilibrium demands, in addition, the existence of appropriate conditions which were not formulated in the traditional theory. As an appropriate condition can be considered either the assumption that the supply elasticity is lower than that of demand, which might not be deduced from the basic assumptions of the economic theory, or the assumption that the entrepreneurs not only adapt production to a given market price, but also to anticipated future prices.

The same problem, which we have discussed in the example of partial equilibrium, also exists in the theory of general economic equilibrium. General economic equilibrium is brought about, on the one hand, by the fact that consumers and entrepreneurs maximize their utility, or their profits, while, on the other hand, the supply and demand for each commodity is the same. Under the latter condition, prices become fixed. These prices are for the consumers and entrepreneurs, however, constant parameters (therefore quasi "data"), on the basis of which they take decisions aiming at maximum utility, or maximum profits. This "parametric" character of the price, it is true, exists fully not only in a state of free competition, but also under monopoly, and in restricted competition it will only be partially suspended since no individual can systematically influence all prices. If the prices are equilibrium prices, i.e. prices for which supply and demand for each commodity are balanced, there is no reason to lift the economy out of its equilibrium. If, however, for some reason (e.g. owing to an unforeseen change in the factors), they are not equilibrium prices, then a process of oscillation begins. Owing to the discrepancy between supply and demand, the prices change, and accordingly the parameters, on whose bases the entrepreneurs and the consumers have taken their decisions, also change. These

---

[1] If the curves of supply and demand are not of a constant elasticity, or straight line curves, then the result of the process of oscillation depends also on the point at which it is fixed. Cf. V. V. Leontief, Delayed Supply Adjustment and Partial Equilibrium (Verzögerte Angebotsanpassung und partielles Gleichgewicht) in *Zeitschrift für Nationaloekonomie*, Vol. V, No. 4, Vienna, 1935.

decisions must, therefore, be altered, and this changes the supply and demand for various goods. As a result, however, prices change which leads to a further change in the decisions on the part of the entrepreneurs and consumers. Prices change again, etc. That these price oscillations and the quantity of goods will arrive at an equilibrium position is not at all *a priori* certain. In order to be able to make any valid statement in this respect additional information is required either on the supply and demand elasticities, or on the individual anticipations concerning the future price-level.

2. It seems that the idea of the economic equilibrium as a state towards which, in the absence of a change in essential factors, the actual movement of the economy tends, has only a restricted meaning, and that the delay of supply adjustment to the price obtaining at the time causes oscillations which only under special conditions lead to an equilibrium. This conclusion is, however, too hasty; for it can be shown that oscillations do not originate in the course of delay in supply adjustments, but they are more commonly brought about by quite a special kind of delay in supply adjustment.

It is tacitly assumed by all authors, in the discussion of the "cob-web theorem", that supply adjustment is not only delayed, but can also take place all at once, as is chiefly the case in agricultural production, for example. If the market price of potatoes is higher than the equilibrium price, then it must remain so for the whole year, for (apart from imports) the supply of potatoes cannot be increased at all before the next harvest. After the harvest, all the potatoes come onto the market, and if the market price now falls below the equilibrium price, it must remain so (apart from speculative influences) until the next harvest. In the case of the majority of industrial products, however, the supply, even if delayed, may be varied gradually, and where a gradual variation in supply takes place, there follows an adjustment to an equilibrium quite different from the case of the "cob-web theorem". This will be illustrated in Fig. 2.

Let AA be the supply curve, which we consider as a supply curve of a total adjustment of the production factors, therefore, as a Marshall "long period" supply curve, and N_1N_2 the demand curve. Then E_1 is the equilibrium point and M_1E_1 and OM_1 are the equilibrium price and the equilibrium quantity. Now the demand curve shifts into the position N_1N_2. The new equilibrium point is, therefore, E_2 and M_2E_2 and OM_2

are the new equilibrium price and the new equilibrium quantity. Supposing that a gradual supply adjustment is possible, how will the process of adjustment to a new equilibrium take place? When the quantity OM_1 cannot immediately be increased, the market price immediately climbs to a height of M_1P_1. If the entrepreneurs adapt their production to the market price, they will wish to produce the quantity OQ'. A specified period of time, e.g. four months, is necessary to expand the supply to OQ'. However, the profits from their goods, resulting from the high

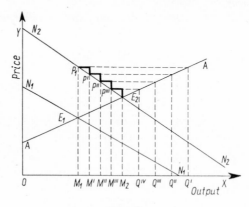

Fig. 2.

market price, cause the entrepreneurs to expand production as much as possible in as short a time as possible. This is feasible by increased purchases of raw materials and labour, and extended use of available factory capacity. By these means, production can be raised to OM', for example. In consequence, however, the market price falls to $M'P'$, and the entrepreneurs will wish to produce the quantity OQ'' only. After a further month, new machines may be installed and, in consequence, production may be increased to OM''. As a result of this, the market price falls to $M''P''$, and the entrepreneurs now wish to produce only the quantity OQ'''. After a further month, the additional buildings are completed and production climbs to OM''' and the price falls to $M'''P'''$. Thus, the adjustment process continues until finally, after four months for example, the adjustment is completed and the equilibrium point E_2 is reached.

Adjustment, therefore, does not proceed by oscillations, but by steps plotted on the P_1E_2 section of the demand curve. If one imagines the number of adjustment stages increased and their length shortened, then the step-graph is always approaching the demand curve N_1N_2, and in a marginal case will merge with it. If the adjustment takes place by a continuous expansion of production from one moment to the next, then the market price slides down the demand curve N_1N_2, until finally it reaches the equilibrium point E_2. The equilibrium point is reached at each slope of the supply and demand curves.

A sketch appropriately illustrating this would show that the above is true also in the case of a displacement of the supply curve. Similarly, it is true in the case when the displacement of the demand or supply curve leads to a limitation of production. If a gradual adjustment is possible, then the price rises along the line formed in steps and in the marginal case of a continuous decrease in supply, the price slides along the demand curve up to a new equilibrium point.

3. The process of gradual or continuous supply adjustment to the new conditions of equilibrium can be summarized theoretically by an extension of the Marshall theory on short-period supply. As is well known, Marshall differentiates between short- and long-period curves, according to whether the adjustment embraces only individual production factors in the so-called variable expenses, or the entire production factors. However, the border-line between constant and variable production factors is not absolute. It is according to the length of the period of adjustment that definite factors are constant and the supply is a vertical straight line. When the period of adjustment is quite short, the raw materials and the number of workers are variable and all other factors are constant. Then the costs, which can include additional raw materials and labour are dependent, too, on the length of the adjustment period. When the adjustment period is longer, machines for example would be variable factors, but buildings would be constant factors. When the period is further extended, buildings finally would also become variable factors. There are, therefore, not just two supply curves, one short- and one long-period, but as many as there are stages of adjustment.

Certain theoretical statements can be made about the slope of the different supply curves. In Fig. 3, AA is the Marshall long-period supply curve, i.e., the curve after a completed total adjustment of all the production factors to an optimum combination. The supply curve of that moment is a vertical straight line passing through the equilibrium

·point E_1, since available supply is limited by the quantity at the given
moment (M_1P_1 in Fig. 3). All other short-period curves have the following
qualities: they all pass through the intersection point of the supply
curve of the given moment and the long-period supply curve, since all
these curves concern either an expansion, or a decrease in supply which
was determined by the old equilibrium point. The supply curves climb
the more steeply, the shorter they are in period. This follows the law of
diminishing returns. The shorter the adjustment period, the fewer factors
serve as a basis for the adjustment and the more factors are constant.
The marginal cost curves on which the supply curves are based climb
the steeper the fewer the factors involved in the adjustment, for then
the law of diminishing returns applies the more strongly. The effect of
the law of diminishing returns will be minimal if an optimum combination of production factors is attained in the long-period supply curve.
All the short-period supply curves are, therefore, contained between
the supply curve of the given moment (M_1P_1 in Fig. 3) and the long-
period supply curve (AA in Fig. 3) and their slope is the greater, the
longer the adjustment period.

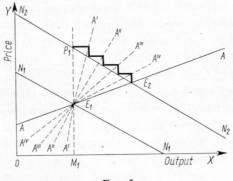

FIG. 3.

From the foregoing consideration on the slope of the short-period
supply curves, one can conceive the graduated line along which the
gradual process of price adjustment takes place as determined by the
short-period curves of supply, as it follows from Fig. 3. If the adjustment
process is continuous and the price slides along the demand curve, then
the process can be considered as caused by the short-period supply
curves which turn around the equilibrium point E_1, whereby the short-

period supply curve runs through all the positions from M_1P_1 to AA (thus also changing its form), and the movement of the intersection point of the short- and long-period supply curves N_1N_2 results in the market price sliding along the demand curve.

4. The process of the continuous (or gradual) supply adjustment may also be expressed mathematically. Let p be the price, x the quantity produced and τ the completed adjustment period. Further let τ_0 be the entire adjustment period, i.e., the time necessary for the creation of the optimum combination of all the production factors, and x_0 the quantity determined by the supply curve at a given moment. Thus, for each value of τ, i.e., for each adjustment period there corresponds a supply curve. Therefore, if one considers τ as a parameter, one obtains a group of supply curves which may be expressed by the equation

$$p = \varphi(x, \tau, x_0). \tag{1}$$

This equation contains not only the parameter τ, but also the parameter x_0, since all these curves must pass through the intersection point of the supply curve at the given moment and the long-period supply curve. Assuming $\tau = 0$, the equation (1) shows the supply curve at the given moment; with $\tau \geqslant \tau_0$ it shows the long-period supply curve. With $0 < \tau < \tau_0$ we obtain the group of short-period supply curves.

The slope of the supply curves is determined by the differential quotient $\dfrac{\partial p}{\partial x}$. The supply adjustment takes place continuously, if $\dfrac{\partial p}{\partial x}$ is a stable function of τ, otherwise, it takes place gradually. From what has been said about the slope of the supply curves it follows for all relevant values of x:

$$\frac{\partial^2 p}{\partial x \partial \tau} < 0 \tag{2a}$$

given $0 < \tau < \tau_0$ and:

$$\frac{\partial^2 p}{\partial x \partial \tau} = 0 \tag{2b}$$

given $\tau \geqslant \tau_0$. In particular, given $\tau = 0$ there is:

$$\frac{\partial p}{\partial x} = \infty \tag{3a}$$

and if one expresses the long-period supply curve by $p = \varphi(x, \tau_0)$, the parameter x_0 can be omitted here since the intersection point of the supply curve of the given moment and the long-period supply curve lies on the long-period supply curve), then, given $\tau \geqslant \tau_0$, we have:

$$\frac{\partial p}{\partial x} = \frac{\partial \varphi(x, \tau_0)}{\partial x}. \tag{3b}$$

If, now, $p = f(x)$ is the demand function, then the adjustment process may be expressed by the equation

$$f(x) = \varphi(x, x_0). \tag{4}$$

For each value of τ one obtains a definite value of x; and by substituting this value in the demand function, a definite value of p is obtained. If one allows τ to vary from zero to τ_0, one obtains the course of the adjustment process. Equation (4) assuming $\tau \geqslant \tau_0$ gives the new equilibrium position. Therefore, equation (4) expresses both the adjustment process and the final equilibrium position.

The same reasoning concerning a continuous or gradual adjustment can easily be extended to the theory of general economic equilibrium. One is dealing, then, with continuous or gradual flow of capital and labour from one branch of production to another, and with a corresponding continuous or gradual supply adjustment which produces the general economic equilibrium. A mathematical presentation of this process would, of course, be very complicated.

5. It appears, therefore, that it is not the fact, in itself, that the supply adjustment requires time which causes oscillations in the quantities produced and in the prices around the new equilibrium point. Such oscillations arise only in special circumstances, namely, when the supply adjustment takes place only all at once, after a constant period. If, however, a gradual or even continuous supply adjustment is possible, then there are no oscillations, and prices and quantities rather approach the equilibrium point along a graduated line, or, if the adjustment is continuous, along the demand curve. This explains why one comes across cyclical fluctuations which arise as a result of supply delay in only certain branches of production. In the majority of cases, this is inherent in agricultural production. There exists, in agriculture, a constant period of production from harvest to harvest or a relatively constant growing period for animals and trees. Here a gradual or even continuous supply adjustment is not possible. Similarly, this is true of some branches

of industry, as shipbuilding, where there is a constant building period. The greater part of industrial production, however, is capable of a gradual or even continuous supply adjustment.

In consequence, the problem of the stability of the economic equilibrium created by the delayed supply adjustment is vastly diminished. For, in the majority of production branches, the stability of the economic equilibrium is guaranteed by a gradual or continuous supply adjustment. Special assumptions on the supply and demand elasticities or the anticipated future price-level by entrepreneurs are not necessary here. It is quite sufficient that the entrepreneurs should adapt their production to the relative market price. This is obvious with regard to a continuous supply adjustment, when the price slides along the demand curve and cannot avoid the equilibrium point. If the supply adjustment is not continuous but rather shows gradual discontinuities, then small oscillations may arise in the area of the equilibrium point; these, however, will never be important, since the gradual adjustment process is in operation. Moreover, in the majority of production branches, the number of adjustment stages is so large that one may consider supply adjustment practically as continuous and may restrict the theoretical analysis to the case of a continuous supply adjustment. Classical economists followed this reasoning when they imagined capital and labour flowing continuously into more profitable production branches, until market prices became equal to equilibrium prices by a process of continuous adjustments. The assumption of continuous adjustment underlies the well-known water tank example of Irving Fisher. In this, it is assumed that the theory holds good and that if the entrepreneurs adapt their behaviour to the relative market prices, the market economy automatically attains a new equilibrium. The formulation of the "cob-web theorem" has brought to light an interesting exception which is, however, restricted to quite definite production branches, mainly to certain agricultural products. In so far as the major part of production in the national economy is capable of a continuous or, at least, a gradual supply adjustment, the classical theory still holds good today.

6. Finally, some comments upon the role of anticipation of the future price level by entrepreneurs are relevant here. In so far as this anticipation is adapted, so to speak, to the tangent of the actual price development, its influence on supply is most usefully demonstrated by the Evans supply function. This supply function reads $x = \varphi\ (p, p')$, where x is

the quantity offered, p the price and $p' = \dfrac{dp}{dt}$ is the differential quotient

of the price over time.[2] According to Evans, the assumption is generally

made that $\dfrac{\partial x}{\partial p} > 0$ i.e. the larger the supply, the greater the price in-

crease.[3] This might be true as the "natural" reaction of most entrepreneurs. However, in the case when delay in the supply adjustment leads
to oscillations, these are aggravated by the "natural" reaction of the
entrepreneurs. Should the anticipation of the future price level check the
oscillations, then the entrepreneurs must react in an opposite manner;
for example, the farmers must immediately decrease pig production,
when prices of pigs rise. Therefore, in Evans' supply function it is re-

quired that $\dfrac{\partial x}{\partial p} < 0$.[4] It is otherwise if the supply adjustment follows

continuously, or gradually. If the market price is above the equilibrium
price, then there is a period of falling prices during the adjustment
process. The "natural" reaction of the anticipating entrepreneurs (there-

fore in the case of $\dfrac{\partial x}{\partial p} > 0$) is, thus, one of caution as far as the expansion

of production is concerned. In consequence, the length of the adjustment
process is increased, but the danger that supply will exceed the equilibrium quantity is diminished. By analogy, it also holds good for the
case, *mutatis mutandis*, when the market price is below the equilibrium
price. This causes a period of rising prices and the anticipation prevents
an excessive fall in production. Thus, with a continuous or gradual
supply adjustment the economic equilibrium is strengthened by anticipation taking place along the tangent of the actual price developments.

---

[2] G. C. Evans, *Mathematical Introduction to Economics*, p. 36 ff, New York, 1930.
Evans deals only with the special case in which the supply function is linear, i.e. of

the form $x = ap + \beta + \gamma \dfrac{dp}{dt}$.

[3] In the special case dealt with by Evans this means that $\gamma > 0$.

[4] I.e. $\gamma < 0$ in the special case dealt with by Evans.

A NOTE ON INNOVATIONS[1]

The present article is concerned with the concept and some of the implications of innovations which play such a dominant role in Professor Schumpeter's theory of economic development. Our analysis of innovations will be based on the theory of the firm. We shall consider the firm as planning its activities over a certain period of time, with the purpose of maximizing the discounted present value of the profit it expects to make during this period. The period over which the firm plans its activities will be called its economic horizon.[2] The expected profit consists of the sum of the differences between expected receipts and expected expenses at all moments (or intervals) of time within the economic horizon. It also includes the difference between receipts and expenses at the current (i.e., present) moment of time.[3]

As a rule, future receipts and future expenses are anticipated with a minor or major degree of uncertainty, and this uncertainty is taken into account by the firm when planning its activities. The uncertainty is due to the fact that the receipts and expenses realized at some future date may take different possible values, and which of the different values they will take cannot possibly be foreseen. But not all these values appear to the firm as equally probable. Thus, the firm may be considered as

---

[1] This term is due to Dr. J. Tinbergen. See his article, The Notions of Horizon and Expectancy in Dynamic Economics, *Econometrica*, I, p. 247 (1933).

[2] Let $R(t)$ be the receipt and $E(t)$ the expense expected at the moment t. Then $S(t)$, the surplus expected at t, is $S(t) \equiv R(t)/E(t)$. Let, further, $i(t)$ be the continuous rate of interest expected at t, and denote by H the length of the economic horizon. The discounted present value of the profit expected during the period H is

$$P = \int_0^H s(t)e - \int_0^t i(t)dt_{dt}$$

where $t = 0$ stands for the "present" moment of time.

[3] This assumption seems to us quite realistic. It merely implies that in making any decision the firm has an idea of the most probable outcome of the decision and of the range within which the actual outcome may deviate from the most probable one. For instance, it thinks that a certain action will cost, most probably, $1000, but in any case not less than $800 and not more than $1500.

135

being confronted with a (subjective) probability distribution of receipts and of expenses at each future date. For our purpose, it is sufficient to assume that the firm is aware of only two characteristics of this distribution, namely, of the most probable value (mode) and of the range.[3] The first indicates the most probable of the receipts or expenses expected; the other expresses the degree of uncertainty of the expectation.[4] Firms prefer, as a rule, expectations which can be held with little uncertainty to expectations to which a larger degree of uncertainty is attached.[5] Consequently, two equal, most probable values are not equivalent when the degree of uncertainty (as expressed by the range of possible outcomes) is different. A firm is ready to "pay" for a reduction in the degree of uncertainty with a reduced most probable value of expected receipts or with an increased most probable value of expected expenses. In other words, an indifference map, as between most probable values and ranges of the probability distributions of receipts and of expenses anticipated at any future date, can be drawn for the firm. This is done in Fig. 1 for receipts, and in Fig. 2 for expenses.

The most probable receipt or expense is measured along the axis OY, and the range is measured along the axis OX. For receipts the indifference curves are rising, because greater uncertainty must be compensated by a larger most probable receipt; for expenses, they are falling because greater uncertainty must be compensated by a smaller most probable expense. The concavity or convexity of the curves expresses the increasing unwillingness to bear uncertainty. The indifference curves indicate the reduction in most probable receipts, or the increase in most probable expenses, with which the firm is ready to "pay" in order to get rid of all uncertainty; we shall call it the risk premium. Thus, if the firm ex-

---

[4] In most cases, the firm will not consider the whole range but will disregard the outcomes at both tails of the distribution, the joint probability of which is too small to bother about. Thus, if the most probable cost of a certain action is $1000, with a practical range of $800–$1500, the firm may be well aware of the fact that the cost may turn out to be below $800 or above $1500, but the joint probability of larger deviations is so small (e.g., less than one per cent) that the firm is ready to take the chances of disregarding them in its planning. This "practical" range is similar to the concept of a "confidence interval" used in statistical estimation.

[5] Up to a certain point, firms may prefer the opposite because they like to gamble. However, the great majority of business planning involves such a large degree of uncertainty that there is definitely a readiness to "pay" for its reduction. Cf. on this point A. C. Pigou, *The Economics of Welfare*, 4th ed., p. 776, London, 1938.

pects a most probable receipt, or expense, *OA*, with a range, *OB*, of possible outcomes, it is ready to accept instead a receipt or expense, *OC*, expected with (subjective) certainty, i.e., with a range of possible outcome equal to zero. We shall call *OC* the *effective* receipt or expense and *CA* is the risk premium. The effective receipt or expense is thus the

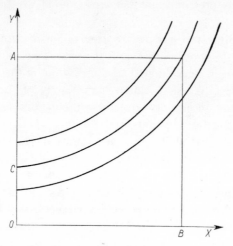

FIG. 1.

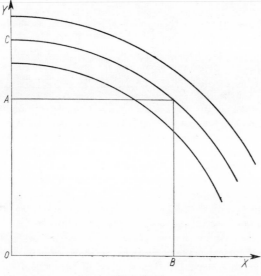

FIG. 2.

most probable value actually expected minus the risk premium (which is positive for receipts and negative for expenses). Taking into account the firm's readiness to "pay" for a reduction in the degree of uncertainty of its expectations, we shall assume that the firm attempts to maximize the discounted value of its *effective* profit, i.e., the expected profit calculated after risk premiums are deducted from all expected receipts and expenses.

The uncertainty involved in the expectation of future receipts and expenses is due to two causes. One is the uncertainty of the expectation of future prices (or, under imperfect competition, of future demand and supply schedules). We shall call it "uncertainty of the market". The other cause is the uncertainty concerning the quantitative relations between current and future inputs and future outputs. We shall call it "technological uncertainty".[6] Both uncertainty of the market and technological uncertainty are the greater, the more distant in the future the action planned by the firm (at least from a certain date on). Thus the risk premium increases as the planned receipts and expenses are more distant in the future. This imposes a limit upon the dates for which receipts and expenses are planned. The firm finds that beyond a certain date effective receipts are less than effective expenses, and stops planning receipts and expenses beyond that date. In this way the economic horizon of the firm is determined.[7]

[6] Cf. G. Tintner, The Pure Theory of Production under Technological Risk and Uncertainty, *Econometrica*, IX, pp. 305–12 (1941). Technological uncertainty arises either when the production function has to be considered directly as a stochastic relationship between outputs and inputs (as, for instance, in agriculture), or when, though the production function is not stochastic, the quantitative input–output relationships are subject to changes because of unforeseen changes in inputs or outputs or of the scale of the operation of the plant (lack of adaptability and flexibility of the firm's production plan). On the latter see G. Stigler, Production and Distribution in the Short Run, *Journal of Political Economy*, XLVII, pp. 312 ff (1939), and A. G. Hart, Imputation and the Demand for Productive Resources in Disequilibrium, in *Explorations in Economics*, pp. 114ff, New York, 1936. Cf. also A. J. Nichol, Production and the Probabilities of Cost, *Quarterly Journal of Economics*, LVII, pp. 69–89 (1942–3).

[7] Cf. J. R. Hicks, *Value and Capital*, p. 225, Oxford, 1939. Provision for the future, however, extends beyond the length of the economic horizon, but it does not take the form of planning specific receipts and expenses. Provision for the future which extends beyond the economic horizon is made by planning to wind up at the end of this period with a certain amount of assets. Cf. Hicks, *op. cit.*, pp. 193–94 and 229–30, and P. N. Rosenstein-Rodan, The Role of Time in Economic Theory, *Economica*, I, pp. 80–84 (New Series, 1934).

Innovations are such changes in production functions, i.e., in the sche-
dules indicating the relation between the input of factors of production
and the output of products, which make it possible for the firm to increase
the discounted value of the maximum effective profit obtainable under given
market conditions.[8] By market conditions we mean the prices and, under
imperfect competition, the demand and supply schedules, respectively,
of the relevant products and factors. Discounted expected prices and
schedules as well as current ones are included. An increase in the discounted effective maximum profit means an increase in the sum of the
surpluses of effective receipts over effective expenses. This can be achieved
either by an increase in the sum of the surpluses unadjusted for risk
premiums, or by a decrease of the risk premiums, or by both. The increase in the (discounted) effective profit implied in an innovation may
thus result also from a diminution of technological uncertainty. A reduction in uncertainty about the market, however, is excluded from our
concept of innovation, because innovation is defined with regard to
given market conditions. The economic impact of an innovation depends
on the way in which it affects the marginal cost of the output as well as
the marginal physical productivity of the input planned for any (current
or future) moment of time. This provides a basis for the classification of
innovations in terms of their effect upon the firm's supply of products
and demand for factors of production.

The marginal cost of any given current output, as well as the expected marginal cost of any output planned for some future date, may
or may not be affected by an innovation in either direction.[9] If the

---

[8] Professor Schumpeter says: "We will simply define an innovation as the setting
up of a new production function". See his *Business Cycles, A Theoretical, Historical,
and Statistical Analysis of the Capitalist Process*, Vol. 1, p. 87, New York, 1939.
This definition, however, is too wide. A large (possibly even infinite) number of ways
always exists in which production functions can be changed. But an innovation appears only when there is a possibility of such a change, which increases the (discounted)
maximum effective profit the firm is able to make. All other possible changes are disregarded by the firms.

[9] This holds true even in the case where the firm maximizes merely the current
profit, as happens when the current profit and the profits expected at later time-inter-
vals are independent of each other (for when the profits in two or several sub-intervals
of a period are independent of each other the total profit over the whole period is
maximized by maximizing separately the profit in each sub-interval). The direction
of change of the current marginal cost depends then on how the innovation affects

marginal cost of the current output which maximizes the discounted value of the firm's profit before adoption of the innovation is reduced by the innovation, the current output of the firm increases. In the opposite case it decreases. Similarly, with regard to the output planned for any future date and the corresponding discounted marginal cost. An innovation will be called output-neutral, output-increasing, or output-decreasing, at the date *t* according as it increases, leaves unchanged, or decreases the output planned for that date.

An innovation increases a firm's current demand for a factor of production, or the demand planned for a certain future date, when the marginal physical productivity of the quantity of the factor used on that date, or planned for that date, before the introduction of the innova-

---

the total cost of the current output and the current "elasticity of productivity". Let all factors currently employed be increased in the same ratio λ, and let x be the current output. The elasticity of productivity is

$$\frac{Ex}{E\lambda} = \frac{dx}{d\lambda} \times \frac{\lambda}{x}$$

[Cf. R. G. D. Allen, *Mathematical Analysis for Economists*, p. 263, London, 1938; cf. also S. Carlson, *A Study in the Pure Theory of Production*, p. 10, Vienna, 1934. The concept was introduced by Dr. Schneider.] According to a theorem established by Dr. Schneider (*op. cit.*, pp. 42–43) we have, for any output, x, the relation $k(x)$ $= k'(x)x\dfrac{Ex}{E\lambda}$, where $k(x)$ is the total cost and $k'(x)$ is the marginal cost of the output

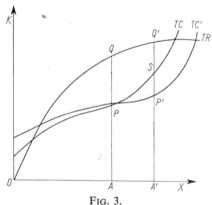

FIG. 3.

---

x. Thus, an innovation reduces or increases the marginal cost of output x according as it increases or decreases the elasticity of productivity relative to the change in total cost which it causes. Clearly, the elasticity of productivity may or may not be

tion is raised. It diminishes this demand when the opposite is the case. This holds under monopoly and monopsony (including monopolistic and monopsonistic competition) just as well as under perfect competition. The marginal revenues and the marginal expenditures[10] corresponding to the output and input plan preceding the innovation are all given. A change in the marginal physical productivity of the corresponding (current or planned) quantity of a factor thus implies a proportional change of its marginal value productivity.[11] Before introduction of the innovation, the marginal value productivity was equal to the marginal expenditure. Now it exceeds it or falls short of it, and the demand for the factor increases or decreases accordingly. An innovation will be called "using" or "sav-

---

affected by an innovation in either direction. The same holds for the total cost, $k(x)$, except when x is the output which maximizes the firm's profit after adoption of the innovation. In the last mentioned case, $k(x)$ is always reduced in consequence of an innovation. This can be seen from Fig. 3. *TR* is the total revenue curve, and *TC* is the total cost curve before the innovation is introduced. *PQ* is the maximum profit obtainable, and *OA* is the corresponding output. After the innovation has been adopted, the total cost curve becomes *TC'*, with *P'Q'* and *OA'* the maximum profit and corresponding output. From the definition of an innovation, it follows that $P'Q' > PQ$. But $PQ > SQ'$ because *PQ* is the maximum profit before the introduction of the innovation. Consequently, $P'Q' > SQ'$. But for any output other than *OA'* (or, if the cost curves are continuous, for any output not in the neighbourhood of *OA'*), total cost need not be less after the adoption of the innovation than before the adoption. The argument is independent of the shape of the *TR* curve and, therefore, holds for imperfect competition as well as for perfect competition. Thus, both the total cost corresponding to *OA*, and the elasticity of productivity for output *OA* may be affected by the innovation in either direction. In view of Dr. Schneider's relation, the marginal cost of the output *OA* may thus be affected in either direction. In the diagram, *A'* is at the right of *A*, and the innovation reduces the marginal cost of *OA*. When the marginal cost of *OA* is increased or left unchanged, *A'* is at the left of *A* or coincides with *A*, respectively.

[10] By marginal expenditure for a factor of production we understand the increment of the firm's total expenditure for the factor resulting from the purchase of an additional unit of the factor. If p is the price of the factor and ε its elasticity of supply to the firm, the marginal expenditure is $p\left(1+\dfrac{1}{\varepsilon}\right)$. The concept of marginal expenditure is similar to the concept of marginal revenue which is $P\left(1-\dfrac{1}{\eta}\right)$, where P is the price of the product and η is its elasticity of demand.

[11] The marginal value productivity is the marginal physical productivity of the factor multiplied by the marginal revenue of the product, i.e., by $P\left(1-\dfrac{1}{\eta}\right)$.

ing" a given factor at the date *t* according as it increases or diminishes the demand planned for that date. Thus innovation will be labelled, e.g., labour-saving after a year, currently steel-using, etc.[12] An innovation which is neither factor-using nor factor-saving will be called factor-neutral.

When an innovation does not "save" any of the factors which the firm employed or planned to employ before its adoption, it is either output-increasing at some (at least) date within the firm's economic horizon, or, instead, it reduces the technological uncertainty attached to the production plan. Under given market conditions an increase, or absence of change, of the quantities of the different factors entering into the firm's production plan implies an increase, or at best an absence of change, in the discounted value of the total effective cost planned by the firm.[13] An innovation, however, by definition increases the discounted value of the total effective profit which the firm expects to make during the period covered by its economic horizon. Therefore, the discounted value of the total effective revenue must increase by more than the discounted value of the total effective cost. The market conditions being given, any increase in the first requires either an increase in the output planned for (at least) some date,[14] or a reduction of the technological

---

[12] The classification of innovation as "using" or "saving" a factor given in the text is in terms of the absolute change in the factor's marginal physical productivity. Professor Pigou (*The Economics of Welfare*, 4th ed., p. 674, London, 1938), Dr. Hicks (*The Theory of Wages*, pp. 121–2, London), and Mrs. Robinson (The Classification of Inventions, *Review of Economic Studies*, V, pp. 139–40 (1938)) have given other classifications which, though differing among themselves, are all in terms of relative changes in the marginal physical productivity (i.e., in terms of changes of the marginal rate of substitution of factors). The difference between our classification and theirs is due to the fact that whereas we are interested in the effect of innovations upon the demand and the employment of a factor, Professor Pigou is interested in the effect upon the aggregate real income, and Dr. Hick and Mrs. Robinson in the effect upon the relative shares of the factors under the assumption (common to all three of them) that full employment of all factors is retained or restored after the innovation. Mrs. Robinson's and Dr. Hick's classifications are related and, with the aid of the concept of the elasticity of substitution, translatable one into the other.

[13] We assume that none of the supply schedules of the relevant factors are negatively sloped.

[14] The discounted marginal revenue corresponding to the output planned for each date is considered as not negative, while for some date at least it is assumed to be positive. Since at each date the planned discounted marginal revenue is equal

risk-premium. Conversely, an innovation which is not output-increasing at all cannot be all-round factor-using or even factor-neutral, unless it causes a decrease in technological uncertainty. It must "save" at least some factor at some date. Subject to these two restrictions, any combination between the output-increasing or output-decreasing effect and the factor-using or factor-saving nature of an innovation is possible. In particular, an innovation can be at the same time output-increasing at all dates and factor-saving with regard to all factors and dates. Our empirical knowledge seems to indicate that the major part of innovations "use" at least some factors (chiefly investments goods) currently and in the near future and are output-increasing at some more remote future. The economic effects of such innovations can be divided roughly in two periods: a factor-using period of "gestation" and an output-increasing period of "operation" of the innovation.[15]

In order to assertain the effect of an innovation upon the output of a commodity and the demand for various factors of production in the whole economy, we have to consider, in addition to the points just discussed, its effect upon the number of firms in an industry. When the industry, producing the commodity under consideration, operates under conditions of perfect competition and, in addition, is subject to free entry,[16] the increase in the discounted value of the effective profit attracts new firms to the industry. The influx of new firms continues until the aggregate output of the industry planned for some or all dates increases[17] sufficiently to reduce the discounted value of the effective profit of the firms to zero level.[18] Thus, under condition of free entry, any innovation must, with respect to the whole economy, be output-increasing at some

---

to the planned discounted marginal cost, the first can be negative only when the latter is so.

[15] This has been pointed out by Professor Schumpeter, who explains on this basis the mechanism of the business cycle, the factor-using period being responsible for the prosperity and the output-increasing period for the recession. Cf. *op. cit.*, Vol. 1, pp. 93 ff.

[16] Free entry may be absent even though the competition is perfect in the sense of being atomistic (i.e., no firm being able to influence prices by individual variation of its outputs and inputs).

[17] The demand schedules of the product are all assumed to be negatively sloped.

[18] "Normal" profit is equal to the sum of all the risk premiums. Thus *effective* profit, which is profit after deduction of the risk premiums, is zero when profit unadjusted for uncertainty is "normal".

date, even though it be exclusively output-decreasing from the point of
view of the individual firms.[19] Free entry, by leading to an increase in
the number of firms in consequence of an innovation, also exercises a
factor-using influence. The net effect of an innovation upon the demand
for factors of production by a competitive industry with free entry, however, may be in either direction. When competition is monopolistic or
monopsonistic in the Chamberlin sense, the concept of free entry has
no meaning,[20] and it is sufficient to analyse the effects of an innovation
upon the decisions of the firm. A superficial analogy to free entry exists
when the innovation leads to the establishment of new firms producing
new commodities. This case, however, can be treated as the extreme case
of output-increasing and factor-using innovations.

Some special consideration is due to the nature of innovations in
firms which operate under conditions of *oligopoly* and *oligopsony*. Oligopoly or oligopsony occurs when the firm's responses to changes in market
conditions are based on conjectures as to how other firms will react to
an action of the firm and how this, in turn, will affect the demand or
supply schedules confronting the firm which contemplates the response.
As a rule, determinate conjectures are possible only if the firms agree
openly or tacitly (often even only subconsciously) upon certain rules of
group behaviour. The uncertainty concerning the reaction of other firms
makes each firm afraid to change its price and thus to "start the ball
rolling". This leads to the establishment of a conventional price (or price
structure) and of conventional patterns of behaviour which become
endowed with the halo of ethical norms. Each member of the group is
allowed to take actions which do not impinge upon the "rights" of other
members, but is penalized for actions which constitute such an infringe-
ment. Thus, when an oligopolistic firm raises the price of its product
above the conventional level, the other firms in the group do not react;
but when it lowers its price below the conventional level, the others
follow suit to "keep their own" or to penalize the transgressor against
the social consensus. In consequence, the demand curve confronting

---

[19] In the special case where the firms maximize only current profit (see footnote 9, p. 139 above), only innovation increases the current output of the industry.

[20] In this case each firm must be considered as selling a separate product or using
separate factors. The concept of an industry thus loses its meaning. Cf. Robert Triffin,
Monopolistic Competition and General Equilibrium Theory, pp. 81–96, Cambridge,
Mass., 1940.

each firm has a kink at the level of the conventionally established price; and the marginal revenue curve is discontinuous at the corresponding output.[21] Under oligopsony the price paid for a factor may be lowered below the conventional level without the other prices reacting, while an increase in this price above the conventional level "spoils the market" and makes the others follow suit. Thus, at the level of the conventionally established price of the factor, the supply curve has a kink and the marginal expenditure curve is discontinuous at the corresponding input.

The demand under oligopoly and the supply conditions under oligopsony are illustrated in Fig. 4 and Fig. 5, respectively. In Fig. 4, *ON* is the conventional price and *OM* is the corresponding output. The demand curve has a kink at *P*, and the marginal revenue curve, *MR*, is discontinuous between *G* and *H*. In Fig. 5, *OB* is the conventional price of the factor, and *OA* is the corresponding output. The supply curve has a kink at *P* and the marginal expenditure curve, *ME*, is discontinuous between *G* and *H*.

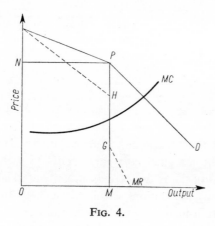

FIG. 4.

Because of the discontinuity of the marginal revenue curve under oligopoly, output and price of the product do not respond to shifts in the marginal cost curve, *MC*, within the range of discontinuity of the former (*GH* in Fig. 4). Similarly, under oligopsony the discontinuity of

---

[21] Cf. Paul M. Sweezy, Demand Under Conditions of Oligopoly, *Journal of Political Economy*, XLVII, pp. 568–73 (1939); and R. L. Hall and C. J. Hicks, Price Theory and Business Behavior, *Oxford Economic Papers*, No. 2, 1939. Unlike Dr. Sweezy's article, the kink is here assumed to be real, not merely imaginary.

the marginal expenditure curve is the reason that price and input of the factor do not respond to shifts in the marginal value productivity curve, *MP*, of the factor within the range of discontinuity of the former (*GH* in Fig. 5). This lack of response (within limits) of price and output to changes in marginal cost or of price and input to changes in marginal value productivity has an important effect upon the nature of innovations in an oligopolistic or oligopsonistic group.

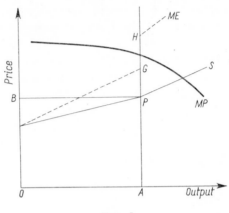

FIG. 5.

Under oligopoly an innovation cannot be output-increasing unless the diminution of marginal cost caused by it is sufficiently great to induce the firm to break the "discipline" of the group. The last mentioned case happens when the marginal cost curve shifts to such an extent as to make it move out of the range of discontinuity of the marginal revenue curve.[22] Thus, only innovations which reduce marginal cost to a great extent can be output-increasing under conditions of oligopoly. Therefore, under oligopoly, an innovation cannot be all-round factor-using, or even all-round factor neutral, unless it causes a sufficiently large reduction of marginal cost or, instead, a decrease in technological uncertainty; it must "save" at least some factor at some date in the firm's production plan. Except for *greatly* marginal cost-reducing innovations and innovations which reduce technological uncertainty, oligopoly exerts a se-

---

[22] Cf. Fig. 4. In order to cause an increase in output, marginal cost must fall below *MG*.

lective action against output-increasing and in favour of factor-saving innovations.

Oligopsony favours factor-neutral innovations, since the demand for a production factor changes under oligopsony only when the marginal value productivity curve of the factor is shifted to such an extent as to exceed the range of discontinuity of the marginal expenditure curve.[23] The demand for factors of production under oligopsony is, therefore, affected only by innovations which produce changes in their marginal physical productivity sufficiently *large* to induce the firm to break the "discipline" of the group. But innovations which do not affect the quantity of factors entering into the firm's production plan must be output-increasing at some date or, instead, must reduce technological uncertainty. This type of innovation seems to be favoured by oligopsonistic conditions.

The type of competition and the entrepreneurial responses associated with innovations thus exercise an important selective influence upon them. Under perfect competition with free entry of firms, all innovations are output-increasing at some date at least, with regard to the whole industry, but may be either output-increasing or output-decreasing with regard to single firms.[24] Oligopsony favours innovations which are output-increasing with regard to the firm, as well as the industry,[25] but which

---

[23] Cf. Fig. 5. The range of discontinuity here is *GH*.

[24] When the innovation is output-decreasing with regard to the firm, it causes, in this case, a deconcentration of the industry.

[25] Unlike under monopolistic or monopsonistic competition, the concept of an industry can be applied under conditions of oligopoly or oligopsony. An industry can be defined in the same way as under perfect competition, i.e., as all the firms which produce the same product (or products) or as all the firms which use the same factor. A commodity, whether a factor or a product, is defined as all the "objects" (including services), the prices of which vary in the same proportion (equality of prices is a special case of it). Cf. Triffin, *op. cit.*, p. 138. Oligopolistic or oligopsonistic group behaviour establishes a "price structure" i.e., certain ratios of the prices changed by the various sellers or paid by the various buyers, maintained by the "discipline" of the group. Thus all the oligopolists can be considered as selling the same commodity and all the oligopsonists as buying the same commodity, i.e., as forming an industry. As here defined, the extent of an industry coincides with the extent of the oligopolistic or oligopsonistic group. It should be noticed, however, that the industry defined in terms of sales of products is not identical with the industry defined in terms of factor-purchases. A firm may belong to one industry with respect to its product and to a different industry with respect to each of its factors. If it is a multi-product firm it

at the same time are factor-neutral. Oligopoly favours output-neutral innovations which, with regard to the firm as well as the industry, necessarily have factor-saving effects.

---

may also belong to a different industry with respect to each of its products. Under perfect competition, however, all firms are alike and belong to the same industry, whether the latter is defined in terms of any of the products or of any of the factors.

SAY'S LAW: A RESTATEMENT AND CRITICISM

1. Say's law is the proposition that there can be no excess of total supply of commodities (general oversupply) because the total supply of all commodities is *identically* equal to the total demand for all commodities. Under certain assumptions as to the nature of the demand for money, this proposition appears as a simple corollary of the general theory of prices. Associated with it is the proposition that there cannot be such a shortage of total entrepreneurial receipts relative to total entrepreneurial cost as to cause losses throughout the whole economy (general over-production). The present paper intends to investigate the relation of these propositions to each other and to study the implications of Say's law with regard to the problem of underemployment, to the general theory of prices, and to the theory of money.

2. Let us consider a closed system in which n commodities are exchanged, one of them, say, the nth commodity, functioning as medium of exchange as well as *numéraire*, i.e., as money. Denote by p_i the price of the ith commodity. We have $p_n \equiv 1$. Let $D_i = D_i(p_1, p_2, ..., p_{n-1})$ and $S_i = S_i(p_1, p_2, ..., p_{n-1})$ be the demand function and the supply function, respectively, of the ith commodity. The equilibrium prices are determined by the $n-1$ equations

$$D_i(p_1, p_2, ..., p_{n-1}) = S_i(p_1, p_2, ..., p_{n-1})$$
$$(i = 1, 2, ..., n-1). \tag{2.1}$$

The condition of stability of the equilibrium of the price system is expressed by the $(n-1)^2$ inequalities and equations[1]

$$\frac{dD_j}{dp_i} < \frac{dS_j}{dp_i} \quad \text{when} \quad j = i \quad (i \text{ and } j = 1, 2, ... n-1)$$

$$\frac{dD_j}{dp_i} = \frac{dS_j}{dp_i} \quad \text{when} \quad j \neq i. \tag{2.2}$$

---

[1] Cf. J. R. Hicks, *Value and Capital*, Oxford University Press, London, 1939, pp. 66–7. This condition is sufficient. Hicks gives additional conditions for what he calls "perfect stability". The concept of perfect stability, however, refers to the way in which the stability of the system is maintained and need not occupy us here.

There are only $n-1$ independent demand functions and $n-1$ independent supply functions, the demand and the supply function for the commodity which functions as money being deducible from the other ones. We have

$$\sum_{i=1}^{n-1} p_i D_i \equiv S_n \qquad (2.3)$$

and

$$\sum_{i=1}^{n-1} p_i S_i \equiv D_n. \qquad (2.4)$$

Taking account of the last two relationships, we obtain the total demand (measured in money value) for all n commodities

$$\sum_{i=1}^{n} p_i D_i \equiv \sum_{i=1}^{n-1} p_i D_i + D_n \equiv S_n + D_n. \qquad (2.5)$$

Similarly the total supply (measured in money value) of all n commodities is

$$\sum_{i=1}^{n} p_i S_i \equiv \sum_{i=1}^{n-1} p_i S_i + S_n \equiv D_n + S_n. \qquad (2.6)$$

Therefore

$$\sum_{i=1}^{n} p_i D_i \equiv \sum_{i=1}^{n} p_i S_i, \qquad (2.7)$$

i.e., total demand and total supply are identically equal.

I propose to call this identity Walras's law because Walras was the first to recognize its fundamental importance in the formulation of the mathematical theory of prices. It should be noted that Walras's law does not require that the demand and supply of each commodity, or of any of them, be in equilibrium. The identity of (2.7) holds independently of whether the equations (2.1) are satisfied or not.[2]

---

[2] Walras's law holds also in the absence of a uniform medium of exchange, i.e, in a moneyless system. Let D_{ij} and S_{ij} be that part of the demand or supply, respectively, of the ith commodity for which the jth commodity is offered or demanded in exchange. Let, further, p_{ij} be the price of the ith commodity in terms of the jth. We have then

$$S_{ji} \equiv D_{ij} p_{ij} \qquad (1)$$

3. Now let us consider all commodities exclusive of money. To simplify the exposition, the term "commodity" will be henceforward understood to exclude money. Thus we shall oppose "commodities" to "money".

The total demand for commodities (exclusive of money) is $\sum_{i=1}^{n-1} p_i D_i$

and the total supply of commodities (exclusive of money) is $\sum_{i=1}^{n-1} p_i S_i$.

---

and
$$D_{ji} \equiv S_{ij} p_{ij} \quad (i \text{ and } j = 1, 2, ..., n). \tag{2}$$

Taking (arbitrarily) one of the commodities as *numéraire* and expressing all prices in terms of it, we have

$$p_{ij} = \frac{p_i}{p_j}$$

where p_i and p_j are the price of the ith and of the jth commodity in terms of *numéraire*. Thus

$$p_j S_{ji} \equiv p_i D_{ij} \tag{3}$$

and

$$p_j D_{ji} \equiv p_i S_{ij}. \tag{4}$$

Total demand, expressed in *numéraire* units, for all n commodities is $\sum_{i=1}^{n} \sum_{j=1}^{n} p_i D_{ij}$ and

total supply, similarly expressed, for all n commodities is $\sum_{i=1}^{n} \sum_{j=1}^{n} p_i S_{ij}$. On account of (4) we have

$$\sum_{i=1}^{n} \sum_{j=1}^{n} p_i S_{ij} \equiv \sum_{i=1}^{n} \sum_{j=1}^{n} p_i D_{ji}. \tag{5}$$

Because of symmetry of subscripts $(i = 1, 2, ..., n; j = 1, 2, ..., n)$ we have also

$$\sum_{i=1}^{n} \sum_{j=1}^{n} p_j D_{ji} \equiv \sum_{i=1}^{n} \sum_{j=1}^{n} p_i D_{ij}$$

and substituting this in (5) we obtain

$$\sum_{i=1}^{n} \sum_{j=1}^{n} p_i D_{ij} \equiv \sum_{i=1}^{n} \sum_{j=1}^{n} p_i S_{ij}, \tag{6}$$

i.e., Walras's law. Walras's proof is somewhat different. He has proved the theorem that if demand equals supply for $n-1$ commodities it does so also for the nth commodity (cf. *Éléments d'économie politique pure*, "edition definitive", 1926, pp. 120–1), Paris and Lausanne. This implies that total demand equals identically total supply of all n commodities and is, therefore, equivalent to (6).

From (2.3) and (2.4) it follows directly that

$$\sum_{i=1}^{n-1} p_i D_i = \sum_{i=1}^{n-1} p_i S_i \tag{3.1}$$

when and only when

$$D_n = S_n, \tag{3.2}$$

i.e., when the demand for money is equal to the supply of money.

But D_n and S_n are the demand for and the supply of money in a particular sense, namely, the money demanded in exchange for the commodities offered and the money offered in exchange for the commodities demanded. It is more convenient to express (3.2) in relation to the existing stock of money and to the demand for cash balances. A difference between the money demanded in exchange for commodities and the money offered in exchange for commodities implies a desire to change cash balances relative to the amount of money available. The desired change is equal to that difference. Let us denote by ΔM the total increase of cash balances (in excess of a possible increase of the quantity of money) desired by all individuals. We have then:[3]

$$D_n - S_n \equiv \Delta M. \tag{3.3}$$

Condition (3.2) may now be written in the form:

$$\Delta M = 0, \tag{3.4}$$

i.e., there is no desire to change the total sum of cash balances relative to the quantity of money. This means that the total demand for cash balances is equal to the existing stock of money. Thus, the necessary and sufficient condition that the total demand for commodities be equal to the total supply of commodities is that the total demand for cash balances be equal to the available amount of money. We may call the fulfilment of this condition *monetary equilibrium*.

The total demand for commodities is equal to total supply of commodities only in a state of monetary equilibrium.

4. Say's law makes a much stronger claim than either Walras's law or the equality of total demand for commodities and total supply of commodities under conditions of monetary equilibrium. It states that

---

[3] D_n and S_n are, like all quantities demanded or supplied, measured per unit or period of time. Consequently, ΔM is measured in the same way.

the total demand for commodities (exclusive of money) is *identically* equal to their total supply:

$$\sum_{i=1}^{n-1} p_i D_i \equiv \sum_{i=1}^{n-1} p_i S_i \tag{4.1}$$

From (2.3) and (2.4) we see immediately that, for Say's law to hold, it is necessary and sufficient that

$$D_n \equiv S_n \tag{4.2}$$

which because of (3.3) can also be written

$$\Delta M \equiv 0, \tag{4.3}$$

i.e., the total demand for cash balances must be identically equal to the available amount of money.

Thus, Say's law implies a peculiar nature of the demand for money, namely, that the individuals in our system, taken together, are always satisfied with the existing amount of money and never wish to hold either more or less. There is never a desire to change the total cash balances otherwise than to adapt them to changes in the amount of money available. Under these circumstances, purchases of commodities are never financed from cash balances nor do sales of commodities serve to increase cash balances.

This peculiar nature of the demand for money implied in Say's law was clearly understood by its original proponents. They assumed it explicitly by stating that money is only a medium of exchange, abstracting from its function as a "store of value". In the *Traité d'économie politique*[4] Say states explicitly that, when there is an oversupply of certain commodities, the difficulty in selling them is only seemingly the lack of money to buy them. The lack of money, says Say, is but an expression of the lack of other commodities because the money to be offered for the purchase of the commodities of which there is an oversupply can be acquired only by the sale of other commodities. This view excludes the use of cash balances for financing purchases of commodities. The same view is also expressed by Ricardo: "Productions are always bought by productions, or by services; money is only the medium by which the exchange is effected."[5]

---

[4] See pp. 347–8 of the *Traité*, Paris, 1861.

[5] *Principles of Political Economy and Taxation*, chap. XXI.

5. From its very first enunciation, Say's law has been associated with the proposition that there can be no "universal glut" or "general over-production" in the sense of all entrepreneurs suffering losses. As Ricardo puts it, in a sequel to the passage just quoted: "Too much of a particular commodity may be produced, of which there may be such a glut in the market as not to repay the capital expended on it; but this cannot be the case with respect to all commodities."[6] Total entrepreneurial receipts are thought of as being identically equal to total cost plus some measure of profit (to be discussed later), and a deficiency of receipts with respect to one commodity must, therefore, be accompanied by a surplus of receipts with respect to some other commodity (or commodities). "Over-production" can be only "partial", each partial overproduction being accompanied by a partial underproduction somewhere else in the economic system. We shall investigate the relation of this proposition to Say's law, with special regard to the nature of the "measure of profit" involved.

Let us distinguish between commodities bought by entrepreneurs and commodities sold by entrepreneurs. We shall call the first "factors" and the other "products". A commodity may be both a factor and a product, or it may be neither. Thus, we have the following four classes of commodities: commodities which are only factors, commodities which are both factors and products, commodities which are only products, and, finally, commodities which are neither factors nor products. We shall call these four classes "primary factors", "intermediate products", "final products" and "direct services", respectively. To simplify the notation, let us denote the total demand for and the total supply (both measured in money value) of a class of commodities by D and S with a subscript indicating the class. Use the subscripts F, I, P, and C to denote primary factors, intermediate products, final products, and direct services, respectively. Let us further split up the demand for intermediate products into demand for the replacement of intermediate products used up during the period in question (i.e., the period over which the demand is measured) and the demand for a net increase in the stock of intermediate products (new investment),[7] using the subscripts IR and IN to

---

[6] *Principles of Political Economy and Taxation*, chap. XXI.

[7] Thus, if less than the amount of intermediate products used up during the period is replaced, the demand for a net increase of stock (new investment) is negative.

indicate the two types of demand for intermediate products. Finally, let us denote, as before, by D_n and S_n the demand and supply of money in exchange for commodities.

Since our classification is exhaustive, we have

$$\sum_{i=1}^{n} p_i D_i \equiv D_F + D_{IR} + D_{IN} + D_P + D_C + D_n$$

and

$$\sum_{i=1}^{n} p_i S_i \equiv S_F + S_I + S_P + S_C + S_n.$$

By Walras' law we have

$$(D_F + D_{IR}) + D_{IN} + D_P + D_C + \Delta M \equiv S_F + (S_I + S_P) + S_C, \qquad (5.1)$$

where $\Delta M \equiv D_n - S_n$, as before. The part in parentheses on the left-hand side of this equation is the demand, measured in money value, of entrepreneurs for primary factors and for replacement of the intermediate products used up, i.e., the total cost entrepreneurs are ready to incur. The part in parentheses on the right-hand side is the supply of products, measured in money value, i.e., the total receipts planned by entrepreneurs. The difference between the two,

$$\pi \equiv (S_I + S_P) - (D_F + D_{IR}), \qquad (5.2)$$

is the total profit entrepreneurs plan to receive.[8] This is the total profit implied in the entrepreneurs' decisions to offer $(S_I + S_P)$ worth of products and to use $(D_F + D_{IR})$ worth of factors.[9] We shall call it *planned* total profit.

The demand for replacement represents what Keynes calls "user cost" and "supplementary cost" (cf. J. M. Keynes, *The General Theory of Employment, Interest and Money*, pp. 53 and 56, New York, 1936). The actual demand for intermediate products is the demand for replacement plus the demand for a net increase of stock.

[8] It is assumed here that entrepreneurs supply exactly the quantities designed, i.e., the quantities indicated by the supply functions. If entrepreneurs' supply is different from what was designed by them (as, e.g., in case of fluctuating crops), i.e., differs from the profit entrepreneurs plan to receive by the difference between the actual supply and the supply originally designed.

[9] S_I and S_P are expressions of the type $\sum p_i S_i$, the summation extending over all intermediate products and all final products, respectively. D_F and D_{IR} are expressions of the type $\sum p_i D_i$, the summation extending over the respective class of commodities. The S_i's and D_i's are functions of prices. The prices are taken as (arbitrarily) given.

Taking into account (5.2), we can re-write (5.1) in the form

$$(\pi - D_{IN}) - (D_P - S_F) \equiv \Delta M - \Delta C \tag{5.3}$$

where

$$\Delta C \equiv S_C - D_C.$$

Each of the terms in this identity, except ΔM, represents an independent set of decisions. The terms in the first parentheses represent entrepreneurial decisions, and the terms in the second parentheses represent decisions to buy from entrepreneurs and to sell to entrepreneurs. We shall call these decisions the *capitalistic sphere* of decisions. On the right-hand side, the term ΔC represents decisions to sell and to buy direct services. As the offers to sell and to buy direct services are not directed to entrepreneurs, we shall call these decisions the *non-capitalistic sphere* of decisions. On account of (5.2)

$$\pi - D_{IN} \equiv (S_I + S_P) - (D_F + D_{IR} + D_{IN})$$

which is the difference between the stream of money demanded and the stream of money offered by entrepreneurs. It is the *net* stream of money demanded by entrepreneurs. The expression $(D_P - S_F)$ is the difference between the stream of money offered to entrepreneurs and the stream of money demanded from entrepreneurs. It is the *net* stream of money offered to entrepreneurs. On the right-hand side, $\Delta C \equiv S_c - D_c$ is the difference between the stream of money demanded and the stream of money offered in exchange for direct services, or the demand for increased cash balances arising in the non-capitalistic sphere of decisions. As ΔM is the total demand for increased cash balances (relative to the quantity of money available), $\Delta M - \Delta C$ is the demand for the increase in cash balances (relative to the quantity of money) arising in the capitalistic sphere of decisions. We shall say that there is monetary equilibrium in the capitalistic sphere of decisions when $\Delta M - \Delta C = 0$.

When $(D_P - S_F) = (\Pi - D_{IN})$, the net stream of money offered to entrepreneurs is equal to the net stream of money demanded by them, and entrepreneurs can realize their planned total profit and their demand for new investment. However, when $(D_P - S_F) < (\Pi - D_{IN})$, the net stream of money offered to entrepreneurs is less than the net stream of money demanded by them. Given their demand for new investment, entrepreneurs cannot realize their planned total profit. They must either accept a smaller total profit than planned or, instead, increase D_{IN}, i.e., their demand for new investment. Demand for new investment is an offer by entrepreneurs to buy from themselves. Therefore, an increase in the demand for new investment diminishes the net stream of money demanded by entrepreneurs. Finally, when $(D_P - S_F) > (\Pi - D_{IN})$, the net stream of money offered to entrepreneurs is greater than the net stream, of money demanded by them. Entrepreneurs can either realize a greater total profit than planned or, alternatively diminish their new investment.

Thus, given the entrepreneurs' demand for new investment, D_{IN}, a profit less than, equal to, or greater than planned can be realized according as to whether $(D_P - S_F) \lesseqgtr (\Pi - D_{IN})$ or, because of (5.3), according as to whether $\Delta M - \Delta C \gtreqless 0$. It should be noticed that the condition which permits entrepreneurs to realize exactly their planned total profit and their demand for new investment is not equivalent to monetary equilibrium for the whole system ($\Delta M = 0$) but to monetary equilibrium in the capitalistic sphere of decisions (i.e., $\Delta M - \Delta C = 0$). However, in a purely capitalistic system (i.e. in a system in which there are no direct services), ΔC disappears and $\Delta M = 0$ is the condition equivalent with the equality between the net stream of money offered to entrepreneurs and the net stream of money demanded by entrepreneurs.

Under Say's law $\Delta M \equiv 0$, and if the economic system is purely capitalistic we have

$$(D_P - S_F) \equiv (\Pi - D_{IN}). \tag{5.4}$$

The net stream of money offered to entrepreneurs is *always* equal to the net stream of money demanded by them. Whatever the total profit and new investment planned by entrepreneurs, the net stream of money offered to them is always such as to enable them to realize their planned profit and new investment, irrespective of whether there is equilibrium of demand and supply for each separate commodity. Thus, total entrepreneurial receipts are, under Say's law, identically equal to total cost plus planned total profit.[10] Consequently, an impossibility of realizing planned profit in one part of the system must be compensated by a possi-

---

[10] This is subject to the qualification stated in footnote 8. It should also be noticed that Say's law implies nothing as to the level of planned total profit. Planned total profit may be even negative, as, e.g., when there is large fixed capital equipment.

bility of realizing more than planned profit in some other part of the system. It is in this sense that "overproduction" can be only "partial".

This holds, however, only for a purely capitalistic system. If direct services are present, the condition $\Delta M \equiv 0$ does not suffice to make total entrepreneurial receipts equal to total cost plus planned total profit. It is necessary, in addition, that $\Delta C = 0$, i.e., that the market for direct services be in equilibrium. Disequilibrium in the market for direct services may cause a discrepancy between the net stream of money offered to entrepreneurs and the net stream of money demanded by entrepreneurs. Thus Say's law implies the impossibility of a "universal glut" only for a purely capitalistic system.

6. Say's law, however, does *not* imply that the total demand and the total supply of products are identically equal. Neither does it imply an identity of the total demand and the total supply of primary factors and direct services.

We can rewrite (5.1) in the form

$$(S_F+S_C)-(D_F+D_C) \equiv (D_{IR}+D_{IN}+D_P)-(S_I+S_P)+\Delta M. \quad (6.1)$$

The left-hand side is the excess supply of factors and direct services (measured in money value). On the right-hand side the two parts in parentheses give the excess demand for (intermediate and final) products (also measured in money value).[11] The identity (6.1) shows that primary factors and direct services are offered in exchange for products and money, while products and money are offered in exchange for primary factors and direct services. Under conditions of monetary equilibrium $\Delta M = 0$, and an excess supply of factors implies an excess demand of equal size for products, and vice versa. This is clear, because, when monetary equilibrium exists, primary factors and direct services are offered in exchange for products alone, and products alone are offered in exchange for primary factors and direct services. In this case, an excess supply of the one means an excess demand for the other.

Under Say's law $\Delta M \equiv 0$, and we obtain

$$(S_F+S_C)-(D_F+D_C) \equiv (D_{IR}+D_{IN}+D_P)-(S_I+S_P). \quad (6.2)$$

The two sides of this identity need not be zero. The total supply of primary factors and direct services may, therefore, differ from the total

---

[11] By "excess supply" we mean the excess of supply over demand; by "excess demand", the excess of demand over supply.

demand for primary factors and direct services. Similarly, the total demand for products may differ from the total supply of products. Neither of the two discrepancies is precluded by Say's law. But (6.2) shows that under Say's law an excess supply of primary factors and direct services *always* implies an excess demand of equal amount for products, and vice versa. This tends directly to restore equilibrium. An excess demand for products causes product prices to rise. This stimulates a decrease in demand and an increase in the supply of products. A decrease in the demand for products is, however, equivalent to a decrease in the supply of primary factors and direct services; and an increase in the supply of products is equivalent to an increase in the demand for primary factors and direct services. Thus, equilibrium is restored simultaneously between demand and supply of products and between demand and supply of primary factors and direct services. In a similar way, equilibrium is restored directly in case of an excess supply of products.

When Say's law does not hold, an excess supply of primary factors and direct services need not be associated with an excess demand for factors. From (6.1) we see immediately that an excess supply of products may coexist with an excess supply of factors and direct services, and vice versa, as long as $\Delta M > 0$. Such a coexistence happens when

$$\Delta M > (S_I + S_P) - (D_{IR} + D_{IN} + D_P) > 0$$

and

$$\Delta M > (S_F + S_C) - (D_F + D_C) > 0,$$

i.e., when there is a desire to increase cash balances (relative to the quantity of money available) by more than the excess supply of products, and also by more than the excess supply of factors and direct services. In this case, there is no direct tendency to restore equilibrium by the simple mechanism of exchange between primary factors and direct services on one side, and products on the other side. Equilibrium can be restored only by abatement of the desire to increase cash balances relative to the quantity of money (i.e., by ΔM's becoming again equal to zero). This will happen only if the fall in prices, resulting from the excess supply, tends to make $\Delta M = 0$. We may say that in such cases the conditions for a stable monetary equilibrium are satisfied. Otherwise, there is no tendency to reach an equilibrium, and the general stability conditions (2.2) are not satisfied. However, the satisfaction of all the stability conditions (2.2) is not implied in Say's law. Say's law implies only that enough of the stability conditions of the system hold to ensure the existence of a stable equilibrium for two broad classes of commodities, namely, the class of products and the class of primary factors and direct services.

This discussion takes us back to the original controversy between Malthus and Ricardo. In his *Principles of Political Economy* Malthus stated: "If commodities were only to be compared and exchanged with each other, then indeed it would be true that, if they were all increased in their proper proportion, to any extent, they would continue to bear among themselves the same relative value".[12] But this is not a correct account, Malthus argued, because "it is by no means true, as a matter of fact, that commodities are always exchanged for commodities. The great mass of commodities is exchanged directly for labour, either productive or unproductive; and it is quite obvious that this mass of commodities, compared with the labour for which it is to be exchanged, may fall in value from a glut just as any one commodity falls in value from an excess of supply, compared either with labour or money".[13] Malthus means here by the term "commodity" (as distinguished from "labour") what is designated in this paper as "product". Remembering this, and substituting "primary factors and direct services" for the more restricted concept of "labour" used by Malthus, the statement quoted expresses the relationship stated in (6.1) when $\Delta M = 0$. It states that products are exchanged not only for products but that "the great mass" of products is exchanged for primary factors and direct services. In consequence, there may be a general excess supply of products which leads to a decline of product prices as compared with prices of primary factors and direct services.

This statement is quite correct, because an excess supply of products implies under these conditions an excess demand for factors and direct services. Malthus, however, thought that by pointing out this correct relationship he had proved *eo ipso* the possibility of a "general over-production" (as defined above on p. 53). The effect of an excess supply of products would be, according to Malthus, that "commodities (i.e., products) would necessarily fall in value, compared with labour (primary

---

[12] T. Malthus, *Principles of Political Economy*, p. 355, London, 1820.

[13] *Ibid.*, pp. 353–4. Cf. also the note on pp. 317–8 of the second edition, London, 1836.

factors and direct services), so as to lower profits almost to nothing, and to check for a time further production. But this is precisely what is meant by the term glut, which, in this case, is evidently general not partial".[14] It is true, as we have seen, that the prices of products would fall relatively to the prices of primary factors and direct services. But, as is clearly seen from (5.3), no "general glut" in the sense of realized total profit falling below planned total profit follows, unless $\Delta M - \Delta C > 0$.

Ricardo's[15] answer to Malthus was: "It is quite true that commodities may exist in such abundance, compared with labour, as to make their value so (to) fall, (estimated) in labour, as not to afford any inducement to their further production. In that case, labour will demand a great quantity of commodities."[16] Keeping in mind our preceding observation concerning terminology, this passage simply states that an excess supply of products is accompanied by an excess demand for primary factors and direct services, which causes a rise in their prices. This is correct under the assumptions of Say's law. Malthus, however, denied that an excess supply of products must be associated with an excess demand for primary factors and direct services. He maintained that there will be

---

[14] *Ibid.*, p. 354.

[15] Say's reply to the same point made by Malthus was merely a terminological evasion: "Commodities, you say, are not only exchanged for commodities: they are also exchanged for labour. If this labour be a produce that some persons sell, that others buy, and that the latter consume, it will cost me very little to call it a commodity, and it will cost you very little more to assimilate other commodities to it, for they are also produce. Then, comprising both under the generic name of 'Produce', you may perhaps admit that produce is bought only with produce" (cf. *Letters to Thomas Malthus on "Political Economy and Stagnation of Commerce"*, London, 1821, reprinted in 1936 by Harding Ltd., Letter 1, pp. 21–22). In this translation the word "not" is omitted in the first sentence. This is obviously a misprint (cf. the French original in *Oeuvres diverses de J. B. Say, Petit volume*, ed. Guillaumin, Paris, 1848, p. 456). The word "produce" obviously means here commodities in general, i.e., primary factors and direct services as well as products.

At a later stage of the controversy Say fell only deeper into his terminological tautologies and defined "produce as a product the receipts for which cover its costs" (see the *Letter to Malthus of July, 1827*, in *Oeuvres diverses*, p. 513, and *Cours complet d'économie politique pratique*, 2nd ed., 1840, vol. I, pp. 347–48); cf. also E. von Bergmann, *Geschichte der nationalökonomischen Krisentheorien*, Kohlkammer, Stuttgart, 1895, pp. 74–76). Thus the proposition that total cost of "produce" cannot exceed total receipts of entrepreneurs became with Say a mere tautology.

[16] *Notes on Malthus' "Principles of Political Economy"*, ed. Jacob H. Hollander and T. E. Gregory, p. 163, Baltimore, 1928.

also an excess supply of primary factors and direct services, i.e., unemployment.[17] This requires, as we have seen, absence of monetary equilibrium, namely, a desire to increase cash balances (relative to the quantity of money available) by more than the excess supply of products, and more than the excess supply of factors and direct services. In such a case, a "universal glut" may occur, indeed, provided that some of the demand for an increase in cash balances arises in the capitalistic sphere of decisions (i.e., that $\Delta M - \Delta C > 0$).

Malthus had clearly something like this in his mind as is shown by the following statement in a footnote:

Theoretical writers in political economy, from the fear of appearing to attach too much importance to money, have perhaps been too apt to throw it out of their consideration in their reasonings. It is an abstract truth that we want commodities, not money. But, in reality, no commodity for which it is possible to sell our goods at once, can be an adequate substitute for a circulating medium, and enable us in the same manner to provide for children to purchase an estate, or to command labour and provisions a year or two hence. A circulating medium is absolutely necessary to any considerable saving; and even the manufacturer would get on but slowly, if he were obliged to accumulate in kind all the wages of his workmen. We cannot therefore be surprised at his wanting money rather than commodities.[18]

But the fact that he had relegated to a footnote this crucial monetary consideration made his argument unconvincing to Ricardo, who argued throughout on the basis of the assumption that money is only a medium of exchange (i.e., $\Delta M \equiv 0$). Because Malthus had failed to make fully explicit his assumption concerning the demand for money, the discussion between him and Ricardo was carried on at cross-purposes.

7. Now let us study the implication of Say's law for the theory of prices. In the general case the $n-1$ equilibrium prices are determined ·

---

[17] *Ibid.*, pp. 361–2. The excess supply of primary factors and direct services is, however, not the same as "involuntary unemployment" in the Keynesian sense. "Involuntary unemployment", as defined in the Keynesian theory, is not an excess of supply of labour but an equilibrium position obtained by intersection of a demand and of a supply curve, the supply curve, however, being infinitely elastic with respect to money wages over a wide range, and the point of intersection being to the left of the region where the elasticity of supply of labour with respect to money wages becomes finite. Thus the left-hand side of (6.1) is always zero in the Keynesian theory. The different levels of employment refer to different levels of the demand and supply of labour (cf. Keynes, *op. cit.*, p. 15; and also my article, The Rate of Interest and the Optimum Propensity to Consume, *Economica*, February, 1938, p. 31).

[18] T. Malthus, *Principles of Political Economy*, ed. cit., pp. 361–2.

by the $n-1$ equations (2.1) which express, for each commodity, the equality of demand and supply. If the stability conditions (2.2) are satisfied, the actual prices tend towards the equilibrium prices given by (2.1). However, when Say's law holds, the number of independent equations is reduced by one. According to Say's law

$$\sum_{i=1}^{n-2} p_i D_i + p_{n-1} D_{n-1} \equiv \sum_{i=1}^{n-2} p_i s_i + p_{n-1} S_{n-1} \tag{7.1}$$

(where the commodity $n-1$ is chosen arbitrarily). This expression shows that, if $D_i = S_i$ for the $n-2$ first commodities, we have necessarily $D_{n-1} = S_{n-1}$. We also have $D_n \equiv S_n$ by Say's law. The number of independent equations is only $n-2$, while the number of equilibrium prices to be determined is $n-1$. Thus, when Say's law holds, the equilibrium prices are indeterminate. The equations (2.1) determine in this case $n-2$ prices as functions of the price of the commodity $n-1$ (which is chosen arbitrarily), i.e., $p_i = f_i(p_{n-1})$, $(i = 1, 2, ..., n-2)$.[19]

---

[19] Denoting $F_i(p_1, p_2, ..., p_{n-1}) = D_i - S_i$, the $n-2$ independent equilibrium equations of the set (2.1) can be written in the form:

$$F_i(p_1, p_2, ..., p_{n-1}) = 0 \quad (i = 1, 2, ..., n-2). \tag{1}$$

A solution with respect to $p_1, p_2, ..., p_{n-2}$ exists if

$$\frac{\delta(F_1, F_2, ..., F_{n-2})}{\delta(p_1, p_2, ..., p_{n-2})} \neq 0,$$

$p_1, p_2, ..., p_{n-2}$ being then functions of p_{n-1}. The Jacobian has the required property when the stability conditions are satisfied. The stability conditions of the system (1) are (see eq. 2.2 above and also Hicks, *op. cit.*, p. 315):

$$\frac{dF_1}{dp_i} = \sum_{r=1}^{n-2} \frac{\delta F_1}{\delta p_r} \frac{dp_r}{dp_i} = 0,$$

$$\cdots\cdots\cdots\cdots\cdots$$

$$\frac{dF_i}{dp_i} = \sum_{r=1}^{n-2} \frac{\delta F_i}{\delta p_r} \frac{dp_r}{dp_i} < 0, \quad (i = 1, 2, ..., n-2) \tag{2}$$

$$\cdots\cdots\cdots\cdots\cdots$$

$$\frac{dF_{n-2}}{dp_i} = \sum_{r=1}^{n-2} \frac{\delta F_{n-2}}{\delta p_r} \frac{\delta p_r}{\delta p_i} = 0.$$

Solving the system (2) with respect to dF_i/dp_i, we obtain

$$\frac{dF_i}{dp_i} = \frac{\delta(F_1, F_2, ..., F_{n-2})}{\delta(p_1, p_2, ..., p_{n-2})} \times \frac{\delta(F_1, ..., F_{i-1}, F_{i+1}, ..., F_{n-2})}{\delta(p_1, ..., p_{i-1}, p_{i+1}, ..., p_{n-2})}. \quad (i = 1, 2, ..., n-2)$$

Since this must be negative the numerator must be different from zero.

This indeterminateness of equilibrium prices which results from the acceptance of Say's law is, however, reduced considerably by taking account of the consequences of the peculiar nature of the demand for money implied in Say's law. Say's law precludes substitution between money and commodities because it implies that purchases of commodities cannot be financed from cash balances and that cash balances cannot be increased out of the receipts from the sale of commodities.[20] This has an important consequence for the structure of the demand and supply functions of commodities. These functions are derived from the theory of substitution. According to the principles of the theory of substitution, a change of the ratios of the prices of the different commodities leads, as a rule,[21] to a substitution of commodities, the prices of which are relatively lowered, for commodities the prices of which are relatively increased.[22] A proportional change of the prices of all commodities, i.e., of $p_1, p_2, ..., p_{n-1}$, implies a change of the exchange ratio of commodities for money (the price of money $p_n \equiv 1$ by definition). In the general case, this would result in a substitution of money for commodities or vice versa. Say's law, however, precludes such a substitution. Thus, in the case in which Say's law holds, a proportional change of the prices of all commodities cannot affect the demand and supply of commodities relative to the demand and supply of money. But a proportional change of all prices does not induce a substitution between different commodities either. Therefore, the demand and supply functions of commodities are, when Say's law holds, homogeneous of zero degree, i.e., a proportional change of *all* prices does not affect the quantities demanded or offered. These quantities depend merely on the *relative prices*, i.e., on the ratios of the prices

$$\frac{p_1}{p_{n-1}}, \frac{p_2}{p_{n-1}}, ..., \frac{p_{n-2}}{p_{n-1}},$$

where the commodity $n-1$ is chosen arbitrarily.

Denoting the relative prices by $\Pi_i = \dfrac{p_i}{p_{n-1}}$ $(i = 1, 2, ..., n-2)$, the

---

[20] Cf. p. 53 above.

[21] This rule may be counteracted by complementarity.

[22] This holds also for the substitution between factors and products if factors are considered as negative products (cf. Hicks, *op. cit.*, p. 93 and pp. 319–22).

equations expressing, for each commodity, the equilibrium of demand and supply can be written

$$D_i(\Pi_1, \Pi_2, ..., \Pi_{n-2}) = S_i(\Pi_1, \Pi_2, ..., \Pi_{n-2}). \quad (i = 1, 2, ..., n-2) \quad (7.2)$$

They take the place of the $n-2$ independent equations among the equilibrium equations (2.1), and the equilibrium values of the $n-2$ relative prices are determinate.

Thus, it is possible to determine the equilibrium values of the relative prices, i.e., of the ratios of the money prices of commodities. The money prices, however, remain indeterminate.

8. Under Say's law the relative prices of commodities are found to be independent of the quantity of money in the system. Money is "neutral",[23] or, to use the phrase of the classical economists, it is merely a "veil" which can be removed and relative prices can be studied as if the system were based on barter. Indeed, by precluding the substitution of money for commodities or vice versa, Say's law constructs a system which is equivalent to a barter economy. Money in such a system is merely a worthless medium of exchange and a standard of value.

The money prices of commodities are indeterminate in a system in which Say's law is satisfied. In order to determine them, we need to know the price p_{n-1} (the commodity $n-1$ being chosen arbitrarily). If this is known, the money prices can be obtained from the relative prices by the relation $p_i = p_{n-1} \pi_i$ ($i = 1, 2, ..., n-2$). The price p_{n-1}, however, cannot be obtained under Say's law because we have only $n-2$ independent equations of equilibrium for demand and supply. This has led the traditional theory of money to determine the price p_{n-1} from a supplementary equation—the "equation of exchange"—introduced into the system. This equation can be written

$$k \sum_{i=1}^{n-1} p_i S_i = M \quad (8.1)$$

where k is a constant, expressing the proportion of the total supply of commodities, measured in money value, which people want to hold in cash balances, i.e., k is the reciprocal of the velocity of circulation of money. M is the quantity of money.

---

[23] Cf. the definition of "neutral" money in J. Koopmans, *Das neutrale Geld* (*Beiträge zur Geldtheorie*), ed. F. A. Hayek, p. 228, (Vienna, Springer, 1933).

Since $p_i = p_{n-1}\pi_i$ (for $i = 1, 2, ..., n-2$; for $i = n-1$ we put $\pi_i \equiv 1$ by definition), the equation (8.1) transforms into

$$kp_{n-1} \sum_{i=1}^{n-1} \pi_i S_i = M. \tag{8.2}$$

The equilibrium values of the relative prices π_i are determined by the equations (7.2) and the equilibrium quantities of commodities supplied S_i ($i = 1, 2, ..., n-1$) are obtained by substituting the π_i's into the supply functions.[24] The π_i's and S_i's thus given, p_{n-1} is determined from (8.2).

This is the procedure of the traditional theory of money. It implies a division of the theory of prices in two separate parts: (1) the determination of relative prices and (2) the determination of a multiplier (the "price level") by a monetary equation distinct from the system of equilibrium equations. It results in money being "neutral".[25]

This procedure, however, is self-contradictory. Equation (8.2) is not compatible with Say's law. The left-hand side of this equation is the total demand for cash balances, and the right-hand side is the existing stock of money. The difference is the desired change in cash balances (relative to the quantity of money). We have thus:[26]

$$kp_{n-1} \sum_{i=1}^{n-1} \Pi_i S_i - M = \Delta M. \tag{8.3}$$

If p_{n-1} has a value which does not satisfy (8.2), there is a discrepancy between the amount of money people want to hold and the quantity of money in existence. This implies a discrepancy between the total demand and the total supply of commodities (see eq. [3.3]). Say's law, however, requires that $\Delta M \equiv 0$ (see eq. [3.4] above). In this case we obtain

---

[24] S_{n-1} is also obtained because we have $n-1$ supply functions of commodities, although there are only $n-2$ independent equilibrium equations.

[25] Except for "frictions" and time lags, which is in this case the only way in which money can influence the relative prices of commodities.

[26] In order that the ΔM here be the same as the ΔM in (3.3), it is necessary that the unit or period of time over which the change is contemplated, be the same as the unit or period of time over which the quantities demanded and supplied are measured. See footnote 3 above.

$$kp_{n-1} \sum_{i=1}^{n-1} \Pi_i S_i \equiv M,\tag{8.4}$$

i.e., an identity, which holds for any value of p_{n-1} and, therefore, cannot serve to determine p_{n-1}. But k cannot be constant and must be indeterminate to adjust itself to any value of p_{n-1} so that the identity be satisfied. Say's law implies an indeterminate velocity of circulation $(1/k)$ and the money prices are indeterminate.

Thus, the traditional procedure of the theory of money involves a contradiction. Either Say's law is assumed and money prices are indeterminate or money prices are made determinate, but then Say's law and hence the "neutrality" of money must be abandoned. Say's law precludes any monetary theory.

9. We have seen that Say's law precludes any monetary theory. The theory of money must, therefore, start with a rejection of Say's law. Instead of assuming that total demand and total supply of commodities are identically equal or, what is equivalent, that the total demand for cash balances is identically equal to the amount of money available, these identities have to be replaced by genuine equations. The objective of the theory of money is then to study the conditions under which equilibrium of total demand and of total supply of commodities (or, instead, equilibrium of total demand for cash balances and the quantity of money available) obtains and the processes by which such equilibrium is attained.

This objective was expressed very clearly by Wicksell: "Any theory of money worthy of the name must be able to show why the monetary or pecuniary demand for goods exceeds or falls short of the supply of goods in given conditions".[27] Wicksell also observed the difficulty of reconciling this with Say's law. He finally appeased his conscience by stating that total demand and total supply must be equal only "ultimately" but may differ "in the first place".[28] With this observation Wicksell, and with him all monetary theorists, gave up Say's law by substituting for the identity an equation which holds only in equilibrium. The statement that total demand and total supply tend to be equal "ultimately" is nothing but an assertion that the stability conditions for the system are satisfied. If the stability conditions (2.2) are satisfied, any disturbance of

[27] J. P. Wicksell, *Lectures on Political Economy*, Vol. II, 159–60, London, 1935.
[28] *Ibid.*, p. 159.

equilibrium will make the demand and supply of each commodity tend toward equality again; and since this happens for each commodity in the system, it also implies that the total demand and total supply of commodities tend toward equality. But this tendency toward equilibrium, implied in the stability conditions, should not be confused with Say's law.

Since the homogeneity of the demand and supply functions of commodities disappears when Say's law is abandoned, we find that the theory of money cannot be separated from the theory of relative prices. The very basis of monetary theory proves to be incompatible with "neutrality" of money. The money prices of all commodities have to be determined directly from the general system of equilibrium equations (2.1).

10. The above implications of Say's law for the theory of prices and the theory of money hold also with regard to a dynamic theory of prices which is based on consideration of substitution of goods at different moments of time as well as of substitution of different goods at a given moment of time.

For simplicity, let us divide the span of time under consideration into $m+1$ small and equal intervals indicated by the indices $0, 1, 2, ..., m$, where the index 0 refers to the "present" interval, the other indices referring to "future" intervals. Denote, further, the price of the ith commodity expected in the tth interval by p_{it} and let it be understood that p_{i0} $(i = 1, 2, ..., n-1)$ are the prices actually obtaining in the "present" interval. We shall call the latter the "current prices". Let r_t be the rate of interest (per interval) on loans of a duration of t intervals. The discounted value of the expected price p_{it} is $q_{it} = p_{it}/(1+r_t)^t$. This definition yields $q_{i0} = p_{i0}$ for $i = 1, 2, ..., n-1$. Current demand and supply of a commodity, i.e., demand and supply in the "present" interval, is a function of all current prices as well as of the discounted values of all expected future prices[29]

$$D_{i0} = D_{i0}(q_{10}, q_{20}, ..., q_{n-1,0}; \quad q_{11}, q_{21}, ..., q_{n-1,1}; ...,$$

$$q_{1m}, q_{2m}, ..., q_{n-1,m}) \quad (i = 1, 2, ..., n-1)$$

and

$$s_{i0} = S_{i0}(q_{10}, q_{20}, ..., q_{n-1,0}; q_{11}, q_{21}, ..., q_{n-1}; ...; q_{1m}, q_{2m}, ..., q_{n-1,m}).$$

---

[29] Cf. Gerhard Tintner, The Theoretical Derivation of Dynamic Demand Curves, *Econometrica*, October, 1938; and Hicks, *op. cit.*, chap. XVIII.

The equations of equilibrium are

$$D_{i0}(p_{10}, p_{20}, ..., p_{n-1,0}; q_{11}, q_{21}, ..., q_{n-1,1}; ...; q_{1m}, q_{2m}, ..., q_{n-1,m})$$
$$= S_{i0}(p_{10}, p_{20}, ..., p_{n-1,0}; q_{11}, q_{21}, ..., q_{n-1,1}; ...; q_{1m}; q_{2m}; q_{n-1,m}). \quad (10.1)$$

They determine the equilibrium values of the $n-1$ current prices p_{i0} ($i = 1, 2, ..., n-1$), as functions of the discounted values of the expected future prices. The latter may be regarded as functions of the current prices

$$q_{it} = f_{it}(p_{10}, p_{20}, ..., p_{n-1,0}). \quad (i = 1, 2, ..., n-1; t = 1, 2, ..., m) \quad (10.2)$$

We shall call these functions the "expectation functions" and their partial elasticities the "elasticities of expectation".[30] Thus, together with the expectation functions, which are $(n-1)m$ in number, the equations (10.1) determine the equilibrium values of the current prices.

When Say's law holds, we have, as before, only $n-2$ independent equations among the equations (10.1), and the demand and supply functions are homogeneous of zero degree because Say's law precludes substitution between money and commodities. In the dynamic theory of prices it is, however, all the money prices q_{it}, the discounted values of the expected future prices as well as the current prices, a proportional change of which does not affect the quantities demanded and offered. The demand and supply functions depend then only on the relative prices, i.e., on the ratios of the q_{it}'s. This, however, does not suffice to make the relative prices determinate because of the expectation functions (10.2). In order that the relative prices be determinate, the expectation functions, too, must involve only relative prices and not money prices. Thus, the expectation functions must be homogeneous of the first degree, i.e., a proportional change of all current prices must change the discounted values of the expected future prices in the same proportion. In this case, a proportional change of all current prices leaves the quantities demanded and supplied unaffected. The demand and supply functions of commodities depend now only on the ratios of the current prices, and the relative prices are determined by the $n-2$ independent equations of the system (10.1) and by the expectation functions (10.2). The money prices, however, remain indeterminate.

---

[30] The latter term was introduced by Hicks, *op. cit.*, p. 205.

In the dynamic theory of prices Say's law implies thus, in addition to homogeneity of the demand and supply functions of commodities, homogeneous expectation functions. This additional assumption makes Say's law much more unrealistic in the context of a dynamic theory of prices than it is in the context of a static theory. Both in static and in dynamic theory Say's law leaves money prices indeterminate.

SOME PROBLEMS CONCERNING ECONOMIC PLANNING IN UNDERDEVELOPED COUNTRIES

The Basic Problem of an Underdeveloped Economy

An underdeveloped economy is an economy in which the available stock of capital goods is not sufficient to employ the total available labour force on the basis of modern production techniques. In consequence, two alternatives are open to such an economy. One alternative is to employ the available labour force in conditions of backward, primitive production techniques. This implies low productivity of labour and thus low *per capita* real income. The other alternative is to adopt more advanced production techniques and higher productivity of labour. This implies, however, unemployment or underemployment of part of the labour force, because the capital goods available do not suffice to employ the whole labour force in conditions of modern techniques of production. The failure to utilize fully the labour force leads to low *per capita* national income.

Usually, both situations are found in underdeveloped economies. The first prevails in fields where the capitalist mode of production has not yet penetrated or has come into use only in the form of cottage industries, organized by capitalist merchants. The second exists wherever capitalist factory production has replaced handicrafts or cottage industries and led to the ruin of small independent producers. The second situation develops also in agriculture where feudal types of landownership exclude small peasant holdings or individual peasant production which is replaced by the capitalist plantations system.

The dilemma of an underdeveloped economy may be presented as follows. Let c be the value of the total stock of capital goods available, and v the value of the total labour force employed. Denote by α the average degree of "capital intensity" of production (the organic composition of capital, according to Marx). We have then

$$\alpha = \frac{c}{v}.$$
(1)

171

If N is the total labour force employed (measured, for instance, in man-hours) and w is the average wage-rate, we have

$$v = Nw. \tag{2}$$

The total employment is thus

$$N = \frac{c}{\alpha w}. \tag{3}$$

Denote by N_0 the total available labour force. The economy is underdeveloped whenever $N < N_0$; the ratio N/N_0 may be considered as a measure of the degree of underdevelopment.

As w cannot be reduced below a certain minimum corresponding to the biological and sociological requirements of maintenance of the working population (cost of reproduction of labour power), total employment can be raised to the full employment level only in one of the following two ways. Either α is reduced sufficiently and the economy is kept at a low level of productivity, or c must increase sufficiently to make possible full employment with a value of α corresponding to modern techniques of production. The latter requires capital accumulation. The relative increase in the necessary stock of means of production is proportional to $(N_0-N)/N$, as can be easily seen from formula (3).

Obviously, only the road of capital accumulation leads the economy out of its state of underdevelopment. The essential problem of underdeveloped economies consists in capital accumulation being insufficient to make c increase to the required level within a reasonably short time. In consequence of the low productivity of labour, or of unemployment or underemployment, the surplus of the national income over what is needed for the reproduction of the labour force—we shall call it simply the economic surplus—is small. This, however, is not the most important obstacle to capital accumulation. The fundamental obstacle is the fact that such economic surplus as is available is not utilized for capital accumulation in the underdeveloped economies.

The causes which have prevented the utilization of that surplus for capital accumulation are basically the following.

One cause is the feudal mode of production and the corresponding way of life of the old feudal ruling classes. The feudal mode of production is characterized by low productivity and correspondingly, a low economic surplus. The feudal ruling class, however, use the small surplus produced for conspicuous consumption, i.e., for unproductive purposes. In this connection, the distinction of the classical English economists, particularly Smith and Ricardo, between productive and unproductive labour may be recalled. The landed aristocracy was accused by Smith and Ricardo of squandering the nation's resources in conspicuous consumption and unproductive employment of labour services, instead of utilizing their incomes for capital accumulation and consequent productive employment of labour.

As a major part of the underdeveloped countries became subject to colonial rule, this drain on the small economic surplus was increased by the very expensive colonial administration. When an underdeveloped country remained independent, the same drain was usually pursued by the domestic monarchy and its officials.

In the period of monopoly capitalism which started towards the end of the nineteenth century, the unproductive drain on the economic surplus of the underdeveloped countries was reinforced by the profits of foreign capital. Foreign capital came to the underdeveloped countries under colonial or semi-colonial conditions, i.e., it treated these countries as sheltered reserves for monopoly exploitation. The monopoly profits thus realized were on the whole, not reinvested in a way conducive to economic progress of the underdeveloped countries. A major part of the profit of foreign capital was taken out from the underdeveloped countries and used for the economic development of the metropolitan countries (this manifested itself, among others, in such forms as the continuous excess of imports over exports in the leading capitalist countries of Western Europe), or were invested in such ways as not to create competition for the basic industries owned by the same monopolistic groups in the metropolitan countries. As these are—as a rule—heavy industries, such capital as was reinvested in the underdeveloped countries was chiefly directed to consumer goods industries, extraction of raw materials and the production of staple foodstuffs.

This leads to the well-known one-sided character of the economy of underdeveloped countries: capital-intensive techniques of production yielding low incomes on the one side, large-scale unemployment and underemployment of small producers ruined by the competition of capitalist factory production and by the import of manufactured goods from the capitalist industrial countries on the other side; at the same time insufficient capital accumulation.

From the foregoing it follows that intensified capital accumulation, which is the only solution for underdeveloped economies, requires the removal of the following obstacles:

(i) abolition of all remnants of feudal modes of production and feudal ways of life, which produce a low economic surplus and divert the surplus produced to non-productive uses.

(ii) liberation from colonial rule or domestic monarchies and their officialdom which use up for unproductive purposes part of the economic surplus, and

(iii) liberation from dependence on foreign monopoly capital which deprives the underdeveloped countries of part of the surplus by the draining of profits and preventing balanced economic development.

These are essential prerequisites for a rate of capital accumulation sufficient to raise the degree of employment, the productivity of labour and consequently the national income.

Accumulation by Planned Economic Development

The conditions stated above aim at preventing the major part of the economic surplus being used for consumption purposes or being utilized outside the underdeveloped countries. In addition to these measures removing the obstacles to rapid capital accumulation, positive measures must be taken in order to ensure the desired capital accumulation.

Under the present historical circumstances of monopoly capitalism and imperialism, rapid capital accumulation cannot be realized in underdeveloped countries by private capital. A characteristic feature of the underdeveloped countries is the absence of a sufficiently broad and wealthy class of domestic industrial capitalists having available the necessary resources for substantial investments in industrial development. It is impossible to repeat here the process of the countries of Western Europe at the beginning of the nineteenth century where capital accumulation was carried out with private resources of the industrial middle class. In Western Europe this process was also supplemented by resources derived from colonial exploitation. Even under these favourable circumstances, the process of industrial development was relatively slow, too slow to satisfy the social needs of modern times.

Neither is industrialization and economic development possible by the influx of foreign capital. Foreign capital, on the whole, is ready to come to the underdeveloped countries only as monopoly capital under colonial or semi-colonial conditions. This would only provide a new drain on the economic surplus of the underdeveloped countries and handicap their economic development in the way which was described above.

However, under certain favourable conditions, as in the case of a large and strong country such as India, with potent rivalries among different groups of foreign monopoly capital and with economic aid from non-capitalist countries, foreign capital may be utilized to a certain extent for economic development. The extent to which this can be done is, however, strictly limited. For the very conditions of such an advantageous utilization of foreign capital require development of the internal resources of the country in order to make it sufficiently independent and strong to accept foreign capital on its own terms.

Under the circumstances stated, economic development can take place only on the basis of public investment, i.e., of accumulation performed by the State and other public institutions (municipalities, co-operatives, etc.). Public investments thus become the strategic lever of economic development in underdeveloped countries.

The physical resources for public investments exist in the form of unemployed or underemployed labour and of underdeveloped natural resources. The problem of accumulation is essentially that of exploiting these resources for the purpose of producing capital goods, i.e., means of production. This implies the utilization of available resources for the development of producer goods industries. The development of these industries is the basic instrument of economic progress in underdeveloped countries.

It may prove, as in the case of India, that even a rapid development of producer goods industries is not sufficient to absorb all the unemployed and underemployed labour force. The surplus must be absorbed in the following two ways; by land reform leading to the distribution of land to landless peasants and to peasants who have not enough land to absorb all their labour power, coupled with resettlement schemes on land reclaimed by irrigation projects or, alternatively, by the development of labour-intensive handicraft and small industries. Increased demand for the products of these industries generated by the employment created in consequence of public investment in heavy industries, and by the rise in peasants' incomes as a result of land reform provides the market for the increased output of crafts and small-scale industries.

The methods of financing public investments necessary for rapid industrial development will vary according to circumstances. Since the physical resources for such public investments are available, the financing problem is soluble in principle. In the Soviet Union and in the People's Democracies of Europe and Asia the financial resources were furnished by: (i) the profits (including turnover tax) of the nationalized industries, (ii) contributions of the peasants in the form of part of their produce delivered to the State at reduced prices. Nationalization of large industries (chiefly foreign-owned) and of the banking system provided the initial financial resources for public investment. The land reform enabled the peasants to contribute their share of produce for the industrialization of the country. These means of financing were supplemented by taxation and by State loans subscribed for by the population.

In other countries which, like Iran and certain Latin American countries, tried to liberate themselves from exploitation by foreign monopoly capital without having had a People's Democratic revolution, an attempt was made to acquire the resources for financing public investment for economic development by means of nationalization of foreign-owned natural resources (such as oil, copper, etc.). These attempts miscarried because of foreign political intervention.

If India does not resort to any major nationalization of industries in the near future, financial resources for public investment will have to be derived largely from taxation, state loans and a certain amount of deficit financing. In order to be effective, these must tap the economic surplus available. However, when a major nationalized sector has been created by means of public investment, its profits will have to become an important source of further public investment and consequently, of further growth of the nationalized sector.

The Role of the Nationalized Sector

Industrialization and economic development by means of public investments imply the development of a nationalized sector in the economy. This sector becomes the driving force in the development of the whole national economy. It is in the nationalized sector that the major part of the new investment is taking place. It is the nationalized sector which initiates the process of creating new employment and generating new incomes. It is the development of the nationalized sector which—either directly by its own purchases or indirectly by the personal incomes generated in it—creates additional demand and an expanding market for consumer goods produced by the private sector of the national economy. The development of the private sector takes place via the development of the nationalized sector brought about by public investments.

If, considerable unutilized capacity is available in the private capitalist sector, as is the case in most underdeveloped countries (it seems to be the case in India), profits in this sector increase considerably because production expands without entailing much additional investment. These profits can be partly utilized, by means of taxation or borrowing or in other ways, for investment in the nationalized sector.

Industrialization of an underdeveloped country by public investment implies that the output and the capital invested in the nationalized sector increases faster than the output and the capital invested in the private sector. Thus, the importance of the nationalized sector in the national economy increases.

Socialism and State Capitalism

The development of a nationalized sector and its more rapid growth than that of the private sector of the national economy is, under present historical circumstances, a necessary condition for the industrialization of underdeveloped countries. Where the political and social conditions for the establishment by means of public investment of a nationalized sector and of its more rapid growth are non-existent, economic progress of the underdeveloped country is impossible; the country must remain backward until the political and economic conditions mature.

The development and more rapid growth of the nationalized sector does not yet by itself determine the nature of the economic and social development of the country. This depends on the purpose which a nationalized sector is made to serve.

The national sector may be used to serve the economic, social and cultural development of the whole nation. In this case, it becomes the nucleus and starting point of development in the direction of a socialist society. The nationalized sector, however, may also be made subservient to the interests of existing concentrations of private economic power, i.e., of domestic and foreign monopoly capital and the remnants of the old feudal ruling class. In this case, it is an instrument of state capitalism, i.e., of the use of the economic activity of the State for the promotion of capitalist interests.

State capitalism is a usual component of modern monopoly capitalism. In the U.S.A. it takes chiefly the form of an armaments economy, the State acting as a large-scale purchaser of armaments from private corporations, sold to the State at monopoly prices. In this way part of the national income is transferred from the taxpayers to private monopoly capital as profits.

In many countries of Western Europe, particularly France and England, an extensive nationalized sector was created after the Second World War. This sector, however, is put at the service of private monopoly capitalism and frequently serves as an instrument of additional exploitation of the people by monopoly capital. Many nationalized industries are operated at a deficit or at a low profit in order to provide capitalist industries with cheap raw materials (i.e., coal, electric power, transport, etc.). The operating deficits and costs of equipment are covered by taxes paid by the people. In this situation, the nationalized sector is an instrument for the transformation of part of the income earned by the people into profits of monopoly capital.

The difference between a state-capitalist sector of the national economy and a nationalized sector acting as the starting point of a development towards socialism thus consists in the purposes which the nationalized sector serves. State-capitalist public investment and state-capitalist enterprise serve to cover out of the taxpayers', i.e., the people's money, the social overhead costs of private capitalist business, to provide private capitalist enterprise with conditions of external economies and with sources of increasing profits. Socialist public investment and socialist nationalized enterprise serve the needs of the nation as a whole, to develop the national economy in a balanced way and to free it from the domination of private concentration of economic power.

Public investment and growth of a nationalized sector indispensable for the progress of an underdeveloped economy may, thus, inaugurate either the development of state capitalism or the development in a socialist direction. Which way the actual development goes depends on the relations of the various social classes in the political power which becomes the prevailing influence in the State.

It may be said that, compared with the inherited stage of backwardness, public investment and the creation of a nationalized sector in the nature of state capitalism are a step forward for an underdeveloped country. The creation by public investment of a state-capitalist sector means a certain amount of industrialization and general economic development which otherwise would not be forthcoming. It also implies diminishing dependence of the native capitalists on foreign monopoly capital and thus a certain degree of freedom of the country from the domination of imperialism. For this reason, the development of state capitalism in an underdeveloped country is on the whole a progressive phenomenon.

State capitalism, however, though it may initiate progress in an underdeveloped country, cannot sustain such progress for a long time. As we have seen, the nationalized sector must develop faster than the private sector because public investment is, under the conditions peculiar to a modern underdeveloped country, the driving force in the development of the whole national economy. If the nationalized sector acquires a state-capitalist character, it becomes reduced to a subsidiary of private capitalism. Its leading economic role ceases and so does the economic development of the country. Furthermore, it ceases to serve the balanced development of the whole national economy. Consequently, in the long run, it ceases to promote economic development altogether. In the long run the economic progress of an underdeveloped country can be sustained only by the development of the economic foundations of a socialist society.

AN INTRODUCTION TO THE THEORY
OF ECONOMIC DEVELOPMENT

Problems involving the theory of economic development, and thus dynamic problems, are not new to the science of economics. Some basic problems of economic development, and more especially the determination of those factors which influence this development, were already established by classical political economy. The important achievement introduced into the history of economic thought by classical political economy was the basic discovery, that the driving force behind economic development is the accumulation of part of the social product and its allocation for productive investment. Classical economy was also concerned with the question of the factors influencing the size of accumulation and of productive investment.

It was in connection with these problems that Adam Smith and David Ricardo introduced the distinction between productive labour and non-productive labour. The research, involving problems of economic development, carried out by the creators of classical political economy, is connected historically with the formation of a new social system—capitalism.

The criticism levelled against feudalism by classical political economy grew out of the fact, among others, that in this system a large part of the social product was consumed unproductively and spent on luxury consumption by the feudal class and on non-productive work of their servants. William Petty described the contemporary ruling class as a class that wasted the social product, maintaining that there are people who "do nothing other than eat, drink, sing, dance and occupy themselves with metaphysics".[1] On the other hand, in a capitalist system the bourgeoisie leads a thrifty life and allocates what it accumulates for productive investment.

Thus, the idea that accumulation constitutes the source of economic development was introduced by classical political economy. To this basic

---

[1] William Petty, *Political Arithmetic*, chapter IV.

180

factor of economic development, a second one was soon added, i.e., technical progress as expressed in the appropriate division of labour. The significance of the division of labour as a factor of economic development was fully expressed by Adam Smith.

Ricardo was the first to formulate a systematic theory of economic development. According to Ricardo the process of economic development can be presented in the following way.

The source of economic development is accumulation and productive investment of a part of the social product. Under the conditions of capitalism, the surplus product takes on two forms: profit from capital, and land rent. Ricardo believed that in practice the only basis for economic development is profit. Land rent is in general consumed by land owners in a non-productive way. It then follows that the greater the profit, the greater the corresponding accumulation. Although Ricardo did not indicate any closer relationship between accumulation and profit, it follows from his theory that the problem of economic development leads to the problem of defining the size of profit within the division of the social product.

What are the factors which influence the division of the product, among wages, profit and land rent? Wages are fixed by the costs of the reproduction of the labour force.[2] Ricardo explains the mechanism of this process, on the basis of Malthus' *Law of Population*. There is a constant tendency for the population to increase to such an extent that the possibility of producing sufficient means of subsistence is exceeded. An increase in the population leads to a fall in wages, which, however, cannot fall below the costs of subsistence, since the population would then decrease. An increase in wages above the costs of subsistence will, after a certain time, be counter-balanced by an increase in population. Thus a mechanism exists which maintains wages at a certain level corresponding to the minimum costs of subsistence.

Land rent is defined as the excess value of the product over and above the costs of production in the least fertile ground (i.e., over and above the marginal costs of agricultural production). Ricardo then takes into consideration the effects of "the law of diminishing returns from land" and this postulates that the marginal costs of agricultural production increase. This means that the expansion of agricultural production

---

[2] In discussing "labour", Ricardo draws no distinction between labour and the labour force, Cf. D. Ricardo, *The Principles of Political Economy and Taxation*.

takes place by the cultivation of poorer and poorer land or else by continually less efficient investment.

Finally, profit from capital is the residue left over when workers' wages and land rent have been deducted from the social product.

In analysing the mechanism of economic development, Ricardo assumes a constant growth of population, which leads to a growth of agricultural production with increasing marginal costs of this production. As a result, the portion of the social product assumed by land rent increases, i.e., land rent absorbs an increasingly greater part of the social product. On the other hand, the real value of wages does not change, although nominal wages increase more or less proportionally to the increase in costs of maintenance (which are due to the increase in the marginal costs of agricultural production). Consequently, the difference between the social production on the one hand, and land rent and wages on the other, i.e., profit, diminishes.

Thus, the mechanism of economic development, according to Ricardo, leads to a constant growth of the share of the land-owning class in the national income, and to a decrease in the share of the capital owners. Since profit is both the source and the stimulus for accumulation as a result of the capital owners' decreasing profits, Ricardo foresaw that after a certain time the process of economic development would come to an end, and would lead to a state of stagnation within the national economy.

The view that the process of economic development ends in a state of stagnation is common to all classical economic literature. This is associated with another phenomenon which results from the above process of economic development, namely: a fall in the profit rate due to the fact that the portion of profits within the division of the social product diminishes with an increasing amount of capital.

Taking the factor of technical progress into consideration has little effect on the process of economic growth presented above. Ricardo himself considered technical progress to be weakest in agriculture and incapable of fundamentally influencing the process of economic development.

Later, bourgeois economics, especially the neo-classical school, gives a picture of the process of economic development which is essentially similar, but without the pessimistic prognosis as given by Ricardo and the classical political economy of his time.

In neo-classical economics, accumulation, which flows from income derived from property, is still considered to be the driving force of economic development. The difference between the role of capital owners and landowners in the process of accumulation here disappears. Historically, this corresponds to the process by which land owners were drawn into the orbit of the capitalist means of production. Profits and land rent are thus the main source of accumulation, and it is in connection with this that the argument for the fitness of unequal incomes developed, since relatively high incomes from property are necessary for economic development. This type of argument is to be found in the work of Alfred Marshall.[3] As Joan Robinson describes it, capitalists according to Marshall, should be given incomes so high that they cannot entirely consume them and thus part will remain for accumulation.[4]

The most essential problem dealt with in the neo-classical school's theory of economic development is the division of the incomes of the owners of land and capital between consumption and accumulation. In considering this problem, Marshall and neo-classical economics introduce certain elements of psychology. According to the neo-classical school of economics there exists a so-called productivity of capital: production investments will give a net income in the future, while at some time there exists a certain reluctance to refrain from the consumption of present incomes in favour of future incomes (time preference).

The division between investment and consumption depends— according to marginal calculation—on the marginal income from capital and the marginal reluctance to refrain from present consumption. It follows that if capital increases, then the marginal productivity of capital will diminish; on the other hand, the marginal reluctance to refrain from the consumption of present income grows since saved income has increased. The curves indicating the relation between these magnitudes and the increase in capital, i.e., investment on the one hand and savings on the other intersect, and the point of their intersection indicates the division of income between the part to be consumed and the part allocated for accumulation. With people whose incomes are small, the marginal

---

[3] Alfred Marshall, *Principles of Economics*, pp. 712–13, London, 1936.

[4] "They have to be 'rewarded for waiting' and they will not save, or even preserve wealth accumulated in the past, unless they are fattened to a certain point by a high standard of life for themselves". Joan Robinson, *Marx, Marshall and Keynes*, in *Collected Economic Papers*, Vol. II, Basil Blackwell, p. 10, Oxford, 1960.

reluctance to refrain from the consumption of present income in favour of future incomes is so great that these people accumulate nothing.

Thus, according to the neo-classical school, a marginal psychological calculation establishes the division of income between consumption and investment, and consequently defines the rate of economic development.

Similar views are to be found among the economists of the Austrian school, and especially in the work of Böhm-Bawerk. In this or in other forms, it was a characteristic theory of bourgeois economics up to the appearance of J. M. Keynes' work.

Neo-classical economics also considered other factors which influence the development of the national economy, e.g., the growth of population, changes in consumer preferences, and technical progress. Technical progress, however, is treated as a phenomenon outside the field of economics, influencing the process of economic development only by chance, and not being involved with it organically.

Keynes' theory did not fundamentally change any of the views which concern the mechanism of economic development. According to Keynes, the division between accumulation and consumption is also determined on the basis of a marginal psychological calculation. But in his theory, another factor is taken into account, namely, the tendency for capital owners to hold back a certain part of their incomes in a liquid form i.e., as money and other means of payment. This introduces certain complications, since besides the decision as to what part of the income should be allocated for consumption and what part for accumulation, a third consideration is brought in, namely, what is to be done with accumulated wealth: should it be saved or invested, or should it be retained in a monetary form. The great differences in the division of incomes in the capitalist system in principle accelerate economic development. However, according to Keynes, complications arise since some of the capital owners hold back money in a liquid form. Part of the labour force and of the productive capacity are thus made to lie idle, and the productive forces of society are squandered.

A common characteristic of decisions of this type is that they are all a result of a certain marginal psychological calculation. Technical progress is a phenomenon which in general favours investment since the productivity of capital consequently increases, and thus counteracts the retarding influence due to money being held back in a liquid form by some of the capital owners. However, technical development is still treated as a "historical chance", and as something existing outside the field of economics.

Briefly, that is how economic development was seen in contemporary capitalist economics. Karl Marx introduced a different conception of the process of economic development. In Marx's works, a systematic theory of economic development, as a self-generating process, is developed for the first time; in fact, Marx's whole economic theory is a theory of economic development and more particularly a theory of the development of the capitalist mode of production.

Marx bases his deductions on the discoveries of classical economics according to which accumulation and productive investments are the source of economic development, and the mechanism of equilibrium within the process of production depends on the action of the law of value. On the basis of these fundamental assumptions Marx goes on to show that accumulation and production investment are not things which, under capitalism might or might not take place. Accumulation and production investment are indispensable to the capitalist mode of production and are a result of objective necessity and the economic laws of this system.

In a capitalist system the size of accumulation and, in turn, the size of productive investment are not established on the basis of any psychological calculation, as neo-classical economics and Keynes maintained they were, but are the necessary result of the action of objective economic laws. Marx also showed that in the capitalist system, constant technical progress is a necessity determined by economic laws.

Thus, the process of capitalist economic development is defined by economic laws independently of any psychological calculation; and constant technical progress does not take place extraneous to economic processes, but is connected organically with the economic processes of which it is an inseparable and constituent part.

The process of economic development can, according to Marx's theory, be presented briefly as follows.

The process of capitalist competition is the basis of economic development and ensures that the law of value is brought into force in the specific form which it assumes in capitalism—the profit rates in different branches are levelled out as a result of the flow of capital from branches with a lower profit rate to those with a higher profit rate.

The mechanism by which the profit rates are equalized was, in principle, known to Ricardo. Marx's contribution in presenting his theory of economic development was to associate competition with technical progress. Marx showed that capitalist competition leads to an equalizing of the profit rate. The question then arises of how it is possible that particular capital owners, who manage to achieve the maximum profit rate, can in the long run and as a result of competition only achieve the average profit rate.

A particular capital owner can avoid the influence of the law that the profit rate is equalized only in one way: that is by the technological improvement of technical methods and the consequent lowering of his own costs of production. By producing more cheaply, the capital owner achieves extraordinary (surplus) profits which, however, are only temporary. At the moment when other capital owners introduce similar or other improvements, the supply of a given article increases, its price falls, and the surplus profit disappears.[5] The price of goods establishes itself on the capitalist market spontaneously and the individual capital owner has no influence on it.

Better organization of labour or better technical methods of production, i.e., technical progress or, as defined by Schumpeter, innovations, and a consequent lowering of costs of production are the only means of procuring temporary surplus profit.

Marx showed that constant technical progress exists within a capitalist economy of necessity. A capital owner who does not introduce it not only denies himself surplus profits, but is liable to be eventually excluded from the production process. As a competitor introduces technical improvements into his production plant and lowers the costs of production, the price of the given article falls to a level equal to the sum of the new lowered cost of production plus an average rate of profit. Bankruptcy threatens capital owners who do not carry out innovations in their plant because the price which they can obtain on the market will be lower than the costs of their own production.

---

[5] Cf. Karl Marx, *Hired Labour and Capital*: "By applying new and better means of production, the capital owner will be able to sell his goods at a price exceeding the actual cost of production... However, our capitalist's privilege will not last long; other capitalists in rivalry with him will introduce the same machinery and the same division of labour... Such is the law which again and again forces capitalist production off the beaten track and forces capitalists to put strain on the productive forces of labour since capital has previously created this tension; it is a law which gives the capitalist no rest, and continually whispers: forward! forward!"

Consequently, every capital owner is compelled to introduce innovations. Technical methods used in the capitalist production process are liable to continual changes towards greater productivity of labour and towards lowered costs of production. Consequently, there exists an objective and universal compulsion to achieve technical progress. This creates an enormous need for new improved techniques, and all productive forces must be directed towards ensuring constant technical progress in all fields of production. Thus, under the conditions of capitalism a favourable environment and climate are created for new inventions and for continuously improving means of production. Basically, these exigencies are satisfied since under normal conditions it is possible to find people capable of meeting such requirements and of bringing about major innovations; scientific development ensues, especially in the natural sciences and technology to an extent previously unknown in history.

This explains the great technical development within the capitalist system. There could be no such fast technical development within the feudal system because there was no economic stimulus which would ensure technical progress.

The compulsion to achieve technical progress within the capitalist system carries with it one further effect which can be defined as the compulsion to accumulate. Technical progress demands accumulation since its introduction demands new means of production. Thus, compulsion to accumulate is the consequent result of the compulsion to achieve technical progress. It can be said that every capital owner is subject to the compulsion to accumulate.

In this way Marx shows that in capitalism, accumulation is an objective necessity and not the result of some psychological calculation. The rate of accumulation, i.e., the relative part of profits allocated for accumulation, is determined by the pressure of the compulsion to accumulate existing at the moment. The above statement is an essential, and even fundamental element in Marx's theory. One of its consequences is that stagnant capitalism, i.e., capitalism without accumulation, is impossible.

Forced technical progress is the cause of constant growth of the organic structure of capital.[6] This leads to a series of further conse-

---

[6] The organic structure of capital is the relation of the amount of "crystallized" social labour, i.e., that embodied in the means of production to the amount of live labour engaged in production. In other words, the organic composition of capital

quences. In the first place, within the capitalist process of production a permanent army of jobless arises (unemployed labour force) as a result of the constant revolutionizing of technical methods and the conversion of live labour into crystallized labour. This has been called "the industrial reserve army". The existence of this reserve army of unemployed plays an important role in Marx's theory, from which it follows that it is then impossible for wages to rise over a long period of time to such an extent that they entirely absorb the capital owners' profits.

The next result of forced technical progress and of the growth of the organic structure of capital is the centralization of capital. If technical progress is to be achieved efficiently, capital must be concentrated within large economic units. This either limits or eliminates free competition, which is replaced by varying degrees of monopoly.

As is well known, the results of the centralization of capital were analysed in detail by classical Marxist literature, and above all in the work of V. I. Lenin. The development of imperialism as the socio-political extension of monopoly type of capitalist means of production has also been discussed in these works.

In Marx's theory, the above problem is connected with the historical limits to the development of the capitalist economy. Marx maintained that the process of accumulation raises obstacles in the path of its own further development, and is in the end retarded. However, Marx did not complete his work dealing with this problem. This subject is widely discussed in later Marxist literature. There has been much divergence of opinion as to what is the cause and character of the obstacles which retard the process of accumulation in the declining phase of capitalism.

In connection with Marx's theory of economic development under capitalism, it is interesting to note the views of Josef Schumpeter[7] which deal with this problem.

Schumpeter's theory developed from the Austrian variation of the marginal school. However, Schumpeter consciously added to his theory many conclusions taken from Marx's work. Against this background, he developed his own theory of economic development within the capitalist system.

---

expresses the amount of social labour embodied in means of production per unit of live labour mobilized by the means of production.

[7] J. Schumpeter, *The Theory of Economic Development*.

The point of departure of Schumpeter's theory is the assumption that under the conditions of economic equilibrium there is no profit from capital, and thus the price of capital goods is equal to the cost of their production. In a state of equilibrium competition reduces the price of capital goods to a level equal to their cost of production. Schumpeter here bases his argumentation on the theory of the Austrian school, according to which the value of capital goods is equal to the value of the consumer goods which they produce.

In dealing with accumulation Schumpeter, however, dismisses the psychological calculation of the marginal school. He maintains, as does Marx, that a particular enterprise can obtain surplus profits by lowering its costs of production. Thus, there is a stimulus for capital owners to introduce new methods of production or innovations which will lower the costs of production and enable surplus profits to be achieved. Under conditions of equilibrium there is no profit from capital, and the only source of profit is innovation; as a result, this stimulus has a fundamental significance for the capitalist economy. Under such conditions, enterprises must improve their production techniques and introduce new and better methods of production.[8] This process of "manufacturing" profits by introducing innovations into the production process is the driving force behind the development of the capitalist economy.

Analysing further the problem of economic development, in precisely the same way as Marx had done, Schumpeter arrives at the conclusion that surplus profits are of a temporary character. In a capitalist economy there is a continual race between innovation and competition. The economy tends towards an equilibrium under which profits disappear. The equilibrium is disturbed by innovations which lead to the temporary appearance of profits; these in turn disappear as the economy returns to a new state of equilibrium, etc. Profits only exist because in this race, competition tending to re-establish equilibrium, does not keep pace with the flow of innovations.

Consequently, the course of economic development takes the form of trade cycles. Innovations in production appear in waves because the introduction of new improvements and inventions in one enterprise facilitates the introduction of similar innovations in other production

---

[8] Schumpeter limits the term "enterprise" exclusively to innovators. Other producers who do not gain surplus profits, but receive a definite income for their work, are called "administrators".

plants. Thus, we can observe a period of great investment in the national economy followed by the fast growth of production. Increased supply leads to a fall in prices and a lower profit rate. Then an economic crisis follows. In turn, under pressure of the falling profit rate, a new wave of increasing innovations and investments begins, and a new period in the cycle of economic development follows.

In his theory Schumpeter ascribes particular importance to the role of the credit system as an important factor in economic development. In general, the innovators' own accumulation is insufficient to provide the investment indispensable for the improvement of the enterprise. They must, therefore, make use of bank credit. In the modern banking system of capitalist countries it is possible to obtain inflationary credit, i.e., credit exceeding bank deposits. Thanks to this, enterprises which obtain credit are in a position to undercut prices of the means of production and of the less efficient producers of their production. The rise in prices, which is a result of inflationary credit, leads to a fall in the real value of the public's incomes and to a decrease in their consumption. Accumulation has thus increased by compulsory savings in the form of decreased real incomes and decreased consumption of the public. That is to say, a constant process of original accumulation takes place in the form of inflationary taxation of the general public.

The similarity of certain aspects of Schumpeter's theory with the theory of Marx is apparent. But there is one fundamental difference. The difference is that: in Schumpeter's theory, accumulation and technical progress do not proceed with the same objective compulsion as in Marx's. The creator of technical progress is the enterprise which, as it were, revolutionizes the production process by its own inspiration. Economic progress is ultimately due to the fact that not all capital owners are static administrators of their fortunes, but that innovators are to be found among them who are discontented with the existing state of affairs.

Schumpeter's theory is, therefore, an idealistic theory of economic development, for it maintains that from time to time outstandingly clever and creative people make their appearance and revolutionize industry, thus becoming the motors of economic progress. This theory follows the idealistic structure of the German historical school and belongs to "the spirit of capitalism" rather than to the objective materialistic-historical approach which characterizes Marx.

POLITICAL ECONOMY

Political Economy (derived from the Greek, oikos—house, nomos—law), is the science of the social laws governing the production and distribution of material goods to meet human needs. Production, that is, the manufacture of material goods for the purpose of satisfying these needs and the division of these goods among members of the society, also called distribution, is defined by the general term economic activity or, in a more restricted sense, management. This is why it is often said that political economy is the science of economic activity or of management (here it is a question of economic activity carried out by human beings living within the bonds of a society). Production takes place in conditions of social co-operation between people, involving not only co-operation but also division of labour which by its very nature, is a social act. The social nature of management implies that methods of management are the product of historical development. The laws governing production and distribution are also of a historical nature. The historical scope of economic laws varies; some laws act at all (or almost all) stages of social development, others have a very narrow historical scope. But first and foremost are the laws specific to certain social and economic systems, such as feudalism, capitalism and socialism. Political economy investigates these laws, taking their historical scope into account. It tries more particularly to throw light on the functioning of the various methods of production shaped by history and on their relative social systems. For this, it uses the method applied in all empirical sciences: abstraction, based on experience, gradual concretization, bringing the results of this abstraction nearer to reality, and verification by confrontation of results with the practice of economic life. In political economy experience is historical in character; thus abstraction leads to a logical generalization of historical material in the form of economic categories and laws. This generalization reflects the dialectic character of development through internal contradictions of social processes. Political economy sets itself the task of investigating all social and economic systems and of embracing the whole economic development

191

of mankind within its scope. However, so far, only the analysis of capitalist methods of production has been fully developed. It is only recently that political economy has started studying the economic laws of socialist methods of production. Now, alongside with the political economy of capitalism, the political economy of socialism is emerging as a new aspect of the science of political economy.

Aristotle used the word "economy" to define the science of the laws of household management. The term "political economy" was first used at the beginning of the seventeenth century by the French author A. Montchrétien in his book *Traité de l'économie politique*, published in 1615, in which he dealt with problems of the economic activity of the state, and for this reason added the adjective "political" to the term "economy". From that time on, the term political economy was mainly used in France and England to denote the science of management not only of the state but of the whole human society. This was due to the broad interpretation of the word "political", meaning not only "state" but also "social". W. Petty, for instance, gave the title of *Political Arithmetic* to the book he wrote in 1676-7 dealing with the quantitative processes taking place in human society, including demographic processes. In view of the fact that the meaning of the term "political" was not clear, the term "social economy" began to be used at the end of the nineteenth century. Even earlier, at the end of the eighteenth century, the term "science of the national economy" began to be used (the outstanding Polish economist F. Skarbek, 1859, called his book *Ogólne zasady gospodarstwa narodowego*—General Principles of the National Economy). This term began to be widely used, particularly in Germany (*Nationaloekonomie, Volkswirtschaftslehre*). At the end of the nineteenth century, under the influence of A. Marshall, the term "economics", which had also been used previously from time to time, began to be adopted. This term is today generally accepted in the universities of the Anglo-Saxon countries, where it has almost completely ousted the traditional term of political economy. Under the influence of Anglo-Saxon science, it was also adopted in other countries, among others, in Poland during the inter-war period (A. Krzyżanowski, E. Taylor). However, this term rather narrows down the subject, as it underestimates the social nature of economic activity. For this reason, a reaction developed in the Anglo-Saxon countries and a trend appeared towards rehabilitating the term "political economy". This designation is today in general

use in Poland and the other socialist countries, and also in circles connected with progressive social movements whose main interest is precisely
the social nature of economic activity.

The Birth and Development of Political Eocnomy

The birth of the science of political economy is closely connected
with the foundation and development of capitalist methods of production. True, writers of ancient times did give some attention to economic
problems, but they were mostly problems of household economy, in
accordance with the original meaning of the term "economy". Only
Xenophon dealt more extensively with the problem of the division of
labour and Aristotle devoted quite a lot of attention to problems of
exchange; he even introduced a special term "chrematistics" to define
the science of exchange as distinguished from economy, which dealt
with household economy. In the field of studies on economic problems,
Aristotle did not have any successors. In any case, the works of the
ancient authors on this subject had the character of ethical evaluations
and not of scientific analysis. Studies of economic subjects in the
Middle Ages were of the same character. The authors of the Middle
Ages, whose most outstanding representative was Thomas Aquinas,
dealt with economic problems from the point of view of normative
moral evaluations based on theological doctrines. The economic studies
of those times were a component part of moral theology. The question
of the so-called just price (*iustum pretium*) and the problem of usury
were given special importance in these studies. It was only the broad
development of the commodity and money-currency economy and trade-
capital in the Netherlands, northern France, and England, and then the
beginnings of capitalist production in industry that awakened interest in
research on the regularities occurring in the national economy that was
then taking shape and in utilizing knowledge of these regularities in
the economic policy of the state. At first, attention was paid to the
financial processes connected with the development of trade, particularly
foreign trade. The writers dealing with these problems were given the
name of mercantilists (mercantilism). The earliest mercantilists, the
so-called bullionists (bullionism), considered that the wealth of the
country depended on the amount of metal ore it possessed and they

worked out ways of getting as much of this metal ore into the country as possible. The means to this end was to be foreign trade. The later mercantilists (in the strict sense of the word) paid more attention to the development of commodity production and to producing surpluses of this for foreign trade. The most outstanding of the mercantilists were: in England T. Mun, who in the years 1628–30 wrote *England's Treasure by Foreign Trade* (1664); and in ¦France A. de Montchrétien. The first systematic analysis of the course of the process of production and distribution in society was made in the eighteenth century by French authors known as the physiocrats (physiocratism). They maintained that this process was governed by certain laws (laws of nature), hence the name physiocracy, or the rule of nature. The most outstanding of them, F. Quesney, published his *Tableau économique* in 1758. It was a schematic presentation of production as a constantly repeated process of reproduction, the distribution of products among the various classes of the society of that time being shown against this background.

It is generally thought that the real development of the economic sciences began with the so-called classical political economy, which was born and developed mainly in England alongside with the development of capitalist production. It began simultaneously in France too, and its influence subsequently extended to many other countries. The precursor of classical economics in England was W. Petty and in France P. Bois-guillebert. The main subject of interest were the conditions for the development of productive forces. The first systematic presentation of classical economics was A. Smith's work *An Inquiry into the Nature and Causes of the Wealth of Nations* published in 1776 (Polish edition 1954). The source of the development of productive forces in England, partic-ularly in the eighteenth century, was, according to A. Smith, the division of labour connected with the new capitalist organization of production (manufacture), the accumulation of capital and the investment of accumulated wealth with the aim of employing labour in production. Adam Smith also formulated the law of value, showing the dependence of the value of goods on the amount of labour used to produce them. He considered that the production and exchange of goods automatically led to equilibrium directed by an "invisible hand", as it were, (auto-regulation). In connection with this, he regarded interference in economic life on the part of the state, guilds or other economic institutions as harmful, and maintained that feudal landowners were wasting wealth in a non-productive way. Thus, Smith's teachings were the expression of the aspirations of the industrial bourgeoisie towards unhampered initiative in economic activity.

The most mature and concise presentation of classical economics was given by D. Ricardo in his *Principles of Political Economy and Taxation* published in 1817 (Polish edition 1957). In his opinion, the subject of political economy is the study of the way the products of the community are distributed among the landowners, capitalists and workers. With this end in view, he elaborated a consistent theory of value, determined by the labour needed to manufacture a product and demonstrated how competition between capitalists leads to an exchange of goods at prices corresponding in principle to their value. He explained the land rent as the result of the difference between the amount of labour needed on soils of varying fertility and the diminishing productivity of successive contributions of labour on the same soil (differential rent). In this way, for the first time, he reconciled the theory of land rent with the theory of value. He considered that physical labour was determined by the physiological minimum necessary to maintain a manual worker and his family. If wages fell beneath that minimum figure, there was a drop in the number of working population; on the other hand, a rise in wages above the minimum was accompanied by an increase in the working population (in accordance with the theory of R. T. Malthus). An increase in the population was, according to Ricardo, to lead to a steady increase in the share of land rent in the division of the social income and to a drop in the share of profits, which in turn was to weaken the incentive to accumulate capital and develop productive forces. So Ricardo regarded the landowners as the main obstacle to economic development, which was in agreement with the views of the radical elements of the English bourgeoisie of that time, who were aiming at a reduction of land rent by efforts to lift customs duties on the import of grain. Ricardo devoted a number of his works to problems of money. He also pointed to certain contradictions between the interests of the working class and those of the capitalists, stating that technical progress could have an adverse effect on the conditions of the working class.

The contradictions of class interests appearing in the capitalist methods of production were also noted by the outstanding Swiss representative of classical economics, J. C. Sismondi (*New Principles of Political Economy*, 1815, Polish edition 1955). He also drew attention to the contradictions between the increase in productive forces and the purchasing power of the population in conditions of capitalist distribution of the national product. The doctrine of classical economics was closely linked with the struggle of the industrial bourgeoisie in England and France against the remnants of feudal relations and the constraints imposed upon its economic activity, and its aspirations to occupy a leading place in social and political life. The bourgeoisie was interested in the scientific analysis of the functioning of the capitalist way of production and the conditions for economic development of which it was the main promoter at that time. However, the political victory of the bourgeoisie brought a change in conditions, all the more so as conclusions began to be drawn from the principles of classical economics, showing the exploitation of the working class by the capitalists and the hampering action of capitalism on social development. This was done by the so-called Ricardian socialists (the most eminent of these was T. Hodgskin, *Labour Defended Against the Claims of Capital,* 1825). As a result, the scope of interest of the bourgeoisie in economic sciences changed. It considered that capitalist production relations were established once and for all, needing no further discussion, and at most calling for justification (apologetics) against growing criticism from the working class movement then taking shape (the mass movement of the Chartists in England, the first workers' rebellion in France). The economic interests of the bourgeoisie then turned to circulation problems, such as the mechanism of market prices, circulation of money, credit, foreign trade, etc. An expression of this change in interests was the appearance of a group of economists whose theories were contemptuously defined by K. Marx as vulgar economics. They considered themselves the followers of classical economics, but in fact they narrowed down the scope of their interest to superficial market phenomena and replaced scientific analysis of production relations by apologetics.

In these conditions, a new approach was made to political economy in connection with the developing working class movement; this new approach came from Karl Marx. Marx transformed all the achievements of classical political economy (and also of the physiocrats). At the same time, he studied the criticisms of capitalist production relations contained in the works of the utopian socialists in France and England and also the literature of the Ricardian socialists. He also drew inspiration from the practical activity of the working class movement, in which he personally took part. From Hegel's school, he gained a thorough knowledge of philosophy and the approach to human society as the product of historical development. Taking as his point of departure Hegel's view of development as a dialectical process, actuated by its internal contradictions, Marx gave dialectics a material interpretation and used it to explain the historical development of mankind. In this way he created a materialistic approach to history, which enabled him to take a new view of the achievements of classical economics and the works of socialist writers. He did this jointly with his friend F. Engels, with whom he maintained close scientific and political contacts till the end of his life, and who later did much to popularize Marx's teachings.

The first mature work resulting from Marx's economic studies was *Critique of Political Economy* (1859, Polish edition 1955). Marx gave a systematic presentation of his economic theory in *Capital*. Only the first volume of *Capital* was published in Marx's lifetime (1867), the second and third volumes were published by Engels from his unfinished manuscripts in 1885 and 1894. The fourth volume *The Theory of Surplus Value* was published for the first time (1905–10) by K. Kautsky. Marx included political economy in the general theory of social development, based on the materialistic interpretation of history. This led him to the thesis of the historically transitional character of capitalist production methods and the historical nature of economic categories and laws. The economic categories and laws discovered by classical economics are the laws of the functioning of the capitalist economy. But capitalism is subject to the development determined by the economic laws peculiar to it and has, as Marx puts it, its own "law of movement". In order to investigate this "law of movement" Marx used the economic categories and laws discovered by classical economics, at the same time, subjecting them to a more precise and thorough analysis. A more thorough analysis of the law of value enabled Marx to explain the source of income coming from the possession of capital, which neither A. Smith nor D. Ricardo had been able to do. The key to the discovery of that source was the distinction between labour and manpower and the statement of the fact that the value produced by the labour of the worker is greater than the value of products necessary for the reproduction of manpower in the conditions determined by the social and historical level of development of a society. The wages for work are determined by the value of these products, while the surplus of the value produced by the workers over and above their wages is a surplus value appropriated by the capitalists owning the means of production. In this way, Marx discovered the basic economic reason for the antagonism between the working class and the capitalist class in the bourgeois society. At the same time he pointed to the similarity of that antagonism with the fundamental class antagonisms occurring in the feudal and slave societies in which the ruling class also appropriated the surplus product produced by the peasants or slaves.

In the bourgeois society, the surplus product assumes the form of a surplus value and is obtained by the action of the law of value. The whole of the surplus value produced by the society is divided between the different capitalists in proportion to their capital in production as a result of which there is a certain constant deviation of the price of goods from their value (cost of production). The different categories of capital participate in the division of the whole surplus value in the form of specific categories of income (profits of industrialists, trade profits, interest). Monopoly in land ownership enables the landowners to appropriate part of the surplus value for themselves in the form of the land rent. In demonstrating the mechanism of appropriation of surplus value by the capitalists, by different parts of capital and by the landowners in capitalism, Marx clarified the economic relations between the different classes and strata of the bourgeois society.

The mechanism of production and division of surplus value is the basis of the theory of the development of the capitalist method of production. The competition between the capitalists, the struggle for increased profits and the threat of ousting industrialists producing at higher cost forces the capitalists to introduce technical and organizational improvements, reducing costs of production. The introduction of such improvements calls for additional capital, and as a result the capitalists are forced to transform part of their profits into additional capital; that is accumulation. Accumulation and technical progress become a vital necessity to the capitalists. On the other hand, this leads to replacement of live labour by machines, which in capitalism leads to unemployment in the form of the so-called industrial reserve army. Accumulation of capital, combined with the ousting of the less competitive enterprises, leads to the concentration of capital into big enterprises. The next consequence is the centralization of capital in the hands of a small oligarchy of big capital. An ever-larger part of the society is turned into hired workers of big capital or made dependent on it in some other way, and this creates conditions for the means of production to be taken over by the whole society, the majority of which is exploited by big capital. The taking over of the means of production becomes a historical necessity as a result of the growing internal contradictions involved in capitalist method of production.

Capitalism led to socialization of the process of labour, organizing it in big industrial enterprises. With private ownership of the means of production, the relations between the various enterprises (co-operation and division of labour) are, however, spontaneously regulated by the action of the law of value. This accounts for the irrational, anarchical character of the capitalist methods of production. Its development is not subject to the conscious management of the society and this leads to breakdowns and catastrophies in the shape of economic crises. This is true in particular when demand fails to keep pace with the growth of production which is a characteristic feature of the capitalist economy. Concentration and centralization of capital augment these contradictions. Finally, the development of productive forces comes into ever greater contradiction with capitalist ownership of the means of production—private-capitalist monopoly ownership of means of production. At the same time, these same economic processes lead to an ever better organization of the working class, which heads the resistance against growing exploitation and capitalist anarchy. A socialist social revolution becomes essential to ensure the society conditions for further development.

Beginning with Marx, the development of political economy went forward in two different trends associated with separate and antagonistic social spheres. Marx's economic theory and the materialist approach to history became the basis of scientific socialism, the social and political doctrine of the revolutionary working class movement. The trend in political economy which grew out of Marx's theory was called the Marxist trend, or simply Marxist political economy. On the other hand, the political economy in bourgeois milieux and milieux connected with the bourgeoisie, (for instance, at universities in capitalist countries) was already called bourgeois economy by Marx. Each of these trends reflected the interest and scope of thought of the social milieux with which it was associated.

Marxist economics became a powerful factor in awakening and shaping the consciousness of the working class; it became a scientific basis on which the organized working class movement based its strategy of action. The main subject of its interest were the laws of development of capitalist methods of production, their internal contradictions and development prospects and criticism of the doctrines of bourgeois economics, which attempted to present capitalism as a harmonious and rational social system serving the interests of all the social classes, including the working class. There was a particular enlivenment of Marxist political economy at the turn of the present century. At that time, new problems matured and called for solution, particularly the problems of cartels and trusts, the growing intervention of the state in economic life and the reasons for the easing of crises and the rise in real wages. In view of this, a revisionist trend came into being in the working class movement, which questioned the Marxist thesis that the internal contradictions of capitalism were becoming more acute (E. Bernstein, C. Schmidt, E. David, M. Tuhan-Baranowski). Another incentive enlivening Marxist economics was the dispute between the Marxists and the nationalists in Russia as to whether capitalism could master Russia's economy and raise it from its economic and social backwardness. This directed the interest of Marxist economists to problems of capitalist reproduction and accumulation which found their foundation in theoretical schemes, contained in the second volume of *Capital*. This was directly connected with the problem of crises and the question of their lessening or increasing intensity, and also the role of the big capitalist monopolies that were becoming ever more widespread at that time. The dispute with the revisionists was also about the development tendencies of agriculture in capitalism. Extensive Marxist economic literature on this subject appeared, the authors including such names as K. Kautsky, G. Plekhanov, R. Luxemburg, V. Lenin, L. Krzywicki and others.

The final transition of capitalism to the monopolist-imperialist phase of development and the first conflict between powers due to their colonial policies brought the working class movement face to face with problems, the analysis of which could not be conducted without taking into account Marxist economic thinking. This marked a new stage in the development of that science. The first event was the publication in 1910 of R. Hilferding's book *Financial Capital* (Polish edition 1958), which contains an analysis of capitalist monopoly organizations (joint stock companies, banks, cartels and trusts) and the process of the merging of industrial capital with bank capital into a new form of capital—financial capital. Hilferding's book also contains an analysis of the influence of capitalist monopolies on the division of social income, on the relations between social classes, on the course of crises and the economic cycle, on foreign trade and export of capital. He shows the new role of the capitalist state in the protection of the interests of big monopolies (mainly the tariffs policy) and the tendency of that state towards imperialist expansion, the new social role of nationalism and the big powers policy. On the eve of the outbreak of the First World War, in 1913, R. Luxemburg's book *Accumulation of Capital* appeared (Polish edition 1963) with its significant sub-title *An Economic Explanation of Imperialism*. R. Luxemburg saw the source of imperialism in the very process of capital accumulation and focussed interest on the importance backward countries had in the development of capitalism. She also pointed to the importance of the production of munitions as a new field of accumulation. The struggle for colonies, war and revolution are an inseparable feature of the epoch of imperialism. They accelerated the socialist social revolution. The theoretical foundations of R. Luxemburg's concepts, and particularly her interpretation of Marx's scheme of reproduction, called forth much criticism among Marxist economists (O. Bauer, N. Bukharin, H. Grossman and others).

Then, in 1916, when the imperialist war was being waged to the full, Lenin wrote *Imperialism as the Highest Stage of Capitalism* (1917, Polish edition 1949). This book was preceded by a number of theoretical articles about imperialism, written in the early years of the war. Lenin linked imperialism directly with the monopoly phase of the development of capitalism, defining imperialism as being identical to monopoly capitalism. The epoch of imperialism is marked by the domination of monopolies, oligarchy of financial capital, the great role played by export of capital, and economic division of markets between big international capitalist combinations and the territorial and political division of colonial regions and spheres of influence between the big powers. The uneven development of the various capitalist countries and groups makes this division unstable, and this leads to attempts at revision, resulting in imperialist wars. The epoch of imperialism was synonymous with the epoch of the disintegration of capitalism. The leading imperialist countries turned into rentier-parasite countries, exploiting the peoples of the backward countries. Part of the working class (the working class aristocracy) of the imperialist countries also shared in the fruits of this exploitation, which, according to Lenin, was the source of reformism and nationalism in the working class movement of these countries. In later works, Lenin points to the further consequences of imperialism, namely, the growth of the national liberation movements among the colonial and dependent peoples. These movements became the allies of the international working class movement. Lenin's works on imperialism and the national liberation movements became the basis for the new strategy, adopted by the revolutionary working class movement, on a world-wide scale.

The development of the bourgeois economy progressed along quite different lines. In principle it was marked by a constant narrowing down of the field of interests. Two trends can be distinguished here. The subjectivist trend continued the tradition of the vulgar economists, further narrowing down its field of interests. The historical trend (the historical school in political economy) went part of the way to negating the existence of economic laws and to transforming political economy into descriptive economic history, and part of the way to an idealistic construction, attributing economic development to changes in the mental attitude of the people. The subjectivist trend was initiated in 1871 by K. Menger and W. S. Jevons. Menger was the initiator of the most consistent version of this trend, namely, the so-called Austrian school, the most outstanding representatives of which were F. Wieser and E. Böhm-Bawerk. In explaining market exchange, the representatives of this school concentrated their attention on the subjective attitude of the participants in this exchange towards the goods purchased or sold. They claimed that this attitude was determined by the marginal utility value the goods had for the individual and the measure of marginal utility was also applied to determine the consumption of goods in the process of production. According to this approach, economics became a science of the disposal of goods according to their marginal utility and the subject of its research was the attitude of man towards things; social relations between people, which were the central problem of classical and Marxist political economy were lost sight of. The same approach to the subject of economics was made in the theory of marginal productivity of the means of production. The most outstanding representative of this theory was J. B. Clark. Like the theory of marginal utility, it often served in practice to justify the capitalist division of the national income, in which the owners of various production factors allegedly received an amount equal to the contribution of the factors they owned to the value of the social product. The problem of the historical-social character of capitalist means of production was completely overlooked. Subjective elements in the form of evaluation of goods according to their marginal utility are also found in the so-called Lausanne school, the most eminent representatives of which were L. Walras and V. Pareto, and in the so-called neo-classical school, founded by A. Marshall, which won a dominant position for itself in the Anglo-Saxon countries. Walras and Marshall investigated market processes in their entirety according to the pattern of vulgar economics. But they did try to make a deeper analysis of these processes. They sought a means to this end in the application of the theory of marginal utility to explain the demand for consumer goods. Marshall gave a subjectivist interpretation to the cost of production, being of the opinion that the "real social cost" would result in disutility in connection with the labour effort and waiting for the results of the production process. The price paid by the market for this disutility comprises the wages paid for labour and the interest on capital. On the other hand, land rent does not correspond to any social cost. It is "unmerited income". In this, Marshall regarded himself as a follower of classical economics (hence the name neo-classical), particularly of Ricardo's school. Walras, on the other hand, linked the cost of production with the outlays in means of production, determined by the given technical level of development (so-called coefficients of production). Thus, he was nearer to the classical school, which regarded the cost of production as an expression of the objective conditions determining the outlays of labour necessary to produce a given product. Both Marshall and Walras dealt with the theory of money and credit. Using graphic and mathematical aids, Marshall made a detailed analysis of the process of the shaping of market prices (elasticity of demand and supply, market equilibrium—short- and long-term), and also international exchange (terms of trade); he also investigated the influence of interest rates and of credit policy on investments and the level of prices. This type of investigation was continued by other representatives of the neo-classical school, who developed an ingenious technical and analytical apparatus to this end. This was research that suited the practical interests and needs of the bourgeoisie of that time, whose economic decisions called for accurate information on market and money–credit processes. However, the technical and analytical apparatus set up in this way can also be applied for research in other historical and social conditions.

In Germany, the historical trend came into being as criticism of classical political economy. Unlike the latter, it took a favourable view of the historical heritage and the social role of the feudal elements and the state apparatus of the Prussian monarchy, which contributed to the development of capitalism in Germany (the so-called Prussian way of the development of capitalism). But it also separated itself from the historical-materialist theory of social development that was the basis of Marxist political economy. In the first stage of its development (the so-called old historical school: W. Roscher, B. Hildebrandt, K. Knies), this trend negated the existence of economic laws and to an ever greater extent confined its work to historical monographs. This was also the point of departure of the second stage (the so-called young historical school: G. Schmoller, K. Bücher, L. Brentano). The fruits of the activity of the representatives of this trend were important achievements in the field of historical-economic knowledge; they do not, however, belong to the subject of economics proper as a theoretical science. At the end of the first decade of the twentieth century, the historical trend produced the great historical-synthetic works of W. Sombart and M. Weber dealing with the foundation and development of capitalism. Both authors drew on Marx's scientific work from whom they took the concept of the historical category of capitalism and the related problems raised by him. They tried to give a different answer to these problems than that of Marx, basing themselves on the idealistic interpretation of social systems as a result of autonomous development of mental attitudes, expressed in the so-called spirit of the epoch. The problem of the foundation and development of capitalism was thus reduced to the foundation and development of the so-called spirit of capitalism. Another work that was produced under the influence of Marx's theory was *Theory of Economic Development* (1912, Polish edition 1960) by J. Schumpeter, of the Austrian school. Schumpeter, like Marx, saw the source of the dynamics of the capitalist economy in the endeavours of enterprises to achieve technical and organizational progress, to manufacture new products and to introduce other innovations in the process of production. But unlike Marx, he attributed these endeavours to the creative mental attitude of the leading entrepreneurs who were the pioneers of technical progress. A near relation to the historical trend is institutionalism (T. Veblen, W. C. Mitchell, J. R. Commons and others), which originated at the end of the last century and developed at the beginning of the present century in the

United States. Its representatives rejected the theory of the classical school as barren theorizing and concentrated their attention on monographic description of the institutional organization of economic life. Special attention is due to Veblen's work, which contains a critical analysis of the social and economic role of big business. Veblen followed in the footsteps of the specific group of the bourgeois economists associated with bourgeois criticism of capitalism, the views of which were already to be found in the works of Sismondi, and which were next represented by P. Proudhon and J. S. Mill. In the second half of the nineteenth century, this criticism died down; it was revised at the turn of the present century as a reaction against big business monopolies which were expanding and becoming more powerful. This criticism was expressed by J. A. Hobson's book *Imperialism* (1902), which was highly valued and utilized by Lenin in his work on imperialism.

The Science of Political Economy Today

The foundation of the first socialist state in the world, as a result of the victorious October Revolution, and the internal processes going on in monopoly capitalism, created new conditions for the development of political economy. Further developments of these conditions came after the Second World War, when the process of building the socialist social system spread to more countries of Europe and Asia and when the national liberation movements in the colonial and dependent countries became stronger and their peoples made efforts to overcome their backwardness as quickly as possible and to start out along the road of accelerated economic development. The rivalry between these two economic systems, socialism and capitalism, and the problem of the underdeveloped countries brought political economy face to face with entirely new problems.

The establishment and development of socialist production relations as well as the management of the socialist economy and the planning of its development gave rise to the need for a new branch of economic knowledge—a political economy of socialism. The Marxist scientific apparatus, which had been used almost exclusively for research on capitalism, now had to be adapted to the problems of the socialist economy. This was a pioneer task, all the more so because the possibility and need for a political economy of socialism had been questioned previously. R. Hilferding was of the opinion that in socialism, political economy would be replaced by the science of "the wealth of the nations", the main subject of which would be the organization and development of productive forces. R. Luxemburg considered that the disappearance of the anarchy of capitalist production would make the separate science of political economy unnecessary, the only need being to investigate the regularities connected with the requirements of the reproduction process. Finally, N. Bukharin completely negated the possibility of such a science, saying that in conditions of socialism the science of economic laws would be replaced by a system of descriptions and norms of practical activity. The socialist economy was born and developed in the difficult conditions of countries that were either underdeveloped, from the economic point of view, or simply backward (and not in the leading industrial countries, as was envisaged by Marx and Engels), and, in addition, they were countries devastated by war. As a result, the experience and the laws of the socialist economy took shape gradually and thus their theoretical generalization by science could also only take shape gradually. Scientific analysis of the socialist economy was initiated by Lenin in numerous publications which appeared during the first years after the revolution. It was further developed in the twenties by the lively discussion carried on at that time on the industrialization of the Soviet Union and the socialist reconstruction of agriculture. Other problems raised at the time were the functioning of the socialist economy, the role of commodity and money relations and economic calculus in socialism. Two of the most outstanding economists of that period were N. Bukharin and J. Preobrazhensky. The simultaneous revolutions in Germany and Austria raised the problem of socializing means of production. In connection with this, a number of bourgeois economists (L. Mises, F. Hayek and others) put forward the thesis that rational economic calculus was impossible in a socialist economy. In the discussion on this subject, which took on a fresh lease of life in the capitalist countries during the great economic crisis, the socialist side was represented by O. Leichter, M. Dobb, O. Lange and others. It was then that the question of the role of prices and of the market in regulating the socialist economy was dealt with systematically for the first time.

In connection with the preparation of the first five-year plan for the economic development of the Soviet Union (1928–32), the basic principles of methodology for planning the national economy were elaborated. G. Krzyżanowski, W. Bazharov, G. Feldman participated in this work and in the discussions, and so did S. Strumilin, who is still carrying on his rich scientific activity to this very day. In the thirties, the view was prevalent that commodity–money relations were a lasting feature of the socialist economy (as distinct from communism). However, the development of political economy was hampered by an atmosphere of dogmatism. The voluntarist system of economic and political management created by Stalin was not conducive to objective investigations of economic regularities. Apologetics of the current economic policy, were substituted for scientific analysis to an ever increasing degree. The apologetics attempted to present the voluntarist system of management as a result of unavoidable, objective economic laws. The most emphatic expression of this was Stalin's work: *Economic Problems of Socialism in the U.S.S.R.*, published in 1952 (Polish edition 1952). But drawing attention in that work to the objective nature of economic laws and to the appearance of contradictions between production relations and productive forces in socialism opened the way towards a scientific analysis, particularly in the people's democracies where the processes of dogmatization were not so advanced. After these obstacles had been overcome, there was a new enlivenment of activity in 1956. Several textbooks on the political economy of socialism appeared.

The subject of political economics of socialism is the investigation of specific properties and regularities of socialist methods of production. Its basic conceptions are based on the Marxist theory of social development ("the materialistic interpretation of history") and on Marxist economics inasmuch as it deals with economic laws of a scope going beyond capitalist methods of production. However, the specific economic laws of socialism are different from the specific economic laws of capitalism and in this field political economics of socialism must go beyond the theoretical works of Marx and of Marxists who followed him in later times. In particular, there is the new problem of rational management of means of production and manpower. Traditional Marxist economics did not, in principle, deal with this problem, only touching upon it marginally in its criticism of the irrationality of the capitalist economy. The results achieved by bourgeois economics, which only dealt with the problem of rational management in individual enterprises, and if it did go beyond these limits, created an apologetic myth about the rational nature of the capitalist economic system as a whole, were not very useful either. The achievements of political economy of socialism to date consist first and foremost in the analysis of accumulation and the conditions for economic growth, the creation and distribution of the national income, the fundamental principles of the calculus of investment efficiency and the role of commodity money relations. The problem of the role of the law of value, problems of the theory of money and the principles of the price mechanism and structure in the socialist economy are still the focal points of discussion. The variety of forms of organization and management of the national economy in various socialist countries and the changes in these forms in individual countries supply rich material for comparative observations and studies furthering the development of political economy of socialism.

An essential part of the economy of socialism is the science of planning the national economy. Two distinct stages can be seen in the development of the science of planning. In the first stage, the main, almost exclusive subject of interest was the question of the internal consistency of plans, guaranteeing proportional growth of the different sectors and branches of the national economy. The instrument of internal co-ordination of the plan is the balance account, drawing up the balance of the national economy and its various parts (balances of materials, manpower, etc.). In this first stage, methods of accounting which were developed in capitalist enterprises were applied in the national economy. This general application of economic accounting was foreseen by Marx, and Lenin postulated that it be put into practice. The theoretical basis for the construction of the balances of the national economy is provided by Marx's theory of reproduction, its basic principles being applied exclusively to the capitalist economy. The beginning of the second stage in the development of the science of planning was relatively recent. The main problem here was the question of optimum plans (internal consistency of plans is the condition for its implementation), but it still does not ensure the best possible utilization of the forces and means of the national economy. The choice of the optimum plan calls for comparison of different variants of these plans, which has only now become practically possible thanks to the development of electronic computers enabling the quick and efficient solution of numerous and complicated calculations. These computers also make possible efficient social economic balance accounting. This results in the mathematical formulation of many problems of the economy of socialism, particularly, the analysis of the process of reproduction.

As can be seen, the development of political economy of socialism to date deals above all with the material and balance aspects of the socialist economy. On the other hand, less attention has been paid to the scientific analysis of problems connected with the internal dialectics of the development of socialist production relations, the problems of the social contradictions latent in these relations and the driving force of economic development. At first, most attention was given to descriptions of the building up of new socialist production relations and its practical problems. It was only in the fifties that attention began to be turned to the question of the economic and non-economic incentives involved in the various ways of shaping socialist production relations and distribution relations (forms of payment, workers share in profits, workers self-government, co-operatives, economic ties between the peasants and the working class, role of the market, etc.).

The foundation of the socialist economy and its rapid development, particularly the foundation of a whole system of socialist states created a new situation, both for monopoly capitalism and for the development of bourgeois thought. The scope of capitalist rule was reduced by one third of the world population, and later the national liberation movements and the formation of a large number of independent states in the former colonial territories reduced the area under the domination of imperialism even more. Capitalism ceased to be the only system in the world economy and was forced to coexist with the quickly developing rival—the socialist system. This weakened the social resistance of capitalism to withstand crises and shocks and created a social need to strive for greater stability of the capitalist economy. In these conditions apologetic justifications of production methods supported by economic theories were no longer enough. Bourgeois political economy was forced to make a critical analysis of the most glaring weaknesses of the capitalist system and to seek methods of remedying the situation. A direct incentive was provided by the big economic crisis of 1929–33 and the great depression that followed it, lasting right up to the outbreak of the Second World War with a few exceptions and short intervals. This depression made all the more evident by the great industrialization of the Soviet Union in this period, did not only strengthen and spread revolutionary tensions among the working class and the so-called middle strata, but also undermined the confidence of the bourgeoisie in its own strength. And it was in this situation that J. M. Keynes's new economic theory was born. In his book *General Theory of Employment, Interest and Money* (1936, Polish edition 1956), he stated that a mature capitalist economy in which accumulation led to a low profitability of capital due to the rentier-like tendencies of capitalists to evade investment risks, did not usually provide employment for the whole available manpower. Unemployment thus became a structural feature of capitalism. According to Keynes's theory, the way out of this situation was active intervention by the state. This intervention was to consist in encouraging private investments by lowering the rate of interest and increasing demand for consumer goods by social redistribution in favour of the strata with lower incomes, and, if necessity arose, also in direct state investments with the aim of increasing employment and enlivening economic life as a whole. This theory of Keynes, which had its precursors among the Swedish economists of K. Wicksell's school and in the theories of stimulating the business cycle, born in the time of the great depression, initiated the development of a whole trend, usually called the Keynes school. Various factions crystallized clearly within this trend. The so-called Keynes right wing, which came forward in the United States, after the Second World War, justified the state outlays on armaments by the need to provide full employment. The so-called Keynes left wing, the most eminent representative of which was J. Robinson, put forward a wide-scale programme of social reforms and state investments aimed at the state taking over important fields of economic life. Some of the representatives of this faction went as far as to make postulates of a socialist character.

In the middle of the fifties, in the period of relative stabilization of the capitalist economy, the problems dealt with by Keynes were put in the shade (particularly in the United States and the G.F.R.) by views regarding this stability as a lasting achievement of contemporary capitalism, which did not call for any particular intervention on the part of the state, as was thought by Keynes and his followers. On the other hand, there are some who raise the social and psychological problem of the absorption of the "abundance of goods" by the contemporary industrial society. This is the main trend of contemporary capitalist apologetics, although some of its representatives (for instance, J. K. Galbraith: *The Affluent Society*, 1958) criticize capitalism for its inability to satisfy the collective needs of the society (culture and science, health protection, conservation of natural resources, etc.) and suggest the intervention of the state with the aim of directing part of the national income to the satisfaction of these needs.

The development of political economy of socialism, particularly the science of planning the national economy, and the practical achievements of the socialist economy have had an influence on economic thought and practice of capitalist countries. This has aroused interest in the problems of economic planning, which was also stimulated by the programme postulates of the working class movement in those countries. The method of social economic balance accounting (so-called social accounting), the need for which was also shown by Keynes's policy for the stabilization of the national economy, has been widely applied. The national liberation movements and the endeavours of the economically underdeveloped countries to free themselves from their economic backwardness have aroused interest in the problems of the development of the national economy. This meant going beyond the bounds of bourgeois economics to-date, which mainly investigated the market processes and presented economics (often for the purpose of defending it) as an automatic mechanism for maintaining equilibrium. It did not interest itself in the problem of economic development (particularly the dependence of this development on the system of production relations), which is a basic problem of Marxist economics, nor did it deal with problems of the conditions and possibilities for accumulation, which was the subject of so many discussions in Marxist literature. The topical question of the underdeveloped countries forced it to take an interest in these problems. And this brought about the economics of growth, which has now become one of the main subjects of interest of bourgeois economics. The very nature of the subject called for investigation of problems which so far had been almost the exclusive domain of Marxist economics. This led to the rediscovery of theoretical categories and approaches that have been known for a long time in Marxist literature and partially also to conscious borrowings from Marxist scientific works. The economics of growth has become the subject of special interest in underdeveloped countries, which are seeking knowledge in it about accelerating economic development. In the highly developed capitalist countries, the interest in it stems from the understanding of the importance of the problem of the underdeveloped countries for world economy and politics, and particularly for the rivalry between capitalism and socialism. But in some circles in imperialist countries theories of growth are being proclaimed which seek to justify the lack of an active policy for accelerating the progress of underdeveloped countries. This is connected with the problem of planning the economic development of these countries. The experience of the socialist states, the majority of which began as underdeveloped countries, has aroused lively interest in problems of planning in all the underdeveloped countries. Many of these countries have now already their own plans for economic development in which the decisive role is played by state investments. The previously mentioned apologetics negate the need for directive planning and postulate that the development of the underdeveloped countries should be based on private capital, particularly capital imported from imperialist countries.

With regard to the economics of growth and also the problems of planning economic development and national economic balances, many economists nurturing traditional bourgeois economic theory, partic- ularly the neo-classical school, started criticizing the usefulness of these theories in gaining an understanding of the basic economic processes. Then came a drive towards going beyond the bounds of market phe- nomena and towards investigating the process of reproduction and accumulation and of linking the process with the distribution of the national income. As a result, tendencies developed towards a return to the basic conceptions of classical political economy and to those of Marx. This tendency is evidenced by J. Robinson's book *Accumulation of Capital* (1958). P. Sraffa made the boldest move in this direction (*Pro- duction of Commodities by Means of Commodities*, 1960). He had already criticized the basic principles of the neo-classical theory earlier. In this situation, wide interest began to be shown in Marx and Marxist economic theory.

After the First World War there was also another wave of criticism of capitalist monopolies, which came from economists with the petty bourgeois and also the middle bourgeois approach. This tendency was strengthened by the growing role of the university intellectuals in making economic studies and publishing their results. It led to a far-reaching professionalization of the science of political economy, making the study of economics into a profession. To some extent, this made economic research independent of the direct interests of the bourgeoisie. A large percentage of the professional economists were members of the so-called new middle class, whose inclinations were linked with the attitudes of the petty bourgeois and middle bourgeois milieux. In these conditions, the criticism of capitalist monopolies' activity took two forms. One was the theory of imperfect competition (E. Chamberlain and J. Robinson). The second was welfare economics (welfare), the chief representative of which is A. C. Pigou (*The Economics of Welfare*, 1920). The point of departure in the criticism of monopolies by the theoreticians of welfare economics is the ideal model of the functioning of free competition, any departure from which is regarded as waste of the economic resources of the society. The petty bourgeois and middle bourgeois social scope of this approach is very evident. These theoreticians recommended the intervention of the state (sometimes very far-reaching intervention) with the aim of removing or neutralizing the harmful activity of monopolies.

In the same period, socialist criticism of the capitalist system also increased, mostly based on Marxist economics. The Russian revolution, the construction of socialism in the Soviet Union, the serious crisis and the long depression of the capitalist economy in the thirties were a new incentive for the criticism. Numerous Marxist economists engaged in it, both in the Soviet Union (e.g. J. Varga) and in capitalist countries (O. Bauer, P. Sweezy, M. Dobb). Special mention is due to the works of M. Kalecki, *Studies in the Theory of Business Cycles 1933–1939* and others, who taking the Marxist theory of reproduction as a point of departure formulated the theory of the business cycle in an original way and explained the source of the instability of the capitalist system. His explanation is somewhat similar to R. Luxemburg's theory of accumulation. Critical Marxist analysis of monopoly capitalism was continued after the Second World War. On the one hand, it showed the inability of capitalism to industrialize underdeveloped countries (P. Baran), and, on the other hand, it was investigating the new changes in the economic and social structure of the advanced capitalist countries (relation of class forces, international division of labour, neo-colonialism and others). The last mentioned line of research is still in the initial stage. And so far we are still waiting for a systematic theory explaining the basic economic laws of monopoly capitalism, the specific forms that the functioning of the law of value assumes in monopoly capitalism, the process of expanded reproduction and its cyclical character, the distribution of the national income among the various classes and strata, international division of labour and many other problems.

The fact that the socialist system and the capitalist system coexist in the world economy also raises new problems for political economy. So far, this fact has only been taken into account in the political economy of socialism, in the form of emphasizing the significance of the hostile attitude of capitalist circles towards the economy of the first socialist countries and the possibility of learning methods of management from the highly developed capitalist countries (particularly V. Lenin). On the other hand, very little has been done so far in the field of investigating the influence of the existence of the socialist system on the course and functioning of the capitalist economy. It is a question of such problems as the influence of the world socialist market on the course of the business cycle in capitalist countries, the reduced social resistance of capitalism to shocks and crises, and learning methods of planning the national economy from the socialist countries. The existence of the socialist system has an influence on the regularities of the functioning and development of the capitalist economy, which can no longer be investigated separately from the dialectics of the mutual connections and rivalry between socialism and capitalism on a world scale. This dialectics is specifically reflected in the problems of the underdeveloped countries, in the clash of capitalist and socialist influences, which, depending on the internal relation of class forces in these countries and the relation of forces in world politics and economy, determine the direction of the development of these countries. Here political economy has some new fields of action.

The Auxiliary Sciences of Political Economy

Political Economy is a theoretical science; it derives knowledge of concrete economic phenomena from descriptive economics, which embraces also economic history, economic geography and economic statistics. Various fields of applied economics are linked with political economy (economics of industry, of agriculture and of trade, the economics of finance and accounting, and others). They apply the results achieved by theoretical economics and descriptive economics in detailed investigations of certain fields or aspects of economic life. The practical application of the results achieved by economics is called economic policy. It embraces various sectors of industry, agriculture, finance, and others. Descriptive economics and applied economics are economic sciences together with political economy. They are auxiliary sciences of political economy. In addition, political economy avails itself of the aid of mathematics, particularly mathematical statistics and of philosophy and sociology. The connection of political economy with philosophy is seen above all, in methodology; political economy is particularly closely associated with sociology, which investigates all problems of social links and helps in understanding the links between economic processes and social life as a whole.

Several new auxiliary sciences of political economy have come into being of late. This was the result of the new needs in management of the economy, both in capitalism and in the socialist economy. Econometrics applies mathematical methods (particularly mathematical statistics) for exact and concrete determination of the interrelation of economic phenomena (elasticity of demand, technical coefficients of production, efficiency of investment, etc.). The first stimulus for the development of econometrics was the demand of the monopolies and the capitalist states for more accurate analysis of market processes. This was because the monopolies were able to set prices at a level guaranteeing maximum profit, which could not be done by enterprises in conditions of free competition, for they had to accept the price level set by the spontaneous market mechanism. Interventionist activity by the state also called for a knowledge of the concrete results of such activity, defined quantitatively. Hence, the first econometric works concerned problems of the statistical determination of the elasticity of demand and supply. Further demands for econometric research resulted from such problems as analysis of the factors entering into production costs, forecasts of future demands for various goods, and other problems. In recent years, econometrics has also been applied in socialist countries. The planned character of the socialist economy creates a special demand for a mathematical-quantitative analysis of economic interrelations. Apart from the traditional field of analysis of demand, knowledge of the technical coefficients of production and investments (so-called technical and investment norms) is a matter of primary importance in the planned economy. Knowledge of these coefficients is necessary in drawing up national balances and different parts of these balances. Here, the balance accounting method, known as input–output analysis, is applied. This method, invented by V. Leontief, was inspired by balance accounting introduced in the

Soviet Union, and is much more widely applied in practice in the socialist economy than in the capitalist countries, where it was originally elaborated. The application of econometrics in planning the national economy is sometimes called planometrics (V. Nemchinov). It is worth mentioning that long before econometrics came into being, in the seventeenth and eighteenth centuries, and particularly in the nineteenth century, mathematics, particularly mathematical statistics, was applied in life insurance and other fields of insurance (insurance mathematics, also called actuarial data). But it was only in econometrics that mathematics was applied to a wide range of economic problems.

The science of programming, which is becoming an important branch of contemporary mathematics, is linked with econometrics. It deals with methods of determining optimum programmes for systems embracing a large number of interdependent human activities. In the economic field, its scope of interest is drawing up plans for the work of enterprises and national economic plans (for instance, optimum distribution of investments). The first to develop and apply the science of programming was L. Kantorovich (*Mathematical Methods of Organization and Production*, 1939, Polish edition 1960). Immediately after the Second World War, the science of programming and the so-called operations research, associated with it, were developed in the United States and Great Britain, largely in connection with military problems. Of late, it is being increasingly applied in the Soviet Union and other socialist countries. The widespread practical application of econometrics and the science of programming, and also operations research calls for the use of electronic computers. Only with electronic computers can such a large number of calculations be carried out (e.g. the solution of hundreds of simultaneous equations in a short enough space of time to guarantee that the results will be of current use in the management of the economy). The science of programming and operations research can be regarded as part of praxiology, the general science of rational activity, the actual founder of which was T. Kotarbiński. Praxiology is also of great importance for the methodology of political economy (problems of the so-called principle of good management, or the principle of rational management). But its application is not possible without clear formulation of the tasks and criteria of economic calculus, which econometrics and programming are to serve. This often calls for the extension of the economic theory itself. Thus, econometrics and programming set new problems to be solved by political economy and require a more precise definition of old problems, in this way contributing to its development.

Lastly, possibilities are opening up for the application of the science of cybernetics in the economic sciences. Cybernetics was founded in 1948 and is the science of controlling and regulating systems composed of elements mutually interacted upon each other and linked by a complicated network of chains of causes and effects. Such problems arise in automatic industrial installations, computers, biological organisms, and also in social systems where a great number of human actions are interlaced with each other. The theoretical apparatus of cybernetics throws new light on problems of the spontaneity of social processes, the possibilities and ways of controlling social processes, the role of information in shaping social processes and others. The planned character of the socialist economy makes cybernetics particularly useful in looking for ways of ensuring efficient management of the national economy and its proper functioning.

The above-mentioned new auxiliary sciences enrich the arsenal of political economy, particularly the political economy of socialism, with precision research tools of high cognitive efficiency. This enhances the role of political economy as an instrument for directing the economic development of the society. Socialism has set us the historic task of overcoming the spontaneity that has characterized social and economic processes in the history of man so far. It has set us the task of creating conditions in which social development will be shaped by man consciously and purposefully according to rational principles based on scientific knowledge. Political economy has a fundamental part to play in this task, as a source of knowledge with which the society can consciously mould its historic destinies. In this way, political economy and the auxiliary sciences that serve it are becoming a factor in the process of mastering the blind play of spontaneous forces by the human mind, conscious of its aims.

Part IV

ECONOMIC-MATHEMATICAL MODELS, ECONOMETRICS AND STATISTICS

THE STABILITY OF MARKET EQUILIBRIUM

The Hicksian Conditions

The theory of stability of economic equilibrium is based on the assumption that an excess demand for a good causes a rise in its price, while an excess supply causes a fall in price. The equilibrium is thus said to be stable when, in the neighbourhood of the equilibrium position, a price above the equilibrium price causes excess supply and a price below the equilibrium price causes excess demand. This condition was first stated by Walras; however, he formulated it in a way which limits its applicability to partial-equilibrium analysis. Within the framework of general-equilibrium theory the stability conditions must take into account the repercussions of the change in price of a good upon the prices of other goods as well as the dependence of excess demand (or excess supply) of a good on the prices of the other goods in the system. This has been done by Professor Hicks.[1]

According to Professor Hicks, the economic system is in stable equilibrium if a rise of the price of any good above the equilibrium price causes an excess of supply and a fall of the price below the equilibrium price causes an excess demand for that good, *when the prices of all other goods in the system are so adjusted as to maintain equilibrium in all other markets*. Otherwise, the system is either in unstable or in neutral equilibrium. The former is the case when a rise of the price above the equilibrium price produces excess demand and a fall of the price produces excess supply; the latter is the case when no excess demand or excess supply is produced. In both cases, adjustment of all other prices maintaining equilibrium in the other markets is presupposed. This formulation of the theory of stability of equilibrium leads to a series of conditions which are best formulated mathematically.

Let there be $n+1$ goods in the economy and let one of them, say the $(n+1)$th, serve as money and *numéraire*. Denote by $p_r(r = 1, 2, ..., n)$

---

[1] See *Value Capital*, pp. 66 ff. and pp. 315-6.

the price of the rth good; $p_{n+1} = 1$ by definition. Write further D_r $(p_1, p_2, ..., p_n)$ for the demand function and $S_r(p_1, p_2, ..., p_n)$ for the supply function of the rth good. We have then n independent excess-demand functions X_r defined by

$$X_r(p_1, p_2, ..., p_n) \equiv D_r(p_1, p_2, ..., p_n) - S_r(p_1, p_2, ..., p_n) \qquad (1.1)$$
$$(r = 1, 2, ..., n).$$

The system is in equilibrium when $X_r = 0 (r = 1, 2, ..., n)$. The equilibrium is stable when, at the equilibrium point,

$$\frac{dX_r}{dp_r} < 0,$$

$$(r \quad \text{and} \quad s = 1, 2, ..., n). \qquad (1.2)$$

$$\frac{dX_s}{dp_r} = 0 \quad (s \neq r).$$

The inequality indicates negative excess demand (i.e., excess supply) when the price rises above equilibrium, and positive excess demand when the price falls below equilibrium. The equations indicate that the prices in the other markets are adjusted to maintain equilibrium in these markets.[2]

Let us write

$$a_{sr} \equiv \frac{\partial X_s}{\partial p_r} \qquad (r \text{ and } s = 1, 2, ..., n).$$

---

[2] The stability conditions can also be expressed in terms of excess demand for money. The aggregate value of the excess demand in all n markets is the excess supply of money, i.e.,

$$-X_{n+1} \equiv \sum_{s=1}^{n} p_s X_s.$$

All other markets remaining in equilibrium, we have $X_s = 0$ for $s \neq r$ and

$$-\frac{dX_{n+1}}{dp_r} = X_r + p_r \frac{dX_r}{dp_r}.$$

At the equilibrium point $X_r = 0$ and, by virtue of (1.2),

$$\frac{dX_{n+1}}{dp_r} > 0 \qquad (r = 1, 2, ..., n). \qquad (1.3)$$

Thus the excess demand for money must become positive when the price of a good other than money rises above equilibrium, and become negative when the price falls below equilibrium.

We have

$$\frac{dX_s}{dp_r} = a_{s1}\frac{dp_1}{dp_r} + a_{s2}\frac{dp_2}{dp_r} + \cdots + a_{sr} + \cdots + a_{sn}\frac{dp_n}{dp_r} \quad (s = 1, 2, \ldots, n). \quad (1.4)$$

Exchanging places between $\frac{dX_s}{dp_r}$ and a_{sr}, and taking into account (1.2), we obtain the equations

$$-a_{1r} = a_{11}\frac{dp_1}{dp_r} + a_{12}\frac{dp_2}{dp_r} + \cdots + 0 + \cdots + a_{1n}\frac{dp_n}{dp_r},$$

$$\cdots \cdots \cdots \cdots \cdots \cdots \cdots$$

$$-a_{rr} = a_{r1}\frac{dp_1}{dp_r} + a_{r2}\frac{dp_2}{dp_r} + \cdots - \frac{dX_r}{dp_r} + \cdots + a_{rn}\frac{dp_n}{dp_r}, \quad (1.5)$$

$$\cdots \cdots \cdots \cdots \cdots \cdots \cdots$$

$$-a_{nr} = a_{n1}\frac{dp_1}{dp_r} + a_{n2}\frac{dp_2}{dp_r} + \cdots + 0 + \cdots + a_{nn}\frac{dp_n}{dp_r}.$$

Write

$$J \equiv \begin{vmatrix} a_{11} & a_{12} & \ldots & a_{1n} \\ a_{21} & a_{22} & \ldots & a_{2n} \\ \cdot & \cdot & \cdot & \cdot \\ a_{n1} & a_{n2} & \ldots & a_{nn} \end{vmatrix} \quad (1.6)$$

and denote by J_{rs} the cofactor of a_{rs}. Solving the equations (1.5) we get

$$\frac{dX_r}{dp_r} = \frac{J}{J_{rr}} < 0 \quad (r = 1, 2, \ldots, n). \quad (1.7)$$

This is negative because of (1.2).

Amplifying and modifying Professor Hicks's terminology, we introduce the concept of *partial stability* of different order and rank. The system is said to be partially stable of order $m (1 \leqq n)$ if (1.2) is satisfied when only m other prices are adjusted and the *remaining prices are kept constant*.[3] By a procedure analogous to that leading to (1.7) we obtain as a condition of partial stability of order m

$$\left(\frac{dX_r}{dp_r}\right)_{n-m} = \frac{J_{nn, \ldots, n-m}}{J_{nn, \ldots, n-m, rr}} < 0 \quad (r = 1, 2, \ldots, m), \quad (1.8)$$

---

[3] In this case (1.2) holds for r and $s = 1, 2, \ldots, m$.

where the numerator and the denominator are cofactors of J of order m and $m-1$ respectively. The subscript on the left-hand side indicates which prices are kept constant (namely, $m+1, m+2, ..., n$). The concept of partial stability is always relative to the prices which are kept constant. The system may be partially stable of order m if certain $n-m$ prices are held constant but may fail to be so if $n-m$ other prices are kept constant. When the system is partially stable of order n (n being the number of goods, exclusive of money), we say that it is totally stable. The condition (1.8) then turns into (1.7).

The system is said to be stable of *rank m* (and *unstable or neutral of rank n−m*) if it is partially stable of order m but not of any higher order. The rank of the stability of the system is thus the highest order of partial stability it possesses. A totally stable system has stability of rank n.

Partial stability of order m is said to be *perfect* when the system shows partial stability of *all* lower orders with respect to *any* prices being held constant. Otherwise, the partial stability is said to be imperfect. This definition of perfect partial stability applies also to partial stability of order n, i.e., to total stability. In virtue of (1.8) the condition for perfect stability of order m can be written

$$a_{11} < 0, \begin{vmatrix} a_{11} & a_{12} \\ a_{21} & a_{22} \end{vmatrix} > 0, \; ..., \; \text{sign} \begin{vmatrix} a_{11} & a_{12} & ... & a_{1m} \\ a_{21} & a_{22} & ... & a_{2m} \\ . & . & . & . \\ a_{m1} & a_{m2} & ... & a_{mm} \end{vmatrix} = \text{sign} \, (-1)^m, \quad (1.9)$$

the numeration of the goods being, of course, arbitrary. These are the Hicksian conditions for perfect stability.[4]

Dynamic Stability Conditions

The reader will have noticed that in the mathematical formulation of the theory of stability of economic equilibrium the basic assumption of that theory, namely that excess demand for a good makes its price rise and excess supply makes it fall, does not appear explicitly. This assumption, however, is tacitly implied in the choice of the condition

---

[4] Professor Hicks limits the concept of perfect stability to total stability. The conditions for perfect stability given by him are thus only for the case $m = n$.

that excess demand should occur when the price is below equilibrium and excess supply should occur when it is above equilibrium. In order to clarify all the implications of stability analysis the basic assumption mentioned must be explicitly introduced into the mathematical formulation of the theory of stability equilibrium. When this is done, stability analysis becomes part of a dynamic theory, as was shown recently by Professor Samuelson.[5] The traditional method of treating the stability of economic equilibrium, as applied by Walras, Marshall, and Hicks, is but an implicit (and therefore imperfect) form of dynamic analysis.

The basic assumption of stability analysis, i.e., that excess demand causes the price to rise and excess supply causes it to fall, can be formulated as follows:

$$\text{sign}\frac{dp_r}{dt} = \text{sign} X_r \quad (r = 1, 2, ..., n),\tag{2.1}$$

where $\frac{dp_r}{dt}$ is the rate of change of price over time. Let

$$\frac{dp_r}{dt} = F_r(X_r) \quad (r = 1, 2, ..., n)\tag{2.2}$$

be a set of functions which satisfy the relations (2.1). Then by (2.1) we have

$$F_r(0) = 0 \quad (r = 1, 2, ..., n)\tag{2.3}$$

as the equilibrium conditions of the system.

In (2.2) we have a normal system of n differential equations which has the solutions $p_r(t)(r = 1, 2, ..., n)$.[6] The functions $p_r(t)$ are the adjustment paths of the prices and the equilibrium is stable when these paths lead back to the equilibrium prices, unstable when they lead away from them, and neutral when neither is the case.[7] Expressing all prices in terms of deviations from the equilibrium prices, i.e., putting the latter equal zero, we thus have stable equilibrium when

$$\lim_{t=\infty} p_r(t) = 0 \quad (r = 1, 2, ..., n).\tag{2.4}$$

---

[5] The Stability of Equilibrium: Comparative Statics and Dynamics, *Econometrica*, April, 1941, Vol. 9, pp. 97–120.

[6] It is assumed that the existing conditions are satisfied. This is always the case when the functions F_r and $X_r(r = 1, 2, ..., n)$ and their first derivatives are continuous.

[7] These definitions are broader than those on the first page of this paper and include the latter as a special case.

In order to solve the equations we expand, on the right-hand side of (2.2), F_r and X_r by Maclaurin's theorem and retain only the linear part of the expansion. Expanding F_r, we have

$$\frac{dp_r}{dt} = F'(0)X_r \qquad (r = 1, 2, ..., n),$$

and then expanding X_r, we obtain

$$\frac{dp_r}{dt} = F'_r \sum_{s=1}^{n} a_{rs} p_s \qquad (r = 1, 2, ..., n), \tag{2.5}$$

where p_s is expressed as a deviation from the equilibrium price $p_s^0 = 0$. $F'_r \equiv F'_r(0) = \text{const.}$, and $a_{rs}^0 = a_{rs}(p_1^0, p_2^0, ..., p_n^0) = \text{const.}$ We have now a system of linear equations with constant coefficients.

It will be noticed that in view of (2.1)

$$F'_r(0) > 0 \qquad (r = 1, 2, ..., n). \tag{2.6}$$

Thus, when the functions on the right-hand side of (2.2) are taken as linear in X_r the basic assumption of stability analysis implies necessarily that the *speed of increase of price is the greater the larger the excess demand.* $F'_r(0)$ may serve as a measure of the flexibility of the price p_r. In general it will be said that the price is flexible when $F'_r(0) > 0$, inflexible or rigid, when $F'(0) = 0$, and negatively flexible when $F'_r(0) < 0$. The last two cases are excluded by (2.6).

The solution of the linear system (2.5) is given by the set of functions

$$p_r(t) = \sum_{s=1}^{k} q_{rs}(t) e^{\lambda_s t} \qquad (r = 1, 2, ..., n), \tag{2.7}$$

where the λ_s $(s = 1, 2, ..., k)$ are the k $(k \leq n)$ distinct roots of the characteristic equation[8]

$$f(\lambda) \equiv \begin{vmatrix} F'_1 a_{11}^0 - \lambda & F'_1 a_{12}^0 & ... & F'_1 a_{1n}^0 \\ F'_2 a_{21}^0 & F'_2 a_{22}^0 - \lambda & ... & F'_2 a_{2n}^0 \\ \cdot & \cdot & \cdot & \cdot \\ F'_n a_{n1}^0 & F'_n a_{n2}^0 & ... & F'_n a_{nn}^0 - \lambda \end{vmatrix} = 0 \tag{2.8}$$

---

[8] Professor Samuelson (*op. cit.*, pp. 109–110) leaves out the factors F'_r in the characteristic determinant. This can be done only when $F'_1 = F'_2 = ... = F'_n$. His results thus hold only for the special case where the flexibility of all prices in the system is the same.

and the $q_{rs}(t)$ are polynomials in t of degree one less than the multiplicity of the root λ_s.[9] If the coefficients of the polynomials n are arbitrary and determined by the initial conditions (i.e., by the initial disturbance of equilibrium), the remaining coefficients are found from a system of homogeneous linear equations with the matrix of coefficients as given in (2.8).

Let the roots be complex and write

$$\lambda_s = R(\lambda_s) + I(\lambda_s) \quad (s = 1, 2, ..., k), \tag{2.9}$$

where the two terms on the right-hand side indicate the real and the imaginary part respectively. This includes real roots as a special case in which $I(\lambda_s) = 0$. Writing $I(\lambda_s) = \beta i$, we have

$$e^{\lambda_s t} = e^{R(\lambda_s)t}(\cos \beta t + i \sin \beta t). \tag{2.10}$$

The equilibrium is thus stable, i.e. (2.4) is satisfied, when

$$R(\lambda_s) < 0 \quad \text{for} \quad s = 1, 2, ..., k. \tag{2.11}$$

This is the stability condition which in the dynamic theory replaces the static condition (1.7). If some $R(\lambda_s) > 0$ we get $\lim_{t=\infty} p_r(t) = \pm \infty$ ($r = 1, 2, ..., n$), and the equilibrium is unstable. If some $R(\lambda_s) = 0$ and no $R(\lambda_s) > 0$ the equilibrium is neutral.

As in the static theory, we introduce the concepts of *partial stability* of a given order and rank of stability of the system. The dynamic system is partially stable of *order m* if it is stable when only m prices are allowed to adjust themselves and the other $n-m$ prices are kept constant. This implies that

$$F'_r \equiv 0 \quad \text{for} \quad r = m+1, ..., n \tag{2.12}$$

and

$$p_s \equiv p_s^0 = 0 \quad \text{for} \quad s = m+1, ..., n. \tag{2.13}$$

The system of equations (2.5) turns into

$$\frac{dp_r}{dt} = F'_r \sum_{s=1}^{m} a_{rs} p_s \quad (r = 1, 2, ..., m) \tag{2.14}$$

and the solutions become

$$p_r(t) = \sum_{s=1}^{k} q_{rs}(t) e^{\lambda_s t} \quad (r = 1, 2, ..., m; \ k \leqq m). \tag{2.15}$$

---

[9] Thus when λ_s is a simple root, the corresponding polynomials $q_{rs}(t) \, (r = 1, 2, ..., n)$ reduce to constants.

The condition for partial stability of order m is given, as before, by (2.11) except that the λ_s are roots of a characteristic equation of order m. The characteristic determinant of this equation is a principal minor of order m of the characteristic determinant in (2.8).

When the dynamic system is partially stable of order n we say that it is *totally* stable. The highest order of partial stability of the system is called the *rank of the stability* of the system.

When the characteristic determinant is symmetric all roots are real.[10] In order that they be all negative it is necessary and sufficient[11] that the Hicksian conditions (1.9) be satisfied. Dynamic partial stability of order m thus requires and implies *perfect* Hicksian stability of the same order. This is clear: symmetry of the characteristic determinant of order m implies (and requires) symmetry of all its principal minors.

Implications of the Validity of the Hicksian Conditions

The Hicksian conditions for perfect stability are equivalent to the dynamic stability conditions when the characteristic determinant of order m is symmetric. Let us examine the economic meaning of such symmetry. We have from (2.2)

$$F_r' = \frac{d}{dX_r}\left(\frac{dp_r}{dt}\right) \quad (r = 1, 2, ..., m). \tag{3.1}$$

Taking into account (1.3) we obtain

$$F_r' a_{rs} = \frac{\partial}{\partial p_s}\left(\frac{dp_r}{dt}\right) \quad (r \text{ and } s = 1, 2, ..., m). \tag{3.2}$$

The symmetry $F_r' a_{rs} = F_s' a_{sr}$ thus implies

$$\frac{\partial}{\partial p_s}\left(\frac{dp_r}{dt}\right) = \frac{\partial}{\partial p_r}\left(\frac{dp_s}{dp_t}\right) \quad (r \text{ and } s = 1, 2, ..., m), \tag{3.3}$$

---

[10] We assume that the $F_r' a_{rs}$ are all real, and apply the well-known theorem about the characteristic (or secular) equation proved in the theory of determinants. Cf., for instance, G. Kowalewski, *Einführung in die Determinantentheorie*, Berlin and Leipzig, 1925, pp. 114 ff.; H. W. Turnbull and A. C. Aitken, *An Introduction to the Theory of Canonical Matrices*, London and Glasgow, p. 101. A very simple proof is given by F. R. Moulton, *Differential Equations*, pp. 298–299, New York, 1930.

[11] This is the fundamental theorem about definite Hermitian forms. Cf. Kowalewski, *op. cit.*, p. 199.

i.e., *the marginal effect of a change in the price p_s upon the speed of adjustment of the price p_r equals the marginal effect of a change in the price p_r upon the speed of adjustment of the price p_s.*[12]

The symmetry of the marginal effect of a change in one price upon the speed of adjustment of another price can be clarified further by a mathematical consideration. The symmetry conditions (3.3) are the sufficient conditions for the integrability of the total differential equation

$$\sum_{r=1}^{m} \frac{dp_r}{dt} \, dp_r = 0. \tag{3.4}$$

When conditions (3.3) hold, there exists a function (or rather a class of functions)[13]

$$P[p_1(t), p_2(t), ..., p_m(t)] \tag{3.5}$$

---

[12] It has been held by some economists that, in order that static equilibrium and stability analysis be applicable, the speed of adjustment must be the same in each market. This view was expressed by S. Kohn (On the Problems of the Modern Theory of Price and Value, *Economista* (The Economist), 1925, in Polish); by P. N. Rosenstein-Rodan (Das Zeitmoment in der Mathematischen Theorie des wirtschaftlichen Gleichgewichtes, *Zeitschrift für Nationalekonomie,* Vol. 1, 1930, pp. 129–142, and The Role of Time in Economic Theory, *Economica,* NS., Vol. 1, February 1934, pp. 90–91); and by Simon Kuznets (Equilibrium Economics and Business-Cycle Theory, *Quarterly Journal of Economics,* Vol. 44, February 1930, p. 404). As shown above, this is wrong. The condition of applicability of static analysis is not equality of the speed of price adjustment in each market, but the symmetry of the cross effects of a change in one price upon the speed of adjustment of the other, as indicated in (3.3). This symmetry is similar to the Hotelling conditions in the pure theory of demand or supply without budget limitations (Edgeworth's Taxation Paradox and the Nature of Demand and Supply Functions, *Journal of Political Economy,* Vol. 40, October 1932, pp. 591 and 594). These conditions are

$$\frac{\partial D_r}{\partial p_s} = \frac{\partial D_s}{\partial p_r}$$

and $(r \text{ and } s = 1, 2, ..., n);$

$$\frac{\partial S_r}{\partial p_s} = \frac{\partial S_s'}{\partial p_r}$$

If these conditions are satisfied we have, on account of (1.1) and (1.3), $a_{rs} = a_{sr}$ $(r \text{ and } s = 1, 2, ..., n).$ If $F_r' = F_s'$ $(r \text{ and } s = 1, 2, ..., n)$ this implies the fulfilment of the condition (3.3). Thus, when the flexibility of all prices is the same, the condition of applicability of static-equilibrium and stability analysis is identical with the Hotelling conditions for demand and supply functions.

such that

$$\frac{dp_r}{dt} = \frac{\partial P}{\partial p_r(t)} \quad (r = 1, 2, ..., m), \tag{3.6}$$

i.e., such that the speeds of adjustments are its partial derivatives. The equation (3.4) can be interpreted as the maximum condition of this function (or class of functions).[14] The adjustment paths $p_r(t)$ $(r = 1, 2, ..., m)$ are then co-ordinated into a consistent system maximizing this function. The function P may, therefore, be called the adjustment potential, and a dynamic system for which an adjustment potential exists will be called an *integrated system*; m will be called the *order of integration* of the system. From (3.3) we see that when the system is integrated of order m it is also integrated in all lower orders. The Hicksian conditions provide sufficient[15] conditions of (partial) stability (of order m; $m \leq n$) for integrated (of order m) dynamic systems.

The economic meaning of an integrated system can be illustrated as follows. Suppose that the m adjustment paths $p_r(t)$ $(r = 1, 2, ..., m)$ are determined by a planning authority that wants to maximize at each moment the total welfare of the community. The adjustment paths must then satisfy the maximum conditions of a function like (3.5). As atomistic competition automatically totals welfare within a static system, similarly a dynamic system *may*, under appropriate circumstances, imply the maximization of a potential function which serves as an indicator of total welfare.

---

[13] If P is a solution of the equation then any function $\Phi(P)$ such that $\Phi'(P) \neq 0$ is also a solution.

[14] The second-order maximum conditions are given by the Hicksian inequalities (1.9). In order to satisfy these, the functions $\Phi(P)$ must be restricted to cases where $\Phi'(P) > 0$.

[15] The conditions of integrability of (3.4) are that $\frac{1}{2}(m-1)(m-2)$ equations of the form

$$\frac{dp_r}{dt}\left[\frac{\partial}{\partial p_t}\left(\frac{\partial p_s}{\partial t}\right) - \frac{\partial}{\partial p_s}\left(\frac{\partial p_t}{\partial t}\right)\right] + \frac{dp_s}{dt}\left[\frac{\partial p_s}{\partial t}\left(\frac{\partial p_t}{\partial t}\right)\right.$$

$$\left. - \frac{\partial}{\partial p_t}\left(\frac{\partial p_r}{\partial t}\right)\right] + \frac{dp_t}{dt}\left[\frac{\partial}{\partial p_s}\left(\frac{\partial p_r}{dt}\right) - \frac{\partial}{\partial p_r}\left(\frac{\partial p_s}{\partial t}\right)\right] = 0$$

are satisfied; for this, (3.3) is sufficient but not necessary.

Homogeneous Systems

Consider a system consisting of $n+1$ goods and suppose that the $(n+1)$th good functions as money. Let the excess-demand functions of m goods other than money ($m < n$) be homogeneous of zero degree in the prices of these goods,[16] and let the excess-demand functions of the remaining $n-m$ goods other than money be homogeneous of first degree in the same prices. We shall prove that such a system has the following properties:

(1) The excess-demand function for money is homogeneous of first degree in the same m prices.

(2) The system is neutral of rank not less than one and the rank of stability of the system does not exceed $n-1$.

(3) The equilibrium value of one of the m prices in which the excess-demand functions are homogeneous of zero degree is arbitrary and the equilibrium values of the other $m-1$ of these prices are proportional to the arbitrary equilibrium price.

In order to fix ideas, assume that the excess-demand functions $X_1, X_2, \ldots, X_m$ are homogeneous of zero degree in the prices $p_1, p_2, \ldots, p_m$ and that the excess-demand functions $X_{m+1}, X_{m+2}, \ldots, X_n$ are homogeneous of first degree in the same variables. We observe that the relation

$$\sum_{r=1}^{m} p_r X_r + \sum_{r=m+1}^{n} p_r X_r + X_{n+1} \equiv 0 \qquad (4.1)$$

holds between the $n+1$ excess-demand functions. This relation is an identity in the p's and may be called Walras's law.[17] If the prices $p_1, p_2, \ldots, p_m$ are multiplied by an arbitrary number k and the prices $p_{m+1}, \ldots, p_n$, are kept constant, each of the expressions under the summation sign in (4.1) is increased k-fold, for in the first expression

---

[16] A function $f(x_1, x_2, \ldots, x_m; x_{m+1}, \ldots, x_n)$ is said to be homogeneous of the Rth degree *in the variables* $x_1, x_2, \ldots, x_m$ if, for every $k, f(kx_1, kx_2, \ldots, kx_m; x_{m+1}, \ldots, x_n) = kf(x_1, x_2, \ldots, x_m; x_{m+1}, \ldots, x_n)$.

[17] For a special case (the foreign-exchange markets) this relation was known already to Cournot (cf. *Researches into the Mathematical Principles of the Theory of Wealth*, transl. by T. Bacon, Macmillan, pp. 33–34, New York, 1927). Walras, however, was the first to give it a general mathematical formulation and to recognize its importance for the theory of prices. See his *Eléments d'économie politique pure* (édition definitive; pp. 120–121, Paris and Lausanne, 1926).

the p's are increased k-fold and the X's are unchanged, while in the second expression the p's are unchanged and the X's are increased k-fold. It follows from the identity that X_{n+1} is also increased k-fold. This proves the first property of our system.

Applying Euler's theorem, we have

$$\sum_{s=1}^{m} a_{rs} p_s = 0 \quad \text{for} \quad r = 1, 2, \ldots, m \tag{4.2}$$

and

$$\sum_{s=1}^{m} a_{rs} p_s = X_r \quad \text{for} \quad r = m+1, m+2, \ldots, n, \tag{4.3}$$

where a_{rs} is defined as in (1.3). Putting the equilibrium prices $p_r^0 (r = 1, 2, \ldots, n)$ into (4.2) and (4.3) and remembering that $X_r(p_1^0, p_2^0, \ldots, p_n^0) = 0 (r = 1, 2, \ldots, n)$ we obtain

$$\sum_{s=1}^{m} a_{rs}^0 p_s^0 = 0 \quad (r = 1, 2, \ldots, n), \tag{4.4}$$

where $a_{rs}^0 = a_{rs}(p_1^0, p_2^0, \ldots, p_n^0)$.

Consider now the determinant

$$J^0 = \begin{vmatrix} a_{11}^0 & a_{12}^0 \ldots a_{1n}^0 \\ a_{21}^0 & a_{22}^0 \ldots a_{2n}^0 \\ \cdot & \cdot \quad \cdot \quad \cdot \\ a_{n1}^0 & a_{n2}^0 \ldots a_{nn}^0 \end{vmatrix} \tag{4.5}$$

Multiply the first column by p_1^0, add the second column multiplied by p_2^0, etc., finally add the mth column multiplied by p_m^0. The result is the determinant

$$\begin{vmatrix} \sum_{s=1}^{m} a_{rs}^0 p_s^0 a_{12}^0 \ldots a_{1n}^0 \\ \sum_{s=1}^{m} a_{rs}^0 p_s^0 a_{22}^0 \ldots a_{2n}^0 \\ \sum_{s=1}^{m} a_{rs}^0 p_s^0 a_{n2}^0 \ldots a_{nn}^0 \end{vmatrix} = p_1^0 J^0. \tag{4.6}$$

On account of (4.4) this determinant vanishes and so does J^0, because the origin of the price co-ordinates can always be chosen so that $p_1^0 \neq 0$. Thus J^0 is at most of rank $n-1$. The same procedure cannot be repeated with all of the first minors of J^0 and it is impossible to show that they must all vanish. They may vanish, of course, but need not do so. All that can be asserted is, therefore, that the rank of J^0 cannot exceed $n-1$.

The determinant

$$D^0 = \begin{vmatrix} F_1' a_{11}^0 & F_1' a_{12}^0 & \dots & F_1' a_{1n}^0 \\ F_2' a_{21}^0 & F_2' a_{22}^0 & \dots & F_2' a_{2n}^0 \\ \cdot & \cdot & \cdot & \cdot \\ F_n' a_{n1}^0 & F_n' a_{n2}^0 & \dots & F_n' a_{nn}^0 \end{vmatrix} = F_1' F_2' \dots F_n' J^0, \qquad (4.7)$$

where $F_r' = F_r'(0) > 0 (r = 1, 2, \dots, n)$ by virtue of (2.6), is at most of the same rank as J^0, i.e. $n-1$.

The characteristic equation (2.8) can be written in the polynomial form

$$\lambda^n - S_1 \lambda^{n-1} + S_2 \lambda^{n-2} + \dots + (-1)^n S_n = 0, \qquad (4.8)$$

where $S_r (r = 1, 2, \dots, n)$ is the sum of all principal minors of order r in D^0. D^0 being of rank not higher than $n-1$, at least the last term of the polynomial vanishes and we have

$$\lambda[\lambda^{n-1} - S_1 \lambda^{n-2} + S_2 \lambda^{n-3} + \dots + (-1)^{n-1} S_{n-1}] = 0. \qquad (4.9)$$

The characteristic equation thus has at least one root $\lambda = 0$ and the system is, therefore, neutral at least of rank one. Since at least one of the roots equals zero, at most $n-1$ roots can have negative real parts, i.e., the order of stability of the system cannot be higher than $n-1$. This proves the second property of our system.

The equilibrium equations are

$$X_r(p_1, p_2, \dots, p_n) = 0 \qquad (r = 1, 2, \dots, n). \qquad (4.10)$$

In view of the fact that $X_1, X_2, \dots, X_m$ are homogeneous of zero degree and $X_{m+1}, X_{m+2}, \dots, X_n$ are homogeneous of the first degree in the variables $p_1, p_2, \dots, p_m$, the equations can be written in the form

$$\Phi_r\left(1, \frac{p_2}{p_1}, \dots, \frac{p_m}{p_1}; p_{m+1}, \dots, p_n\right) = 0 \qquad \text{for} \quad r = 1, 2, \dots, m,$$

$$p_1 \Phi_r\left(1, \frac{p_2}{p_1}, \dots, \frac{p_m}{p_1}; p_{m+1}, \dots, p_n\right) = 0 \qquad\qquad (4.11)$$

$$\text{for} \quad r = m+1, m+2, \dots, n.$$

We see immediately that if the set of prices $p_1^0, p_2^0, \dots, p_m^0, p_{m+1}, \dots, p_n^0$

is a solution of (4.11),[18] the set of prices $kp_1^0, kp_2^0, ..., kp_m^0, p_{m+1}, ..., p_n^0$, where k is an arbitrary number, is also a solution. This proves the third property of our system.

A practical application of the system under discussion is found by interpreting the goods $1, 2, ..., m$ as commodities and stocks and the goods $m+1, m+2, ..., n$ as fixed-income-bearing securities. Our system then describes the case where the excess-demand functions of commodities and stocks are homogeneous of zero degree in the prices of commodities and stocks, interest rates (or the prices of fixed-income-bearing securities) being constant. Under these circumstances the demand and supply functions, and, consequently, also the excess-demand functions, of fixed-income-bearing securities are homogeneous of first degree in commodity prices, because if all commodity and stock prices increase k-fold the real earning power of the securities mentioned decreases in inverse proportion and it takes k times as many securities to represent the same real earning power as before.[19] The properties of such a system have been discovered by Lord Keynes in his doctrine of the effect of changes in money wages upon employment and upon product prices.[20] Lord Keynes's theory presupposes a system in which interest rates are kept constant and in which the demand and supply functions of all commodities are homogeneous of zero degree in money wage rates and commodity prices. Professor Hicks has developed further this doctrine in application to general-equilibrium theory under conditions where all price expectations are of unit elasticity.[21] A mathematical proof of Professor Hicks's conclusion was given by Dr. Mosak.[22] Dr. Mosak uses the Hicksian stability conditions in his proof. His proof is, therefore, restricted to systems in which these conditions are valid. The results established in this section contain those of Keynes, Hicks, and Mosak as special cases.

---

[18] The existence of a solution of the equilibrium equations is assumed.

[19] Cf. p. 16 above.

[20] *The General Theory of Employment, Interest and Money*, Harcourt, Brace, pp. 257–271, New York, 1936.

[21] *Op. cit.*, pp. 254–255. It seems, however, that he was not aware of the fact that his analysis and conclusions presuppose a neutral monetary system. Cf. footnote 10 on p. 228 above.

[22] Jacob Mosak, *General-Equilibrium Theory in International Trade*, Cowles Commision Monograph No. 7, Principia Press, pp. 162–164, Bloomington, Indiana, 1944.

The Law of Composition of Goods

The rank of stability of economic equilibrium indicates the maximum number of flexible prices compatible with the stability of the system. To secure stability, the remaining prices must be rigid. Any argument, however, which attaches importance to the number of goods or prices presupposes the existence of a way of classifying goods and determining their number which is not purely arbitrary. From experience we know that there is no unique way of classifying goods. A commodity can be split up into several subcommodities; for instance, wheat into wheat of different grades. On the other hand, several commodities can be combined into one composite commodity. The classification of goods occurring in practical economic life is to a certain degree conventional. In economic science, however, the classification of goods cannot be made on a purely arbitrary basis, because the laws of economics would then be dependent on the particular classification adopted. This would restrict the significance of the propositions of economics to a degree that would make them practically valueless. Each proposition might be changed into its opposite by a mere reclassification of goods. We adopt, therefore, the following *Principle of Invariance*:

The criterion of classification of goods must be such that reclassification of any group of goods in the economic system leaves invariant (1) all propositions of economic theory which relate to the subsystem consisting of the remaining goods, and (2) the formal mathematical structure of the propositions relating to the goods which are reclassified.

In equilibrium and stability theory the criterion required is obtained by means of the following consideration: Take a system consisting of $n+1$ goods (including money). Let $q(q < n)$ goods be such that their prices vary always in the same proportion. Combine these goods into one composite good and define the price of the composite good as a linear combination of the prices of the q goods. Without loss of generality, we can assume that these are the goods $1, 2, ..., q$, and the composite good may be represented by the symbol $(1q)$. We have

$$p_r(t) \equiv b_r p_q(t) \quad (r = 1, 2, ..., q-1). \tag{5.1}$$

where $b_r = $ const. $> 0 (r = 1, 2, ..., q-1)$. Denoting the price of the composite good by $p_{(1q)}$, we shall write

$$p_{(1q)}(t) \equiv \sum_{r=1}^{q} w_r p_r(t) \quad (w_r = \text{const.} > 0). \tag{5.2}$$

Combining (5.1) and (5.2) we find

$$p_r(t) \equiv c_r p_{(1q)}(t) \qquad (r = 1, 2, ..., m), \tag{5.3}$$

where

$$c_r = \frac{b_r}{\displaystyle\sum_{s=1}^{q} w_s b_s} > 0 \qquad (b_q = 1). \tag{5.4}$$

The excess demand $X_{(1q)}$ for the composite $(1q)$ will be defined by the relation

$$p_{(1q)} X_{(1q)} \equiv \sum_{r=1}^{q} p_r X_r . \tag{5.5}$$

Together with (5.2), this leads to the relations

$$X_r = w_r X_{(1q)} \qquad (r = 1, 2, ..., q). \tag{5.6}$$

Taking into account (5.3), we write this in the form

$$X_r(p_1, p_2, ..., p_q; p_{q+1}, ..., p_n)$$
$$\equiv X_r[c_1 p_{(1q)}, c_2 p_{(1q)}, ..., c_q p_{(1q)}; p_{q+1}, ..., p_n] \equiv w_r X_{(1q)}[p_{(1q)}, p_{q+1}, ..., p_n].$$

Following our previous notation, let us write

$$a_{(1q)s} = \frac{\partial X_{(1q)}}{\partial p_s} \qquad [s = (1q), q+1, q+2, ..., n], \tag{5.7}$$

and we obtain the relations

$$\sum_{s=1}^{q} a_{rs} c_s = w_r a_{(1q)(1q)} \qquad (r = 1, 2, ..., q). \tag{5.8}$$

$$a_{rs} = w_r a_{(1q)s} \quad \text{for} \quad s = q+1, q+2, ..., n.$$

Consider the system of differential equations

$$\frac{dp_r}{dt} = F'_r \sum_{s=1}^{n} a^0_{rs} p_s \qquad (r = 1, 2, ..., n), \tag{5.9}$$

i.e., the system (2.5) discussed above. Because of (5.3) and (5.8) this system can be written in the following form:

$$\frac{dp_{(1q)}}{dt} = \frac{F'_r w_r}{c_r} \left[a^0_{(1q)(1q)} p_{(1q)} + \sum_{s=q+1}^{n} a^0_{(1q)s} p_s \right] \quad \text{for} \quad r = 1, 2, ..., q,$$

$$\tag{5.10}$$

$$\frac{dp_r}{dt} = F'_r \sum_{s=1}^{n} a^0_{rs} p_s \quad \text{for} \quad r = q+1, q+2, ..., n.$$

Since the system (5.10) is equivalent to the system (5.9), the prices of the goods $q+1, q+2, ..., n$ are not affected by the combination of the goods $1, 2, ..., q$ into a composite good. We see from (5.10) that the differential equations for $s = q+1, q+2, ..., n$ are not affected either. The prices $p_1, p_2, ..., p_q$ are transformed into $p_{(1q)}$ through multiplication by a constant. By writing

$$F'_{(1q)} = \frac{F'_r w_r}{c_r} \qquad (r = 1, 2, ..., q), \qquad (5.11)$$

the system (5.10) can be written in the reduced form

$$\frac{dp_r}{dt} = F'_r \sum_s a^0_{rs} p_s \quad [r \text{ and } s = (1q, q+1, q+2), ..., n]. \qquad (5.12)$$

Comparing this reduced system with the original system (5.9) we find that the first q differential equations in (5.9) are reduced to one equation which retains the mathematical structure of the original equations (i.e., is a linear equation with constant coefficients). We see also that the composite good behaves exactly as if it were a single good and that the composition does not affect the other goods in any way.

The passage from the system (5.9) to the system (5.10) or (5.12) is equivalent to subjecting the system (5.9) to the algebraic transformations

$$\frac{dp_r}{dt} \equiv \frac{c_r}{w_r} \frac{dp_{(1q)}}{dt} \quad \text{for } r = 1, 2, ..., q,$$

$$\frac{dp_r}{dt} \equiv \frac{dp_r}{dt} \quad \text{for } r = q+1, q+2, ..., n, \qquad (5.13)$$

and

$$p_s(t) \equiv c_s p_{(1q)}(t) \quad \text{for } s = 1, 2, ..., q,$$

$$p_s(t) \equiv p_s(t) \quad \text{for } s = q+1, q+2, ..., n. \qquad (5.14)$$

These transformations are nonsingular and can be inverted. In economic terms the inverse transformations mean the splitting up of the composite good $(1q)$ into q separate goods. The inverse transformations change neither the prices of the goods $q+1, q+2, ..., n$ nor the corresponding differential equations. The price of the separated goods $1, 2, ..., q$ are obtained by multiplying the price of the composite good by a constant structure of the original equation.

Thus the transformations (5.13) and (5.14) as well as their inverses satisfy our *Principle of Invariance*. This consideration leads us to the following criterion of classification of goods:

Any goods the prices of which always vary in the same proportion can be combined into one composite good; and, conversely, any good can be split up into an arbitrary number of separate goods with prices varying always in the same proportion.

We shall call it the *law of composition of goods*. By applying this law the number of goods in the theoretical system can be reduced to a certain minimum. This minimum is attained when no two goods in the system are such that their prices vary always in the same proportion. In this case the theoretical system will be said to be *canonical*. In a canonical system the number of goods is arbitrary and need not even be finite. For any good can be split up into several goods with prices always varying proportionally. By succesive application of transformations of this kind the number of goods can be increased indefinitely.

Constant prices are a special case of prices which always vary in the same proportion, namely in the same proportion as the price of money, which equals unity by definition. Thus, all goods with rigid prices can be combined with money into one composite good. In a canonical system the introduction of rigid prices is synonymous with a reduction of the number of goods. This suggests an interpretation of the rank of stability of economic equilibrium. Stability of rank $n-q$ of a system containing $n+1$ goods (including money) means that q prices must be kept rigid in order to secure stability. This means that the corresponding canonical systems cannot contain more than $n-q+1$ goods and still be stable. The instability is due to there being q goods too many. In order to secure stability q goods must be combined with money into one composite good. Thus stability short of total stability, can be interpreted as indicating an excessive number of goods in the canonical system.

Imperfect Competition

With some reinterpretation of the economic meaning of symbols, our analysis can be extended to systems containing forms of imperfect competition where sellers or buyers are confronted with determinate and differentiable demand or supply functions. These forms are monopoly and monopsony, monopolistic and monopsonistic competition.[23] This presupposes that each seller deals with atomistic buyers and each buyer deals with atomistic sellers. Each non-atomistic seller or buyer must be regarded as dealing in a separate good. Equilibrium obtains in the system when all prices are such that every seller and every buyer maximizes his profit or utility. If perfectly competitive markets are present, excess demand must vanish in them.

That atomistic buyers and sellers maximize their profit or utility is implied in the construction of their demand and supply functions. The demand and supply functions of the atomistic buyers and sellers being given, the profit or utility U_r, which the non-atomistic seller or buyer of the good r maximizes, can be considered as a function of the prices, i.e., $U_r = U_r(p_1, p_2, ..., p_n)$. Of these prices the non-atomistic seller or buyer controls only p_r, and, under the forms of imperfect competition under consideration, he does not take into account a possible influence of a change in p_r upon other prices. We define now for each non-atomistic seller and buyer a function $X_r(p_1, p_2, ..., p_n)$, such that

$$X_r \equiv \frac{\partial U_r}{\partial p_r} \tag{6.1}$$

(r running through any values of the sequence $1, 2, ..., n$).

We shall call it the *marginal-gain function*.

$X_r = 0$ when the non-atomistic seller or buyer of the good r maximizes his profit or utility. The second-order maximum condition requires that $X_r \gtrless 0$ according as his price is less or greater than the price which maximizes his profit or utility. Thus when $X_r > 0$ the non-atomistic seller or buyer raises his price. He lowers his price when $X_r < 0$. The functions X_r thus conform to the equations (2.1) and, consequently, the differential equations (2.2) and (2.5).[24] In these equations the functions X_r can, therefore, be interpreted as excess-demand functions when the market for the good r is subject to perfect competition, and as marginal-gain functions when competition is imperfect. In this way, our analysis can be extended to systems which contain imperfections of competition

---

[23] Oligopoly and oligopsony based on group behaviour are excluded because the demand or supply functions, though determinate, are not differentiable at the point of the conventionally established price.

[24] They also satisfy the inequalities (1.2) which are Professor Hicks's conditions for "imperfect" stability.

of the type mentioned. The conclusions of Sections 1–3 and 5 hold fully for such systems.

The properties of homogeneous systems established in Section 4 hold in systems which contain imperfect competition in any of the goods $1, 2, ..., m$ (i.e., commodities and stocks), provided the non-atomistic buyers and sellers are firms.

Suppose that the assumptions of Section 4 are satisfied in the atomistic markets. Since in non-atomistic markets excess demand is always zero, irrespective of whether these markets are in equilibrium or not, the corresponding terms in identity (4.1) vanish. This identity is thus restricted to terms relating to atomistic markets and the first property of homogeneous systems follows immediately.

Suppose further that in each atomistic market the demand function confronting the monopoly or the supply function confronting the monopsonist is homogeneous of zero degree in the prices $p_1, p_2, ..., p_m$. Denote the demand function or supply function confronting the non-atomistic seller or buyer of the rth good by $\left(D_r(p_1, p_2, ..., p_n)\right)$ or $S_r(p_1, p_2, ..., p_n)$, respectively. The firm's profit can be expressed in the form

$$U_r(p_1, p_2, ..., p_n) \equiv p_r D_r + \sum_{s \neq r} p_s q_s \tag{6.2a}$$

or

$$U_r(p_1, p_2, ..., p_n) \equiv -p_r S_r + \sum_{s \neq r} p_s q_s, \tag{6.2b}$$

according as the firm sells or buys the rth good in a non-atomistic market. The q_s are quantities of goods sold or bought in atomistic markets and can be any of the goods $1, 2, ..., m$. The q_s which stand for goods bought are negative. Given all prices except p_r, the quantities q_s are chosen so as to maximize the firm's profit. These quantities are thus determined by the set of equations

$$\frac{\partial U_r}{\partial q_s} = \frac{\partial D_r}{\partial q_s}\left(p_r + D_r \frac{\partial p_r}{\partial D_r}\right) + p_s = 0 \qquad (s \neq r), \tag{6.3a}$$

or

$$\frac{\partial U_r}{\partial q_s} = -\frac{\partial S_r}{\partial q_s}\left(p_r + S_r \frac{\partial p_r}{\partial S_r}\right) + p_s = 0. \tag{6.3b}$$

In these equations $\frac{\partial D_r}{\partial q_s}$ or $\frac{\partial S_r}{\partial q_s}$ is derived from the firm's transformation function and is the marginal rate of transformation of the sth into the rth good, or vice versa. $\frac{\partial p_r}{\partial D_r}$ or $\frac{\partial p_r}{\partial S_r}$ is the reciprocal of the partial derivative of the demand function or supply function, respectively.

Since D_r or S_r is homogeneous of zero degree in $p_1, p_2, ..., p_m$, $\frac{\partial p_r}{\partial D_r}$ or $\frac{\partial p_r}{\partial S_r}$ is homogeneous of first degree in the same variables $\left(\frac{\partial D_r}{\partial p_r} \right.$ or $\frac{\partial S_r}{\partial p_r}$ is homogeneous of degree $-1 \big)$. The price p_r and p_s being among the variables $p_1, p_2, ..., p_m$ the equations in (6.3) are invariant under a proportional change of these variables. Consequently, the quantities q_s, which are the solutions of these equations, are not affected by a proportional change in the prices $p_1, p_2, ..., p_m$. It follows that the expression (6.2) is homogeneous of first degree in $p_1, p_2, ..., p_m$, because the q_s as well as D_r or S_r remain constant when p_r and the p_s all change in the same proportion. The marginal gain function $X_r \equiv \frac{\partial U_r}{\partial p_r}$ is, therefore, homogeneous of zero degree in $p_1, p_2, ..., p_m$. The second and third property of a homogeneous system follow from the results of Section 4 by mere reinterpretation of symbols.

ON THE THEORY OF THE MULTIPLIER

The multiplier is the marginal effect of a change of one economic variable, upon another economic variable of which the first variable is a component; for instance, the marginal effect of a change in primary employment upon total employment, or of a change in investment upon national income. In recent years multipliers of various kinds have been applied as tools of analysis in a number of fields of economic inquiry, such as the theory of employment, the evaluation of the national income, and foreign trade. However, some misunderstandings and confusions have arisen in this connection. The present paper intends to clear up many of the difficulties involved by surveying briefly the main types of multipliers and their correct interpretation.

Simple Multipliers

Simple multipliers are those which involve only one marginal relationship. The most important of them are the *investment multiplier* and the *consumption multiplier*. The first has gained great prominence on account of its introduction by Keynes; the second is a symmetric counterpart of the first.

Let C be the rate of consumption, I—the rate of investment, and Y—the national income per unit of time. Write $C = C(Y)$ for the consumption function and $I = I(Y)$ for the investment function. The marginal propensity to consume is $C' = C'(Y)$ and the marginal propensity to invest is $I' = I'(Y)$. From the relation $Y \equiv C + I$, we derive

$$\frac{dC}{dY} + \frac{dI}{dY} \equiv 1,$$

whence, if I is a free variable and $C = C(Y)$,

$$\frac{dY}{dI} = \frac{1}{1 - C'} \tag{1}$$

242

and, if C is a free variable and $I = I(Y)$,

$$\frac{dY}{dC} = \frac{1}{1-I'}. \tag{2}$$

(1) is the investment multiplier and is equal to the reciprocal of the marginal propensity to save; (2) is the consumption multiplier and is equal to the marginal reluctance to invest.

These two multipliers can also be obtained, by the Kahn–Clark method, as sums of infinite geometric progressions, namely:

$$\frac{dY}{dI} = 1+C'+(C')^2+ \ \dots$$

and

$$\frac{dY}{dC} = 1+I'+(I')^2+ \ \dots$$

If $(C') < 1$ or $(I') < 1$, these sums are equal to the expressions (1) and (2), respectively. The first condition is implied in the well established empirical fact $0 < C' < 1$; the second condition holds when the system is stable. The stability condition of the system is $C'+I' < 1$,[1] which, given $0 < C' < 1$, implies $0 < I' < 1$.

The interpretation of the consumption multiplier is similar to that of the investment multiplier. The consumption multiplier indicates the marginal effect upon national income of an increase in the rate of consumption, in the same way as the investment multiplier indicates the marginal effect upon national income of an increase in the rate of investment.

---

[1] Denoting the marginal propensity to save by $S' = S'(Y)$ we have $S' \equiv 1-C'$, and the stability condition can be stated in the form $S' > I'$ (the marginal propensity to save is greater than the marginal propensity to invest). In this form

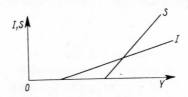

it can be represented by means of the familiar diagram expressing the equilibrium of (planned) saving and (planned) investment. The S-curve must intersect the I-curve from below.

In the relations

$$dY = \frac{1}{1-C'} dI \qquad\qquad (1')$$

and

$$dY = \frac{1}{1-I'} dC \qquad\qquad (2')$$

the multiplicand dI or dC, respectively, indicates the *total* increment in the rate of investment or in the rate of consumption in the economy. As a rule, any initial *autonomous* increment in investment leads to (positive or negative) additional investments, which are *induced* by the increase in national income resulting from the increase in consumption generated by the initial investment. In a similar way, any *autonomous* increment in consumption leads to *induced* additional consumption, due to the increase in national income resulting from the increase in investment generated by the initial increase in consumption. The multiplicands dI and dC have to be interpreted as representing not the initial increment in I or C, but the total increment, which includes all induced increments, in addition to the initial one. This imposes a serious limitation upon the practical application of the multipliers (1) and (2).

Thus, our formulae cannot be applied to as simple a problem as the effect of a given government expenditure upon national income. An initial government investment leads, as a rule, to induced private investment and the multiplicand dI must include the latter. Unless the amount of induced private investment is known to us, we cannot calculate dI, and our formula of the investment multiplier is practically useless. This uselessness of the investment multiplier formula was particularly apparent during the period 1936–40. At that time, many economists held the belief that, because of its allegedly adverse effect upon business confidence, government investment causes a diminution of private investment to such an extent that it results in a fall of the national income. This argument was frequently expressed in the form of the statement that the multiplier is negative. This statement was a wrong formulation of a basically meaningful (though empirically unfounded) proposition. What the critics of government spending meant to say was that the multiplicand dI, not the multiplier $\frac{1}{1-C'}$, is negative, because the (allegedly) negative induced private investments outweigh the positive initial increment of investment made by the government.[2]

The same limitation of the multiplier arises with regard to the effect upon national income of an initial increment in government consumption expenditure (e.g., for relief, or for the armed forces). The multiplicand dC includes, in addition to the increase in the government's expenditure, all the induced increases in private consumption. Unless the latter are already known, dC cannot be calculated and the multiplier formula $\frac{1}{1-C'}$ is of no practical use.

The difficulty mentioned can, however, be overcome by means of an extension of the multiplier technique, which leads to multipliers involving two or more marginal relationships.[3] Such multipliers will be called compound multipliers.

Compound Multipliers

Let dI_0 be an initial autonomous increment in the rate of investment. This implies an equal increase in the national income and leads to induced consumption equal to $C'dI_0$ and to induced investment equal to $I'dI_0$. The result is an induced increase in income $(C'+I')dI_0$ which, in turn, leads to a further induced increase in income $(C'+I')(C'+I')dI_0$, etc. The total increase in national income is thus

$$dY = [1+(C'+I')+(C'+I')^2+ \;...]dI_0$$

and the *compound investment multiplier* is[4]

---

[2] This and many other points of the theory of the multiplier have been elucidated by Professor Paul A. Samuelson. Cf. his articles The Theory of Pump-Priming Re-examined, *American Economic Review*, Vol. 30, September 1940, p. 500, and Fiscal Policy and Income Determination, *Quarterly Journal of Economics*, Vol. 56, August 1942, pp. 576–577.

[3] This idea seems to have been first suggested by Professor James W. Angell (*Investment and Business Cycles*, McGraw-Hill Book Co., p. 196, New York, 1941) and by the present writer (Review of Professor Schumpeter's Business Cycles, in the *Review of Economic Statistics*, Vol. 23, November 1941, p. 191. Both of us used the term "cumulative multiplier".

[4] This formula has been given by Professor Samuelson, *Fiscal Policy and Income Determination*, p. 578.

$$\frac{dY}{dI_0} = \frac{1}{1-(C'+I')},$$ (3)

provided $C'+I' < 1$.

An initial autonomous increment dC_0 in the rate of consumption implies an equal increase in the national income and leads, through induced investment and consumption, to further increments in income $(C'+I')dC_0$, $(C'+I')(C'+I')dC_0$, etc. Thus we have

$$dY = [1+(C'+I')+(C'+I')^2 \ldots]dC_0$$

and, if $|C'+I'| < 1$, the *compound consumption multiplier* is

$$\frac{dY}{dC_0} = \frac{1}{1-(C'+I')}.$$ (4)

In (3) and (4), dI_0 and dC_0 are the autonomous increments in investment or consumption, respectively. These multipliers measure the marginal effect of such an autonomous increment upon the national income and can thus be used for the problems mentioned in the preceding section, for which the simple multiplier formulae proved inadequate. Induced investment and consumption are not included in the multiplicands dI_0 and dC_0, but are taken care of by the multiplier formula.

The argument about the alleged negative effect of goverment spending upon national income can be stated correctly in the form of the statement that the multiplier is negative, if the multiplier in question is the compound multiplier (3) or (4). Such a multiplier can be negative, indeed, if the marginal propensity to invest is negative and outweighs the effect of the positive marginal propensity to consume. Such a situation, however, is incompatible with the stability condition of the system. In order that the multiplier be negative, we must have $1-(C'+I') < 0$, while the stability condition requires $1-(C'+I') > 0$. Thus only in unstable systems can the compound multiplier (3) or (4) be negative. In this case it cannot be finite either, because the convergence condition $|C'+I'| < 1$ is not satisfied in an unstable system.

From (3) and (4) we obtain

$$\frac{dY}{dI_0} \equiv \frac{dY}{dC_0},$$ (5)

i.e., the compound investment multiplier and the compound consumption multiplier are identical. Thus, any given autonomous increment in expenditure has exactly the same effect upon national income, irrespective of whether the expenditure is for investment or for consumption. The identity of the two multipliers suggests combining them into one simple multiplier expressing the marginal relationship between national income and expenditure. For this purpose we need only define $E' = E'(Y) \equiv C' + I'$ as the *marginal propensity to spend*, and (3) and (4) turn into

$$\frac{dY}{dE} = \frac{1}{1-E'}.$$ (6)

This may be called the *spending multiplier;*[5] dE is the autonomous increment in the rate of spending. The denominator $1 - E'$ is the marginal reluctance to spend (propensity to hoard[6]). The stability condition can be expressed in the form $1 - E' > 0$, i.e., that the reluctance to spend is an increasing function of national income.

A comparison of (6) with (1) and (2) gives the relation between the simple investment multiplier and the simple consumption multiplier on the one side and the spending multiplier (or the two compound multipliers) on the other side. The relation is

$$\frac{dY}{dI} = \frac{dY}{dE} \bigg/ \frac{dI}{dI_0}$$ (7)

and

$$\frac{dY}{dC} = \frac{dY}{dE} \bigg/ \frac{dC}{dC_0}.$$ (8)

The denominators are multipliers too, namely,

$$\frac{dI}{dI_0} = \frac{1-C'}{1-E'}$$ (9)

and

$$\frac{dC}{dC_0} = \frac{1-I'}{1-E'}.$$ (10)

----

[5] This is the "cumulative multiplier" of Professor Angell, who also has given the formula (6). Cf. *op. cit.*, p. 196.

[6] It may also be called the "marginal propensity to hoard", "hoarding" meaning the difference between planned receipts and planned expenditure. Since $1 - C' \equiv S'$, i.e. the marginal propensity to save (see footnote 1 above), we find that $1 - E' \equiv S' - I'$ i.e., the marginal reluctance to spend (propensity to hoard) is the difference between the marginal propensity to save and the marginal propensity to invest.

Formula (9) states that the marginal effect of autonomous investment upon the rate of investment in the economy is equal to the ratio of the marginal reluctance to consume (the marginal propensity to save) and the marginal reluctance to spend.[7] Formula (10) states that the marginal effect of an autonomous change in consumption upon the rate of consumption in the economy is equal to the ratio of the marginal reluctance to invest and the marginal reluctance to spend.

In order to evaluate the effect upon national income of any given autonomous change in spending, we can use either the spending multiplier (6), or any of the two simple multipliers (1) or (2). The use of the latter, however, requires a knowledge of the multipliers (9) or (10), which presupposes the same data as the spending multiplier.

Multipliers in Open Systems

In a closed system, the reluctance to spend (propensity to hoard) is the only leakage in the effect of an autonomous change in the rate of spending upon national income. In open systems other leakages exist; the cause of these is that part of the spending is done in such a way that it does not flow back to other income-receivers in the system. We shall call it *external spending* as distinguished from *internal spending*, which flows back to income-receivers within the system. External spending, however, may be offset by receipts of income-receivers in the system derived from external spending in other systems. Such receipts will be called *external receipts*. Two outstanding examples of open systems are (1) a country or region in trade relations with other countries or regions (international or inter-regional trade), and (2) the relation between a country's private economy and the government's Treasury. Another example might be the relation between the private sector and the socialized sector of a "mixed economy". We shall use the first two examples for the illustration of multipliers in open systems.

Denote by Y the aggregate income of the open system and by E, E_1, and E_2, the rate of total spending, internal spending, and external spending of the system, respectively. $E \equiv E_1 + E_2$. By hypothesis, $E_1 = E_1(Y)$ and $E_2 = E_2(Y)$. Denote further by R the rate of external

---

[7] Or, in other words, the ratio of the marginal propensity to save and the marginal propensity to hoard.

receipts of the system, and assume that $R = R(E_2)$, i.e., external receipts are a function of external spending. This function may be called the other systems' *propensity to spend back,* $Y \equiv E_1 + R$.

Let dE_1 be an autonomous increment in the rate of internal spending. The aggregate income of the system increases by dE_1 but of this, only $E_1' dE_1$ is spent within the system and leads to a further increase in the system's income. $E_2' dE_1$ is spent externally, but, of this $R' E_2' dE_1$ flows back to the system and contributes to an increase in the system's income. The initial increment dE_1 in the system's income thus leads to a further increase equal to $(E_1' + R' E_2') dE_1$. Out of this further increase, $E_1'(E_1' + R' E_2') dE_1$ is spent internally and $R' E_2'(E_1 + R' E_2') dE_2$ of the external expenditure flows back. Thus the system's income increases again by $(E_1' + R' E_2')^2 dE_1$, and so forth. The total increase in the system's income, therefore, is

$$dY = [1 + (E_1' + R' E_2') + (E_1' + R' E_2')^2 + \ldots] dE_1$$

and the *internal spending multiplier* is

$$\frac{dY}{dE_1} \equiv \frac{1}{1 - (E_1' + R' E_2')}, \tag{11}$$

provided $|E_1' + R' E_2'| < 1$.[8]

In the case of a country engaged in international trade, Y has to be interpreted as the country's national income, E_1' as the marginal propensity to spend for domestic goods, and E_2' as the *marginal propensity to import.*[9] R' is the other countries' marginal propensity to spend back. If the multiplier is applied to the relation between the private economy and the Treasury, Y can be interpreted as aggregate private income, E_1 as the private marginal propensity to spend (net of taxes and loans to the Treasury), and E_2' as the Treasury's *marginal propensity to tax* and borrow. R' is then the Treasury's marginal propensity to spend.

---

[8] The stability condition is in this case $E_1' + R' E_2' < 1$. If we accept $E_1' + R' E_2' > 0$ as a property empirically established, the convergence condition is satisfied for stable systems. It should be noted that the stability of an open system does not presuppose that the system shall be stable when isolated, i.e., that $E_1' + E_2' < 1$. If R' is sufficiently small the open system may be stable even though the aggregate marginal propensity to spend $E_1' + E_2' \geqq 1$. For a detailed treatment of this question see Lloyd A. Metzler, Underemployment Equilibrium in International Trade, *Econometrica*, Vol. 10, April 1942, pp. 102–103.

[9] This includes the propensity to buy foreign securities.

The multiplier (11) can also be written in the form

$$\frac{dY}{dE_1} = \frac{1}{1-[E'-(1-R')E_2']},$$ (12)

which shows clearly that the internal spending multiplier is the smaller the larger the marginal propensity to import or the marginal propensity to tax and borrow, and the larger the other countries', or the Treasury's, marginal reluctance to spend back, i.e., $1-R'$. It shows thus the income-reducing effect of imports and of taxation and government borrowing,[10] as well as the income-increasing effect of exports and of government spending. When $R' = 1$, formula (12) becomes identical with (6), i.e., with the simple spending multiplier of a closed system, while for $R' = 0$ it becomes

$$\frac{dY}{dE_1} \equiv \frac{1}{1-E'+E_2'},$$ (13)

in which form it is well known in the treatment of foreign trade problems.[11]

If, instead of an autonomous increment dE_1 in the rate of internal spending, we start with an autonomous increment dE in the rate of total spending, we find that the first increment in the system's income is $(E_1'+R'E_2')dE$, which is followed up by the increments $(E_1'+R'E_2')^2 dE$, $(E_1'+R'E_2')^3 dE$, etc. The total increase in the system's income is thus

$$dY = (E_1'+R'E_2')[1+(E_1+R'E_2')+(E_1'+R'E_2')+...]dE$$

---

[10] Imports, taxation, and borrowing have this effect only if $E_2'(Y) > 0$, i.e., if they are out of income. For imports, taxation, and borrowing which are out of wealth (i.e., stocks of goods or of money) $E_2'(Y) = 0$ and there is no income-reducing effect.

[11] The marginal propensity to import, or to tax and borrow, is taken here as a function of income, i.e., $E_2 = E_2(Y)$. If it is treated as a function of internal spending, i.e., $E_2 = E_2(E_1)$, we have $E_2'(Y) = E_2'(E_1)E_1'(Y)$ and (13) must be written in the form

$$\frac{dY}{dE_1} = \frac{1}{1-E'(1-E_2')},$$

where $E' = E'(Y)$ and $E_2' = E_2'(E_1)$. Cf., for instance, D. H. Robertson, Mr. Clark and the Foreign Trade Multiplier, *Economic Journal*, Vol. 48, 1939, pp. 354–356. See also G. Haberler, *Prosperity and Depression*, League of Nations, third edition, pp. 464–465, Geneva, 1941. In this form the formula is also used by Professor Samuelson for the study of the income-reducing effects of taxation (*Fiscal Policy and Income Determination*, p. 584).

and

$$\frac{dY}{dE} = \frac{E'_1 + R'E'_2}{1 - [E'_1 + R'E'_2]},$$ (14)

the convergence condition being taken as satisfied. This is the *total spending multiplier* of an open system. Comparing (14) with (11), we obtain

$$\frac{dY}{dE} = (E'_1 + R'E'_2)\frac{dY}{dE'_2},$$ (15)

i.e., the total spending multiplier is the internal spending multiplier times the sum of the marginal propensity to spend internally and the marginal inducement of other systems to spend back.

The effect of internal spending upon external spending can be calculated as follows. An autonomous increase dE_1 in the rate of external spending raises the system's income by dE_1 and leads to external spending $E'_2 dE_1$. The system's income, however, increases further by $(E'_1 + R'E'_2)dE_1$, which leads to new external spending $E'_2(E'_1 + R'E'_2)dE_1$. The system's income increases again, now by $(E'_1 + R'E'_2)^2 dE_1$, and external spending, in turn, increases by $E'_2(E'_1 + R'_2E'_2)^2 dE_1$, and so forth. The total increase in external spending is, consequently,

$$dE_2 = E'_2[1 + (E'_1 + R'E'_2) + (E'_1 + R'E'_2)^2 + \ldots]dE_1,$$

and, in view of (11) we obtain

$$\frac{dE_2}{dE_1} = E'_2\frac{dY}{dE_1}$$ (16)

In a similar way, we find that an autonomous increment dE of the rate of total spending causes an increase of external spending equal to

$$dE_2 = E'_2(E'_1 + R'E'_2)[1 + (E'_1 + R'E'_2) + (E'_1 + R'E'_2)^2 + \ldots]dE,$$

whence, on account of (14) we derive

$$\frac{dE_2}{dE} = E'_2\frac{dY}{dE}.$$ (17)

The multipliers (16) and (17) indicate the marginal effect upon the rate of external spending and, consequently, upon the external receipts of the systems to which the external spending is diverted. They may, therefore, be called the *inter-system* internal spending or total spending multiplier, respectively. Thus, for instance (16) or (17) measures the marginal effect of a change in a country's rate of (internal or total) spending upon its imports (and thus upon the external receipts of other countries).[12] Another application of (16) or (17) is the marginal effect of a change in private spending (net or gross of taxes and government loans) upon the receipts of the Treasury. The formulae (16) and (17) show that the inter-system multiplier is equal to the product of the marginal propensity to spend externally and the internal or total spending multiplier.

The effect of an autonomous increment in the rate of external receipts upon the system's income is the same as the effect of an increment of equal size in the rate of internal spending. Therefore, interpreting dE_1 as an autonomous increment in the rate of external receipts, we can use formula (11) to evaluate the marginal increase in the system's income.[13] The internal spending multiplier can thus be used also as an external receipts multiplier, e.g., as an export multiplier or government spending multiplier. With the same interpretation of dE_1, the inter-system multiplier (16) indicates the marginal effect of an increase in the system's rate of external receipts upon its external spending. The multiplier (16) may thus be used to study the marginal effect of a change in the rate of imports upon the country's foreign balance, or of a change in the rate of government spending upon the budget deficit (or surplus). As we see from the formula, this effect is equal to the internal spending multiplier times the marginal propensity to spend externally (i.e., times the marginal propensity to import, or times the marginal propensity to tax and borrow). An autonomous increase dE_1 in the rate of imports, or in the rate of government spending, increases, leaves unchanged, or diminishes, the foreign balance or the budget deficit,[14] according as $\frac{dE_2}{dE_1} \lessgtr 1$ or according as the reciprocal of the marginal propensity to import, or of the marginal propensity to tax and borrow, is greater than, equal to, or less than the internal spending multiplier.

---

[12] Formula (17) is used for the determination of the effect of investment upon imports by J. J. Polak, Balance of Payments Problems of Countries Reconstructing with the Help of Foreign Loans, *Quarterly Journal of Economics*, Vol. 57, February 1943, p. 233.

[13] Such use of (11) as well as of other more complicated formulae is made by Professor Machlup in his book *International Trade and the National Income Multiplier*, The Blakiston Co., Philadelphia, 1943, which appeared after the present article was written.

[14] A surplus can be considered as a negative deficit.

An interesting case arises when a mechanism or a policy exists that tends to equalize changes in external spending and in external receipts of the system, as, for instance, in international trade in the absence of capital movements, or under a fiscal policy which maintains a constant budget deficit or surplus (a policy which maintains a balanced budget is a special case of it). In this case, $\frac{dE_1}{dE_2} = 1$ and the formula (16) becomes

$$\frac{dY}{dE_1} = \frac{1}{E_2'}. \tag{18}$$

Applied to international trade, this is Roy F. Harrod's multiplier which expresses the effect of a change in the rate of exports upon the country's income and which is equal to the reciprocal of the marginal propensity to import.[15] The multiplier (18) may also be used to estimate the marginal effect of government expenditure upon private income under a fiscal policy of maintaining a constant budget deficit or surplus (including, as a special case, a policy of a balanced budget). This effect is the reciprocal of the marginal propensity to tax and to borrow out of income[16] and is *independent of the size of the deficit or surplus.*

Dynamic Multipliers[17]

The multipliers treated in the preceding section are all static. The marginal effect expressed by the multiplier formulae does not refer to any specific moment or period of time, it is undated. The multiplier formulae give a comparison of the values the dependent variable has in two equilibrium positions of the system, differing in the values of the independent variable. Nothing is said about the time it takes to pass from one equilibrium position to another, nor about the path of the transition. The procedure is merely one of comparative statics. But whether we recognize it in our formulae or not, the effect of a change of one economic variable upon the value of another does operate in time. If this fact is taken into consideration explicitly, multiplier formulae

---

[15] See *International Economics*, Cambridge University Press, pp. 122–123, New Edition, 1939.

[16] It is not influenced by taxation and borrowing out of wealth.

[17] I am indebted to Professors Abraham Wald, Paul A. Samuelson, and Harold T. Davis for valuable suggestions concerning this and the following parts of the article.

can be obtained which measure the effect produced at any given moment of time as well as the final limit which the effect tends to approach. The effects produced at successive moments of time are the path by which the system reaches equilibrium. The multipliers which measure the effects in time and the limit these effects tend to approach will be called *dynamic multipliers*.[18] For the sake of brevity, our exposition will be confined to the examination of the dynamic spending multiplier. But the same, or similar, formulae can be applied for setting up dynamic counterparts to all the other multipliers discussed in the present article.

Suppose that the rate of spending responds to a change in the national income with a simple time lag equal to one unit of time. Let us denote by α the dynamic marginal propensity to spend, i.e., the marginal effect of a change in (the flow of) income at any moment of time upon the rate of spending one unit of time later. We have $\alpha = \frac{dE/t}{dY(t-1)}$. An autonomous permanent increment $dE(0)$ in the rate of spending, starting at the moment $t = 0$, produces, at the moment $t = n$, where n is an integer, an increase in the flow of income equal to

$$dY(n) = (1 + \alpha + \alpha^2 + \ ... \ + \alpha^n)\,dE(0)$$

whence

$$\frac{dY(n)}{dE(0)} \equiv \frac{1 - \alpha^{n+1}}{1 - \alpha} \ (n \text{ integer}). \tag{19}$$

The left-hand side of this expression will be called the *truncated*[19] *dynamic multiplier* corresponding to the period of adjustment n. It measures the marginal effect of a change in the rate of spending upon the flow of national income n units of time hence. The *dynamic multiplier* will be defined as

$$\frac{dY}{dE(0)} = \lim_{n \to \infty} \frac{dY(n)}{dE(0)}, \tag{20}$$

---

[18] Professor J. M. Clark's multipliers are, unlike those of Mr. Kahn and Mr. Keynes, dynamic. See *Economic Planning of Public Works*, U.S. Government Publication, pp. 85–96, Washington, D.C., 1935. The dynamic investment multiplier has been discussed also by Professor Fritz Machlup, Period Analysis and Multiplier Theory, *Quarterly Journal of Economics*, Vol. 54, pp. 11 ff, November 1939.

[19] This term is due to Professor Samuelson. Cf. his article A Fundamental Multiplier Identity, in Vol. 10, April, 1942, pp. 221–226, *Econometrica*.

and measures the final marginal effect of a change in the rate of spending. It is finite if $|\alpha| < 1$ and its value is, in this case,

$$\frac{dY}{dE(0)} \equiv \frac{1}{1-\alpha}. \tag{21}$$

In order to simplify the notation let us write $y(t) = dY(t)$ and $e(t) = dE(t)$. The truncated dynamic multiplier (19) can then be interpreted as a special solution of the difference equation

$$y(t) = \alpha y(t-1) + e(t) \quad (t \text{ integer}). \tag{22}$$

This equation expresses the marginal increment in income at any moment of time as the additive result of (a) an induced increase in income caused by the increase in income $y(t-1)$ which took place one unit of time back, and (b) a simultaneous autonomous increase in spending $e(t)$. The solution of (22) can be obtained by superposition from solutions of the reduced equation

$$y(t) = \alpha y(t-1).$$

The special solution of the latter, corresponding to the initial condition $y(s) = e(s)$, is

$$y_s(t) = \alpha^{t-s} e(s) \quad (s \text{ and } t \text{ integer}). \tag{23}$$

An initial *single* increase in spending $e(s)$ taking place at the moment s produces at the moment $t(t \geq s)$ an increase in income indicated by (23). A set of autonomous increments in spending $e(0), e(1), ..., e(n)$, taking place at the moments $0, 1, ..., n$, respectively, produces thus at the moment $t = n$ an increase in the flow of income equal to

$$y(n) = \sum_{s=0}^{n} \alpha^{n-s} e(s). \tag{24}$$

This is the desired solution of (22). If the autonomous increase in spending is constant, i.e., $e(0) = e(1) = ... = e(n)$, the solution obtained can be written as

$$y(n) = e(0) \sum_{t=0}^{n} \alpha^t. \tag{25}$$

If we put $e(0) = 1$, $y(n)$ becomes the truncated dynamic multiplier.

Suppose now that the rate of spending responds to a change in income with a distributed time-lag equal to $1, 2, ..., k$ units of time. Denote the marginal propensities to spend corresponding to the distri-

buted time-lag by $\alpha_1, \alpha_2, ..., \alpha_k$, respectively. For instance, α_1 is the
marginal effect of a change in income upon the rate of spending i units
of time hence (i is a positive integer). A change in income at the moment
t is made up of the induced change resulting from changes in income at
moment $t-1, t-2, ..., t-k$, and of an autonomous rate of spending
at the moment t. This relation is described by the difference equation

$$y(t) = \alpha_1 y(t-1) + \alpha_2 y(t-2) + \ ... \ + \alpha_k(t-k) + e(t). \tag{26}$$

The characteristic equation of this difference equation is

$$\lambda^k - \alpha_1 \lambda^{k-1} - \alpha_2 \lambda^{k-2} - ... - \alpha_k = 0. \tag{27}$$

Let $\lambda_1, \lambda_2, ..., \lambda_r$ be the r different roots of (27) ($r \leq k$) with multiplici-
ties $v_1, v_2, ..., v_r$, respectively

$$(v_1 + v_2 + ... + v_r = k).$$

The particular solutions of the reduced equation are then of the form

$$\lambda_i^t, t\lambda_i^t, ..., t^{v_i-1}\lambda_i^t \quad (i = 1, 2, ... r), \tag{28}$$

and the general solution of the reduced equation is

$$\sum_{i=1}^{r} q_i(t)\lambda_i^t \quad (t \text{ positive integer}),$$

where the $q_i(t)$ are polynomials of degree v_i-1. Since only integer values
of t are considered here, the coefficients of the polynomials are constant.
Consider the initial conditions $y(s) = e(s)$,

$$y(s-1) = y(s-2) \ ... \ = y(s-k+1) = 0.$$

These conditions allow us to set up the k equations

$$\sum_{i=1}^{r} q_i(0) = e(s),$$

$$\sum_{i=1}^{r} q_i(t-s)\lambda_i^{t-s} = 0 \quad (t = s-1, s-2, ..., s-k+1), \tag{29}$$

which are linear in the coefficients (k in number) of the polynomials
$q_i(t-s)$ and which serve to determine the values of these coefficients.[20]
Inspecting (29) we see that these values can be expressed as products of

---

[20] Since (28) is a fundamental system of solutions, the solving matrix of (29) is
non-singular.

$e(s)$.[21] Taking this into account, we shall denote the polynomials with the values of their coefficients as determined from (29) by $\bar{q}_1(t-s)e(s)$. The special solution of the reduced equation conforming to the initial conditions is thus

$$y_s(t) = \sum_{i=1}^{r} \bar{q}_i(t-s)\lambda_i^{t-s}e(s) \qquad (t \text{ and } s \text{ integer}). \tag{30}$$

It indicates the effect of a single increase in spending at the moment s upon the income at the moment $t(t \geq s)$.

The effect of a set of autonomous increments in spending $e(0), e(1), \ldots, e(n)$ taking place at the moments $0, 1, \ldots, n$, respectively, upon the income at the moment $t = n$ (where $n \geq k$) is obtained from (30) by superposition. It is

$$y(n) = \sum_{s=0}^{n} \sum_{i=1}^{r} \bar{q}_i(n-s)\lambda_i^{n-s}e(s). \tag{31}$$

This is a solution of the complete equation (26). If $e(0) = e(1) = \ldots e(m)$, i.e., if the autonomous increase in the rate of spending is constant, (31) can be written as

$$y(n) = e(0) \sum_{t=0}^{n} \sum_{i=1}^{r} \bar{q}_i(t)\lambda_i^t. \tag{32}$$

If we put $e(0) = 1$, we find that $y(n)$ is the value of the truncated dynamic multiplier, i.e.,

$$\frac{dY(n)}{dE(0)} \equiv \sum_{i=1}^{r} \sum_{t=0}^{n} \bar{q}_i(t)\lambda_i^t \tag{33}$$

and that the value of the dynamic multiplier is

$$\frac{dY}{dE(0)} \equiv \sum_{i=1}^{r} \sum_{t=0}^{\infty} \bar{q}_i(t)\lambda_i^t. \tag{34}$$

The inner sum in (34) is a power series and the dynamic multiplier is finite when this series converges. The coefficients $\bar{q}_i(t)$ of the power series being polynomials, we find[22]

$$\lim_{n \to \infty} \frac{q_i(t)}{q_i(t+1)} = 1 \qquad (i = 1, 2, \ldots, r).$$

---

[21] The determinant in the numerator of the solutions can be written as a product of $e(s)$ and the corresponding cofactor.

[22] This follows immediately by repeated application of de l'Hopital's rule.

The power series converges when[23]

$$|\lambda_i| < 1 \quad (i = 1, 2, ..., r). \tag{35}$$

Thus the condition for a finite multiplier reduces to the well-known problem that the absolute values of the roots of a polynomial be less than unity.[24] If the α's are assumed to be not negative, it can be shown[25] that this condition is verified when and only when

$$\sum_{i=1}^{k} \alpha_i < 1. \tag{36}$$

---

[23] For real roots $|\lambda_i|$ is the absolute value, for complex roots the modulus of the root.

[24] Cf. Paul. A. Samuelson, Conditions that the Roots of a Polynomial be less than Unity in Absolute Value, *The Annals of Mathematical Statistics*, Vol. 12, September 1941, pp. 360–364.

[25] The necessity of (36) is established in the following way. Suppose $\sum_{i=1}^{k} \alpha_i = 1$. In this case the characteristic equation

$$F(\lambda) = \lambda^k - \sum_{i=1}^{k} \alpha_i \lambda^{k-i} = 0$$

has a root $\lambda = 1$. If $\sum_{i=1}^{k} \alpha_i > 1$ then $F(1) < 0$. But $F(\lambda)$ is a continuous function of λ with $\lim_{\lambda = \infty} F(\lambda) = +\infty$. Thus there exists a root $\lambda > 1$. In order to establish the sufficiency of (36) write $\lambda = re^{\sqrt{-1}z}$. We have

$$r^k e^{\sqrt{-1}kz} = \sum_{i=1}^{k} \alpha_i r^{k-i} e^{\sqrt{-1}(k-i)z},$$

whence

$$r^k = \left| \sum_{i=1}^{k} \alpha_i r^{k-i} e^{\sqrt{-1}(k-i)z} \right| \leq \sum_{i=1}^{k} \alpha_i \left| r^{k-i} e^{\sqrt{-1}(k-i)z} \right|.$$

Supposing $r \geq 1$, we get

$$r^k \leq r^{k-1} \sum_{i=1}^{k} \alpha_i < r^{k-1}$$

which contradicts the supposition. Consequently, $r = |\lambda| < 1$. This is an adaptation of the proof given by A. Smithies, The Stability of Competitive Equilibrium, *Econometrica*, Vol. 10, July–October 1942, p. 269.

Continuous Dynamic Multipliers

When the time-lag of the response of the rate of spending to a change in income is distributed continuously over the closed interval of time $[0, k]$ the marginal propensity to spend after τ units of time (counting from the change in income) is $\alpha(\tau)$ a continuous function of time. Instead of the difference equation (26) we obtain the integral equation

$$y(t) = e(t) + \int_0^k y(t-\tau)\alpha(\tau)d\tau \quad (t \text{ and } \tau \text{ real}). \quad (37)$$

This is the well-known equation of hereditary phenomena.[26] By a suitable change of variables it can be transformed into the integral equation of the "closed cycle", which is readily solved.[27] For our purpose, however, it is most instructive to consider a procedure of solving analogous to that which we have adopted in solving the difference equation (26).

Consider the reduced equation

$$y(t) = \int_0^k y(t-\tau)\alpha(\tau)d\tau.$$

By means of trial substitution we find that this equation has the particular solutions (fundamental functions)

$$e^{\mu_1 t}, e^{\mu_2 t}, \dots,$$

where the μ's are simple roots of the characteristic equation

$$f(\mu) = \int_0^k e^{-\mu\tau}\alpha(\tau)d\tau = 1. \quad (38)$$

If multiple roots occur, the particular solutions are

$$e^{\mu_i t}, te^{\mu_i t}, \dots, t^{\nu_i - 1}e^{\mu_i t} \quad (i = 1, 2, \dots), \quad (39)$$

ν_i being the multiplicity of the root μ_i.[28] The roots of the characteristic

---

[26] Cf. Vito Volterra, *Leçons sur la théorie mathématique de la lutte pour la vie*, Gauthier-Villars, pp. 148 ff, Paris, 1931.

[27] Cf. Harold T. Devis, *The Theory of Linear Operators*, The Principia Press, p. 484, Bloomington, Indiana, 1936.

[28] The root μ_i of the transcendental equation $f(\mu) = 1$ is *defined* as being of multiplicity ν_i if $f'(\mu_i) = f''(\mu_i) = \dots f^{(\nu_i - 1)}(\mu_i) = 0$ and $f^{(\nu_i)}(\mu_i) \neq 0$. We have

equation form an enumerable set. As a rule there is an infinite number of distinct roots.[29] The general solution of the reduced equation is, therefore, given by the infinite series

$$\sum_{i=1}^{\infty} q_i(t)e^{\mu_i t},\qquad(40)$$

where the $q_i(t)$ are polynomials of degree v_i-1. We shall assume that $\alpha(\tau)$ is such that this series converges uniformly.[30]

The values of the coefficients of the polynomials are determined by the initial conditions $y(s) = e(s)$ and $y(t) = 0$ for $s-k \leq t < s$. Let us write the polynomials with coefficients thus determined in the form $\bar{q}_i(t)$ $-s)e(s)$. The special solution of the reduced equation conforming to the initial conditions is then

$$y_s(t) = \sum_{i=1}^{\infty} \bar{q}_i(t-s)\lambda_i^{t-s}e(s),\qquad(41)$$

where $\lambda_i = e^{\mu_i}$. This solution gives the effect of a momentary increase in spending at the moment s upon the income at the moment $t(t \geq s)$.

$$f^{(n)}(\mu) = (-1)^n \int_0^k \tau^n e^{-\mu\tau}\alpha(\tau)\,d\tau.$$

By virtue of this relation we can verify by substitution that (39) are solutions of the reduced equation.

[29] The roots form an enumerable set because $f(\mu)$ is an entire analytic function not constant. At $\mu = \infty$ this function has an essential singularity. According to Picard's theorem the equation $f(\mu) = c$ has then an infinite number of roots in the neighbourhood of $\mu = \infty$ except for at most one single value of c. Unless $c = 1$ this is the exceptional value, the characteristic equation has an infinite number of roots. In the special case, in which $c = 1$ turns out to be the exceptional value, there are no roots in the neighbourhood of $\mu = \infty$. All the roots are then contained in some bounded region and their number must be finite. In this special case the series (40) becomes finite.

[30] The present writer has been unable to ascertain the exact conditions which $\alpha(r)$ must satisfy in order to ensure the convergence of this series. For any given value of t the $q_i(t)$ in (40) reduce to constants and all their partial sums are bounded. The series thus converges (by Dirichlet's test) absolutely if the real parts of the roots μ_i can be ordered in a monotone sequence $R(\mu_i) \to -\infty$. For in this case $\left|e^{\mu_i t}\right| = e^{R(\mu_i)t} \to 0$ monotonically for any $t > 0$. Since the absolute convergence, if established, holds for any $t > 0$ it can be shown to be uniform. In the exceptional case in which the number of roots is finite, the convergence is, of course, trivial.

The effect of a continuous increase in spending, following the time pattern $e(t)$, upon the income at the moment $t = n(n \geq k)$ is given by superposition of the results (41). It is

$$y(n) = \int_0^n \sum_{i=1}^\infty \bar{q}_i(n-s)\lambda_i^{n-s}e(s)ds. \qquad (42)$$

If $e(s) = e(0)$ for $0 \leq s \leq n$, this reduces to

$$y(n) = e(0)\int_0^n \sum_{i=1}^\infty \bar{q}_i(t)\lambda_i^t dt. \qquad (43)$$

When $e(0) = 1$, $y(n)$ is the value of the truncated dynamic multiplier

$$\frac{dY(n)}{dE(0)} \equiv \int_0^n \sum_{i=1}^\infty \bar{q}_i(t)\lambda_i^t dt \qquad (44)$$

and the value of the dynamic multiplier is

$$\frac{dY}{dE(0)} \equiv \int_0^\infty \sum_{i=1}^\infty \bar{q}_i(t)\lambda_i^t dt. \qquad (45)$$

If integrated by terms, (45) can be written in the form

$$\sum_{i=1}^\infty \int_0^\infty \bar{q}_i(t)\lambda_i dt.$$

This expression is finite when the integral converges. Since $\bar{q}_i(t)$ is a polynomial, this happens when

$$|\lambda_i| < 1. \quad (i = 1, 2, ...). \qquad (46)$$

It can be shown[31] that, if $\alpha(\tau)$ is not negative (as we assume to be the case), the necessary and sufficient condition for this inequality to hold is

$$\int_0^k \alpha(\tau)d\tau < 1. \qquad (47)$$

---

[31] The proof is similar to that in the finite case given in footnote 25 above, integration being substituted for summation.

Cumulated Multipliers

The dynamic multipliers discussed measure the effect of a permanent change in the rate of spending upon the flow of national income some (finite or infinite) time hence. They measure the effect of a permanent change of one rate of flow upon another rate of flow and may be designated as *horizontal*[32] multipliers. In addition to these, we have *cumulated*[32] multipliers, which measure the sum, over any period of time, of all the marginal increments of income generated by a *single dose* of additional spending made in the first interval of time.

A single dose of spending, extending over the interval of time $[0, 1]$ or $\Delta t \to 0$ respectively, at the rate $e(0)$ per unit of time, produces in the tth unit of time an increment in income as indicated by (30) or (41), respectively, i.e.,

$$y_0(t) = e(0) \sum_{i=1}^{\tau} \overline{q}_i(t)\lambda_i^t, \quad \text{or} \quad y_0(t) = e(0) \sum_{i=1}^{\infty} \overline{q}_i(t)\lambda_i \Delta t. \quad (48)$$

The sum of all these increments over the period $[0, n]$ is

$$e(0) \sum_{t=0}^{n} \sum_{i=1}^{\tau} \overline{q}_i(t)\lambda_i^t, \quad \text{or} \quad e(0) \int_0^n \sum_{i=1}^{\infty} \overline{q}_i(t)\lambda_i^t dt. \quad (49)$$

If we set $e(0) = 1$, this expression gives the value of the cumulated truncated multiplier. But (49) is identical with (32) or (43). Thus, the cumulated truncated multiplier equals identically the horizontal truncated multiplier. Consequently, the cumulated multiplier, too, is identically equal to the horizontal multiplier.[33]

---

[32] These terms are due to Professor Samuelson. Cf. A Fundamental Multiplier Identity, in *Econometrica*, Vol. 10, April 1942.

[33] The identity of the cumulated and horizontal multipliers (as well as of the corresponding truncated multipliers) has been proved by Professor Samuelson, *A Fundamental Multiplier Identity*, pp. 222–3. In the case of a simple time-lag it was known already to Professor Clark. See *op. cit.*, pp. 90–1. Cf. also Haberler, *op. cit.*, p. 458.

THEORETICAL DERIVATION OF ELASTICITIES OF DEMAND AND SUPPLY: THE DIRECT METHOD

The Purpose of this Paper

The usual method of deriving theoretically the elasticities of demand and supply consists in finding first the partial derivatives. These are subsequently multiplied by the ratio of the independent to the dependent variable and the elasticity is obtained. Thus, in order to arrive at the elasticity of the quantity x_s, with respect to the price p_r, the derivative $\frac{\partial x_s}{\partial p_r}$ is found and multiplied by $\frac{p_r}{x_s}$. The result is the elasticity $\frac{Ex_s}{Ep_r}$ $= \left(\frac{\partial x_s}{\partial p_r}\right)\left(\frac{\partial p_r}{x_s}\right)$. The results appear in rather complicated and awkward algebraic form and the expression obtained is simplified by means of the concept of the partial elasticity of substitution (usually denoted by σ_{rs}). This concept too is represented by a rather complicated algebraic expression. The whole procedure, however, can be shortened considerably and the results put in a much simpler and more elegant form by a direct method of derivation which makes use of the algorithm of the calculus of elasticities.[1] This is the purpose of the present paper.

The Elasticity of Demand for a Factor of Production

Consider a firm under conditions of atomistic competition. The production function is $x = f(a_1, a_2, ..., a_n)$, where x is the output and the a's are the quantities of the different factors used. Let p be the price of the product and p_r the price of the rth factor. Further, write $f_r = \frac{\partial x}{\partial a_r}$.

---

[1] The fundamental theorems of this calculus were given first by Ragnar Frisch in an appendix to his article, Méthodes nouvelles pour mésurer l'utilité marginale, *Révue d'Economie Politique*, 1932, pp. 20–22. A statement of them is found in R. G. D. Allen, *Mathematical Analysis for Economists*, Macmillan Company, London, pp. 252–254, 1938.

The first-order maximum conditions (of profit) are given by the n equations

$$pf_s = p_s \quad (s = 1, 2, ..., n). \tag{2.1}$$

From these equations we derive the equivalent set

$$\log(pf_s) = \log p_s \quad (s = 1, 2, ..., n). \tag{2.2}$$

The left-hand side of each of these equations can be considered as a function of the logarithms of the a's. The logarithms of the a's are, in turn, functions of the logarithms of the prices $p_r(r = 1, 2, ..., n)$, because the a's are functions of the prices by virtue of the demand functions derived from (2.1).

We differentiate the equations (2.2) partially with respect to $\log p_r$, taking into account two theorems of the calculus of elasticities.[2] One theorem is that the elasticity of a function is the product of the two elasticities $\left[\text{thus, e.g., } \frac{Ey}{Ex} = \left(\frac{Ey}{Eu}\right)\left(\frac{Eu}{Ex}\right) \text{ when } y = y(u) \text{ and } u = u(x)\right]$. The other theorem is that a multiplicative constant can be left out of an elasticity (i.e., $\frac{E\alpha y}{Ex} = \frac{Ey}{Ex}$ when $\alpha = \text{const.}$). We obtain, therefore,

$$\frac{Ef_1}{Ea_1} \times \frac{Ea_1}{Ep_r} + \frac{Ef_1}{Ea_2} \times \frac{Ea_2}{Ep_r} + \cdots + \frac{Ef_1}{Ea_n} \times \frac{Ea_n}{Ep_r} = 0,$$

$$\cdots \cdots \cdots$$

$$\frac{Ef_r}{Ea_1} \times \frac{Ea_1}{Ep_r} + \frac{Ef_r}{Ea_2} \times \frac{Ea_2}{Ep_r} + \cdots + \frac{Ef_r}{Ea_n} \times \frac{Ea_n}{Ep_r} = 1, \tag{2.3}$$

$$\cdots \cdots \cdots$$

$$\frac{Ef_n}{Ea_1} \times \frac{Ea_1}{Ep_r} + \frac{Ef_n}{Ea_2} \times \frac{Ea_2}{Ep_r} + \cdots + \frac{Ef_n}{Ea_n} \times \frac{Ea_n}{Ep_r} = 0.$$

Solving these equations we obtain immediately

$$\frac{Ea_s}{Ep_r} = \frac{D_{rs}}{D} \quad (r \text{ and } s = 1, 2, ..., n), \tag{2.4}$$

where

$$D = \begin{vmatrix} \dfrac{Ef_1}{Ea_1} & \dfrac{Ef_1}{Ea_2} & \cdots & \dfrac{Ef_1}{Ea_n} \\[2ex] \dfrac{Ef_2}{Ea_1} & \dfrac{Ef_2}{Ea_2} & \cdots & \dfrac{Ef_2}{Ea_n} \\[2ex] \cdots & \cdots & \cdots & \cdots \\[2ex] \dfrac{Ef_n}{Ea_1} & \dfrac{Ef_n}{Ea_2} & \cdots & \dfrac{Ef_n}{Ea_n} \end{vmatrix} \tag{2.5}$$

---

[2] Cf. R. G. D. Allen, *Mathematical Analysis for Economists*, p. 253.

and D_{rs} is the cofactor of the element $\dfrac{Ef_r}{Ea_s}$ in D. The elements of the determinant D are the partial elasticities of the marginal productivities of the different factors. It should be noticed that D is *not* symmetric and hence $D_{sr} \neq D_{rs}$.

The formula (2.4) is extremely simple and is quite similar to the expression obtained for the partial derivative. The latter is[3]

$$\frac{\partial a_s}{\partial p_r} = \frac{1}{p} \times \frac{F_{rs}}{F}$$

where

$$F = \begin{vmatrix} f_{11} & f_{12} \cdots f_{1n} \\ f_{21} & f_{22} \cdots f_{2n} \\ \cdot & \cdot \quad \cdot \quad \cdot \\ f_{n1} & f_{n2} \cdots f_{nn} \end{vmatrix}$$

and F_{rs} is the cofactor of f_{rs} in F (the notation $f_{rs} = \dfrac{\partial f_r}{\partial a_s}$ is used here). The determinant in the partial, derivative formula contains the (partial) derivatives of the marginal productivities. The elasticity formula is even simpler than the formula for the partial derivative, the factor $1/p$ being absent in the former.

By the usual indirect method we obtain[4]

$$\frac{Ea_s}{Ep_r} = k_r \sigma_{rs} \tag{2.6}$$

---

[3] See H. v. Stackelberg, *Angebot und Nachfrage in der Produktionswirtschaft*, Archiv für mathematische Wirtschafts- und Sozialforschung, Bd. IV, Heft 2, p. 87, 1938; and Jacob Mosak, Inter-relations of Production, Price and Derived Demand, *Journal of Political Economy*, December 1938.

[4] We have

$$\frac{Ea_s}{Ep_r} = \frac{\partial a_s}{\partial p_r} \times \frac{p_r}{a_s} = \frac{p_r}{a_s p} \times \frac{F_{rs}}{F}.$$

Multiplying and dividing the last term by $a_r \sum_{s=1}^{n} p_s a_s$ we obtain

$$\frac{Ea_s}{Ep_r} = \frac{p_r a_r}{\sum_{s=1}^{n} p_s a_s} \times \frac{\sum_{s=1}^{n} p_s a_s}{a_r a_s p} \times \frac{F_{rs}}{F}.$$

where

$$k = \frac{p_r a_r}{\sum\limits_{s=1}^{n} p_r a_r}$$

and

$$\sigma_{rs} = \frac{\sum\limits_{s=1}^{n} f_s a_s}{a_r a_s} \times \frac{F_{rs}}{F}$$

(the partial elasticity of substitution).

Confronting (2.6) and (2.4) we obtain

$$\sigma_{rs} = \frac{1}{k_r} \times \frac{D_{rs}}{D} \tag{2.7}$$

as an expression for the partial elasticity of substitution.

The Elasticity of Supply of a Product

In order to obtain the elasticity of supply of x we rewrite the equations (2.2) in the form

$$\log f_s = \log p_s - \log p \qquad (s = 1, 2, ..., n). \tag{3.1}$$

Differentiating partially with respect to $\log p$ we get

$$\frac{Ef_1}{Ea_1} \times \frac{Ea_1}{Ep} + \frac{Ef_1}{Ea_2} \times \frac{Ea_2}{Ep} + \cdots + \frac{Ef_1}{Ea_n} \times \frac{Ea_n}{Ep} = -1$$

$$\frac{Ef_2}{Ea_1} \times \frac{Ea_1}{Ep} + \frac{Ef_2}{Ea_2} \times \frac{Ea_2}{Ep} + \cdots + \frac{Ef_2}{Ea_n} \times \frac{Ea_n}{Ep} = -1 \tag{3.2}$$

$$\cdots \cdots \cdots \cdots \cdots$$

$$\frac{Ef_n}{Ea_1} \times \frac{Ea_1}{Ep} + \frac{Ef_n}{Ea_2} \times \frac{Ea_2}{Ep} + \cdots + \frac{Ef_n}{Ea_n} \times \frac{Ea_n}{Ep} = -1.$$

By virtue of (2.1) $p_s = f_s p$. Hence

$$\frac{Ea_s}{Ep_r} = -\frac{p_r a_r}{\sum\limits_{s=1}^{n} p_s a_s} \times \frac{\sum\limits_{s=1}^{n} f_s a_s}{a_r a_s} \times \frac{F_{rs}}{F}.$$

This reduces to (2.6) by the substitution of the symbols k_r and σ_{rs} as defined in the text.

Solving, we have

$$\frac{Ea_s}{Ep} = \frac{1}{D} \begin{vmatrix} \dfrac{Ef_1}{Ea_1} & \cdots & -1 & \cdots & \dfrac{Ef_1}{Ea_n} \\[2mm] \dfrac{Ef_2}{Ea_1} & \cdots & -1 & \cdots & \dfrac{Ef_2}{Ea_n} \\[2mm] \cdot & \cdot & \cdot & \cdot & \cdot \\[2mm] \dfrac{Ef_n}{Ea_1} & \cdots & -1 & \cdots & \dfrac{Ef_n}{Ea_n} \end{vmatrix}.$$

Expanding the last determinant according to the column with the elements -1 (which is the sth column) we arrive at

$$\frac{Ea_s}{Ep} = -\frac{\sum\limits_{r=1}^{n} D_{rs}}{D} \tag{3.3}$$

or, on account of (2.4),

$$\frac{Ea_s}{Ep} = -\sum_{r=1}^{n} \frac{Ea_s}{Ep_r} \quad (s = 1, 2, \ldots, n). \tag{3.4}$$

This is the partial elasticity of demand for a factor with respect to the price of the product.

We have $x = f(a_1, a_2, \ldots, a_n)$. Thus the partial elasticity of supply of the product is obtained by

$$\frac{Ex}{Ep} = \sum_{s=1}^{n} \frac{Ex}{Ea_s} \times \frac{D_{rs}}{D}. \tag{3.5}$$

On account of (3.3) this can be written

$$\frac{Ex}{Ep} = -\frac{1}{p} \sum_{r=1}^{n} \sum_{s=1}^{n} \frac{Ex}{Ea_s} \times \frac{D_{rs}}{D}. \tag{3.6}$$

$\frac{Ex}{Ea_s}$ is the partial elasticity of the production function.

The last formula is similar to that for the partial derivative of the product with respect to its price, i.e.,[5]

$$\frac{\partial x}{\partial p} = -\frac{1}{p} \sum_{r=1}^{n} \sum_{s=1}^{n} f_r f_s \frac{F_{rs}}{F}.$$

[5] H. v. Stackelberg, *op. cit.*, p. 88.

Elasticities of Demand and Supply in Joint Production

In the theory of joint production which, incidentally, includes as a special case that of a one-product firm treated above, it is most convenient to use a transformation function. Using the same symbols $x_r (r = 1, 2, ..., N)$ for both factors and products, the transformation function will be written

$$\Phi(x_1, x_2, ..., x_N) = \text{constant.} \tag{4.1}$$

Products are considered to be positive and factors to be negative. We denote $\Phi_r = \frac{\partial \Phi}{\partial x_r}$. The first-order maximum conditions are given, jointly with (4.1), by the equations

$$\mu \Phi_s = p_s \quad (s = 1, 2, ..., N), \tag{4.2}$$

where μ is a Lagrange multiplier.

Write for (4.1) and (4.2) the equivalent set of equations

$$\begin{cases} \log \Phi(\log x_1, \log x_2, ..., \log x_N) = \text{constant,} \\ \log \mu + \log \Phi_s = \log p_s \quad (s = 1, 2, ..., N). \end{cases} \tag{4.3}$$

Differentiating partially with respect to $\log p_r$ we have

$$\frac{E\Phi}{Ex_1} \times \frac{Ex_1}{Ep_r} + \frac{E\Phi}{Ex_2} \times \frac{Ex_2}{Ep_r} + \ ... \ + \frac{E\Phi}{Ex_N} \times \frac{Ex_N}{Ep_r} = 0,$$

$$\frac{E\mu}{Ep_r} + \frac{E\Phi_1}{Ex_1} \times \frac{Ex_1}{Ep_r} + \frac{E\Phi_1}{Ex_2} \times \frac{Ex_2}{Ep_r} + \ ... \ + \frac{E\Phi_1}{Ex_N} \times \frac{Ex_N}{Ep_r} = 0,$$

$$\cdot \ \cdot \ \cdot \ \cdot \ \cdot \ \cdot \ \cdot \ \cdot \ \cdot \ \cdot \ \cdot \ \cdot \ \cdot \ \cdot \ \cdot \ \cdot \ \cdot \ \cdot \ \cdot \tag{4.4}$$

$$\frac{E\mu}{Ep_r} + \frac{E\Phi_r}{Ex_1} \times \frac{Ex_1}{Ep_r} + \frac{E\Phi_r}{Ex_2} \times \frac{Ex_2}{Ep_r} + \ ... \ + \frac{E\Phi_r}{Ex_N} \times \frac{Ex_N}{Ep_r} = 1,$$

$$\frac{E\mu}{Ep_r} + \frac{E\Phi_N}{Ex_1} \times \frac{Ex_1}{Ep_r} + \frac{E\Phi_N}{Ex_2} \times \frac{Ex_2}{Ep_r} + \ ... \ + \frac{E\Phi_N}{Ex_N} \times \frac{Ex_N}{Ep_r} = 0.$$

Solving, we have

$$\frac{Ex_s}{Ep_r} = \frac{\Delta_{rs}}{\Delta} \quad (r \text{ and } s = 1, 2, ..., N), \tag{4.5}$$

where

$$\Delta = \begin{vmatrix} 0 & \dfrac{E\Phi}{Ex_1} & \dfrac{E\Phi}{Ex_2} & \cdots & \dfrac{E\Phi}{Ex_N} \\[2ex] 1 & \dfrac{E\Phi_1}{Ex_1} & \dfrac{E\Phi_1}{Ex_2} & \cdots & \dfrac{E\Phi_1}{Ex_N} \\[2ex] 1 & \dfrac{E\Phi_2}{Ex_1} & \dfrac{E\Phi_2}{Ex_2} & \cdots & \dfrac{E\Phi_2}{Ex_N} \\[2ex] \cdot & \cdot & \cdot & & \cdot \\[1ex] 1 & \dfrac{E\Phi_N}{Ex_1} & \dfrac{E\Phi_N}{Ex_2} & \cdots & \dfrac{E\Phi_N}{Ex_N} \end{vmatrix} \tag{4.6}$$

and Δ_{rs} is the cofactor of $\dfrac{E\Phi_r}{Ex_s}$ in Δ.

The formula (4.5) compares with

$$\frac{\partial x_s}{\partial p_r} = \frac{\Phi_{rs}}{\mu\Phi}$$

where

$$\Phi = \begin{vmatrix} 0 & \Phi_1 & \Phi_2 & \ldots & \Phi_N \\ \Phi_1 & \Phi_{11} & \Phi_{12} & \ldots & \Phi_{1N} \\ \Phi_2 & \Phi_{21} & \Phi_{22} & \ldots & \Phi_{2N} \\ \cdot & \cdot & \cdot & & \cdot \\ \Phi_N & \Phi_{N1} & \Phi_{N2} & \ldots & \Phi_{NN} \end{vmatrix}$$

and Φ_{rs} is the cofactor of Φ_{rs} in Φ.[6]

Using the indirect method, the elasticity is given by[7]

$$\frac{Ex_s}{Ep_r} = -k_r'\sigma_{rs}', \tag{4.7}$$

where

$$k_r' = \frac{p_r x_r}{\displaystyle\sum_{r=1}^{N} p_r x_r}$$

---

[6] See J. R. Hicks, *Value and Capital*, Clarendon Press, p. 321, Oxford, 1939. I have changed the notation.

[7] See J. R. Hicks, Théorie mathématique de la valeur, *Actualités Scientifiques et Industrielles*, No. 580, Paris, Herman et Cie., 1937, p. 45. Hicks's notation is somewhat different.

and

$$\sigma'_{rs} = \frac{\sum\limits_{r=1}^{n} \Phi_r x_r}{x_r x_s} \times \frac{\Phi_{rs}}{\Phi}.$$

Confronting (4.7) and (4.5) we get as an expression for the partial elasticity of transformation

$$\sigma'_{rs} = -\frac{1}{k'_r} \times \frac{\Delta_{rs}}{\Delta}. \tag{4.8}$$

An Alternative Treatment of Joint Production

Joint production can also be treated in a way which does not involve the bordered determinant Δ and leads to the formulae (2.4) and (3.5). For this purpose we solve the transformation function (4.1) for (any) one of its variables, say for x_N. The result is a production function with x_N as the dependent variable, i.e.,

$$x_N = f(x_1, x_2, \ldots, x_n), \tag{5.1}$$

where $n = N-1$. Our treatment can be reduced to that of the earlier sections of this article through an appropriate change of symbols. Let us write $x = x_N$ and $a_r = x_r$ $(r = 1, 2, \ldots, n)$. The production function (5.1) is now

$$x = f(a_1, a_2, \ldots, a_n). \tag{5.2}$$

The a's are positive or negative, according as to whether they stand for products or for factors. Similarly x may be either positive or negative.

Denoting the price of x by p and the price of a_r by p_r $(r = 1, 2, \ldots, n)$, the net profit of the firm is

$$px + \sum_{s=1}^{n} p_s a_s. \tag{5.3}$$

The first-order maximum conditions are[8]

$$pf_s + p_s = 0 \quad (s = 1, 2, \ldots, n). \tag{5.4}$$

---

[8] Cf. Stackelberg, *op. cit.*, p. 91.

These can be written in the equivalent form

$$\log(-pf_s) = \log p_s \quad (s = 1, 2, ..., n). \tag{5.5}$$

Differentiating partially with respect to $\log p_r$ and remembering that a multiplicative constant ($-p$ on the left-hand side) can be left out of an elasticity, we obtain the equations (2.3) and the solution (2.4).

Thus, this method of treatment of joint production leads to the same formal solution as in the case of a single-product firm. The difference is only one of economic interpretation and of the algebraic sign of the variables. In the case of a single-product firm, (2.4) is the elasticity of demand for a factor and a_s is always positive. In the case of joint production, a_s is positive when it represents a product and is negative when it represents a factor. In the first instance, (2.4) is the elasticity of supply of a product, in the second instance (2.4) is the negative of the elasticity of demand for a factor.

The whole argument of Section 3 applies in our present case and we obtain for $\frac{Ex}{Ep}$ the expressions of the formulae (3.5) or (3.6). In the case treated in Section 3 this is the elasticity of supply of the product and x is always positive. In our present case, x may be either a product or a factor and positive or negative accordingly. In the first instance (3.5) or (3.6) gives, as before, the elasticity of supply of a product. In the second instance they give the negative of the elasticity of demand for a factor.

The Elasticity of Demand for a Consumption Good

Let the utility function be $u(x_1, x_2, ..., x_n)$, where the x's are the amounts of the different consumption goods. Denote further $u_r = \frac{\partial u}{\partial x_r}$ and p_r is the price of the rth good. The first-order maximum conditions for the consumer are given by the equations

$$\begin{cases} \displaystyle\sum_{s=1}^{n} p_s x_s = M, \\ u_s - \mu p_s = 0 \end{cases} \quad (s = 1, 2, ..., n). \tag{6.1}$$

The first equation is the budget equation and M is the income; μ in the second group of equations is a Lagrange multiplier (the marginal utility of income).

Transform (6.1) into the equivalent set of equations

$$\log \sum_{s=1}^{n} p_s x_s = \log M,$$

$$(s = 1, 2, ..., n), \qquad (6.2)$$

$$-\log \mu + \log u_s = \log p_s$$

and differentiate partially with respect to $\log M$.

The differentiation of the first equation gives

$$\frac{E \sum_{s=1}^{m} p_s x_s}{EM} = 1.$$

Making use of the theorem that the elasticity of a sum is the weighted mean of the elasticities of the summands $\left(\text{i.e., } \frac{E\Sigma y}{Ex} = \Sigma y \left(\frac{Ey}{Ex}\right) \Sigma y\right)$,[9] and leaving out of the elasticities the multiplicative constants $p_r (r = 1, 2, ..., n)$, we have

$$\frac{E \sum_{s=1}^{m} p_s x_s}{EM} = k_1 \frac{Ex_1}{EM} + k_2 \frac{Ex_2}{EM} + ... + k_n \frac{Ex_n}{EM},$$

where

$$k_r = \frac{p_r x_r}{\sum_{s=1}^{n} p_s x_s} \qquad (r = 1, 2, ..., n).$$

On account of (6.1) we have $p_s = \frac{u_s}{\mu}$. Substituting this into the expression for k_r we obtain

$$k_r = \frac{u_r x_r}{\sum_{s=1}^{n} u_s x_s} \qquad (r = 1, 2, ..., n), \qquad (6.3)$$

i.e., k_r can be expressed in terms which do not involve prices.

---

[9] Cf. Allen, *op. cit.*, p. 252.

Thus, the differentiation of the equations (6.2) yields

$$k_1 \frac{Ex_1}{EM} + k_2 \frac{Ex_2}{EM} + \ldots + k_n \frac{Ex_n}{EM} = 1,$$

$$-\frac{E\mu}{EM} + \frac{Eu_1}{Ex_1} \frac{Ex_1}{EM} + \frac{Eu_1}{Ex_2} \frac{Ex_2}{EM} + \ldots + \frac{Eu_1}{Ex_n} \frac{Ex_n}{EM} = 0,$$

$$-\frac{E\mu}{EM} + \frac{Eu_2}{Ex_1} \frac{Ex_1}{EM} + \frac{Eu_2}{Ex_2} \frac{Ex_2}{EM} + \ldots + \frac{Eu_2}{Ex_n} \frac{Ex_n}{EM} = 0, \qquad (6.4)$$

$$\cdots \cdots \cdots \cdots \cdots \cdots \cdots \cdots$$

$$-\frac{E\mu}{EM} + \frac{Eu_n}{Ex_1} \frac{Ex_1}{EM} + \frac{Eu_n}{Ex_2} \frac{Ex_2}{EM} + \ldots + \frac{Eu_n}{Ex_n} \frac{Ex_n}{EM} = 0.$$

Solving, we have

$$\frac{Ex_s}{EM} = \frac{R_s}{R} \ (s = 1, 2, \ldots, n), \qquad (6.5)$$

where

$$R = \begin{vmatrix} 0 & k_1 & k_2 & \ldots & k_n \\ 1 & \dfrac{Eu_1}{Ex_1} & \dfrac{Eu_1}{Ex_2} & \cdots & \dfrac{Eu_1}{Ex_n} \\ 1 & \dfrac{Eu_2}{Ex_1} & \dfrac{Eu_2}{Ex_2} & \cdots & \dfrac{Eu_2}{Ex_n} \\ \cdot & \cdot & \cdot & \cdot & \cdot \\ 1 & \dfrac{Eu_n}{Ex_1} & \dfrac{Eu_n}{Ex_2} & \cdots & \dfrac{Eu_n}{Ex_n} \end{vmatrix} \qquad (6.6)$$

and R_s is the cofactor of k_s in R.

This is the income elasticity of demand. Formula (6.5) compares with the analogous expression

$$\frac{\partial x_s}{\partial M} \equiv \frac{\mu U_s}{U}$$

where $\left(\text{using the notation } u_{rs} = \frac{\partial u_r}{\partial x_s}\right)$

$$U = \begin{vmatrix} 0 & u_1 & u_2 & \dots & u_n \\ u_1 & u_{11} & u_{12} & \dots & u_{1n} \\ u_2 & u_{21} & u_{22} & \dots & u_{2n} \\ \cdot & \cdot & \cdot & \cdot & \cdot \\ u_n & u_{n1} & u_{n2} & \dots & u_{nn} \end{vmatrix}$$

and U_s is the cofactor of u_s in U.[10]

The price elasticity of demand is obtained by differentiating partially the equations (6.2) with respect to log p_r. For the first equation:

$$\frac{E \sum_{s=1}^{n} p_s x_s}{E p_r} = 0.$$

On account of the theorem about the elasticity of a sum

$$\frac{E \sum_{s=1}^{n} p_s x_s}{E p_r} = k_1 \frac{E p_1 x_1}{E p_r} + \dots + k_r \frac{E p_r x_r}{E p_r} + \dots + k_n \frac{E p_n x_n}{E p_r}.$$

All the p's, except p_r, are constant. Dropping the multiplicative constants from the elasticities,

$$\frac{E p_s x_s}{E p_r} = \frac{E x_s}{E p_r} \quad \text{for} \quad s \neq r.$$

The elasticity of a product is the sum of the elasticities of the factors,[11] therefore

$$\frac{E p_r x_r}{E p_r} \equiv \frac{E x_r}{E p_r} + 1.$$

In consequence we have

$$\frac{E \sum_{s=1}^{n} p_s x_s}{E p_r} = k_1 \frac{E x_1}{E p_r} + k_2 \frac{E x_2}{E p_r} + \dots + k_n \frac{E x_n}{E p_r} + k_r.$$

Thus, the partial differentiation of (6.2) with respect to log p_r gives

$$k_1 \frac{E x_1}{E p_r} + k_2 \frac{E x_2}{E p_r} + \dots + k_n \frac{E x_n}{E p_r} = -k_r,$$

[10] See Hicks, *Value and Capital*, p. 308.
[11] Cf. Allen, *op. cit.*, pp. 252–253.

$$-\frac{E\mu}{Ep_r}+\frac{Eu_1}{Ex_1}\frac{Ex_1}{Ep_r}+\frac{Eu_1}{Ex_2}\frac{Ex_1}{Ep_r}+ \ \cdots \ +\frac{Eu_1}{Ex_n}\frac{Ex_n}{Ep_r}=0,$$

$$\cdots \cdots \cdots \cdots \cdots \cdots$$

$$-\frac{E\mu}{Ep_r}+\frac{Eu_r}{Ex_1}\frac{Ex_1}{Ep_r}+\frac{Eu_r}{Ex_2}\frac{Ex_2}{Ep_r}+ \ \cdots \ +\frac{Eu_r}{Ex_n}\frac{Ex_n}{Ep_r}=1, \quad (6.7)$$

$$\cdots \cdots \cdots \cdots \cdots \cdots$$

$$-\frac{E\mu}{Ep_r}+\frac{Eu_n}{Ex_1}\frac{Ex_1}{Ep_r}+\frac{Eu_n}{Ex_2}\frac{Ex_2}{Ep_r}+ \ \cdots \ +\frac{Eu_n}{Ex_n}\frac{Ex_n}{Ep_r}=0.$$

Solving, we have

$$\frac{Ex_s}{Ep_r}=\frac{1}{R}\begin{vmatrix} 0 & k_1 & \cdots & -k_r & \cdots & k_n \\ 1 & \dfrac{Eu_1}{Ex_1} & \cdots & 0 & \cdots & \dfrac{Eu_1}{Ex_n} \\ \cdot & \cdot & \cdot & \cdot & \cdot & \cdot \\ 1 & \dfrac{Eu_r}{Ex_r} & \cdots & 1 & \cdots & \dfrac{Eu_r}{Ex_n} \\ \cdot & \cdot & \cdot & \cdot & \cdot & \cdot \\ 1 & \dfrac{Eu_n}{Ex_n} & \cdots & 0 & \cdots & \dfrac{Eu_n}{Ex_n} \end{vmatrix}.$$

Expanding the last determinant according to the column containing the right-hand side of (6.7) we arrive at

$$\frac{Ex_s}{Ep_r}\equiv\frac{-k_rR_s+R_{rs}}{R},$$

where R_s has the same meaning as in (6.5) and R_{rs} is the cofactor of $\frac{Eu_r}{Ex_s}$ in R. Because of (6.5) our result can be written

$$\frac{Ex_s}{Ep_r}=-k_r\frac{Ex_s}{EM}+\frac{R_{rs}}{R} \quad (r \text{ and } s=1, 2, \ldots, n). \quad (6.8)$$

The first term on the right-hand side is the income term, the second is the substitution term.

The formula obtained compares with[12]

$$\frac{\partial x_s}{\partial p_r}=-x_r\frac{\partial x_s}{\partial M}+\mu\frac{U_{rs}}{U}.$$

[12] See Hicks, *Value and Capital*, p. 309.

The expression for the price elasticity of demand arrived at by the indirect method is[13]

$$\frac{Ex_s}{Ep_r} = -k_r \frac{Ex_s}{EM} + k_r \sigma''_{rs},$$
(6.9)

where

$$\sigma''_{rs} = \frac{\sum\limits_{s=1}^{n} u_s x_s}{x_r x_s} \times \frac{U_{rs}}{U}.$$

Confronting (6.9) with (6.8) we obtain an expression for the elasticity of substitution

$$\sigma''_{rs} = \frac{1}{k_r} \times \frac{R_{rs}}{R}.$$

Conclusion

We see that the direct method of deriving the elasticities of demand and of supply leads throughout to much simpler expressions than the indirect method usually applied. All the elasticities derived are found to be (or can be reduced to) ratios of the type $\frac{D_{rs}}{D}$, $\frac{\Delta_{rs}}{\Delta}$, and $\frac{R_{rs}}{R}$ (in the case of consumption goods the matter is complicated by the addition of an income term). They are analogous to the expressions for the partial derivatives of demand or supply with respect to price which involve similar ratios, i.e., $\frac{F_{rs}}{F}$, $\frac{\Phi_{rs}}{\Phi}$, and $\frac{U_{rs}}{U}$, but they are simpler in so far as they do not contain the multiplicative constant of the latter. The income elasticity of demand for a consumption good is given by the ratio $\frac{R_s}{R}$ while the partial derivative of this demand with respect to income is $\frac{U_s}{U}$ times a multiplicative constant. The determinants and cofactors in the elasticity formulae contain as elements the partial elasticities of the marginal productivities or utilities. The determinants appearing in the partial-derivative formulae contain as elements the partial derivatives

---

[13] See Hicks, *Théorie mathématique de la valeur*, p. 14. The double prime has been added in our paper in order to avoid confusion with the elasticities of substitution (or transformation) in the theory of production which appear in the preceding sections.

of the marginal productivities or utilities. In the bordered determinants the elasticities of the production (or transformation) function and of the utility function appear in the first instance, the partial derivatives of these functions in the second instance. Finally, the direct methods lead to a simple formula for the partial elasticity of substitution (or transformation).

Appendix: Matrices and the Calculus of Elasticities

The results of this paper can be obtained in a much shorter way by means of a generalization of the calculus of elasticities which makes it applicable to matrices and vectors.[14] Matrices and vectors will be denoted by bold-face print. In order to distinguish between matrices and vectors we shall also use parentheses to indicate matrices, brackets to indicate row vectors, and braces to indicate column vectors.

Consider the set of functions $y_s = y_s(x_1, x_2, ..., x_n)$ where $s = 1, 2, ..., m$. We define and denote the elasticity matrix of the set as

$$\frac{Ey}{Ea} = \begin{vmatrix} \dfrac{Ey_1}{Ex_1} & \dfrac{Ey_1}{Ex_2} & \cdots & \dfrac{Ey_1}{Ex_n} \\[2mm] \dfrac{Ey_2}{Ex_1} & \dfrac{Ey_2}{Ex_2} & \cdots & \dfrac{Ey_2}{Ex_n} \\[2mm] \cdot & \cdot & \cdots & \cdot \\[2mm] \dfrac{Ey_m}{Ex_1} & \dfrac{Ey_m}{Ex_2} & \cdots & \dfrac{Ey_m}{Ex_n} \end{vmatrix}. \tag{1}$$

The inverse of the elasticity matrix is written $\left(\frac{Ey}{Ex}\right)^{-1}$.

Rows and columns of an elasticity matrix will be called elasticity vectors and are distinguished by superscripts indicating the row or column. Row vectors have a superscript in the "numerator", column vectors have a superscript in the "denominator".[15] Thus

$$\frac{Ey^{(s)}}{Ex} = \left[\frac{Ey_s}{Ex_1}, \frac{Ey_s}{Ex_2}, ..., \frac{Ey_s}{Ex_n} \right] \tag{2}$$

---

[14] The idea of such a generalization has been suggested to me by Mr. Leonid Hurwicz to whom I am also indebted for advice in matters of notation.

[15] These words are put in quotation marks because, strictly speaking, the elasticities are not ratios but limits of ratios.

and

$$\frac{Ey}{Ex^{(r)}} = \left\{ \frac{Ey_1}{Ex_r}, \frac{Ey_2}{Ex_r}, \ldots, \frac{Ey_m}{Ex_r} \right\}. \tag{3}$$

In cases when the vectors do not refer to a specific row or column of an elasticity matrix, or when the row or column is not identified by an index, the superscripts are left empty but the small parentheses embracing the superscript are retained in order to distinguish the vectors from matrices. Thus we write

$$\frac{Ey^{(\ )}}{Ex} = \left[\frac{Ey}{Ex_1}, \frac{Ey}{Ex_2}, \ldots, \frac{Ey}{Ex_n} \right]$$

and

$$\frac{Ey}{Ex^{(\ )}} = \left\{ \frac{Ey_1}{Ex}, \frac{Ey_2}{Ex}, \ldots, \frac{Ey_m}{Ex} \right\}.$$

We state the following propositions concerning elasticity matrices.

Proposition I. If $\alpha = $ const., then

$$\frac{E(\alpha y)}{Ex} = \frac{Ey}{Ex}.$$

Proposition II. Take two sets of functions $y_s = y_s(u_1, u_2, \ldots, u_l)$ and $u_t = u_t(x_1, x_2, \ldots, x_n)$ where $s = 1, 2, \ldots, m$ and $t = 1, 2, \ldots, l$. We have

$$\frac{Ey}{Ex} = \frac{Ey}{Eu} \frac{Eu}{Ex}.$$

Proposition III. Denote two sets of functions of the same variables by $u_s = u_s(x_1, x_2, \ldots, x_n)$ and $v_s = v_s(x_1, x_2. \ldots, x_n)$ where $s = 1, 2, \ldots, m$. Write

$$\frac{E(uv)}{Ex} = \left| \begin{array}{ccc} \dfrac{E(u_1 v_1)}{Ex_1} & \cdots & \dfrac{E(u_1 v_1)}{Ex_n} \\ \cdot \quad \cdot \quad \cdot & \cdot \quad \cdot & \cdot \quad \cdot \\ \dfrac{E(u_m v_m)}{Ex_1} & \cdots & \dfrac{E(u_m v_m)}{Ex_n} \end{array} \right|,$$

then

$$\frac{E(uv)}{Ex} = \frac{Eu}{Ex} + \frac{Ev}{Ex}.$$

Proposition IV. Writing

$$\frac{E\left(\frac{u}{v}\right)}{Ex} = \begin{vmatrix} \dfrac{E\left(\dfrac{u_1}{v_1}\right)}{Ex_1} & \cdots & \dfrac{E\left(\dfrac{u_1}{v_1}\right)}{Ex_n} \\ \cdot & \cdots & \cdot \\ \dfrac{E\left(\dfrac{u_m}{v_m}\right)}{Ex_1} & \cdots & \dfrac{E\left(\dfrac{u_m}{v_m}\right)}{Ex_n} \end{vmatrix}$$

we have, for the two sets of functions under III,

$$\frac{E\left(\frac{u}{v}\right)}{Ex} = \frac{Eu}{Ex} - \frac{Ev}{Ex}.$$

The propositions I, III, and IV follow immediately from the corresponding rules of the calculus of elasticities. Proposition I can also be regarded as a special case of III or IV. Proposition II follows from the function-of-function rule,

$$\frac{Ey_s}{Ex_r} = \sum_{t=1}^{l} \frac{Ey_s}{Eu_t} \frac{Eu_t}{Ex_r}.$$

For the sake of completeness we mention a further proposition which follows from the rule about the elasticity of a sum or difference.

Proposition V. Writing

$$\frac{E(u \pm v)}{Ex} = \begin{vmatrix} \dfrac{E(u_1 \pm v_1)}{Ex_1} & \cdots & \dfrac{E(u_1 \pm v_1)}{Ex_n} \\ \cdot & \cdots & \cdot \\ \dfrac{E(u_m \pm v_m)}{Ex_1} & \cdots & \dfrac{E(u_m \pm v_m)}{Ex_n} \end{vmatrix}$$

and denoting by U and V the diagonal matrices

$$U = \begin{vmatrix} u_1 & \ldots & 0 \\ \cdot & \cdot & \cdot \\ 0 & \ldots & u_m \end{vmatrix}$$

and

$$V = \begin{vmatrix} v_1 & \ldots & 0 \\ \cdot & \cdot & \cdot \\ 0 & \ldots & v_m \end{vmatrix}$$

we have, for the two sets of functions under III,

$$(U \pm V) \frac{E(u \pm v)}{Ex} = U \frac{Eu}{Ex} \pm V \frac{Ev}{Ex}.$$

Thus the rules of the calculus of elasticities apply also to matrices. Vectors can be considered as special cases of matrices and these rules can, therefore, be applied also to vectors. We can, therefore, add superscripts to the "numerators" or "denominators" of the elasticity matrices in our five propositions.

Now let us consider the set of equations (2.1) of the text. It is

$$pf_s(a_1, a_2, \ldots, a_n) = p_s, \tag{4}$$

where $p = $ const. and $a_t = a_t(p_1, p_2, \ldots, p_n)$ (s and $t = 1, 2, \ldots, n$). We want the vector

$$\frac{Ea}{Ep^{(r)}} = \left\{ \frac{Ea_1}{Ep_r}, \frac{Ea_2}{Ep_r}, \ldots, \frac{Ea_n}{Ep_r} \right\}.$$

Taking elasticities of (4) with respect to p_r and applying the propositions I and II, we obtain the matrix equation

$$\frac{E(pf)}{Ep^{(r)}} = \frac{E(f)}{Ea} \frac{Ea}{Ep^{(r)}} = e_r. \tag{5}$$

Here

$$\frac{E(pf)}{Ep^{(r)}} = \left\{ \frac{Epf_1}{Ep_r}, \frac{Epf_2}{Ep_r}, \ldots, \frac{Epf_n}{Ep_r} \right\}, \quad \frac{Ef}{Ea} = \left(\frac{Ef_s}{Ea_r} \right),$$

where r and $s = 1, 2, \ldots, n$. The right-hand side is the n-rowed unit vector in the direction of p_r, i.e., $e_r = \{0, 0, \ldots, 0, 1, 0, \ldots, 0\}$.

Solving the matrix equation,

$$\frac{Ea}{Ep^{(r)}} = \left(\frac{Ef}{Ea} \right)^{-1} e_r. \tag{6}$$

Denoting $D = Ef/Ea$ we obtain (2.4) as in the text.

When p is a variable and elasticities are taken with respect to p we get (applying the propositions II and III)

$$\frac{Epf}{Ep^{()}} = 0, \quad \text{or} \quad \frac{Ef}{Ea} \times \frac{Ea}{Ep^{()}} = -1 \tag{7}$$

where $0 = \{0, 0, \ldots, 0\}$ and $1 = \{1, 1, \ldots, 1\}$. This leads to the results of Section 3.

For joint production we have the equations (4.1) and (4.2) of the text. These are

$$\Phi(x_1, x_2, ..., x_N) = \text{const.},$$
$$\mu\varphi_s(x_1, x_2, ..., x_N) = p_s \tag{8a}$$

where $x_t = x_t(p_1, p_2, ..., p_N)$ (s and $t = 1, 2, ..., N$).

Taking elasticities with respect to p_r we have

$$\begin{bmatrix} \dfrac{E\varphi}{Ep_r} \\[2mm] \dfrac{E(\mu\varphi)}{Ep^{(r)}} \end{bmatrix} = e_r \tag{9a}$$

where

$$\frac{E(\mu\varphi)}{Ep^{(r)}} = \left\{ \frac{E\mu\varphi_1}{Ep_r}, \frac{E\mu\varphi_2}{Ep_r}, ..., \frac{E\mu\varphi_N}{Ep_r} \right\},$$

i.e., an N-rowed column vector; e_r is here the $(N+1)$-rowed unit vector in the direction of p_r [which now corresponds to the $(r+1)$th row].

Applying the propositions III and II as well as the rules of matrix algebra we obtain

$$\begin{bmatrix} \dfrac{E\varphi}{Ep_r} \\[2mm] \dfrac{E(\mu\varphi)}{Ep_r} \end{bmatrix} = \begin{bmatrix} 0 + \dfrac{E\varphi}{Ep_r} \\[2mm] \dfrac{E\mu}{Ep^{(r)}} + \dfrac{E\varphi}{Ep^{(r)}} \end{bmatrix} = \frac{E\mu}{Ep_r}\begin{pmatrix}0\\1\end{pmatrix} + \begin{bmatrix} \dfrac{E\varphi^{(\ )}}{Ex} \\[2mm] \dfrac{E\varphi}{Ex} \end{bmatrix}\frac{Ex}{Ep^{(r)}}$$

$$= \begin{bmatrix} 0 & \dfrac{E\varphi^{(\ )}}{Ex} \\[2mm] 1 & \dfrac{E\varphi}{Ex} \end{bmatrix}\begin{bmatrix} \dfrac{E\mu}{Ep_r} \\[2mm] \dfrac{Ex}{Ep^{(r)}} \end{bmatrix}. \tag{10a}$$

In the last expression $E\varphi/Ex$ is the N-rowed square matrix $(E\varphi_s/Ex_t)$, $E\varphi^{(\ )}/Ex$ is the N-columned row vector

$$\left[\frac{E\varphi}{Ex_1}, \frac{E\varphi}{Ex_2}, ..., \frac{E\varphi}{Ex_N} \right],$$

$Ex/Ep^{(r)}$ is the n-rowed column vector

$$\left\{ \frac{Ex_1}{Ep_r}, \frac{Ex_2}{Ep_r}, ..., \frac{Ex_N}{Ep_r} \right\}, \quad 1 = \{1, 1, ...\},$$

i.e., an N-rowed column vector. The remainder are isolated elements.

The second matrix in this expression represents the $(N+1)$-rowed column vector

$$\left\{\frac{E\mu}{Ep_r}, \frac{Ex_1}{Ep_r}, \dots, \frac{Ex_N}{Ep_r}\right\}.$$

This leads to the matrix equation

$$\begin{bmatrix} 0 & \dfrac{E\varphi^{(\ )}}{Ex} \\[2ex] 1 & \dfrac{E\varphi}{Ex} \end{bmatrix} \begin{bmatrix} \dfrac{E\mu}{Ep_r} \\[2ex] \dfrac{Ex}{Ep^{(r)}} \end{bmatrix} = e_r \qquad (11a)$$

which can be solved for the column vector. Denoting by Δ the determinant of the first matrix in (11a) we arrive at (4.5) of the text.

The elasticity of demand for consumption goods is found from the equations (6.1) of the text. We write them

$$\varphi = \sum_{s=1}^{n} p_s\, x_s = M,$$

$$\frac{u_s(x_1, x_2, \dots, x_n)}{\mu} = p_s, \qquad (8b)$$

where $x_t = x_t(p_1, p_2, \dots, p_n)$ (s and $t = 1, 2, \dots, n$).

Taking elasticities with respect to M, we have

$$\begin{bmatrix} \dfrac{E\varphi}{EM} \\[2ex] E\left(\dfrac{u}{\mu}\right) \\[2ex] \dfrac{}{EM^{(\ )}} \end{bmatrix} = e_0 \qquad (9b)$$

where $e_0 = \{1, 0, 0, \dots, 0\}$, an $(n+1)$-rowed column vector.

Applying the propositions IV and II,

$$\begin{bmatrix} \dfrac{E\varphi}{EM} \\[2ex] E\left(\dfrac{u}{\mu}\right) \\[2ex] \dfrac{}{EM^{(\ )}} \end{bmatrix} = \begin{bmatrix} 0 + \dfrac{E\varphi}{EM} \\[2ex] -\dfrac{E\mu}{EM^{(\ )}} + \dfrac{Eu}{EM^{(\ )}} \end{bmatrix} = -\frac{E\mu}{EM}\begin{pmatrix}0\\1\end{pmatrix} + \begin{bmatrix} \dfrac{E\varphi^{(\ )}}{Ex} \\[2ex] \dfrac{Eu}{Ex} \end{bmatrix} \frac{Ex}{EM^{(\ )}}$$

$$= \begin{bmatrix} 0 & \dfrac{E\varphi^{(\ )}}{Ex} \\[2ex] 1 & \dfrac{Eu}{Ex} \end{bmatrix} \begin{bmatrix} -\dfrac{E\mu}{EM} \\[2ex] \dfrac{Eu}{EM^{(\ )}} \end{bmatrix}. \qquad (10b)$$

Here

$$\frac{Eu}{Ex} = \left(\frac{Eu_s}{Ex_t}\right),$$

where s and $t = 1, 2, ..., n$;

$$\frac{E\varphi^{(\ )}}{Ex} = \left[\frac{E\varphi}{Ex_1}, \frac{E\varphi}{Ex_2}, ..., \frac{E\varphi}{Ex_n}\right];$$

$$\frac{Eu}{EM^{(\ )}} = \left\{\frac{Eu_1}{EM}, \frac{Eu_2}{EM}, ..., \frac{Eu_n}{EM}\right\};$$

and $1 = \{1, 1, ..., 1\}$, i.e., n-rowed.

From the first equation of (8b) we have (in virtue of the rule on the elasticity of a sum)

$$\frac{E\varphi}{Ex_r} = k_r \quad \text{where} \quad k_r = \frac{p_r x_r}{\sum\limits_{s=1}^{n} p_s x_s} = \frac{u_r x_r}{\sum\limits_{s=1}^{n} u_s x_s},$$

see (6.3) in the text. Consequently

$$\frac{E\varphi^{(\ )}}{Ex} = [k_1, k_2, ..., k_n] = k.$$

Thus we obtain, finally, the matrix equation

$$\begin{bmatrix} 0 & k \\ 1 & \dfrac{Eu}{Ex} \end{bmatrix} \begin{bmatrix} -\dfrac{E\mu}{EM} \\ \dfrac{Eu}{EM^{(\ )}} \end{bmatrix} = e_0 \tag{11b}$$

which serves to determine the income elasticity of demand and the income elasticity of the "marginal utility of money".

The price elasticity of demand (and of the "marginal utility of money") is obtained by taking elasticities with respect to p_r. This gives

$$\begin{bmatrix} \dfrac{E\varphi}{Ep_r} \\ E\left(\dfrac{u}{\mu}\right) \\ \dfrac{}{Ep^{(r)}} \end{bmatrix} = e_r \tag{9c}$$

with meanings similar to those in (9a) and (9b).

Because of the rule on the elasticity of a sum, we have

$$\frac{E\varphi}{Ep_r} = \sum_{s=1}^{n} k_s \frac{Ex_s}{Ep_r} k_r.$$

Substituting this in (9c) we obtain

$$\left[\begin{array}{c} \sum\limits_{s=1}^{n} k_s \dfrac{Ex_s}{Ep_r} + k_r \\[2ex] \dfrac{E\left(\dfrac{u}{\mu}\right)}{Ep^{(r)}} + 0 \end{array} \right] = e_r,$$

or

$$\left[\begin{array}{c} \sum\limits_{s=1}^{n} k_s \dfrac{Ex_s}{Ep_r} \\[2ex] \dfrac{E\left(\dfrac{u}{\mu}\right)}{Ep^{(r)}} \end{array} \right] = -k_r e_0 + e_r. \tag{9c$'$}$$

By steps analogous to those under (10a) and (10b) we reach

$$\left[\begin{array}{c} \sum\limits_{s=1}^{n} k_s \dfrac{Ex_s}{Ep_r} \\[2ex] \dfrac{E\left(\dfrac{u}{\mu}\right)}{Ep^{(r)}} \end{array} \right] = \left[\begin{array}{cc} 0 & k \\[2ex] 1 & \dfrac{Eu}{Ex} \end{array} \right] \left[\begin{array}{c} -\dfrac{EM}{Ep_r} \\[2ex] \dfrac{Ex}{Ep^{(r)}} \end{array} \right] \tag{10c}$$

with a meaning similar to (10b).

This gives us the matrix equation

$$\left[\begin{array}{cc} 0 & k \\[2ex] 1 & \dfrac{Eu}{Ex} \end{array} \right] \left[\begin{array}{c} -\dfrac{E\mu}{Ep_r} \\[2ex] \dfrac{Ex}{Ep^{(r)}} \end{array} \right] = -k_r e_0 + e_r. \tag{11c}$$

Solving, we obtain

$$\begin{bmatrix} -\dfrac{E\mu}{Ep_r} \\ \dfrac{Ex}{Ep^{(r)}} \end{bmatrix} = -k_r \begin{bmatrix} 0 & k \\ 1 & \dfrac{Eu}{Ex} \end{bmatrix}^{-1} e_0 + \begin{bmatrix} 0 & k \\ 1 & \dfrac{Eu}{Ex} \end{bmatrix}^{-1} e_r. \qquad (12)$$

Taking into account (11b), the solution can be written

$$\begin{bmatrix} -\dfrac{E\mu}{Ep_r} \\ \dfrac{Ex}{Ep^{(r)}} \end{bmatrix} = -k_r \begin{bmatrix} -\dfrac{E\mu}{EM} \\ \dfrac{Eu}{EM^{()}} \end{bmatrix} + \begin{bmatrix} 0 & k \\ 1 & \dfrac{Eu}{Ex} \end{bmatrix}^{-1} e_r, \qquad (13)$$

which indicates the decomposition of the price-elasticity vector into an income term and a substitution term.

THE FOUNDATIONS OF WELFARE ECONOMICS

1. Welfare Economics is concerned with the conditions which determine the total economic welfare of a community. In the traditional theory the total welfare of a community was conceived as the sum of the welfares (utilities) of all constituent individuals. The problem of maximization of total welfare thus involved the weighing against each other the losses of utility and gains of utility of different individuals. This implies inter-personal comparability of utility, as is seen in the dictum about the marginal utility of a dollar for the poor man and for the rich man. Such implication, however, is open to epistemological criticism on the ground of it lacking in operational significance. In consequence a restatement of the principles of welfare economics is in progress[1] which tries to dispense with the inter-personal comparability of utility. Such restatement, however, entails a narrowing down of the field of welfare economics. The aim of this paper is to give a precise statement of the basic assumptions and propositions of welfare economics and to discuss their operational significance.

2. In order to dispense with inter-personal comparability of utility the total welfare of a community has to be defined not as the sum of the utilities of the individuals (a scalar quantity) but as a vector. The utilities of the individuals are the components of this vector. Let there be θ individuals in the community and let $u^{(i)}$ be the utility of the ith individual. Total welfare is then the vector

$$u = (u^{(1)}, u^{(2)}, ..., u^{(\theta)}). \tag{2.1}$$

---

[1] Some of the recent literature: A. P. Lerner, The Concept of Monopoly and the Measurement of Monopoly Power, *Review of Economic Studies*, June, 1934; A. Burk, A Reformulation of Certain Aspects of Welfare Economics, *Quarterly Journal of Economics*, February, 1938; H. Hotelling, The General Welfare in Relation to Problems of Taxation and of Railway and Utility Rates, *Econometrica*, July, 1938; L. Robbins, Interpersonal Comparisons of Utility, *Economic Journal*, December, 1938; N. Kaldor, Welfare Propositions and Inter-personal Comparison of Utility, *Economic Journal*, September, 1939; J. R. Hicks, The Foundations of Welfare Economics, Economic Journal, December, 1939; T. de Scitovsky, A Note on Welfare Propositions in Economics, *Review of Economic Studies*, November, 1941.

It is convenient for our purpose to order vectors on the basis of the following definition: a vector is said to be greater than another vector when at least one of its components is greater than the corresponding component of the other vector, and none is less.[2] Thus, a vector increases when at least one of its components increases and none decreases. According to the definition adopted, a maximum of total welfare occurs when conditions cannot be changed so as to increase the vector u, i.e., when it is impossible to increase the utility of any person without decreasing that of others.[3] We have, therefore, $u = \max$ when

$$u^{(i)} = \max \quad (i = 1, 2, ..., \theta) \tag{2.2}$$

subject to

$$u^{(j)} = \text{const} \quad (j = 1, 2, ..., i-1, i+1, ..., \theta). \tag{2.3}$$

3. Let the utility of each individual be a function of the commodities in his possession. Denoting by $x_1^{(i)}, x_2^{(i)}, ..., x_n^{(i)}$ the quantities of n commodities in the possession of the ith individual, his utility is $u^{(i)} = u^{(i)}(x_1^{(i)}, x_2^{(i)}, ..., x_n^{(i)})$. Denote further by $X_r = \sum_i^{\theta} {}_1 X_r^{(i)}$ the total amount of the rth commodity in the community. These amounts are not constant but subject to technological transformation the possibilities of which are circumscribed by a transformation function $F(X_1, X_2, ..., X_n) = 0$. Our problem is to maximize total welfare subject to the constraint of the transformation function.

We thus have the following maximum problem:

$$u^{(i)}(x_1^{(i)}, x_2^{(i)}, ..., x_n^{(i)}) = \max \quad (i = 1, 2, ..., \theta)$$

subject to the side relations

$$u^{(j)}(x_1^{(j)}, x_2^{(j)}, ..., x_n^{(j)}) = \text{const} \quad (j = 1, 2, ..., i-1, i+1, ..., \theta), \tag{3.1}$$

---

[2] The ordering of vectors according to this definition must be distinguished from the ordering of vectors according to their length (defined as usual). When a vector is greater than another in the above sense, then its length is also greater than the length of the other vector, but the reverse does not hold. According to our definition the vectors form a partially ordered system which does not have the "chain" property: given u and v, either $u \geqq v$ or $v \geqq u$.

[3] In the language of the theory of partially ordered systems a maximum of total welfare is a "maximal" element of the set of admissible vectors u. Cf. Garrett Birkhoff, *Lattice Theory*, American Mathematical Society, *Colloquium Publications*, Vol. XXV, 1940, p. 8. The set of admissible vectors is given by the conditions (3.2) and (3.3) in the text.

$$X_r = \sum_{i=1}^{\theta} x_r^{(i)} \quad (r = 1, 2, ..., n), \tag{3.2}$$

$$F(X_1, X_2, ..., X_n) = 0. \tag{3.3}$$

This is equivalent to maximizing the expression

$$\sum_{i=1}^{\theta} \lambda_i u^{(i)}(x_1^{(i)}, x_2^{(i)}, ..., x_n^{(i)}) + \sum_{r=1}^{n} \nu_r \left(\sum_{i=1}^{\theta} x_r^{(i)} - X_r \right) + \nu F(X_1, X_2, ..., X_n), \tag{3.4}$$

where the λ's and the ν's are Lagrange multipliers and $\lambda_i \equiv 1$ successively for $i = 1, 2, ..., \theta$. The result obtained is the same for each i.

The first-order maximum conditions yield, after elimination of the Lagrange multipliers, the $(n-1)\theta$ equations[4]

$$\frac{u_r^{(i)}}{u_s^{(i)}} = \frac{F_r}{F_s} \quad (r \text{ and } s = 1, 2, ..., n; \; i = 1, 2, ..., \theta), \tag{3.5}$$

which together with the equations (3.1) and (3.3) serve to determine the $n\theta$ quantities $x_r^{(i)}$. The equations (3.5) can also be written in the form

$$\frac{\partial x_s^{(1)}}{\partial x_r^{(i)}} = \frac{\partial X_s}{\partial X_r} \quad (r \text{ and } s = 1, 2, ..., n; \; i = 1, 2, ..., \theta). \tag{3.6}$$

The latter form shows clearly the economic interpretation and the operational significance of our maximum conditions. The left-hand side of (3.6) is the marginal rate of substitution of two commodities (the amounts of the remaining commodities being kept constant) which leaves the individual's utility unaffected. The right-hand side is the marginal rate of technological transformation of the two commodities and must be equal to the marginal rate of transformation of these commodities. Both rates can be determined empirically, the second from the technological conditions of transformation, the first by offering each individual choices between different "bundles" of commodities and adjusting the "bundles" so as to make his choice indifferent.

The derivation of (3.5) or (3.6) does not imply interpersonal comparability of utility. This can be seen also in the following way. From (3.5) we have

$$\frac{u_r^{(i)}}{u_r^{(j)}} = \frac{u_s^{(i)}}{u_s^{(j)}} \quad (r \text{ and } s = 1, 2, ..., n; \; i \text{ and } j = 1, 2, ..., \theta; \; j \neq i). \tag{3.7}$$

---

[4] These subscripts stand for partial derivatives. Thus, e.g.,

$$u_r^{(i)} = \frac{\partial u^{(i)}}{\partial x_r^{(i)}} \quad \text{and} \quad F_r = \frac{\partial F}{\partial X_r}.$$

Each side is the ratio of the marginal utilities of different individuals. The numerical value of these ratios is indeterminate.

This treatment of the maximum total welfare problem does not imply the measurability of the individuals' utility either. The equations (3.5)–(3.7) are invariant with regard to any positive transformation $\Phi^{(i)}(u^{(i)})$ (where $\Phi^{(i)} > 0$)[5] of the utility functions of the individuals. Only the projective properties of these functions are used. This implies only ordering, not measurement, of each individual's utility.

The equations (3.5) or (3.6) contain *in nuce* most theorems o welfare economics,[6] e.g., all the propositions in Pigou's *Economics of Welfare*. The only theorems not contained in these equations are those which relate to the optimum distribution of incomes. This limitation and the problem of how it can be overcome in a way which is operationally significant will be the subject of the remaining part of this paper.

4. The solution given by (3.5) or (3.6) contains arbitrary parameters, namely the constants of the right-hand side of (3.1). These parameters express the level at which the utilities of all the other individuals are held constant while the utility of the ith individual is being maximized. Thus, our solution is *relative* to the values chosen for these parameters. It gives, for instance, the conditions under which the poor man's utility cannot be increased any more without diminishing the rich man's utility (or vice versa), but the level at which the rich man's utility is held constant is arbitrary. Obviously, the poor man's utility corresponding to a situation of maximum total welfare will be different when the level of the rich man's utility is chosen differently.

In an exchange economy the constants on the right-hand side of (3.1) are uniquely related to the money incomes of the respective individuals. This follows from the maximization of the individuals' utility.

Let $u^{(i)}(x_1^{(i)}, x_2^{(i)}, ..., x_n^{(i)}) = \max$ subject to $\sum_{r}^{n} = {}_1 p_r x_r^{(i)} = M^{(i)}$ where $M^{(i)}$ is the individual's income and the p's are the prices of the commodities. The value of $u_{\max}^{(i)}$ depends on $M^{(i)}$ and on the p's as parameters. The p's can be determined from equations which express the equality of

---

[5] In fact, they are invariant with respect to any transformation such that $\Phi^{(i)\prime} \neq 0$. But the second-order maximum conditions admit only positive transformations. Negative transformations would change the maximum into a minimum.

[6] For a somewhat fuller treatment of this point see the Appendix.

demand and supply of each commodity, but $M^{(i)}$ remains arbitrary.[7] Thus, the problem of determining the constants on the right-hand side of (3.1) is reduced, in an exchange economy, to that of determining the distribution of incomes. The conditions of maximum total welfare expressed in (3.5) or (3.6) leave this distribution arbitrary.

5. In order to arrive at the optimum determination of the constants on the right-hand side of (3.1) it does not suffice to maximize the vector u. We must be able to choose between different vectors u which cannot be ordered in the way defined above.[8] This can be done in two ways. One is to weigh against each other the gains of utility and the losses of utility of different individuals. This need not, however, imply the acceptance of the traditional definition of total welfare as the sum of the utilities of the individuals. The weighting can be based, instead, upon a social valuation of the importance of the individuals, the subject exercising the valuation being an agency of the organized community (e.g., Congress).[9] The other way is to establish directly a social valuation of the distribution of commodities or incomes between the individuals, without reference to the individuals' utilities. In the first case, the optimum distribution of incomes (and of commodities) is determined by a social valuation of the individuals' utilities. In the second case, the utilities of the individuals appear as a more or less accidental by-product of the direct social valuation of the distribution of incomes (or of commodities).

In both cases the social valuation can be expressed in the form of a *scalar function of the vector* u, i.e., $W(u)$, except that in one case the community (or rather its agency) chooses the most preferred vector u and adjusts the distribution of incomes and of commodities among the individuals so as to obtain the desired vector, while in the other case it chooses the most preferred distribution of incomes (or commodities) directly and the vector u adjusts itself to this choice. We shall call the function W the *social value function*.

---

[7] The $M^{(i)}$ must, however, satisfy the relation $\sum\limits_{i=1}^{\theta} M^{(i)} = \sum\limits_{r=1}^{n} p_r X_r$ which follows from (3.2) and from the budget equations $\sum\limits_{r=1}^{n} p_r X_r^{(i)} = M^{(i)}$.

[8] I.e., we need now the "chain" property mentioned in footnote 2 above.

[9] In a democratically organized community these agencies will have to reflect the valuations of the majority.

It is convenient to give names to the different derivatives of this function. We shall call them *marginal social significances*. Let $W_i = \frac{\partial W}{\partial u^{(i)}}$ and call it the marginal social significance of the ith individual. As $u^{(i)} = u^{(i)} (x_1^{(i)}, x_2^{(i)}, ..., x_n^{(i)})$, we can form the derivative $\frac{\partial W}{\partial x_r^{(i)}}$. It will be called the marginal social significance of the rth commodity in the hands of the ith individual. In the preceding section it was shown that in an exchange economy a unique relation exists between $u^{(i)}$ and the individual's money income $M^{(i)}$. Hence, we can form $\frac{\partial W}{\partial M^{(i)}}$ which will be called the marginal social significance of the ith individual's income.

Between these derivatives there are the relations

$$\frac{\partial W}{\partial x_r^{(i)}} = W_i u_r^{(i)}, \tag{5.1}$$

$$\frac{\partial W}{\partial M^{(i)}} = W_i \mu_i \quad \text{where} \quad \mu_i = \frac{\partial u^{(i)}}{\partial M^{(i)}}; \tag{5.2}$$

u_i is called the marginal utility of income.[10] We have also

$$\frac{\partial W}{\partial x_r^{(i)}} = \frac{\partial W}{\partial M^{(i)}} \frac{\partial M^{(i)}}{\partial x_r^{(i)}}.$$

---

[10] μ_i is also the Lagrange multiplier used in maximizing $u^{(i)}$ subject to $M^{(i)} = \text{const.}$ The first-order maximum conditions are in this case (omitting the superscript i in order to simplify the notation) $u_r = \mu p_r (r = 1, 2, ..., n)$. Write $\frac{\partial u}{\partial M} = \sum_{r=1}^{n} u_r \frac{\partial x_r}{\partial M}$. It can be shown (cf. J. R. Hicks, *Value and Capital*, Clarendon Press, 1939, p. 308) that

$$\frac{\partial x_r}{\partial M} = \frac{\mu U_r}{U}$$

where

$$U = \begin{vmatrix} 0 & u_1 & ... & u_n \\ u_1 & u_{11} & ... & u_{1n} \\ .... \\ u_n & u_{n1} & ... & u_{nn} \end{vmatrix}$$

and U_r is the cofactor of the element u_r in the first row. Thus we get

$$\frac{\partial u}{\partial M} = \mu \sum_{r=1}^{n} \frac{u_r U_r}{U} = \mu.$$

But $M^{(i)} = \sum_{r=1}^{n} p_r x_r^{(i)}$ (*vide* Section 4) and $\frac{\partial M^{(i)}}{\partial x_r^{(i)}} = p_r$. Consequently, we have the relation

$$\frac{\partial W}{\partial x_r^{(i)}} = \frac{\partial W}{\partial M^{(i)}} p_r. \tag{5.3}$$

Our problem is now to maximize W subject to the side relations (3.2) and (3.3). This leads to the maximizing of the following expression

$$W(n^{(1)}, n^{(2)}, \ldots, n^{(\theta)}) + \sum_{r=1}^{n} v_r \left(\sum_{i=1}^{\theta} x_r^{(i)} - X_r \right) + v F(X_1, X_2, \ldots, X_n) \tag{5.4}$$

where the v's are Lagrange multipliers.

Eliminating the Lagrange multipliers, we obtain the first-order maximum conditions

$$\frac{\partial W}{\partial x_r^{(i)}} \div \frac{\partial W}{\partial x_s^{(j)}} = \frac{F_r}{F_s} \tag{5.5}$$

$$(r \text{ and } s = 1, 2, \ldots, n; \quad i \text{ and } j = 1, 2, \ldots, \theta).$$

For $j = 1$ and $s \neq r$ these equations become, taking account of (5.1),

$$\frac{u_r^{(i)}}{u_s^{(i)}} = \frac{F_r}{F_s}; \tag{5.6}$$

for $j \neq i$ and $s = r$ they become

$$\frac{\partial W}{\partial x_r^{(i)}} = \frac{\partial W}{\partial x_r^{(j)}}. \tag{5.7}$$

The conditions (5.6) are identical with (3.5) and have the same economic interpretation. Their operational significance has already been established. The equations (5.7) state that each commodity must have the same marginal social significance in the hands of each individual. The operational significance of this condition requires further inquiry.

6. In virtue of (5.1)–(5.3) the equation (5.7) can be written in the following alternative forms:

$$\frac{\partial W}{\partial M^{(i)}} = \frac{\partial W}{\partial M^{(j)}}, \tag{6.1}$$

$$W_i u_r^{(i)} = W_j u_r^{(j)}, \tag{6.2}$$

$$W_i u_i = W \cdot u_j. \tag{6.3}$$

(6.1) states that the marginal social significance of each individual's income must be the same. According to (6.2) the weighted marginal utility of each commodity, and according to (6.3) the weighted marginal utility of income, must be the same for each individual, the marginal social significance of the individual serving as weight.

The operational significance of the maximum conditions obtained depends on which of the two types of social valuation is used. When the communal agency makes its valuation directly in terms of the distribution of commodities or incomes among the individuals, the equations (5.7) and (6.1) can be used. They have, in this case, an immediate operational significance. The communal agency need not bother about the individuals' utilities and it considers W as a direct function of the x's or of the M's, i.e., as being in the form $W(x_1^{(1)}, ..., x_n^{(1)}; ...; x_1^{(\theta)}, ..., x_n^{(\theta)})$ or $W(M^{(1)}, ..., M^{(\theta)})$. A direct valuation in terms of the distribution of commodities is in practice a very complicated affair. It requires a separate evaluation of the marginal social significance of each commodity in the hands of each individual. Therefore, it is rarely fully practised, except in times of emergency, e.g., during war, when practice comes pretty close to it. A direct valuation in terms of the distribution of incomes does not present the same technical obstacles. It requires only an evaluation of the marginal social significance of each individual's income. This can be done by means of one or a few simple principles and is actually practised, for instance, in framing income-tax legislation.

When the social valuation is made in terms of weighting the individuals' utilities, the equations (6.2) and (6.3) have to be used. This requires a knowledge of the marginal utilities of the different individuals. There exists no operational procedure by which such a knowledge can be gained. To that extent (6.2) and (6.3) lack operational significance. This, however, does not make them completely meaningless. It is possible to form certain *a priori* hypotheses about the relationships between individuals' marginal utilities and to investigate the resulting consequences in terms of the distribution of incomes or of commodities. Thus, it is possible to control the valuations made directly in terms of incomes or commodities in the light of these hypotheses.

The most interesting of such hypotheses is the hypothesis that the function $\mu_i(M^{(i)})$ which expresses the marginal utility of income is the same for each individual. In this case (6.3) becomes

$$W_i \mu(M^{(i)}) = W_j \mu(M^{(j)}) \quad (i \text{ and } j = 1, 2, ..., \theta), \qquad (6.4)$$

where μ is written without subscript because the function is the same for all individuals. Let us also assume that the community adopts an egalitarian social ideal, i.e., the marginal social significance of each individual is the same. Then $W_i = W_j$ for all i's and j's, and we obtain from (6.4)

$$M^{(i)} = M^{(j)} \quad (i \text{ and } j = 1, 2, ..., \theta). \tag{6.5}$$

Each individual has to receive the same income.[11]

In this way, it is possible to check the consistency of the social valuation with the professed ideal of an economic society which, like ours, claims to attach to each individual the same marginal social significance. Upon the hypothesis that the marginal-utility-of-income function is the same for all individuals, the inequalities in the distribution of incomes are inconsistent with the equalitarian ideal professed. In a similar way, the actual distribution of incomes (or of commodities) can be checked against other hypotheses made and other social valuations of the individuals' utilities.

7. It is seen from (5.5) that the maximum conditions are invariant under a transformation $\Phi(W)$ of the social-value function, where $\Phi' > 0$.[12] Thus only the projective properties of W are used. Only the ordering, not the measurement, of the social valuations is involved.

The utilities of the individuals need not be measurable either. Let us subject the utility functions of the individuals to the transformation $\Phi^{(i)}(u^{(i)})$, where $\Phi^{(i)} > 0$[13] and $i = 1, 2, ..., \theta$. We obtain, instead of (6.2),

$$\frac{\partial W}{\partial \Phi^{(i)}} \, \Phi_r^{(i)} = \frac{\partial W}{\partial \Phi^{(j)}} \, \Phi_r^{(j)}. \tag{7.1}$$

---

[11] This does not imply that each individual's money earnings must be the same. In the goods $x_r^{(i)}$ are included leisure, safety and attractiveness of different occupations, social prestige, etc., and prices have to be assigned to them. If an individual prefers, for the reasons indicated, an occupation in which he earns less money than he could earn in some other one, he can be considered as purchasing certain goods associated with the occupation he chooses and as paying a price for them. Thus, differences in money earnings which correspond to the individuals' preferences for the various occupations are not in contradiction with the equality of incomes discussed in the text. This takes care of the question of incentives. Cf. on this subject the present writer's essay, *On the Economic Theory of Socialism*, University of Minnesota Press, pp. 101–102, Minneapolis, 1938.

[12] Cf. footnote 5 above.

[13] Cf. footnote 5 above.

This can be written

$$\frac{\partial W}{\partial \Phi^{(i)}} \, \Phi^{(i)\prime} u_r^{(i)} = \frac{\partial W}{\partial \Phi^{(j)}} \, \Phi^{(j)\prime} u_r^{(j)}, \qquad (7.2)$$

whence

$$\frac{\partial W}{\partial u^{(i)}} \, u_r^{(i)} = \frac{\partial W}{\partial u^{(j)}} \, u_r^{(j)}, \qquad (7.3)$$

which is identical with (6.2). In a similar way, it can be shown that (6.3) is invariant under the transformation $\Phi^{(i)}$.

8. Let us restate our conclusions. The propositions of welfare economics can be divided into two parts. One part is based on maximizing the vector u and is concerned with conditions which permit to increase the utility of one individual without diminishing the utility of any other individual. It comprises all propositions of welfare economics except those which relate to the optimum distribution of incomes. These propositions are all operationally significant. The other part requires the setting up of a social value function $W(u)$ which is maximized. The maximum conditions thus obtained may be expressed either directly in terms of the commodities and incomes allowed to different individuals or in terms of the marginal utilities of the individuals. In the first case, propositions of immediate operational significance are obtained, but each individual's utility is determined quasi-accidentally as a by-product of the valuations made in terms of commodities or incomes. In the other case, the optimum distribution of incomes must be derived from certain *a priori* hypotheses concerning the functions expressing the marginal utility of incomes of the different individuals. Although these hypotheses have no direct operational significance, they lead to definite conclusions as to the appropriate distribution of incomes. They may, therefore, be used as check-ups on a distribution of incomes established by direct valuation.

Neither the social valuations nor the utilities of the individuals need be measurable; it is sufficient that they can be ordered.

Appendix

In order to simplify the exposition, the transformation function introduced at the beginning of Section 3, is assumed to refer to the whole economy. This is a strong oversimplification of reality, admissible

only under special circumstances. Actually the technological transformation of commodities is performed by individuals ("firms"; even in
a socialist society there would be separate productive establishments)
and each individual is confronted with a transformation function of his
own. Only when the transformation functions of the individuals are
all the same can they be combined in a unique way into a transformation
function for the economy as a whole. Otherwise, the conditions of
transformation in the economy as a whole depend on how the transformation of commodities is distributed among the individuals (i.e., the
relation between total "outputs" and total "inputs" depends on how
much "output" and "input" is obtained from each individual). Thus, in
order to give a better picture of an actual economic system, we must
assume each individual to be confronted with a separate transformation
function.

Denote by $f^{(i)}(y_1^{(i)}, y_2^{(i)}, ..., y_n^{(i)}) = 0$ the transformation function of
the ith individual, where $y_r^{(i)}$ is the quantity of the rth commodity he
transforms. Denote, as before, by $x_r^{(i)}$ the quantity of the rth commodity
which the ith individual possesses. The amount of a commodity which
an individual possesses need not be equal to the amount he obtains or
gives up through transformation, for he may acquire commodities or
get rid of them by means other than technological transformation
(e.g., by exchange or gift). But for the economy as a whole these amounts
are equal. We have, therefore, $\sum\limits_{i=1}^{\theta} x_r^{(i)} = \sum\limits_{i=1}^{\theta} y_r^{(i)}$ for $r = 1, 2, ..., n$.

In place of the maximum problem in Section 3, we now have

$$u^{(i)}(x_1^{(i)}, x_2^{(i)}, ..., x_n^{(i)}) = \max \quad (i = 1, 2, ..., \theta),$$

subject to the side relations

$$u^{(j)}(x_1^{(j)}, x_2^{(j)}, ..., x_n^{(j)}) = \text{const} \quad (j = 1, 2, ..., i-1, i+1, ..., \theta), \tag{1}$$

$$f^{(i)}(y_1^{(i)}, y_2^{(i)}, ..., y_n^{(i)}) = 0 \quad (i = 1, 2, ..., \theta), \tag{2}$$

$$\sum_{i=1}^{\theta} x_r^{(i)} = \sum_{i=1}^{\theta} y_r^{(i)} \quad (r = 1, 2, ..., n). \tag{3}$$

This leads to the expression

$$\sum_{i=1}^{\theta} \lambda_i u^{(i)} + \sum_{i=1}^{\theta} \gamma_i f^{(i)} + \sum_{r=1}^{\theta} \nu_r \left(\sum_{i=1}^{\theta} x_r^{(i)} - \sum_{i=1}^{\theta} y_r^{(i)} \right), \tag{4}$$

where the Greek letters stand for Lagrange multipliers and $\lambda_i \equiv 1$ successively for $i = 1, 2, ..., \theta$.

Eliminating the Lagrange multipliers, we arrive at the first-order maximum conditions

$$\frac{u_r^{(i)}}{u_s^{(i)}} = \frac{f_r^{(j)}}{f_s^{(j)}} \qquad (r \text{ and } s = 1, 2, ..., n; \ i \text{ and } j = 1, 2, ..., \theta), \qquad (5)$$

which take the place of (3.5) in the text.

The propositions usually found in the literature on welfare economics are special cases of the conditions (5). We obtain from (5)

$$\frac{f_r^{(i)}}{f_s^{(i)}} = \frac{f_r^{(j)}}{f_s^{(j)}} \qquad (6)$$

$$\frac{u_r^{(i)}}{u_s^{(i)}} = \frac{u_r^{(j)}}{u_s^{(j)}} \qquad (i \neq j). \qquad (7)$$

The relation (6) states that the marginal rate of transformation of any two commodities must be the same for each individual (i.e., "firm").[14]

---

[14] The relation (6) can be interpreted as the condition of maximum total physical output. In a similar way as total welfare was defined as the vector u, total physical output can be defined as the vector $X = (X_1, X_2, ..., X_n)$, where $X_s = \sum_{i=1}^{\theta} x_s^{(i)} = \sum_{=1}^{\theta} y_s^{(i)}$. We have then the problem

$$X_r = \max \qquad (r = 1, 2, ..., n)$$

subject to the side relations

(i) $$X_s = \text{const} \qquad (s = 1, 2, ..., r-1, r+1, ..., n),$$

(ii) $$X_s = \sum_{i=1}^{\theta} y_s^{(i)} \qquad (s = 1, 2, ..., n),$$

(iii) $$f^{(i)}(y_1^{(i)}, y_2^{(i)}, ..., y_n^{(i)}) = 0 \qquad (i = 1, 2, ..., \theta),$$

which leads to the conditions (6). The maximum total output is determined purely by the technological transformation possibilities without any reference to utility. Since the relation (6) is part of any maximum-welfare conditions, whether involving the social-value function W or only the vector u, the maximization of total physical output may be considered as the most narrow type of a concept of maximum total welfare. It is concerned only with the possibility of increasing the output of some commodities without diminishing the output of any other commodity, regardless of who is to be the recipient of the commodities (cf. Lerner, *op. cit.*, p. 57). We may thus consider the problem of maximum total welfare in three stages (instead of in two, as in the text): (1) maximizing the vector X, (2) maximizing the vector u, (3) maximizing the scalar function W. The maximum conditions in each stage include the maximum conditions of the preceding one.

If the commodities are both factors, this means that the ratio of their marginal productivities (in terms of any given product) must be the same for each firm in the economy. If they are both products, the ratio of their marginal factor cost (in terms of any given factor) must be the same in all firms. If one is a factor and the other a product, the marginal productivity of the factor in terms of that product must be the same in each firm.[15] These are all theorems well known in welfare economics. The relation (7) indicates the well known theorem that the marginal rate of substitution of any two commodities must be the same for each individual. With these relations in mind, we see that, according to (5), any individual's marginal rate of substitution of two commodities has to be equal to the ratio of the marginal factor costs of these commodities in any firm of the economy. The last is the most widely known theorem of welfare economics.

It was assumed here that each commodity appears as a variable both in the utility functions and in the transformation functions. However, this need not be the case. It may appear only in the utility functions as, for instance, a "gift of nature" which is not the product of human activity. Then the relation (7) still applies to it, but the other relations do not. Or, what is of greater practical importance, it may appear in the transformation functions without appearing in the utility functions, i.e., it is a factor of production which has no direct utility. In this case the relation (6) alone applies to it.

By proper interpretation, the relations (5), or (6) and (7) which are derived from it, can be taken as giving the dynamic conditions of maximum total welfare over a period of time. For this purpose, we consider the period over which total welfare is maximized as being divided into a finite number of discreet intervals (e.g., "days" or "weeks"); the first of these intervals constitutes the "present", the other ones are in the

---

[15] This condition implies the absence of unemployment. An unemployed factor can be considered as being employed by an "industry" or "firm" where its marginal productivity is nil. Any shift of the factor to an industry or firm where its marginal productivity is positive increases total physical output (as defined in the preceding footnote). The distinction between two types of propositions of welfare economics. one dealing with the allocation of resources and the other dealing with the degree of utilization of resources, which has been recently proposed by Mr. Scitovsky (*op. cit.*, p. 77), while useful pedagogically, is unnecessary from an analytical point of view. All propositions of welfare economics concerned with the degree of utilization of resources can be treated as allocational propositions.

future.[16] The same physical good in different time intervals is considered to constitute different commodities. The utility functions $u^{(i)}(x_1^{(i)}, x_2^{(i)}, \ldots \ldots, x_n^{(i)})$ and the transformation functions $f^{(i)}(y_1^{(i)}, y_2^{(i)}, \ldots, y_n^{(i)}) = 0$ are taken as covering the whole period of time over which total welfare is maximized. These functions thus contain among their variables commodities in different future time intervals as well as commodities in the "present". The relations (5)–(7) refer then to inter-temporal as well as intra-temporal substitution and transformation. Condition (5) states, among other things, that the inter-temporal marginal rates of substitution must be equal to the corresponding inter-temporal marginal rates of transformation.

Thus, condition (5) implicitly determines the rate of capital accumulation which maximizes total welfare over time. The result is very much along the lines of the traditional theory. The inter-temporal marginal rate of substitution is the marginal rate of time preference [which, according to (7), for any given commodity must be the same for each individual] and the inter-temporal marginal rate of transformation is the marginal productivity of waiting [which, according to (6), for any given commodity must be the same for each firm] of the traditional theory.[17] The two must be equal when total welfare is maximized over time. It should be noticed, however, that though for any given commodity and any given two time intervals these rates are the same for each individual (and firm), they need not be the same for different commodities or different pairs of time intervals. We have a separate rate of time preference and of (equal to the former) marginal productivity of waiting for each commodity[18] and for each pair of time intervals. Nor need the

---

[16] Cf., for instance, Hicks, *Value and Capital*, pp. 122–127, Clarendon Press, 1939.

[17] Speaking more precisely, the marginal rate of time preference and the marginal productivity of waiting differ by unity from the marginal rate of inter-temporal substitution or transformation, respectively. The marginal rate of time preference is usually defined as $\dfrac{u_r^{(i)}}{u_s^{(i)}} - 1$. Cf. R. G. D. Allen, *Mathematical Analysis for Economists*, Macmillan and Co., p. 344, London, 1938. Correspondingly, the marginal productivity of waiting may be defined as $\dfrac{f_r^{(i)}}{f_s^{(i)}} - 1$. The subscripts r and s refer here to different time intervals.

[18] Using Keynes's terminology of *The General Theory of Employment, Interest, and Money*, p. 223, New York: Harcourt Brace Co., 1937, we obtain a system of optimum (from the social point of view) "own rates" of interest.

time preference and the marginal productivity of waiting be necessarily positive.[19]

Our treatment can be generalized further by assuming that the transformation function of each individual (or firm) depends also on the quantities transformed by other individuals (or firms) in the economy. Taking the most general case, the transformation functions are then of the form $f^{(i)}(y_1^{(i)}, \ldots, y_n^{(i)}, \ldots, y_n^{(\theta)}) = 0$.

The maximum conditions (5) become

$$\frac{u_r^{(i)}}{u_s^{(i)}} = \frac{f_r^{(j)} + \sum_{k \neq j} f_r^{(k)}}{f_s^{(j)} + \sum_{k \neq j} f_s^{(k)}}. \tag{8}$$

The terms under the summation signs represent "external economies" and "external diseconomies" which play such a distinguished role in the analysis of Professor Pigou.

---

[19] The proposition made in the traditional treatment of the theory of interest that under conditions of zero capital accumulation these rates are positive rests on empirical assumption, not on theoretical deduction. The empirical assumption is either that the marginal rate of time preference is positive under these conditions and determines a positive value of the marginal productivity of waiting (time-preference theory of interest), or, conversely, that the latter is positive and determines a positive value of the first (marginal-productivity theory of interest). Whether any of these assumptions (and which one) is true is an empirical, not a theoretical question.

ON STATISTICAL REGULARITIES

Statistical Regularity and Causality

By mass processes we understand those processes which, when considered as a whole, show a certain regularity not to be observed in one particular case. How does this type of mass regularity, also called statistical regularity, manifest itself?

It appears in a process taking place in nature or in human society in which every case is subject to the same complex of causes, every individual case also being subject to special additional causes which are different for each case. We can divide the causes which affect mass processes into two categories: those which affect all cases and which we call main causes, and those which only have an effect on individual cases and which we call incidental causes.

Let us consider an example, concerning mortality. The life-span of an individual depends on his particular biological constitution and on the given social conditions in which he grew up, and this follows a definite pattern. Thus, the organism of a young child is very delicate and offers little resistance to harmful influences; consequently, at this age there is a high mortality rate. Then, during old age the organism has grown weak and offers little resistance, and again there is a high rate of mortality. Generally speaking, the organism shows certain biological characteristics according to age, which can be observed in every individual. The factors which constantly affect people's ages are the main causes.

Apart from these, the life of a particular individual is also affected by a vast number of specific additional causes, One individual is born more physically fit than another; one is subject to the danger of infection, another is not. One grows up and lives under better economic and social conditions than another. Another meets with an accident, e.g. is knocked down by a car. These are incidental causes, differing in the case of each individual.

If main causes were operative only, i.e. if each individual were affected only by main causes which always were the same, the regularity would be absolute. It could be observed in each particular case, and thus all people would live for precisely the same number of years. We could say when someone is born that he will live exactly so many years and die at a definite age. On the other hand, if exclusively incidental causes were to operate, differing in each case, there would be no regularity, only chaos. Statistical regularity arises when we are dealing with a main cause together with incidental causes. Regularity exists as a result of main causes, while incidental causes make this regularity only an approximation which exists *en masse*, since particular individual cases may deviate from the general regularity.

Particular cases can deviate appreciably from the general regularity, but in large groups the regularity, which is a result of the constant effect of main causes, prevails over and above the influence of the various incidental causes.

The Role of Statistics

Statistics are necessary in order to analyse processes involving mass regularity. If main causes alone were involved and there were no incidental causes, then every individual case would follow the same course and there would be no need to analyse the whole group. It would be enough to take one case and from this to draw conclusions covering the whole group. If all people lived equally long, then, in order to see what the expectancy of life in a given country is, we could take one individual, observe how long he lives, and conclude that all people live for the same length of time as the individual in question. If all people married at the same age, we could observe one case which would serve as a generalization for the rest.

This is how we proceed in many sciences, for example in chemistry, where we assume that one drop of water is similar to another. By analysing one test-tube filled with water, we can make a generalization as to the chemical composition of water. In zoology and anatomy we generally proceed in a similar way. We assume that one dog is basically similar to another. After examining the anatomical structure of one dog we draw conclusions as to the anatomical structure of all dogs. On the other hand, when the regularity imposes itself over the effects of incidental causes, we must examine a whole group of cases in order to be able to establish a regularity. A single case is now insufficient. In such cases, the examination of single examples can lead to false conclusions. From the fact that one person dies at the age of three we cannot draw the conclusion that all people live only three years, or if one person marries at the age of seventy, we cannot conclude that all men marry at this age.

Such incorrect methods are often used in economic analyses. From a single example general conclusions are drawn. Other examples could equally well be taken which would lead to quite contrary results. We arrive at general conclusions only by examining a whole group with the aid of statistics.

This was clearly demonstrated by Lenin. Shortly before his death he began to write a book called Statistics and Sociology which he did not finish. In this work Lenin clearly formulated the methodological conclusions which result from the mass character of social regularities.

"In the field of sociological phenomena no concept is more widespread and more incorrectly applied than the singling out of particular facts, i.e. playing with examples. To take facts in general may not entail any difficulties, but they may be of no significance, or else point to completely negative results, since everything depends on the concrete historical situation in which the particular cases are to be found. Facts, if they are examined in their entire context and in their relation to each other, are not only 'stubborn' to denial, but are entirely convincing. Facts examined without regard to their entire context, gathered together at random, disregarding related facts are mere play or even worse.

"The result is clear: It is necessary to build a foundation of exact and irrefutable facts on which it would be possible to depend and with which it would be possible to confront these 'general' and 'exemplary' views which are so excessively misused today in certain countries. In order that this be a real foundation, it is absolutely necessary to take instead of particular facts a complex of facts connected with the question under consideration, with no exception. Taking the above into consideration, we have decided to begin with statistics..."[1]

The Structure of Mass Processes

Mass processes which show the type of regularity described above are often called statistical processes, since this regularity can only be observed after a whole group of examples has been studied with the use

---

[1] V. Lenin, *The Works*, vol. 23.

of statistics. As a rule, two elements can be distinguished in mass processes: systematic and chance elements. The systematic element is that part of a mass process which is the result of the effect of a group of main causes; the element of chance is that part which is the result of incidental causes. In many cases it is possible to make a mathematical distinction between these two elements. The systematic element is then represented by that numerical value which would be given by each part of the mass process if main causes alone were operative, and the element of chance is represented by the deviation from this value which is due to the effect of incidental causes.

Let us take, for example, the number of boys born per 1000 births. The table of male and female births during various decades from 1820 to 1909 in Berlin, shows that out of 1000 children born, the number of boys varies between 512 and 516. Here some group of main causes must be operative, otherwise the stability which we can observe would not exist. However, this ratio changes from decade to decade. The deviation is the result of various incidental causes. Observation suggests that main causes produce a certain constant ratio of boys to the total number of births. We do not know exactly what that ratio is, but we know it lies somewhere between $\frac{512}{1000}$ and $\frac{516}{1000}$, and that during a given year of a given decade, the deviation is due to a set of incidental causes which may not act during another period or may act to a varying degree.

If we denote the ratio of boys to the total number of births by $\frac{m}{n}$, this ratio can be presented as the sum of two components: the systematic element which we call p, plus the element of chance which is usually denoted by the Greek letter ε (epsilon). We sometimes call the element of chance the random deviation or accidental disturbance.

Thus we get:

$$\frac{m}{n} = p + \varepsilon.$$

In our example, between 1820 and 1829 there are 515 boys per 1000 births. If we make a hypothetical estimate of the systematic element, e.g., 513 per 1000, we then get

$$\frac{515}{1000} = \frac{513}{1000} + \frac{2}{1000},$$

where 2 per 1000 is the random deviation.

Chance and Necessity

By defining the deviation from the systematic element as being accidental, we do not mean that we consider it to be produced independently of any cause. This definition means that it is not a result of those causes which are constantly brought into play in every particular example, i.e. of main causes, but that it is a result of causes which act differently in every single example, i.e., of incidental causes. The result of incidental causes is in general defined as chance.

Let us illustrate this with an example. A man is ill with cancer and dies. We can then say that this death is the necessary consequence of the illness because we know that every man who has cancer dies when the illness reaches a certain state. If the cancer sufferer returning from the doctor and walking along a street is hit and killed by a brick dislodged by the wind, this is not the necessary consequence of the illness. We then say that his death is accidental. This does not mean that it is not the result of some cause, but that it is due to a cause which is not usually connected with cancer. Cancer involves certain constant anatomical and physiological changes which lead to death, but it is not a permanent characteristic of that disease for someone to be hit by a brick while walking along a street. This is the result of a completely different chain of events, entirely independent of cancer, which just happens to coincide with another chain of events, i.e., the patient after a visit to the doctor happens to be walking along a certain house at the moment when a brick dislodged by the wind falls and hits him.

We say that something happens by chance when it is the result of a chain of events which is not normally and constantly connected with a phenomenon in question, but which is the result of an incidental chain of events coinciding with the normal chain of events. This we describe as happening by chance, while what happened in the first case was of necessity.

Chance and necessity are the two forms in which the law of regularity manifests itself. The character of both is objective. Things which happen of necessity are the result of a chain of events which always take place in every individual example, and things which happen by chance are the result of a chain of incidental events which normally are not connected and do not appear within the set of main causes.[2]

---

[2] A more exact explanation of the connection between causality and chance is to

It is necessary to be aware of two things. Firstly, chance does not mean a lack of causality. On the contrary, it is the result of definite but incidental causes, not connected with the system of main causes. Secondly, chance is something which takes place quite objectively and does not depend on undefinable subjective causes, as some people suppose. On the other hand, there exists the contrary view that everything happens of necessity and that we only talk about chance because we do not know the cause; that chance is merely our subjective ignorance. This view is wrong. Chance is the objective result of the effect of causes which for a given process are incidental; nevertheless, these causes can be established. After the causes have been understood, the result of incidental causes does not cease to be chance.

It is precisely in this sense that we speak of historical chance. Take for instance a battle, the result of which is determined by many main causes such as the strength and quality of the armies. During the battle there is an earthquake which changes the whole course of the battle. This is historical chance. Here, we can see the result of certain incidental causes which are not usually connected with the course of the battle: an earthquake does not coincide with every battle.

The Law of Great Numbers

Statistical regularities appear when we examine a whole mass of phenomena but not when we examine single examples, because incidental causes play such an important role in single examples that they counteract the effect of the main causes. However, if we examine a process *en masse*, the random deviation from the systematic element is positive in one case and negative in another, and throughout the whole mass it tends to cancel itself out.

Thus, if we take particular families, in one there will be just girls, in another just boys, and in others boys and girls in the most varying ratios. Here the effect of various incidental causes can be seen. It is only when we take a large number of examples, several thousand or several tens of thousands, that we see a more or less constant relationship between both the number of boys and the number of girls born.

---

be found in Professor A. Schaff's book, *Wstęp do teorii marksizmu* (An Introduction to the Theory of Marxism), pp. 112–120, Warsaw, 1950.

The consequences of incidental causes or random deviations often cancel themselves out as the number of the mass of observed phenomena increases. We then say that the law of great numbers is in operation.

An example of the law of great numbers is given in Table I. This example, taken from the sphere of games of chance has a great significance for the theory of statistics because in general it depends on the law of great numbers. We toss a coin 1000 times. Sometimes it falls heads up, sometimes tails up. If we know the structure of the coin we can define the systematic element precisely. On the basis of mathematical calculation we can say that if the coin is symmetrical then the systematic element will come to $\frac{1}{2}$, i.e. from half the tosses we will get heads up and from half tails. From a single throw we will either get heads or tails depending on the effect of incidental causes for the given toss. The incidental causes depend on the way we hold the coin, the force with which we toss it, the unevenness of the floor on which it falls, in what place we toss it, etc. If we throw the coin many times we get approximately half heads and half tails, as a result of which the relation of heads to tails tends towards one-half as the number of tosses increases. This can be seen in Table I which gives the results of an experiment carried out at the Warsaw Statistical Institute of the Central School of Planning and Statistics. In the first 50 tosses there were 23 heads and the portion of heads came to 0·460. In the next 50 throws there were 23 heads. Taking the first 100 throws together we got 46 heads and the proportion of heads came to 0·460. As we went on tossing, the proportion of heads came closer and closer to a half. Thus after 500 tosses we got the relation 0·512 and after 1000 tosses 0·501.

The law of great numbers does not, however, operate for every increase in the number forming the mass. Certain conditions must be fulfilled. Above all, as the number of parts increases, groups from other masses, not homogeneous with the first, should not be added to the mass under examination. A mass is homogeneous if each of its parts is subject to the same main causes.

If we add groups from a different mass, (i.e., which are subject to another set of main causes) to the increasing number of the first mass, the regularity will not only be disturbed but will be obliterated. This is illustrated by Table 2.

This table shows the mortality among employers and workers in Holland according to age groups. It is evident that the mortality differs in various social classes. All the figures concerning employers and workers involve a certain systematic element plus a certain element of chance. As the figures for an examined mass of workers or employers within a given age group increase, so the element of chance decreases and these figures tend towards the value of the systematic element. However, if we increase the figures in the mass by mixing employers and workers or the various age groups, we do not arrive at a better elimination of the incidental causes. On the contrary, the regularity disappears.

TABLE 1

No. of series	Number of heads in the series	nth toss	Number of heads m	Relation $\dfrac{m}{n}$
1	23	50	23	0·460
2	23	100	46	0·460
3	23	150	69	0·460
4	21	200	90	0·450
5	32	250	122	0·488
6	21	300	143	0·476
7	28	350	171	0·488
8	29	400	200	0·500
9	28	450	228	0·506
10	28	500	256	0·512
11	26	550	282	0·514
12	22	600	304	0·506
13	25	650	329	0·506
14	26	700	355	0·507
15	22	750	377	0·502
16	21	800	398	0·497
17	27	850	425	0·500
18	25	900	450	0·500
19	27	950	477	0·502
20	24	1000	501	0·501

We cannot establish whether or not a given statistical mass is homogeneous on the basis of statistical examination alone. Some sort of analysis must be made having recourse to the science which deals with the given subject, e.g., economics, medicine, etc.

The second condition which must be fulfilled if the law of great numbers is to be effective is that the incidental causes which act on the various groups within the mass process must be independent of each other, or only "vaguely connected" in the sense that only a small number of the interconnected groups are subject to their effect. In the last example we can divide the parts of the mass process into a few groups so that the incidental causes acting on each of the groups are independent of each other. Finally, it is possible that the effect of an incidental cause, acting on a large number of groups within the mass process be "divorced" by increasing in the number of these groups to such an extent that its result is reduced to a minimum and in practice does not enter into the calculation. In this example, the incidental causes acting on the various parts of the mass process can be considered as being independent. If such independence does not exist the tendency for the effects of incidental causes to compensate each other is not improved by increasing the numbers of the mass which is being examined.

TABLE 2. MORTALITY IN HOLLAND*—NUMBER OF DEATHS PER 100 PERSONS AMONG EMPLOYERS AND WORKERS IN INDUSTRY IN HOLLAND 1908–1911

Age	Mortality among employers	Mortality among workers
18–24	3·76	3·97
25–34	3·70	4·36
35–44	5·06	5·59
45–54	9·83	10·64
55–64	23·68	26·43
65 and over	75·81	82·61

* S. S. Ostroumov, *Sudiebnaya Statistika* (Legal Statistics), p. 82, Moscow, 1949.

The condition in which the incidental causes affecting the various parts of a mass process are independent of each other or only "vaguely connected", or the condition in which the effect of incidental causes is "divorced" as the number of groups is increased, is often not fulfilled in mass socio-economic processes. The groups within a process form the links connecting the development of a historical chain of events, and, as a rule, the incidental causes affect the majority of these links and only with difficulty can they be separated into groups of independent incidental causes. This is why the law of great numbers is often deceptive in mass socio-economic processes. Such processes should not be examined by mechanically increasing the mass under consideration, but through a quantitative social and economic analysis based on the dialectics of Marxism.

Types of Mass Processes

Mass processes were first observed and appear most distinctly in the field of social phenomena. However, they also appear in nature, e.g., in biology. We make a generalization about all dogs on the basis of an analysis of one, and in a zoological textbook on the anatomy of the dog we say that the structure of all dogs is the same. We follow this type of procedure when we are dealing with certain characteristics which on the whole are true of the entire mass. On the other hand, if we examine the growth of dogs, we find that even in the same race there is some difference in each individual case. Let us take, for example, the length of pods growing on the same plant. There is an apparent inclination for them to reach a certain definite length, but there are individual deviations depending on various incidental causes.

Mass processes are also to be found among inorganic substances. The laws of molecular physics (e.g. the laws of thermodynamics) and the laws of atomic physics follow certain regularities which appear in a mass of particles or atoms, but not in each particular one.

Here we will be mainly concerned with mass social economic processes. However, we will consider one type of mass process of a physical nature which has a great economic significance in the economy. This is the type of mass technological process which takes place in mass production, and is involved in the statistical control of production quality. For example, let us say, we are producing metal rods which should be 37 mm thick. In actual fact, however, the rods which come out of the machine are a little more or a little less than 37 mm. They are not entirely identical because, apart from the main cause, which is the construction of the machine, other incidental causes have an effect during the production of the rods. One load of metal is a little harder than another, the machine vibrates, its parts expand or contract depending on the temperature, etc. Each rod thus differs somewhat from the standard of 37 mm. A limit of tolerance is, therefore, fixed which defines which rods are to be accepted for use. Let us suppose that the tolerance is

1 mm; thus rods which are 36 and 38 mm are accepted for use, but rods which are thicker or narrower must be rejected as faulty.

Table 3 gives the results of production on various days.

Every day 150 rods are selected and examined to determine how many are faulty. If the machine works normally, the systematic element in the width of the rods comes to 37 mm and the actual thickness can be considered as the sum:

$$37+\varepsilon,$$

where ε is the random deviation. If ε falls within the limits of tolerance, the rods are accepted; otherwise they are rejected. In general, the number of rods found to be faulty during each test falls between 0 and 2. We consider this as the random deviation.

TABLE 3. CONTROL CARD OF PRODUCTION QUALITY FOR THE MONTH ...*

Day of the month	Number of faulty rods per test	Day of the month	Number of faulty rods per test
1	1	14	1
2	0	15	0
3	1	16	2
4	0	17	0
5	7	18	0
6	0	19	1
7	1	20	1
8	1	21	1
9	0	22	0
10	0	23	2
11	0	24	1
12	6	25	0
13	1		

* J. Oderfeld, *Statystyczna kontrola jakości produkcji* (Statistical Quality Control of Production), p. 16, Warsaw, 1949.

On the fifth and twelfth days, however, the number of faulty rods suddenly rises. It is difficult to consider this as accidental; something must have happened to the machine or to the raw material, the systematic element has changed. In this case the cause turned out to be bad material.

Mass processes appearing in the statistical control of agricultural experiments are also important for us. Statistical quality control of agricultural production and of experiments affects the productive forces of society, and is closely connected with socio-economic statistics.

Socio-economic Mass Processes

We will consider now socio-economic mass processes. Mass processes appear quite spontaneously in capitalist economy just as in general the course of all processes in human history has been spontaneous.

The course of historical processes throughout the entire length of human history preceding socialism was described by Engels as follows: "Those things which have taken place have seldom been just what people wanted. In most cases, their aims have crossed and opposed each other, or were forestalled in advance, or the means necessary for their realization were inadequate. This obliteration of innumerable individual intentions and individual factors has led to a state entirely analogous with that which prevails in nature. Individuals act with the intention of achieving certain aims, but in reality the results of their actions are something unintended, and although at first they might seem to satisfy the intended aims, in the end they unfortunately turn out to be quite different. Thus, the events of history seem, in the main, to be equally governed by chance. Whenever on the surface events pass for chance, hidden internal laws are always in control; what is important is to discover these laws. People create their own history, regardless of its consequences, by each of them endeavouring to achieve his own consciously intended aims; and history is simply the result of all these aims, taking effect under various conditions, and of their multifarious influence on the outside world".[3]

In Engel's letters on historical materialism, this thought is expressed even more clearly as follows:

"People create their own history, but up to now even within the limits of a given, strictly defined society, their actions have not been directed by the general will and they have not acted according to a general plan; their endeavours conflict with each other because necessity prevails throughout such a society although externally its complement, and the form in which it reveals itself, is chance".[4]

---

[3] F. Engels, *Ludwig Feuerbach.*
[4] F. Engels, K. Marx, *On Historical Materialism.*

Thus, historical processes are the spontaneous result of conflicting human activities. Regularity in historical processes is due to the fact that human activity takes place under certain definite social conditions. The activity of each individual, of each group of individuals, and of each social class is determined by a certain group of main causes which control this activity and form the basis of historical regularity. These are joined by numerous incidental causes, as a result of which the regularity appearing in socio-historical processes takes on a statistical character.

The Spontaneity of Mass Processes in a Capitalist Economy

An example of this type of mass process is the way in which the law of value works. The market price of particular goods does not always cover their value as established by the costs of production. The market price deviates from this value with each monetary fluctuation of supply and demand occurring in the market.

Throughout the entire process, however, there is a tendency for prices to exceed the value established by the cost of production. The value of an article, established by the cost of its production, can be considered as the systematic element in the mass process, which establishes the price of goods; the deviation of the market price from this value can be considered as the random deviation due to incidental causes.

The law of value penetrates the mass process, establishing market prices spontaneously, automatically and of necessity.

The statistical character of the way in which the law of value takes effect was confirmed by Marx who, in the first volume of *Capital*, writes:

"The possibility, therefore, of quantitative difference between price and magnitude of value, or, in other words, the deviation of the former from the latter is inherent in the very form of price. This is no defect, but, on the contrary, admirably adapts the form of price to a mode of production whose inherent laws impose themselves only as apparently lawless irregularities that offset one another".[5]

In the third volume of *Capital* Marx writes:

"But in reality this sphere is the sphere of competition, which, considered in each individual case, is dominated by accident. In other words,

---

[5] Karl Marx, *Capital*, vol. I, ch. 3, section I.

the internal law, which enforces itself in these accidents and regulates them, does not become visible until large numbers of these accidents are grouped together. It remains invisible and unintelligible to the individual agents of production".[6]

Lenin also emphasized the statistical character of the regularity in capitalist economy:

"It is quite natural that the regularity, which appears in the total activity of separate producers connected with one market, cannot be other than a mean and a mass social regularity from which individual deviations, whatever the direction, have been eliminated".[7]

With the coming of socialism, historical social processes have taken on the form of mass statistical regularity. The economic laws of capitalism are of the same nature. In the theory of political economy we ignore random deviations and consider economic processes as though only main causes were acting. It is on this point that the method of political economy depends. We establish economic laws by ignoring the elements of chance.

TABLE 4. THE CORN MARKET PRICE OF CEREALS—AVERAGE PRICES IN ZLOTYS PER 100 KG*

		1928	1929	1930	1931	1932	1933	1934	1935	1936	1937
Wheat											
	Warsaw	52·6	45·3	35·8	27·6	27·4	29·5	19·9	17·9	22·8	30·2
	Poznań	47·4	42·8	33·5	24·9	24·6	27·2	17·8	16·1	21·6	28·7
	Berlin	49·7	48·2	54·6	52·8	48·7	39·7	—	—	—	—
	Prague	57·3	48·5	44·3	41·4	41·7	41·8	36·8	39·4	38·0	32·7
	Liverpool	48·5	45·0	35·7	22·6	20·1	17·3	15·0	16·4	20·9	27·3
	Chicago	43·3	40·5	31·9	22·1	17·5	19·3	19·2	20·2	—	—
	Buenos Aires	40·7	36·8	29·9	14·9	14·9	12·1	11·0	12·7	18·4	21·1
Rye											
	Warsaw	42·6	29·6	19·4	23·9	21·9	17·2	14·8	13·2	15·2	24·2
	Poznań	40·9	28·4	19·1	23·3	20·7	16·3	15·4	13·3	15·1	23·1
	Berlin	50·7	40·8	34·5	38·7	37·8	32·0	—	—	—	—
	Prague	55·7	38·6	26·0	36·0	33·0	22·9	27·1	30·3	29·2	25·2
	Paris	46·9	40·2	28·1	30·7	31·2	23·9	—	—	—	—
	Chicago	39·9	36·4	23·3	13·7	13·0	15·5	—	—	—	—

* *Mały Rocznik Statystyczny (Concise Statistical Year Book) 1938*, p. 232.

---

[6] Karl Marx, *Capital*, vol. III, part 2, ch. 48, section III.

[7] V. Lenin, *Works*, vol. 23.

In practice, however, the action of economic laws is always disturbed by accidental deviation and only appears as a statistical mass regularity.

Table 4 will serve as an example of the regularity which appears in the spontaneous mass processes taking place in a capitalist economy.

The table gives the pre-war market price of cereals on several cereals markets in Poland and in other countries. It can be seen that for each year the price of wheat on the various corn markets is similar. There are certain differences: prices varied between Poznań and Warsaw, between Berlin and Chicago, and between Liverpool and Buenos Aires, but they did not deviate much from each other. For instance, in 1928 they fluctuated between 40 and 57 zlotys per 100 kg. The prices changed from year to year, but on all the corn markets these changes were in the same direction. The prices of rye behaved in a similar way.

The prices of wheat and rye were more or less similar everywhere because during this period there was a world market for cereals. Had prices in a particular country been considerably higher than in other countries, importers of corn would have shifted their orders from the country with higher prices to a country with lower prices. Consequently, there was a tendency for prices of corn to be levelled out in various countries. During the period after 1930 the prices in Berlin and Prague were considerably higher than on other cereals markets. This is due to the intervention of the state in those countries which maintained the price of cereals at a higher level and protected it from the fluctuations of the world market. Wherever there was a free world market, we find a statistical regularity. This regularity was established spontaneously as a result of competition on the world market.

Another example of spontaneous regularity in the capitalist economy can be seen in Table 5. This table gives an index of steel production for various countries in which at that time there was a capitalist economy. The close relationship between the indices and the trade cycle can be clearly seen. The rise and fall of steel production is the same in all the countries; there was a rise in production up to 1929 (in Poland up to 1928), then a fall until 1932, and then again a rise. Various accidental deviations appear between particular countries, but in principle the course is the same. This is connected with the course of the economic cycles, which is a spontaneous process.

TABLE 5. INDEX OF STEEL PRODUCTION* (1928 = 100)

Country	1925	1926	1927	1929	1930	1931	1932	1933	1934	1935	1936
Poland	54	55	87	96	86	72	39	58	60	66	79
England	87	42	107	113	86	61	62	82	104	116	138
France	78	89	88	103	98	81	61	71	70	66	71
Germany	84	85	113	112	79	57	39	52	82	113	131
U.S.A.	88	94	87	109	79	50	27	45	51	66	91
Italy	91	91	81	108	89	72	71	90	93	109	100
Czechoslovakia	75	68	86	111	92	77	34	37	48	60	79
Rumania	66	73	85	105	103	74	67	95	114	139	145
Hungary	48	67	97	106	76	65	37	47	65	92	114

* *Mały Rocznik Statystyczny* (Concise Statistical Yearbook), 1938, p. 4.

Mass Processes in a Planned Economy

Economic processes in a planned socialist economy are also mass processes, but they are not spontaneous. The doctrine of the "obsolescence of statistics" in a socialist planned economy was at one time widespread in the Soviet Union. The adherents of this doctrine argued that statistics is the science of mass processes. They then identified mass processes with spontaneous processes, and argued as follows: in a planned economy there are no spontaneous processes because the economic processes are planned, and, therefore, the statistical regularity to be found in economic life disappears. There is then neither need nor place for the scientific analysis of these processes. There remains merely the reporting of economic processes which gives results undisturbed by accidental deviations and does not require the science of statistics for their analysis and interpretation.

The doctrine of the "obsolescence of statistics" in a planned economy is false. It was eventually discarded in the Soviet Union. This doctrine connects statistical regularity with spontaneity. Mass processes, however, are not identical with spontaneous processes. Planned social economic processes may also be considered as mass processes. Processes in a planned economy as a rule contain a certain element of chance and are, therefore, mass processes.

This is the result of an economic plan being carried out by millions of people, and is due to the fact that it is not realized mechanically but by human activity and by human effort. The millions of people who carry out the plan work well or badly, their work differs, and consequently the realization of the plan varies. In one plant the plan is realized well, in another not so well, depending on the organization, management, and the effort put in. The millions of people carrying out the plan work under varying conditions. One plant has better technical equipment or natural conditions, others have worse. In this way, the implementation of the plan involves a certain element of chance which fluctuates from worker to worker, from plant to plant, and from one type of industry to another.

This fact is well known in the Soviet Union and was described as follows by Stalin:

"Essentially, the production plan is the living practical activity of millions of people. The reality of our production plan is millions of working people who are creating a new life[8]".

Because the carrying out of the plan is not a mechanical process, and because it is the result of the activity and efforts of millions of people, the realization of the plan takes on the character of a mass process, the regularities of which are statistical.

The next two examples demonstrate that the realization of the plan is a mass statistical process. One example (Table 6) gives data connected with the carrying out of the industrial plan in Czechoslovakia in 1948.

The percentage of the production plan achieved in various industries is given in the first column. However, within each industry, the various plants fulfil the plan differently. The minimum and maximum achievements of the plan in the given industry are shown in the second and third columns. It is evident that there are great differences. For instance, in the mining industry some plants only completed 10 per cent of the plan, while others completed 124 per cent. In the power industry the achievement of the plan was more uniform and varied between 88 per cent and 112 per cent. In the smelting industry it varied between 72 per cent and 105 per cent, in the metal industry the achievement of the plan was very varied, in the ceramic industry it was more uniform, etc. Thus, deviations in the carrying out of the plan occur within each industry. In this example, the deviations tend to be abnormal, which is explained by the fact that this was the first year in which economic planning in

---

[8] J. Stalin, *Problems of Leninism.*

TABLE 6. INDICATORS AND ACHIEVEMENT OF THE INDUSTRIAL PLAN IN
CZECHOSLOVAKIA FOR 1948[*]

Industry	Indicators of the average achievement of the plan in %	% of the plan achieved	
		minimum	maximum
Mining	96·1	10·8	124·3
Power	99·4	88·2	112·3
Smelting	98·8	75·2	105·4
Metal	96·5	30·0	444·9
Ceramic	117·9	103·1	132·7
Chemical	114·1	25·6	332·9
Mineral	97·8	37·9	248·9
Paper	100·6	63·1	238·0
Wood	104·6	83·4	225·1
Textile	126·6	13·6	206·8
Leather	119·1	96·9	157·7

* *Podnikova Statistika*, No. 1, p. 4, Prague, 1949.

Czechoslovakia really began seriously; socialization of heavy and medium industries only began in February 1948.

Table 7 shows the achievement of the industrial production plan in Poland in 1950.

The achievements of the plan are given for various industries. The percentage of the plan achieved varies: in one industry the plan is carried out better, in others less so.

It would be interesting to try to estimate the systematic element here. As we have already said, the systematic element is the result which we attribute to the action of main causes, i.e. causes which affect all cases. The element of chance is the result of the action of incidental causes which vary in each type of industry. At a first glance, one could imagine that the standard set in the plan is the only main cause operative everywhere. The plan should then be completed to 100 per cent and any instances of the plan being exceeded or not attained should be interpreted as random deviations due to incidental causes. According to this assumption, the systematic element in the carrying out of the plan should come to 100 per cent. This, however, is not the case. A more precise analysis of the figures of the completed plan shows that quantitatively those cases which exceed the plan predominate over those cases in which the plan is not achieved, and that, if we consider industrial production

TABLE 7. COMMUNIQUE OF THE STATE COMMISSION FOR ECONOMIC PLANNING ON THE ACHIEVEMENT OF THE PLAN. IMPLEMENTATION OF THE PLAN IN 1950 VALUES

Products	Implementation of plan in %	Products	Implementation of plan in %
Pit coal	102	Valve-type radio sets	112
Brown coal	93	Cotton	100
Oil	101	Wool	105
Rock salt	104	Silk	101
Electrical power	105	Linen	106
Steel	100	Rayon	101
Rolled products	100	Leather footwear	109
Zinc	101	Cellulose	100
Iron ore	90	Paper	104
Refined lead	102	Solid and perforated	
Pig iron	96	bricks	87
Sodium hydroxide	104	Lime	99
Soda ash	92	Cement	102
Sulphuric acid	85	Electrical and table	
Nitro chalk from		porcelain	105
nitrate of ammonia	105	Pane glass	109
Carbon electrodes	103	Suites of furniture	89
Goods locomotives	86	Matches	103
Goods wagons	96	Cigarettes	110
Tractors	112	All types of soap	107
Lorries	116	Sugar	115
Motorcycles	109	Beer	130
Bicycles	104	Wine	117
Tooling machines for		Confectionery and	
metal and wood	96	chocolates	115
Agricultural machines	116	Flower products	103
Cables	102	Pork	121
High and low tension		Cured pork products	130
transformers and		Best quality butter	104
safety apparatus	97		

as a whole, the plan was carried out to 107·4 per cent. We ought, therefore, to assume that the systematic element is here greater than 100 per cent. This is due to the fact that within the group of main causes, and, besides the standard of 100 per cent set by the plan, an important role is played by the systematic campaign to exceed the plan. Under the guidance of the Party, this campaign affects every kind of industry and every plant. The results of the campaign form a part of the systematic element, and they are the basis on which it is possible to raise the standard in the next plan.

In a socialist planned economy the achievement of particular standards involving productivity of labour, quality of production, use of materials, prime costs, etc., is similar. The result involves a systematic element which is due to the set standard and the systematic campaign to exceed it, and an element of chance which is due to incidental causes, varying in each plant, in each workshop and with each worker. As a result of the campaign to exceed the standard, the systematic element is greater than the standard 100 per cent, and this forms the basis of progress by the successive raising of the norm.

We can now see that the implementation of the plan and the fulfilment of the norm in a socialist planned economy is a mass process, and that the analysis of this process demands scientific and statistical examination. Because of this, it is ridiculous to talk about the "obsolescence of statistics" in socialism.

It should be also added that, apart from the plan being the result of the activity of millions of people working under varying conditions, many other factors influence the way in which it is carried out, such as the agricultural harvest.

At the moment, there still exist certain spontaneous market processes in Poland's economy. Moreover, it should be noticed that in a society in which socialism has been fully developed there still exist aspects of social life which are spontaneous and are not subject to planning. Here we might mention, for instance, changes in population (births, deaths, marriages), illness, crime, and many other aspects of life not planned by the state. The course of these processes continues to be spontaneous, although the character of this spontaneity has changed fundamentally with the changed socio-economic conditions.

Statistical analysis plays different roles in a socialist economy and in a capitalist economy. In a capitalist economy statistics can only passively register and describe the spontaneous course of economic processes; it cannot, however, influence this course. On the other hand, in a planned economy, statistics fulfil two functions: statistical material and analysis provide the basis for planning, and at the same time are the fundamental means of controlling plan fulfilment.

AVERAGES AND MEANS

Averages

The average represents a statistical synthesis, abstracting from differences between particular units. All units are treated as though they were of the same numerical value, i.e. the average value. In this way, instead of examining the original group, we examine a representative synthesis, in which all units are equal.

In this way, we are able to compare different statistical groups. For instance, we can compare the productivity of labour in two plants. In both plants, under examination, various workers show a different productivity; it is, therefore, impossible to compare the productivity of an individual worker in one plant with that of an individual worker in another. We can calculate the average productivity in both plants, and we then proceed as though all the workers employed in either of the two plants showed the same, i.e. the average productivity. On the basis of this comparison, we say that the productivity of labour in one plant is greater than that in the other, although some workers in the plant with the greater productivity might be less productive than certain workers in the plant with lower productivity. In gauging the differences between the workers in a particular plant we must take into account the mutability and asymmetry of these differences.

We have described the average as the means by which statistical groups can be compared. Consequently, it can be defined in the following way:

Let $x_1, x_2, ..., x_n$ be the particular units of a group made up of n units. Let us take any function of these values $F(x_1, x_2, ..., x_n)$. We then say that this function is the average value of $x_1, x_2, ..., x_n$ for cases in which

$$x_1 = x_2 = ... = x_n = c.$$

It then follows that

$$F(c, c_1, ..., c) = c. \tag{1}$$

321

In other words, the function $F(x_1, x_2, ..., x_n)$ is the average value of the units of the statistical group, and, in cases in which all the units of the group are equal, the function is also their common value. This definition lays emphasis on the average as being the basis by which we examine and compare representative syntheses, in which we ignore the differences between the units of the group and treat all units as being the same.

The function fulfilling condition (1) is of an unlimited size. We can also construct an unlimited number of various averages. In practice, when dealing with statistics, we limit ourselves to two types of averages which seem to be most useful. One of these is the average obtained by breaking down the total value of the units in the group (or this value put in another form) uniformly so that each unit participates in the total sum to the same extent. This type of average we call the mean. The second type is a positional average. This depends on the choice of the value of a particular unit due to its position in the statistical group, e.g., the value which is most often repeated or a value which in some particular way divides the group in half.

A Generalization of the Concept of the Mean

All means which we examine can be reduced to an arithmetic mean by transforming the values of the units in the statistical group; the geometric mean is obtained with the aid of logarithms, the harmonic mean by inversion, and the quadratic mean by squaring. Here, the idea suggests itself of constructing a general definition of the mean so that each particular definition would be a particular case of this general definition.

This can be done in the following way. Let $x_1, x_2, ..., x_n$ be the values of individual units in a statistical group, the number of which is n. These values can be treated as the particular values of the changing x. We then introduce the function $f(x)$ which is called the transformation function, and take the arithmetical mean of the value $f(x)$, i.e.

$$\frac{\sum f(x)}{n} .$$

We can consider this mean to be a particular value of the transformation function $f(x)$ corresponding to a certain definite value of $x = S$, i.e.

$$f(S) = \frac{\sum f(x)}{n}. \tag{2}$$

S, defined in this way, is the generalized mean of the value x.

So far, we have mentioned means which satisfy various types of transformation functions $f(x)$. We now give the formulae of the various means. From $f(x) = x$ we obtain the arithmetical mean; from $f(x) = \log x$—the geometric mean; from $f(x) = \frac{1}{x}$ — the harmonic mean; and from $f(x) = x^2$ we obtain the quadratic mean. It is evident that formula (2) defines an unlimited number of various means. Those which we have mentioned are most often used.

From formula (2) it follows that all means are averages, i.e. they fulfil condition (1). Indeed, let $x_1 = x_2 = \ldots = x_n = c$. Then

$$f(x_1) = f(x_2) = \ldots f(x_n) = f(c),$$

and

$$f(S) = \frac{\sum f(c)}{n} = \frac{nf(c)}{n} = f(c)$$

(since $f(c)$ is added in the numerator n times). Therefore,

$$S = c.$$

In cases, therefore, in which all the units of the statistical group are equal, all the means are equal to each other and are equal to the common value of the units. In other cases, the values of the various means differ and depend on the transformation function, $f(x)$.

The relation between the various means can be obtained from a graph in the following way (see Fig. 1). We mark the changing values of x along the axis of abscissae and the values of the transformation function $f(x)$ along the axis of ordinates, and plot the curve given by the function $f(x)$. Let $OA = M$ be the arithmetical mean of the x's, and OB the arithmetical mean of values of $f(x)$. It then follows that $OB = f(S)$. The point P which has both means as co-ordinates lies on the vertical line AL. This point is the centre of gravity of the curve $f(x)$ and lies within the concave field of this curve. In the particular case in which all values of x are equal, these values will all be equal to M, and as we have seen $f(S) = f(M)$, i.e., the point P will then lie on the curve $f(x)$. The value of the mean S can be found in the following way: we draw a horizontal line through the point P and extend it until it bisects the curve $f(x)$. The point of intersection Q has the same ordinate value as the point P, i.e., $f(S)$. Consequently, the abscissa OC of the point Q equals S.

If the point Q lies to the right of the point P, then $OC > OA$ or $S > M$; if, on the other hand, Q lies to the left of P, then $OC < OA$ or $S < M$. The first case is true when the concave field of the curve $f(x)$ lies to the left (as in Fig. 1), and the second case is true when the concave field of the curve $f(x)$ lies to the right.

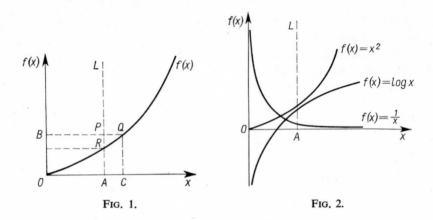

FIG. 1. FIG. 2.

The curves formed by the transformation functions

$$f(x) = \log x, \quad f(x) = \frac{1}{x}, \quad f(x) = x^2$$

are given in Fig. 2.

As before, we will denote the arithmetical mean of the x's by OA. The points P which correspond to the various transformation functions $f(x)$ all fall on the line AL within the concave field of the corresponding curve. From the graph it can be seen that

$$H < G < M < K,$$

---

[1] Here, H denotes the harmonic mean, G the geometric mean, M the arithmetic mean, and K the quadratic mean, i.e. $K = \sqrt{\dfrac{\sum x^2}{n}}$.

unless all values of x are equal.[1] Then, as we already know,

$$H = G = M = K$$

and the points Q lie on the curves given by the transformation functions.

Appendix

The argumentation already given in the text shows that the point P in Fig. 1 is the centre of gravity of the curve formed by the transformation function $f(x)$ and lies within the concave field of this curve. Denoting the frequency with which the values $x_1, x_2, ..., x_s$ repeat themselves, or the quantities of these values, by $m_1, m_2, ..., m_s$, we can then note that the co-ordinates of the point P are:

$$OA = M = \frac{\sum mx}{\sum m}, \tag{1}$$

$$OB = AP = \frac{\sum mf(x)}{\sum m}. \tag{2}$$

The point P is, therefore, the centre of gravity of the curve for which the quantities $m_1, m_2, ..., m_s$ are masses of points corresponding to the abscissa values of $x_1, x_2, ..., x_s$ (other points have masses equal to zero). We can now show that the point P lies within the concave field of the curve.

To do this we must examine the difference between the ordinate values of the points P and R. The ordinate of the point P is OB, and the ordinate of the point R is $f(M)$. By applying the Maclaurin formula we have

$$f(x) = f(0) + f'(0)x + \frac{1}{2}(f''(0)x^2 + 0(x)^3 \tag{3}$$

where $0(x)^3$ is infinitely small and of the third order. For the particular case in which $x = M$ we have

$$AR = f(M) = f(0) + f'(0)M + \frac{1}{2}f''(0)M^2 + 0(M^3). \tag{4}$$

Substituting (3) in (2) we arrive at

$$BO = \frac{\sum m[f(0)+f'(0)x+\frac{1}{2}f''(0)x^2+0(x^3)]}{\sum m}$$

$$= f'(0)+f'(0)\frac{\sum mx}{\sum m}+\frac{1}{2}f''(0)\frac{\sum mx^2}{\sum m}+0(x^3).$$

Using formula (1), this can be rewritten as:

$$AP = OB = f(0)+f'(0)M+\frac{1}{2}f''(0)\frac{\sum mx^2}{\sum m}+0(x^3). \tag{5}$$

Subtracting (4) from (5) we obtain

$$AP-AR = \frac{1}{2}f''(0)\left(\frac{\sum mx^2}{\sum m} - M^2\right)+0(x^3)-0(M^3).$$

Since $0(x^3)$ and $0(M^3)$ are infinitely small and of a higher order than the rest of the expression, the sign of the expression, therefore, depends on the sign of

$$\frac{1}{2}f''(0)\left(\frac{\sum mx^2}{\sum m}-M^2\right).$$

Let us note that

$$\frac{\sum mx^2}{\sum m}-M^2 = S^2,$$

i.e., this is the dispersion of the values $x_1, x_2, ..., x_s$.[2] The sign of the

---

[2] The proof of this formula is as follows. By definition

$$S^2 = \frac{\sum m(x-M)^2}{\sum m}.$$

Therefore,

$$S^2 = \frac{\sum mx^2-2M\sum mx+M\sum m}{\sum m}.$$

However, since

$$M = \frac{\sum mx}{\sum m},$$

difference $AP - AR$, therefore, depends on the sign of

$$\frac{1}{2} f''(0) S^2.$$

In all cases $S^2 \geqslant 0$. If $S^2 = 0$, which is the case when and only when $x_1 = x_2 = \ldots = x_s$, then $AP - AR = 0$. The point P then coincides with the point R. This means that for each transformation function $f(x)$

$$\frac{\sum mf(x)}{\sum m} = f(M),$$

or, using the notation used in the text,

$$f(S) = f(M),$$

therefore,

$$S = M.$$

All the means are then equal to the arithmetic mean.

If, on the other hand, $S^2 > 0$, then $AP \lessgtr AR$ depending on whether $f''(0) \lessgtr 0$. This means that the point P lies within the concave field of the curve formed by the transformation function $f(x)$. The difference $AP - AR$ and, if the transformation function $f(x)$ is monotonic, the difference $S - M$, becomes greater as the dispersion S^2 becomes greater.

---

we have

$$S^2 = \frac{\sum mx^2}{\sum m} - 2M^2 + M^2,$$

or

$$S^2 = \frac{\sum mx^2}{\sum m} - M^2.$$

STATISTICAL ESTIMATION OF PARAMETERS IN MARKOV PROCESSES

1. *Methods of estimation.* Consider a simple Markov process with the transition function

$$f(t_0, x_0; t_k, x_k; \theta_1, \theta_2 \ldots). \tag{1.1}$$

The transition function expresses the conditional probability (for discrete processes), or the conditional probability density (for continuous processes), that the random variable $\theta(t)$ will assume the value x_k at the moment t_k if its value is x_0 at the moment t_0. This function contains certain parameters $\theta_1, \theta_2, \ldots$ the values of which have to be determined from statistical observation.

In Markov processes this can be done by the method of maximum likelihood, which consists in choosing the estimators of the parameters $\theta_1, \theta_2, \ldots$, so as to maximize the probability or probability density of an observed set of realizations of the stochastic process. The method of maximum likelihood can be applied in several ways.

If the realizations of the stochastic process can be repeated many times (as, for instance, in the laboratory or in industrial production), we take n independent realizations of the process and perform on each realization a pair of observations at the moments, say, $t_0^{(r)}$ and $t_k^{(r)}$. The superscript r stands for the rth realization $(r = 1, 2, \ldots, n)$. Denote by $x_i^{(r)}$ the result of the observation carried out on the rth realization at the moment $t_i^{(r)}$, where $i = 0, k$. Since the pairs of observations are independent, their likelihood function is

$$L_1 = \prod_{r=1}^{n} f(t_0^{(r)}, x_0^{(r)}; t_k^{(r)} x_k^{(r)}; \theta_1, \theta_2 \ldots). \tag{1.2}$$

The estimators of $\theta_1, \theta_2, \ldots$, which will be denoted by $\hat{\theta}_1, \hat{\theta}_2, \ldots$, are determined from the condition $L_1 = \max$.

This way of using the method of maximum likelihood will be called *cross section estimation*, or *space estimation* (over the space of realizations of the process). The estimators thus derived will be called *cross section* or *space estimators*.

In cases, however, where the realization of the stochastic process cannot be repeated (as, for instance, in meteorological processes, in processes of growth of human populations, in socio-economic processes), we have to use the method of maximum likelihood in a different way, which will be called *historical estimation* or *time series estimation*. The estimators thus obtained will be called, accordingly, *historical* or *time estimators*.

Historical or time series estimation consists in performing a number of observations on a single realization of the stochastic process. Let the observations be made at the moments $t_0^{(r)}$, $t_1^{(r)}$, ..., $t_k^{(r)}$. The results of the observations then form the time series $x_0^{(r)}$, $x_1^{(r)}$, ..., $x_k^{(r)}$. The superscript r serves to identify the realization on which the observations are performed; since, in this case, only one realization is accessible to observation it may also be omitted. In view of the process being Markovian, the likelihood function of the observed time series is

$$L_2 = \prod_{i=1}^{k} f(t_{i-1}^{(r)}, x_{i-1}^{(r)}; t_i^{(r)}, x_i^{(r)}; \theta_1, \theta_2 \ldots). \tag{1.3}$$

The estimators $\hat{\theta}_1$, $\hat{\theta}_2$, ... are determined from the condition $L_2 = \max$.

Finally, situations may occur where it is possible to perform historical observations on a set of independent realizations of the same stochastic process. Let there be n such realizations and $k+1$ observations performed on each at the moments $t_0^{(r)}$, $t_1^{(r)}$, ..., $t_k^{(r)}$, respectively. Denoting, as before, by $x_i^{(r)}$ the result of the observation performed on the rth realization at the moment $t_i^{(r)}$, we have the following observation matrix:

$$\begin{vmatrix} x_0^{(1)} & x_1^{(1)} \ldots x_k^{(1)} \\ x_0^{(2)} & x_1^{(2)} \ldots x_k^{(2)} \\ \cdot & \cdot \quad \cdot \quad \cdot \quad \cdot \\ x_0^{(n)} & x_1^{(n)} \ldots x_k^{(n)} \end{vmatrix}. \tag{1.4}$$

The rows of the matrix are time series corresponding to the various realizations of the process, the columns are cross sections of observations performed on different realizations. It should be noted that the observations corresponding to a given column need not be simultaneous, for the $k+1$ observations performed on each realization may be effected on different realizations at different moments. Thus, the $t_i^{(r)}$ corresponding to a given subscript i but to different superscripts r may be different.

The likelihood function of the above observation matrix is

$$L = \prod_{r=1}^{n} \prod_{i=1}^{k} f(t_{i-1}^{(r)}, x_{i-1}^{(r)}; t_i^{(r)}, x_i^{(r)}; \theta_1, \theta_2 \ldots). \tag{1.5}$$

The estimators $\hat{\theta}_1, \hat{\theta}_2, \ldots$ are determined from the condition $L = \max$. This way of determining the estimators will be called *complete estimation* and the estimators thus obtained will be called *complete estimators*.

Complete estimators maximize the probability or probability density of the whole observation matrix (1.4), while historical and cross section estimators maximize only the probability or probability density of a particular row or column, respectively. Historical estimation and cross section estimation may thus be treated as special cases of complete estimation corresponding to $n = 1$ and $k = 1$, respectively. We shall, therefore, henceforth consider the general case of complete estimation.

In the present paper we shall consider the statistical estimation of parameters in the following elementary Markov processes: the simple Poisson process, the Gaussian process with stationary independent increments which is usually called the Brownian motion process, the linear "birth process" and the linear "death process". Finally, we shall consider the case of estimating transition probabilities in simple Markov chains.

2. *The simple Poisson process.* For the simple Poisson process the transition function (1.1) takes the form

$$f(t_i - t_{i-1}, z_i; \lambda) = \frac{[\lambda(t_i - t_{i-1})]^{z_i}}{z_i!} \exp[-\lambda(t_1 - t_{i-1})]. \tag{2.1}$$

Here

$$z_i = x_i - x_{i-1} \tag{2.2}$$

denotes the number of changes of state occurring during the period $t_i - t_{i-1}$; x_i and x_{i-1} denote the number of changes of state taking place during the periods from 0 to t_i and from 0 to t_{i-1}, respectively. Obviously x_i and x_{i-1} are integers. The number of changes of state expected during the period $t_i - t_{i-1}$ is

$$Ez_i = \lambda(t_i - t_{i-1}),$$

where λ is a constant. The simple Poisson process is a homogeneous process with independent increments.

The logarithm of the likelihood function is

$$\log L = \sum_{r=1}^{n} \sum_{i=1}^{k} \log f(t_i^{(r)} - t_{i-1}^{(r)}, z_i^{(r)}; \lambda)$$

$$= \sum_{r=1}^{n} \sum_{i=1}^{k} [z_i^{(r)} \log \lambda + z_i^{(r)} \log (t_i^{(r)} - t_{i-1}^{(r)}) - \log (z_i^{(r)}!) - \lambda(t_i^{(r)} - t_{i-1}^{(r)})].$$

(2.3)

Putting

$$\frac{\partial \log L}{\partial \lambda} = 0$$

and taking account of (2.2), we find the estimator of λ:

$$\hat{\lambda} = \frac{\sum_{r=1}^{n} (x_k^{(r)} - x_0^{(r)})}{\sum_{r=1}^{n} (t_k^{(r)} - t_0^{(r)})}.$$

(2.4)

The estimator $\hat{\lambda}$ depends only on the results of the observations performed at the moments $t_0^{(r)}$ and $t_k^{(r)}$ and on the length of the periods $t_k^{(r)} - t_0^{(r)}$ elapsing between these observations. The results of observations carried out at intermediate moments $t_1^{(r)}, t_2^{(r)}, \ldots, t_{k-1}^{(r)}$ do not affect the value of the estimator. Thus, it is sufficient to perform on each realization of the process only one pair of observations; all intermediate observations are redundant.

In view of the reproductive property of the Poisson distribution, the sampling distribution of

$$\sum_{r=1}^{n} (x_k^{(r)} - x_0^{(r)}) = \hat{\lambda} \sum_{r=1}^{n} (t_k^{(r)} - t_0^{(r)})$$

is given by the probability function

$$\frac{\left[\lambda \sum_{r=1}^{n} (t_k^{(r)} - t_0^{(r)})\right]^{\hat{\lambda} \sum_{r=1}^{n} (t_k^{(r)} - t_0^{(r)})}}{\left[\hat{\lambda} \sum_{r=1}^{n} (t_k^{(r)} - t_0^{(r)})\right]!} \exp \left[-\lambda \sum_{r=1}^{n} (t_k^{(r)} - t_0^{(r)})\right].$$

(2.5)

Consequently, the expectation of $\hat{\lambda}$ is

$$E\hat{\lambda} = \lambda$$

(2.6)

and the variance of $\hat{\lambda}$ is

$$V\hat{\lambda} = \frac{\lambda}{\sum\limits_{r=1}^{n}(t_k^{(r)}-t_0^{(r)})}. \tag{2.7}$$

The estimator $\hat{\lambda}$ is thus unbiased and consistent. Its sampling variance depends only on the number of realizations and the length of the periods $t_k^{(r)}-t_0^{(r)}$, and is not affected by observations at intermediate moments. Introducing the average period between the pairs of observations performed on each realization

$$t_k-t_0 = \frac{1}{n}\sum\limits_{r=1}^{n}(t_k^{(r)}-t_0^{(r)}), \tag{2.8}$$

we have

$$V\hat{\lambda} = \frac{\hat{\lambda}}{n(t_k-t_0)}. \tag{2.9}$$

The efficiency of the estimator, therefore, can be increased either by augmenting the number of realizations considered or by lengthening the average period between the two observations carried out on each realization. Additional observations at intermediate moments are useless.

3. *The Brownian motion process.* In the Brownian motion process the transition function (1.1) is

$$f(t_i-t_{i-1}, z_i; \mu, \sigma^2) = \frac{1}{\sigma\sqrt{2\pi(t_i-t_{i-1})}}\exp\left\{-\frac{[z_i-\mu(t_i-t_{i-1})]^2}{2\sigma^2(t_i-t_{i-1})}\right\}, \tag{3.1}$$

where z_i is the change of state taking place during the period t_i-t_{i-1}. Denoting the state at the moments t_i and t_{i-1}, respectively, we have

$$z_i = x_i-x_{i-1}. \tag{3.2}$$

Here x_i and x_{i-1} may be real numbers.

The expected change of state during the period t_i-t_{i-1} is

$$Ez_i = \mu(t_i-t_{i-1})$$

and the variance of the change of state during that period is

$$E[z_i-\mu'(t_i-t_{i-1})]^2 = \sigma^2(t_i-t_{i-1}),$$

where μ and σ^2 are constants. The Brownian motion process is thus a Gaussian process with stationary independent increments.

The logarithm of the likelihood function is

$$\log L = \sum_{r=1}^{n} \sum_{i=1}^{k} \log f(t_i^{(r)} - t_{i-1}^{(r)}, z_i^{(r)}; \mu, \sigma^2) \tag{3.3}$$

$$= \sum_{r=1}^{n} \sum_{i=1}^{k} \left\{ -\log \sigma - \frac{1}{2} \log (2\pi) - \frac{1}{2} \log (t_i^{(r)} - t_{i-1}^{(r)}) \right.$$

$$\left. - \frac{[z_i^{(r)} - \mu(t_i^{(r)} - t_{i-1}^{(r)})]^2}{2\sigma^2(t_i^{(r)} - t_{i-1}^{(r)})} \right\}.$$

Putting

$$\frac{\partial \log L}{\partial \mu} = 0$$

and taking account of (3.2), we obtain the estimator of μ:

$$\hat{\mu} = \frac{\sum_{r=1}^{n} (x_k^{(r)} - x_0^{(r)})}{\sum_{r=1}^{n} (t_k^{(r)} - t_0^{(r)})}. \tag{3.4}$$

The estimator of σ^2 is obtained by putting

$$\frac{\partial \log L}{\partial \sigma^2} = 0$$

and substituting $\hat{\mu}$ for μ in this equation. We obtain

$$\hat{\sigma}^2 = \frac{1}{nk} \sum_{r=1}^{n} \sum_{i=1}^{k} \frac{[(x_i^{(r)} - x_{i-1}^{(r)} - \hat{\mu}(t_i^{(r)} - t_{i-1}^{(r)})]^2}{t_i^{(r)} - t_{i-1}^{(r)}}. \tag{3.5}$$

Similarly to the estimator $\hat{\lambda}$ in the Poisson process, the estimator $\hat{\mu}$ is independent of the results of observations carried out at moments intermediate between $t_0^{(r)}$ and $t_k^{(r)}$. By virtue of the reproductive property of the normal distribution it is normally distributed with expectation

$$E\hat{\mu} = \mu \tag{3.6}$$

and variance

$$V\hat{\mu} = \frac{\sigma^2}{\sum_{r=1}^{n} (t_k^{(r)} - t_0^{(r)})}. \tag{3.7}$$

The estimator $\hat{\mu}$ is thus unbiased and consistent. Its sampling variance depends only on the number of realizations and on the length of the periods $t_k^{(r)} - t_0^{(r)}$, and is not affected by additional observations at intermediate moments. By writing it in the form

$$V\hat{\mu} = \frac{\sigma^2}{n(t_k - t_0)}, \tag{3.8}$$

where $t_k - t_0$ is, as in (2.8), the average period between the pairs of observations performed on each realization, we find that the sampling variance of $\hat{\mu}$ is inversely proportional to the number of realizations taken into account and to the average period mentioned.

Unlike $\hat{\mu}$, the estimator $\hat{\sigma}^2$ depends on the results of the observations at all moments in the intervals $t_k^{(r)} - t_0^{(r)}$, as well as on the choice of these moments. It is distributed according to the χ^2 law with $nk - 1$ degrees of freedom. In view of the known properties of the χ^2 distribution, the expectation and the sampling variance of $\hat{\sigma}^2$ are, respectively,

$$E\hat{\sigma}^2 = \frac{nk-1}{nk}\sigma^2, \tag{3.9}$$

$$V\hat{\sigma} = \frac{2\sigma^4}{nk-1}. \tag{3.10}$$

Thus the estimator $\hat{\sigma}^2$ is not unbiased. An unbiased estimator, however, can be obtained by taking

$$\frac{nk}{nk-1}\hat{\sigma}^2. \tag{3.11}$$

Because of (3.10), $\hat{\sigma}^2$ as well as the expression (3.11), are consistent estimators. Their efficiency increases (roughly) in proportion both to the number of realizations considered and to the number of observations performed on each realization.

4. *Testing hypotheses.* Since the sampling distribution of the estimator $\hat{\lambda}$ in the simple Poisson process and of the estimators $\hat{\mu}$ and $\hat{\sigma}^2$ in the Brownian motion process are known, hypotheses concerning values of the corresponding parameters can be tested by means of the Neyman–Pearson procedure.

In the simple Poisson process and in the Brownian motion process the number of changes of state or the magnitude of the change of the state, respectively, occurring in not overlapping time intervals are independent. Consequently the χ^2 criterion can be applied to test the hypothesis that one or several observed time series are realizations of a simple Poisson process or of a Brownian motion process. Furthermore, the hypothesis that a set of observed time series are realizations of the same Poisson or Brownian motion process, i.e., of a process with the same parameter values, can be tested by the usual procedure of analysis of variance.

5. *Linear "birth" and "death" processes.* The transition function of the linear "birth process" is

$$f(t_{i-1}, x_{i-1}; t_i, x_i; \alpha)$$

$$= \binom{x_i-1}{x_i-x_{i-1}} e^{-\alpha x_{i-1}(t_i-t_{i-1})} [1-e^{-\alpha(t_i-t_{i-1})}]^{x_i-x_{i-1}}. \tag{5.1}$$

Here x_i and x_{i-1}, which must be integers, denote the number of individuals in the "populations" at the moments t_i and t_{i-1}, respectively. The probability of any one individual "giving birth" to a new individual during the infinitesimal period dt is αdt, where α is a constant. It can be shown that the number of individuals expected at the moment t_i is

$$Ex_i = x_{i-1} e^{\alpha(t_i-t_{i-1})}. \tag{5.2}$$

The logarithm of the likelihood function is

$$\log L = \sum_{r=1}^{n} \sum_{i=1}^{k} \log f(t_{i-1}^{(r)}, x_{i-1}^{(r)}; t_i^{(r)}, x_i^{(r)}; \alpha) = \sum_{r=1}^{n} \sum_{i=1}^{k} \left\{ \log \binom{x_i^{(r)}-1}{x_i^{(r)}-x_{i-1}} \right. \tag{5.3}$$

$$\left. - \alpha x_{i-1}^{(r)}(t_i^{(r)}-t_{i-1}^{(r)}) + (x_i^{(r)}-x_{i-1}^{(r)}) \log \left[1-e^{-\alpha(t_i^{(r)}-t_{i-1}^{(r)})}\right] \right\}.$$

The estimator $\hat{\alpha}$ is obtained from the equation

$$\frac{\partial \log L}{\partial \alpha} = 0. \tag{5.4}$$

In order to obtain a workable solution of (5.4) we shall assume that all observations are carried out at equal intervals of length τ. We have then

$$t_i^{(r)}-t_{i-1}^{(r)} = \tau$$

for all r's and i's, and we obtain

$$e^{\hat{\alpha}\tau} = \frac{\displaystyle\sum_{r=1}^{n} \sum_{i=1}^{k} x_i^{(r)}}{\displaystyle\sum_{r=1}^{n} \sum_{i=1}^{k} x_{i-1}^{(r)}} \tag{5.5}$$

whence

$$\hat{\alpha} = \frac{1}{\tau} \left(\log \sum_{r=1}^{n} \sum_{i=1}^{k} x_i^{(r)} - \log \sum_{r=1}^{n} \sum_{i=1}^{k} x_{i-1}^{(r)} \right). \qquad (5.6)$$

This result was obtained by David G. Kendall.[1]

For the linear "death process" the transition function is

$$f(t_{i-1}, x_{i-1}; t_i, x_i; \beta) = \binom{x_{i-1}}{x_i} e^{-\beta x_{i-1}(t_i-t_{i-1})} [e^\beta (t_i-t_{i-1})-1]^{x_{i-1}-x_i} \quad (5.7)$$

where x_i and x_{i-1} have the same meaning as before. Note, however, that in the "death process" $x_i \geqslant x_{i-1}$, whereas in the "birth process" $x_i \leqslant x_{i-1}$. The constant β is defined by βdt being the probability that any one individual "dies" during the infinitesimal period dt. The number of individuals expected at the moment t_i is

$$Ex_i = x_{i-1} e^{-\beta(t_i-t_{i-1})}. \qquad (5.8)$$

By a procedure similar as in the "birth process" we find that the estimator $\hat{\beta}$ satisfies the relation

$$e^{\hat{\beta}\tau} = \frac{\displaystyle\sum_{r=1}^{n} \sum_{i=1}^{k} x_{i-1}^{(r)}}{\displaystyle\sum_{r=1}^{n} \sum_{i=1}^{k} x_i^{(r)}} \qquad (5.9)$$

whence

$$\hat{\beta} = \frac{1}{\tau} \left(\log \sum_{r=1}^{n} \sum_{i=1}^{k} x_{i-1}^{(r)} - \log \sum_{r=1}^{n} \sum_{i=1}^{k} x_i^{(r)} \right). \qquad (5.10)$$

The exact sampling distributions of $\hat{\alpha}$ and $\hat{\beta}$ are as yet unknown. Neither do we know whether these estimators are unbiased. However, the known asymptotic properties of maximum likelihood estimators allow us to find their asymptotic sampling variance. The observed realizations of the process being independent, we have, for $n \to \infty$, asymptotically

$$V\hat{\alpha} = -\frac{1}{E \dfrac{\partial^2 \log L}{\partial \alpha^2}}. \qquad (5.11)$$

---

[1] D. G. Kendall, Stochastic Processes and Population Growth, *Journal of the Royal Statistical Society*, Series B, p. 250, 9 (1949).

From (5.3) we find, treating $t_i^{(r)} - t_{i-1}^{(r)} = \tau = $ const,

$$\frac{\partial^2 \log L}{\partial \alpha^2} = \frac{\tau^2 e^{\alpha \tau}}{(e^{\alpha \tau} - 1)^2} \sum_{r=1}^{n} (x_k^{(r)} - x_0^{(r)}). \qquad (5.12)$$

By virtue of (5.2) we have

$$Ex_k^{(r)} = x_0^{(r)} e^{\alpha T},$$

where $T = k\tau$ is the total observation period. Consequently,

$$E\frac{\partial^2 \log L}{\partial \alpha^2} = -\frac{\tau^2 e^{\alpha \tau}(e^{\alpha T} - 1)}{(e^{\alpha T} - 1)^2} \sum_{r=1}^{n} x_0^{(r)}$$

and, according to (5.11),

$$V\hat{\alpha} = \frac{1}{N_0(e^{\alpha T} - 1)} \cdot \frac{(e^{\alpha T} - 1)^2}{\tau^2 e^{\alpha \tau}},$$

where $N_0 = \sum_{r=1}^{n} x_0^{(r)}$ is the total initial "population" of all the realizations considered.

This can be brought into the form

$$V\hat{\alpha} = \frac{\alpha^2}{N_0(e^{\alpha T} - 1)} \left(\frac{\sinh \frac{1}{2} \alpha \frac{T}{k}}{\frac{1}{2} \alpha \frac{T}{k}} \right)^2, \qquad (5.13)$$

a formula which was obtained by D. G. Kendall.[2]

By an analogous procedure we get asymptotically

$$V\hat{\beta} = \frac{\beta^2}{N_0(1 - e^{-\beta T})} \left(\frac{\sinh \frac{1}{2} \beta \frac{T}{k}}{\frac{1}{2} \beta \frac{T}{k}} \right)^2. \qquad (5.14)$$

The sampling variance of the estimators $\hat{\alpha}$ and $\hat{\beta}$ is thus inversely proportional to the total initial "population" of all the realizations considered. It also decreases rapidly with the length of the observation period T. Furthermore, it depends on the number of observations performed on each realization (which is $k+1$). From (5.13) and (5.14) it is seen

---

[2] D. G. Kendall, *loc. cit.*, p. 250.

immediately that the variance decreases with the number k, reaching asymptotically a minimum value for $k \to \infty$ when the squared factor becomes unity. Thus the estimators $\hat{\alpha}$ and $\hat{\beta}$ become most efficient under conditions of continuous observation of each realization of the process.

6. *The influence of intermediate observations.* The estimators $\hat{\alpha}$ and $\hat{\beta}$ in the linear "birth" and "death" processes are, so to speak, on the opposite pole of the estimators $\hat{\lambda}$ and $\hat{\mu}$ in the simple Poisson process and the Brownian motion process, respectively. The latter two, as we know, depend only on the first and on the last observation performed on each realization. So does their efficiency. Neither their value nor their efficiency is affected by intermediate observations.

In order that an estimator $\hat{\theta}$ be independent of the intermediate observations the derivative of the logarithm of the likelihood function must be separable into two factors

$$\frac{\partial \log L}{\partial \theta} \tag{6.1}$$

$$= gh(x_0^{(1)}, x_0^{(2)}, \ldots, x_0^{(n)}; x_k^{(1)}, x_k^{(2)}, \ldots, x_k^{(n)}; t_0^{(1)}, t_0^{(2)}, \ldots, t_0^{(n)}; t_k^{(1)}, t_k^{(2)} \ldots t_k^{(n)}; \theta)$$

in such a way that the factor g may depend on all or some of the observations $x_0^{(r)}, x_1^{(r)}, \ldots, x_k^{(r)}$ and corresponding moments $t_0^{(r)}, t_1^{(r)}, \ldots, t_k^{(r)}$, as well as on other parameters, but does not depend on the parameter θ (or, if it depends, the equation $g = 0$ has no admissible solution for θ; for instance, the solution is complex while θ is postulated to be real), whereas the factor h, which depends on the parameter θ, depends only on the first and the last observation performed on each realization, i.e., on $x_0^{(r)}, x_k^{(r)}$ and $t_0^{(r)}, t_k^{(r)}$ $(r = 1, 2, \ldots, n)$. This is obviously sufficient as well as necessary.

We assume that the equation

$$h(x_0^{(1)}, x_0^{(2)}, \ldots, x_0^{(n)}; x_k^{(1)}, x_k^{(2)}, \ldots, x_k^{(n)}; t_0^{(1)}, t_0^{(2)}, \ldots, t_0^{(n)}; t_k^{(1)}, t_k^{(2)}, \ldots, t_k^{(n)}; \theta) = 0 \tag{6.2}$$

is uniquely solvable with regard to θ. The solution yields the estimator $\hat{\theta}$. This estimator does not depend on the intermediate observations.

The condition (6.1) implies

$$\log L = gH(\theta) + C, \tag{6.3}$$

where $H(\theta)$ is the primitive function of h with regard to θ, and g and C do not depend on θ.

The condition (6.3) is satisfied with regard to the parameter $\hat{\lambda}$ in the simple Poisson process. It is satisfied in the Brownian motion process with regard to the parameter μ but not with regard to the parameter θ^2. It is not satisfied with regard to the parameters α and β, respectively, in the linear "birth process" and the linear "death process".

The conditions for independence from intermediate observations of the sampling variance of the estimator $\hat{\theta}$ require separate investigation. In view of the relation

$$V\hat{\theta} = -\frac{1}{E\dfrac{\partial^2 \log L}{\partial \theta^2}} \tag{6.4}$$

which holds asymptotically for $nk \to \infty$, we find that the sampling variance of $\hat{\theta}$ does not depend on the intermediate observations, at least asymptotically for $n \to \infty$, when

$$E\frac{\partial^2 \log L}{\partial \theta^2} \tag{6.5}$$

is a function of $x_0^{(r)}$, $x_k^{(r)}$ and $t_0^{(r)}$, $t_k^{(r)}$ $(r = 1, 2, ..., n)$ only. This condition is necessary as well as sufficient.

As can easily be verified, the condition (6.5) is satisfied for the estimator $\hat{\lambda}$ in the simple Poisson process and for the estimator $\hat{\mu}$ in the Brownian motion process. In these cases (6.4) is satisfied not asymptotically but exactly. In the Brownian motion process the sampling variance of $\hat{\theta}^2$ depends on the number of intermediate observations, but is independent of their timing. This can also be seen directly from (3.10).

7. *Relation to least squares estimation.* The maximum likelihood estimators obtained in this paper are identical with the corresponding least squares estimators. Using the same notation as before, we find the following.

The estimator $\hat{\lambda}$ for the simple Poisson process can be obtained by minimizing the expression

$$\sum_{r=1}^{n} \sum_{i=1}^{k} \frac{(\tau_i^{(r)} - E\tau_i^{(r)})^2}{t_i^{(r)} - t_{i-1}^{(r)}}, \tag{7.1}$$

where

$$E\tau_i^{(r)} = \lambda(t_i^{(r)} - t_{i-1}^{(r)}).$$

The estimator $\hat{\mu}$ for the Brownian motion process can be obtained by minimizing the expression

$$\sum_{r=1}^{n} \sum_{i=1}^{k} \frac{(\tau_i^{(r)} - E\tau_i^{(r)})^2}{t_i^{(r)} - t_{i-1}^{(r)}}, \tag{7.2}$$

where

$$E\tau_i^{(r)} = \mu(t_i^{(r)} - t_{i-1}^{(r)}).$$

The estimator $\hat{\sigma}^2$ is then the mean square of the residuals of the least squares estimation, i.e.

$$\sigma^2 = \frac{1}{nk} \sum_{r=1}^{n} \sum_{i=1}^{k} \frac{[\tau_i^{(r)} - \hat{\mu}(t_i^{(r)} - t_{i-1}^{(r)})]^2}{t_i^{(r)} - t_{i-1}^{(r)}}. \tag{7.3}$$

The estimators $\hat{\alpha}$ and $\hat{\beta}$ for the linear "birth process" and linear "death process" can be obtained by minimizing the expression

$$\sum_{r=1}^{n} \sum_{i=1}^{k} \frac{(x_i^{(r)} - Ex_i^{(r)})^2}{x_{i-1}^{(r)}}, \tag{7.4}$$

where

$$Ex_i^{(r)} = x_{i-1}^{(r)} e^{\alpha\tau}$$

in the "birth process" and

$$Ex_i^{(r)} = x_{i-1}^{(r)} e^{-\beta\tau}$$

in the "death process".

Notice should be taken of the fact that in the expression (7.1) and (7.2) the squares of the deviation from the expected value are weighted by the reciprocals of the length of time $t_i^{(r)} - t_{i-1}^{(r)}$ elapsing between successive observations. In the expression (7.4), instead, the squares of the deviations from the expected value are weighted by the reciprocal of the size of the "population" at the beginning of each successive observation period. In other words, in (7.1) and (7.2) the squares of the deviations are taken as "per unit of time", whereas in (7.4) they are taken as "per unit of population".

8. *Estimation of transition probabilities in simple Markov chains.* Finally, we consider the problem of estimating transition probabilities in simple Markov chains with a finite number of states. We assume the transition probabilities to be stationary.

Denote the states by the numbers $1, 2, ..., s$, and denote by p_{ij} the probability of transition from state i to state j. The probabilities of transition form the transition matrix

$$\begin{pmatrix} p_{11} & p_{12} \cdots p_{1s} \\ p_{21} & p_{22} \cdots p_{2s} \\ \cdot & \cdot \quad \cdot \quad \cdot \quad \cdot \\ p_{s1} & p_{s2} \cdots p_{ss} \end{pmatrix}. \tag{8.1}$$

In this matrix

$$0 \leqslant p_{ij} \leqslant 1 \quad \text{for} \quad i, j = 1, 2, ..., s$$

and

$$\sum_{j=1}^{s} p_{ij} = 1 \quad \text{for} \quad i = 1, 2, ..., s. \tag{8.2}$$

Let N changes of state be observed and denote by m_{ij} the observed frequency of changes from state i to state j. Denote further

$$n_i = \sum_{j=1}^{s} m_{ij}, \tag{8.3}$$

i.e., the total frequency of changes starting from state i. Obviously

$$\sum_{i=1}^{s} n_i = N.$$

We have the observation matrix

$$\begin{pmatrix} m_{11} & m_{12} \ldots m_{1s} \\ m_{21} & m_{22} \ldots m_{2s} \\ \cdot & \cdot \quad \cdot \quad \cdot \quad \cdot \quad \cdot \\ m_{s1} & m_{s2} \ldots m_{ss} \end{pmatrix}. \tag{8.4}$$

The logarithm of the likelihood function of this matrix is, according to the multinomial law,

$$\log L = \log(N!) - \sum_{i=1}^{s} \sum_{j=1}^{s} (m_{ij}!) - \sum_{i=1}^{s} \sum_{j=1}^{s} m_{ij} p_{ij}. \tag{8.5}$$

The estimators $\hat{p}_{ij}$ are found by putting

$$\frac{\partial \log L}{\partial p_{ij}} = 0 \tag{8.6}$$

subject to the side relations (8.2). Introducing the Lagrange multipliers $l_1, l_2, ..., l_s$, we arrive at the equations

$$m_{ij} = l_j p_{ij} \quad (i, j = 1, 2, ..., s). \tag{8.7}$$

Summing over j and taking into account (8.3) as well as (8.2), we find

$$l_i = n_i \quad (i = 1, 2, ..., s)$$

and, consequently,

$$\hat{p}_{ij} = \frac{m_{ij}}{n_i} \quad (i, j = 1, 2, ..., s). \tag{8.8}$$

The estimator of the probability of transition from state i to state j is the relative frequency of changes ensuing in state j among all changes starting from state i. This result was first obtained by V. I. Romanovski.[3]
The expectation and the sampling variance of $\hat{p}_{ij}$ are, respectively,

$$E\hat{p}_{ij} = p_{ij} \quad \text{and} \quad V\hat{p}_{ij} = \frac{1}{n_i} p_{ij}(1 - p_{ij}). \tag{8.9}$$

The estimator $\hat{p}_{ij}$ is thus unbiased and consistent.
The observation matrix (8.4) being given, we can by virtue of (8.8) estimate the transition matrix (8.1). By means of the χ^2 criterion the hypothesis can be tested that an observation matrix (8.4) is the result of the realization of a simple Markov chain with some theoretical transition matrix (8.1). In this case

$$\chi^2 = \sum_{i=1}^{s} \sum_{j=1}^{s} \frac{(m_{ij} - n_i p_{ij})^2}{n_i p_{ij}}, \tag{8.10}$$

the number of degrees of freedom being $s^2 - 1$.

[3] V. I. Romanovski, *Markov's Discreet Chains* (in Russian), p. 393, Moscow, Leningrad, 1949.

MICHAŁ KALECKI'S MODEL OF THE BUSINESS CYCLE

There are many mathematically based economic models which attempt to explain the cyclical nature of the development of the capitalist economy. Here we shall describe and then critically discuss one of them which has gained a notable place in economic literature.

The model with which we shall be concerned is now a classic of its type and was formulated by the Polish economist, Michał Kalecki. Kalecki changed and improved his model many times. He first presented it in his book (*Próba teorii koniunktury*) *Studies in the Theory of Business Cycles*, which was published in 1933, and work was published in English as an article in the journal *Econometrica* in 1935. This marked the beginning of Kalecki's international career. A modified version of the original work appeared in 1943 as Studies in Economic Dynamics. Continuing to develop further his theory, Kalecki published in 1954, in English, his *Theory of Economic Dynamics*.

Kalecki's first work appeared in 1933, before Keynes published his important work *The General Theory of Employment, Interest and Money* in 1936, and is often considered as a precursor of Keynes's theory. This is not strictly true. Kalecki's work contains many elements which appear in Keynes's theory, but in principle it is derived from Marx. In this article we shall deal with Kalecki's model in its original form. Later modifications mainly consisted in the introduction of certain complicating elements which, however, did not exhaust all the possibilities either of improving or of bringing the model nearer to reality; but this did not change the fundamental idea of the model. Because of this it will be easier and simpler to deal with Kalecki's model in its original form in which the principal thoughts are expressed most clearly.

Kalecki assumes the entire demand, Y_t at a particular moment t to be the sum of consumption, C_t and investment, I_t (by which in the future we will understand, for the sake of simplification, only net investment, assuming that autonomous investment is equal to zero), plus a certain additional element, k_t. This last element represents a linear

343

trend of general development and changes taking place within the process which is being examined. The significance of this type of trend in the mechanism of Kalecki's model will be discussed later. It would appear, for instance, if the coefficient of consumption were not constant but changed in the course of time.

Ignoring this element of trend for the moment, we can express the entire demand Y_t by the formula

$$Y_t = C_t + I_t$$

or, if we introduce a coefficient of consumption c:

$$Y_t = cY_t + I_t. \tag{1}$$

We must now determine the demand for investment, I_t.

An essential element in Kalecki's theory is the distinction which he makes between investment decisions and their realization. Between the moment in which a decision concerning some investment is made and the moment in which the carrying out of the decision is completed, a certain time elapses which we will denote by the letter θ. Consequently we have the following relation:

$$I_{t+\theta} = B_t; \tag{2}$$

this means that the size of investments carried out at the point of time $t+\theta$ is equal to the size of investment decisions made at the moment t, which we will denote by B_t. The making of investment decisions is influenced by certain economic conditions, and the length of time which is necessary for the carrying out of these decisions depends on the technical conditions prevailing at the time this investment is being implemented.

Kalecki endeavoured to estimate the period θ. At first he took θ to equal 1/2 year, and later $\theta = 1$ year. By and large, we can, therefore, assume that $1/2 \leqslant \theta \leqslant 1$.

The period θ as defined by Kalecki is the average period which elapses between the moment in which a decision is made and the moment in which the investment is completed. This means, for instance, that if 2 years elapse between the moment in which the building of a factory is begun and its completion, then the mean $\theta = 1$ year. In his work Kalecki gives an extensive argumentation of how this average period, in which the investment process takes place, should be established. Here, in order to simplify the problem, we will take the period θ to be the same for all investments.

Our further considerations will be based on the following observations:

1. There is a certain relation between investments and the growth of capital (by which we understand stocks of the means of production, or, in Marx's terminology, durable capital).

That is to say, investment, I_t equals the growth in capital K_t during a given period or in a given moment, and, therefore,

$$\frac{dK_t}{dt} = I_t. \tag{3}$$

In other words, during a continual process, investments are equal to the rate of growth of capital at a given moment.

2. There is a certain level which determines investment decisions.

Kalecki considers that investment decisions are determined by a foreseeable risk which depends on two factors: the total demand and the entire stock of capital goods; as stocks of capital goods for a given demand increase profits will decrease; on the other hand, for a given amount of capital, profits will increase as demand increases.

Kalecki reaches the conclusion that investment decisions B_t, made in a given moment t, are linearly dependent on the size of capital owners' savings, S_t, during the given period, and also on the stock of capital goods already in existence, K_t. The following relation, therefore, obtains:

$$B_t = aS_t - bK_t, \tag{4}$$

where a and b are the corresponding positive coefficients of the linear dependence of B_t on S_t and K_t.

Kalecki assumes that only capital owners save, and that their savings are proportional to their profits. Workers either do not save at all, or their savings amount to so little that they have no influence on the course of the investment process.

Using a longer mathematical argument, Kalecki supports the soundness of formula (4) in the following way:

The total profit of capital owners, Z_t, can be divided into the capital owners' consumption, D_t, which depends on the size of profits, and savings S_t, i.e.,

$$Z_t = D_t + S_t,$$

where $D_t = vZ_t + \text{constant}$, and v is the coefficient of capital owners' consumption. It then follows that $Z_t = vZ_t + S_t + \text{constant}$ or $Z_t(1-v) = S_t + \text{constant}$, and, therefore, $S_t = Z_t(1-v) - \text{constant}$.

This equation means that the savings of capital owners, S_t, are proportional to profits, Z_t, taking into consideration a certain correction which corresponds to the minimum consumption by capital owners, or, one could say, to the normal living standard of capital owners.

Since it has been assumed that investment decisions, B_t are proportional to profits which are in turn proportional to savings, investment decisions can be expressed as follows:

$$B_t = aS_t - bK_t + \varepsilon_t \tag{4a}$$

This formula also indicates the linear relation (in the opposite direction) of investment decisions to capital. As stocks of capital goods increase, so, for a given Z_t, profits yielded per unit of capital decrease, i.e., the profit rate decreases.

The component ε_t is an increasing or decreasing trend which indicates the changes in the dependence of investment decisions on capital owners' savings and stocks of capital goods, which take place in the course of time.

If we assume that $\varepsilon_t = 0$, then formula (4a) becomes the same as (4).

It follows from our assumptions that $0 \leqslant a \leqslant 1$ since capital owners cannot invest more than all their savings. Kalecki assumes $a < 1$. As a rule, it is also assumed that $0 < b < a$, since, as we know from observation, the reaction of capital owners to changes in total assets is weaker than their reaction to changes in the total sum of savings. This can be explained as follows. A relatively small change in the total sum of capital owners' savings can have an important influence on the increase of foreseen investments, while, on the other hand, the same relative change in total assets will produce an insignificant decrease in future investments.

On the basis of statistical research which he himself carried out, Kalecki reached the conclusion that for the United States (i) $a = 0.95$, which means that 95% of capital owners' savings are used for investment, and (ii) $b = 0.12$, which means that if total assets increase by 100, then planned investments will decrease by 12, i.e., by 12% of the growth in total assets.

As a result of the theoretical asumptions accepted by Kalecki we obtain four equations: (1), (2), (3), and (4) which can be combined to form two or even one new equation.

From equation (4) and taking into account the equality $S_t = (1-c)Y_t$, it follows that

$$B_t = a(1-c)Y_t - bK_t,$$

from which, on the basis of equation (1), we have

$$B_t = aI_t - bK_t.$$

By combining this last equality with (2), we arrive at the following difference equation:

$$I_{t+\theta} = aI_t - bK_t.$$

To simplify, let us assume that $\theta = 1$; this means that we accept the period θ as being one unit of time (equal for instance to 1/2 year or 1 year). We can then rewrite the last equation as:

$$I_{t+1} = aI_t - bK_t. \tag{5}$$

For the cases already discussed, in which the trend ε_t does not equal zero, equation (5) assumes the form

$$I_{t+1} = aI_t - bK_t + \varepsilon_t. \tag{5a}$$

Equation 5 or 5a, together with the remaining equation, from the group of four,

$$I_t = \frac{dK_t}{dt}, \tag{3}$$

determines the process of investment development.

The first of these, i.e., the difference equation (5) was derived from the relation between "present" investment decisions and "future" investments. Equation (3) is a differential equation of the simplest type and shows how total assets change during the course of the process under examination.

Equations (5) and (3) can be combined to form one equation by determining the value of K_t from equation (3) and inserting it in equation (5). However, it will be more convenient to consider equations (5) and (3) separately, because essentially they represent independent processes, the combined action of which, as will be seen, determines the trade cycle.[1]

In order to examine the growth of investments, I_t, as indicated by equation (5), let us look at the graph given in Fig. 1.

---

[1] The course of changes in investments I_t, during time t, can be determined from equations (5) and (3), and by using the multiplier $Y_t = \frac{I_t}{1-c}$, which follows from equation (1), we can establish the development of total demand, i.e. the national income.

"Present investments" I_t are plotted along the abscissa, and "future investments" I_{t+1}, along the axis of ordinates. The straight line L is a graphical representation of the line of investments defined by equation (5a). If the trend $\varepsilon_t = 0$, then the graph of the *line of investments*, which is then defined by equation (5), is the straight line L_1, parallel to L.

The straight line M, positively inclined at a 45° angle, is a *line of stationary investments* since at every point on this line "present investments" are equal to "future investments" ($I_t = I_{t+1}$).

We should note that when the value of capital K changes, the line of investments L shifts, always parallel downwards as K increases and upwards as K decreases. Some of the possible positions of the line of investments have been drawn in Fig. 1 as broken lines.

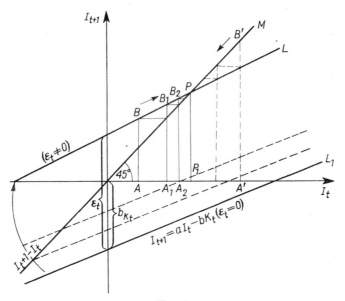

FIG. 1.

Since for the time being we are examining the course of investment development given by equation (5), we can assume that $K_t = $ constant.

If at a particular moment (period) t investments $I_t = OA$ are less than OP_1, i.e., less than the abscissa of the point of intersection P of the line of investments L and the line of stationary investments M, there then follows, as can easily be confirmed, a process of increasing investment which tends towards the point of equilibrium P, the abscissa of which $I_t = OP$.

Indeed, if present investments $I_t = OA$, then future investments $I_{t+1} = AB$.

Again, as a result of investments which in the second period equal $OA_1 = AB$, investments in the third period will be $A_1 B_1$ etc. In this way investments increase from period to period and tend towards the value of the ordinate $P_1 P$.

The situation would be analogous if at the moment (period) t investments $I_t = CA_1$ were greater than the abscissa of the point of equilibrium, P. A period of decreasing investments would then follow, as a result of which investments would also adjust to the level $I_t = OP$, as can be seen from Fig. I.

We should note that the level of investments will always reach a state of permanent equilibrium if the parameter $a < 1$, i.e., if the slope of the line of investments is less than that of the line of stationary investments. When the opposite situation prevails, i.e., if $a > 1$, the process will by no means tend towards equilibrium, as can easily be demonstrated graphically; in this case the level of investment would rise (or fall) from period to period (without any restriction). The significance of the assumption $0 < a < 1$ is therefore essential in the mechanism of Kalecki's model.

Thus we can see that the investment process established by equation (5), assuming $0 < a < 1$, tends towards a state of equilibrium. The tendency for the level of investments to reach a state of permanent equilibrium is, however, disturbed by the relation defined in the equation

$$I_t = \frac{dK_t}{dt}. \tag{3}$$

From this equation it follows that if investments are subject to change, then capital K_t also changes, and this, as we know, shifts the line of investments L, always parallel upwards if K_t decreases or downwards if K_t increases.

In order to really understand the course of the process, which is simultaneously a result of equations (3) and (5), we ought to put the changes, produced by each of these equations in successive short periods, on a film strip. By projecting this film we would have an objective picture of the mechanism of the process which we are examining.

Nevertheless, we will try to visualize and to analyse the course of this process with the aid of an ordinary graphic representation. In Fig. 2, as in Fig. 1, the magnitudes of "present investments" I_t are plotted along the abscissae, and magnitudes of "future investments" along the axis of ordinates. The relation between these two quantities is $I_{t+1} = aI_t - bK_t$.

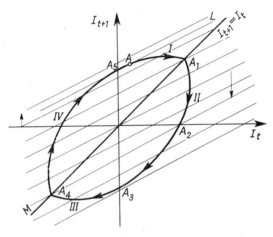

FIG. 2.

The straight line M is the line of stationary investments. The straight line L and the series of straight lines parallel to it represent the lines of investments corresponding to the differing sizes of total assets K_t; the inclination of these lines to the positive direction of the horizontal axis is less than 45° because, as we know, the coefficient of the inclination of these lines a is less than unity.

Let us assume that at a certain initial moment we are at point A; this means that the size of present investments is equal to the abscissa of the point A and that total assets, K, are such that the line of investments corresponding to them passes through point A. We know that if total assets, K, were not subject to change, i.e., if the line of investments were to be constant, then, according to the results of the previous analysis (Fig. 1), the process would tend towards the point of equilibrium, P. However, at the moment in which A begins to move towards point P and investments begin to increase, an increase takes place in total assets K_t, according to equation (3). Consequently, the line of investments $I_{t+1} = aI_t - bK_t$ is lowered, and its position shifts from the level represented by line L to another position, e.g. line L_1.

Thus, in the first period, point A does not, as would be expected, move along line L towards point P, but, moving to the right, it falls to L_1. This process continues in a similar way until A has moved to point A_1, which lies on the line of stationary investments. There is then a momentary stabilization of investments at a positive level, which means that total assets continue to rise and that the line of investments continues to fall. The movable point, representing the course of the process we are examining, will continue to fall as long as the investments corresponding to this point are positive, i.e., until this point reaches A_3.

But equilibrium will not occur at the point A_3. The point whose movement illustrates the process we are examining will move on in the direction of A_4. In the meantime investments are constantly negative, and, therefore, the size of total assets, K_t, decreases, which means that the position of the line of investments shifts upwards. The point consequently moves along a curve from position A_3 to position A_4. The course which the process continues to follow is similar. Investments continue to be negative, the line of investments also continues to rise and the point follows the arc of the curve from A_4 to A_5, and then moves on, as we have temporarily assumed, to the exact point of departure. The second cycle of the process, identical with the one described above, begins at this moment, etc.

The cycle we have described can be divided into 4 phases.

During the first phase, which corresponds to the arc of the curve A_0A, (Fig. 2) investments rise, i.e., $\frac{dI_t}{dt} > 0$. Since investments, during this phase, are constantly positive, capital also increases, i.e., $\frac{dK_t}{dt} > 0$.

During the second phase, represented by the arc of the curve stretching from point A, to point A_3, investments decrease $\frac{dI_t}{dt} < 0$, but capital continues to rise $\frac{dK_t}{dt} > 0$ because investments during this phase, as in the first phase, are constantly positive.

Throughout the third phase, which stretches from point A_3 to point A_4, investments continue to decrease $\frac{dI_t}{dt} < 0$; capital also decreases $\frac{dK_t}{dt} < 0$ since in this phase investments are negative.

Finally, during the fourth phase of the cycle, represented by the arc $A_4 A_5$, investments rise $\frac{dI_t}{dt} > 0$ and are constantly negative; therefore capital decreases, and $\frac{dK_t}{dt} < 0$.

Figure 2 shows that the lines which divide the cycle, we have been considering, into the phases described above are the line of stationary investments and the axis of ordinates, I_{t+1}.

Several points arise from the description of the cyclical changes of investments and capital given in Kalecki's model. Firstly, the level of investments and capital can never reach a state of constant equilibrium. It might be supposed that stability could be achieved at the points A_1, or A_4 which lie on the line of stationary investments. At these points, however, equilibrium is disturbed by the relation defined in the equation $I_t = \frac{dK_t}{dt}$ as a result of which the value of K_t changes, and this in turn displaces the line of investments.

Equilibrium also cannot be achieved at the points A_5 and A_3 since the process of investment defined by the equation $I_{t+1} = aI_t - bK_t$ does not permit this.

Equilibrium could only be achieved under one set of conditions, i.e. if investments I_t were equal to zero, and total assets were consequently constant. This means that the point, illustrating the course of this process, would be at the origin of the system of coordinates shown in Fig. 2.

This particular case would correspond to a process of simple reproduction, because the condition $I_t = I_{t+1} = 0$ means that total assets are constant (K_t = constant), i.e., the means of production are merely renewed.

The cyclical process described above and illustrated in Fig. 2 will be set in motion, however, if the equilibrium corresponding to the conditions $I_t = I_{t+1} = 0$ and K_t = constant is disrupted by some disturbance.[2]

From our analysis it follows that it is impossible for equilibrium to be achieved in the process under examination because it is impossible for the process of investment and the process by which changes in capital take place to be stabilized at the same time. The essential in the mechanism of this process is that the cycle is made up of two parts: one in which investments are constantly positive and total assets in-

---

[2] In reference to this remark someone once jokingly said that the Napoleonic wars, for instance, could be the cause of cycles in capitalist economy, as described by Kalecki.

crease (phases I and II), and the second in which investments are negative and total assets decrease (phases III and IV).

In examining the mechanism of this process with reference to profit we can see that as capital increases, the profitableness of production decreases, and vice versa, as capital decreases, profitableness increases.

Consequently, the fall in profitableness during the first part of the cycle (phases I and II) is restored in the second half of the cycle (phases III and IV).[3]

We should also note that in reality such periods of economic development in which investments are negative have rarely existed, i.e., periods in which the decapitalization of the national wealth has taken place.[4]

In order to make allowance for this phenomenon, which has been established historically, a certain correction must be introduced into Kalecki's model. Kalecki does this by introducing the element ε_t into the equation of the process of investment. This element denotes a trend which raises the line of investments. The equation of investments now assumes the form

$$I_{t+1} = aI_t - bK_t + \varepsilon_t . \tag{5a}$$

Thus, in Kalecki's model, a third process appears, besides the process of the development of investments and capital, which ensures that the line of investments constantly shifts upwards as the cycle continues.

Consequently, after the cycle of fluctuations of investments and total assets has completed one full cycle, it does not return to the point of departure, just as it can never pass through the values of negative investments. A picture of this process is given by the spiral line or the rising circle to be seen in Figs. 3a and 3b.

The actual cause of the appearance of the trend ε_t in the equation of the investment process might be technical progress, for instance, which produces an additional need for investment.

A further criticism which may be levelled at the mechanism of Kalecki's model is whether, in fact, even if we assume that the trend ε_t does not exist, the cycle will return to the point of departure after one

---

[3] Similar deductions were obtained by Marx from his analysis of the fluctuation of profit and the trade cycle.

[4] Such an exception was the period of the great economic depression in the United States between 1929 and 1932.

full cycle. It is possible that in reality, instead of a closed cycle, in which the final point (point A_5 in Fig. 2) coincides with the point of departure (point A_0 in Fig. 2), we will be faced with a damped cycle (represented graphically in Fig. 4a) or with a cycle in which the oscillations are constantly increasing (Fig. 4b).

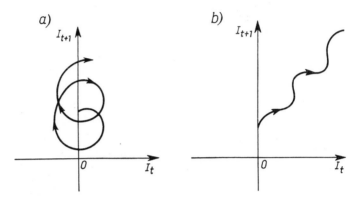

FIG. 3.

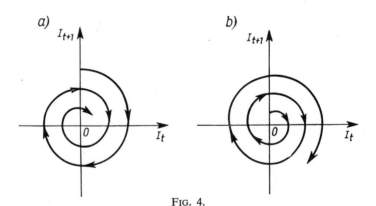

FIG. 4.

In order to find an answer to this problem it must be analysed mathematically and we must solve the equation of differences (5) and the differential equation (3). As we shall see, the process of the development of investments and total assets, which we are examining here, depends on the parameters a and b which appear in equation (5).

In general, the actual examples examined by Kalecki turned out to be damped cycles (Fig. 3) which theoretically tend to reach a state of constant equilibrium. In reality, however, equilibrium was not achieved due to some new disturbance, e.g., war, the discovery of new sources of raw materials, technical changes, etc., as a result of which a state of equilibrium was avoided and which kept the cycle alive and did not allow it to become entirely damped.

Kalecki dealt with this type of problem in his latest work. He had previously considered the cycle corresponding to his model to be a cycle of constant oscillations.

We will begin our mathematical analysis of Kalecki's model by combining equations (3) and (5), which determine the course of the cycle, to form one equation, and go on to solve this new equation with respect to K_t.[5]

By combining equation (3) and (5) we obtain the following differential equation of differences:[6]

$$\frac{dK_{t+1}}{dt} = a\frac{dK_t}{dt} - bK_t. \tag{6}$$

How is this equation to be solved? To do this, as an analogy for solving differential equations we will try to solve an equation of the form

$$K_t = K_0 e^{\varrho t}. \tag{7}$$

This can be verified by substituting this expression $K_0 e^{\varrho t}$ for K_t, and the expression $K_0 e^{\varrho(t+1)}$ for K_{t+1} in equation (6); then

$$K_0 \varrho e^{\varrho(t+1)} = aK_0 \varrho e^{\varrho t} - bK_0 e^{\varrho t}.$$

Dividing both sides of this last equation by $K_0 e^{\varrho t}$, we have

$$\varrho e^{\varrho} = a\varrho - b. \tag{8}$$

It therefore follows that function (7) can be a solution to equation (6), if ϱ has a definite value which satisfies equation (8). This type of equation, which fulfils the condition in which a difinite expression is the solution of a given (differential) equation of differences, is called the *characteristic equation* of the given (differential) equation of differences. Thus, equation (8) is the characteristic equation of equation (6).

---

[5] We are devoting this space to the method used in Kalecki's cycle, because with only minor changes, they can eventually be applied to other cycles of economic growth.

[6] Besides the derived functions, the differential equation of differences also contains, the various sizes of a given change at different moments.

Let us examine this characteristic equation more closely, and define what values ϱ will assume in order that function (7) be a solution of equation (6).

There can be two possibilities, which we will examine in turn: (a) ϱ can be a real number or (b) ϱ can be a complex number.

In the first case there are again three possibilities: $\varrho > 0$, $\varrho < 0$ and $\varrho = 0$.

If $\varrho > 0$, then, according to the exponential function $K_t = K_0 e^{\varrho t}$, capital increases constantly with increasing t. Investments also increase constantly to the same order since $I_t = \dfrac{dK_t}{dt} = K_0 \varrho e^{\varrho t} = I_0 e^{\varrho t}$ (Fig. 5a). Similarly, according to the exponential functions, when $\varrho < 0$, then capital, K_t, and investments, I_t decrease (Fig. 5b). Finally, when $\varrho = 0$, K_t and I_t are constant.

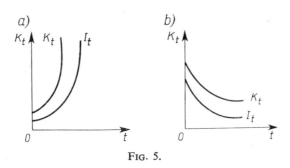

FIG. 5.

Thus, if ϱ is a real number, there is a constant and not a cyclic increase (decrease) in capital and investment.

By examining the second possibility, i.e., when ϱ is a complex number, we obtain a more interesting result.

If ϱ is a complex number, it can be expressed in the form $\varrho = \alpha + i\beta$, where $i = \sqrt{-1}$. Solution (7) of equation (6) can then be put in the following form:

$$K_t = K_0 e^{(\alpha + i\beta)t} = K_0 e^{\alpha t} c^{i\beta t}$$

or[7]

$$K_t = K_0 e^{\alpha t} (\cos \beta t + i \sin \beta t). \qquad (9)$$

---

[7] Here we have applied Euler's theorem. An explanation and proof of this theorem can be found in any textbook of mathematical analysis.

Function (9), which defines the value of capital K_t, is a periodic function with respect to time t, and its fluctuation is sinusoidal, i.e., it fluctuates in a way similar to $y = \sin x$.

In this way, we are able to show that if the characteristic equation (8) has a complex solution, the function which is a solution to equation (6) is then an oscillatory periodic function. Consequently in this case, capital, K_t, and investments, I_t, are subject to periodic fluctuations.[8]

We must now examine what type of functions these are: whether they are increasing, decreasing, or constant. This depends on parameter α.

If $\alpha > 0$, then the factor $e^{\alpha t}$, which appears in equation (9) increases with time t, and, therefore, the amplitude of the oscillations of K_t increases from period to period (Fig. 6a).

If $\alpha < 0$, then $e^{\alpha t}$ decreases and the oscillations of capital K_t decrease (Fig. 6b).

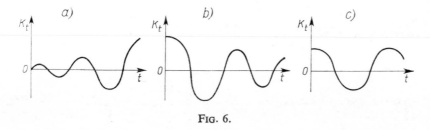

FIG. 6.

When $\alpha = 0$, then $e^{\alpha} = 1$, and the oscillations are therefore of an unchanged amplitude (Fig. 6c).

We must now proceed to solve the characteristic equation (8), and in this case the simplest way will be to use a graphic method. Let us treat each side of equation (8) as a function of ϱ. We then have the functions $y_1 = \varrho e^{\varrho}$ and $y_2 = a\varrho - b$ which we can plot graphically (Fig. 7).

It can be seen that the function $y_1 = \varrho c^{\varrho}$ passes through the intersection of the two axes (if $\varrho = 0$, then $y_1 = 0$), and, as an exponential function with respect to ϱ, increases very quickly. For $\varrho > 0$, the inclination of the curve given by the function $y_1 = \varrho e^{\varrho}$ is greater than 1.

Indeed,

$$\frac{dy_1}{dp} = e^{\varrho} + \varrho e^{\varrho} = e^{\varrho}(\varrho + 1).$$

---

[8] We also get $I_t = I_0 e^{\varrho t} = I_0 e^{\alpha t}(\cos \beta t + i \sin \beta t)$.

For $\varrho = 0$, we have $\frac{dy_1}{d\varrho} = 1$; to the right of the origin of the system we have $\frac{dy_1}{d\varrho} > 1$ since the slope of the curve y_1 is constantly increasing.

We might also note that the function of y_1 reaches its minimum point when $\varrho = -1$, and that, moving to the left, it tends asymmetrically towards the axis of the abscissae.

Indeed, when $p = -1$, the derivative $\frac{dy_1}{dp} = e^{\varrho}(\varrho + 1) = 0$, and for $p = -1$, the second derivative $\frac{d^2y_1}{dp^2} = e^{\varrho}(\varrho + 2) > 0$.

We can prove that $y_1 = \varrho e^{\varrho} \to 0$ when $p \to -\infty$ by applying l'Hopital's rule to the indefinite value $-\infty \cdot 0$. However, that $\varrho e^{\varrho} \to 0$ when $\varrho \to -\infty$ follows directly from the properties of the exponential function e^{ϱ} which changes more rapidly than any other elementary function, and therefore more rapidly than ϱ. Consequently, the influence of the function e^{ϱ} in the expression ϱe^{ϱ} is dominant and $\varrho e^{\varrho} \to e^{\varrho} \to 0$ when $\varrho \to \infty$.

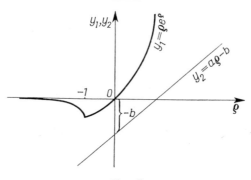

FIG. 7.

The graph of the function $y_1 = \varrho e^{\varrho}$, the properties of which we have just examined, and the graph of the linear function $y_2 = a\varrho - b$ are given in Fig. 7.

The graphic solution of the characteristic equation $\varrho e^{\varrho} = a\varrho - b$, or the equation $y_1 = y_2$ involves finding the abscissa of the point of intersection of the graphs representing the functions of y_1 and y_2. Where can these lines intersect? They cannot intersect in the first quadrant of the system of coordinates because the slope of the straight line $y_2 = a\varrho - b$, and therefore the coefficient a is, as we already know, less than 1, and for $\varrho > 0$, the slope of the curve $y_1 = \varrho e^{\varrho}$ is greater than 1.

But perhaps the lines can intersect in the third quadrant of the system of co-ordinates. From Fig. 7 it is evident that this is impossible if b is sufficiently small. Let us now establish the value of the coefficient b for which the lines $y_1 = \varrho e^\varrho$ and $y_2 = a\varrho - b$ have a common point. The function of y_1 assumes its minimum value when $\varrho = -1$, i.e. when
$$y_1 = -e^{-1} = -\frac{1}{e} \approx -0.368.$$

For the same value of ϱ, $y_2 = -(a+b)$.

It then follows that if $-(a+b) = -0.368$, i.e., $a+b = 0.368$, then the lines satisfying functions y_1 and y_2 are tangent.

When $a+b < 0.368$, the lines intersect at two points, and when $a+b > 0.368$ they do not intersect.

We know that, according to the statistical data gathered by Kalecki, $a = 0.95$ and $b = 0.12$; therefore $a+b = 1.07$.

It therefore follows that the solutions of the characteristic equation $\varrho e^\varrho = a\varrho - b$, satisfying conditions which can appear in reality, are complex values of ϱ. Therefore, the process of growth in capital and investments, which we are examining here, is a cyclical process.

It should be noted that the essential factor for this process of growth is b, and that the process is cyclical only when $b > 0$.

If $b = 0$, the solution to the characteristic equation (8) is a real number, since the line determined by the equation $y_2 = a\varrho - b = a\varrho$ passes through the origin of the system of coordinates and intersects the line $y_1 = \varrho e^\varrho$. We can then determine the root of the characteristic equation, which when $b = 0$ assumes the form $\varrho e^\varrho = a\varrho$, and therefore $e^\varrho = a$, and consequently $p = \ln a$. Because coefficient $a < 1$, therefore, $\varrho = \ln a < 0$. We are then dealing with a process in which capital is constantly decreasing: $K_t \to K_0$ and $I_t \to 0$. In the exceptional case in which $a = 1$, $p = \ln a = 0$. The process of extended reproduction then becomes a process of simple reproduction. Capital, K_t, remains unchanged, and, therefore, the economic system is stable.

If coefficient b were negative, the line $y_2 = a\varrho - b$ would shift upwards and intersect the line $y_2 = \varrho e^\varrho$ at two real points. But the inequality $b < 0$ means that the growth of capital leads to an increase in investment decisions. In this case, therefore, K_t constantly increases and the process is not cyclical.

We have already shown that for values of the coefficient a and b, which can be verified statistically, the process taking place according to Kalecki's model cannot be cumulative but cyclical. Let us see whether the cyclical solution, corresponding to the complex value of the rate of growth, ϱ, satisfies real conditions.

In the case when the complex value of $\varrho = a + i\beta$, the characteristic equation (8), given in the form $e^\varrho = a - \frac{b}{p}$ can be rewritten as follows:

$$e^\alpha e^{i\beta} = a - \frac{b}{\alpha + i\beta}.$$

Applying Euler's formula $e^{i\beta} = \cos\beta + i\sin\beta$ and the equality $(\alpha + i\beta)(\alpha - i\beta) = \alpha^2 + \beta^2$, we have

$$e^\alpha(\cos\beta + i\sin\beta) = a - b\frac{\alpha - i\beta}{\alpha^2 + \beta^2}.$$

In order that this equation be fulfilled, the real component on the left side of the equation must be equal to the real component on the right side. The same is true for the imaginary parts. We therefore have the following equations:

$$e^\alpha\cos\beta = a - \frac{b\alpha}{\alpha^2 + \beta^2}, \quad e^\alpha\sin\beta = \frac{b\beta}{\alpha^2 + \beta^2}. \tag{10}$$

The algebraic solution of the system of these two equations would be complicated. We shall, therefore, confine ourselves to examining certain general properties of the equations, i.e. the limits of possible values of α and β, and the relation between their values.

From the second of the two equations mentioned above (10) it follows that

$$e^\alpha = \frac{b}{\alpha^2 + \beta^2} \times \frac{\beta}{\sin\beta}.$$

Since $e^\alpha > 0$ and $b > 0$, $\frac{\beta}{\sin\beta}$ must also be positive.

The condition $\frac{\beta}{\sin\beta} > 0$ sets certain limitations on β. Since we take β to be always positive, it must always happen that $0 < \beta < \pi$.

On the basis of the condition $0 < \beta < \pi$, we can go on to say something about the length of the cycle we are examining. Let us denote the period of the sinusoidal fluctuations of the quantity K_t as defined by equation (9), by T. Then $T\beta = 2\pi$, therefore $T = \frac{2\pi}{\beta}$, and since $\beta < \pi$, it follows that the period $T > 2$.

Since we have taken the period which elapses between the moment in which an investment decision is made and the moment in which the investment is completed to be a unit of time, the condition $T > 2$ means that, if the time necessary for carrying out planned decisions comes for instance to $\frac{1}{2}$ year, then the period of the cycle comes to more than 1 year. If this time came to 1 year, then the period of the cycle would come to more than 2 years.

From equation (10), however, we can deduce something more, i.e., the relation between α and the length of T.

We have assumed that $\alpha > 0$, i.e., that the cycle is damped. Since $a > 0$ and $b > 0$, the right side of the equation

$$e^{\alpha} \cos \beta = a - \frac{b\alpha}{\alpha^2 + \beta^2}$$

is then positive. Therefore $\cos \beta$ must be positive and $0 < \beta < \frac{1}{2}\pi$. Since $T = \frac{2\pi}{\beta}$, therefore $T > 4$.

If the cycle is damped ($\alpha < 0$), the period of the cycle T must be more than 4 times the unit in which time is expressed.

If $\alpha = 0$, i.e., if the cycle is constant (neither increasing nor decreasing), then $e^{\alpha} = 1$ and

$$\frac{b}{\alpha^2 + \beta^2} \times \frac{\beta}{\sin \beta} = 1 \, .$$

From this it follows that $\beta \sin \beta = b$. Remembering that $b < 1$, we can show that in this case β must be less than $\frac{1}{2\pi}$, and therefore again $T > 4$.

β can be greater than $\frac{1}{2\pi}$ only when $\alpha > 0$, i.e., when the fluctuations of the cycle are increasing; then the period of cycle $T < 4$.

This analysis has enabled us to define a certain relation between the amplitude of the cycle and the period of the cycle. We can see that only longer cycles can be damped; shorter cycles increase.

From statistical calculations it follows that the period of Kalecki's cycle lasts 9 years: it ought therefore to be a cycle of decreasing amplitude. This cycle, however, does not come to an end because—according to Kalecki—certain accidental changes (accidental disturbances) take place which set the fading cycle in motion again, and continue to keep it alive.

This briefly gives us a picture of Kalecki's theory. What attitude should we assume towards it and towards other similar models? Firstly, we should say that many models of this type can be constructed. They will all illustrate a certain cyclical process of growth, on the condition that the solution of the characteristic equation is complex. Models of this type which have a practical significance are those in which the period of the cycle—due to the application of real values taken from statistical data at the appropriate stages of the model—corresponds to real conditions, i.e., when the period comes to about 8 years. Models which do not fulfil this condition should be discarded in advance.

The famous model of economic growth, based on the Harrod–Domar theory, leads to a process of growth in which the trend is constant, but in which there is no cycle. Kalecki's theory leads to a cyclical process of growth devoid of trends, and assumes the action of accidental disturbances which ensure that the cycle does not fade out.

Marx's theory of extended reproduction suggests the idea of building some kind of general model in which the cycle and trend are elements of the same process of growth. There are such models, but they must be based on sufficiently accidental psychological assumptions, e.g. that demand is a function of incomes received in previous years.

It should be considered whether or not a model of extended reproduction could be constructed in such a way as to represent a process of economic growth in which both trend and cycle appear together as they do in the reality of the capitalist economy.[9]

---

[9] An attempt made by me to construct such a model is to be found in Model wzrostu gospodarczego (A Model of Economic Growth), *Ekonomista*, No. 3/1959.

A NEW VERSION OF KALECKI'S MODEL

Let us once again briefly examine the principal lines of thought in Kalecki's model of the dynamics of economic growth in its original form.

As we know, from the mathematical point of view, Kalecki's model contains four equations which can be combined to form two equations or even one. As has already been explained in the previous paper, these four relations can be expressed as follows:

$$X_t = cY_t + I_t, \tag{1}$$

$$I_{t+1} = B_t, \tag{2}$$

$$I_t = \frac{dK_t}{dt}, \tag{3}$$

$$B_t = aI_t - bK_{t+\varepsilon t}. \tag{4}$$

The first of these equations means that the entire demand in a certain period, t, is equal to the sum of consumption, $C_t = cY_t$, and investments, I_t. For the sake of simplification, it has been assumed that autonomous investments are equal to zero. Similarly, it has also been assumed that the coefficient of consumption, c, is constant, i.e., it does not change with time. As a result of this, an element of trend, representing changes taking place in the given process, does not appear in equation (1).

Equation (2) expresses the basic assumption on which the mechanism of Kalecki's model is based, i.e., that investment decisions, β_t, after a certain time, θ, are converted into investments $I_{t+\theta}$, and that here the period, θ, which elapses between the moment in which investment decisions are made and the moment in which the carrying out of these decisions is completed, is taken to be one unit of time; thus, it is assumed that $\theta = 1$.

The third equation means that throughout the process, investments are equal to the rate of growth of capital at a given moment.

Finally, equation (4) is the second basic assumption and, at the same time, this relation is, as it were, the motor of the economic development which takes place according to Kalecki's model. It means, as we already

363

know, that investment decisions B_t taken at the moment t, are linearly dependent on the size of capital owners' savings S_t and on the stocks of capital goods already in existence. It should be noted here that in equation (4) the size of investments I_t has been introduced instead of the size of savings, S_t. This follows from the assumption that investments, or at least the decisive part of investments, are made from the savings of capital owners. Furthermore, the element ε_t appears in equation (4); this is a certain trend (increasing or decreasing), representing changes in the dependence of investment decisions, B_t, on savings, S_t, and on stocks of capital goods, K_t. The element ε_t plays an essential role in Kalecki's model, because without it each cycle, given by this type of model, would have to pass through a period of decapitalization of the national economy.

As we have shown in the previous paper, the four relations given above can be combined to give the two following equations:

$$I_{t+1} = aI_t - bK_t + \varepsilon_t, \tag{5}$$

$$I_t = \frac{dK_t}{dt}, \tag{3}$$

from which in turn we can derive a differential difference equation:

$$\frac{dK_{t+1}}{dt} = a\frac{dK_t}{dt} - bK_t + \varepsilon_t. \tag{6}$$

However, it is more convenient to analyse the mechanics of Kalecki's model by dealing with the equations (3) and (5) which represent the two forces acting in this process. We can then clearly see that this process has, as it were, its own dialectic of development. Each investment raises demand and encourages new investments, but at the same time each investment also increases capital and thus simultaneously discourages further investments. As a result of the interplay between these two opposing forces we are faced with the cycle of 4 phases described in the previous paper.

In order to arrive at a better understanding of the mechanism of Kalecki's model, we shall describe it with the aid of a cybernetic diagram.

From the upper part of the diagram, given in Fig. 1, it follows that demand, Y_t, determines the size of consumption, cY_t, which is entirely absorbed by demand. On the other hand, investments, I_t, are absorbed in the demand, which consequently, as indicated by equation (1), is determined by the sum of $C_t + I_t$.

According to equation (4), if we ignore the element ε_t, the size of investment decisions, B_t, is determined by two factors aI_t and $-bK_t$. Bearing in mind that the size of investments (savings) $I_t = Y_t(1-c)$, we can obtain the first of these two factors by multiplying Y_t by $a(1-c)$. The second factor, which has a reducing influence on investment decisions, can be obtained by multiplying stocks of capital goods, K_t, by the coefficient $-b$. The influence of both these factors on investment decisions is denoted in the diagram by the arrows pointing towards the circle with the letter B in it.

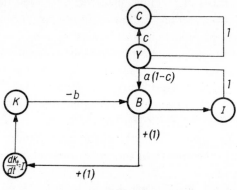

Fig. 1.

Investment decisions, B_t, in turn, act in two directions. In the first place, they determine the size of investments, with the reservation, however, that the size of investment decisions in the period, t, fix the size of investments in the period $t+1$. Thus, investment decisions take place one period in advance. In other words, investment decisions are entirely fulfilled in the form of investments, but only in the following period. Secondly, investment decisions, once they have been converted into the form of investments I_t in the following period, influence the changes in stocks of capital goods K_t, so that based on equation (3) $\frac{dK_t}{dt} = I_t$.

Then, from equation $\frac{dK_t}{dt} = I_t$, we can determine by integration the growth of capital which is entirely absorbed in stocks of capital goods and affects investment decisions in the way described above.

The cybernetic diagram of Kalecki's model could be supplemented by adding autonomous investments A_t which would be entirely absorbed in the demand Y, and the internal factor, which is the trend ε_t, and which, as is shown by equation (4), influences the size of investment decisions.

The cybernetic diagram of Kalecki's model, described above, shows that the characteristic of this scheme is that the reaction and time lag which take place in it are twofold: investment decisions in a given period are converted into equivalent investments in the following period, and similarly investment decisions in a given period produce an increase in capital in the next period.

As we know, Kalecki later changed his first model thus losing its lucidity. The aim of this was to introduce a distinction between durable capital, which consists of buildings machinery etc., and turnover capital which includes raw materials, unfinished products, and finished goods. This was to bring the model closer to reality.

The effect of this modification lies mainly in equation (2), in which investments for a given period, I_t, are divided into two parts: investments in durable means, I'_t, and investments in turnover capital, I''_t. Investments in durable means, I'_t are equal to investment decisions made in the period $t-\tau$, i.e. $I'_t = B_{t-\tau}\tau$.

Investments in turnover capital, on the other hand, are assumed to be proportional to the growth of the entire demand, also after a certain time lag equal to θ.

Consequently the modified version of Kalecki's model is based on the following equations:

$$Y_t = cY_t + I_t \tag{7}$$

$$I_t = I'_t + I''_t \tag{8}$$

$$I'_t = \frac{dK_t}{dt} = B_{t-\tau} \tag{9}$$

$$I''_t = v_1 \frac{dY_{t-\theta}}{dt} \tag{10}$$

$$B_t = aI_t + v_2 \frac{dY_t}{dt} - b \frac{dK_t}{dt} + \varepsilon_t. \tag{11}$$

The first of these equations is equation (1) from Kalecki's original model, unchanged. As before, in this equation, autonomous investments, A_t, are assumed to be zero for the sake of simplicity. Equation (8) means that in a given period total investments are equal to the sum of investments in durable means I'_t and in turnover means I''_t. Equations (9) and (10) express the investments I'_t and I''_t in terms of investment decisions and in terms of increased total demand. ν_1 in equation (10) is a coefficient of proportionality; thus bearing in mind that $Y_t = \frac{I_t}{1-c}$, we can rewrite equation (10) in the form

$$I''_t = \nu_1 \frac{I}{1-c} \times \frac{dI_{t-\theta}}{dt}. \tag{10a}$$

Equation (11) corresponds to equation (4). In the modified version of his model, Kalecki assumes that investment decisions are linearly dependent on (i) the size of capital owners savings, i.e., $S_t = I_t$, (ii) the rate of growth of total demand (ν_2 is a coefficient of proportionality), and (iii) the rate of change in the stocks of capital goods (and not the level of capital as in the original model) so that an increase in the rate of change in stocks of capital goods leads to a decrease in the size of investment decisions. The factor of trend ε_t which appears in equation (11) plays an identical role to the role it played in the original model.

Thus, we can see that the assumptions made in the latest version of Kalecki's model differ from the assumptions in the original model. It is characteristic that two different time lags appear in the mechanism of the new version of the model, the sizes of which mutually affect each other: (i) investments in durable means in the period t are equal to investment decisions from the period $t-\tau$, and (ii) the size of investments in turnover means in period t are influenced by the change in the growth of total demand which appeared in period $t-\theta$.

Equations (7)–(11) can, after suitable transformation, be combined to form one equation which can then be solved with respect to I_t. This, in turn, would enable us to determine the size of total demand, $Y_t = \frac{I_t}{1-c}$.

Indeed, to simplify, let us assume that the trend $\varepsilon_t = 0$. Then, bearing in mind that $I_t = I'_t + I''_t$ and $I'_{t+\tau} = B_t$, from equation (11) it follows that

$$I'_{t+\tau} = aI'_t + aI''_t + \nu_2 \frac{dY_t}{dt} - b \frac{dK_t}{dt}$$

and from equation (10) and (9):

$$I'_{t+\tau} = aI'_t + a\nu_1 \frac{dY_{t-\tau}}{dt} + \nu_2 \frac{dY_t}{dt} - bI'_t.$$

Therefore, since

$$I_{t+\tau}-I''_{t+\tau} = I_{t+\tau}-v_1\frac{dY_{t+\tau-\theta}}{dt} = I'_{t+\tau},$$

it follows that

$$I_{t+\tau}-v_1\frac{dY_{t+\tau-\theta}}{dt} = a\left(I'_t+v_1\frac{dY_{t-\theta}}{dt}\right)+v_2\frac{dY_t}{dt}-b(I_t-I''_t).$$

By applying equations (8) and (10), we can rewrite the last expression as follows:

$$I_{t+\tau} = aI_t+v_2\frac{dY_t}{dt}-b\left(I_t-v_1\frac{dY_{t-\theta}}{dt}\right)+v_1\frac{dY_{t+\tau-\theta}}{dt}.$$

From equation (7), from which it follows that $dI_t = (1-c)dY_t$, and by substitution we obtain the following equation:

$$I_{t+\tau} = (a-b)I_t+\frac{v_2}{1-c}\times\frac{dI_t}{dt}+\frac{bv_1}{1-c}\times\frac{dI_{t-\theta}}{dt}+\frac{v_1}{1-c}\times\frac{dI_{t+\tau-\theta}}{dt}. \quad (12)$$

The above expression can be written in the form:

$$I_{t-\tau} = \alpha I_t+\beta\frac{dI_t}{dt}+\gamma\frac{dI_{t-\theta}}{dt}+\delta\frac{dY_{t+\tau-\theta}}{dt}, \quad (13)$$

where α, β, γ and δ are the corresponding coefficients depending on the parameters a, b, c, v_1 and v_2.

Assuming, as in solving the differential difference equation (6) in the previous paper, that the solution to equation (13) takes the form $I_t = I_t e^{rt}$, then after simplification we have the following characteristic equation:

$$c^{r\tau} = \alpha+\beta r+\gamma re^{-r\theta}+\delta re^{r(\tau-\theta)}. \quad (14)$$

Taking the time lag τ to be one unit of time measured, i.e., $\tau = 1$, the characteristic equation assumes the form

$$e^r = \alpha\beta r+\gamma re^{-r\theta}+\delta re^{r(1-\theta)}. \quad (14a)$$

Kalecki assumes that the time lags θ and τ are equal, i.e., $\theta = \tau$; equation (13) can then be written as follows:

$$I_{t+\tau} = \alpha I_t+(\beta+\delta)\frac{dI_t}{dt}+\gamma\frac{dI_{t-\tau}}{dt}, \quad (13a)$$

and, when $\theta = \tau = 1$, the corresponding characteristic equation takes on the form:

$$\theta^r = \alpha + (\beta + \delta)r + \gamma r e^{-r}. \tag{14b}$$

The further course of analysis is identical with the analysis made on the original model in Kalecki's previous paper. When the solution to the characteristic equation *r* is a real number, we are dealing with a constant process of growth (or fall) in investments and capital. On the other hand, if *r* is a complex number, the process is cyclical.

It should be added that the new version of Kalecki's model has not the elegance which was characteristic of the original version. It is also doubtful if the new expanded version grasps the process of development as realistically as its author maintained. Kalecki's original model is indisputably far from realistic. Nevertheless, it presents clearly and simply the active forces in the process of economic development.

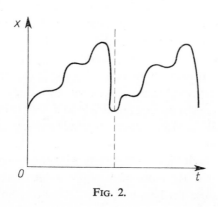

Fig. 2.

The question then arises: why did Kalecki change his original model? This is connected with a certain property of the trade cycle in the United States of America which began to draw attention in economic literature shortly after the first version of Kalecki's model appeared. In the United States, a special role is played by stocks of commodities in the course of the trade cycle, i.e., by a factor which is less significant in Europe. Closer examination shows that the trade cycle in the United States has other characteristics, for instance, differing from those in France or England. When we talk about trade cycles in European countries we usually have in mind cycles of 8–10 years which are connected with the periods of

renewal of durable capital. Consequently, it is for this reason that Kalecki's original model led to an 8-year cycle.

During the period after the Second World War American economic
literature began to deal with shorter cycles, and the theory was put forward that in reality the period of the cycle lasts 3 to 4 years, i.e., a period
of two years elapses between the period of expansion and depression.
Closer examination shows that the curve of the trade cycle (e.g., the
curve of overall production) assumes the form shown schematically in
Fig. 2. This graph shows two great cycles of 8–10 years which, with
respect to time, correspond to European cycles. The curve of the trade
cycle also shows that, within a great cycle of 8–10 years, there appear
two or three shorter cycles of a 3–4 year period, which follow the movement of the larger cycle.

According to most theories, the additional 3–4 year cycles which
appear in the United States are connected with the accumulation and
dwindling of inventories. When inventories rise above a fixed norm, there
is a fall in orders and in production until they have been exhausted. In
turn, there then follows a rise in orders and a boost in production, etc.

The course of the trade cycle, therefore, consists of two processes of
reproduction: the process of renewal of durable capital which leads to
an 8–10 year cycle, and the process of the reproduction of inventories
of materials and commodities which leads to a 3–4 year cycle. The entire
discussion now taking place among economists examining the American
economy is to ascertain whether the recession taking place this year
(1958) involves a cycle connected merely with the reproduction of commodities or also with the reproduction of durable capital. This question
is important because predictions as to the course the trade cycle will
take in the future, and the preventive means which will be applied to
counteract the negative results of the deterioration in the trade cycle
will depend on the answer given.

As a result of these remarks concerning the American trade cycle,
there arises the question of why we do not observe cycles of stocks of
commodities in European countries. Perhaps this is simply because
European economic statistics are not elaborate enough and do not
register their appearance. However, this is probably to be better explained by a different economic structure in European countries in which
inventories of materials and commodities do not play the same role as
in the United States. In that country larger inventories are depended

upon, and production is carried out to a greater extent for inventory than for actual orders.

In modifying this theory, Kalecki wanted to add to his original model a cycle of commodities, and to answer the question as to the way in which the reproduction of inventories of materials and commodities influences the process of economic development. In the end, however, the new version of Kalecki's model does not give an answer to this question. In fact, the process of the creation and diminution of materials does influence the general course of the trade cycle, but again the new model only gives one cycle of an 8–10 year period. The real solution to this problem should involve two independent cycles of different periods. Attempts have been made in economic literature to develop such theories of growth (Schumpeter, for example, said that there are two and even three cycles developing within each other); they did not lead, however, to the desired results.

SOME OBSERVATIONS ON INPUT–OUTPUT ANALYSIS

The Scope of Inter-industry Analysis

The analysis of inter-industry relations, usually referred to as input–output analysis, serves the purpose of establishing the quantitative relations between various branches of production which must be maintained in order to ensure a smooth flow of production in the national economy. It studies the conditions of mutual consistency of outputs in various branches of the economy which result from the fact that the output of one branch is the source of input in other branches.

The idea that certain proportions must be maintained between outputs of various branches of the economy is at the basis of the equilibrium analysis of classical political economy and neo-classical economics. The proportions referred to are, however, conceived by classical and neo-classical economic theory basically in "horizontal" terms, i.e., as proportions between final products designed to satisfy the wants of consumers. Under conditions of competitive capitalism, i.e., of free mobility of capital, the tendency of the rate of profit towards a "normal" level in each branch of the economy leads towards an equilibrium in output of the various branches. In equilibrium, output is adjusted to demand for various products. In a planned economy, it is believed, proper planning should ensure the establishment of equilibrium proportions.

While this idea of "horizontal" equilibrium proportions undoubtedly points to an important aspect of the relations between output of various branches of the economy, it overlooks the need for maintaining another kind of proportion, determined not by conditions of consumer demand, but by conditions of technological relations associated with the fact that the output of certain products serves—entirely or in part—as input in the process of producing other products. We shall call this the problem of "vertical" proportions.

This problem of "vertical" proportions is the subject matter of input–output analysis. The problem was first posed by Quesnay in his famous *Tableau Economique*. Its implications escaped the attention of classical and neo-classical economic theory. A systematic treatment as well as a fundamental solution of the problem was given by Marx in his schemes of reproduction of capital contained in volume II of *Capital*. Outside Marxist political economy the problem was scarcely touched upon, neo-classical economics confining their studies to equilibrium conditions of the "horizontal" type.

However, in business cycle theory of bourgeois economists the problem of "vertical relations" between investment goods and consumer goods was bound to reappear, for it is this type of relation which is at the root of the phenomenon of crises and depressions. Consequently, it plays an important role in Keynesian theory. The "vertical" character of the relations involves "disproportionalities" in this field which are not automatically solved by the process of competition entailing the movement of capital from less profitable to more profitable branches of the economy. It also explains why smooth economic development is not automatically ensured under conditions of capitalism, even if the constraints resulting from the specific features of monopoly capitalism were disregarded.

The importance of a study of "vertical" relations between various branches of the economy, i.e., of input–output analysis, is not limited to conditions of a capitalist economy. As was already pointed out by Marx, since input–output relations are based on technological conditions of production, proper proportions in this respect must be maintained in any economic system. A study of such relations is, therefore, necessary for purposes of socialist economic planning as well as for the understanding of the mechanics of the capitalist economy. Under conditions of socialism, input–output analysis is a necessary tool for ascertaining the internal consistency of economic plans.

In socialist countries, input–output analysis takes the form of various "statistical balances" which are the basis of economic planning. These balances are conceived as concretizations of the general idea underlying Marx's reproduction schemes. In the U.S.A., Professor Leontief has developed a type of input–output analysis which, too, can be conceived as a concretization of Marx's idea of input–output relations taking place in the process of reproduction of the national product. Professor Leontief's analysis takes explicitly into account the technological relations between output and input. Though applied first to the economy of the U.S.A., this analysis like all input–output analyses is also applicable to a socialist economy. Indeed, it seems to me that this analysis achieves its full justification only if applied as a tool of economic planning. Its technique, though first applied to a capitalist economy, points beyond the historical limitations of capitalism, and can come fully into its own only under conditions of a planned economy.

The Marxian Schemes

Marx's analysis of reproduction is based on two devices. First, the value of the total national product during a period of time, (e.g., a year), is considered as being composed of three parts—the value of the means of production used-up during this period (to be denoted by c—in Marx's terminology the used up constant capital), the value of the labour power directly engaged in production (to be denoted by v—in Marx's terminology the variable capital, i.e., the revolving wage fund), the generated surplus value (to be denoted by s). Thus, the

$$\text{total national product} = c+v+s.$$

Here, c is the replacement of the used-up means of production, $v+s$ is the total value added (or national income).

Secondly, the economy is divided into two departments: one producing means of production, the other producing consumer goods. Using the subscripts 1 and 2 to indicate the two departments, respectively, we write:

$$\text{total output of means of production} = c_1+v_1+s_1;$$
$$\text{total output of consumer goods} = c_2+v_2+s_2;$$
$$\text{gross national product} = c+v+s$$

where

$$c = c_1+c_2, \quad v = v_1+v_2, \quad s = s_1+s_2.$$

In a stationary economy (Marx's simple reproduction):

$$\text{total demand for means of production} = c_1+c_2;$$
$$\text{total demand for consumer goods} = v_1+v_2+s_1+s_2.$$

The total demand for means of production is equal to the joint replacement requirements of both departments; the total demand for consumer goods is equal to the joint wage fund and surplus of both departments.

Putting equal demand and output of means of production, we obtain

$$c_1+c_2 = c_1+v_1+s_1; \tag{2.1}$$

this can be simplified to

$$c_2 = v_1+s_1. \tag{2.2}$$

The same result is obtained from putting equal total demand and output of consumer goods. That is,

$$v_1+v_2+s_1+s_2 = c_2+v_2+s_2. \tag{2.3}$$

This is so, because the gross national product $c+v+s$ is given. Equation (2.3) can be derived from equation (2.1).

Equation 2.2 indicates an input–output relation between the two Departments of the national economy. Indeed, let us write,

$$\frac{c_1 + \boxed{v_1+s_1}}{\boxed{c_2} + v_2+s_2}. \tag{2.4}$$

Department 1 produces means of production. Part of its output, equal in value to c_1, is retained within the Department to replace the used-up means of production. The remainder (in the rectangle), equal in value to v_1+s_1, is exchanged with Department 2 for consumer goods. Department 2 produces consumer goods. Part of its output, equal in value to v_2+s_2, is retained within the Department for consumption. The remainder in the rectangle, equal in value to c_2, is exchanged with Department 1 for means of production needed to replace the used-up means of production. For production to proceed smoothly, the output of the two departments must be co-ordinated in such a way that a balanced exchange takes place between the two Departments, i.e., $c_1 = v_1+s_1$. The above table (2.4) thus indicates the input–output relations between the two Departments: equation (2.2) gives the condition of a proper balance between the two Departments.

In an expanding economy (Marx's expanded reproduction) not all the surplus is consumed; part of it is accumulated to increase the amount of means of production and of labour. We shall express this by writing,

$$s = \bar{s}+s_c+s_v,$$

where $\bar{s}$ is the part of the surplus consumed, s_c the part of the surplus used to increase the amount of means of production, s_v the part of the surplus used to increase the labour force.

Dividing as before, the economy into two Departments, we have

total output of means of production $\quad = c_1+v_1+\bar{s}_1+s_{1c}+s_{1v};$

total output of consumer goods $\quad\quad = c_2+v_2+\bar{s}_2+s_{2c}+s_{2v};$

gross national product $\quad\quad\quad\quad\quad = c+v+\bar{s}+s_c+s_v.$

Furthermore:

total demand for means of production $= c_1+c_2+s_{1c}+s_{2c};$

total demand for consumer goods $\quad = v_1+v_2+s_{1v}+s_{2v}+\bar{s}_1+\bar{s}_2.$

The total demand for means of production is equal to the joint replacement and expansion requirement of both Departments. The total demand of consumer goods is equal to the joint wage fund, the joint expansion wage fund and the joint surplus consumed in both Departments.

Equality of demand and output of means of production implies

$$c_1+s_{1c}+c_2+s_{2c} = c_1+v_1+\bar{s}_1+s_{1c}+s_{1v} \tag{2.5}$$

which leads to

$$c_2+s_{2c} = v_1+\bar{s}_1+s_{1v}. \tag{2.6}$$

The same result can be obtained from the condition of equality of demand and output of consumer goods.

Equation (2.6) indicates the input–output relation between the two Departments in an expanding economy. It can be presented by means of the following table:

$$\frac{c_1+s_{1c} \quad +\boxed{v_1+\bar{s}_1+s_{1v}}}{\boxed{c_2+s_{2c}}+ v_2+\bar{s}_2+s_{2v}}. \tag{2.7}$$

In Department 1 part of the product, equal in value to c_1+s_{1c}, is retained within the department to replace the used up means of production and to expand further the means of production in the department. The remainder (contained in the rectangle) is transmitted to Department 2 in exchange for consumer goods. In Department 2 part of the product, equal in value to $v_2+\bar{s}_2+s_{2v}$, is retained for consumption. The remainder (contained in the rectangle) is exchanged with Department 1 for means of production required to replace the used-up means of production and to expand further the means of production in the department. The proper balance between the two departments is thus expressed by equation (2.6).

Input–Output Relations in a Multi-sector Model

Professor Leontief's input–output tables are designed to study the relations between a larger number of sectors of the national economy. Let the economy be divided into n production sectors denoted by the indices $1, 2, ..., n$. Denote by X_i the total or gross output of the ith sector, by X_{ij} the quantity of the product of the ith sector transmitted to the jth sector where it is used as input. Further, denote by x_i the net output of the ith sector, viz., that part of the gross output X_i which is net allocated to other sectors to be used there as input. The net output x_i can be consumed, exported, or accumulated for the purpose of investment.

We have thus,

$$X_i = \sum_{j=1}^{n} x_{ij} + x_i \quad (i = 1, 2, ..., n). \tag{3.1}$$

It is convenient to represent the input–output relations between the sectors of the economy in the form of a table as follows:

$$
\begin{array}{c|ccccccc|c}
X_1 & x_{11} & x_{12} & \cdots & \cdots & \cdots & \cdots & \cdots & x_{1n} & x_1 \\
X_2 & x_{21} & x_{22} & \cdots & \cdots & \cdots & \cdots & \cdots & x_{n2} & x_2 \\
\cdot\,\cdot & \multicolumn{8}{c|}{\cdot \quad \cdot \quad \cdot \quad \cdot \quad \cdot \quad \cdot \quad \cdot \quad \cdot \quad \cdot \quad \cdot \quad \cdot} & \cdot\,\cdot \\
X_n & x_{n1} & x_{n2} & \cdots & \cdots & \cdots & \cdots & \cdots & x_{nn} & x_n
\end{array}
\tag{3.2}
$$

The items in the square matrix in the centre of the table represent the input–output relations, or the "inter–flows" between the various branches of the national economy (also called "intersector deliveries") The column on the right-hand side represents the net outputs, and the column on the left-hand side the gross outputs of the various products. The rows are subject to the balance relation given by equation (3.1).

Since the process of production requires not only the use of means of production but also labour, we complete the table by introducing the amounts of labour force employed in production. Let us denote the total labour force available in the national economy by X_0, the labour force employed in producing the output of the ith sector of the economy by X_{0i} and, finally, by x_0 the unproductive labour force. The latter may be either unemployed (labour reserve) or employed in nonproductive activities, i.e., in activities which do not produce material goods, (e.g., personal services). With regard to the allocation of the total labour force, the following equation holds:

$$X_0 = \sum_{i=1}^{n} x_{0i} + x_0. \qquad (3.3)$$

Introducing the allocation of the labour force into the input–output table, we obtain the following table:

X_0	x_{01}	x_{02}	...	...	...	...	x_{0n}	x_0
X_1	x_{11}	x_{12}	...	...	...	...	x_{1n}	x_1
X_2	x_{21}	x_{22}	...	...	...	...	x_{2n}	x_2
$\cdot\;\cdot$	$\cdot$	$\cdot$	$\cdot$	$\cdot$	$\cdot$	$\cdot$	$\cdot$	$\cdot\;\cdot$
X_n	x_{n1}	x_{n2}	...	...	...	...	x_{nn}	x_n
	Y_1	Y_2	...	...	...	...	Y_n	

(3.4)

The items in the square matrix in the centre of the table are "interflows" or "intersector deliveries". The upper row in the centre represents the allocation of the labour force to the various branches of the economy. Similarly as before, the column on the right represents the remainder of the labour force not allocated productively (x_0), and the net outputs of the various products (x_i; $i = 1, ..., n$). The column on the left-hand side represents the total labour force X_0 and the gross outputs X_i($i = 1, 2, ..., n$) of the various branches.

The entries in the table may be expressed either in physical or in value units. In the latter case, the table is sometimes called a "transaction table" rather than our input–output table. Whatever the units used, the rows of the table can always be summed up, for each row is expressed in the same units, (e.g., man-hours, tons, gallons, yards, pieces). Thus, the equations (3.1) and (3.2) hold under all circumstances. We may call them the "allocation equations".

The columns, however, can only be summed if the entries of the table are expressed in value units (e.g., rupees), i.e., if the table is a transaction table, otherwise the items of a column would be non-homogeneous. We shall represent these sums in the following form:

$$Y_j = x_{0j} + \sum_{i=1}^{n} x_{ij} \quad (i = 1, 2, ..., n). \tag{3.5}$$

Obviously, Y_j is the cost of the output of the jth branch, x_{0j} being the cost of the labour force employed, and $\sum_i x_{ij}$ the cost of the means of production used up in producing the output. We may call the equations (3.5) the "cost equations". The costs of producing the output of the various branches of the economy are given in the row at the bottom of table (3.4).

The excess output value of a branch of the economy over the cost of producing the output is the surplus produced in this branch. Denoting the surplus produced in the jth branch by s_j, we have:

$$s_j = X_j - Y_j \tag{3.6}$$

and in view of (3.5)

$$X_j = x_{0j} + \sum_{i=1}^{n} x_{ij} + s_j \quad (j = 1, ..., n). \tag{3.7}$$

This is the relation which in a multi-sector model corresponds to the Marxian decomposition of the value of the output of a branch of the national economy into $c_j + v_j + s_j (j = 1, 2)$. Here $\sum_i x_{ij}$ stands for c_j and x_{0j} stands for v_j in the Marxian notation. The value added in the sector is $X_{0j} + S_j$.

Introducing the surplus produced in the various branches of the economy into the transaction table, and taking account of the relation (3.7) we obtain the following transaction table:

X_0	x_{01} x_{02} ... ... x_{0n}	x_0
X_1	x_{11} x_{12} ... ... x_{1n}	x_1
...	. . . .	...
X_n	x_{n1} x_{n2} ... ... x_{nn}	x_n
	s_1 s_2 ... ... s_n	
	. . . .	
	X_1 X_2 ... ... X_n	

(3.8)

From Table 3.8 it is apparent that the gross output of a branch, say X_i, can be obtained either by summation of the entries of a row or by summation of the entries of a column. Consequently, we have

$$\sum_{j=1}^{n} x_{ij} + x_i = x_{0i} + \sum_{j=1}^{n} x_{ji} + s_i \quad (i = 1, ..., n). \quad (3.9)$$

This results directly from the equations (3.1) and (3.7). On both sides of equation (3.9) x_{ii} is appearing under the summation sign: it is the part of the output retained in the sector for replacement. Eliminating x_{ii} from the equation, we obtain

$$\sum_{j \neq i} x_{ij} + x_i = x_{0i} + \sum_{j \neq i} x_{ji} + s_i \quad (i = 1, ..., n). \quad (3.10)$$

This equation states that (measured in value units) the outflow from the sector to other sectors—plus the net output is equal to the inflow from other sectors plus the value added in the sector.

Equation (3.10) is the analogue, in a multi-sector model, of the Marxian equations (3.2) and (3.6) of the previous sections which hold in a two-sector model. The aforementioned Marxian equations are obtained similarly to equation (3.10)—by making the value of the output of the sector equal the total allocation of the sector's output and by eliminating on both sides the part of the output retained in the sector.

In order to see the exact analogy of equation (3.10) with the equations of the Marxian two-sector model, let us transform equation (3.10) in the following way. Suppose that the net output x_1 is partly reinvested in this sector and partly consumed or allocated to other sectors; the corresponding parts will be denoted by x_i' and x_i'' respectively. Thus we have

$$x_i = x_i' + x_i'' \quad (i = 1, ..., n). \quad (3.11)$$

Further, suppose that the surplus produced in the sector is used partly for consumption, partly for employment of additional labour in the sector, and partly for increasing the means of production used in this sector. Denote these quantities by $\bar{s}_i$, s_{i0} and x_i' respectively. Thus

$$s_i = \bar{s}_i + s_{i0} + x_i'. \quad (3.12)$$

Substituting (3.11) and (3.12) in equation (3.10) and eliminating x_i' on both sides, the equation reduces to

$$\sum_{j \neq 1}^{n} x_{ji} + x_i'' = \sum_{j \neq i} x_{ji} + x_{0i} + s_{i0} + \bar{s}_i \quad (i = 1, ..., n). \quad (3.13)$$

In this form both the quantities x_{ii} retained in the sector for replacement and the quantity retained in the sector for expansion are eliminated. Equation (3.13) states that the net outflow to other sectors and to consumption is equal to the inflow from other sectors and to the part of the value added not retained in the sector. This is the exact counterpart—in a multi-sector model—to the Marxian equation (2.6) of the previous section.

If the number of sectors is reduced to two, equation (3.13) becomes identical with equation (2.2) of the preceding section. In this case (3.13) reduces to

$$x_{12}+x_1'' = x_{21}+x_{01}+s_{10}+\bar{s}_1. \qquad (3.14)$$

The corresponding transaction table takes the form:

X_0	x_{01}	x_{02}	$x_{01}'+x_{02}'+x_0''$
X_1	x_{11}	x_{12}	$x_1' +$	x_1''
X_2	x_{21}	x_{22}	$x_2' +$	x_2''
	$\bar{s}_1$	$\bar{s}_2$	
	s_{10}	s_{20}	
	x_1'	x_2'	

(3.15)

Sector 1 produces means of production and sector 2 produces consumer goods. As consumer goods are not means of production, $x_{21} = 0$, and as means of production are not consumed, x_1'' is the means of production allocated to sector 2 for expansion. Using the notation of the preceding section, we shall write:

$$x_{01} = v_1; \qquad x_{02} = v_2$$
$$x_{11} = c_1; \qquad x_{12} = c_2; \qquad x_{21} = 0$$
$$x_1'' = s_{2c}; \qquad s_{10} = s_{1v}.$$

Thus equation (3.14) takes the form

$$c_2+s_{2c} = v_1+s_{1v}+\bar{s}_1,$$

which is identical with equation (2.6) of the preceding section. In a stationary economy, $s_{2c} = s_{1v} = 0$, and the equation reduces to $c_2 = v_1+s_1$, i.e., to equation (2.2) of the preceding section.

It should also be noticed that of the equations (3.10) or (3.13)—which are equivalent to (3.10)—only $n-1$ are independent. From the transaction table (3.8) it is apparent that

$$\sum_i \left(\sum_j x_{ij} + x_i\right) = \sum_i \left(x_{0i} + \sum_j x_{ji} + s_i\right) = \sum_i x_i. \qquad (3.16)$$

This implies directly that one of the equations (3.10) can be derived from the remaining $n-1$. This corresponds to the property of the Marxian two-sector model where only one relation such as equation (2.6) or (2.2) of the preceding section holds between the two sectors.

Eliminating the double sums on both sides of the identity (3.16), we obtain

$$\sum_i x_i = \sum_i x_{0i} + \sum_i s_i, \qquad (3.17)$$

which shows that the net product of the national economy, or national income is equal to the total value added during the period under consideration.

Technological Relations and Value Relations

In order to study the effect of the technological conditions of production upon input–output relations we have to distinguish clearly between input–output tables expressed in physical units and transaction tables which are expressed in value units. For this purpose we shall use a separate notation.

The physical output of the ith sector will be denoted by Q_i, the physical net output by q_i and the physical interflow from the ith to the jth sector by $q_{ij}(i, j = 1, ..., n)$. The physical total labour force (measured, for instance, in properly weighted man-hours) will be denoted by Q_0, the physical labour power employed in the ith sector by q_{0i} and the remainder not employed productively by q_0. The physical input–output table can thus be written in the form

Q_0	q_{01}	q_{02} $\cdots$ q_{0n}	q_0
Q_1	q_{11}	q_{12} $\cdots$ q_{1n}	q_1
Q_2	q_{21}	q_{22} $\cdots$ q_{2n}	q_2
.	.	. . . .	.
Q_n	q_{n1}	q_{n2} $\cdots$ q_{nn}	q_n

$$(4.1)$$

The rows of the table are subject to the allocation balance

$$Q_i = \sum_j q_{ij} + q_i \quad (i = 0, 1, 2, ..., n).$$ (4.2)

The technological conditions of production can be described by the technical coefficients, also called production coefficients:

$$a_{ij} = q_{ij}/Q_j \quad (i = 0, 1, ..., n; \; j = 1, ..., n).$$ (4.3)

The coefficient a_{0j} indicates the labour power employed in producing a unit of output in the jth sector, the remaining coefficients a_{ij} indicate the amount of output of the ith sector needed to produce a unit of output in the jth sector.

In the socialist countries the values of these coefficients are generally available in the form of "technical norms" used in planning and administration of production. These norms indicate the amounts of labour power, raw materials, etc., which are allowed to be used per unit of output. In the absence of such "technical norms" in industries, the technical coefficients can be obtained approximately from statistical input–output tables, according to formula (4.3). This method was employed by Professor Leontief.

Introducing the technical coefficients (4.3), the allocation equations (4.2) become

$$Q_i = \sum_j a_{ij}Q_j + q_i \quad (i = 0, 1, ..., n).$$

It is convenient to separate the first equation relating to labour power from the remaining ones. We have then

$$Q_0 = \sum_j a_{0j}Q_j + q_0$$ (4.4)

and the remaining equation can be written in the form

$$(1 - a_{ii})Q_i - \sum_{j \neq 1} a_{ij}Q_j = q_i \quad (i = 1, ..., n).$$ (4.5)

Thus the equations (4.5) can be solved separately from equation (4.1). The matrix of the coefficients of these equations

$$\begin{bmatrix} 1 - a_{11}, & -a_{12}, & \cdots & \cdots & -a_{1n} \\ \cdot & \cdot & \cdot & \cdot & \cdot \\ -a_{n1}, & -a_{n2}, & \cdots & \cdots & 1 - a_{nn} \end{bmatrix}$$ (4.6)

is called the "technical matrix". It describes the technological conditions of production.[1]

In the system (4.5) there are n equations and $2n$ variables, i.e., the gross outputs $Q_1, ..., Q_n$, and the net outputs, $q_1, ..., q_n$. If the technical matrix is non–singular, as we shall assume it to be the case, there are thus n degrees of freedom. We can fix in the national economic plan the net outputs $q_1, ..., q_n$, and the gross outputs $Q_1, ..., Q_n$ are then uniquely determined by the equations (4.5). Or, instead, we can fix in the plan the gross outputs and the net outputs available which will result uniquely from the equations. Or, finally, we can fix in the plan a number of gross outputs and of net outputs, together n in number, and the remaining n gross and net outputs are determined by the equations.

If the technical matrix happens to be singular, the number of degrees of freedom is increased according to the order of nullity of the matrix. Thus if the rank of the matrix is $m(m < n)$, the order of nullity is $n-m$, and the number of degrees of freedom is $n+n-m$. Thus, we must fix in the plan $2n-m$ variables, the remaining m variables being then obtained from the equations (4.5).

Having the gross outputs $Q_1, ..., Q_n$ either from the equations (4.5) or directly from the plan, we can substitute them into equation (4.4). This gives us the total labour force employed $\sum_{j=1}^{n} a_{0j}Q_j$, and taking the total labour force Q_0 as a datum, we can calculate q_0, i.e., the labour force remaining outside productive employment.

To show the relation between the transaction table and the physical input–output table (1), we must explicitly take account of prices. Denote by p_0 the remuneration per unit labour force, and by $p_1, p_2, ..., p_n$ the prices of the products of the various sectors. Further p'_0 denotes the earning of the labour force not employed in production. We have then

---

[1] It should be noticed that this technical matrix differs from the matrix used by Professor Leontief in so far as in Professor Leontief's matrix the coefficients a_{ii} in the diagonal are absent; his diagonal consists only of unities. This is due to the fact that he does not take into account that part of the output is retained in the sector as means of production, e.g., part of the output of agriculture is retained as seed and as fodder for breeding animals, part of the coal is retained in the coal mines as fuel, etc. If the number of sectors in the model is small, the sectors being accordingly large, this omission may be serious.

$$X_i = p_i Q_i, \quad x_i = p_i q_i,$$
$$x_0 = p_0' q_0, \tag{4.7}$$
$$x_{ij} = p_i q_{ij}.$$

We shall also denote by π_i the surplus per unit of gross physical output in the sector, i.e.,

$$S_i = \pi_i Q_i \quad (i = 1, ..., n). \tag{4.8}$$

By introducing these relations into the transaction table (3.8) of the preceding section we obtain the following form of the transaction table:

$$
\begin{array}{|c|cccc|c|}
\hline
p_0 \sum q_{0j} + p_0' q_0 & p_0 q_{01} & p_0 q_{02} \cdots p_0 q_{0n} & & p_0' q_0 \\
\hline
p_1 Q_1 & p_1 q_{11} & p_1 q_{12} \cdots p_1 q_{1n} & & p_1 q_1 \\
p_2 Q_2 & p_2 q_{21} & p_2 q_{22} \cdots p_2 q_{2n} & & p_2 q_2 \\
\cdot \ \cdot & \cdot & \cdot \ \cdot \ \cdot \ \cdot \ \cdot \ \cdot & & \cdot \ \cdot \\
p_n Q_n & p_n q_{n1} & p_n q_{n2} \cdots p_n q_{nn} & & p_n q_n \\
\hline
 & \pi_1 Q_1 & \pi_2 Q_2 \ldots \pi_n Q_n & & \\
\hline
 & p_1 Q_1 & p_2 Q_2 \cdots p_n Q_n & & \\
\hline
\end{array}
\tag{4.9}
$$

Summing the columns we obtain the equations

$$p_0 q_{0i} + \sum_j p_j q_{ji} + \pi_i Q_i = p_i Q_i$$

which are identical with equations (3.7) in the preceding section. Taking account of the technical coefficients (a_{ij}), these equations can be written as

$$a_{0i} p_0 + \sum_j a_{ji} p_j + \pi_i = p_i$$

or, more conveniently,

$$(1 - a_{ii}) p_i - \sum_{j \neq i} a_{ji} p_i - a_{0i} p_0 = \pi_i. \tag{4.10}$$

The matrix of the coefficients is

$$
\begin{bmatrix}
1 - a_{11}, & -a_{21}, & \ldots \ldots, & -a_{n1}, & -a_{01} \\
\cdot \ \cdot & \cdot \ \cdot \ \cdot \ \cdot \ \cdot & \cdot \ \cdot \ \cdot \ \cdot & \cdot \ \cdot & \cdot \\
-a_{1n}, & -a_{2n}, & \ldots \ldots, & 1 - a_{nn}, & -a_{0n}
\end{bmatrix}.
\tag{4.11}
$$

There are n equations and $2n+1$ variables, i.e., n prices $p_1, ..., p_n$, the wage rate p_0 and n per unit surpluses, $\pi_1, ..., \pi_n$. If the matrix is of rank n, there are thus $n+1$ degrees of freedom. We can fix, for instance, the wage rate p_0 and the per unit surpluses $\pi_1, ..., \pi_n$, the n prices are then uniquely determined. Or, instead, we can fix the n prices mentioned and the wage rate, the per unit surpluses are then uniquely determined, or any other combination of $n+1$ variables can be fixed, the n remaining ones resulting from the equations.

If the rank of the matrix is less than n, the number of degrees of freedom increases correspondingly. The important point to be noticed is that these relations between prices of products, wage rate and per unit surpluses are entirely determined by the technological conditions of production as represented by the technical matrix of the coefficients of equations (4.10). The $n \times n$ submatrix containing the first n columns is simply the transpose of the technical matrix (4.6).

Now we can show the relation between the physical input–output relations and the input–output relations in value terms as expressed in a transaction table. The rows of the transaction table (4.9) are subject to the allocation balance

$$p_i Q_i = \sum_j p_i q_{ij} + p_i q_i$$

or, introducing the technical coefficients according to (4.3),

$$p_i Q_i = \sum_j p_i a_{ij} Q_j + p_i q_i.$$

This can also be written in the form

$$p_i Q_i = \sum_j a'_{ij} p_j Q_j + p_i q_i \tag{4.12}$$

where

$$a'_{ij} = \left(\frac{p_i}{p_j}\right) a_{ij} \quad (i, j = 1, ..., n). \tag{4.13}$$

In view of (4.7), the equations (4.12) can be written in the form

$$X_i = \sum_j a'_{ij} X_j + x_i$$

or

$$(1 - a'_{ii}) X_i - \sum_{j \neq i} a'_{ij} X_j = x_i \quad (i = 1, ..., n). \tag{4.14}$$

These equations establish the relations between the value of the net outputs $x_1, ..., x_n$, and the value of the gross outputs of the various sectors.

The matrix of the coefficients of these equations is

$$\begin{bmatrix} 1-a'_{11}, & -a'_{12}, & ...., & -a'_{1n} \\ \cdot & \cdot \quad \cdot \quad \cdot \quad \cdot \quad \cdot \quad \cdot \quad \cdot \quad \cdot & \cdot \\ -a'_{n1}, & -a'_{n2}, & ...., & 1-a'_{nn} \end{bmatrix}, \tag{4.15}$$

i.e., analogous to the matrix (4.6), only that the coefficients a'_{ij} appear instead of the coefficients a_{ij}.

The coefficients a'_{ij} can be written in the form

$$a'_{ij} = \frac{x_{ij}}{X_j} \qquad (i, j = 1, ..., n). \tag{4.16}$$

They indicate the value of the input of the product of the ith sector ($i = 1, ..., n$) required to produce a unit of output value of the jth sector. We shall call these coefficients—"input coefficients".

In addition, input coefficients of the type

$$a'_{0j} = \frac{x_{0j}}{X_j} \tag{4.17}$$

can be introduced which indicate the value of direct labour power needed to produce a unit of product value in the jth sector. With the aid of these coefficients the value of the total labour force employed in production can be calculated, i.e.,

$$X_0 - x_0 = \sum_j a'_{0j} X_j. \tag{4.18}$$

The input coefficients derive their significance from their simple behaviour with regard to aggregation of two or several sectors into one single sector. For instance, let us aggregate the jth sector and the kth sector and denote the new sector thus obtained as the lth sector. The value of the gross output of the new sector is then

$$X_l = X_j + X_k \tag{4.19}$$

and the value of the part of the product of the ith sector allocated as input to the new sector is

$$x_{il} = x_{ij} + x_{ik}. \tag{4.20}$$

The new input coefficient is, consequently,

$$a'_{il} = \frac{x_{il}}{X_l} = \frac{x_{ij}+x_{ik}}{X_j+X_k}.$$

In view of the definition (4.16), this is equal to

$$a'_{i1} = \frac{a'_{ij}X_j+a'_{ik}X_k}{X_j+X_k}, \tag{4.21}$$

i.e., the new input coefficient is the weighted mean of the input coefficients before aggregation.

The input coefficients can be given a simple interpretation on the basis of the Marxian theory of value. If the prices of the products express the amount of socially necessary labour required to produce a physical unit of output, the input coefficients indicate the quantity of social labour engaged in one sector necessary to produce in another sector a value unit, (i.e., an amount representing a unit of social labour). This quantity is entirely determined by the technological conditions of production. The transaction table indicates the allocation of the social labour among the various sectors of the national economy and shows the interflow of social labour between the various sectors of the economy. Aggregation of sectors can be performed by mere summation and the input coefficients are transformed under aggregation by simple averaging.

The Marxian theory, however, points out that in a capitalist economy prices do not exactly reflect the amount of social labour necessary to produce a unit of output. Systematic deviations arise between the "prices of production", i.e., equilibrium prices under competitive capitalism, and the values of products measured in labour. These deviations are the result of the technologically determined differences in ratios of capital goods and direct labour employed, on the one hand, and the equalization of the rates of profit by competition, on the other hand. Monopoly produces further systematic deviations. Consequently, transaction tables of a capitalist economy give only an approximate picture of allocation of social labour. In a socialist economy transaction tables give a picture of the allocation of social labour to the extent that prices express the amount of social labour required in production. Therefore, in a socialist economy, a proper system of prices reflecting the amounts of social labour required in production is a necessary instrument of effective accounting of the allocation of society's labour force among the various branches of the economy.

Consumption and Investment

The net output of any sector of the national economy may be consumed, exported or accumulated for future use. Accumulated output may be designated for future consumption or allocated to increase the quantity of means of production, i.e., invested in the process of production. In the first case, we shall consider it as another form of consumption; the last mentioned use will be called productive investment. The part of the net output exported can be considered as destined for consumption or productive investments in proportion as the goods imported, in turn, consist of consumer goods or means of production. Thus, the total net output of a sector may be divided into a part to be consumed and a part to be utilized for productive investment.

Consider the net physical output q_i of the ith sector and denote the part consumed by $q_i^{(1)}$ and the part invested productively by $q_i^{(2)}$. Then

$$q_i = q_i^{(1)} + q_i^{(2)}. \tag{5.1}$$

Further, let

$$k_i = \frac{q_i^{(i)}}{Q_i}; \qquad \alpha_i = \frac{q_i^{(2)}}{Q_i}. \tag{5.2}$$

Thus, k_i is the proportion of the gross output Q_i of the sector i to be consumed, and α_i is the proportion of the gross output Q_i to be used for productive investment. We shall call them the "rate of consumption" and "rate of investment", respectively.

Obviously,

$$q_i = (k_i + \alpha_i)Q_i. \tag{5.3}$$

The allocation equations (4.5) of the preceding section can then be written as homogeneous equations of the form

$$(1 - a_{ii} - k_i - \alpha_i)Q_i - \sum_{j \neq i} a_{ij}Q_j = 0 \quad (i = 1, \ldots, n). \tag{5.4}$$

In order that these have a non-trivial solution it is necessary that

$$\begin{vmatrix} 1 - a_{11} - k_1 - \alpha_1, & -a_{12}, \ldots \ldots & -a_{1n} \\ \cdot \cdot \cdot \cdot \cdot \cdot \cdot \cdot \cdot \cdot \cdot \cdot \cdot \cdot \cdot \cdot \cdot \cdot \cdot \cdot \cdot \cdot \\ -a_{n1}, & -a_{n2} \ldots \ldots & 1 - a_{nn} - k_n - \alpha_n \end{vmatrix} = 0, \tag{5.5}$$

i.e., the rates of consumption and rates of investment of the various sectors cannot be fixed independently of each other. Their mutual relations depend on the rank of the matrix of (5.5).

This may be conveniently illustrated by the example of a two-sector model. Taking the sector 1 and 2, the determinantal equation (5.4) becomes

$$(1-a_{11}-k_1-\alpha_1)(1-a_{22}-k_2-\alpha_2) = a_{12}a_{21} \qquad (5.6)$$

or,

$$\frac{1-a_{11}-k_1-\alpha_1}{a_{12}} = \frac{a_{21}}{1-a_{22}-k_2-\alpha_2}. \qquad (5.7)$$

This means that the fractions of the gross output of each sector going to the other sector for current use in production, i.e., $1-a_{ii}-k_i-\alpha_i$ is proportional to the technical coefficients relating the two sectors to each other. It is seen from (5.6) that if the rates of consumption are kept constant, the rate of investment of one sector can be increased only at the expense of reducing the rate of investment of the other sector. A similar relation holds for the rates of consumption of the two sectors, if the rates of investment are kept constant.

Now, suppose that sector 1 produces means of production and sector 2 produces consumer goods. Means of production are needed to produce consumer goods but are not consumed themselves; consequently, $a_{12} > 0$ and $k_1 = 0$. Consumer goods are only used for consumption; they are neither needed currently to produce means of production nor are they investable in production. Consequently, $a_{21} = 0$ and $\alpha_2 = 0$. Thus the equation (5.6) becomes:

$$(1-a_{11}-\alpha_1)(1-a_{22}-k_2) = 0.$$

As consumer goods are not invested, their total net output is consumed, i.e., $1-a_{22}-k_2 = 0$. Consequently, $1-a_{11}-\alpha_1$ is arbitrary and the rate of investment, α_1, can be arbitrarily fixed.

In a communist economy distribution of the national product is divorced from the input of labour and follows the principle, "to each according to his need". Under such circumstances, the rates of consumption can be set by policy, provided their mutual relations resulting from (5.5) are observed. These relations are expressed in physical terms only and no value relations are involved; they depend entirely on the technical coefficients.

In a socialist economy distribution of the national product is based on the remuneration for labour performed. Under capitalism it depends also on property in means of production which permits certain classes to appropriate the surplus generated in production. Therefore, in a socialist economy the rates of consumption are related to the remuneration of the labour force both in productive and non-productive employment. In a capitalist economy they depend also on the use property owners make of the surplus they appropriate.

In order to determine the rates of consumption, it is best to start from a transaction table. We have seen in section 3, equation (3.17), that the net product of the national economy is equal to the total value added in production, i.e.,

$$\sum_i x_i = \sum_i x_{0i} + \sum_i s_i.$$

Introducing the rates of consumption and of investment, we can write this in the form

$$\sum_i k_i X_i = \sum_i x_{0i} + \sum_i s_i - \sum_i \alpha_i x_i. \tag{5.8}$$

The left-hand side of this equation represents the part of the total value of the net product of the economy (national income) devoted to consumption.

Let W_i be the fraction of the part of the national income devoted to consumption spent for the product of the ith sector $(i = 1, ..., n)$. We consider these fractions to be "behavioural data" and shall call them "consumption parameters". Then,

$$k_i X_i = W_i \left(\sum_j X_{0j} + \sum_j S_j - \sum_j \alpha_j X_j \right), \quad \left(i = 1, ..., n; \quad \sum W_i = 1 \right). \tag{5.9}$$

(The subscripts in the summation signs on the right-hand side are denoted by j in order to avoid confusion with the subscript i on the left-hand side.)

Introducing input coefficients and writing

$$S_j = \pi_j X_j \quad (j = 1, ..., n) \tag{5.10}$$

we can write

$$k_i X_i = W_i \left(\sum_j a'_{0j} X_j + \sum_j \pi'_j X_j - \sum_j \alpha_j X_j \right) \quad (i = 1, ..., n). \tag{5.11}$$

Substituting this in the allocation equations (4.14) of the preceding section which indicate the allocation balances in the rows of the transaction table, we obtain

$$1-a'_{ii}-\alpha_i-W_i(a'_{0i}+\pi'_i-\alpha_i)X_i-\sum_{j\neq i}[a'_{ij}+W_i(a'_{ij}+\pi'_j-\alpha_j)]X_j = 0,$$

$$(i = 1, \ .., n). \tag{5.12}$$

In order that these equations have a non-trivial solution we must have the determinant

$$\begin{vmatrix} 1-a'_{11}-\alpha_1-W_1(a'_{0i}+\pi'_1-\alpha_1) \ \dots \ \cdots \ a'_{1n}-W_1(a'_{0n}+\pi_n-\alpha_n) \\ \dots \ \dots \ \dots \ \dots \ \dots \ \dots \ \dots \ \dots \ \dots \ \dots \ \dots \ \dots \ \dots \ \dots \ \dots \ \dots \\ -a'_{n1}-W_n(a'_{01}+\pi_1-\alpha_1) \ \dots \ 1-a'_{nn}-\alpha_n-W_n(a'_{0n}+\pi'_n-\alpha_n) \end{vmatrix} = 0. \tag{5.13}$$

This condition establishes the relations which must be maintained between the rates of investment $\alpha_1, \ ..., \ \alpha_n$ when the rates of consumption are determined by the "demand equations" (5.1).

The expressions

$$a'_{0j}+\pi'_j-\alpha_j \quad (j = 1, \ ..., n) \tag{5.14}$$

which occur in the determinant (5.13) indicate the part of the value added per unit output value in the sector which is devoted to consumption. By multiplying these expressions by W_i, we obtain the fraction of it which goes into consumption of the product of the ith sector.

For illustration, let us consider a two-sector model. The determinantal equation can then be written in the fcrm

$$\frac{1-a'_{11}-\alpha_1-W_1(a'_{01}+\alpha_1-\pi'_1)}{a'_{12}+W_1(a'_{02}+\pi'_2+\alpha_2)} = \frac{a'_{21}+W_2(a'_{01}+\pi'_1-\alpha_1)}{1-a'_{22}-\alpha_2-W_2(a'_{02}+\pi'_2-\alpha_2)}. \tag{5.15}$$

This equation indicates that the fraction of the value of gross output of each sector, remaining after deduction of the part retained in the sector for replacement (a'_{ii}), and for consumption $W_1(a'_{0i}+\pi'_i-\alpha_i)$ and of the part devoted to investments (α_i), is proportional to the total demand (per unit value of its output) of the other sector for the product of the first. The latter is equal to the sum of the input coefficient ($-a'_{ij}$) and the output of the other sector required for consumption, i.e., $W_i(a'_{0j}+\pi'_j-\alpha_j)$.

Transforming the input coefficients into technical coefficients according to formula (4.13) of the preceding section and observing that

$$\pi_j' = \frac{\pi_j}{p_j}, \quad (j = 1, \ldots, n) \tag{5.16}$$

we can write the determinantal equation (5.13) in the abbreviated form

$$\left| \delta_{ij} - \frac{p_i}{p_j} a_{ij} - W_i \frac{p_0}{p_j} a_{0j} + \frac{\pi_j}{p_j} - \alpha_j \right| = 0 \tag{5.17}$$

where $\delta_{ij} = 1$ for $i = j$ and $\delta_{ij} = 0$ for $i \neq j$. This equation contains the wage rate p_0, the product prices $p_1, \ldots, p_n$, and the per unit surpluses $\pi_1, \ldots, \pi_n$. These quantities cannot be eliminated from the equation.

Thus, when the rates of consumption are determined by "demand equations" as in (5.11), linking them to the national income, the relation between the rates of investment in the various sectors of the national economy cannot be expressed in purely physical and technological terms. They have to be expressed in value terms and are found, according to (5.13), to depend on the input coefficients, the rates of surplus $\pi_1', \ldots, \pi_n'$ and the consumption parameters $W_1, \ldots, W_n$ of the various sectors.

As the input coefficients in the light of the Marxian theory of value can be interpreted as indicating technological conditions of production, the relations between the rates of investment are found to depend, in addition to technological conditions of production, on behavioural parameters relating consumption of the various products to national income, and on the per unit surpluses in the various sectors. The latter can be considered as "sociological parameters". In a capitalist economy they are equal to the proportion of the value of each sector's output appropriated by the owners of means of production. In a socialist economy the surpluses are set by considerations of social policy, providing the resources for productive investment and for society's collective consumption.

Investment and Economic Growth

The part of the net outputs of the various sectors invested in production is added to the means of production available in the next period. This makes it possible to increase the output of the various sectors of the national economy in the next period. Investment realized in one period adds to the amount of means of production in operation in the next period. In consequence, a larger output is obtained in the next period. The output of successive periods (years, for instance) are linked into a chain by the investments undertaken in each period. Thus, productive investment generates a process of growth of output.

Let $Q_i(t)$ be the gross physical output of the ith sector of the economy during the time period indicated by t, e.g., the year 1955, and let α_i be the rate of investment of the ith sector as defined by (5.2) in the preceding section. The quantity of the sector's output invested is thus $\alpha_i Q_i(t)$. The stock of products of the ith sector available in the economy as means of production is thus increased by this amount.

This increment is partly retained in the sector and partly allocated to other sectors. Denote the increment allocated to the jth sector by $\Delta q_{ij}(t)$, $(i, j = 1, \ldots, n)$; and the period during which the allocation takes place by t.

We have

$$\alpha_i Q_i(t) = \sum_j \Delta q_{ij}(t). \tag{6.1}$$

However, not all the increment allocated is used up by the various sectors during a single unit time. For instance, if it consists of machines or other durable equipment, it will last for several units of time (years) and only a fraction of it is used up during a unit period of time. Let the durability of the part of the output of the ith sector allocated to the jth sector, as additional means of production, be T_{ij} units of time. T_{ij} is taken as a parameter given by the technological conditions of production and may be called the "turnover period" of the particular type of productive equipment. The reciprocal of the turnover period, $\frac{1}{T_{ij}}$ is the rate of used up productive equipment per unit time; it is also called "rate of replacement" or "rate of depreciation".

In order to produce a unit of physical output of the product of the jth sector during a unit period of time the quantity a_{ij} of the product of the ith sector must be used up during the time period; a_{ij} is the technical coefficient. Thus to increase in the next period the output of the jth sector by an additional unit, the quantity of output of the ith sector $a_{ij} \cdot T_{ij}$ must be allocated to the jth sector. Then, exactly $[a_{ij}$ of output of the ith sector will be used up in the next unit period in the sector, and this will produce one unit of output.

The quantities

$$b_{ij} = a_{ij} T_{ij} \quad (i, j = 1, ..., n) \tag{6.2}$$

may be called the "investment coefficients". The investment coefficients give the quantity of output of one sector which must be invested in the other sector in order to increase by one unit the output of the other sector in the next unit period.

Both the investment coefficients and their reciprocals reflect technological conditions of production; given the technical coefficients, the investment coefficients are proportional to the turnover periods of the various types of means of production.

Write $Q_i(t)$ for the physical gross output of the jth sector in the unit period under consideration, and $Q_j(t+1)$ for the physical gross output of this sector in the next unit period. An increment of output of the jth sector equal to $Q_j(t+1) - Q_j(t)$ requires the investment in the sector of the following quantity of the output of ith sector:

$$\Delta q_{ij} = b_{ij}[Q_j(t+1) - Q_j(t)] \quad (i, j = 1, ..., n). \tag{6.3}$$

In view of (6.1), we have

$$\alpha_i Q_i(t) = \sum_j b_{ij} Q_j(t+1) - Q_j(t) \quad (i = 1, ..., n). \tag{6.4}$$

These equations express the relations between the allocation of the part of the net product of each sector devoted to investment in the various sectors of the economy and the increments of output obtained in the various sectors in the next unit period.

If the amounts of product of the various sectors invested during the unit period t, i.e., $\alpha_i Q_i(t)$ are given $(i = 1, ..., n)$, the increments of output in the next unit period can be calculated from the equations (6.4). Denote by

$$B = \begin{bmatrix} b_{11}, & b_{12}, ..., b_{1n} \\ b_{21}, & b_{22}, ..., b_{2n} \\ \cdot & \cdot \quad \cdot \quad \cdot \quad \cdot \\ b_{n1}, & b_{n2}, ..., b_{nn} \end{bmatrix} \tag{6.5}$$

the matrix of the investment coefficients. The increments of output in the various sectors are then

$$Q_j(t+1) - Q_j(t) = \frac{1}{|B|} \sum_i B_{ij} \alpha_i Q_i(t) \tag{6.6}$$

where $|B|$ is the determinant of the matrix B and $|B_{ij}|$ is the co-factor of the element b_{ij}.

It is convenient to write

$$B_{ji} = \frac{B_{ij}}{|B|} \tag{6.7}$$

and express (6.6) in the form

$$Q_j(t+1) - Q_j(t) = \sum_i B_{ji}\alpha_i Q_i(t) \quad (j = 1, \ldots, n). \tag{6.8}$$

The coefficients B_{ji} indicate the increment of output obtained in the jth sector from an additional unit of the ith sector's product invested in the jth sector. They may be called "intersector output–investment ratios". The matrix of the coefficients B_{ij}, is the inverse of matrix B.

The increments of output in the various sectors depend on the investment coefficients and on the amounts of product of the various sectors invested. The investment coefficients, in turn, depend on the technical coefficients and turnover periods. By virtue of (6.2), the matrix of investment coefficients can be presented as follows:

$$B = \begin{bmatrix} a_{11}T_{11}, & a_{12}T_{12}, & \ldots a_{1n}T_{1n} \\ \cdots & \cdots & \cdots \ \cdots \\ \cdots & \cdots & \cdots \ \cdots \\ a_{n1}T_{n1}, & a_{n2}T_{n2}, & \ldots a_{nn}T_{nn} \end{bmatrix}. \tag{6.9}$$

In this way, the investments made in one unit period lead to an increase of output in the next period. If the rates of investment remain constant, the investments in the successive unit periods are

$$\alpha_i Q_i(t+1), \ \alpha_i Q_i(t+2), \ \ldots, \quad (i = 1, \ldots, n).$$

The investment of the first unit period t is the initial "impact" which sets in motion the process of economic growth. The investments in the successive unit periods carry the process forward from one stage to another.

The course of the process of economic growth can be derived from the equation (6.4) or, for that matter, also from the equivalent equations (6.8). These are linear difference equations with constant coefficients. The characteristic equation of the system (6.4) is

$$0 = \begin{vmatrix} \alpha_1 + b_{11}(1-\lambda), & b_{12}(1-\lambda), & \ldots & b_{1n}(1-\lambda) \\ \cdot \ \cdot \ \cdot \ \cdot \ \cdot \ \cdot & \cdot \ \cdot \ \cdot \ \cdot \ \cdot & \cdot \ \cdot \ \cdot \ \cdot \\ b_{n1}(1-\lambda), & b_{n2}(1-\lambda), & \ldots & \alpha_n + b_{nn}(1-\lambda) \end{vmatrix}. \tag{6.10}$$

The solution of the difference equations indicating the gross output in the unit period t_s can be written in the form

$$Q_j(t_s) = \sum_k C_k h_{jk} \lambda_k^{ts} \quad (j = 1, ..., n) \tag{6.11}$$

where the λ_k are the roots of the characteristic equation, the C_k are constants determined by the output $Q_j(t_s)$ in the initial unit period t_s, the h_{jk} are constants determined by the matrix of the coefficients of equation (6.4), i.e., by the matrix

$$\begin{bmatrix} \alpha_1 + b_{11}, b_{12}, ..., b_{1n} \\ \cdot \quad \cdot \quad \cdot \quad \cdot \quad \cdot \quad \cdot \quad \cdot \\ b_{n1}, b_{n2}, ..., \alpha_n + b_{nn} \end{bmatrix}. \tag{6.12}$$

Thus, the constants C_k reflect the initial situation of the national economy, while the constants h_{jk} depend on the technological structure of the economy as expressed by the technical coefficients and the turn-over periods as well as on the rates of investment.[2]

This analysis can be generalized by considering the rates of investment as variable in time, i.e., considering functions $\alpha(t)$ instead of constants $\alpha_i (i = 1, ..., n)$. In a similar way, changes in technical coefficients and turnover periods can be investigated. Instead of the constant investment coefficients, we would have to consider functions of time $b_{ij}(t)$, where $i, j = 1, ..., n$. The difference equations (6.4) then become

$$\alpha_i(t) Q_i(t) = \sum_j b_{ij}(t)[Q_j(t+1) - Q_j(t)]. \tag{6.13}$$

Since the coefficients in these equations are not constant, the equations require more complicated methods of treatment.

The increments in output from one unit period to the next one can, however, be easily computed. They are, in analogy with (6.8),

$$Q_j(t+1) - Q_j(t) = \sum_i B_{ji} \alpha_i(t) Q_i(t), \tag{6.14}$$

---

[2] In the above, the roots λ_k are assumed to be all distinct. In the case of a multiple root the corresponding h_{jk} on the right-hand side of (6.11) is not a constant but a polynomial of degree one less than the multiplicity of the root. The coefficients of this polynomial are determined by the technological structure of the economy expressed by the matrix and the rates of investment. The coefficients C_k remain determined by the initial situation.

the matrix of the coefficients B_{ji} being now the inverse of the matrix

$$B(t) = \begin{bmatrix} b_{11}(t), b_{12}(t), \ldots \ldots, b_{1n}(t) \\ \ldots \quad\quad \ldots \quad\quad \ldots\ldots\ldots \quad \ldots \\ \ldots \quad\quad \ldots \quad\quad \ldots\ldots\ldots \quad \ldots \\ b_{n1}(t), b_{n2}(t), \ldots \ldots, b_{nn}(t) \end{bmatrix}. \tag{6.15}$$

The relations between investment and the process of growth of output are here presented entirely in physical terms. They are found to depend solely on the technological structure of the economy and on the rates of investment chosen. The process of economic growth, however, can also be presented in value terms.

In such a case, the technological investment coefficients b_{ij} are replaced by a set of coefficients,

$$b'_{ij} = \frac{\Delta x_{ij}}{X_j(t+1) - X_j(t)} \quad (i, j = 1, \ldots, n), \tag{6.16}$$

indicating the value of the output of the ith sector which must be invested in the jth sector in order to obtain in the latter a unit increment of output value. These coefficients may be called "investment–outlay coefficients" or simply "outlay coefficients".[3]

In view of the relations (4.7) in section 4, the outlay coefficients are related to the investment coefficients as follows:

$$b'_{ij} = \frac{p_i}{p_j} b_{ij}. \tag{6.17}$$

Taking into account (6.2), they can also be written in the form:

$$b'_{ij} = a'_{ij} T_{ij} = \frac{p_i}{p_j} a_{ij} T_{ij}. \tag{6.18}$$

Using the relations (4.7) of section 4, the difference equations (6.4) expressing the relations between investments in the various sectors of

---

[3] Usually the term "capital coefficients" is used to denote the outlay coefficients. For reasons exposed by the Marxian theory the term "capital" is not appropriate in a socialist economy because it covers up the fundamental difference between the role of capital as value of means of production used to appropriate by their owners the surplus produced in the national economy and the role of means of production as an instrument in the physical process of production. We, therefore, prefer to use the term "outlay coefficients", meaning by "outlay" the money value of the physical investments.

the economy and the increments of output obtained can be written in the value form:

$$\alpha_i X_i(t) = \sum_j b'_{ij}[X_j(t+1) - X_j(t)], \tag{6.19}$$

and the solutions of these equations are obtained by means of their characteristic equation, which is

$$0 = \begin{vmatrix} \alpha_1 + b'_{11}(1-\lambda), & \ldots \ldots & b'_{1n}(1-\lambda) \\ \cdots & \cdots & \cdots \cdots & \cdots \\ \cdots & \cdots & \cdots \cdots & \cdots \\ b'_{n1}(1-\lambda), & & \ldots \alpha_n + b'_{nn}(1-\lambda) \end{vmatrix}. \tag{6.20}$$

The process of growth of the value of the output of the various sectors of the economy is thus determined—given the values of the initial outputs $X_1(t_0), \ldots, X_n(t_0)$—by the outlay coefficients b_{ij} and the rates of investment α_{ij}.

The outlay coefficients behave, under aggregation of two or several sectors into one sector, in a similar way as the input coefficients. The outlay coefficients of the new sector, resulting from aggregation, are the weighted means of the outlay coefficients of the sectors aggregated.

Indeed, denote by the subscript l the sector resulting from aggregation of the jth sector and the kth sector. The outlay coefficients of the new sector are then

$$b'_{il} = \frac{\Delta x_{il}}{X_l(t+1) - X_l(t)}.$$

Since

$$\begin{cases} \Delta X_{il} = \Delta X_{ij} + \Delta X_{ik} \\ X_l(t) = X_j(t) + X_k(t) \\ X_l(t+1) = X_j(t+1) + X_k(t+1) \end{cases} \tag{6.21}$$

we obtain, taking into account the definition (6.16),

$$b'_{il} = \frac{b'_{ij}[X_j(t+1) - X_j(t)] + b'_{ik}[X_k(t+1) - X_k(t)]}{[X_j(t+1) - X_j(t)] + [X_k(t+1) - X_k(t)]}. \tag{6.22}$$

The merit of presenting the growth of output, resulting from investment, in value terms is that it enables to aggregate sectors. But it must be pointed out that the outlay coefficients do not reflect the technological structure of the economy alone. As seen from (6.17), they depend also on the relative prices of the products. The result of their averaging under aggregation also depends on the relative prices of the products of the sectors aggregated.

However, on the basis of the Marxian theory of value, the outlay coefficients may, under appropriate circumstances, be interpreted as indicating the quantity of social labour employed in the sector of the economy which must be "stored up" in order to increase the output of another by an amount representing one unit of social labour. By such interpretation, which requires that prices reflect the amounts of social labour necessary to produce a physical unit of product, the outlay coefficients too represent the technological structure of the economy.

The way in which the growth of output set in motion by investment depends entirely on the technological structure of the economy is further elucidated by the fact that the investment coefficients are, according to (6.2), products of the technical coefficients and the turnover periods, or that the outlay coefficients, according to (6.8), are the products of the input coefficients and the turnover periods.[4] Thus the technological conditions, determining the growth of output, resulting from investment, consist entirely of two factors. One are the technical coefficients indicating current input–output relations during a unit period. The other are the turnover periods which simply indicate the durability of the various means of production and, consequently, the rate of depreciation of the means of production in a single unit period of time.

This disposes definitely of any mystical notions about the "productivity" of a mythical entity "capital" conceived as a separate factor of production distinguished from the physical means of production. Such metaphysical entity is proved to be nonexistent.

In a capitalist economy "capital" consists of private property rights to means of production which permit the owners of the means of production to appropriate the surplus produced in the national economy. "Capital" is the power to appropriate surplus. This power, under capitalism, is measured by the money value of the means of production

---

[4] The fact that the investment coefficients are not independent of the technical coefficients but are derived from them by multiplication by the turnover periods seems to have been pointed out first by David Hawkins, Some conditions of macroeconomic stability, *Econometrica*, 1948, p. 313. Usually they are wrongly taken as independent data, like, for instance, by Professor Leontief in, *Studies in the Structure of the American Economy*, Oxford University Press, New York 1953, p. 56.

and hired labour power a person (or corporation) can command. In a socialist economy such property rights are absent. There exist simply physical means of production and certain technological conditions expressed by the technical coefficients and turnover periods. From these technological conditions there result certain consequences concerning the quantity of social labour which must be "stored up" in order to achieve a planned increase in output. Thus, there is no need in a socialist economy for any concept of "capital". Such concept would only obscure the technological character of the conditions of the process of economic growth.

Effects of Investment on National Income and Employment

The equations (6.19) of the preceding section can be transformed into a form analogous to equation (6.8), i.e., which presents the increment of the output value of a sector of the national economy as a linear combination of the investment undertaken in the various sectors. For broader treatment it is convenient to consider the rates of investment, α_i, as variable in time, i.e., $\alpha_i(t)$. We then obtain

$$X_j(t+1) - X_j(t) = \sum_j B'_{ji} \alpha_i(t) X_i(t) \qquad (j = 1, ..., n). \qquad (7.1)$$

The coefficients B'_{ji} are the elements of a matrix $(B'_{ij})^{-1}$ which is the inverse of the matrix of the outlay coefficients

$$B' = \begin{bmatrix} b'_{11}, \ b'_{12} \ ... \ ..., \ b'_{1n} \\ \cdot \quad \cdot \quad \cdot \quad \cdot \quad \cdot \quad \cdot \quad \cdot \\ b'_{n1}, \ b'_{n2}, \ ... \ ..., \ b'_{nn} \end{bmatrix}. \qquad (7.2)$$

This means that

$$B'_{ji} = \frac{B'_{ij}}{B'} \qquad (i, j = 1, ..., n), \qquad (7.3)$$

where $|B'|$ is the determinant of B' and $|B'_{ij}|$ is the co-factor of the element b'_{ij}.

The coefficients B'_{ji} may be called "inter-sector output–outlay ratios". They indicate the increment of the output (measured in value) of the jth sector resulting from a unit increase of investment outlay on the product of the ith sector.

Summing the equation (7.1) over all sectors of the national economy, we obtain

$$\sum_j [X_j(t+1)-X_j(t)] = \sum_j \sum_i B'_{ji}\alpha_i(t)X_i(t)$$

or, writing

$$\beta_i = \sum_j B'_{ji} \quad (i = 1, ..., n), \tag{7.4}$$

$$\sum_j (X_j(t+1)-X_j(t)) = \sum_i \beta_i\alpha_i(t)X_i(t). \tag{7.5}$$

The left-hand side of equation (7.5) is the increment of the gross national product from one unit period to the next. The coefficients β_i, on the right-hand side show the effect of a unit increase in investment outlay of the products of the various sectors of the economy on the gross national product. They can be called simply "output–outlay ratios" of the products of the various sectors.

A further simplification of equation (7.5) can be achieved by expressing the investment outlays in the various sectors as a fraction of the total investment outlay in the national economy. Denote by $\alpha(t)$ the overall rate of investment in the national economy during the unit period t. The total investment outlay during the unit period is

$$\alpha(t) \sum_i X_i(t).$$

Denoting further by $\mu_i(t)$ the proportion of the total investment outlay which consists of the product of the ith sector of the economy, we have

$$\alpha_i(t)X_i(t) = \mu_i(t)\alpha(t) \sum_i X_i(t). \tag{7.6}$$

We shall call the $\mu_i(t)$ investment structure fractions and observe that

$$\sum_i \mu_i(t) = 1.$$

Substituting the relation (7.6) into equation (7.5) and observing that

$$\sum_i X_i(t) = \sum_j X_j(t),$$

we arrive at

$$\sum_j (X_j(t+1) - X_j(t)) = \alpha(t) \sum_j X_j(t) \sum_i \beta_i \mu_i(t),$$

which can also be written as

$$\frac{\sum_j (X_j(t+1) - X_j(t))}{\sum_j X_j(t)} = \alpha(t) \sum_i \beta_i \mu_i(t). \tag{7.7}$$

The left-hand side of (7.7) is the rate of increase of gross national product and will be denoted by $R(t)$. In order to simplify the right-hand side we shall put

$$\beta(t) = \sum_i \beta_i \mu_i(t). \tag{7.8}$$

Since $\sum_i \mu_i(t) = 1$, β can be interpreted as the average output–outlay ratio of the national economy, equation (7.7) can thus be expressed in the simple form

$$R(t) = \alpha(t)\beta(t). \tag{7.9}$$

Thus the rate of increase of the gross national product is the product of the overall rate of investment and of the average output–outlay ratio.

We can now calculate the effect of a given investment programme upon gross national income after a number of unit periods of time. Let $\sum_j X_j(t_0)$ be the gross national product in the initial unit period t_0, and let the investment programme be given by the overall rates of investment $\alpha(t_0), \ldots, \alpha(t_n)$ and the fractions $\mu_i(t_0), \ldots, \mu_i(t_n)$ of the total investment outlay of products of the various sectors of the economy, $(i = 1, \ldots, n)$. We obtain, then, the average output–outlay ratios, $\beta(t_0), \ldots, \beta(t_n)$. The gross national product in unit period $t_s (t_s > t_0)$ is

$$\sum_j X_j(t_s) = \prod_{t=t_0}^{t_s} [1 + \alpha(t)\beta(t)] \sum_j X_j(t_0). \tag{7.10}$$

If the overall rate of investment $\alpha(t)$ and the allocation fractions $\mu_i(t)$ are the same during each unit period, say α and μ_i, this reduces to

$$\sum_j X_j(t_s) = (1 + \alpha\beta)^{t_s - t_0} \times \sum_j X_j(t_0). \tag{7.11}$$

National income is the value of the total net output of the national economy. The value of the net output of the *i*th sector in unit period, *t*, is according to the allocation equation (4.12) or (4.14)

$$x_i(t) = X_i(t) - \sum_j a'_{ij} X_j(t), \qquad (7.12)$$

where the a'_{ij} are input coefficients.

The rate of increase in national income is equal to the rate of increase of the gross national product only when the change taking place in replacement is neglected. Taking account of the latter, we obtain the following result.

Using the same notation, national income in unit period *t* is

$$\sum_i x_i(t) = \sum_i X_i(t) - \sum_i \sum_j a'_{ij} X_j(t).$$

The double sum on the right-hand side represents that part of the gross national product which is used for the replacement of means of production used up during the unit period, i.e., depreciation. Let us denote the rate of replacement (rate of depreciation) during unit period *t* by

$$\sigma(t) = \frac{\sum_i \sum_j a'_{ij} X_j(t)}{\sum_i X_i(t)}.$$

We then can write

$$\sum_i x_i(t) = \sum_i X_i(t)[1 - \sigma(t)).$$

Denoting by $r(t)$ the rate of increase of national income and by $R(T)$ the rate of increase of the gross national product, we obtain

$$\frac{\sum_i x_i(t+1)}{\sum_i x_i(t)} = 1 + r(t) = \frac{\sum_i X_i(t+1)[1 - \sigma(t+1)]}{\sum_i X_i(t)[1 - \sigma(t)]}$$

whence the relation

$$1 + r(t) = [1 + R(t)] \frac{1 - \sigma(t+1)}{1 - \sigma(t)} \qquad (7.13)$$

between the rate of increase of national income $r(t)$ and the rate of increase of the gross national product $R(t)$.

In the relation obtained $1+r(t)$ is the growth coefficient of national income, $1+R(t)$ is the growth coefficient of the gross national product. $1-\sigma(t)$ and $1-\sigma(t+1)$ represent the fraction of the gross national product in the respective unit periods t and $t+1$ which does not serve for replacement; it may be called the net output ratio. Thus relation (7.13) states that the growth coefficient of national income is equal to the growth coefficient of the gross national product multiplied by an expression giving the change in the output ratio.

National income in unit period t_s is related to national income in the initial unit period $t_0(t_s > t_0)$ by formulae analogous to (7.10) and 7.11), namely

$$\sum_i x_i(t_s) = \prod_{t=t_0}^{t_s} [1+r(t)] \times \sum_i x_i(t) \tag{7.14}$$

and, in the case when $r(t) = r = $ constant,

$$\sum_i x_i(t_s) = (1+r)^{t_s-t_0} \sum_i x_i(t_0).$$

In view of (7.9) and (7.14) in this paper, the expression (7.14) can also be written in the more explicit form

$$\sum_i x_i(t_s) = \prod_{t=t_0}^{t_s} \left\{ [1+\alpha(t)\beta(t)] \frac{1-\sigma(t+1)}{1-\sigma(t)} \right\} \sum_i x_i(t). \tag{7.15}$$

The total employment generated by the gross national product is calculated as follows. Denote as in section 4 by a'_{0j} the input coefficients indicating the value of direct labour needed to produce a unit of product value in the jth sector. We shall call them for convenience "employment coefficients". The total employment (in value units) corresponding to the gross national product in unit period t is, according to the balance equation (4.1),

$$\sum_j a'_{0j} X_j(t).$$

Consequently, the increment of total employment from one unit period to the next is $\sum_j a'_{0j}[X_j(t+1)-X_j(t)]$. Taking into account equation (7.1), we find

$$\sum_j a'_{0j}[X_j(t+1)-X_j(t)] = \sum_j a'_{0j} \sum_i B'_{ji}\alpha_i(t)X_i(t),$$

or, in view of (7.6),

$$\sum_j a'_{0j}[X_j(t+1)-X_j(t)] = \sum_j a'_{0j} \sum_i B'_{ji}\mu_i(t)\alpha(t) \sum_i X_i(t). \quad (7.16)$$

This expression can be simplified as follows. Write

$$\gamma_i = \sum_j a'_{0j} B'_{ji} \quad (i = 1, ..., n), \quad (7.17)$$

where γ_i is the additional amount of employment (in value units) created in the national economy by a unit increase in investment outlay on the product of the ith sector of the economy. We may call it the "employment–outlay ratio" of the product of the ith sector. Then we obtain

$$\frac{\sum_j a'_{0j}[X_j(t+1)-X_j(t)]}{\sum_j X_j(t)} = \alpha(t) \sum_i \gamma_i\mu_i(t),$$

or, by introducing the average employment–outlay ratio of the national economy,

$$\gamma(t) = \sum_i \gamma_i\mu_i(t) \quad (7.18)$$

$$\frac{\sum_j a'_{0j}[X_j(t+1)-X_j(t)]}{\sum_j X_j(t)} = \alpha(t)\gamma(t). \quad (7.19)$$

The left-hand side of (7.19) indicates the increment of total employment from one unit period to the next in relation to the value of the gross national product in the initial unit period. Let us write,

$$a'_0(t) = \frac{\sum_j a'_{0j}X_j(t)}{\sum_j X_j(t)}, \quad (7.20)$$

i.e., the average employment coefficient of the national economy. Substituting this into (7.19), we obtain the rate of increase in total employment from one unit period to the next;

$$\frac{\sum_j a'_{0j}[X_j(t+1)-X_j(t)]}{\sum_i a'_{0j}X_j(t)} = \frac{\alpha(t)\gamma(t)}{a'_0(t)},$$

or, denoting the left-hand side by $\varrho(t)$,

$$\varrho(t) = \frac{\alpha(t)\gamma(t)}{a_0'(t)}. \tag{7.21}$$

Thus, we find that the rate of increase in total employment is the product of the rate of investment and the average employment–outlay ratio divided by the average employment coefficient of the national economy.

The total employment in unit period t is related to the total employment in the initial unit period $t_0(t_s > t_0)$ by the formula

$$\sum_j a_{0j}' X_j(t_s) = \prod_{t=t_0}^{t_s} \left[1 + \frac{\alpha(t)\gamma(t)}{a_0'(t)}\right] \sum_j a_{0j}' X_j(t_0). \tag{7.22}$$

Comparing (7.21) with (7.9), we can establish a relation between the rate of increase in employment and the rate of increase of the gross national product. Denote by $\nu(t)$ the ratio of these two rates, i.e.,

$$\nu(t) = \frac{\varrho(t)}{R(t)}; \tag{7.23}$$

we have

$$\nu(t) = \frac{1}{a_0'(t)} \times \frac{\gamma(t)}{\beta(t)}, \tag{7.24}$$

i.e., this ratio is proportional to the ratio of the average employment–outlay ratio and the average output–outlay ratio.

Total employment grows faster, equal or slower than the gross national product according as to whether

$$\frac{\gamma(t)}{a_0'(t)} \gtreqless \beta(t). \tag{7.25}$$

However, $\gamma(t)$ and $\beta(t)$ are averages depending on the structure of the total investment outlay. Remembering (7.8) and (7.18) we have

$$\nu(t) = \frac{1}{a_0'(t)} \frac{\sum_i \gamma_i \mu_i(t)}{\sum_i \beta_i \mu_i(t)}. \tag{7.26}$$

Since the coefficients γ_i and β_i are determined by technological conditions and $a_0'(t)$ is determined by the employment coefficients a_{0j}' and by the way the national product is composed of outputs of the various sectors, $v(t)$ can be influenced only by a proper choice of the structure of investment fractions $\mu_i(t)$.

In order to obtain the greatest rate of increase of national income (or of the gross national product), the structural fractions $\mu_i(t)$ have to be chosen so as to maximize the average overall output–outlay ratio $\beta(t)$. In order to achieve this, investment outlays must be composed of products of the sectors with the highest overall outlay ratios, β_i.

To obtain the greatest possible rate of increase in total employment, the structural fractions $\mu_i(t)$ have to be chosen so as to maximize the average employment outlay ratio $\gamma(t)$. This requires that the investment outlays be composed of products of sectors with the highest overall employment outlay ratio γ_i.

These considerations refer to the rate of increase of the gross national product or of total employment in a given unit period t. If the goal of the policy is to obtain the greatest possible increase of total employment after a longer period of time, an additional factor has to be brought into consideration. From (7.21) we see that the rate of increase in total employment is proportional to $\alpha(t)$, i.e., to the rate of investment in the unit period. The rate of investment, however, may depend on the national income, because an increase in national income makes it possible to have a greater rate of investment.

Consequently, it may be possible to obtain in the long run a greater increase in total employment by allocating investment outlays not in a way which produces immediately the greatest rate of growth in total employment, but in a way which produces the greatest increase in the rate of growth of national income. The slower rate of increase in employment in the earlier period is then over-compensated by a more rapid rate of increase of employment in the later period due to an increased rate of investment.

For instance, let

$$\alpha(t) = cI(t), \qquad (7.27)$$

where $I(t) = \sum x_j(t)$ is the national income in unit period t and c is a factor of proportionality ($0 < c < 1$). Then,

$$\varrho(t) = \frac{cI(t)\gamma(t)}{a_0'(t)} . \qquad (7.28)$$

Taking into account relation (7.14), we find that in any given unit period $t_k(t_k > t_0)$ the rate of increase of total employment is

$$\varrho(t_k) = c\,\frac{\gamma(t_k)}{a_0'(t_k)}\,I(t_0)\prod_{t=t_0}^{t_k}(1+r(t)), \tag{7.29}$$

where $I(t_0)$ is the national income in the initial unit period, t_0.

Thus, the rate of increase in total employment in any given unit period is proportional to the increase of national income which took place between the initial unit period and the unit period under consideration.

In equation (7.29) $\gamma(t_k)$ depends on the values of the investment structure fractions $\mu_i(t_k)(i = 1, ..., n)$ in unit period t_k, whereas $r(t)$ depends on the values of the allocation of investment structure fractions $\mu_i(t)$ in all the unit periods from t_0 to t_k. This can be seen immediately from the formulae (7.8), (7.15), and (7.18). A change in the values of the investment structure fractions in each period from t_0 to t_k thus produces a change in the rate of increase of total employment in unit period t_k equal to

$$d\varrho(t_k) = \frac{c}{a_0'(t_k)}\,I(t_0)\left[\prod_{t=t_0}^{t_k}(1+r(t)\,d\gamma(t_k)+\gamma(t_k)d\prod_{t=t_0}^{t_k}(1+r(t)\right]. \tag{7.30}$$

The change is positive, zero or negative, according to the sign of the expression in braces on the right-hand side, i.e., according as to whether

$$\frac{d\prod_{t=t_0}^{t_k}(1+r(t))}{\prod_{t=t_0}^{t_k}(1+r(t))} \gtrless \frac{d\gamma(t_k)}{\gamma(t_k)}. \tag{7.31}$$

The left-hand side of (7.31) can be written in the form

$$d\log\prod_{t=t_0}^{t_k}(1+r(t)) = \sum_{t=t_0}^{t_k}\frac{dr(t)}{1+r(t)}.$$

Hence, the expression (7.31) becomes

$$\sum_{t=t_0}^{t_k}\frac{dr(t)}{1+r(t)} \gtrless -\frac{d\gamma(t_k)}{\gamma(t_k)}. \tag{7.32}$$

Let us start with values of the investment structure fractions which in each unit period from t_0 to t_k maximize the average employment–outlay ratio $\gamma(t)$. Then change these fractions so as to maximize $r(t)$. In each unit period $dr(t) > 0$ and $d\gamma(t_k) < 0$ (except in the trivial case when $\gamma(t) = \beta(t)$ in each unit period, in which case $dr(t) = 0 = d\gamma(t)$). Thus the left-hand side of (7.32) increases monotonously with the value of t_k. By choosing t_k large enough it is possible to make the left-hand side in (7.32) greater than the right-hand side, i.e., to achieve a greater rate of increase in total employment than would be the case if the investment allocation fractions were chosen so as to maximize in each unit period the immediate effect on total employment.

Total employment in the unit period $t_s (t_s \geqslant t_k \geqslant t_0)$ is according to (7.22)

$$\sum_j a'_{0j} X_j(t_s) = \prod_{t_k=t_0}^{t_s} [1+\varrho(t_k)] \sum_j a'_{0j} X_j(t_0). \qquad (7.33)$$

Taking logarithms, we find

$$d \log \sum_j a'_{0j} X_j(t_s) = \sum_{t_k=t_0}^{t_s} \frac{d\varrho(t_k)}{1+\varrho(t_k)} + \text{constant}. \qquad (7.34)$$

As we have seen, a change in the investment structure fractions designed to maximize $r(t)$ in each unit period leads to $d\varrho(t_k) > 0$ from a certain unit period onwards. Beginning with that unit period, the right-hand side of (7.34) increases monotonously with the value of t_s. By choosing t_s large enough, it is possible to make (7.34) positive, i.e., to make total employment larger than would be the case if the rate of increase of national income were not maximized in each unit period.

Denote by t_c the critical value of t_s at which the expression starts becoming positive. Over planning periods which are shorter than $t_c - t_0$, the greatest possible total employment is obtained by composing investment outlays of products of the various sectors of the national economy so as to maximize in each unit period $\gamma(t)$ by using always products of the sectors with greatest employment–outlay ratios. Over planning periods exceeding $t_c - t_0$, the greatest possible total employment is obtained by maximizing, in each unit period, $r(t)$, i.e., by composing investment outlays always of products of the sectors with the greatest output–outlay ratios.

More complicated conditions for the structure of investment outlays are obtained when the principal goal of the policy, i.e., the greatest possible increase in national income or in total employment during a period of time, is subject to additional constraints such as, for instance, a certain predetermined rate of growth of consumption. Such problems can be solved on the basis of the relations established in this paper by means of the techniques of linear programming.

Part V

ECONOMIC SCIENCE IN THE SERVICE OF PRACTICE

CURRENT PROBLEMS OF ECONOMIC SCIENCE IN POLAND

The present Conference of Polish economists is taking place more than five years after the previous Conference in December 1950. The latter took place shortly after the adoption of the Six-Year Plan for the economic development and construction of the foundations of Socialism in Poland. The present conference is taking place on the eve of adopting a new Five-Year Plan which maps out new lines of economic and social development for our country.

The period between the two conferences was one of strenuous efforts to carry out the Six-Year Plan. It was a period of great transformations in the social and economic structure of our country. Great progress has been made in the industrialization of Poland and in transforming her from an economically backward and weak country into one playing an increasing part in international economic affairs. In this period, the foundations of the socialist society have taken shape and the Polish nation has been changing into a socialist nation. This was also a period of tremendous efforts on the part of the working class, the working peasantry, the intellectuals and of the entire nation, a period of great pressure arising from the Plan, of difficulties and contradictions which had to be overcome, and of serious disproportions which developed in the national economy. It was a period of great achievements and, at the same time, of new problems which to a large extent were the results of these achievements.

The previous Congress of Polish economists, as well as the First Congress of Polish Science for which the former was a preparation, were an expression of and also an incentive for a turn to Marxism in Polish science. It was no accident that this was associated with the introduction of the Six-Year Plan for laying the foundations of socialism in Poland. It constituted a necessary condition for Polish economic science to join in the work of building the foundations of Socialism.

Bourgeois economics along with other bourgeois social sciences did not contribute to the understanding of the fundamental laws governing

415

social development. With one-sided concentration on the process of exchange and of monetary and commodity circulation, it failed to see the connection of the phenomena it investigated with the system of production relations existing in a given social system. Moreover, bourgeois economics made use of diverse idealist and subjective concepts which were not an adequate reflection of objective reality as expressed in production relations. Bourgeois economics, therefore, failed to comprehend the laws of development of contemporary capitalism and in particular the essence of imperialism and the anti-imperialist forces surging up throughout the world. Similarly, it barred the way to a lucid definition of the tasks and means for the construction of socialism, which consists precisely in changing the existing production relations.

Bourgeois political economy proved to be practically useless for the transformation of the social and economic structure of the country and for the planning of the nation's economic development. For this reason, the building of the foundations of socialism in Poland which found expression in the Six-Year Plan, called for an economic science firmly based on Marxism–Leninism. The bankruptcy of bourgeois science in front of the practical tasks of socialist construction was becoming increasingly evident to the majority of social scientists in Poland.

The practice of the social revolution in Poland opened the way to Marxism in Polish economic science as in Polish science generally. Here of special significance have been the great ideological discussions which preceded the unification of the Polish working class movement and the founding of the Polish United Workers Party. In these discussions and at the First Congress of the Polish United Workers' Party, Poland's social and economic structure, the alignment of class forces, and the progress of the class struggle in the course of building the foundations of socialism were analysed, the class character of the people's democratic state and the role of the Soviet Union in the building of socialism in the people's democracies were elucidated. Upon this basis, a great programme was formulated for the socialist industrialization of the country, for the initial steps in the socialist transformation of agriculture and for laying of the foundations for a socialist culture.

This programme could only be carried out on the basis of a theoretical generalization of the practical experience of building a new social system. And such generalization could only be effected by the collective effort of the party which is the leader and organizer of the process of building socialism, the repository of the historical experience of the working class and all progressive forces of the nation. The analysis of the basic processes of socialist construction made by the party laid the foundations for detailed economic research work on the social changes and problems inherent in this construction.

To what extent did Polish economic science fulfil this task? First of all, it should be noted that the move towards Marxism in the years 1949–1951 brought about greatly increased activity in the field of economic science. This became apparent, primarily, in educational and organizational spheres. The reorganization of the Central School of Commerce in Warsaw into the Central School of Planning and Statistics, the establishment of the Institute for Training Scientific Cadres under the Central Committee of the Polish United Workers' Party (now the Institute of Social Sciences), the organization of the faculty of Political Economy at Warsaw University, the establishment of the Institute of Agricultural Economics, of the Institute of Industrial Economy and Organization, and later also of the Economic Section of the Polish Academy of Sciences, and finally the reorganization of the higher economic schools throughout the country—these were the main features of this activity. As a result, economic science in Poland now has at its disposal a substantial educational and scientific research apparatus. It embraces nine higher schools of economics and of advanced studies of economics in other educational institutions.

In total, over 23,000 students study economics, i.e., 13·3 per cent of the total number of students in Poland. Advanced schools of economics employ 64 professors, 151 assistant professors, 134 fellows and 210 assistants. There are now 94 graduate students in economic science. Furthermore, there are five economic research institutes at present. There is also the Committee for Economic Science of the Polish Academy of Sciences to promote and co-ordinate the development of economic studies. A number of scientific economic periodicals are published; the leading among them is *Ekonomista* (The Economist). Finally, the Polish Economic Society plays an important part in popularizing economic studies and in organizing and inspiring scientific discussions.

Never before have economic studies in Poland enjoyed such favourable material conditions for development. And never before has so much been expected from economic science as regards its practical participation in the development and guidance of the national economy. For socialism is a system of planned guidance of social and economic development, based on scientific knowledge of objective economic and social laws. And under socialism, as well as in the period of building the foundations of socialism, economic science is a necessary tool for directing the processes of social development.

That task—it must be said openly—economic science in Poland has not fulfilled. It had not fulfilled it in other socialist countries either, as evidenced by the criticism of the state of economic science at the 20th Congress of the Communist Party of the Soviet Union.

In the early stages of socialist construction, it is sufficient to know the general laws of social and economic development and the analysis of social and economic transformations based upon this knowledge. However, with the advance of socialist construction, new social and economic realities emerge. A basic transformation in all spheres of social and economic life takes place. These processes, as all other social processes, have their own objective laws.

Effective guidance of these processes requires a knowledge of the underlying laws. The knowledge of the general laws of social and economic development and the general analysis of the basic problems of socialist construction are no longer adequate. It is necessary to make a detailed, concrete, scientific analysis of social and economic processes developing in our system and to understand their objective laws. Without such analysis, there is no way of controlling and guiding these processes.

The process of socialist construction is subject to the general laws of dialectical and historical materialism. Contradictions and difficulties, therefore, are inseparable from this process. The Marxist method of overcoming them consists in finding out their social causes and inner laws of development, as well as in creating new conditions where these causes have no more scope for action and the laws of social processes are utilized for the benefit of socialist construction.

The contradictions and obstacles emerging on the road to socialism are of three kinds. First, obstacles resulting from the historical heritage of capitalism, and in Poland from the still persisting feudal remnants within the framework of capitalism. This heritage has been holding back for a long time the emerging socialist society. Frequently it is intensified by the processes of ideological and political infiltration from capitalist countries.

The second kind are contradictions of both an antagonistic and non-antagonistic nature, specific to the very process of building socialism. This is a process of intensive struggle of the new against the old, a process of basic transformation of all social relations. It takes place under conditions of class struggle with the capitalist classes or elements which strive to stop or to retard the process of socialist revolution. It is featured by numerous "difficulties of growth" which arise from the well-known phenomenon of "lagging behind", i.e., the protracted process of adaptation to new development needs. Institutions and organizational principles of the old society often cease to operate before socialist institutions and principles of organization which are to replace them have become stabilized and developed. Examples of this are found in some branches of small-scale production and services where the capitalist forms no longer operate and the socialist forms have not yet developed sufficiently. Then, the peculiar phenomenon of "social vacuum" occurs. This often has been holding back our economic development. It must be said that errors in our economic policy have amplified this phenomenon.

The third kind of contradictions and difficulties stems from the fact that the development of a socialist society is also subject to the laws of dialectics. We know that the contradictions between the development of productive forces and production relations do appear under socialism. Even more frequent are the contradictions between the needs of the economic base and the political and administrative superstructure, particularly the methods of administering the national economy. Socialism does not mean the absence of contradictions in social and economic development. Such a viewpoint would be the negation of the fundamental principles of dialectical and historical materialism. The difference between socialism and earlier social systems does not consist in the absence of contradictions in social development, but in their different nature and in the way of overcoming them. Since there are no class contradictions in a socialist society, the existing contradictions are non-antagonistic and they are eliminated gradually without upheavals and "explosions". But they are not overcome without struggle. On the contrary, they call for struggle against the inertia of old habits of thought and organizational practice. They even call for struggle against the vested interests of certain social groups which have found a comfortable place for themselves within obsolete forms of organization and administration. Under socialism, contradictions mounting in the course of development are not overcome spontaneously because there is the possibility to master them by means of a conscious policy of the leading bodies of socialist society. This requires, however, scientific analysis of the social causes of these contradictions and a skilful utilization of the objective laws governing the processes of socialist society. In our conditions, the three types of contradictions and difficulties are entangled. They must be perceived and scientifically analysed no matter whether they are inherited from the past, peculiar to the period of transition (the latter are the most numerous) or whether they arise from the inner dialectics of existing and developing socialist institutions.

For some time a tendency prevailed of acknowledging only the first type. This was justified in the initial stages of socialist construction, since the difficulties stemming from the heritage of the past (including the war and occupation) were predominant; the difficulties of the second and third kind had not yet become apparent at that time. But as socialist construction advanced, this tendency became in practice a dangerous oversimplification. It led to the shifting of responsibility for all our shortcomings on to the capitalist heritage. From this it was concluded that these shortcomings must automatically disappear with the progress of socialist construction. This failure to see the dialectical nature of the process of socialist construction led to renouncing any detailed Marxist analysis of the process of building socialism and of the development of a socialist society. In the absence of scientific marxist analysis, idealistic, subjective voluntarism made its way. Marxist policy based on a scientific analysis was replaced by subjective appeals, by moralizing and by administrative measures.

This process grew in intensity, particularly during the Six-Year Plan which was a vast programme of reshaping Poland's social and economic structure and of development of her productive forces. It was one of the greatest undertakings in the history of our nation. Full stress must be laid on the fact that the essential objectives of the Six-Year Plan were attained. We have built a powerful industry. Poland has ceased to be an economically backward and weak country. She is now a country with a fair level of industrial production, with rapidly growing productive forces and today she holds an important place in the world economy and politics. Socialist ownership of the means of production is the irrevocable basis of our national economy and of its dynamic development; the economic base of a socialist society is taking shape.

At the same time, however, serious disproportions have arisen which hinder further development of our economy. These are widely recognized today as the disproportions between the development of agriculture and industry, between capital investment and the supply of raw materials, between the quantitative development of industrial production and its quality and cost, between investment and production programmes and technically obsolete conditions of many industrial establishments. These disproportions show themselves in the serious difficulties of our foreign trade, in the lack of material reserves and in the shortcomings in the supply of goods to meet the requirements of the population. But the most serious aspect was that they were responsible for the failure to carry out the targets of the Six-Year Plan with regard to raising the living standards of the people, i.e., in the field which constitutes the social justification of socialist construction.

The aforementioned disproportions have not been the result of the heritage of the past. They appeared in the course of carrying out the Six-Year Plan as one of its effects. An important contributory element in creating these disproportions was the revision of the Six-Year Plan in 1951 as a result of growing international tension and the necessity of diverting part of the resources for the purposes of national defence.

No doubt, there were also serious mistakes in the very premises of the plan relating to the high pressure investment programme. But these mistakes were unavoidable. Lenin said that he who wants a "pure" revolution, that is, one without excesses and aberrations actually gives up the revolution. It may be equally rightly said that he who wants a plan of such vast social and economic transformations as envisaged by the Six-Year Plan, without mistakes in the planning, in fact renounces both the plan and the social transformations. Being Marxists, we renounce neither the revolution nor the great plans of social and economic transformation, and therefore assume the responsibility for mistakes and aberrations.

It is not a question of whether or not the Six-Year Plan contained faults in its premises. The essential issue is that the mistakes and disproportions which occurred in the course of fulfilling the plan had not been rectified in good time. These disproportions grew and accumulated until they reached such magnitude that they became an important obstacle to the further development of the national economy. This is related to the system of administering the national economy which developed during the realization of the Six-Year Plan.

The heavy investment programme called for tight centralization of economic leadership of the country in order to ensure that the modest means available are used in conformity with the plan. Centralized economic leadership was also required for the revolutionary reconstruction of the social system, for the struggle against capitalist elements and for the policy of restricting and gradually eliminating the capitalist sector. It was also required for the struggle to liberate the sector of small-scale commodity production from the exploitation and influence of the capitalist sector in order to link it up with the expanding socialist economy. Lastly, the high rate of industrialization had created a serious problem of cadres for the industry as well as for other branches of the rapidly expanding national economy. The cadres of managers of the socialist economy were formed from elements which formerly had no practical executive experience. These cadres were weak and inexperienced and this made it necessary to centralize all important decisions.

All these factors taken together produced an administrative apparatus for the national economy, based on methods characteristic of a "war economy". We have in fact waged a war against backwardness and the sad heritage of the past, a war against capitalist elements, a war for winning the small commodity producers, a war for higher productivity and greater efficiency in the national economy. With time, the methods of administering the national economy which developed in the course of this "war", and which constituted a revolutionary medium for the transformation of the social and economic structure had become an obstacle to further economic development.

They consisted in one-sided application of moral and political appeals and administrative measures which to an increasing degree replaced the utilization of economic incentives. Since these measures were not based on the skilful utilization of objective economic laws, they merely produced temporary effects (e.g., in the case of cost reduction or improved quality of production) and had to be repeated periodically. This resulted in economic processes functioning on the basis of consecutive moral, political and administrative "upsurges" while uncontrolled spontaneous processes developed in our economic life.

The consequence was an enormous expansion of the bureaucratic apparatus which, once it gathered its own momentum, enmeshed the national economy in a web of regulations and instructions hampering its development. Moreover, this apparatus excelled in producing optimistic reports from "the battlefield" obscuring the real state of affairs in the national economy and hindering speedy rectification of mistakes and adaptation to new situations. Excessive centralization and bureaucratization deprived the national economy of flexibility and this became a source of waste and a brake on technical progress.

Under these conditions, economic science had only restricted opportunities for studying the concrete processes taking place in our national economy. There was no social demand on the part of the economic administration for a Marxist analysis of our economic processes. Marxism was replaced by a subjective voluntaristic and administrative-legalistic conception of the course of social processes. A turning point in this respect might have been, and should have been, Stalin's essay *The Economic Problems of Socialism in the U.S.S.R.* But in practice it all ended in general declarations on the existence of objective economic laws and on the need to study and use them. The unaltered system of administration of the national economy could not create the right conditions for applying these principles in practice.

In addition, the students of economic problems encountered difficulties in getting access to the material on their subjects. The extensive use of the principle of state secrecy, which was justified in the period of tense international relations and especially at the time when the national economy was being re-geared in 1951 to meet the needs of national defence, had been distorted by shutting off from the public all information concerning the problems of the national economy. In practice, it turned into a camouflage under which bureaucracy and bad management could operate freely. To what absurd proportions the application of this principle had been carried is demonstrated by the many instances of statistical data being labelled "confidential" while at the same time they were being printed in foreign publications from materials officially supplied by our government (e.g. to the United Nations or to foreign trade agencies). For economic science this was a deadly situation. The economist found himself in the position of a chemist cut off from his laboratory, a physician without access to his hospital or an astronomer forbidden to observe the skies.

The sterility of economic study of the laws of concrete socialist construction processes, however, was not exclusively due to the above

external causes. A fair share of the responsibility rests upon economic
science itself which was loaded down by a ballast of dogmatism and
schematism. Live scientific thought was frequently replaced by dogmatic
and schematic reiteration of tarnished, officially approved formulae.
This phenomenon was closely related to the aberrations in the political
and ideological life of the socialist countries and which were known
as the "personality cult".

These aberrations were not the product of "ill will" or any other
subjective causes. They had an objective substratum in the complex
social processes occurring in the course of socialist construction in countries which were industrially backward amidst a hostile capitalist environment. This process took place, though with various degrees of
intensity, in all the countries building socialism. The rapid process of
socialist industrialization brought about a mass influx of peasant and
some petty bourgeois elements into the working class. In addition, the
old cadres of the working class were weakened by the war; part of
them became uprooted during the war and the dislocation of the national
economy under the Nazi occupation. When the workers and peasants'
rule was set up in this country the most experienced working class cadres
entered the state apparatus. Thus, the old revolutionary working class
cadre as well as the old revolutionary intelligentsia were replaced by
new peasant and petty bourgeois elements. This had weakened the
political consciousness and activity of the working class at a time when
the requirements of socialist construction demanded the reverse. The
widening of inner-party democracy, the widening of democracy in trade
unions and in other social organizations of the working people was the
result. And in this way the effectiveness of social control over the state
apparatus was reduced. The tendency of this apparatus towards bureaucratization following the centralization of the economic administration
of the country and of social life, indispensable in the early period of
socialist construction, did not encounter the resistance of a democratic
social control which effectively checks these tendencies.

At the same time, the existence of a hostile capitalist environment
and the sacrifices called for by socialist industrialization, created the
necessity for social discipline which could have only been realized by
centralized leadership. In these conditions, some sections of the state
apparatus, both political and economic, had rendered themselves independent of Party control and of the elected representatives of the

working people. It was against this background that all the phenomena grew which we denote as the "personality cult".

Dogmatism and schematism were the ideological reflection of this social process and the result of the reluctance to come face to face with reality and to stand up to criticism following this confrontation. The reluctance to make a Marxist analysis of the concrete processes of socialist construction, the cultivation of a subjective–voluntarist and legal–administrative conception of these processes—to put it in a nutshell: an idealist conception—were also ideological reflections of the same trend. Apologetics was frequently substituted for Marxist analysis. It was not apologetics of socialism, for socialism being a progressive social system corresponding to the requirements of contemporary development of productive forces does not need any apologetics. Apologetics is alien to the needs of socialism and to the very nature of Marxism. Apologetics, instead of scientific analysis, is demanded only by social institutions and the vested interests attached to them which have outlived their social usefulness and retard social progress. Instead, apologetics was flourishing as evidenced by phenomena such as the "personality cult" which is contrary to the idea of socialism and re presents a force retarding further social development.

The dialectics of socialist construction and development of socialist society, however, have the quality of making such aberrations only transitory. The successes of socialist construction create conditions which make it possible and imperative to correct the incidental aberrations. Following socialist industrialization, not only has the strength of the working class grown numerically but its consciousness and social and political activity have grown as well. The alliance between the working class and the peasantry and the socialist transformation of agriculture raises the consciousness and activity of working peasants. A new intelligentsia is emerging which has its roots in the working people. In becomes an important factor in crystallizing social consciousness of the emerging socialist society. It breaks the system of the so-called "personality cult", and we see now a renaissance of Marxist and Leninist principles.

In Poland, the third Plenary Session of the Central Committee of the Polish United Workers' Party paved the way for such a renaissance. But it first found full expression at the 20th Congress of the Communist Party of the Soviet Union. The results of the 20th Congress facilitate the process in the people's democracies and enable its acceleration. The inexhaustible impact of the ideas of the October Revolution, the dynamic strength of Soviet socialist society are an incentive for Marxists in all countries building socialism. The return to Leninist principles opens new vistas for the advance of economic studies. It also creates new possibilities and imposes new duties upon them in Poland. First and foremost our science must take up concrete current problems of socialist construction in this country. And there are many such problems on record. Foremost is the present system of economic administration of the country and the problems of initiating and introducing proper economic incentives. This is connected with the problem of socialist economic accounting in all its aspects, i.e. proper determination of prices both for consumer goods and means of production in conformity with the law of value, effectiveness of investments and correct economy of investment goods, the system of wages and salaries, a closer than hitherto interconnection between the material welfare of the personnel of socialist establishments and the financial effects of its activity, the link between the socialist economy and the small-scale commodity sector of our national economy, stronger economic incentives for the promotion of socialist reform in agriculture. All these problems are by no means exhaustive and they can be brought down to the common basic question of how the law of value operates in our economic system. This question has been frequently discussed in Poland and, on the whole, correctly assessed, but so far in broad terms only. The pertinent issue now is to render our theoretical Marxist knowledge concrete, to apply it to all spheres of our economic life and draw appropriate practical conclusions.

Other problems which require serious scientific elaboration concern economic planning. In this connection the problem of proportions in the development of the national economy, the discovery of scientific criteria for the proper establishment of these proportions are of great importance. Another problem here is the methodology of planning and how the system of management is related to the methods of planning, how to simplify and decentralize planning and how to combine effective planning with the full utilization of automatic incentives inherent in the national economy, without infringing upon the directional nature of planning.

It should be noted that scientific discussion on all these questions has gathered momentum in the last years. Several works have been published and constituted an important contribution to this discussion. The discussion must be deepened and extended, and converted into a programme of creative scientific work. Such a programme will be of fundamental significance for the solution of the major problems facing our national economy today.

In the studies and discussions of concrete problems of socialist construction in our country, it is necessary for us to be in close touch with economic research conducted in the Soviet Union and other socialist countries. We must be accurately informed on major problems of economic life in other socialist countries and on research work and scientific discussions associated with these problems. We must learn by their experience, both good and bad, offering in exchange the knowledge of our own experience and the results of our discussions and scientific studies. It must be stated that our contacts with economists of other socialist countries, including the Soviet Union, are still weak. They are mostly confined to reading their literature. We publish a great deal of economic literature, especially Soviet, but personal contacts for the purpose of joint research work are few and there are almost no joint scientific discussions. Our contacts, therefore, need livening up. In particular, this applies to scientific discussions with economists from the Soviet Union and the people's democratic countries. I believe that we, too, could make a contribution to such discussions. The problems of socialist construction in Poland cannot be treated in isolation from the problems of development of the Soviet economy or the building of socialism in other people's democracies.

The capitalist system still prevails over large areas of the world. We have now entered the period of peaceful rivalry between socialism and capitalism. In the light of this, we must closely observe and learn to know the processes developing within the capitalist economy. General ready-made formulae on the progressive disintegration of capitalism will not suffice here. We must concretely study the processes of contemporary capitalism with due regard to new phenomena because, obviously, the capitalist system is not stationary; it is subject to continuous and various transformations.

Specifically, attention should be focussed on the new forms of imperialist expansion evolved after the Second World War, chiefly in the United States, where so-called economic aid has played a dominant

part. The role of the state in the countries of highly developed monopoly capitalism calls for a thorough examination, especially with regard
to the social and economic role of nationalization of some branches
of industry. The differences in the development and structure between
different capitalist countries should also be investigated.

A special analysis is required of the economic problems of the underdeveloped countries. Owing to the fact that in many of these countries,
the local bourgeoisie is unable to raise sufficient capital resources,
industrialization is attempted by state-capitalist means, i.e., the industry
is being developed by the state ruled by the national bourgeoisie. This
is a state capitalism varying from its counterpart in the highly developed
capitalist countries. The latter serves to consolidate the rule of the
big monopolies, while the former serves to liberate the underdeveloped
countries from their dependence on foreign monopoly capital, which may
also lead to the liberation from own monopoly capital linked with
foreign big business. State-capitalist industrialization in underdeveloped
countries, e.g. India, often works under the slogan of building a socialist
pattern of society. It is supported by the working class and all the working
people, it seeks the aid of the socialist countries. The study of this process, its social contents and prospects of development opens an important
and interesting field for investigation.

Finally, we have the problems associated with the coexistence of
the socialist system and the capitalist system at different levels of its
development within the present day world economy. In this field, Marxist
thought has already something on its record in the form of the theory
of two world markets. This theory, however, needs to be further developed and made concrete. First of all, a study should be made of how
the existence of the socialist world market may influence the course of
economic processes in the capitalist world. For example, trade relations
with the socialist countries, where economic crises are non-existent,
may influence the course of the trade cycle, at least in some capitalist
countries; the aid granted by the Soviet Union and other socialist
countries to the underdeveloped countries for their industrialization,
forces imperialism to revise its methods and policy in the underdeveloped countries. This is already becoming evident in India. Thus, a whole
range of new problems has emerged which requires elucidation by
Marxist economic analysis.

The study of the contemporary capitalist economy and of the prob-

lems arising from the coexistence of the two systems in the world economy calls for co-operation with Marxist economists and other progressive economists from capitalist countries, including those of Asia
and Africa. They may prove helpful to us in grasping these problems.
In this connection, it is necessary to observe the development of bourgeois economic thought. Bourgeois economics performs two functions.
One is the apology of capitalism. With the end of the progressive role
of the Western European bourgeoisie, classical political economy
gave way to "vulgar economics" which is pure apology of the bourgeois
society, devoid of any true scientific understanding. The development
of monopoly capitalism and imperialism has extended the apologetic
tasks of bourgeois political economy.

But, on the other hand, the resistance of the petty bourgeoisie and
frequently also of the middle bourgeoisie, as well as the present-day
resistance of the progressive national bourgeoisie in Asia, Africa and
Latin America against their own and foreign big monopolies has also
caused resistance among some sections of bourgeois economists against
the apologetics of big monopolies and imperialists. New trends have
appeared in bourgeois economics which with considerable objectivity
investigate the economic processes of monopoly capitalism.

We must take due note of this inner differentiation of bourgeois
economics and learn to use judiciously the contributions of bourgeois
economists as a source for better understanding the internal problems
of the contemporary capitalist economy. But bourgeois economic
science performs yet another function. This bourgeoisie, including big
monopolies, lay out big funds on higher schools of economics and research institutes not merely to secure assistance in the apologetics of
the capitalist system. They expect something more from their economists,
namely, their help in solving diverse problems related to the administration of the capitalist economy.

In the period of free competitive capitalism the tasks of economists
were confined to such problems as the administration of the monetary
system, credit policy, tariff policy, transport, etc. But under conditions
of monopoly capitalism and particularly under conditions of growing
state–capitalist interference in the economic life, these tasks have also
grown. Here such questions are arising as the analysis of markets to
aid monopolies in determining their price policy, the methods of administration of large complexes of establishments under joint management,

planned co-ordination of operations and of development of such establishments and their suitable location, inter-plant accounting, depreciations and investment policies. In addition, there are the problems of operating a contemporary capitalist state, including the principles of operating nationalized undertakings, of their investment and location policy (e.g. in respect of power plants), the methods of economic policy and of influencing the course of the national economy as a whole.

Considerable technical–economic insight has been acquired here. In some fields as, for example, market research, co-ordination of activity of integrated establishments, inter-departmental or inter-plant economic accounting, principles of depreciation and so on, this knowledge may be partly utilized by us in the process of building socialism, just as, undoubtedly, in the future, the working class of the present capitalist countries will utilize this experience. It is a known fact that bourgeois economists display keen practical interest in our record in kindred fields, if only to mention the visit of French economists to Poland. Lack of interest on our part in the achievements concerning the technique of organization and of management of the economic life in the capitalist countries would be equally wrong as a lack of interest in their development of production techniques. The 20th Congress of the Communist Party of the Soviet Union, the rebirth of Leninist principles, place a new duty on economic science in the socialist countries, the duty of genuine concrete, and not merely verbal and general correlation of the theory with practice. Economic science must take its due place in the process of socialist construction. It must acquire honest and concrete knowledge of the laws governing the operation of a socialist economy and its construction, and of the processes occurring in the contemporary capitalist world, both in the metropolis of capitalism and in the countries fighting for liberation from imperialist domination. Only with such knowledge can economic science serve the construction of socialism and the entire international working class movement. These tasks face also Polish economic science. Their fulfilment demands bold and inquisitive scientific thinking, bold and pertinent discussions in which more than one mistaken view will be voiced. By collective effort in honest service of socialism, scientific truth will be produced, which is indispensable for effective victorious action.

Perhaps there are some who are afraid of such bold discussions, who long for the easy but sterile period of dogmatism and schematism.

They are the people for whom the great idea of the October Revolution had become vague and distant, who fail to see the powerful creative force of socialism. But socialism, as demonstrated by the experience of recent years, cannot be enclosed in dogmas and dead patterns, as those people would like to have it.

There are probably some, both here and abroad, who pin vain hopes on our discussions expecting that it will reverse the course of history, who think that the outcome of this discussion may be the return to the vanquished ideas of bourgeois economics and the renunciation of Marxist knowledge acquired by our science in recent years. These hopes are equally vain as the hopes of those who believe that bold criticism of the methods of managing our national economy may lead to a retreat from the road of socialist construction.

We are in the process of a great social revolution which is transforming to the very depth the social and economic structure of our country. It is also transforming to the very depth the psychology and the mode of thinking of our nation. It is further transforming science by harnessing it in the service of building a new social order. Only science based on the principles of Marxism–Leninism is capable of such a service, because it alone can offer a full understanding of life. The revolution may commit mistakes and yield to aberrations. It corrects such mistakes and aberrations in its own course. Correcting them, however, the revolution does not recede, it reaches out into the future, strengthens its forces to make a new step forward in the construction of socialism. This will be the meaning of the lively discussions and the sharp clash of views in economic science. They will be the point of departure for a new advance of our Marxist–Leninist knowledge by which we want to serve socialist construction in Poland.

CLOSING SPEECH AT THE SECOND CONGRESS
OF POLISH ECONOMISTS, WARSAW, 9th JUNE 1956

This Congress was convened by a resolution of the Committee of the Polish Economics Society. As originally conceived, the Congress was to be a forum for theories to be discussed and developed, and this idea was partly the reason for the absence of a clear programme or purpose. However, the fact that the Congress is being held at a very crucial period for our country and, indeed, for every socialist country, means that it has become the expression of a deep social process which is taking place, namely, the maturing of socialism.

The Congress has reviewed the state of economic science in Poland and has considered several basic problems of our national economy. A considerable part of our discussion has been taken up with the question of the state of economic thought in Poland. The review made by the Congress may have been given various shades of meaning in the contributions of individual speakers, but it has been basically unanimous. I believe, I can say that this Congress has unanimously concluded that economic science in Poland has lately not carried out—and, indeed, has been unable to carry out—its tasks. The great hopes which we have attached to the Marxist turning point in thought, which is taking place in Poland, have not been fulfilled. Our study and teaching have stuck in the morass of dogmatism and schematism which has been closely bound up with the whole socio-political atmosphere known as the "personality cult". In addition, as a result of the progressively increasing bureaucracy in our economy, economic science has not been given a social role in the form of a creative contribution and constructive participation which, according to the basic principles of Marxism, is its task in the process of building socialism.

More than once the discussion has dwelt on the way in which the inaccessibility of statistical and other information on the state of the national economy and its basic problems has prevented independent or constructive work of any kind. The failure to invite economists to participate in basic decision making, affecting the development of the national economy, together with the lack of access to information and material, enabling the basic problems of our economic life to be investigated, has prevented science from fulfilling its role.

Not only has research suffered from this, but so has teaching. In the recent past we have witnessed an enormous growth of the teaching apparatus in the field of economic studies. However, this apparatus has not been able to fulfil its role of making available a new cadre of economists for the national economy because of the absence of the basic factual material or information needed to develop the analytical powers of economics students. In these conditions, the content of what could be taught was strictly limited by the narrow framework of dogmatism and schematism. It was impossible for constructive scientific thought to develop, or to give any effective preparation in forming the new cadre of economists for the national economy. Today we and the whole national economy are paying a high price for these past errors.

As a result of this situation there followed another distortion, which has struck a deep chord at this Congress. I am referring to the neglect of centres of scientific thought and life outside Warsaw. This neglect was the result of the conditions prevailing then, in which even the leading economists in Warsaw had enormous difficulties in obtaining information about the basic problems of our national economy. These difficulties were occasionally overcome when, for instance, someone had an acquaintance in some institution or other establishment, perhaps a young clerk, who had access to information which was denied to our distinguished representatives of Marxist thought. In these conditions, the neglect of provincial centres was a natural consequence.

In conditions which prevented the development of independent economic thought, our teaching and research work were, from the very nature of things, bound to undergo a certain degeneration. It has been held here—and deservedly so—that economic thought in Poland degenerated to the role of apologetics. This is a very serious accusation for a discipline striving to be a Marxist science; but it is a fair one.

It is certainly very serious, for where, and in what conditions, does science degenerate to the role of apologetics? As Marxists we are familiar with these conditions. We know that this occurs when a contradiction arises between the needs of further social development and certain elements in the infrastructure which frustrate this development, and which fear criticism, the disclosure of truth and the understanding of the laws governing social development. Bourgeois political economy underwent such degeneration when the bourgeoisie had played out its progressive historical role, when from the progressive class there grew out a class which prevented further social development.

And so our science has gradually sunk—and let us say it openly— to the level of apologetics. But apologetics for what? For socialism? No. Socialism needs no apologia. Socialism, a system expressing the needs of contemporary social development, is based on a bold and scientific analysis of reality. Indeed, since Marxism is free from any *a priori* considerations, any need to sacrifice scientific laws in order to defend the long-established interests of the ruling class, it has been able to produce a critique exposing the real state of affairs, to formulate real laws of social development which point to the necessity of socialism— and here lies the great role of Marxism in the history of mankind.

Therefore socialism needs no apologia and our study and teaching were not an apologia for socialism. Since it is true to say that at a certain period our scientific thought fell to the level of apologetics, these apologetics were not for socialism, but for certain deviations. These deviations arose during the construction of socialism, and whilst historically understandable, there could be no justification for them in a political evaluation since they hindered the process of development of socialist construction. Certainly, our study and teaching ceased at a certain moment to be science, and became apologetics—apologetics for those deviations which were contradictory to the essence of socialism. Then, there followed the striking phenomenon that we, Marxists, who had managed to analyse the development of capitalist society so critically and with such acuity, did not apply this same keenness of Marxist analysis to the processes taking place in our own society. This apologia was an abdication from Marxism.

I do not need to convince those gathered in this hall of the harmfulness of this degeneration of thought which occurred. We deprived ourselves of the most efficient single instrument for understanding our own reality, the sole instrument for correcting those deviations which have occurred in the process of the construction of socialism. Moreover, there arose those enormous misunderstandings which have so greatly harmed socialism both in our country and in those where the struggle for socialism is only just beginning—that is, misunderstandings resulting from the fact that these deviations have often been put forward as the essence of socialism. This has occurred in economic and social science generally in that the deviations from Marxism, the atrophy of Marxist thought, which have taken place, have been presented as Marxism itself.

This atrophy, this ossification of Marxist thought, has shown itself also in the fact that we ceased to draw from the achievements of our own Marxist tradition. And we must remember that in Poland this tradition had been very much alive, that Polish Marxists—I mention among them great names such as Rosa Luxemburg, Marchlewski and others—have made a great contribution to the ideological wealth of the international workers' movement. In this period we also erased all mention and recollection of the great tradition of our workers' movement, of which the Polish Communist Party was the guide. In this atrophy of Marxist thought and failure to make use of our own great resources, we also neglected to make full use of the wealth provided by such an eminent representative of Polish liberal thought as Ludwik Krzywicki. Today we have rectified this mistake, here at the Congress, with the resolution we have adopted.

However, as I tried to show in my introductory speech, the dialectic of the process of constructing socialism is such that it establishes the conditions for overcoming the deviations which have arisen. We have entered a period in which we can overcome and get rid of these deviations, a period of great revival for socialist Marxist–Leninist principles. This should also be a period of great revival and rapid growth in Marxist economic thought. The road to this revival leads through an analysis of the errors committed, as well as through free and frank discussion. There can be no scientific progress without discussion and this must be free, forthright and to the point. In talking of such discussion, I should like to emphasize one point. In every scientific discussion—and, indeed, not only scientific—erroneous views are, and must be, expressed. We must not fear erroneous statements; we must recognize the right (if I may use the word) to err. This is the condition of every free and forthright discussion. Only by discussion, in the course of which mistakes are bound to be made, can we arrive at scientific truth.

Various views have been expressed here. With some I agree, with others not. At this moment, however, it is not important which speakers were right, and which were not. The important fact is that at this Congress, for the first time for a long time, there has been truly free, open and courageous discussion.

In the same discussion we have also debated how far freedom of scientific discussion is to go. It seems to me that certain misunderstandings have crept in here. Two things must be distinguished: first, scientific discussion which, if it is to be real, must be free and without any constraints, and secondly, something different, namely, the abuse of the name of science for ends which have nothing in common with science. It is clear that in the conditions of constructing socialism and of proletarian dictatorship, it is impossible to allow the abuse of science for the furtherance of a policy which is hostile to the construction of socialism. But this has nothing to do with the question of the freedom of really scientific discussion. Such freedom must be ensured, and I am convinced that in the process of this great revival of Marxist and of Leninist principles, it will be ensured.

Our Congress has dealt not only with the state of study and teaching; it has also expressed its views on certain fundamental problems of our economic life. This is natural. We all, as citizens, constantly do so. Writers, architects and others have expressed their views on the problems of our economic life at their own congresses. All the more is it expected of us as economists—and rightly so—that we should debate these problems. I think that, within the bounds of its modest possibilities, our Congress has fulfilled this task. There has been interesting discussion on a whole series of problems concerning the method of managing our national economy. It is clear that this discussion has not produced, and from its nature could not produce, a programme already worked out for the "repair of the republic" (to use an old Polish expression). This was not the object of our Congress. Our discussion has, however, emphasized those problems of our national economy which need to be worked out. The resolution passed by the Congress covers several suggestions which will be helpful in considering these problems. We have resolved that a Social Commission of Inquiry, composed of workers from both theoretical and practical fields, should be set up; and we have also resolved that an Economic Council, composed of the most eminent representatives of both these fields should be formed under the Chairman of the Council of Ministers. This resolution expresses the concern of our Congress for the development of the national economy. It also expresses our readiness to combine theory with practice in accordance with the old Marxist slogan, which in recent years has unfortunately been a slogan only on paper, but which we now want to put into effect

It is clear that on themes connected with the management of our national economy there are differing views among us, and different attitudes have been adopted during the discussion. All these problems need further investigation and research. Nevertheless, it seems that on certain matters some agreement of views can be shown. There are three such matters. First, the shortcomings which have arisen in our national economy cannot be removed simply by patching them up. As our resolution says, a radical programme is needed to overcome the weaknesses and shortcomings of our economy. To the task of preparing such a programme we, as economists, wish to make our contribution. We regard this as our duty in view of the great task of constructing socialism. Secondly, there is general agreement (I do not wish to go into details at the moment) that to overcome the weaknesses in our national economy requires a certain amount of decentralization in planning and in the methods of managing the national economy. As far as the range of this decentralization is concerned, there will be conflicting views amongst us for a long time yet, and an analysis of views and an examination of facts will have to be carried out for quite some time. Thirdly, we are wholly unanimous in our view (which, indeed, is a result of the preceding point) that our national economy requires full and efficient economic accounting. Bearing in mind that this Congress is attended by people from different economic and professional environments, people with different views, partly even with considerable differences in their assessment of certain situations and political problems — the unanimity reached on these matters is a considerable achievement. This shows the importance of economists as such. In this connection, we have also passed a resolution covering a whole series of claims on the raising of the status of the professional economist in social and economic life.

I think that the value of our Congress can be summed up in one sentence: it has given rise to wide theoretical discussion, it has expressed a fundamentally unanimous view on certain basic problems of our national economy, and it has emphasized the importance of the economist in our economic and social life. In this way, the Congress has fulfilled its responsibility towards the country, the people's State, and towards the great work of constructing socialism, which is the concern of all humanity; it has also opened the way to a new development and flowering of creative Marxist thought in Poland.

HOW I SEE THE POLISH ECONOMIC MODEL

The Polish economic model, the model of a socialist economy, adapted to the historical and geographical conditions of Poland and meeting the needs of the Polish nation, cannot be formulated from above, worked out at a conference table. It stems from the great movement towards socialist democracy which has permeated the country, from the setting up of workers' self-government, from the renewal of the self-governing co-operative movement, from the search for new forms of self-government and of social initiative among farmers. It stems from the ideological quests—passionate and creative—of the young intelligentsia, from the real need to introduce effective economic incentives, to replace management of the national economy by administrative directives.

The experience of this great movement must, however, be analysed scientifically in order to draw practical conclusions from it, and to enable the Party to make use of it and to direct the construction of a Polish model of the socialist economy. The scientific analysis of this experience will be one of the principal tasks of the Economic Council, which will shortly be established under the Council of Ministers. It is as yet difficult to anticipate the results of a detailed analysis of the problems of constructing a new model of the socialist economy, corresponding to Polish conditions and needs, from available theoretical and practical knowledge. The outline of such a model is, however, now crystallizing and further conclusions can be drawn from it.

Central Planning and the Decentralization of Management

The Polish model of the socialist economy will undoubtedly be marked by the link between the central planning of the development of the national economy and the decentralization of management based on self-government of workers and partly also of co-operatives and regions. A further characteristic of this model will be the use of economic

438

incentives as the basic instrument for implementing the national economic plans.

Central planning should cover the general lines of development of the national economy, as well as those areas which are of fundamental importance to the national economy as a whole or whose management must, for technical reasons, be centralized. The subject of central planning should, thus, be: the allocation of national income to investment and consumption and, connected with this, the rate of growth of the national economy, the wages fund and other incomes of the population, the value of goods produced to meet consumer needs, the quantity of currency in circulation. Planning the level of these is necessary to ensure equilibrium in the development of the national economy.

In addition, however, central planning must ensure that the national economy develops on lines consistent with the needs and wishes of the nation which are expressed by the highest organ of State authority, the House of Representatives (the Seym). Therefore, investment should be subject to central planning. Primary investment must be planned directly by the centre; subsidiary investment, of less significance to the whole economy, could be planned by departments, national councils and enterprises, within the framework of general allocations and directives laid down by the central plan. Finally, the national economic plan should cover the production of commodities which are basic to the national economy, such as coal, steel and other important raw materials, fertilizers, machines, transport, equipment and goods for mass consumption. The production of other goods should be determined by autonomous regional plans or directly by individual enterprises.

The national economic plan must also cover the basic means (especially in the form of appropriate investment), needed to ensure technical progress. In branches of production where centralized management is required for technological reasons, as in the steel industry, the national economic plan must itself make specific innovations in production techniques.

The Basis of Management: the Autonomous Enterprise

The basis of the management of the national economy should be the autonomous socialist enterprise. Such enterprises should function as teams of people implementing common social tasks, personally interested in the favourable outcome of these tasks, and linked together by a feeling of friendly co-operation. In a State-owned economy, socialist enterprises are trustees of property belonging to the nation as a whole, which they manage autonomously within the framework of the national economic plan and the general directives of State economic policy. In a co-operative economy the socialist enterprises are themselves property-owners. It is clear, however, that they too should, to a certain extent, be considered as trustees of the nation's business and act within the framework of the national economic plan and the general economic policy of the State.

Since small-scale private production—and even, up to a certain size, small-scale capitalist production in agriculture, in handicrafts and in small-scale local industry—will continue to exist in Poland for a long time yet, national economic plans will have to be able to influence such production, by appropriate manipulation of economic incentives inducing small-scale producers to conform to State economic plans.

It is the task of socialist enterprises, both State-owned and co-operative, to implement the national economic plan, to carry out the production of goods not covered by the plan, to reduce costs, to introduce technological advances, and to attain a suitable profit level. The implementation of these tasks should be based above all on workers' material interest in the profits of the enterprise. Profit should become the basic criterion determining whether the enterprise fulfils its socio-economic tasks.

At present there is often conflict between the profitability of producing a particular assortment of goods and the social demand for such an assortment. Enterprises frequently show a tendency to produce an assortment which is more profitable, but socially less necessary. Such a conflict is the result of a bad price structure, incompatible with the law of value. With a proper price structure an assortment which is socially more necessary should also be more profitable. The socialist enterprise, guided by the profitability of production, would then automatically fulfil its socio-economic tasks.

The relations between socialist enterprises should generally be based on a system of direct contracts which would replace the present system of allocation from above. Allocation from above should be limited to exceptional cases in which the shortage of certain commodities, particularly raw materials, cannot be eliminated by a price increase, since the implementation of the national economic plan requires more selective means than a price policy.

The Principle of Pricing

The basic means of linking socialist enterprises to each other, as well as of linking them to consumers and private producers (peasants and craftsmen), should be prices. In other words, these links should be based on the operation of the law of value. In such conditions pricing will become the essential instrument for guiding the national economy.

Pricing must remain in the hands of the State, i.e. of the central or regional authorities, depending on the nature and general economic importance of a given product. In the case of products of fundamental importance to the whole national economy, whose production is directly controlled by the national economic plan, prices must be set by the central authorities. This is essential for the creation of economic incentives to ensure the implementation of plans. The prices of products decided by regional economic plans, or of products not covered by a plan, can be set by the regional authorities. Only in exceptional cases, in small-scale industry, either social or private, in which there is a large number of enterprises effectively competing with each other, can prices be freely determined by the market mechanism. Here too, however, a certain measure of control by the State authorities is necessary. In the case of agricultural products, prices would be determined partly by the State through purchases by State and co-operative trade organizations, and partly by the open market in direct transaction between peasants and consumers.

The principle of pricing by the State is necessary also to prevent the rise of monopoly syndicates among socialist enterprises. If socialist enterprises could themselves fix prices for their products, they could raise their profits, not by increasing output, reducing costs by technological progress, but, by raising prices, leaving production, costs and techniques unchanged. Socialist enterprises or their associations would then be transformed into monopolistic owners of the means of production and would cease to be trustees of property belonging to and managed in the interest of society in general.

Everyday Experience Will Decide

This is how I think the general outline of a Polish model of the socialist economy will look. It must be emphasized, however, that this picture is only provisional and may be considerably modified as a result of further studies and investigations. For the new model of the Polish socialist economy must grow from experience, and especially from experience gained from the great movement of workers' self-government. It cannot be worked out theoretically. The steel industry must be managed differently from the industry producing leather goods or buttons; managerial methods in industry requiring large central investments must be different from those in local industry. Similarly, the degree of independence must also vary from enterprise to enterprise and even the nature of workers' self-government.

Great help in exchanging experience in the course of constructing the new economic model can be given by conferences of delegates from workers' councils and from the management of factories in particular sectors of the national economy, conferences of representatives from co-operatives, and so on. Such conferences would provide valuable material for the management of the national economy in their policy making. At the appropriate moment, it would be necessary to call a general Polish congress of workers' councils which would define the principles governing the activity of these councils and their role in the management of the national economy. Such a congress would also be of great political significance in formulating and co-ordinating, the activities of the working class, thus furthering the process of industrial democracy.

The new model of the socialist economy will also require certain changes in the political structure of the State. A logical consequence of basing the management of the national economy on the self-government of factory workers, and on co-operatives, and other forms of peasant self-government, which are only just developing, will be to set up a second chamber in the House of Representatives (Seym), representing the self-government of individual industries of the socialist economy. Such a chamber would be an essential organ of socialist democracy constituting, as Marx puts it, "an alliance of free people working with the help of communal means of production".

THE ROLE OF THE CO-OPERATIVE MOVEMENT IN THE CONSTRUCTION OF SOCIALISM

My paper is the last in today's series, and my aim is, therefore, to sum up the role of the co-operative movement in the construction of the socialist system. We all know from experience that in the socialist countries there are two forms of socialist ownership and of socialist management. In addition to ownership by society as a whole, which at the present level of development takes the form of State ownership, there is also the co-operative form of socialist ownership and the form of management corresponding to it. Furthermore, we know from the historical experience of socialist countries that co-operative ownership in these countries is spreading widely to a range of activities assuming dimensions unknown to the co-operative movement under capitalism.

This brings us to the question of the reasons for the existence and growth of co-operative ownership and management in the process of the construction of socialism and of the socialist development of society. The reasons are threefold. It should be pointed out that at the time of a socialist revolution, when the new State i.e., the dictatorship of the proletariat is being established, preceding the construction of a socialist social system, *there already exists a historically based co-operative movement, which has arisen under capitalism as a movement of largely non-capitalist classes and social strata,* namely, the working class, the peasantry and the *petite bourgeoisie.* This movement arises and develops in conditions of capitalism as a movement for the self-defence of these classes and strata against capitalist exploitation, and in particular against some of the more grievous forms of capitalist exploitation, which such a movement of self-defence can to some extent alleviate. This is the origin of the co-operative movement in conditions of capitalism. The new State of proletarian dictatorship finds and takes over this movement of non-capitalist strata and classes, as a historical legacy, when it begins the construction of the socialist system. It is apparent that, because of its social origins, this movement becomes part of the process of socialist construction. This is one of the origins of co-oper-

443

ative ownership and management in this process. The incorporation of this movement within the general framework of socialist construction also changes the movement's appearance; from it develops part of the socialist economy, and co-operative ownership becomes a particular form of socialist ownership.

The second reason for the development and widespread diffusion of co-operative ownership and management during the construction of socialism arises from the fact that *the co-operative movement is a means of socializing small-scale production and services; it is a means whereby this sector can be integrated with the socialist economy.*

Finally the third cause, which I shall discuss at greater length later on, is the fact that the *co-operative movement is also one of the activities giving rise to socialist accumulation and as such contributes to the development of the socialist economy.*

I shall consider first of all the ways in which socialist ownership arises. These ways are basically:

(1) The expropriation of capitalist property, and the establishment of social ownership by society as a whole, namely, State ownership. This act of expropriation establishes the framework for socialist ownership in the form of State ownership. There are various ways of expropriating capitalist property; I shall not examine them in detail. But it is characteristic that this act of expropriating the capitalists gives rise to socialist State ownership.

(2) There is a second way in which socialist ownership arises, namely, by transferring the property of small-scale producers and suppliers of small-scale services to co-operative ownership. The decline of capitalism occurs before capitalism has managed to eliminate all non-capitalist sectors of the economy, especially the small-scale element. Therefore, the socialist revolution is faced not only with the problem of socializing capitalist property by expropriating it, but also with the problem of the socialist transformation of the property of small-scale producers. These latter, in contrast to the bourgeoisie, are not enemies of the working class, which is the leading class, guiding the socialist revolution and the construction of the new social system. On the contrary, they are allies of the working class. It is therefore clear that the problem of expropriating the small-scale producers, the allies of the working class, cannot be considered desirable; there must be a different means of drawing them into the orbit of the socialist economy. Such a means

is the co-operative. Moreover, in certain cases, even part of the capitalist property, expropriated by the revolutionary State for reasons of managerial convenience, may be handed over to co-operatives. This is a rather minor point, but one worth mentioning. Socialist ownership—both ownership by society in general (State ownership), and co-operative ownership—arises, then, in these ways.

The development of a socialist society, or even the earlier process of the construction of socialism, is based on socialist accumulation. Socialist accumulation is of particular historical importance since, with few exceptions, history has been such that the first successful socialist revolutions took place, not in the most highly developed capitalist countries, but in the less developed countries; and this for reasons which were by no means fortuitous, but which were connected with the nature of contemporary imperialism. These less developed countries were faced with the problem of socialist industrialization and of socialist methods of raising agriculture from its backward state. In these conditions socialist accumulation became the vital means for constructing the socialist economy.

Socialist accumulation denotes the creation of new social property, that is, both new State property and new co-operative property, for the term covers the development of both forms of socialist property. As far as socialist State ownership is concerned, development takes place above all by the accumulation of part of the profits earned by the State sector of the national economy. In the case of the growth of co-operative ownership, on the other hand, there are two possibilities. One is the accumulation of the incomes of the co-operatives. However, the requirements of socialist industrialization and modernization of agriculture set such great tasks of accumulation that this method is usually not enough. A State which is building socialism needs to draw upon additional sources of accumulation, namely, the personal incomes of the population; and, above all, the State must call upon the peasant population for their help in this task, in the form of compulsory deliveries and taxes. In this way, the peasant population and other social strata contribute to socialist accumulation, the result of which is the development of socialist ownership.

There is, however, another means of accumulation, based on personal incomes of the population, which forms the financial foundation of the co-operatives. Co-operative ownership can spread not only by the accumulation of these incomes or of part of these incomes, but also by drawing into the co-operative movement ever wider circles of the population which, by their participation in the different activities of co-operatives, contribute monetary assets and in this way transform individual incomes into socialist property. This role of the co-operatives as an instrument for the socialist accumulation of part of the personal incomes of the population is particularly important in economically less developed countries, which have yet to embark on the great task of accumulation. It is particularly important in a country like Poland, with which I shall deal later in greater detail.

In dealing with the role of co-operative ownership in the construction of socialism, in addition to its role as an instrument of socialist accumulation, the significance of co-operatives as a form of economic management must also be mentioned. The co-operative is a form of economic management which activates certain special economic incentives and develops certain special methods of economic administration. As far as economic incentives are concerned, apart from the fact that the co-operative is the only socially acceptable form of socializing small-scale producers and small-scale suppliers of services, there is an additional consideration, namely, the co-operative is able to activate certain economic incentives, which cannot be activated to the same extent by an economy based on ownership by society as a whole. These economic incentives result from the collective nature of co-operative ownership and from the fact that it is a form of socialist ownership which is nearer to private ownership than is ownership by society as a whole. It is, therefore, able to activate certain closer, more direct economic incentives by means of joint ownership and its promotion. It is because the results of the co-operative economy are more directly connected with the given group of co-operative members that the material interest is more direct. As we shall see later, the collective nature of co-operative ownership has a second side too, which limits its possibilities. But its positive side, especially in the initial period of the construction of socialism, is this very possibility of activating direct incentives. This offers advantages which must be exploited to the full in the process of constructing socialism.

Further, the co-operative, because of the communal nature of its property, has established a great tradition of democratic economic management of a social nature. After the activation of certain economic incentives, co-operative self-government is the second specific feature of the co-operative management. This feature, as we shall see, also plays an important role in the process of constructing socialism.

I have discussed certain specific features of co-operative management which give the co-operative movement its particular significance, especially in the initial period of socialist construction. I shall now consider the relationship of co-operative ownership, that is, of the co-operative method of management together with its corresponding economic incentives and administrative method, to ownership by society as a whole in the form of State ownership. What differentiates these two forms of socialist ownership? What are the basic consequences stemming from this distinction? The first difference is the narrower social range of co-operative ownership, that is, its group nature. As I have already mentioned, this produces a more direct operation of incentives towards interest in this kind of ownership and more direct forms of democratic management. In short, co-operative owners administer their joint property directly.

However, for this joint property, managed in such a direct and autonomous way, to be socialist property, certain conditions must be fulfilled. Socialism is management on the basis of the national ownership of the means of production and distribution for the satisfaction of the needs of society as a whole, and not of any particular parts or groups constituting it. Therefore, group ownership can qualify for the name of socialist ownership only if it is part of socialist management in a general sense, that is, of management in the interests of society as a whole. In other words, *co-operative management is socialist management if it is responsible to the whole society, and not only to a group of co-operative members.* In order to be socialist in nature, co-operative management must operate in some measure on trust for the interest of society in general. *Consequently, co-operative ownership in capitalist conditions, even in co-operatives of the working class, is not yet, and cannot be, socialist ownership.* Under capitalism, it is ownership by a group to satisfy the interests of that group, which forms a co-operative and endeavours to decrease capitalist exploitation; but it is not, and cannot as yet be socialist ownership.

The possibility of transforming co-operative ownership into socialist ownership and of developing new co-operative ownership in the form of socialist ownership arises only during the construction of socialism.

This requires the existence of ownership by society in general, that is, by the socialist State. Furthermore, it requires that this socialist State ownership should be a key form of social ownership in the process of constructing socialism. For only in this way is it possible to construct an economy serving the needs of the whole society, and create the conditions in which the group form of social ownership can also be in the nature of socialist ownership. Only in these conditions can the co-operative sector become socialist in form. This is the fundamental requirement for co-operative management to be socialist in nature. This is why the development of socialism cannot be based exclusively on co-operative ownership, but must have ownership by society in general, in the form of State ownership, as its keystone, with the co-operative sector serving only as an auxiliary element. *The transformation of co-operative ownership into socialist ownership, of the co-operative sector into a socialist sector, requires the inclusion of the co-operatives in the planned economy and the implementation by the co-operatives of the general political and economic tasks laid down by the socialist State.* Without the fulfilment of this condition co-operatives have no socialist content.

I have discussed the key role played by State ownership in the construction of socialism. I want now to draw attention to a very important fact, namely, that the difference between socialist co-operative ownership, which forms part of the socialist economy, and ownership by society in general in the form of State ownership, is less significant than would appear. From a purely legal point of view the difference is fundamental. On the one hand, there is ownership by society as a whole vested in the State, as the supreme authority of the whole working society; on the other hand, there is ownership by a group. However, two facts must be pointed out. The group nature of co-operative ownership in conditions of socialism is limited. As I have mentioned, if organization and management are to be socialist in nature, they cannot be only for the satisfaction of the needs of a group of co-operative owners, perhaps at the cost of the rest of society. They must operate in accordance with the interests of society as a whole, in some measure on trust for the interest of society in general. To a certain extent, this diminishes the group element and introduces an element of society in general. On the other hand, management under State ownership of the property belonging to society as a whole, operates in the form of the activity of socialist enterprises. The socialist enterprise is a group of workers entrusted with property, belonging to society as a whole, with the aim of carrying out certain social tasks such as production, services, trade, and so on. With the maturing of socialist society, the activity of these workers is based on the principles of self-government, and their direct influence on the management of the property belonging to the whole society increases. In this or in another form there arises workers' self-government. In Poland and Yugoslavia it takes the form of workers' councils; in other socialist countries the role of trade unions in enterprise management is increased. The working staff acquires a more direct influence in managing the enterprise and, therefore, have greater material interest in the results of the management entrusted to the enterprise by society as a whole.

As we have seen, although the property belongs to the State acting on behalf of society in general, its management is entrusted to the enterprise, and the labour force has some say in the direction of the enterprise. Certain special economic incentives to promote interest in the good management of this property are brought into play, and hence the whole series of factors which I mentioned in discussing the specific features of management under co-operative ownership. Thus, the difference between State and co-operative ownership proves to be less fundamental than it appeared at a first glance on the basis of a purely legalistic approach. I think, I can go even further and say that as socialist society develops, the differences between ownership by society as a whole and co-operative ownership will decrease and finally disappear altogether.

In this country, as in other socialist countries, the process of decentralizing the management of property belonging to society in general, and of making it more democratic, is gradually progressing; and certain economic incentives connected with workers' participation in enterprise management are being introduced. Moreover, the integration of co-operative ownership into the socialist economy as a whole will undoubtedly gradually move forward, so that the differences between these two forms of ownership will gradually decrease.

In the initial period of socialist development, in the field of the management of both State and co-operative property, certain deviations may occur and, as we know, have occurred. I would say that basically there are two possible deviations:

(1) the deviation of bureaucratic centralism; and
(2) the deviation of sectionalism.

The deviation of bureaucratic centralism arose, as we know, during the period of great pressure of socialist industrialization; it was born of the need for a high degree of centralization in the control and management of the national economy during this period. This need gave rise to the deviation of exaggerated bureaucratic centralization which lasted not only when such a high degree of centralization was no longer necessary, but even when it actually obstructed further development of the national economy. This deviation of bureaucratic centralism was evident not only in the sector of the economy based on State ownership, but also in the co-operative sector. This was apparent partly in the trend towards the elimination of the co-operatives, towards their absorption into the State sector in just those areas where the State failed to activate the economic incentives stimulated by the co-operative sector. This was detrimental to the national economy. This deviation appeared also in the elimination of co-operative self-government which deprived the co-operative sector of one of its most characteristic features. Co-operatives remained only in name, for in fact they were assimilated into the State sector, to the detriment both of the co-operatives themselves and of the whole process of the construction of socialism. We have been convinced of this by our own experience in agricultural and other sectors.

The deviation of bureaucratic centralism had further consequences in the lack of democratic control within the economy, particularly in the enterprises. As a result, the socialist nature of production relations was warped, due to the gulf created between the social ownership of the means of production and the working masses which were precluded from exerting any effective influence on the management of these means. This led to bureaucratic inflexibility, waste, and all the phenomena with which we have become familiar in recent times. These, then, are the results of the deviation of bureaucratic centralism.

There is, however, another deviation which must be kept in mind. We seldom think of it since we are only now eliminating the results of bureaucratic centralism. Nevertheless, we must not shut our eyes to the possibility of another deviation and it must be mentioned here. This is the deviation of sectionalism. In the State sector, sectionalism takes the form of attempts to transform socialist State enterprises, *de facto*, into communal property belonging to those who work in these enterprises. We call this the deviation of anarchist syndicalism. It becomes possible in the State sector when the principle of workers' self-government is interpreted as a principle leading to the transfer of the enterprise to the joint ownership of those working in it. In this case, the enterprise ceases to operate as a trustee of the interests of society in general, responsible for the property belonging to society as a whole which is entrusted to it under the management of a board, and instead operates as if independently owned by a group. At the time of the Russian revolution this tendency was manifested by what was known as workers' opposition, against which Lenin campaigned.

In the co-operative field, the deviation of sectionalism takes the form of autonomy. The doctrine of the autonomy of the co-operatives, understood in the sense that a co-operative does not act as a trustee of the interests of society in general, as a part of the planned socialist economy, or as one of the instruments for the realization of the general political and economic tasks of the socialist State, is analogous to the deviation of anarchist syndicalism in the management of State property.

In Poland we have overcome or, strictly speaking, we are in the course of overcoming, the deviation of bureaucratic centralism. I do not think that we are at present threatened with the deviation of sectionalism, although such a danger arose during the bitter struggle against the deviation of bureaucratic centralism. At that time, ideas of an anarchist-syndicalist type were revived and found expression in the press. It seems to me that today we have overcome this danger and that we are on the way to creating an acceptable model of the direction and management of our national economy with a suitable role in it for co-operatives.

I shall now say a few words about the specific tasks of co-operatives in Poland, especially in connection with the current process of forming a new model of the management of the national economy. The October revolution and the gradual realization of the new economic model have opened up for co-operatives in Poland great new possibilities, as well as new tasks. Above all, the elimination of bureaucratic centralism which weighed heavily on the co-operatives, limiting and depriving them of a proper co-operative role, has opened up a new field of activity for them. This field exists in every part of the co-operative movement: in peasant, craft and service co-operatives, in labour, credit, building and consumer co-operatives, etc. As far as rural co-operatives are concerned, this new field of activity and new forms of operation have been opened up by a new political role. This has enabled the distributive and sale co-operatives to develop, and has extended the range of their activity in providing services. There has also arisen the question of widening their activity in the form of certain functions in the sphere of mechanization and other aid for co-operative peasant management. Possibilities have arisen of developing different forms of machinery holding and supplying co-operatives, co-operatives for agricultural amelioration, various forms of simple peasant co-operatives, as they are called, which, indeed, have an ancient tradition in Poland and which, during the deviation of bureaucratic centralism, were suppressed, thereby obstructing socialist development of the rural areas. Finally, opportunities have also arisen for new producer co-operatives, developed on a new basis. Deviation in this sphere consisted, among others, in the limitation of their principle of self-government. This lack of self-government was one, though not the only, factor which obstructed the process of the socialization of agricultural production.

Possibilities have arisen, for the development of various forms of producer co-operatives. At present certain experiments are being carried out in this field. As we know, some State farms have been handed over to producer co-operatives working with State-owned land, buildings and heavy machinery. All these are new fields for the development of rural co-operatives—a development which, as conceived by the new programme of agricultural policy, is an instrument of the long-term policy of building a socialist agriculture by using different methods from those which have in the past proved unsatisfactory. *Great opportunities also face handicraft service and labour co-operatives.* The question of rapidly raising the standard of living of the population is today one of the foremost tasks of economic policy. During the last two years there has been a fundamental revision of investment policy. The rate of accumulation has been reduced for some time, the structure of investment has been changed in favour of directing large sums to investment in agriculture and those branches of industry producing consumer goods which were neglected during the period of forced industrialization. The policy of rapidly increasing the standard of living of the working population requires substantial growth in small-scale production and services, and hence in those areas where the most appropriate form of development is the co-operative. This opens up new tasks for the development of these types of co-operative, especially as the co-operative form of development for small-scale production and services facilitates the mobilization of large areas of hidden reserves which undoubtedly exist but which, due to the failure in the past to appreciate the role of co-operatives, were not made use of.

The question of the labour reserve is very important since, as we know from the resolutions of the XI Plenum of the Central Committee of the Polish United Workers' Party, we are entering a period of increasing efficiency in industrial production by eliminating, among others, excessive growth of employment. The surplus labour force in heavy industry can be absorbed by employing it in co-operatives, which ought to play a more significant role.

Particular importance is attached to co-operatives for housing construction. These are faced with considerable tasks. Indeed the XI Plenum, and even the X Plenum, of the Polish United Workers' Party, put forward certain proposals for speeding up the solution of the housing problem, which is one of the most important social questions in the country. Indeed, after some sort of solution and improvement in the question of pensions, which will be introduced shortly, the main social problem in this country will be housing. The solution of this problem requires the mobilization of the population's own resources, so that State accumulation can be supplemented by the population's own savings for building purposes. In this field, co-operatives have a great role to play as an instrument for mobilizing these resources.

The Resolution of the XI Plenum deals with this in a fair amount of detail and I am not going to repeat it here. The important role which, on the basis of this resolution, falls to housing co-operatives is clear. Apart from this, there is the question of the management of the housing sector of the economy. The old highly centralized form of management has proved unsatisfactory. Certainly, there were also extraneous causes which contributed to the bad state of housing in our economy. The deterioration of the fabric of buildings in towns and cities was due to an extraneous cause, namely, that at the turbulent time of rapid industrialization, there were no resources for proper upkeep and repairs. But that is only one side. There is a second side too: the administration of houses and flats was bad. Hence the problem arises of making such management efficient.

I do not want, at this stage, to prejudge what form the management of the housing sector of the economy should take—whether it should be co-operative or not, although this is one of the forms which must be considered. But one thing is clear: there must be decentralization of management, in which repairs and maintenance costs, such as those for the upkeep of the fabric of buildings, must be borne not only by society as a whole, that is, by the State fund, but also directly by those who enjoy the use of the houses and flats. Forms of such decentralization of management are found in many socialist countries. I am not familiar with all the organizational forms of the housing sector in the different socialist countries, but in the case of our neighbour, the German Democratic Republic, for example, there are decentralized managerial boards which, so far as I know, even issue shares in new house building and sell them to those who are going to live in the buildings. These are formally not co-operatives, but in essence they are close to co-operatives. Thus, there is the problem of total or part transfer of the management of the housing sector to co-operatives, and this problem must be considered carefully. As I say, I do not want to prejudge this issue; I am only presenting it for discussion. It must be considered against the background of the whole complex of problems in our economy. *We may observe a revival of credit co-operatives, which in the past had virtually died out.* They are being revived against a background in which co-operatives are being activated as a means of socialist accumulation of the population's own resources. Credit co-operatives in rural areas will play an increasing role, as will credit co-operatives for handicrafts.

The Central Committee of the Polish United Workers' Party, and particularly Comrade Gomułka in his speech at the XI Plenum, clearly stated that the time has passed when the only source of accumulation was income from the State sector, and that for the solution of many new problems we shall call for a contribution from the population's own resources. In this connection the various forms of credit co-operative can each play its own role. In the past, the role of the co-operative as a medium of socialist accumulation has been completely neglected. We have needlessly ignored wider possibilities for hastening the construction of the socialist economy, possibilities of which we now want to make full use.

Finally, there is the problem of consumer co-operatives. I mention these last of all because they present several specific problems which I shall not be able to answer completely here. If I were asked what the answer is, I could not say, for as yet there is no answer. But certain problems arise. We are faced with the task of making socialist trade efficient. A project for the reform of socialist trade, concerning decentralization and the independence of enterprises, is at an advanced stage of preparation. In connection with this there arises the problem of direct democratic social control in trade. A basic feature of co-operative trade is the democratic control exerted by the members of the co-operative. It is important to realize, however, that in just this field consumer co-operatives are experiencing a crisis. This crisis is partly the result of the deviation of bureaucratic centralism which I have already discussed. Self-government has disappeared from all our social life, and consumer co-operatives have been affected by the general process. We halted this process in October 1956 and reversed it. But there is a second problem. I present it simply as a problem, for its solution requires examination and study. It is this: the trade of our urban consumer co-operatives—as distinct from the rural distribution and sale co-operatives—is based on larger units, for example, the Consumer Co-operative Centre was the only one for the whole of Warsaw. These units have, from their very nature—because of their size—shown centralistic deviations. Because of the size of these units, co-operative self-government is very doubtful. As a result, a person treats consumer co-operatives in basically the same way as the Municipal Retail Trade (MHD). If consumer co-operatives are to be made efficient as a distinct form of socialist trade, they must assert their distinctness in the field of self-government, and in more direct links with the consumer, that is, the member of the co-operative. Here, I see important work for consumer co-operatives. A positive realization of this work could also be a very good influence on State trade, since, as I have already said, with the maturing of the socialist society, the differences between the State sector and the co-operative sector will fade away. In this way, co-operative trade can also play a considerable role in the development of State trade, the other great branch of socialist urban trade.

These are the specific tasks which face co-operatives in Poland today. To sum up, co-operatives can be said to have four tasks in the construction of socialism in Poland:

(1) development of small-scale production, cottage industry and personal services;

(2) socialist transformation of small-scale production;

(3) efficient, cheap and democratic management which may favourably influence the sector of the economy based on State ownership;

(4) attracting personal savings as a contribution to the process of socialist accumulation.

In one sentence, these four tasks for co-operatives can be said to be *the task of mobilizing social initiative of the working masses.*

The construction of a new model for the control and management of the national economy provides the co-operatives with great opportunities. It is up to the co-operatives themselves to make the most of them; because the opportunities are there, it does not follow that they will automatically be used.

So, to conclude, I should like to stress that the co-operatives' place in the economic model which is being drawn up in our country, will depend on the co-operatives themselves, that is, on their initiative and on whether, and how, they manage to seize the opportunities which are opening up before them, and on the efficiency with which they fulfil their social tasks in the process of constructing socialism in Poland.

OBSERVATIONS ON THE SECOND
FIVE-YEAR PLAN IN INDIA

1. Planned economic development requires mobilization of a major part of the country's economic surplus for purposes of productive investment. This is the substance of the planned industrialization and economic development carried out in the Soviet Union and in the countries of Eastern Europe and started in China. The magnitude of the national effort involved is illustrated by the fact that in these countries 20–30 per cent of the national income is assigned to investment. This has yielded a yearly rate of increase of the national income of the order of 14–15 per cent, of industrial production of 18–22 per cent, and of industrial employment of some 10 per cent.

The resources came from contributions by peasants who benefited from the land reform, from profits of nationalized industries, direct taxation, particularly of the capitalist sector, from loans subscribed by the public, and, to some extent also, by deficit financing. The strategic lever of economic development was the construction of basic industries producing means of production to which 40 per cent or more of total investment was devoted. A national effort of such magnitude could be carried out only in the context of a true social revolution.

2. The Draft Plan Frame of Professor Mahalanobis presents a programme of planned economic development under conditions which do not entail such radical changes as in the countries mentioned above. Accordingly, the national effort is set more modestly for a gradual stepping up of the rate of investment from 7 to 11 per cent of the national income and of achieving a yearly rate of growth of national income of 5 per cent.

The strategy of economic development consists in concentrating investments (some 20 per cent) on the construction of industries producing means of production. In view of the inability of private capital to undertake a task of such magnitude, this should be done by public investment. Thus, it follows that the public sector becomes the pivot of the process of industrialization. No nationalization, however, is

457

assumed in the fields of production; development of state activity in the field of banking, insurance and trade is foreseen as a possible subsidiary measure. Additional subsidiary measures are land-reform and special measures for the benefit of home industries on account of their capacity to create employment.

Additional employment to be generated by this programme is estimated at 11 million, of which 20 per cent would take place in industrial development. A weak feature of the Plan is the perfunctory manner in which the problem of financing is treated, entrusting detailed solutions to proper government agencies. This leaves open the question of ways and means of mobilizing the resources necessary for the realization of the economic development envisaged.

3. The Draft Memorandum of December 1955 and the Draft Outline of February 1956 differ in draftsmanship. Their content is almost identical, as can be seen from the enclosed comparative table. It is, therefore, sufficient to consider one of these documents, say, the Draft Outline.

The basic feature of the Draft Outline is that it abandons the main concept, namely, that the strategic lever of industrialization and economic development is the construction of industries producing means of production. This is apparent in reduced allocations for investments in basic producer goods industries and in the shift of expenditure allocation to non-productive (though certainly socially useful) objectives or to such productive activities which do not increase the future national income (e.g., transport). Only 19 per cent of total public development expenditure is allocated to industries and minerals as compared with 26 per cent in the Plan-Frame; 9 per cent is allocated to power as compared with 10·5 per cent in the Frame Plan. The absolute amount of development expenditure allocated to industries and minerals is diminished from 1100 crores in the Plan-Frame to 891 crores in the Draft Outline, i.e., by 20 per cent. There is also a slight reduction in the amount allocated for power (from 450 to 440 crores). Furthermore, of the 19 per cent allocated to development in industries and minerals only 15 per cent of the total are assigned to "large-scale industries, scientific research and minerals", i.e., the field which develops the productive capacity of the national economy.

This change of emphasis stands out even more clearly if we consider the fraction of total investment going to the basic industries. In the

Plan-Frame, 1100 crores of a total of 5600 crores is assigned to these industries; in the Draft Outline it is 691 crores out of a total of 6100 crores. Thus, the portion going to basic industries is reduced from 20 per cent to 11 per cent and the absolute level is reduced by 37 per cent.

This change is not a consequence of an overall curtailing of targets and expenditure. On the contrary, the total expenditure is raised, compared with the Plan-Frame, from 4300 to 4800 crores. The increase is chiefly in the fields of transport and communications (from 950 to 1384 crores) and social services, housing and rehabilitation (from 750 to 946 crores). Thus, there is a change in the basic conception concerning the strategy of economic development. The basic strategic lever is seen not in the concentration of resources for development of means of production, but in the development of transportation facilities. In view of the reduced rate of industrial development envisaged, the burden of creating additional employment is thrown upon the public services, i.e., upon non-productive (though socially useful) activities.

It seems that this difference between the two conceptions is due to different views on the respective roles of the public and the private sectors. According to the Plan-Frame, 66 per cent of total investment was to take place in the public sector. But in industry—which is the pivotal centre of economic development—71 per cent of investment was to take place in the public sector. In the Draft Outline the proportion of investment in the public sector is reduced to 62 per cent. However, a major part of it is assigned to transport, communications and to social services, housing and rehabilitation. Consequently, only a minor fraction of public investment would go to industry and minerals.

Obviously, the idea is that public investment concentrated in transport will create the facilities necessary for the development of private industries and that investment in social services, housing, etc., will create the demand for the products of private industries. The public sector is thus related to fields creating facilities and demand for industrial production being conceived as basically the task of the private sector. Indeed, the Draft Outline concentrates public investment in industry and minerals, in steel, railway and electrical equipment, shipbuilding, coal, coke, etc. Manufacturing of machinery, chemicals, fertilizers, etc., is essentially to be the task of the private sector.

4. The Draft Outline sets the same basic development targets as

the Plan-Frame, i.e., a gradual increase in the proportion of national income invested from 7 to 12 per cent, an annual rate of growth in national income of 5 per cent and the creation of additional employment outside agriculture for some 8 million (as compared with 8·5 million in the Plan-Frame).

It is very doubtful that these targets can be achieved by the methods envisaged. Supposing that the employment targets were achieved (which is doubtful according to critical evaluations), it would be impossible to achieve the production and national income targets. Of the additional employment only 800,000 i.e., 10 per cent of the total, is to be in industries and minerals (not including small-scale and cottage industries), as compared with 1·7 million, i.e., 20 per cent of the total, in the Plan-Frame. The additional employment in industries and minerals has been reduced by more than a half. This corresponds to the reduced investments in this field. Consequently, the growth of productive capacity of the national economy is also reduced.

It is difficult to see how the same rate of increase in national income as in the Plan-Frame (i.e., 5 per cent per annum) can be maintained by reducing investment by 37 per cent and by reducing by over 50 per cent the additional labour force in that sector of the national economy which creates new productive capacity, unless, of course, the Plan-Frame grossly overestimated the output–capital ratio and the productivity of labour. I do not think that this can be proved; if anything, the Plan-Frame errs in the opposite direction.

If investment and additional employment is directed largely into fields which do not contribute to the raising of the productive capacity of the national economy, a much slower rate of increase of national income must result. I think that 3 per cent would be a more realistic expectation.

Another important consequence of the Draft Outline should be pointed out. By increasing investment in industries producing means of production, besides creating new productive capacity, creates the foundations for independence from import of investment goods from abroad. By reducing investment in industries producing means of production, the period of economic dependence on foreign countries and foreign capital is prolonged.

5. However, even these reduced possibilities of increasing the national income are not likely to be realized because of the inadequate provisions

for the financing of the programme. Already the Plan-Frame did not contain an adequate programme of financing economic development. This weakness emerges even more strikingly in the Draft Outline.

The total outlay is increased to 4800 crores (as compared with 4300 crores in the Plan-Frame). This outlay is to be covered by 800 crores of foreign assistance (as compared with 400 crores in the Plan-Frame), 1200 crores of deficit financing, 1200 crores from budgetary sources and 1200 crores of borrowing from the public. An uncovered gap of 400 crores is left. Of these, foreign assistance and the uncovered gap amounting together to 1200 crores i.e., to one fourth of the total outlay, are entirely unspecified, the absorptive capacity of the market for public loans is uncertain, so is the capacity of the national economy to absorb deficit financing. Finally, only 1/4 of the outlay is covered by means which are certain.

The capacity to absorb deficit financing depends upon the ability to increase rapidly the output of consumer goods, particularly food. This, in turn, depends on the unpredictable factor of weather and crops. As 1200 crores presents an increase of about 75 per cent in note circulation, when national income can increase during the period by some 18 per cent (at an annual rate of 3 per cent), the effect is almost certainly to be inflationary. This inflationary effect will be diminished by good crops, and aggravated by bad crops. It also can be mitigated by imports of food. This, however, necessitates either an unproductive use of foreign exchange reserves or acceptance of foreign aid on a credit basis (e.g., surplus food from the USA, practically the only source available).

A rise in prices would increase the cost of investment and necessitate larger outlays than originally planned, thus aggravating the financing difficulties. More likely, the result would be a drastic cut in the investment programme and consequently a further fall in the rate of growth of national income, or, in order to prevent this trend—a frantic search for foreign assistance.

6. The discussions about the Second Five-Year Plan which took place in the press, in scientific gatherings, in political meetings, etc., have aroused public opinion. The public has become, so to speak, "plan conscious". Great expectations have been raised, people have come to think of the Second Five-Year Plan as an instrument of great industrial and economic development. The provisions of the Draft Outline are bound to cause disappointment, even if carried out. They

cannot achieve more than a slow gradual increase of national income at a rate similar to that achieved during the First Five-Year Plan and, in view of the growing population, a rather precarious stabilization of the present level of unemployment. But bearing in mind the unsatisfactory financing provisions mentioned, even this is not likely to be achieved and a serious increase in unemployment has to be feared.

There is a danger that the discrepancy between expectations raised and actual realizations may lead to discrediting the idea of planned economic development. The atmosphere of disillusion may create a favourable ground for the revival of the idea current in traditional economics that economic development should be based upon facilitating the influx of foreign capital. Though countries where this theory has been applied, as, for instance, Turkey, Iran, Pakistan, Thailand, the Philippines, have not established a record of great economic progress or strong national independence, it is by no means obvious that similar ideas would not gain influence in an atmosphere of disillusion with "planning" which failed to satisfy the great expectations raised.

The ideas a nation adopts concerning its economic and social development must be of its own choice. It would be hardly appropriate for a foreign visitor to enter into a discussion of this subject. The writer of these lines, however, frankly admits to have a direct political interest in the outcome. For the outcome will weigh heavily on the balance of the forces making for peace and for war, for progress and for reaction in the whole world. He is deeply conscious of the fact that his own nation will be affected by the balance.

7. It seems that the next two years will not be favourable for starting a bold programme of economic development. This year's budget is basically set and developments for the year are determined by it. Next year is election year which may not be a moment favourable for the implementation of great social changes. During this period, the Draft Outline might be used as a temporary "stop-gap" plan, without, however, making too great commitments for the future in the field of transportation and construction for non-productive purposes. It is important that the provisions of the Draft Outline concerning developments in industry and minerals be carried out. This will require active measures to increase budget revenues. Professor Kaldor's recommendation for tax reform provide such measures which can increase revenue by 100 crores per annum.

As soon as political conditions become more favourable (say, in 1958), a bold programme of economic development should be started. Such a programme, to be really effective and to mobilize the nation on a large scale (and also to counter a certain disillusionment which is most likely to develop in the next two years), must go definitely beyond the targets even of the Plan-Frame. It must be large enough to overcome the "threshold" below which gradual changes dissipate without tangible results, to give emergence to a new qualitative situation where economic development becomes a self-feeding process.

As income from property comprises at least 23 per cent of total national income, it is possible to mobilize some 15 per cent of national income for purposes of investment without imposing sacrifices upon the masses whose income is derived from labour. By concentrating investments in the fields which create productive capacity, i.e., in the production of machines, steel, minerals, power, land improvement, fertilizers, etc., it should be possible to secure a rate of increase of national income of some 10 per cent a year.

The following is a set of measures which may serve to mobilize the nation's economic surplus for such a bold plan of economic development. Each of these measures can be (and, indeed, has been) adopted by a government operating on the basis of capitalist economy. If the political situation is favourable, and if it is so desired, these measures can also be used as a starting point, leading to a development of the national economy on socialist lines. This, however, need not be the case. The measures can stand on their own merit and be implemented without transcending the framework of capitalist society. However, as public investment is the strategic instrument envisaged by these measures, concentrated power of private monopoly capital is not built up. Furthermore, any successful industrialization, combined with the removal of semi-feudal relations, by developing an industrial working class and a peasantry free from feudal dependence, cannot help creating or strengthening democratic social forces aiming towards socialism. Those who fear the risks involved have no choice but to perpetuate economic underdevelopment and social backwardness.

(i) A thorough land reform giving and distributing the land to those who work on it (whether land is nationalized or given into individual ownership seems secondary) with the beneficiaries of land reform paying a revenue directly to the State.

(ii) A moratorium on agricultural debts, part of the debts being cancelled and part taken over by the State.

Both measures are measures of bourgeois reform liquidating semi-feudal social relations. In Western Europe such measures were undertaken in the eighteenth and nineteenth centuries.

(iii) Earmarking part of industrial and commercial profits for investment serving the purposes of planned development. At present, some 30 per cent of the profits are being reinvested, the rest is consumed. At least 50 per cent of profits should be channelled into a "development fund" with the provision that the sums be released to the profit-recipients for purposes of investment approved by the Plan. On funds not invested, the profit-recipients would draw interest, the funds being utilized by the government for investment in the public sector. Such measures have been taken occasionally by capitalist governments during periods of special national effort, e.g., war. In Poland, such a measure was taken with regard to the capitalist sector in 1946 and subsequent years.

(iv) As a special application of the above measure, prohibition of capital exports and blocking (or drastic reduction of) the outflow of dividends of foreign capital. Such a step was taken by many European countries in the nineteen-thirties, e.g., by Great Britain (control of capital exports) and by Germany (blocking the outflow of dividends).

(v) Extension of the nationalization of banking, particularly where foreign capital is involved, and nationalization of foreign trade in commodities particularly important to the country's foreign trade (e.g., tea, jute, ores, etc.) and of such natural resources as are largely foreign-owned. Such measures have been taken by many capitalist governments in Europe and in other continents. Their purpose is to promote independence from such influence of foreign capital as might hamper the realization of a national plan of economic development.

These measures, together with usual taxation provisions, say, on the lines proposed by Professor Kaldor, utilizing savings of the broad public by government borrowing and, within the limits of possibility—some deficit financing, should make it easy to assign 15 per cent of the national income to productive investment and to concentrate a major part of investment on basic industries thus increasing the productive capacity of the national economy.

The resulting rate of economic development would mean a real tangible "break through" in the vicious circle of poverty delaying progress, lack of progress causing poverty, and so on. It would set free the economic potentialities of India which are not less than the economic potentialities of many other countries in Asia or in Europe successfully advancing on the road of planned economic development.

THE TASKS OF ECONOMIC PLANNING
IN CEYLON

The Present State of Planning

Planning in Ceylon has reached a state in which clarity has been achieved concerning the basic lines of development of Ceylon's national economy, the steps necessary to formulate a plan of economic development and the measures required to ensure its successful implementation. The First Interim Report of the National Planning Council issued on July 1, 1957, presents a very clear outline of the fundamental problems of economic development in Ceylon and of the directions in which the solution of these problems must be sought. In a way which can be considered as exemplary, it analyses the possibilities as well as the limitations of the development of the export sector, of the Dry Zone, of improvements in non-estate agriculture. On the basis of an examination of these possibilities and limitations the Interim Report arrives at the conclusions that industrialization is the fundamental dynamic factor in promoting Ceylon's further economic development. The Interim Report then examines the needs for the development of energy supply and of the output of constructional materials as the basic conditions of successful industrialization. This Interim Report and the Reports of the Technical Working Groups, particularly the papers on industrialization, provide the basis for the preparation of a plan of economic development of Ceylon.

The reports by Nicholas Kaldor of April 1958 and, in particular, that by Joan Robinson of August 1958, provide an outline of an economic development policy for Ceylon. In the special field of agriculture, the First Agricultural Plan, formulated in the First Report of the Planning Committee of the Ministry of Agriculture and Food and presented in July 1958, provides such an outline of policy.

It seems that the work done so far as well as such public discussion that took place provide sufficient clarity concerning the basic problems of economic development in Ceylon. On this basis, a concrete plan of economic development can now be formulated. Without wanting to go into the details of the various reports, memoranda and proposals presented, it seems possible to draw certain general conclusions which might be accepted as more or less uncontroversial and which should become the foundation of the plan of economic development in Ceylon.

These conclusions are as follows:

(i) Further economic development of Ceylon rests on industrialization. Industrialization is the factor which alone has the dynamic force of carrying forward this island's economy by increasing national output, providing the necessary outlets for employment, making full use of the country's human and natural resources and producing a rise in the standard of living of the population.

(ii) All other fields of economic activity have to be developed in the light of the contribution they can make to the industrialization of Ceylon. This holds for the export sector, agriculture, transportation, trade and finance.

(iii) The specific position of Ceylon's economy, an economy geared to production for export, should be used as the chief instrument of providing the resources needed for industrialization; Ceylon's export production creates particularly favourable conditions for industrialization. Enjoying a sizeable income derived from export, Ceylon belongs to a category of countries which, because of their possession of exportable products, can undertake an industrialization programme without encountering the major part of the difficulties which in other countries are associated with such programmes.

In the great continental countries, such as the Soviet Union, China and India, industrialization must be based on an all round mobilization of internal resources to provide the economic surplus serving as the source of investment designed to promote industrial development. In other countries which are smaller in size, such as the various countries of Central and Eastern Europe, for instance, Poland, Czechoslovakia, Hungary, etc., the economic surpluses had to be provided by a most austere policy holding down imports and trying with great difficulty to expand exports. Ceylon, similarly to the oil producing countries of the Middle East or oil and mineral producing countries in Latin America, is assured by the very nature of her products of an export surplus. This provides the basic part of the economic surplus needed for industrial investment. This surplus has to be increased, carefully husbanded and properly utilized for industrialization.

(iv) The special role of the economic surplus, generated in the export sector, is to determine the direction of industrial development for the next period. Industrial development must, first of all, increase the export surplus. This can be achieved by developing such lines of industrial production as lead to a diminution of imports of consumer goods, of certain intermediate products and of invisible items. Second, it is necessary to increase the output of export goods as well as the value of export goods by processing them, as far as possible, in Ceylon and using them as intermediate products for the production of high value commodities which could be exported. Thus, the objective of increasing the value of the economic surplus, generated in the export sector, provides the first lines of industrial development in Ceylon.

(v) A further possibility of increasing the value of the economic surplus, generated in exports, is by the creation of new export industries which may even utilize imported raw materials. As such industries require new markets, and as other countries in South-East Asia also have embarked or are at the stage of embarking on industrial development programmes, it would be necessary to base the development of such industries on some co-ordinated industrialization plans for the various countries of the region.

(vi) The increased value of the export surplus would provide the resources for importation of industrial plant, machines, raw materials, and technical assistance needed in the process of industrialization. In addition, however, an effort has to be made to provide, as far as possible, such things from internal resources. This can be done by better utilization of the country's natural resources which might provide raw materials for industrial production. As a preliminary step, a geological survey of the country is needed. It should also be possible to develop domestic production of certain industrial raw materials such as steel and cotton and of certain types of machinery, assembly facilities and industrial plants.

(vii) Finally, industrial production has to be developed to meet the demand for consumer goods resulting from an increase in the standard of living of the population. With industrial facilities and skill increasing in the country, an increasing part of additional demand for consumer goods could be produced in Ceylon. This should contribute toward a further increase in employment and in national income.

(viii) Both industrialization and the increase in the value of the export surplus require further development of agricultural production. Though agricultural production by itself cannot solve Ceylon's economic problems because it lacks the power of expansion necessary to provide full employment and create a noticeable increase in the standard of living, the development of agricultural production is an indispensable complementary factor of industrial development. This is so, because the demand for agricultural products rises with increasing employment and increasing incomes. Furthermore, increased agricultural production and its diversification are needed to meet consumption requirements from home produced agricultural products, in place of imported ones, and to raise in this way the economic surplus derived from foreign trade. The same consideration applies to the needs of increasing the products of the fishing industry. This points to the need for a proper development programme in the fields of agriculture and of fishing. Such a programme should also provide, where possible, for diversification of agricultural export production. Such diversification is needed in order to stabilize the country's export surplus by making it less dependent on fluctuations of demand and prices for the three staple export products.

(ix) Industrial development requires as its foundation an adequate development of energy supply as well as of the supply of constructional materials. These are, therefore, a further requirement of a plan for industrial development. At the same time, they are also required for the development of agricultural production, both directly as well as indirectly, owing to the fact that the supply of hydroelectric power (which is the chief form of power to be envisaged in Ceylon) is closely associated with the development of irrigation facilities. Constructional materials will also be required to meet the additional requirements for housing which accompany industrial development. The general increase in economic activity resulting from industrialization, and from the development of agriculture connected with it, will also require additional investment in transportation.

(x) The above-mentioned possibilities and requirements determine the basic lines of a development plan accounting for the specific economic conditions in Ceylon. Such a plan requires co-ordination of the various lines of development mentioned. Such co-ordination must be twofold. First, the various lines of development must provide a balanced growth of the economy in the sense that the requirement of each sector of the national economy for raw materials, intermediate products and services is met by the output of other sectors of the national economy (including foreign trade). The purpose of balancing the development of the various sectors of the economy is to avoid the development of major bottlenecks which hold up general economic development of the country. Second, it is necessary that economic growth also be balanced inter-temporally. This means that account has to be taken of the fact that development of certain fields of economic activity must be synchronized with or even precede the development of other fields of economic activity. Thus, for instance, an increased supply of power and of constructional materials must be synchronized with other plans of industrial development. Investment in power projects or constructional materials projects may have to precede other industrial investment. Thus the investment plan must be suitably timed.

(xi) A special aspect of balancing economic growth is the balance between physical requirements and financial resources. Finance must be conceived as an instrument of proper implementation of a development plan and not as an independent factor limiting the rate of economic development. The only limits to economic development are set by nature and the given historic heritage of society. They consist of limitations in natural resources, human skills and organizing power. To allow finance to act as a limiting factor would introduce a man-made limit on economic development which has no justification in the state of available natural and human resources.

However, finance is an important medium for ensuring a smooth course of economic development, and for avoiding disturbances. Finance is an instrument by which the needed physical resources are made available for the plan and by which they are directed to their proper allocation. Furthermore, finance is an accounting device which shows whether the total requirement of physical resources balances with the available quantity. Such balance is necessary to avoid bottlenecks and inflationary disturbances in the course of realization of the plan of economic development. Consequently, the plan of economic development must be balanced both in terms of physical and of financial requirements and availabilities.

(xii) The successful realization of a plan of economic development requires the fulfilment of certain social and institutional conditions. One is to remove or control such concentrations of vested interests, foreign or domestic, which for selfish reasons might want to oppose the realization of the national plan of economic development. This implies the concentration by the Government of sufficient economic means, i.e., holding "the commanding heights" of the economy, which would allow it to overcome any resistance to the implementation of the national economic plan. This is largely a political decision affecting the social structure of the country upon which a foreign adviser is not competent to comment. The second condition is a proper organization of the administrative machinery for implementing the plan. Such organization must create an operative centre responsible for the realization of the plan. Finally, in order to be effectively carried out, to overcome various obstacles and difficulties, to induce people to do their best, there must be broad popular support for the plan. For this reason, it is necessary that the plan be understood and accepted by the overwhelming majority of the population so that every citizen considers it to be his duty to contribute to a successful realization of the plan. In other words, the plan must capture the imagination of the people, become a focus which organizes, co-ordinates and concentrates the efforts of the whole nation. It must become a truly national enterprise inspiring in every citizen the ambition to participate in it by doing his share.

Such appear to be the general conclusions which can be accepted as the foundation for the drawing up of a plan of economic development in Ceylon. In so far as these conclusions can be regarded as more or less generally accepted, the situation is now ripe for working out a detailed plan of economic development. Such a plan must be for a period sufficiently long to cover the gestation period of major investment, i.e., the period elapsing from the beginning of the investment until the investment bears fruit in the form of output or services.

Experience has shown that the traditional five-year period of planning which originally was adopted in the Soviet Union, and later became accepted in other countries (not only socialist ones), is too short. Its "rationale" consisted in evening out crop fluctuations during the five-year periods. This was important in the first stage of planning when industry still played a minor part in the national economy. However, as the weight of industry in the structure of the economy increased, it was found that the plan period must be adjusted not so much to evening out crop fluctuations but rather to the period of gestation of major industrial investments. The period of gestation in the fields of basic investment such as power, transportation, mining of minerals, chemicals, etc., lasts usually longer. Consequently, a tendency exists in many countries to have longer range plans, covering longer periods. For instance, in the Soviet Union, Poland and other countries fifteen-year long-term plans are now in preparation.

On the other hand, however, planning over such long periods may become problematic unless reliable data are available for forecasting future possibilities. Such data are absent at the beginning of an industrialization programme. It seems, therefore, that for Ceylon a period of ten years would be most useful for an initial plan of economic development.

Here, mention should be made of Professor Myrdal's useful suggestion to have the ten-year plan remade every two or three years by adding two or three additional years, and revising the years of the old plan which still remain in the light of experience acquired in the preceding two or three years. This would introduce a continuous "moving" ten-year plan.

Successive Steps to Be Taken

The drawing up of a detailed plan of economic development for the next ten years requires considerable time. On the basis of experience of other countries and the preparatory work done by the Planning Secretariat, it seems that about a year would be needed. Consideration of the plan by the Cabinet and by Parliament, public discussion in the Press, journals and other media, would take another half a year; thus, almost two years might possibly elapse before the plan is ready for implementation.

However, it would be unwise to wait all this time before starting activity designed to promote implementation of the plan. Much valuable time would be lost and action for economic development would be delayed unnecessarily by two years. It seems that the country can hardly afford such a loss of opportunity for lack of action. Furthermore, inactivity during the preparatory period for the development plan would undermine the nation's faith in the efficacy of economic planning. This might create a state of apathy and even scepticism towards economic planning which later would make it difficult to mobilize the people's support when the plan is ready. It also would make it difficult to enlist the full active effort of the people in carrying the plan into practice. It might even be used as an argument for discrediting economic planning.

For this reason, the following procedure is proposed:

(i) Preparation within a period of two months of a "Draft Plan" which should indicate the main directions of the development plan and should formulate, in a provisional way, the main targets and tasks without going into too many details. Speed appears here more important than completeness of detail and accuracy of target figures. Such a "Draft Plan" is now being prepared by the Planning Secretariat. The document under preparation will cover a ten-year period in the fields of energy and agriculture, and a five-year period in other industrial investments. Presentation of this draft plan to the Government and its publication should fulfil two functions. First, it should make Government, Parliament and the whole nation conscious of the main tasks involved in the economic development of the country. It should start a fruitful public discussion which, on the one hand, would help to correct certain features of the plan, and, on the other hand, also make the people "plan conscious". This should facilitate the mobilization of public support and effort in carrying out the final plan. Second, it should serve as the basis for an "Immediate Action Programme" which appears to be the most important task of the future.

(ii) The "Immediate Action Programme" should be formulated on the basis of the "Draft Plan". This programme should contain such investments, undertakings, policy measures and changes in administrative machinery as can be started right away.

A large amount of available investments and undertakings as well as of policy measures must form part of any sound plan of economic development. There is no need to wait for their implementation until the plan is ready. They can be started right away because they will have to form part of any plan. Many such investments, undertakings and policy measures may have to precede other investments and undertakings provided for in the plan, which is an additional reason for starting them immediately. This holds for development in the fields of power, irrigation, agricultural policy, certain aspects of export and import policy, promotion of savings, etc. In many fields the necessary preliminary studies are already made. All this makes it commendable and possible to start with them right away.

In this way, the "Immediate Action Programme" would become the nucleus or skeleton around which the future plan of economic development is to be built.

It is suggested that the "Immediate Action Programme" should contain the following items:

(i) Starting with the implementation of the investment projects and schemes contained in the Agricultural Plan of the Ministry of Agriculture and Food, published in July 1958.

(ii) Implementing as rapidly as possible the investment projects in power and irrigation which have been started or prepared. At the same time, preparatory studies in other investment projects in this field should be accelerated.

(iii) Starting with the implementation and preparation of investment projects for production of constructional material. A brick and tile factory should be set up in every province. Several new cement factories must be started.

(iv) Starting a programme of improvement and development of transportation and such investment measures as have to be undertaken immediately in connection with investments in energy, irrigation and industry.

(v) A list should be drawn up of new industrial enterprises where preparations for investment should be started immediately. In particular such investments as are specified in the proposed programme of the Ministry of Industries and Fisheries should be started immediately. The list should include first of all fertilizers and processing of export goods (copra, rubber products, including tyres), processing of imported materials (e.g., refining of oil, cotton spinning and weaving, assembly of radios, bicycles, and other small machinery, a steel plant using scrap iron available in the country). Furthermore, a number of industrial investments designed to supply the home market with products based as far as possible on domestic resources could be started immediately, for instance, in fishing (construction of an efficient fleet) and processing of fish, production of sugar, leather goods, ceramics, glass, paper, simple machine tools, electrical and telecommunication equipment, household, housing and other equipment, iron ore mining and smelting, foundries, production of pipes, etc.

In preparing such a list of new enterprises, projects should be chosen which can be carried out rapidly. It is advisable to avoid in the beginning projects which require a very long period of construction. It is important for reasons both psychological and economic that the products of these enterprises should appear rapidly. This will make soon visible the benefits resulting from the investments made and also serve as a check against possible inflationary development. It is also important to avoid dissipation of resources on too many projects. This would prolong the construction period of the projects and cause unnecessary delay in reaping the fruits of the investments made. In order that some of the products appear in a relatively near future as many of the projects as possible should be started immediately.

(vi) Starting a programme of housing development, of educational activities, particularly in the field of vocational and technical training, and of improving the skills of the population, and of other social services needed to ensure the successful operation of a national plan of economic development.

(vii) A general geological survey of the country as well as a survey of agricultural land utilization.

(viii) Such changes in tariff policy as would have an immediate effect in encouraging the development of home production of commodities which can serve as substitutes for imports. At the same time, measures should be taken to minimize the effect of tariff changes on the cost of living of the broad masses of the people.

(ix) Adequate financial measures to cover public expenditure on investment and adequate savings to cover private investment implied in the "Immediate Action Programme". The programme should include financial measures designed to increase savings, to discourage luxury consumption and unproductive speculation. The expenditure tax and capital gains tax, if adopted, will contribute to this end. At the same time, provisions should be made for financing and procurement of the physical resources (raw materials, machinery, etc.) required for the implementation of the programme.

(x) A statement by the Government concerning the respective roles of the nationalized and of the private sector in the development of the country's national economy. Such a statement should be designed to remove the feeling of uncertainty in the private sector. Such a statement would be similar in form (not necessarily in content) to India's Industrial Policy in this respect. The basis of such a statement was already presented by the Minister of Industries in his speech in Parliament on

July 23, 1957, in which he classified industrial activities in Schedules A, B and C. However, since nationalization of foreign owned plantations forms part of the Government's programme of economic policy, the statement should also be explicit on the Government's intentions in this field.

(xi) Organizational measures to implement public investment in the "Immediate Action Programme", such as formation of the necessary public corporations as well as organizational measures for such subsidization of private investment as will be provided in the "Immediate Action Programme".

(xii) Steps necessary to create executive machinery for successful implementation both of the "Immediate Action Programme" and of a longer range plan for economic development which is in preparation.

The "Immediate Action Programme" on the lines proposed would create in the country a feeling that economic planning has passed from the initial stage of discussion and proposal making to the stage of implementation. It would be a most potent instrument in making the nation conscious that a new period in Ceylon's economic development has started and arouse the people's interest in action designed to promote economic development.

At the same time the "Immediate Action Programme" would really contain the first steps for the implementation of a long range development plan to be worked out within a period of an additional year. The "Immediate Action Programme" could be introduced in July together with the new budget; the financial provisions implied in the programme would actually have to form part of the new budget. Then, in the spring of 1960, the ten-year Plan of economic development could be presented to Parliament and the nation.

Adjustment of Executive Machinery

The successful realization of a plan of economic development requires proper administrative machinery. Such machinery has to be able to work out the plan and also to execute its realization. So far, in Ceylon, only the first part of the machinery has been created, viz., the National Planning Council and the Planning Secretariat. However, as planning proceeds from the stage of drawing up a plan to the stage of its realization, additional machinery must be created both to carry out the plan and to supervise its realization. Such machinery must have the power of independent decision which may become necessary should the realization of the plan meet with delays or difficulties.

Since the realization of the plan is the responsibility of Government, such machinery must be part of the Government's activities. It has to be created on the basis of existing Government agencies. For the purpose of planning, adjustments have to be made in the organization of those Ministries upon which responsibility will rest for carrying out various parts of the plan. In order to ensure full co-ordination in the realization of the various parts of the plan as well as because of the need to allocate in a definite way the responsibility for the realization of the plan as a whole, an appropriate organ must be formed within the framework of the Cabinet.

The realization of various parts of the plan which are entrusted to appropriate Ministries, such as the Ministry of Finance, the Ministry of Industries, the Ministry of Lands and Land Development, the Ministry of Transport and Works, the Ministry of Labour, Housing and Social Services, etc. All Ministries to whom parts of the national plan of economic development are assigned for implementation should have a special Planning Division responsible for the implementation of the plan in the fields assigned to them. Such Planning Division should be directly under the Minister concerned. It should work out measures for the implementation of the part of the plan assigned to the Ministry, inform the Minister currently on the progress made in the realization of the plan, on delays and difficulties which arise and recommend to the Minister remedial action to overcome these.

The Minister's decisions concerning the implementation of the plan must have the highest priority over other activities of the Ministry. As many Ministries have Planning Committees, the Planning Divisions of the Ministries would also perform the services of Secretariat for these Planning Committees. Where experience shows that certain aspects of the plan should be changed, either because of impossibility of realization or because higher targets can be achieved than those contained in the original plan, the Ministry's Planning Committee would have to present to the Cabinet a report proposing changes in the future implementation of the plan.

The Planning Divisions and Planning Committees of the Ministries, where appointed, should keep the Planning Secretariat currently informed on the course of the implementation of the plan in its field. They also should inform the Planning Secretariat of any major proposals and actions suggested by them.

In order to co-ordinate Government activities in the implementation of the plan and to determine in an unambiguous way the boundaries of responsibility in its implementation, it seems necessary to create a Planning Committee within the Cabinet. Such a Committee should consist of the Prime Minister, the Minister of Finance, the Minister of Agriculture and Food, the Minister of Lands and Land Development, the Minister of Industries and Fisheries, the Minister of Transport and Works, the Minister of Trade and Commerce, and the Minister of Labour, Housing and Social Services. Other Ministers should participate in the meetings of the Planning Committee, as required. In view of the great importance of the Committee, it is essential that it be presided over by the Prime Minister, in order to ensure unity of purpose in the Government, although the Prime Minister may want to appoint one of the Ministers as deputy chairman to take care of the minor current business of the Planning Committee.

The Planning Committee of the Cabinet should receive monthly progress reports from all Ministries to whom parts of the plan are assigned for implementation and recommend to the Cabinet immediate action in case of delays or difficulties. Where difficulties require a change in the implementation of a plan, and/or where changes in the objectives of the plan are dictated by necessity, proposals should be sent to the National Planning Council and to the Planning Secretariat with a recommendation to prepare changes in the plan which later would be submitted to the Cabinet.

The Planning Secretariat should serve as secretariat of the Planning Committee, thus fulfilling a double role, i.e., that of the secretariat to the Planning Council and of the secretariat to the Planning Committee of the Cabinet. In this way, the Planning Secretariat would concentrate all information on the progress in the realization of the plan which is needed to prepare future changes in the plan and, finally, a new plan for the next planning period.

The above proposals concerning the creation of adequate executive machinery for the effective realization of the plan of economic development are tentative only. No claim of finality is made on their behalf, because, to make definite proposals, a wider knowledge of the experience or the operation of the various parts of the administrative machinery of the Government of Ceylon would be needed than the writer of this report has been able to acquire in so short a time.

The proposals, however, intend to point out that it is not enough to have a good plan but that appropriate executive means must exist for carrying the plan into practice. Such machinery must satisfy two conditions:

(i) Concentration of decisions and of responsibility for the implementation of the plan must be clearly fixed in the Cabinet. Unity of purpose of the Cabinet must be ensured. Finally, for the proper realization of the plan, it is necessary to make not only right decisions but also quick decisions which are suitably executed.

(ii) In a similar way, a clear concentration of decisions and of responsibility with regard to the realization of the plan is needed in the Ministries. For that purpose it is important that each Minister be currently informed of the progress made in the realization of the part of the plan within his sphere of competence and be able to make quick decisions if delays or difficulties occur.

All changes designed to adjust Government machinery to the requirements involved in the effective realization of the plan can be undertaken within the framework of the existing Constitution, i.e., the Ceylon Independence Order-in Council 1946 and subsequent amendments. There is no need for constitutional changes to implement successfully a plan of economic development. However, changes may be required in administrative procedure designed to allow the Planning Committee of the Cabinet and the Ministries in charge of the implementation of the relevant sectors of the plan to make quick and effective decisions and to carry out certain Government operations on a strict businesslike basis. This seems possible without infringing upon the constitutional rights of Parliament to control activities of the Government. Parliament should receive annual or semi-annual reports on the progress achieved in the realization of the plan which it might discuss subsequently, giving the Government the benefit of its criticism.

Organization and Operation of Public Corporations

Without entering into the question concerning the relative roles of the public and private sectors in the economic development plan of Ceylon, it is generally agreed that public investment and government policy must play a decisive role as the driving force moving forward the national economy. In the fields where private enterprise is relied upon to undertake economic development, financial and other assistance by the Government will be needed to induce private firms to undertake the tasks included in the plan. All this will entail establishing the necessary forms and means of efficient organization of public enterprises, and of providing such assistance to private enterprise as will be called for by the plan.

In both cases, it seems that the best form of organization is that of public development corporations. Such corporations either themselves enter certain fields of production or other economic activities (e.g., trade, finance) or subsidize and assist certain activities in the hands of private enterprise. To be effective, such corporations must be organized on a businesslike basis, without being hampered by traditional regulations of Civil Service activities. Control of the activities of such corporations, which obviously is necessary, must be exercised by methods which have been evolved and have established their usefulness in the control of business firms's standards of honesty in performance.

Appropriate steps in this direction have already been taken by the Industrial Corporations Act, No. 49 of 1957, and the subsequent establishment of a number of industrial corporations, i.e., the Co-operative Wholesale Establishment, the Ceylon Transport Board and the Colombo Port (Cargo) Corporation. The realization of the plan of economic development will undoubtedly require the establishment of further industrial corporations. For the purpose of initiating financial assistance to private enterprise, the Ceylon Development Finance Corporation and the Agricultural and Industrial Credit Corporation may serve as a starting point. However, it is necessary that all public corporations be clearly conceived as agencies for implementing the plan of economic development.

For this purpose, it may be advisable to amend the relevant acts in the direction of stating clearly the obligations of the corporations to implement the objectives of the national plan of economic development which are assigned to them. Correspondingly, the Minister responsible should have the authority to supervise the implementation of the plan objectives by the corporations, and act promptly where delays or difficulties arise. In other words, public corporations, though operating like business enterprises with regard to methods of management and accounting, must be distinguished from private enterprise, being official agencies for the implementation of the national economic plan.

A number of problems arise on the organization, management and policy of public corporations:

(i) As a rule, public corporations should make profits. Part of the profits may remain at the disposal of the corporation, but the major portion of the profits should revert to the budget to be used for purposes of new industrial investment. Such investments may be made within the same corporation from which the profits accrued, or may even be used for the establishment of new corporations. In any case, it is important that the major part of the profits of public corporations be channelled into general revenue, and should serve to finance public investment policy according to the national plan of economic development. Such pooling together of a major part of the profits is essential to ensure industrial development on the lines laid down in the national plan of economic development.

Exceptions to the rule that public corporations should make profits may be allowed in case of activities involving social overhead expenditure on economic development on a national scale. These exceptions, however, should not be allowed to become the cloak for inefficient management. It may even be preferable, in such cases, to assign to the public corporation a subsidy providing that the corporation's losses do not exceed the subsidy granted by the plan.

(ii) In deciding upon industrial and commercial activities under State public corporations, it is important to choose as far as possible such fields which can yield a profit. It would be dangerous to drift into a line of development in which the State undertakes only unprofitable or even deficit activities involving social overhead expenditure and leaves all profitable lines of development in the hands of private enterprises. This would mean indirectly subsidizing private enterprises at the expense of the public which covers, by taxation and otherwise, the deficits of the public sector, while private enterprise benefits from cheap goods and services provided by the public sector. Furthermore, it would mean giving up planning the direction of industrial development. It would also deprive the national economy of an increasingly important source of capital accumulation and self-sustained industrial growth. Finally, it would discredit the public sector as allegedly inefficient. As the development of the public sector is an essential part of planned development and the real dynamic instrument of that development, it would handicap the economic development of the country.

(iii) In order to ensure efficient operation of public corporations it is essential that proper incentives be provided to the personnel employed in such corporations. Contracts with employees must be on a commercial basis and various methods of bonuses, etc., for efficiency, may be applied. Obviously, salaries and wages in different corporations may have to be different, according to the amount of skill, etc., required. It may be advisable to set aside a certain portion of the profits of an enterprise as a fund for bonuses to employees and workers and for expenses contributing to their welfare.

(iv) It seems also advisable that a representative of both the workers and consumers of products or services be included in the boards of public corporations. The representative of consumers would ensure that the products or services of the public corporations are of the quality and kind required. This would also introduce an element directly interested in keeping down the cost of production and operation of public corporations. The representative of workers should create interest in the operation and development of public corporations in which they are employed. It should serve to emphasise the character of the corporation as a national enterprise designed to carry out the objectives of the national plan of economic development. From this point of view, the question might be examined whether it would be advisable to create in the public corporations workers' committees endowed with certain rights and responsibilities with regard to the operation of the enterprise (particularly in matters of social welfare of the employees), and electing their representative to the managing board of the corporation.

The public sector of the national economy, organized in the form of public corporations, must by the very nature of the situation be the dynamic driving force of industrial development. Its role consists in undertaking investments for production and services designed to achieve a breakthrough in the existing economic situation and to create a new structure of the national economy. The profits made in the public sector should become an increasingly important source of capital accumulation. Thus, the public sector should gradually achieve its own means of self-sustained economic growth.

The growth of the public sector will be a source of demand for production of the private sector both directly by requiring all kinds of subsidiary products produced in the private sector and indirectly by creating employment and incomes, which in part will be spent on products and services of the private sector. Consequently, there is no conflict between the development of the public and private sectors of the economy. On the contrary, in an underdeveloped economy, like that of Ceylon, the development of a healthy public sector playing the leading role in the growth of the national economy is indispensible for the development of private activity. In the absence of such development private enterprise would be deprived of expanded markets and would become stagnant. For this reason, special care must be taken to develop sound and profitable public corporations playing a leading role in the realization of the national plan of economic development.

ECONOMIC DEVELOPMENT, PLANNING AND INTERNATIONAL CO-OPERATION

Lecture I. Patterns of Economic Development

The topic of my three lectures is Economic Development, Planning and International Co-operation. I intend to devote the first lecture to patterns of economic development. The second lecture will deal with planning for economic development, and the third will be devoted to the theme of economic development and international co-operation.

Economic development is increasingly becoming the central theme of economic thought. In the period which started with the end of the Second World War, the problem of economic development increasingly occupied the centre of economic thought. Before that time, economic development played a minor role in economic theoretical thinking, particularly among economists of the leading capitalist countries. Their theories at that time were chiefly concerned with problems of economic equilibrium. This was so because development was considered in these countries as something which is taken for granted and which comes about spontaneously, and therefore need not be given special attention.

In more recent times, however, two events happened which had the effect of making economists conscious of questions of economic development. One was the development of the socialist countries which started with the Russian revolution after the First World War, the emergence of a number of socialist economies in Eastern Europe after the Second World War, and, finally, China, the largest nation in the world, embarking upon the road of socialist development. All these countries were formerly to a lesser or greater degree underdeveloped, and only began to develop very rapidly after the social revolution. The most important of them, the Soviet Union, became in a brief period of forty years the second industrial power in the world. This was one factor which drew the attention of economists throughout the world to problems of development.

The other factors were the national-revolutionary movements in the countries which formerly were colonial, semi-colonial or in some other form dependent on the leading capitalist powers. The national revolutions, which in a number of countries were victorious, led to the establishment of new independent states or to the emancipation of existing dependent states from foreign political and economic domination. These countries considered economic development and progress to be their chief problem. The international importance of the national revolutions became so great that the whole problem of underdeveloped countries, of their economic progress, became a major, I may say, the major, international problem. Thus, again attention of economists was drawn to problems of economic development. We may say that today economic science is becoming increasingly development conscious; the theme of development becomes the central theme of economic thought.

As a result of these historical events, which I have outlined here, we can discern three historic patterns of economic development. One is the capitalist pattern which was followed by the countries of Western Europe and the U.S.A. The second is the socialist pattern which was started in the Soviet Union, then extended to a number of countries in Eastern and Central Europe, then to China and some other Asiatic countries. The third is what I shall call the national revolutionary pattern which is establishing itself in countries which emancipated themselves from colonial or semi-colonial dependence. In today's lecture I intend to give a brief comparative analysis of these three patterns of economic development, However, before going into this I have to state what is the central issue of economic development.

The essential feature which appears in all these three patterns and distinguishes a developing economy from one which is more or less stagnant in traditional ways of life—the essential factor of economic development, or in other words, its essential mechanism—is the increase in productivity of labour. This is achieved in three ways. One is the accumulation of part of the product of the economy for purposes of productive investment, the second is technical progress, and the third is the improvement in the organization of economic activities. All these three ways of increasing the productivity of human labour are strictly related one to another. These three factors appear in every developing economy, and are common to all patterns of economic development. The most important of these three is undoubtedly productive investment.

In the older economies, which were stagnant for centuries, there existed various obstacles that hampered economic development. These obstacles essentially consisted in the following: the resources available for productive investment were very small. This was so for two reasons. With a low productivity of labour, the surplus product over what was needed to maintain the labour power of the community was very small. This economic surplus, as I shall call it, was small; but, furthermore, a substantial part, in most cases even the major part of it, was used for non-productive purposes. This non-productive use of the economic surplus was due to the system of social relations, either feudal or in many countries even pre-feudal, like, for instance, in some countries of Africa. Under these conditions, the amount of economic surplus available for productive investment was very small and this was responsible for the stagnant character of these economies. In addition, the ways of economic activity were determined by tradition. An economic mentality existed which was not conducive to innovation, to improvements in the technology of production. This further contributed to the stagnant character of the societies in question.

In all these patterns of economic development mentioned above, development starts with overcoming these obstacles. This implies overcoming the feudal or pre-feudal system of social relations and the mental traditionalism attached to it. This is necessary in order to be able to utilize a major part of the economic surplus for purposes of productive investment. The removal of feudal or pre-feudal social relations marks always the beginning of economic development; it is common to all the patterns of economic development mentioned above. The difference between the three patterns consists in the way in which these traditional obstacles are overcome and broken down, as well as in the way in which part of the economic surplus is mobilized to serve for productive investment. It is here that the difference of these three patterns emerges.

The oldest of these patterns is the capitalist pattern. Up to the First World War it was considered to be the only possible pattern, the pattern which is universal. It was thought that any country which wants to enter the road of economic development must repeat this pattern. Such was the unanimous opinion of the leading economists in the old capitalist countries. But even economists, who were critical of the capitalist system, and who held socialist views, shared the same opinion. The founders of modern scientific socialism, Marx and Engels, believed that all countries will have to pass through a stage of capitalist development which is a precondition to the development of a socialist society.

What was the essential feature of the capitalist pattern of economic development? The essential feature was capital accumulation and productive investment by the urban middle class. In Western Europe, in the towns, a middle class—the bourgeoisie—developed which accumulated a certain amount of wealth. Unlike the feudal classes it did not use its wealth for conspicuous consumption but turned it into productive investment. That was the beginning of capitalist development.

Where did the resources for such investment come from? They came from different sources: in the first place from profits accumulated by the merchants who were the first capitalists. These profits were used for industrial investment and brought further profits already out of industrial activities of the middle class. This again provided a source for new investment. Thus, profits from trade and production, partly also from financial operations of the middle class, became the basis of investments which led to capitalist development. But these were not the only sources. In addition, there were other sources: one, and a very important one in the emergence of capitalist development, was the exploitation of colonies. Such exploitation frequently took the form of direct plunder, to mention only the great plunder of India. Other forms of exploitation were by trade monopolies. At a later stage, capital investment in colonial or semi-colonial countries provided an important source of capital accumulation and productive investment in the countries of Western Europe. It contributed very much to accelerating their economic development. Another source was the ruin of small craftsmen and peasants, whose property was taken over by capitalists and turned into capital.

Finally, a certain amount of capital accumulation was either performed or facilitated by the state. It should not be forgotten that, particularly in the earlier stage of capitalist development, the state played a rather important part, either directly investing in fields such as railroads, public utilities and sometimes even in industrial and commercial enterprises, or subsidizing private enterprise. Particularly in the construction of what is called the infra-structure or the social overheads of productive activity, the state used to be very active as an investor or in subsidizing private investments. Thus, public investment played an important part in the capitalist pattern of development.

Such was the way in which the countries of Western Europe and later the United States of America started upon the capitalist road of economic development. Later, with capitalist enterprise in industry, commerce, and finance already established, the profits derived from these enterprises provided the source of further capital accumulation and self-sustained economic growth.

This process of capitalist development was unequal in various countries. International capital investment came into play as a factor accelerating the development of the less developed countries. In the less developed countries the rate of profit was higher than in the more developed ones. This provided an incentive for capital movements out of the countries with greater capital resources to those where capital resources were relatively scarcer. This helped to speed up the development of the less developed countries.

Such was briefly the capitalist pattern of development which up to the First World War appeared to economists, and as I said to economists of all shades of opinion, as a kind of universal law of economic development, through which all countries must pass. But we know from historic experience that other patterns of economic development have emerged in the socialist countries and, more recently, in countries which I classified as countries undergoing national revolutions.

We may ask what happened? what made the capitalist way of development impracticable to solve the problems of underdeveloped countries and made these countries to embark upon other roads of economic development? The answer is that a new factor entered into the picture. This factor is the development of monopoly capitalism and imperialism. Monopoly capitalism and imperialism made it impossible for the underdeveloped countries to follow the traditional pattern of capitalist development. This is so for a number of reasons. The most important is this: with the development of large capitalist monopolies in the leading capitalist countries, the capitalists of those countries lost interest in developmental investment in the less developed countries because such investment threatened to cause competition to their established monopoly positions. Consequently, investment in underdeveloped countries of capital from the highly developed countries acquired a specific character. It went chiefly into the exploitation of natural resources to be utilized as raw materials by the industries of the developed countries, and into developing food production in the underdeveloped countries to feed the population of the developed capitalist countries. It also went into developing the economic infra-structure such as transportation, ports and other facilities needed to maintain economic relations with the underdeveloped countries.

In consequence, the economies of the underdeveloped countries became one-sided, raw material and food exporting economies. The profits made by foreign capital in these countries were used not for reinvestment in these countries but were exported back to the countries where the capital came from. Or if used for investment in the underdeveloped countries, they were used for investment in the production of raw materials, foodstuffs and in the building up of an infra-structure. These profits were not used for industrial investment on any major scale, which, as we know from experience, is the real dynamic factor of modern economic development. This is the essential reason why the underdeveloped countries were not capable of following the classical capitalist path of economic development.

Furthermore, there were additional reasons. For political reasons, the great capitalist powers supported the feudal elements in the underdeveloped countries as an instrument of maintaining their economic and political influence. This provided another obstacle to the economic development of these countries. The repetition of the classical pattern of economic development in the underdeveloped countries, with a few exceptions, turned out to be impossible. As a result, new patterns of economic development emerged.

What is the essential feature of the new patterns? I shall first describe briefly the socialist pattern of economic development which by now has crystallized into a pretty clear-cut form of economic organization. The socialist revolutions took place in countries under specific historic conditions. They were underdeveloped, the classical capitalist pattern was not workable, though there was some industrialization on capitalist lines. A limited industrialization, as in Russia, produced an industrial working class and a political movement of the working class which became the chief agent of the social revolution.

The socialist revolution started everywhere with two acts. One was the nationalization of capitalist industry, trade, finance, transport, which were in existence, and the creation on that basis of a socialist sector in the economy. The second act was the agrarian reform which abolished feudal social relations in agriculture, divided the land among the peasants, and at a later stage, fostered co-operative development in agricultural production. These two acts provided the basis for the accumulation of resources for productive investment.

The nationalized industries, trade, finance, transport, provided a pool of profits which were used for further industrial investment. As new industrial establishments were constructed, this pool of profits became larger. Again, it was used for new investment and, thus, the nationalized industrial sector of the economy was growing by means of reinvestment of its own profits. In this way, a process of self-sustained growth was started. However, these countries were underdeveloped and industry did not play any major role in their economies to provide adequate resources for the requirements of large-scale investments. An additional source of investment were the contributions from the peasants. The peasants, having received land in the agrarian reform, were made to contribute part of their proceeds by way of taxation, mostly as compulsory deliveries of their products to the state at a lower price. The revenue thus obtained was used for new investment. By reinvesting growing industrial profits and by investing the contributions of the agricultural population, which benefited from the agrarian reform, accumulation on a large scale was started. This made it possible to embark upon economic development; this development then gradually became self-sustained and cumulative.

This is the essential feature of the socialist pattern of economic development. The third pattern which I call the national revolutionary one, is only in the making, it has not yet crystallized as clearly as the capitalist and the socialist patterns have. If you take the various countries which emancipated themselves from colonial or semi-colonial dependence, you find rather large differences. Therefore, it may be somewhat more difficult to give a brief synthetic description of that pattern. None the less, certain general features of that pattern already emerge.

The general features of the national revolutionary pattern are the following. First, similarly to the socialist pattern, it is state and public investment which is the most active, dynamic factor in economic development. The reason is simple. In the countries in question not enough of a capitalist middle class has developed to be capable of providing the capital resources for investment on a scale which is needed to achieve a breakthrough from the old stagnant into a developing economy. Therefore, public investment must become the leading factor of economic development, its very driving force. The second feature of the national revolutionary pattern is that it relies on nationalization in a different way than the socialist pattern. Nationalization of private capital played a very prominent role in the socialist countries. In the national revolutionary countries, nationalization is usually limited to foreign capital or certain parts of it. Very frequently, nationalization of foreign capital is not so much the result of an economic programme, but of a political conflict with the old capitalist countries which make nationalization necessary as a means of political emancipation and of asserting independence of the formerly colonial or semi-colonial countries. Nationalization does not cover as a rule indigenous capital.

The situation in these countries is dominated by the struggle for national emancipation and the assertion of national independence. This creates a broad basis of, national unity in which many capitalist groups participate, and consequently take part in the national revolution. Furthermore, in many countries the amount of existing private capital, particularly in industry, is very small. There is not much to be nationalized, and not much that by nationalization could become a source of capital accumulation. Thus, the national revolutionary pattern, while relying on public investment as the dynamic guiding force of economic development, at the same time, tries to mobilize whatever indigenous private capital is available and to encourage it to take part in the investment serving economic development. It tries to channel private investment into productive activity.

In most of the national revolutionary countries some measure of agrarian reform takes place. These reforms, among others, serve the objective of inducing the revenues coming from agriculture to be invested in industrial activity. Feudal landholding and use of land revenues for conspicuous consumption are removed, former land holders are encouraged to find their way into industrial investment.

Such is roughly the pattern of economic development which begins to emerge, and which I have classified as the national-revolutionary one. Both the socialist and the national-revolutionary patterns have one feature in common. Economic development is not spontaneous as in the classical capitalist pattern but is consciously achieved by planning.

Economic planning was originally an invention of the socialist economy. But now it is gradually spreading throughout the whole world. Planning has been adopted as an instrument of economic development by national-revolutionary countries, and the idea of planning even begins to penetrate the old capitalist economies. Thus, the new patterns of economic development, which I have briefly and very broadly outlined in this lecture, also lead to the development of a new technique of economic development, namely, of economic development by planning. Planning becomes the basic feature and instrument of economic development in our time.

Lecture II. Planning Economic Development

This second lecture will be devoted to the topic of planning economic development. Planning is a relatively new method of economic policy. It originated with the socialist economies and is an essential part of a socialist economy. Under conditions where the major part of the means of production become publicly owned, it is only natural that the utilization of these means and the process of production be subject to a general national economic plan. However, planning as a method of promoting economic development is no longer confined to socialist countries alone. It has spread first to the countries which follow, what I call, the national-revolutionary pattern of economic development. In these countries it has become—in a similar way as in the socialist countries— the main instrument of promoting economic development. More recently, the idea of planning is even spreading to the old capitalist countries as part of their growing preoccupation with economic development.

As was mentioned in my first lecture, in the capitalist countries up to the Second World War the main preoccupation was with problems of economic equilibrium; development was a spontaneous process and was not a subject of particular attention. But the rapid development of the socialist countries and the increasing importance of the problem of underdeveloped countries, which more and more adopt the national revolutionary pattern of economic progress, has created a challenge for the old capitalist countries. The challenge is twofold. First, not to stay behind the rapid rate of development of the socialist countries, to keep pace in the international competition between the socialist and the capitalist economic systems, which increasingly dominates the present world situation. Second, the need to find a solution to the problem of economic underdevelopment which has become a major issue in today's international politics. Thus, the idea of planning even reaches the old capitalist countries. The fact, that planning is connected with many international problems also raises the question of international co-operation in planning for economic development.

This evening I want to concentrate on the question of planning economic development. In the socialist countries and in the countries following a national-revolutionary pattern we plan economic development, because economic development would not, under existing historic conditions, take place by itself automatically. Consequently, it must be planned.

What is the essential of planning economic development? I would say that the essential consists in ensuring an amount of productive investment which is sufficient to provide for a rise of national income substantially in excess of the rise in population, so that *per capita* national income increases. The strategic factor is investment, or, more precisely, productive investment. Consequently, the problem of development planning is one of ensuring that there shall be sufficient productive investment, and, then, of directing that productive investment into such channels as will provide for the most rapid growth of the productive power in the national economy.

These are the essential tasks of development planning. The problems which planning faces can be divided into two categories. One is the mobilization of resources for purposes of productive investment; the other is suitable direction of investment. These are the essential problems involved in planning.

The first problem is that of mobilizing resources for investment. Taking the experience of the socialist countries and of the countries following a national revolutionary pattern, a certain picture of methods employed for that mobilization of resources can be drawn. These methods are: nationalization of industries, finance, trade and the use of the profits, thus derived, for purposes of investment. This method was widely applied in the socialist countries. The other method is nationalization of foreign owned natural resources and the use of the profits from these resources for investment purposes. This method plays a role in the countries following the national-revolutionary pattern.

A further method are the contributions by the peasantry in countries where agrarian reforms have been or are carried out. The peasants are required, in return, to make some contribution to state revenue which is partly used for purposes of investment. This frequently does not suffice and an appeal is made to resources derived from general taxation, public loans, and, in certain cases, also to deficit financing.

These methods of raising funds for investment are applied both in socialist and national-revolutionary countries to a varying degree. There is, also, a method which plays a particularly important role in the national revolutionary countries, and which in certain socialist countries during a transition period played its role too. This is the method of inducing private savers to undertake productive investment. It means inducing private industrialists, traders, landowners, and financial groups, to invest a considerable part of their income in ventures which are likely to lead to the country's rapid economic development; this means, essentially, investment in production. This can be achieved by various ways such as, for instance, taxation of unproductive uses of wealth, compulsory saving, restrictions on the distribution of profits and on uses of profits which do not result in productive investment, compulsory loans and all kinds of other measures. Finally, import of foreign capital may also be a source of financing productive investments. I shall not speak today of the latter source because tomorrow's lecture will deal with it in greater detail.

Thus, there is a whole catalogue of means applied in various proportions in different countries which provide the resources necessary for substantial productive investment. By substantial productive investment I mean investment which is large enough to achieve a breakthrough, or, as some economists call it—to produce the "take-off", the passage from stagnation to intensive development. This obviously cannot be done by small investments which are likely to peter out in a great number of minor projects. Sufficient investment is required to produce a real, a qualitative change in the structure of the national economy. This is one problem of developmental planning, namely, to secure such resources for productive investment.

The second problem is the direction of investment, and here I shall distinguish three sub-problems. The first is how to allocate investment so as to ensure the most rapid growth of production; the second is how to achieve balanced development of the economy, i.e., a balance between the different branches of the national economy; the third is how to ensure efficiency in the use of resources for economic development, and how to avoid their waste. These are three sub-problems of the general problem of directing investment so as to ensure economic development.

The first sub-problem is the most important one. It concerns the choice of investments which would most rapidly increase the productive capacity of the economy. It entails a concentration of investment in fields which increase the capacity of further production; this means building up industries which produce means of production. It is only by developing industries producing means of production that the production capacity of the economy can be raised.

This can be done, however, either directly or indirectly. It is done directly by investing in construction of, say, power plants, steel plants, machine building industries, extraction and processing of raw materials, and so on. It is done indirectly by foreign trade: instead of investing directly in the production, say, of certain machines it may be possible to obtain these machines from abroad by investing in the production of such commodities which can be sold abroad in order to import the machines in question. Thus the productive power of the economy can be increased either directly by investing in the production of means of production, or indirectly by developing export industries which make it possible to import future requirements in means of production. Which of these two methods is used depends on all kinds of circumstances, on existing facilities for developing either directly the output of means of production, or for producing commodities for export. However, if investment in exportable commodities is undertaken, then obviously it must be associated with importation of machinery, steel and other means of production to increase the country's productive power in exchange for these exports.

However, investment in the production of means of production is not the only type of investment needed. There are two complementary types of investment which are necessary. One is investment in agriculture to increase food production. The experience of economic planning, particularly in socialist countries, has shown that with the growth of industrialization, with an increasing number of the population being employed in industries or transport services and so on, a considerable surplus of agricultural products is needed to feed the non-agricultural population. Consequently, complementary to the investment in the development of the output of means of production must be investment in agriculture to increase agricultural output. There is also need for a certain amount of investment in industries producing consumer goods for the population, for the standard of living rises with the expansion of industrial employment and output. These are then the chief directions for developmental investments. The first is the strategic one, which brings about economic development, and the other two are of a complementary nature, necessary in order that economic development may proceed smoothly.

Finally, there is one important field of developmental investment, namely, investment in the general economic infrastructure of the country, such as transport facilities, roads and social services. They, too, are complementary investments needed to ensure smooth economic development. However, they by themselves are not a factor bringing about development. One of the problems in many, if not most, underdeveloped countries was—and this was a feature of the colonial or imperialist system—that construction of this economic infrastructure was pursued on a large scale purely for the needs of colonial exploitation, and not for the development of the productive power of the country.

In choosing various allocations of investment, or rather the right proportions between various allocations of investment, the problem of the choice of technology arises, i.e., the question whether to use labour or capital intensive methods of production. Very frequently it is being argued that since in underdeveloped countries there is available a large supply of unemployed or underemployed labour power, the most labour intensive methods should be chosen so as to bring about a rapid increase in employment.

Usually the situation is such that there is a distinction between the methods of production which employ much labour and those which are more productive in the sense of contributing to the increase of net output of the economy, i.e., of national income. Thus, there emerges a dilemma in underdeveloped countries whether to use methods which are less labour intensive, i.e., provide less employment, but increase rapidly output and national income, or whether to choose methods which are labour intensive but which lead to a slower rate of increase in output and national income. The decision to be made depends on the period for which you plan. If planning is made only for a short period, then one might argue that the most labour intensive method is the best because it leads most rapidly to the absorption of unemployment or underemployment.

However, if you take a longer view on development, then you find the following. By investing in methods, as well as in industries which yield a rapid increase in output, you achieve a more rapid increase in national income. If a certain proportion of national income, for instance 20%, is investment it turns out that by choosing the method and allocation of investment which more rapidly increases national income, even if less labour intensive, after a number of years national income will have grown to such an extent that the total amount of investment will become so great that it will provide more employment. Instead, a more labour intensive method would have led to a slower growth of national income, and consequently also to a slower increase in the absolute amount of investment. Thus, after a certain period it always pays—also from the point of view of employment—to use that method and that allocation of investment which contributes most to increasing the national income, i.e., the net product of society.

This is the basic principle to be observed in a plan which aims at a rapid increase in the productive power of the economy. It may be that a certain amount of unemployed labour can be "on the side" employed in ways which use little capital resources, and thus also be called upon to make some contribution to the increase in production and consequently in national income. This is being done very successfully in China. But still this is, so to speak, a secondary line of activity. The strategic activity in pursuing rapid development must involve such methods of production and such allocation of investments which most rapidly contribute to an increase in net output. In the long run, this proves to be the way which provides more employment than the alternative method of starting with labour intensive, but less productive investments simply in order to diminish underemployment.

In planning economic development, usually the problem of foreign trade turns out to be a major difficulty. The development of industry in any less developed country, requires in the initial stages, a considerable increase in imports of machinery, steel and other means of production. For, in the very beginning of economic development these cannot be produced at home, which immediately puts a burden on the balance of payments. In the second stage, when the basic industries, which create the country's productive potential, are already constructed and start producing, there arises a need for increased imports of various raw materials and also of further imports of machinery to continue the process of industrialization. The process of industrialization requires increased imports.

There are certain countries which are in a particularly fortunate position of having large exportable resources providing considerable revenues in foreign exchange. Before embarking on planned development, these revenues usually were not used, or were used only to a small extent for productive investment. Now they can be used for that purpose. To cite examples: in Iraq export of oil provides such a source of revenue, in Ceylon it is the export of rubber and tea. In the United Arab Republic cotton is such a source of revenue; I would also classify as such an exportable resource the Suez Canal. Countries which are in such a fortunate position have immediately available a certain amount of foreign exchange to import machines and other commodities necessary for industrial development.

Countries where such exportable resources do not exist or exist in small quantities have to go through a period of austerity in imports, cutting down on imports of consumer goods, particularly luxury goods, in order to free the exchange necessary to import producer goods and raw materials. Very frequently, it is exactly this necessity to impose a high degree of austerity on the consumption of imported goods which limits the possibility of rapid economic development. Here, of course, the situation can be aided by foreign capital, foreign loans, but this is a subject with which I want to deal in tomorrow's lecture. These are roughly the directions of investment required to ensure economic development. These investments, however, must be co-ordinated; balancing investment and production in the different branches of the national economy is another important aspect of planning.

There are two kinds of balances which must be established: one is the physical balance and the other is the financial or monetary balance. The physical balance consists in a proper evaluation of the relations between investment and output. In the countries which have already experience in economic planning investment coefficients are computed. These coefficients indicate the amount of investment and also the composition of that investment in terms of various kinds of goods needed in order to obtain an increase in output of a product by a given amount. For example, how much iron, how much coal, how much electric power is needed in order to produce an additional ton of steel. On this basis, the planned increase in output of various products is balanced with the amounts and types of investment. It is also necessary to balance the outputs of the various sections of the economy because, as we know, the output of one branch of the economy serves as input for producing the output of another branch. For instance, the output of iron ore serves as an input in the steel industry. In the last mentioned field a special technique, that of input–output analysis, has been developed.

The physical balancing mentioned is necessary in order that the output of the different branches of the economy proceeds smoothly. This is a condition of the internal consistency of the plan. If this condition is not observed bottlenecks appear. The plan cannot be carried out because of physical obstacles, such as lack of raw materials, of manpower, etc.

The second kind of balancing is monetary balancing, ensuring monetary equilibrium in the economy. This consists in establishing equilibrium between the incomes of the population—wages, incomes of peasants and others—and the amount of consumer goods made available to the population. If the amount of incomes, or, more precisely, that part of the incomes which is spent for purposes of consumption, should turn out to be greater than the amount of available consumer goods, inflationary processes will develop. Thus, the financial or monetary balance must establish an equilibrium between the part of incomes devoted to consumption and the output of consumer goods. Further, it must establish equilibrium between the part of incomes of the population which will be used for private investment and the amount of investment goods made available to private investors. Finally, in the public sector a balance must be established between the financial funds made available for investment purposes and the amount of investment goods which will be produced or imported. In addition to these balances, it is necessary to establish a balance of foreign payments and receipts. The financial balances are an important part of planning. Just as the lack of physical balance leads to physical obstacles in the smooth process of production, so the lack of financial balance leads to disturbances in the supply and demand for commodities, and finally also to physical disturbances in the process of production.

Looking back upon the experience of the countries which applied planning as a tool of economic development, I must say that it usually turned out to be difficult to maintain the proper financial balance. Few of these countries escaped inflationary processes during certain periods. These processes were due to the wage bill rising more rapidly than the output of consumer goods. However, in theory and with the experience which has been gained in earlier years it is today quite possible to plan financial equilibrium of economic development in a way which avoids inflationary processes.

A last point—to be only mentioned briefly—is that of ensuring efficiency in the use of resources in the process of economic development. This is connected with the use of the price system. The function of the price system in economic planning is twofold. Prices serve as a means of accounting, namely, as a means of evaluating the cost of production, the value of output, and of comparing the two. For this purpose it is necessary to have a proper price system which reflects the social cost (and in the short run—scarcity) of the various means of production and the social importance of the various products. Without such a price system, cost accounting would not have any objective economic significance. This is one role of the price system: the other role is that of an incentive.

The plan of economic development has two aspects: in the public sector it is a directive to various public agencies and enterprises to do certain things, e.g., to invest that much in such a way, to produce in such a way at such a cost. With regard to the private sector, the plan has not the power of a directive, but is a desire expressed which must be followed by creating such incentives as will induce private producers to do exactly the things which are required from them in the plan. It is quite clear and does not require any further explanation that, with regard to the private sector, the price system, including interest rates, is an important incentive serving to induce the private sector to do things required of it in the plan. But in the public sector too there is a need for incentives. It is not sufficient just to address administrative directives to public agencies and public enterprises. In addition to this, it is necessary to create such economic incentives that the public agencies, enterprises, etc., find it in the interest of their management and their employees to do the things which are required of them in the plan. This again requires a suitable price system.

Thus, the price system plays in planning a role both as a basis of accounting and as an incentive inducing the people to do the things required of them in the plan. A certain general observation may be made here. It seems rather general historical experience that in the first phase of economic development, particularly of industrialization, the problem of a proper price system is not the most important one. In both the socialist and the national-revolutionary type of economic development we find that in the first period the main problem is not that of the details of accounting or incentives. The main problem is to ensure rapid growth of productive capacity. The question of speed of growth overshadows the more subtle questions of high grade efficiency. It is more important, for instance, to develop at all cost the machine industry than to do it in the most efficient manner. Too much preoccupation with the subtleties of economic accounting may hold up action and slow down progress. It is only at a higher stage of economic development, when the national economy has become more complex and diversified, that the problems of efficiency and incentives become increasingly important. It is then that the subtleties of ensuring the highest efficiency in the economy by suitable cost accounting, by properly established incentives, etc., come into play.

Thus—without wanting to minimize the importance of the problem—I do believe that it is not the most important problem in the first stage of economic development. In this first stage, the take-off stage, the real issue is to mobilize the necessary resources for productive investment, to allocate them to the branches of the economy which most rapidly increase the productive potential of the country, and to do so by the most productive technological methods. At a later stage, more subtle aspects of planning come into play. Thus, a certain crudeness of planning in the early stages of economic development is, I believe, quite justified.

These are briefly the points I wanted to make in today's lecture. I have only very briefly mentioned the international aspects of economic planning and of economic development. These are the aspects with which I want to deal in my next and last lecture.

Lecture III. Economic Development and International Co-operation

I intend to speak this evening of international co-operation and economic development. The problem of international co-operation acquires today new and important features. This is due to the coexistence in the present world economy of the three patterns of economic development of which I have spoken. It is the coexistence of countries with a capitalist system, countries with a socialist system, and countries which follow, what I call, the national revolutionary pattern of development. Coexistence and, at the same time, competition of the capitalist and socialist systems, on the one side, the question of economic underdevelopment and of national revolutions with their economic consequences, on the other side, face the world economy with new problems.

The problems essentially are threefold. One is the problem of international trade under conditions where there are various economic systems and patterns of development in the world economy. The second is the problem of aid, and it is usually formulated in terms of aid to the underdeveloped countries which underwent or are undergoing national revolutions. The third problem is political in origin, but has important economic consequences, namely, the problem of disarmament.

It is this last problem which I shall consider first. I shall consider it first because disarmament has become the paramount political problem of our days and because its economic consequences will have important repercussions on international trade and also on the problem of action on behalf of underdeveloped countries. I do not intend to discuss here the political aspect of the problem of disarmament. With the destructive power of modern weapons, the problem of disarmament has become a problem of life and death for the human race. I think it is sufficient to mention this in so far as its political aspects go. But there are economic problems involved in disarmament. These problems have a different aspect in socialist and in capitalist economies.

Radical and rapid disarmament creates certain economic problems also in a socialist economy. The problems are those of reallocation of large resources—industrial plants, equipment, raw materials and also human manpower—from production for armaments to production for non-military purposes. Obviously, when such reallocation is to take place rapidly on a large scale, there arise certain problems of readjustment, of new directions of production, of transfer of manpower, of organization of economic activities. In a socialist economy these problems are largely problems of proper planning and of management of the national economy. The difficulties are of a character which economists usually denote by the word "frictions". There are all kinds of frictional obstacles involved in the transfer of manpower and in the reallocation of resources. With proper planning, however, and proper managerial skill, they can be overcome.

The problems are more complicated in the capitalist economy. There, too, frictional difficulties arise. But in addition, they entail a special type of problem which is peculiar to the mechanism of the capitalist economy. This is the question of effective demand. A large-scale and rapid reduction in expenditure on armaments reduces the demand for the products of armament industries. These reduce their output and employment, which lead to a reduction in effective demand by the population. A further reduction in the demand for consumer and investment goods usually follows. This, in turn, leads to further falls in output and employment. The process may become cumulative, causing a recession or even a depression and, consequently, mass unemployment. Therefore, we find in the leading capitalist countries, particularly in the U.S.A., serious apprehension concerning the economic consequences of disarmament. Frequently, we observe that whenever the political situation becomes favourable to prospects of disarmament, quotations on the Stock Exchange begin to fall.

This, however, does not mean that it is impossible for the capitalist countries to carry out disarmament without running into recession or even depression. It only means that, under conditions of a capitalist economy, disarmament must be accompanied by certain measures of economic policy which are designed to counterbalance, to compensate the fall-out in effective demand and to prevent the fall-out from generating a cumulative reduction of economic activity. This is possible by means of internal measures activating public or private investment, and also by certain measures in the field of international economic co-operation. It is about the last mentioned measures that I want to speak.

One such measure is the increase in international trade; another is planned action to aid the economic progress of underdeveloped countries. I believe that measures of economic policy in these two fields can compensate in the capitalist economies the fall-out of effective demand caused by disarmament; moreover, they can even overcompensate it, and create new conditions for economic development. At the same time, disarmament in the leading capitalist and socialist countries can free important resources, which could be utilized in an international programme of economic development of the less developed areas of the world. Various proposals have been made to use part of the financial and physical resources saved by disarmament to promote economic development in those areas of the world which are most in need of such development. Consequently, the consideration of the economic implications of disarmament leads us to the problem of international trade and to the problem of planned aid to underdeveloped countries.

Let us consider the question of international trade. After the Second World War international trade suffered extensively by the cold war. The cold war, for a certain period, had greatly reduced, and in certain cases almost stopped, trade between capitalist and socialist countries. It also has affected very strongly the foreign trade possibilities of the underdeveloped countries in Asia, Africa and Latin America. For the trade connections of these countries were subjected, or at least attempts were made to subject them, to considerations of cold war policies imposed by the great capitalist powers. In the last few years the international political atmosphere has improved, there was considerable relaxation of international tension and many of the underdeveloped countries have freed themselves from the influence of cold war pressure. The emancipated countries have used their newly won freedom in economic policy to develop trade relations not only with capitalist but also with socialist countries, thus extending their area of choice of trade partners and thereby gaining a better position in international trade relations.

But, we still are far from having exhausted the opportunities of expanding international trade. In Europe, for instance, trade between the countries of Eastern and Western Europe, though it has increased in the last years, is far below the potential possibilities. The situation is even worse in Asia where many countries are still prevented from maintaining normal trade relationships with socialist countries, particularly with China. Consider the absence of any significant trade between Japan and China, which, from the point of view of economic geography, is sheer nonsense. The development of foreign trade relations, unhampered by consideration of the cold war, can provide for all partners concerned great opportunities of economic progress.

The most important factor in this field is the rapid development of the socialist economies. It may suffice to say that the present five-year plans of the socialist countries signify that by 1965 approximately half of the world's industrial output will be produced in the socialist countries. As socialist countries comprise 35% of the world's population, this means that the *per capita* output in the socialist countries will by 1965 be higher than that in the rest of the world, though not higher, but still lower, than in most highly developed countries of Western Europe and the U.S.A.

Of the whole world population 19% live in the developed capitalist countries, 35% in the socialist countries, and 46% in countries which until recently were dependent on the leading capitalist countries and now are at various stages of their process of emancipation or of struggle for emancipation. Given such a situation, it is obvious that the socialist countries will increasingly provide a market for exports and will become a source of supplies, particularly in the field of industrial products. Thus, if we manage to remove the restrictions on international trade which were built up during the cold war, we may look forward to a substantial increase in international trade.

This is particularly important for the underdeveloped countries, more so for countries which are exporters of raw materials and in whose economic life exports of raw materials play an important part. These countries have suffered in the last few years very heavily from a fall in prices of raw materials. Thus, in the period from 1953 to 1958 raw material prices fell by 7%, while industrial prices rose by 4%. In the two years of the last economic recession in the leading capitalist countries, in 1957 and 1958, the raw materials exporting countries lost in consequence of the fall of their export prices $2 billion each year. This shows the importance of foreign trade conditions for the underdeveloped countries. It turns out that during the years 1957 and 1958 the loss suffered by these countries, due to the fall in prices of exported raw materials, was equal to the amount of loans obtained from the International Bank for Reconstruction and Development over the last 6 years. The loss resulting from the fall in export prices probably counterbalanced, and, may be, even exceeded, the amount of foreign loans the underdeveloped countries received. Thus, regularization and expansion of foreign trade is essential to the economic progress of the underdeveloped parts of the world.

This, however, is not sufficient. In addition, the underdeveloped countries need capital from the more advanced countries. Speaking of the need of foreign capital for the underdeveloped countries, it must be clearly realized that economic development of these countries cannot be based on foreign aid. It must be based on the mobilization of internal resources. If we really want to develop all that part of the world in which 46% of humanity lives, then the capital resources which both the leading capitalist countries and the leading socialist countries can put at the disposal of such a development are insufficient. Therefore, an internal effort for capital accumulation must be the basis of economic development. However, foreign capital may play an important auxiliary role, facilitating the situation particularly in the so-called "take-off" period, and even in the early period of self-sustained development. It is precisely in these early stages of development that machinery and raw materials are needed, but the industries are not yet ready to provide sufficient products for export purposes. In such a transitional period foreign capital aid may be of great and even crucial importance.

With regard to foreign capital, we have to face one very important fact. This is the declining role of private international capital movements. This decline is of a structural and permanent character. It is the result of the very process of emancipation of the former colonial or otherwise dependent countries, of their embarking upon the national-revolutionary road of development. Under these historic conditions, the requirements of private capital ready to be invested in such countries, and the requirements of these countries in terms of what they may expect from foreign investment are very different and not easy to reconcile.

In the imperialist period, which started with the last quarter of the nineteenth century, private capital investment in underdeveloped countries did not follow the classical pattern described in the old textbooks of economics. It was investment of monopoly capital reaping exceedingly high profits not because of its economic contribution but because of political domination over the country in which the investment was made. Political domination provided monopoly privileges and possibilities of excluding competition of capital from other countries. This also led to the consequence that foreign capital investment was largely of a specifically colonial type and did not set in motion a process of economic development of the dependent countries.

With the progress of the movement for emancipation from colonial and imperialist domination, these terms of investment became impossible. The once very important inducement to investment in the less developed countries—the particular privileges foreign capital enjoyed in the undeveloped countries—disappeared. In addition, another problem emerged;

namely, the problem of safety of the foreign investment, safety of private foreign capital. This problem arose already in the early period of capital exports in the nineteenth century. At that time, it was a question of safety for investment from capitalist countries in the less developed countries from arbitrary expropriation and restrictions imposed by pre-capitalist governments of a feudal or even more primitive type. The desire to ensure the safety of investment became a powerful force behind colonial expansion, behind establishing colonial or other forms of domination in the countries where pre-capitalist conditions prevailed.

Later, there came a period when international private investments flourished. These investments, however, increasingly became monopolistic in character. At present, there is concern about the safety of private investments, i.e., concern about their safety from nationalization. The financial circles in the leading capitalist countries, when asked about investment in the underdeveloped areas of the world, always put the question of guarantees; guarantees first of all against nationalization. Here the basic conflict between the requirements of private investors from leading capitalist countries and of the countries entering upon national-revolutionary development becomes apparent.

Of course, certain guarantees can be given by national-revolutionary governments to various foreign capitalist groups. Such guarantees, however, must of necessity be limited to certain groups and in scope. For the national-revolutionary governments cannot give guarantees which would prevent the national-revolutionary states from exercising their sovereignty in determining their own pattern of economic development. The requirements of economic development of the national-revolutionary countries differ from the interests of foreign capital investors. This fact is crucial in the historic period in which we live, and it limits the possibilities of promoting the flow of international private capital to underdeveloped countries on a large scale. Such movements are not entirely excluded, but their role is limited and on the decline. They cannot play any more the historic role of an important factor in economic development. Their significance becomes of secondary or even tertiary importance.

One aspect of international private investments deserves particular attention. The classical type of foreign investment by the leading capitalist countries was direct investment. But precisely for reasons of

maintaining and asserting their national sovereignty, the new independent countries want loans rather than direct investments. This factor
limits very strongly the future of private capital investments.

International investments which increasingly dominate the scene in
the present period are of two types. One is investment based on bilateral
agreements between states. This type of investment is today adopted by
the socialist countries in their relations with the countries following the
national-revolutionary pattern of development, as, for instance, in the
case of the Soviet Union and the United Arab Republic in constructing
the Aswan High Dam. The same type of investment grows in importance
even in relations between capitalist countries and the national-revolutionary countries. Relations of state to state or sometimes relations of
private capitalists in the capitalist countries and the state in the national-
revolutionary countries occur today with increasing frequency.

The type of investment mentioned increasingly replaces in importance
private capital investments of the classical type. Direct investments of
private capitalists in the less developed countries make room for loans
by private capitalists or by the state to the newly independent states. In
the field of international investments a certain important development
has taken place. The socialist countries, in particular the Soviet Union,
the largest of them, have entered the field of aid to countries developing
according to a national-revolutionary pattern. Soviet aid in conjunction
with other socialist countries has already influenced, and will increasingly influence, the types of investment made by capitalist countries in
the countries following the national-revolutionary pattern of development.

This has become quite clear, for instance, in the case of India. The
United Arab Republic may also serve as an example. The active role of
the socialist countries, particularly of the Soviet Union, in promoting
capital aid to the national-revolutionary countries has caused a change
in the investment policy of the leading capitalist states and of the leading
private capitalist groups. It has forced these states and groups to
abandon, to a certain extent, the old type of colonial investments, and to
adopt new types which are directly conducive to the development of the
industrial potential of the new countries. In the case of India, the policy
of the leading capitalist groups in Great Britain was rather adverse to
fostering industrial development, and particularly the development of
heavy industries. But the moment the Indian State started to develop

a steel industry with investment aid from the Soviet Union, British capitalists were quite ready to come in and provide a loan for the development of the Indian steel industry.

The foreign aid policy of the socialist countries has forced capitalist countries and private capitalist monopolies to revise their investment policy in a way beneficial to the development of the national-revolutionary countries. This process is only in its beginnings; it works already in India and in the United Arab Republic; it still does not work in many other underdeveloped countries. I am sure, however, that we are seeing the beginning of this process, and the greater the activity of other socialist countries and of the Soviet Union in this field, the more the leading capitalist groups and their governments will have to revise their investment policies. There arises, however, the problem of co-ordination of such international investment activities, and in particular the problem of an international programme for the development of the widely underdeveloped areas within the world economy. Such a co-ordinated international investment programme would have to be undertaken by, or at least under the auspices of, international organizations.

Since quite some time the countries of Asia, Africa and Latin America have been demanding the United Nations to set up an agency for financing development projects in these countries. Certain steps have been taken in this field by the United Nations, though they are of a very limited character. But should disarmament really be carried out on a large scale, some part of the resources thus saved in the budgets of various countries might be used for purposes of international economic development. If this should happen, the question of international investment projects financed by international agencies will become of increasing importance. Thus, we may look forward to a future where important international economic development will be financed by funds provided by international agencies, which, of course, means by agencies, in one way or another, under the auspices of the United Nations. However, though it seems to me that such a future prospect is clearly on the horizon, I think that the situation at the moment is not yet ripe for it. The last experience of the United Nations' action in the Congo has shown that the United Nations executive organs are not yet a truly international body. They are used to reassert colonial or neo-colonial policies. In the long run, the United Nations undoubtedly will play an increasing role in the planning and financing of international economic development. But at the moment, the United Nations executive machine is still too much under the influence of imperialist and colonial powers to be suitable for such a task. None the less, the process of maturing of the United Nations Organization will proceed. With the growing economic and political significance of the struggle for colonial emancipation of national-revolutionary countries, together with the further growth of the economic potential and of the political significance of the socialist countries, the United Nations will gradually mature to perform this new task.

We can look forward to the United Nations becoming a truly international agency which will no longer be used for purposes of reasserting colonial or semi-colonial policies, as unfortunately was the case recently. Then, the United Nations will be able to play their role as an instrument of international economic co-operation and international planning and financing economic development.

International co-operation for economic development is not limited to action in the underdeveloped areas of the world. Even the most developed countries in the world could benefit from such action. Countries like the United States and the Soviet Union, which today are the leading industrial powers of the world, can too undertake common projects for economic development. Actually, various scientists have already proposed such projects, as for instance connecting the United States, the Soviet Union and Western Europe by a railway through Alaska and the Asiatic and European continents.

I do not want to evaluate the technical or economic feasibility of such projects. I just mention them to show that even the most developed industrial countries can find a useful field for commonly planned economic co-operation. There is also the possibility of economic co-operation in the field of scientific and technical research which will grow in importance. Already we have reached a situation where certain fields of scientific and technical research, such as the utilization of atomic power or the conquest of space, are not accessible to smaller countries simply because they do not have sufficient economic resources for such research.

The time will come when even the largest countries will not be able to afford the expenses in certain fields of scientific and technical research and will have to pull together their resources. But already at the present stage smaller countries which are interested in co-operation in the scientific and technical fields may pull together their resources. In particular, countries which follow the national-revolutionary pattern of development may wish to pull their resources together on a regional basis.

This brings me to the question of regional arrangements in co-operation for economic development. Such regional arrangements may play an important role in bringing together certain countries with their resources to provide for economic development. Co-operation on a broader geographical scale depends on the political situation; it requires relaxation of international tension and peaceful coexistence between countries following different patterns of development. Such coexistence opens great possibilities for concerted action in the field of economic development.

One thing, however, has to be made clear, namely, what peaceful coexistence and co-operation can mean and what it cannot mean. It can mean all that I have said about pulling together resources for international development plans to the benefit of all the partners concerned. It cannot mean halting the processes of social progress and social change. International co-operation is not possible on the terms that the struggle for emancipation from colonial rule must stop, and that nations which have not yet gained their independence must give up their aspirations and objectives. Neither is international co-operation possible on the terms that social changes shall not take place in countries which are mature, where the economic and social structure requires such changes and the population wants them. Economic co-operation cannot mean a freezing of the *status quo* of imperialist, colonial domination or of antiquated economic and social systems.

To nourish such expectations would be unrealistic; we must face the realities of the situation. Peaceful coexistence and international co-operation, however, can mean that such changes which become necessary and cannot be prevented must take place by peaceful means and in a way which does not make them a cause of increasing international tension, and in particular a cause of war. This is what we realistically can aspire to: a situation where by means of international co-operation, necessary political and economic adjustments, national emancipation and economic and social progress are achieved in a peaceful way. To be workable, conditions for continuous progress must be created in which the people of the world will improve their economic, social and cultural position. This is the type of international co-operation we all can look forward to realistically, co-operation which we can expect and which certainly is worth striving for.

PROSPECTS OF ECONOMIC SCIENCE UNDER SOCIALISM

I do not know whether, or to what extent, it is possible to talk of a turning point in political economy or in economic science. This depends partly on the meaning attached to the notion of a turning point in science. There is no doubt, however, that for political economy (I am thinking here of Marxist political economy, since it is the only kind which merits consideration as a science embracing all socio-economic problems) and other economic sciences, such as the economics of particular sectors or economic statistics, significant new problems have arisen, with which these sciences have already begun to deal, or with which they will have to deal in the near future.

There are two types of problems here. One concerns new developments in capitalism; the second concerns the political economy of socialism. Yet a third type of problem might be mentioned, namely, the problem which results from the coexistence in the world economy of capitalist and socialist countries. Here, however, I should like to consider only the problem, which concerns the political economy of socialism. This kind of problem is naturally closest to us and is of greatest immediate practical significance for the direction and management of our economy.

The political economy of socialism is a new feature of political economy if only because the socialist system is itself young. Thus, the political economy of socialism is only at a formative stage. There are several problems which have already arisen in this field and which are today the subject of scientific debate in all the socialist countries. One of these problems is that of priorities in the development of the national economy, which is the basic problem of planning. Next, is the problem of the role of the law of value and prices in a socialist economy; and finally, the problem of economic incentives. These various problems are, moreover, closely connected with each other. Thus, for example, the question of the law of value is both a question of relative priorities of the constituent parts of the national economy and a problem of economic incentives. Undoubtedly, the political economy of socialism has already made certain achievements in these fields. Various problems have been worked out, and others are in the process of being elaborated and discussed, and presumably at some time in the not too distant future we shall have more concrete scientific results.

Connected with this, there is the development of the economics of particular sectors, such as the economics of agriculture, of industry and of trade, and of sciences which are auxiliary to economics, such as the sciences of economic planning, of econometrics, and even of what we may call borderline sciences, such as cybernetics. These subjects are of considerable significance for the development of economic science, and especially for its practical application to the management of the socialist economy.

In dealing with problems of management of the socialist economy and of the methodology of its planning, it must be emphasized that the characteristic feature of the socialist economy—in contrast to the capitalist and pre-capitalist economies—is that it is based on scientific principles. One can state categorically that socialism is the great historical undertaking to give social life a scientific foundation. From this stems the peculiar significance of political economy and other economic sciences, and of the various subsidiary sciences, as far as the direction and management of the socialist economy is concerned. Socialism (that is, socialist relations in production) makes it possible to direct economic life in a way which is rational from the point of view of society as a whole. But this possibility must be turned into reality; and it is precisely here that the nature of economic science is of great importance. Whether the possibilities opened up by socialist relations in production are put to good use or not depends on the state of economic science. In other words, the efficiency with which the socialist economy functions depends, among other things, on the state of the economic sciences.

In this context, an important role can be played by the new methodological elements which are today appearing with increasing frequency. We all know that there is a growing tendency to make economic research more mathematical. This tendency is very much in evidence in this country, and it can also be seen in the Soviet Union and several other socialist countries. It is brought about by the demands made on economic science by the socialist economy. Indeed, we continually have to deal with quantitative factors such as the level of production, costs, profits, and prices, and it is clear that this inescapably calls for a precise mathematical approach. Moreover, there are fields in which the application of mathematical methods plays a particular role. Such a field is the forecasting of what are known as autonomous social processes, a knowledge of which is necessary in planning—for example, the projection of the growth of population and of its age structure in future years. In this case, it is the science of mathematical demography which enables such forecasting to be made. In the realm of forecasting I would also generally include econometric research on the future pattern of demand, and in particular the dependence of demand upon national income.

The new elements in the methodology of economic investigation also include the theory of programming, which is directly connected with planning. A plan must fulfil two conditions: above all, it must be internally consistent; there should be no inconsistencies in it such as would arise, for example, if the planned growth of certain outputs were to result in a greater consumption of coal, say, than its planned output. A plan containing such a contradiction could not be internally consistent. Thus, the planner's first task is to establish methodological criteria which ensure the internal consistency of the plan. This is achieved by means of balancing. Secondly, the plan must be optimal: it must give maximum results for a given expenditure or, which comes to the same thing, achieve a given result with minimum expenditure.

In the context of the effectiveness of planning, the most important problem is the effectiveness of investment, that is, the influence of investment on the growth of national income. Here again, an analysis must be made (partly using mathematical means) of alternative investment projects and their variants from the point of view both of results and how they are obtained, and of the expenditure involved. This is further connected with the problem of value and prices, which must be considered in order to arrive at a true evaluation of this expenditure. This whole field of science is usually called the theory of programming, which applies new methods to the planning and management of the socialist economy.

I have already mentioned cybernetics. This is a science which arose in fields far removed from economic problems, in the course of the automatic processes which occur in organisms. For example, there is an analogy between the automatic process of temperature regulation in the human organism and certain automatic mechanisms used in industry.

Against this background, an entirely new science has been built up which unexpectedly proved to be of great significance in some important problems of management of the socialist economy.

The role of cybernetics can best be explained by an example with which we are all familiar. At one time, we were involved in a very animated discussion on the economic model, and the pertinent theme of centralization and decentralization. We know that on the whole the socialist economy is and must be centrally directed. Without this, it would develop haphazardly, and the conscious shaping of economic development would be impossible. Thus, centralism in the planning of such an economy is essential. On the other hand, we also know that a certain degree of decentralization in everyday management is necessary, if only to ensure flexibility in the operation of the economy. Hence, in the course of this discussion we tried, on the basis of previous experience, to determine empirically the optimum relationship between centralization and decentralization. It is now apparent that for this kind of problem the conceptual apparatus developed by cybernetics gives us certain scientific criteria. Moreover, in our example cybernetics gives a very simple answer: decentralization is necessary where the time needed for the flow of information from the outfield to the centre, for the transformation of this information at the centre into a decision, and the transmission of the decision from the centre back to the outfield is so long that certain irreversible changes many have meanwhile taken place in the outfield, thus rendering the decision inoperative.

Here, we have two problems: the time taken for the information and answer to be relayed, and the capacity of the centre to transform information into decisions. How important this is, is shown by our difficulties prior to 1956. When, towards the end of the six-year plan period, complex, unforeseen problems became apparent to the management of the economy, attempts were made to remedy them by greater centralization. But this not only proved unsuccessful and did not bring the situation under control but increased the number of unforeseen developments, since decisions arrived too late. I give this example in order to show the importance which the problems faced by cybernetics have for the management of the socialist economy. I would say that we are still far from a systematic science for the management of the socialist economy, and hence of its optimal organization, by centralization and decentralization, of the way in which incentives operate within it, and of the methods of choosing optimal variants. But the economists of the socialist countries are already carrying out research into it, and considerable achievements in this field can probably soon be expected.

The more general hypothesis can be postulated of socialism as a young system only just beginning to produce results. We have passed through our painful period of construction in difficult conditions of economic backwardness, war, reconstruction, and so on, and results are only now becoming apparent. Certainly, this is only the beginning of the process. But one of its effects will be, indeed, the development of the science of management of the economy, which is essential if the economy is to be made efficient and if socialist relations in production are to realize all those possibilities which they contain, but which can be realized only by conscious and co-ordinated effort.

Turning to the prediction of the lines along which the economic sciences will develop in the future, I have a vital reservation to make. It is my opinion that no forecast can be made which would be applicable to all countries. I know, for example, that in the Soviet Union at the present time, pride of place in scientific discussion is held by the question of the price system—a rational, scientifically drawn up price system—as the basis of economic accounting and as the means of establishing economic incentives. As far as Poland is concerned, it seems to me that, in the near future, the dominant problems will be in a sense more practical than theoretical. I have in mind the problem of economic incentives. We have already discussed the model at length, at the time of the last elections to the House of Representatives (Seym); and many of these changes in the organization of the economy were carried out. The independence of the enterprise was increased to a considerable extent. The associations were set up as associations of enterprises, and not as agencies of the ministerial organs. An entirely new system of industrial management was established: ministry–association–enterprise. A new investment model was developed, covering the role of central investment, of investment by associations, and of investment by the enterprise. Enterprises and associations were given a certain amount of autonomy in carrying out their investment projects. Further, the administration of the national councils was made independent, and they were provided with their own financial base; in addition, the management of a substantial section of the economy was handed over to them, namely, trade, regional industry, and regional planning. The national councils were even given an advisory voice in the drawing up of plans for key industries situated in their areas, and there is now self-government for workers and co-operatives. On the organizational side, the role of the co-operatives was increased; for example, co-operatives for dairy produce were reintroduced and housing co-operatives were developed. Thus, on the organizational side there were very considerable changes.

To conclude and summarize these changes, we must examine them and see how they look and operate in practice. Here the problem of incentives comes to the forefront, for these organizational changes introduced a certain system of incentives. By granting independence to enterprises, for example, it became necessary to establish incentives for these enterprises to exercise their independence in a desired manner; otherwise, independence would have been harmful. In short, these organizational changes had to be synchronized with a system of incentives. In this field it can be said—from everyday experience without scientific analysis—that we are continually faced with very great difficulties. For this reason, too, the question of organization and incentives will be, in my opinion, one of the most important topics for theoretical and practical development. Indeed, I personally believe that this problem will be a matter for the Economic Council; but in any case, it ought to be.

The last question of our enquiry concerns the evaluation of research staff and of studies. In my opinion, both our research cadres and our system of economic studies are good and up to the required standards. Our economic journals and other publications such as: *Ekonomista* (The Economist), *Gospodarka Planowa* (The Planned Economy), *Przegląd Statystyczny* (Statistical Review) are sufficient evidence of this. It can be justifiably claimed that from the research point of view, Poland today is becoming one of the leading countries in the field of political economy. This is happening even though unfortunately, due to the limited ambit of the Polish language, not everything finds its way abroad. But the interest in Polish economic thought, in both socialist and capitalist countries, is enormous. However, there is the further problem of the proper use of these cadres and their achievements. So far, the contact between research work and economic life and practice is by far too inadequate, resulting in a particular disparity in activity. On the one hand, practice does not benefit from, or does not make sufficient use of, the help which research can give it; and on the other hand, theoreticians often begin to lose contact with practical experience, partly because they are not engaged in practical pursuits. I feel it is essential that a sensible solution to this problem be found quickly. Nevertheless, it must be emphasized that in spite of these difficulties, some progress has been made. As far as econometric methods are concerned, they are today widely applied by the Planning Commission and the Ministries of Internal and of Foreign Trade. One need only recall the last instruction drawn up by the Planning Commission for the purpose of investigating the effectiveness of investment. This is binding on all the larger, more important investors. Without going into a detailed analysis of the merits of this instruction, it should nevertheless be pointed out that it is the result of considerable research which has, I believe, aroused great interest in other socialist countries.

I consider this type of development, which helps to solve major practical problems, to be particularly important and necessary at the present time. I am not referring to the practical requirements of day to day administration, but to the importance of contact between practice and theory. It is precisely in this field of contact between theoretical research work and practice, in the form of directing and managing the economy, that I would look for an overall solution of the tasks which our economic science is at present facing.

Mobilization of Public Effort and Participation in the National Economic Plan

As already indicated, realization of the national plan of economic development requires active participation of all citizens of the country. Such participation is needed in order to make full use of all human, natural and capital resources of the country. This participation must be suitably organized and channelled in the directions contributing to the realization of the national plan of development. It therefore must be part of this plan. The programme of such participation can be considered under the following headings:

(*i*) *A national saving campaign.* The need for such a campaign is obvious. The larger the savings available, the greater are the opportunities of planned developmental investment without causing danger of inflation. Savings campaigns are already being organized in Ceylon. However, it seems that the announcement of the national economic development plan should be connected with a forceful savings campaign. The fact that the campaign is tied up with the larger national plan of economic development which is designed to bring about a basic change in the economic conditions of the country, would have a much greater impact than isolated savings campaigns can have.

(*ii*) *Active participation of rural areas.* As the great majority of the population lives in the rural areas it is of particular importance that the rural population participate actively in the realization of the plan. Only by such participation is it possible to achieve full productive utilization of the many scattered human, natural and capital resources of the country. For this purpose, it is advisable to put immediately into practice proposals laid down in the Report of the Subcommittee on Rural Participation in Development attached to the First Interim Report of the National Planning Council on Village Councils and Village Committees, and the proposals contained in the Agricultural Plan on multi-purpose co-operative societies. Indeed, these proposals should be made part of the "Immediate Action Programme".

According to the proposals mentioned, each village should have a development plan of its own to be carried out under the guidance of the Village Council with the aid of the multi-purpose co-operative society or village development society. In a similar way, district development plans would have to be carried out under the guidance of Regional Councils. However, if the Village Councils and the Regional Councils are really to be capable of organizing active participation of the people, their membership must consist of persons enjoying the confidence of the villagers. Elected representatives of Village Committees and other elected representatives must play a prominent part. They cannot be bodies appointed from above or consisting of only *ex officio* members.

The Village and the Regional plans would have to provide for such possible economic development which can be achieved by the utilization of local resources. The great economic potential entailed in the utilization of local resources by planned development activity on a village and regional level is shown by China's recent experiences. In China, utilization of local resources has become a major factor in the transformation of the economic and social structure of the country.

(*iii*) *Participation of town areas.* In a similar way, as village and regional plans, towns too should have their own economic development plans based on the utilization of local resources. Such plans may refer to the development of schools, sanitation and other civic projects. However, care must be taken that they rely entirely on local resources which would otherwise remain unutilized, and that they do not draw from resources required for the general economic development plan.

(*iv*) *Participation of economic and civic organizations.* Organizations such as Chambers of Commerce, Co-operatives, Trade Unions, and other organizations should be drawn in on a voluntary basis, and made to participate in the national plan by contributing to the utilization of such resources within the domain of their activities which otherwise would remain unutilized.

In organizing the active participation of rural areas, town areas, economic and civic organizations, particular care must be taken that such participation is based on the utilization of local resources, otherwise unutilized. The danger must be avoided that it becomes a drain upon resources of a non-local character which are allocated in the plan to purposes of general economic development.

In this way, all sections of the population of Ceylon might be made to participate actively in the realization of the plan of economic development. Such participation would have a double effect: a direct economic effect consisting in utilizing all potential resources of the nation, and an indirect effect of making the nation plan conscious and thus increase the general effort and individual contribution of every citizen to the realization of the national plan of economic development. Planned economic development to be successful must be designed for the people. In order to be carried out effectively it must be carried out by the people as a great national enterprise, the vision of which captures the imagination of every man and woman and creates in them the ambition to do their best for the development of the country.

THE ROLE OF SCIENCE
IN THE DEVELOPMENT OF A SOCIALIST SOCIETY

Under social systems preceding socialism, the process of man's control over nature developed fortuitously; from the point of view of human aims, it was a chance process. The social effects of this process were even more so fortuitous and unintentional, and often simply contrary to human desires. The development of human societies was a process independent of human will, a result of social forces which evaded control by man and opposed him as an apparently superhuman power. Man was unaware of the operation of these forces, or else he misunderstood them as various kinds of metaphysical mystification.

Socialism changes the nature of social development. Under socialist conditions the development of society becomes purposeful and conscious, and the organized social activity of man is directed to achieving the effective realization of definite purposes. This is expressed by the planning of economic and social development. The transformation of social development from a fortuitous and unconscious process into one which is purposefully and consciously directed by man, constitutes the central idea of scientific socialism. This was expressed by Frederick Engels in the following words: "Social forces operate exactly as do the forces of nature: blindly, violently, destructively—until we understand them and make allowances for them... But when once we have understood them they can, in productive hands, be changed from demoniac masters into docile servants. This difference is the same as that between the destructive force of electricity contained in lightning and the controlled electricity of the telegraph and arc light, or the difference between an outbreak of fire and fire in the service of man."

The historical significance of socialism as a social system lies in the achievement of this transformation. To continue in Engels' words: "In socialism, people's social existence which has hitherto faced them as something imposed by nature and history, becomes thenceforth a free act. Unfamiliar forces, which have hitherto prevailed upon history, become subject to the control of people themselves. Only from this point do people create their own history with full consciousness; only from this point do the social forces activated by them achieve largely and increasingly the results which are aimed at."

Such is the vision of scientific socialism. It is a vision of social development guided by scientific knowledge of the laws governing the phenomena of nature and of the social life of man. Socialism gives science a new importance as the main instrument serving to guide the development of society. In no previous social system has science been so important.

The role of science in the transformation of socialist society is threefold: the transformation of the productive forces, of the economic base, and of the political, organizational and cultural superstructure of socialist society. The role of science in the transformation of the productive forces or, as we usually say, the material and technical base of socialist society, is immediately apparent. This role falls above all onto the natural and technological sciences and, to a limited extent, to the social sciences in so far as they are concerned with questions of the efficient organization and functioning of production processes. In addition to these sciences, there are also the medical and educational sciences, which raise the efficiency and skill of human labour and widen the range of its possibilities. The role of these sciences as a factor transforming the development of the productive forces developed within the framework of capitalism; for within this framework, modern technology was born, based on a scientific knowledge of the laws of nature. Also within this framework were born the modern organizational forms of the enterprise and the rational calculation of the costs and results of production. Under capitalism, however, they are subordinated to the private ends of individual capitalist enterprises, that is, they are generally subordinated to private profit.

The lack of a general social purpose in the capitalist economy makes the planned development of productive forces impossible. Certainly in recent times some efforts have been made to plan the development of science and technology. This has occurred partly under the influence of the planned development of the productive forces in socialist countries, that is, as a result of the need to compete with the socialist system. In capitalist conditions, however, this is generally planning within the framework of individual enterprises or concerns, and in so far as elements of planning exist on a national scale, they concern the development of the theoretical foundations; practical application is left to the private initiative of concerns and enterprises. As a result, the development of the productive forces continues to be haphazard. Only socialism makes the real planned development of the productive forces possible. This does not happen immediately, but is the gradual result both of the transformations in socialist production relations, of the organization of socialist production, and of the experience acquired in the planning of scientific and technological development and its practical application. This does not come about without difficulty. The main source of difficulty is the historical fact that the first socialist societies arose in economically less developed countries, which entered the process of industrialization only in conditions of socialism. In such conditions, in the course of planning the productive forces, it is necessary both to acquire the experience of the old capitalist industrialized countries, and to develop new methods appropriate to a socialist system. To the extent, however, that the socialist countries attain the level of the highly developed industrialized countries, these difficulties disappear, and the superiority of the planned socialist direction of the development of productive forces becomes increasingly apparent.

The more efficiently we plan the development of the productive forces, the greater is the role of science in this field. As a result, as stated in the programme adopted by the XXII Congress of the Communist Party of the Soviet Union, "science will become to the highest degree a direct productive force". This is a considerable change in the social role of those branches of science which are connected with the development of the productive forces. Science was formerly partly connected with the ideological superstructure of a particular social system, and partly—in fields such as most of the natural sciences, mathematics, etc.—represented some of the social culture, not necessarily directly connected with the superstructure of the system. It was not, however, a direct component part of the productive forces of society. It influenced the productive forces indirectly by its practical application. Now, however, when certain branches of science take part in the conscious, planned transformation of the productive forces, these branches become a direct component in the development of the productive forces of society.

The economic and sociological sciences are instrumental in forming the economic base of socialist society, that is, socialist relations in production, and their organization and proper functioning. In capitalism these sciences were condemned to the role of a passive observer of haphazard social processes, and often—generally even in certain periods—they were transformed into mere apologetics for capitalist production relations thereby abandoning their scientific, cognative function. Only Marxist social science, connected with the working-class movement, has reached a true understanding of the objective laws of development of capitalist society. It affects the course of this development by the revolutionary policy of the working-class movement, which is based on this science. The victory of socialism has brought it new tasks of consciously shaping the relations of production and the conditions in which they can function properly.

A new branch of political economy has arisen—the political economy of socialism—the task of which is to examine the characteristics and laws of socialist relations in production. On this basis, these relations are consciously formed. The aim is a system of production relations, of organizational forms of socialist production, such that the incentives resulting therefrom should contribute fully to the development of the productive forces. As with the planned building up of productive forces, this aim is attained not immediately, but gradually, as we master the various elements in production relations, the incentives connected with them, and the ways of responding to these incentives, drawn from the capitalist past, and as the skill of economic management is raised. Examination of problems connected with this is the subject of the political economy of socialism. Various branches of applied sociology also help in this, particularly the science concerned with the organization of labour. The political economy of socialism and those branches of sociology which have been mentioned are as yet young sciences; they are maturing gradually together with the socialist relations of production with which they are concerned, though often lagging behind the requirements for the practical formation of these relations.

Apart from the building up of the socialist production relations and the related incentives for the development of productive forces, there is the problem of directing the development of the socialist economy. This problem arises from the fact that the development of a socialist society is consciously guided, and it is the subject of the science of national economic planning and of the various economic sciences which deal with the management of the different sectors or branches of the national economy. All these sciences are directly connected with the political economy of socialism, being concerned with the detailed and practical application of its basic conclusions.

The science of national economic planning should have special mention. This science derives from the socialist method of production, as does national economic planning itself. This is not altered by the fact that capitalist countries also—particularly the economically less developed countries—have recently shown interest in national economic planning. This interest is the result of the high growth rate of the socialist economy, as well as of the fact that the contemporary development of productive forces goes beyond the framework of private capitalist ownership and requires planned management. The need to plan economic development is particularly great in less developed countries, which are eager to overcome economic and social backwardness.

In this connection, a definite contribution to the science of national economic planning has been made by non-socialist countries, including developed capitalist countries. The fragmentary nature of planning under capitalism, however, and particularly the difficulty of the practical implementation of national economic plans in conditions where the means of production are privately owned, means that a sizeable part of this theoretical contribution has no practical application there. It can be fully applied only in a socialist economy.

There are two distinct stages in the development of the science of national economic planning in socialist countries. In the first stage, the subject of interest has been almost exclusively the problem of ensuring the internal consistency of plans. An increase in the production of steel requires a corresponding increase in the production of coal, iron ore, electrical power, and the training of an appropriate labour force. An increase in the wages fund requires an appropriate increase in the market supply of consumer goods, and an increase in investment expenditure requires an appropriate increase in the quantity of the material means of production. Lack of internal co-ordination of the different parts of the plan disrupts the development of the national economy.

Balance accounting is an instrument for co-ordinating the plan. National and sector economic balances are today applied in capitalist countries too. They were first introduced, however, in the Soviet Union in connection with the drawing up of the first five-year plan. Balance accounting as applied to the national economy is becoming increasingly mathematical, in the form of sets of equations solved with the help of computers. This improves the accuracy of the calculations and, at the same time, allows an increasingly wider range of phenomena to be covered.

The second stage was begun relatively recently. It is mainly concerned with the problem of plan optimization. Internal consistency of the plan is a necessary condition for its implementation, for otherwise the economic processes would be disturbed. There is, however, a great number of internally consistent plans (theoretically an infinite number). From these the optimal plan must be chosen, that is, the one which ensures the highest degree of implementation of the chosen target. In the national economy, as a whole, this target is the growth of national income. In the different economic sectors there are more specific targets, such as minimizing production costs or transport costs, or maximizing the production of a given enterprise or branch of industry. The problem of optimization has become the subject of a separate science—programming theory, and what is known as operations research—which has found application not only in the field of economics but in various other disciplines. Again, this science first developed in the Soviet Union, was afterwards taken up and further developed in Western countries; but it is applied to the planning of the national economy as a whole, only in conditions of socialism.

The possibility of applying programming theory to national economic planning in practice, arose only with the introduction of electronic computers. These have effected a technological revolution which has had a profound influence on the theory and practice of national economic planning. Their use made it possible to develop balance accounting and to apply widely the calculation of programme optimization, which would not be feasible without these machines. We see here how technological development affects not only the productive forces, but also makes it possible to improve planning and management of the national economy.

Efficient planning and management of the national economy require knowledge of the numerical value of various parameters, such as cost norms for the different means of production and for labour per unit of output, investment cost norms for an extra unit of production, the elasticity of demand for particular consumer goods, and so on. These parameters, known as economic parameters, are determined by means of statistical observation or directly by laboratory examination, that is, in a production plant. Mathematical statistics plays an auxiliary role in determining them, and such determination is the subject of econometrics. In connection with the application to national economic planning, the term "planometrics" has recently come into use.

Finally, a few words on the role of science in the formation of the superstructure of a socialist society. The direct impact of science has so far been weakest in this field. In so far as we have begun, to any measurable extent, the conscious, planned formation of production relations and the development of the national economy, and have begun to plan with increasing efficiency the development of productive forces, so the development of the superstructure of the socialist society has continually been carried out empirically, largely on an *ad hoc* basis. A special contribution to the formation of this superstructure falls to the sociological, juristic and human sciences.

The contribution of the juristic and sociological sciences is shown in the formation of the organizational forms and the norms which regulate State and social life, in the formation of the whole set of relations of communal life. The human sciences have a profound influence on social awareness. Knowledge of history, in its widest sense, including social, economic and political history, the history of all aspects of human culture, awakens an understanding of the path followed by society, and of the origins of existing social conditions, and facilitates the definition and formulation of the aims of development which society sets itself. Psychology uncovers the mysteries of human psychological processes, and helps in the formation of the personality of the socialist man.

Finally, the philosophical sciences—logic, scientific method, praxiology, and philosophy itself as a generalized summary of the whole of our theoretical knowledge—develop the capacity for rational thinking, for a precise analysis of situations, clear insight into the structure of means and ends, and form in people a scientific view of the world. This is essential for society, which longs to free itself completely from the blind, haphazard forces which have governed it in the past, to master nature, and become the conscious creator of its own historical destiny.

However, science influences the formation of the superstructure of socialist society not only by the direct action of individual specialized sciences. No less important—indeed, at the present stage even more so— is the effect which general scientific thought, the scientific method of approaching phenomena, has on social consciousness. Science is becoming an increasingly powerful factor in the formation of our culture;

science creates a definite cultural and psychological climate which becomes part of the superstructure of socialist society. A leading role is played here by the human sciences; and the natural sciences, particularly the achievements of technology, influence this climate to an increasing extent.

Marxist social, political and philosophical thought is of particular significance for the formation of both the economic base and the superstructure of socialist society. On the whole, such thought did not originate and develop in the studies or laboratories of professional scholars. It was brought forth and shaped by the immense laboratory of the historical experience of the revolutionary working-class movement and of the construction of socialism. But it is scientific thought in the truest sense of the word. Arising from the practice of transforming things as they are, it generalizes the experience of such practice on the scale of whole nations and on an international scale; it establishes general laws, analyses specific situations, and draws conclusions for effective action. In the process of forming socialist society, Marxist thought acquires great significance for individual specialized sciences—not only for the social sciences and humanities. In generalizing to a national and international level the experience of the construction of socialism—and, later, of communism too—Marxist thought defines the tasks and role of individual sciences in the process of the conscious and purposeful direction of social development. It becomes the organizer of this historical process.

I have presented in turn the role of science in the building up of productive forces, the economic base and the superstructure of a socialist society. In each of these areas the different sciences have a particular role to play. These areas are, however, inter-connected and the influences of these sciences therefore overlap. I have already mentioned how technological development in the field of computers influences the streamlining of planning and management in the national economy. The inter-connection of particular areas of life, of the process of controlling nature and forming social relations, finds expression in the rise and development of sciences, which cover the different areas of both nature and social life. Mathematics is such a science. At first applied principally to the study of nature, but today entering more and more into the economic sciences, it finds its use in the practice of planning and management of the national economy, in sociology and psychology, and recently even in linguistics. The field of mathematics which is most widely applied is probability calculus and mathematical statistics. This covers natural, social and economic processes, and is applicable wherever the laws being studied are what is known as statistical or stochastic laws. The widening of the field of application of mathematics leads increasingly to new branches of this science, such as the game theory and the decision theory.

Of particular significance for the formation of the socialist society is a science which has developed relatively recently and which is today advancing very rapidly. This is cybernetics—the science of the control of complex sets of connections between causes and effects. As in the case of mathematics, with which it is closely connected, it has a wide field of application in technology, biology, economics and sociology, in linguistics, and its range is continuously extending. As in the case of probability calculus and mathematical statistics, it examines natural and social processes which are distinguished by a definite kind of regularity. These are laws in which a decisive role is played by what are known as cause and effect feedbacks, and the automatic regulation and control of processes. This is a further development, in a specific mathematical form, of the basic ideas of Marx and Engels dialectical materialism. It is this which leads to its special connection with Marxist philosophy.

Cybernetics may be applied to automated machines and industrial equipment, autonomic biological processes, and the problems of controlling and regulating economic and social processes. Cybernetics constitutes a scientific basis for the automation of production processes. Automation progresses rapidly in industry, transport and communications, and stretches even to agriculture. Automated equipment makes it possible to conquer cosmic space. Computers make it possible to solve tasks which were previously beyond man's powers. Mechanization and automation today affect the treatment of statistical material, economic reporting and accounting, and the management of production, trade and finance. It has even reached fields such as medical diagnosis, the deciphering of texts (I have in mind the deciphering of the writings of the Mayas with the aid of a computer) and of language translations. There has recently been talk of constructing a machine to deal with legal classification and deduction.

Worthy of special mention are studies in the field which is often called the general theory of organization. In this the conceptual apparatus of cybernetics and praxiology is applied to material from economics and sociology. This is intended to produce methods for the efficient development of social processes. This has obvious application to the problems of planning and distribution (economic cybernetics), to State and social administration, and to many other fields.

The role of mathematics, of mathematical statistics, and especially of cybernetics, presented here also shows the blurring of the boundaries between different sciences. The methodologies of the various sciences are growing more alike, and at the same time the differences in their social functions are disappearing. All the sciences have an increasing influence on the productive forces, the economic base and the superstructure of socialist society, although the immediacy with which a particular science affects different fields may vary.

From this there arises a practical need for increasingly complex scientific studies. These studies must cover wider areas of inter-related problems and mobilize an increasingly large number of sciences, including the technological sciences. Programmes of investigation needing the co-operation of the natural and social sciences are becoming increasingly important. Co-operation cannot be confined to the different natural sciences, or to the different social sciences. Co-operation between the natural and social sciences, technology and the humanities, is essential. All sciences also need (though to varying degrees) the help of mathematics, cybernetics and philosophy. Such co-operation is possible only if investigations take the form of planned teamwork, concentrating material and technical means and human energy on wide sets of those problems which are the key to the development of society.

This leads to far-reaching consequences in the organization of scientific enquiry, and in the education necessary for the research worker of today. The sharp division between those who study the humanities and those who study the natural sciences is a relic of the past, and the numerous public discussions which contrast the humanities with the natural sciences and vice versa are fruitless. In a socialist society, the natural and applied sciences are subordinate to the human purpose of the formation of social relations and social consciousness, and at the same time make it possible to create the technological basis necessary for these human ends to be realized. The combination of a mathematical education with knowledge of the natural sciences, and of a philosophical and historical education with knowledge of the humanities is also a relic of the past. Today the unity of science is revealed in its entirety when mathematics and technology find common ground with the humanities, when the natural sciences and technology raise new philosophical problems, when technology has far-reaching social effects, when the theoretical concepts of cybernetics find increasingly wide application in technology and in the control of social processes. A new kind of scientific preparation becomes necessary and new programmes of school teaching, different from the traditional ones, will also be needed. As a result, new links will be formed between individual sciences, new methods of enquiry, new forms of organizing scientific investigation, and new ways of influencing natural and social processes. All this contributes to the increasingly full realization of the vision of scientific socialism which I have already mentioned: a world in which man will ever more improve his mastery of nature and of the development of his social life, a world in which he will be increasingly effective as the conscious creator of his own fate. It is to this role that science is called by socialism.

THE SITUATION AND TASKS OF THE ECONOMIC SCIENCES

The development of economic sciences in Poland can be divided into three periods.

The first period—lasting more or less until about 1950—was characterized by the fact that teaching of economics was based on prewar bourgeois economics. The publications of that period displayed the same features and content. Marxists were in the minority among our economists. The majority of our economists showed however goodwill in joining in the work of laying the economic foundations of the people's state and many of them took an active and very useful part in that work. As most of the economic tasks of that time were generally national in character and connected with the economic reconstruction and development of the country, this facilitated such an approach. At that time, the tasks of decisive importance were of a general, democratic nature, corresponding to the social views of progressive non-Marxist economists.

However, as the socialist character in the further development of the national economy began to take definite shape, new tasks emerged. Economic knowledge based on the old bourgeois approach was no longer enough. The economic views based on this foundation became an ideological brake, slowing down further participation of economists in the construction of the socialist economy and, in many cases, they played a definitely hostile role.

This situation called for a determined switch-over of the economic sciences into Marxist channels. This was done in the early fifties. The most important element of this switch-over were courses for all economists and student youth on the basic principles of Marxist theory, at the same time revealing the bourgeois ideological sources, the practical inadequacy and even the harmful character of the bourgeois economy. As a result of this process, the majority of economists, particularly those of the younger generation, went over to Marxist teaching. And from that time onwards, Marxism definitely became the basis for the further development of the economic sciences in Poland. But this turn to Marxism

532

in the economic sciences did not create an adequate basis for the further development of the economic sciences and their practical application in the national economy. This was because of the situation as regards Marxist thought at that time.

In the early fifties, Marxist thought was encumbered by serious restrictions imposed on it by dogmatism, which were not conducive either to its further development or to the elaboration of definite concepts needed for practical application in the socialist economy. Marxist economic science of those years was marked by its very abstract and general formulations and did not take enough interest in the concrete conditions in which the economic processes were taking place.

Marxist economics came into being by way of criticism of the capitalist economy, revealing along broad lines its basic development trends and its contradictions. Because of its very nature, it did not go into detailed problems connected with the management of the economy. In capitalist conditions, management of the economy was in the hands of the bourgeoisie and the working class had no influence on it. After the October Revolution, the Marxist economy had to cope with a completely new problem, that of building a socialist economy. In this field, the traditional Marxist theory, being mainly a critical analysis of capitalism, could only give very general guide lines. The task was a new one and called for a creative approach.

In the first years after the October Revolution, there was extensive and widespread theoretical discussion. Later, however, the discussion began to die down, for the political conditions produced dogmatism.

But in these first discussions, too, it was a question of undertaking broad and general political and economic decisions concerning such matters as the rate at which the economy was to develop, the rate of accumulation, the structure of investments, the reform of the agricultural system, etc. The foundations of the political economy of socialism laid at that time were—as one might say—"economics for members of the Political Bureau". They were the organ for fundamental macroeconomic decisions in political economy. In addition, they were helpful in enlightening large sections of the community—particularly the working class and the intelligentsia employed in the economic apparatus—on the importance of the general social and political tasks set by the political leadership.

The foundations of the political economy of socialism laid at that time were not concrete enough to form a basis for decisions at lower levels. "Economics for the members of the Political Bureau" was not supplemented by "Economics for industrial associations and enterprises" or "Economics for farms, transport, banks, etc". An effort to fill these gaps was made by the so-called "detailed economics". In these conditions, "detailed economics" did not, however, have an adequate basis in the political economy of socialism as it was then, but developed as a collection of practical skills which, if the need arose, could include practical skills born of the experience gained by the capitalist economy. Moreover, the highly centralized, administrative system of managing the economy at that time did not create the need for giving a more concrete form to the political economy of socialism, elaborated in such a way as to make it useful in taking micro-decisions at lower level management of the national economy.

This contradiction emerged most acutely in the period which we can set tentatively around 1956. The breakdown of dogmatism in Marxist thought and in our policy coincided with the emergence of new needs in the field of developing the socialist economy. These needs were the result of the growth of the socialist productive forces and the growing complications of the economic system. The need became evident for more subtle and elastic methods of managing the socialist economy, for basing these methods on a detailed scientific analysis of the functioning of both the socialist economy as a whole and of its various sectors. This set a new task before political economy and also before the various economic sciences.

This situation became evident in the powerful protest it brought about against the dogmatic limitations of Marxist thought up to that time and in the search for new lines of development. In these conditions, interest was revived in contemporary bourgeois economics, particularly in the methods of economic analysis developed recently in capitalist countries, such as econometrics, programming, analysis of operations, cybernetics, etc., in so far as they could become useful techniques in the management of the socialist economy.

This led some economists to rather uncritical views of the newest methods of economic analysis developed in the capitalist countries. Their role in making the functioning of the capitalist economy more efficient was often overestimated and their ideological class basis and the resulting limitations, biased and apologetic tendencies were overlooked.

This state of affairs also held the danger of revisionism consisting in attempts to introduce uncritically into the economy elements taken from bourgeois economic ideology. This was depriving Marxist thought of its most essential class-revolutionary aspects and gave birth to liquidation tendencies towards Marxism. Views of this kind were only proclaimed emphatically by very few economists and were quickly and rightly opposed by the majority of them.

And this opposition was not confined to polemics alone; soon positive counter-arguments were formulated and could be found in books and other publications.

The character of Polish economic science, as we know it today, was hammered into shape by discussion. To describe it briefly, its aim is the creative development of Marxist economic thought. The great majority of Polish economists are definitely in favour of Marxism and try to apply Marxist methods in analysing contemporary economic problems, particularly problems of the socialist economy. With this aim in view, efforts are being made to give Marxist economics a more concrete character, so that it can deal not only with great problems of transforming the social structure, but also with specific problems connected with the management of the socialist economy. In this connection, an important role is being played in contemporary Polish economic science not only by the great macroeconomic problems of accumulation and consumption, the rate of development, its planned or spontaneous character, etc., but also by more specific microeconomic problems, such as the structure and efficiency of investments, concrete economic incentives, sound principles of regulating prices, production costs, indices determining the tasks of enterprises, the rate of interest, the efficiency of foreign trade, etc.

This has also made it possible to provide a better link between the various economic sciences and the political economy of socialism because, given this concrete form, the political economy of socialism provides the theoretical foundations for the development of the various economic sciences.

In recent years, Polish economic thought has aroused considerable international interest. Interest in it is also being shown by other socialist countries, particularly the Soviet Union and Hungary, and more recently, by Czechoslovakia, Rumania and the G.D.R. In particular, there is a great convergence in the development of economic thought in Poland and the Soviet Union as regards theory. The subjects discussed in Poland are more and more frequently also being discussed in the Soviet Union with reference to Polish economists. In turn, Soviet economic science can boast of a relatively high degree of practical application of the results of theoretical research in economic life. The works of Polish economists are being published to an ever larger extent in the Soviet Union and in other socialist countries.

The underdeveloped countries of Asia and Africa and of Latin America are also showing great interest in Polish economic thought. In these countries, the problem of economic development and progress is the most fundamental one of their social and political life. In view of this, a great deal of interest is also being shown in the practical experience gained by the socialist countries and socialist economic thought. For the economists of these countries Polish economic thought has a special appeal, as many Polish economists write in languages they understand and deal with problems of development that are of vital interest to them. This interest can be seen, for instance, in the numerous visits paid to Poland by economists from these countries and the quite large number of Polish economists being invited to these countries as advisers. Another proof of this interest is the participation of many economists from these countries in the higher course on planning for foreigners run by the Central School of Economics. The number of students coming to Poland to study economics is also growing.

Much interest is also being shown at present in Polish economic thought by the countries of western Europe and by the United States. This is due to their growing interest in socialist countries and problems of coexistence, as well as Poland's role in the world economy and politics.

Sometimes we are asked to what extent the development of Polish economic science described here can be included within the framework of Marxism. It is impossible to answer this question without first giving an answer to the question: What is Marxism?

From the point of view of the dogmatic concepts that were prevalent in the period of the so-called "personality cult", it is quite easy to see a departure from Marxism in all new ideas. For there was a period when drawing attention to things like the problem of prices and equilibrium of the market in the socialist economy was regarded as a departure from Marxism. Decentralization in management of the national economy, introduction of interest on fixed assets, workers self-government and all the new means of shaping agriculture along socialist lines, the doubts expressed about the dire poverty of the working class in the leading capitalist countries, recognition of such development as the European common market, etc., all this was treated as a departure from Marxism.

However, the Marxist character of the development trends of economic science in contemporary Poland, as well as in contemporary Soviet economic science, is denied not only from the dogmatic point of view. It is also denied by a large number of bourgeois economists, and particularly by bourgeois journalists and politicians. They say that the practical needs of the socialist economy call for a departure from Marxist concepts, which they allege is supported by the contemporary development of economic science in the Soviet Union, Poland and other socialist countries, as well as by the development of new forms of planning and management in the national economy.

This evaluation is related to the thesis of the alleged growing likeness of social systems, according to which the socialist system is acquiring more and more features characteristic of the capitalist system. This thesis confuses the question of socio-economic systems with the question of the level of economic development. Phenomena which are the result of the economic development attained by the socialist countries, the fact that the socialist countries are catching up with the level of the highly developed capitalist countries, are mistakenly taken as a growing likeness between the two systems.

This evaluation also shows a misunderstanding of the very character of Marxism as the first world outlook in history based on scientific and creative cognition. The scientific character of Marxism assumes its constant and creative development, that the Marxist method will embrace more and more historical phenomena and that these methods themselves will be constantly improved. Such was also the process of development of Marx and Engels' thought, and the progress of Marxist thought associated with the name of Lenin and the development of Lenin's thought. And such is the character of the further development of Marxist thought in connection with the construction and development of the socialist economy.

The essential feature of Marxist thought is that analysis is based on the materialist approach to history and on the economic categories formulated by Marx. However, as the socialist economy gives rise to new problems for economic science, the need arises to introduce new categories of economic analysis and new ways of conducting economic research. This means, we must go beyond the economic categories, economic methods and methodology that we find in the works of Marx, Engels and Lenin.

Should this development be described as Marxist in character?

The character of Marxist development of science depends on two factors. Firstly, to what extent it comes organically from the concept of Marxist scientific socialism, from the philosophy of dialectical materialism, from the materialist approach to history and from the foundations of Marxist economic analysis. Secondly, it depends on the extent to which it answers the real needs of the working class and the socialist community, arising from the construction and development of the socialist economy, the needs of the struggle of the working class in the capitalist countries, the needs of the fight against imperialism and the economic development of the underdeveloped countries.

It is Marxist in character to the same degree that the development of economic science grows organically from the Marxist heritage and answers the needs of the construction of socialism and the fight against capitalism and imperialism. When it departs from this heritage and does not answer these needs, then there is a danger of its going astray along revisionist lines and of becoming practically ineffective in the long run. Therefore, the real criterion is that of practice. And from this point of view, the situation in Polish economic science still leaves much to be desired.

The divorce of theory from practice—which was a feature of dogmatism—has, in principle, been overcome. But there is another tendency that renders difficult contact between economic science and the practice of the economy. It is the situation that exists as regards staff. There are certain divergencies between the way of thinking of the economists and that of the people doing the practical economic work. The men with long years of experience in the practical field often take a mistrustful attitude towards the economists as theorists who are not of much use when it comes to practice and often are rather troublesome. The economists, on the other hand, have a tendency to treat the experience of the practical men as being narrowly empirical and as expressing a conservative way of thinking and failure to understand the deeper connections prevailing in the national economy.

This situation is partly a heritage from the preceding period when economic science could not give much concrete assistance in the practical management of economic life and the theorists had not gained enough insight into the practical side of the economy. But this is a dangerous situation. It means that the practical men are in danger of getting into a conservative rut and of failing to take advantage of the new possibilities presented by the development of modern economic science of making the socialist economy more efficient. It means that the scientists are in danger of cutting themselves off from life, of becoming too academic, engaged in barren theorizing. And this in turn spells the danger of a departure from the substance of Marxism, a danger that can best be averted by constant and close links between theory and practice.

Basing the development of economic science on close links with practice, drawing up a suitable programme of research and the practical application of the results of this research is the best way of ensuring that our economic science has sound ideological foundations and guaranteeing its active participation in the construction of socialism. This is the basis for proper Marxist development of economic science.

ECONOMICS IN THE TWENTY YEARS
OF INDEPENDENCE

When Poland was liberated from the Nazi occupation twenty years ago reconstruction in the field of science was, at first, pursued along the old intellectual, cultural and institutional base. This was also the case with the economic sciences, which at that time were dominated by various trends of bourgeois economics and Marxists were clearly in the minority.

However, new tasks were inevitably set by the peoples character of the new Poland. The majority of the intelligentsia and scientists actively participated in the process of building the new state and the new economy. This co-operation was facilitated by the fact that during the period of reconstruction the problems of universally democratic and national character prevailed. This gave possibilities for broad collaboration and drew in large circles of progressive intelligentsia. In these conditions, the majority of Polish economists tried to do their utmost in the reconstruction and development of the national economy. These endeavours, however, were the product of their knowledge, derived from the traditions of bourgeois economic thought.

As time passed, especially between the years 1948–50, the socialist tasks of reconstruction and of the social and economic development of the country began to take shape. In these conditions, the knowledge of the economists proved inadequate and often even a hindrance in dealing with the process of social change, because bourgeois economic science one-sidedly concentrated its attention on the market, monetary and credit processes, accepting without question the alleged rationalism and efficiency of the automatic functioning of the capitalist economy. The problems of economic development and of social and structural changes were either alien to them, or else their ideas on such problems were altogether biased. In this situation, it was necessary to revise economic science, and this could only be done by basing it on the achievements of Marxist thought, where exactly these problems were dominant.

540

The Turning Point

For the reasons mentioned above, Polish economic science came to a situation, which could be called the Marxist turning point. This happened in 1950 and the following years. The First Congress of Polish Science and the preparatory work which preceded it played here a special role.

This turning point consisted, in the first place, in popularizing among a wide circle of scientific workers and students the principles of Marxist economic and social theories.

At the same time, in connection with the intensive industrialization of the country, which had just begun (the great six-year plan started at that time), economics was being taught to an increasing number of students. New schools of economics were opened, old ones reformed and extended. A Department of Political Economy was opened at Warsaw University; various scientific and experimental institutes were established for the study of economics, and to prepare new cadres for the growing needs of expanding industry. Teaching of economics was at the time connected with an extensive campaign to shape the socialist conscience of the society, and especially of the intelligentsia. The result was the general spreading of a knowledge of the principles of Marxism.

However, this spreading of knowledge of Marxist economics was not followed by the development of independent, creative scientific work. This was due to many reasons.

One, was the dogmatism, connected with the system of that time, which we usually refer to as the system of the "personality cult". Efforts were made to squeeze Marxist thought into a narrow pattern, which was recognized as a criterion of political orthodoxy. This did not favour the development of independent, creative work. It was manifest, among others, in the disregard for the rich tradition of Polish Marxist thought (to mention only such great names linked with that tradition as Krzywicki, Rosa Luxemburg, Marchlewski, Keller-Kraus, numerous writers of the Polish Communist Party and others); often this tradition was rejected as not fitting into the established pattern.

But this was not the only reason. There was another, deeper reason, namely the character of Marxist economic science at that time. Marxist economics arose as a critique of capitalism. As such it brought to light, in broad outline, the social substance, the laws of development and the inner contradictions of the capitalist system. On the other hand, it was not interested in particular problems connected with the management of the country. The reasons are clear. The management of the economy was in the hands of the bourgeoisie; the working class, whose aspirations were expressed by Marxist theory, had no influence on the management of the capitalist economy. That was why within the framework of the Marxist theory interest in these problems was not developed. However, the building of socialism brought these problems to the fore. Here Marxist thought had to enter a new field, for which it was not prepared by tradition.

Immediately after the October Revolution great theoretical discussions took place in the Soviet Union. But these discussions followed the lines laid down by traditional Marxist teaching. These discussions were concerned, just as the previous critique of capitalism, with the problems of the broad lines of social reconstruction and economic development. The problems discussed were the rate of economic development and of accumulation, the structure of investments, the relationship between the various branches of the national economy, the reconstruction of agriculture, etc. Out of these discussions there arose, in spite of the later dogmatism and schematism, a new branch of political economy—namely, the socialist political economy.

The framework of this new science of socialist political economy laid the foundation for important decisions, let me call them macro-decisions, on economic policy in the domains, which I have just mentioned. But it was a science, which in view of its subject—the broad lines of social change and social and economic development—was designed for those who had to take decisions. It might be called "political economy for the benefit of members of the Polit-Bureau and Government". Besides, the newly born socialist political economy also helped broad circles of the society, and especially the working class and the intelligentsia, employed in the economic apparatus, to appreciate the importance of the social and economic changes which were taking place. Thus, it became a tool of ideological and psychological mobilization of wide circles of society for their active and conscious participation in the building of socialism.

However, the framework of socialist political economy, as formed at that period, was too general and too vague to serve as a base for decision making at the lower levels of leadership and for directing the national economy. One might put it like this, that the "political economy for the members of the Polit-Bureau and the Government" was not supplemented by a "political economy for industrial concerns and enterprises, for agricultural units, transport, banks, etc." Nevertheless, the practical needs still existed in these domains. The gap was filled by the so-called "detailed economics", which however at the stage of development of socialist political economy did not find sufficient theoretical support in that science. Thus, "detailed economics" developed as an accumulation of practical knowledge, based on experience, to a great extent, earlier than our own, going back to the time of building a socialist economy in the U.S.S.R., and also to the experience of capitalist countries in the management of industry and other domains of the economy.

The early period of socialist industrialization was characterized by a highly centralized system of management. Such a system was necessary in the period of revolutionary reconstruction of the social structure and mobilization of all economic resources for an intensive and rapid industrialization. Management of the national economy in these conditions was mainly carried out by administrative measures for directing the economy. This, however, did not create the necessity for a more concrete socialist political economy to meet the requirements of the lower level leadership. The independence of action at these lower levels was rather limited and as a rule those responsible adhered rather strictly to the directives from the top, and the scope of their own decisions was limited.

Conditions of Renewal

This, however, began to change together with the growth of the socialist economy. The means of production and production itself was growing and with it grew the complexity of socialist economic relations. This required new methods of direction, planning and management and also new scientific knowledge, adequate to these methods. The appraisal of these new needs was also helped by the difficulties which appeared in the last period of the six-year plan. At that time, a strong feeling was growing for the methods of directing the economy that must be renewed and that a deeper understanding and better scientific tools for its direction must be provided. The XX Congress of the Communist Party of

the Soviet Union, the VIII Plenary Meeting of the Central Committee of
the Polish United Workers' Party and the lively discussions which preceded these events, criticised the system of the "personality cult" and
the dogmatism and schematism in social sciences, connected with this
system. Thus both the need and the conditions arose for opening wide
the doors for new economic thinking.

A tendency also appeared for a renewal of Marxist economic thought.
This renewal was directed in the first place to more concrete problems,
introducing detailed investigations of particular problems, connected
with the functioning of the socialist economy. To the fore were brought
such problems as centralization and decentralization of decisions in the
management of the socialist economy, the democratization of management, in particular workers' self-government, the role of economic means,
on the one hand, and of the administrative means, on the other, in the
management of the economy, the role of economic incentives, the principles of price fixing, the problems of balancing the market, etc. In Poland,
these problems were known as "the economic model". The discussions
which followed were called the model discussions.

Simultaneously with these problems, discussion was continued on
the old problems of socialist political economy, which at that period
could already be called traditional. But this was pursued in a new manner,
free from dogmatism and in the light of the more concrete knowledge
obtained. Within the framework of these problems, again first place was
taken by the problem of the rate of development and of the ratios of
the various activities in the socialist economy. These *development problems*, seen in the new light, just as the model problems, stressed the
question of efficiency of the socialist economy: the efficiency of its way
of functionning and of its development mechanism. In the development
sphere, the problem was primarily a question of the effectiveness of
various trends and various kinds of economic progress, such as labour-
saving, capital-saving, etc. At the same time the problems of employment
became important.

In these conditions, interest was renewed in the latest developments
of economic sciences in capitalist countries, and in particular in the
possibility of utilizing some of their methods for raising the efficiency in
the management of the socialist economy. Specially interesting were the
new trends in economic investigations, new techniques developed by
certain detailed sciences (which I would like to define as subsidiary to

political economy), such as: econometry, programming theory, mathematical theory of rational decisions and lately cybernetics.

It is quite understandable that in the reaction against the dogmatism of the previous period, many economists overrated the importance of these new investigating techniques. They thought that in some way they could serve as a substitute for the basic Marxist problems of socialist political economy. Some economists, and especially those, who were still "brought up" in the old school of bourgeois political economy tried to find in it a panacea for directing and managing the socialist economy. But such tendencies were shortlived and quickly vanished, when confronted with the practical needs of the socialist economy. These practical needs proved to be the best school for Marxist thought, and therefore in the course of discussions and disputes a conviction was maturing that all the achievements in the techniques of economic analysis in capitalist countries are of practical value only when mounted in the solid frames of Marxist political economy. Besides, closer investigations showed that in capitalist countries too, the importance of these new investigating techniques is limited by the economic framework of individual private enterprises or concerns, beyond which, in capitalist conditions, they can no longer be applied.

In capitalist conditions, the possibilities of these new techniques are limited, and only within the framework of the socialist planned economy can they be fully applied. This is a fact, of which by the way nowadays a great number of scientists in capitalist countries are also aware; they feel that their technical and research knowledge begins to exceed the possibilities of its application in conditions of the capitalist system.

Thus, we have arrived in our deliberations to the present state of our economic sciences and their tasks. We shall confine ourselves here to socialist political economy and its subsidiary sciences. By this I do not want to underestimate the importance for our economists to study also the problems of modern capitalism. An understanding of the economic changes, of trends of development taking place in modern capitalism, is more than just an intellectual exercise. In our conditions, this knowledge is important also for the practical direction of the socialist economy. This is most obvious in problems of foreign trade and general questions connected with coexistence. It is sufficient to realize how important in the planning of our economic development it is, for instance, to arrive at a correct evaluation of the integration tendencies, observed in the

Western European countries and such developments as the common market. Even of greater importance for us and for the planning of the development of our economy is knowledge of the structural changes and development trends in the countries of the so-called third world.

These problems are therefore also important for our national economy.

At present, the overwhelming majority of Polish economists definitely stand on the ground of Marxist political economy and endeavour to develop Marxist theory in their own individual and creative manner. This is evidenced by the extensive scientific literature which appeared in the last few years. Numerous monographs were written on various aspects and problems of socialist political economy, as well as on problems of economic growth, both under socialism and in countries of the so-called third world. Additionally, our economic literature is concerned with problems of modern capitalism, history of economic thought, etc. There also appeared the first more extensive syntheses on many subjects, and, what is most important, their authors were increasingly young scientists. In previous years, we "invested" in educating young scientific cadres. Today, the results of these investments are visible; we already reap the first fruit, and the harvest is likely to expand and to be more and more interesting.

The greatest interest is aroused by the problems of *planning and directing* the socialist economy and of its growth witnessed by a most abundant scientific production. The problems are examined from the point of view of increasing the efficiency of the socialist economy. Particular attention, especially by younger scientists, is paid to mathematical-economic and econometric analysis as means of greater precision in economic calculations. Lately, economists also turned their attention to cybernetics and its possible role as a tool for more efficient planning and directing of the economy. This is largely due to the general scientific atmosphere prevailing at present, and especially to the development and expected increased practical role of electronic computers. These machines herald a real revolution in the methods of planning and directing the economy; they announce new possibilities in the sphere of co-ordination and optimization of economic planning and rationalization of direction. This new set of problems also found expression in the theses prepared for the IV Congress of the Polish United Workers' Party.

This more detailed economic knowledge, about which I have just been talking, served as a base for the development of the so-called "detailed economics": the economics of industry and of enterprises, the economics of agriculture, transport, finances, etc. Today, conditions already exist for the development of these economic techniques from the achievements of a political economy of a more general character.

World Promotion

In consequence, great interest was aroused by Polish economic science also outside the socialist countries. In the socialist countries, this interest is growing because the development of the problems with which our economists are concerned is convergent with the interests of the other socialist countries, and in particular of the U.S.S.R. The problems raised in scientific discussion in Poland appear also today in the U.S.S.R. and more and more often references are made to Polish economists. The same is also true in other socialist countries. But the interest in Polish economic science is growing also outside the socialist countries. It is sufficient to mention that more than 20 books of Polish economists were translated into foreign languages and further translations are being planned. In the export of Polish scientific thought, the economic sciences take today the second place after mathematics.

Polish economic thought meets with special interest in the countries of the so-called third world, in countries of Asia, Africa and Latin America. It is manifest in numerous visits of economists from these countries, who come to us to become acquainted with the theory and practice of economic planning. The fact that Poland achieved such speedy progress from an economically underdeveloped country into a country where the share of industry is constantly increasing, and that she plays an ever increasing role in the world's economy, is the reason why the economists from developing countries seek in Poland knowledge and methods by which to accelerate their own social and economic development. This contact is made easier by the fact that many of our economists write also in languages understood by economists from developing countries. This interest is also proved by the large participation in a special planning course, arranged two years ago for economists from these countries at the Warsaw Central School of Planning and Statistics. Many Polish economists are invited to the countries of the so-called third world as advisers on problems of planning and economic development. A concrete example, which may be worth mentioning here, is the Republic of Ghana, where the whole department of political economy at Ghana University was staffed, reorganized and in fact formed anew by Polish economists.

Social Problems

These important achievements should not however cover up the shortcomings. The development of interest in and of economic studies in Poland, as in other socialist countries, is directed today to problems of planning and management. These are problems of rational management, i.e., problems of a praxeological character. On the other hand, in Poland and in other socialist countries, economists are less concerned with what are really the traditional but at the same time the basic problems of socialist political economy, namely, the problems of formation of socialist relations in production, of *social* relations taking shape in the socialist economy. The problems of the driving forces in the development of the socialist economy, of the dialectics of its development mechanism, too, come within these categories. Of all these problems, only one became an object of great interest, namely the question of economic incentives. But this is connected with the problem of efficiency in the functioning and development of the socialist economy and this was the reason for its shifting the centre of interest. There is, however, still a lack of wider scientific analysis of the basic historical experiences at various periods of socialist industrialization (both as regards its achievements and failures at that period), of the reconstruction of the rural economics, and first of all, of a comparative analysis of experience gathered from various socialist countries.

Socialist political economy started off from the problems of the broad lines of social and structural reconstruction and the basic social conditions of economic development. At some later stage in the development of the socialist economy, this became insufficient. The need arose for an economic science, capable of dealing with the more detailed problems involved in the broad lines of reconstruction and development of the socialist economy, and in the basic social problems of socialist structural relations. These are the real problems of socialist political economy, in its traditional Marxist conception. I have no doubt, that soon we shall come back to these problems from the new historical perspective and we shall tackle them in the light of new research methods now at our disposal.

Theory and Practice

Talking about the shortcomings, one should also mention the link with practice, which still leaves much to be desired. Often, there is a tendency to develop science and practice as two independent, parallel currents, instead of considering their mutual co-influence and welding one with the other. This leads, on the one hand, to the empirical narrowing down of practice, by not utilizing the possibilities offered by the modern development of economic science; on the other hand, in science, cutting oneself off from practice brings about tendencies to academicism, and setting of problems not according to their practical weight, but on the basis of hypothetical schemes. This needs an analysis of institutional conditions of the economic science, on the one side, and of economic practice on the other. In my opinion, much can be done here by the Scientific and Technical Board. Within the framework of this Board, a commission has already been created to examine the practical applications of mathematical methods and computers to the economy. Also within the framework of the same Scientific and Technical Board a Central Economic Commission is formed, whose special task is to make use of the scientific achievements in the practice of economic life.

An analysis is also necessary of the institutional conditions of research activity within the sphere of economic sciences. The bulk of scientific work is pursued outside the Polish Academy of Sciences, in the chairs of various universities and in various institutes, mainly departmental, such as the Economic Research Institute of the Planning Commission, the Institute of Rural Economy, the Institute of Foreign Trade, the Institute of Internal Trade, the Institute of Organization and Economics of Industry and others.

The Academy of Sciences has only a comparatively small Institute of Economic Sciences. In these conditions, the Commission of Economic Science, established within the framework of the Academy, has only limited possibilities for influencing the development of economic sciences and, once again, the problem arises of the expediency of creating within the framework of the Academy of Sciences a bigger institute of economic sciences; I do not want to say a "large" one, I am modest.

The problem of the Institute of Economic Sciences was already put forward during the I Congress of Polish Science, as a postulate of that Congress. Various reasons hindered its realization. One of them, the most important, was the condition of the cadres. The scientific cadres were too small to staff such an institute adequately. The demand for cadres from higher schools, various economic departments and other organizations engaged in economic practice was too urgent. But there was also another reason: after the experiences of the period of the "personality cult", there was a certain reluctance and anxiety against creating a central institute. There was a fear that such a central institute may again become a centre of some new schematism, imposed on the development of economic sciences. The majority of scientific circles saw in the decentralization of the institute and the creation of a great number of independent institutes a guarantee that freedom in the development of science will be safeguarded. Today, however, the situation is different. Scientific cadres have been formed and are quickly growing in number. From that point of view, the question of the Institute of Economic Science can be solved. And, from the other side, there are no such fears now which might cause doubts as to the expediency of creating a larger economic institute within the framework of the Polish Academy of Sciences. Today, nobody has any intention of giving it a monopolistic position, to remove into the shade the valuable and vital work of many other institutes, which developed in the meantime, or the work performed in the chairs at the higher schools.

It is evident from the foregoing that in the People's Poland economic sciences underwent a tremendous development. This development is strictly linked with the development of the socialist economy, with its maturing and also with the needs which it presented.

Polish economic science is maturing and is more and more called upon to perform the fundamental role assigned to it by scientific socialism, namely, the role of an efficient tool in forming the socialist economy, a tool warranting its efficient functioning and development. This ambition of our economic science is based on its hitherto achievements. With this ambition in mind, Polish economic science enters the second twenty years' period of People's Poland.

PLANNING AND ECONOMIC THEORY

Economic Planning rouses ever growing interest in all countries of the world. It originated in the socialist countries as an essential part of the socialist economy which is by definition a planned economy.

However, we are now faced with a most important phenomenon: the interest in planning has gone beyond the boundaries of socialist countries, spreading first of all to the so-called economically underdeveloped countries. Nowadays, the majority of the countries of Asia, Africa, and Latin America are entering the road of economic and social progress; planning the development of the national economy constitutes the basis of their political economy. The idea of planning has also begun to spread in Europe, e.g., in France, in Scandinavia, and recently in Italy.

The cause of this phenomenon is very simple: Planning has been pursued in the socialist countries as a means of economic development, and it is to be considered as such in all situations in which a conscious policy of economic development is wanted, in other words, when we would not leave the direction of development to spontaneous economic forces alone. I think that the fact that in Italy planning has been initiated with the development of the "Mezzogiorno" is more than a simple historic coincidence. Where spontaneous forces are not able to promote a rapid economic development, it is necessary to resort to planning.

I shall not consider in what way planning is linked to the nature of the economic system in which it is applied—i.e., to the socialist system—or if it could be enforced in different economic and social conditions. This is a very interesting problem; but it goes beyond the proposed argument of this lecture which is: "The instruments of the scientific planning technique". One can say that experience has already proven that these instruments are largely generalizable, in that they are linked to planning, but not necessarily to the economic systems in which planning itself is applied. Within certain limits one can talk of the scientific instruments of planning in a strict sense.

The problem of the role of the economic system places itself, in my opinion, on a different plane, i.e., the means the public authority (the State or other authorities) has at its disposal of positively enforcing the plan. All the discussions dealing with the possibility of applying or not applying planning to a capitalist economy do not consider the technique of planning, but rather the means necessary to make the plan prevail over dominant private interests.

Coming back to the problem of the technical instruments, I shall confine my considerations to the historical experience of the socialist economies. It should not be forgotten, nevertheless, that, as I have already pointed out, planning has a larger and more general application.

There are three aspects of planning which we must consider: first, the goals of the economic plan. By "economic plan" I mean planning on a national scale, which is also the only one that has actually been drawn up to completion. Some socialist countries have begun the study of planning on an international scale, but it would be hazardous to generalize about their attempts at the moment. Planning on a national scale needs, firstly, the definition of the targets aimed at; secondly, the formulation of an organic plan, feasible for the given targets; and thirdly, the choice of means for the execution of the plan. It is at this stage, i.e., in the implementation of the plan, that the different economic systems differ.

In so far as the objective of planning is concerned, one can say that initially it was empirically established by two methods. First, as a consequence of a particular historical situation, plans were drafted for the reconstruction of economies. In the Soviet Union and in other socialist countries, economies were completely destroyed by the war, by civil strife, and by the Nazi occupation. Obviously, the first goal was the reconstruction of all that had been destroyed. But even during this period, some countries, Poland for example, also tried at the same time to renew and to technically modernize their economy within the limits afforded by the particular situation. In these cases, reconstruction plans were already partially plans for economic development.

The second period of planning in the socialist countries is characterized by objectives for economic development. Most of the countries being backward and underdeveloped, these objectives aimed, on the one hand, at industrialization and, on the other, at the modernization of agriculture. The economic policy acquired preeminent importance by concentrating on problems of accumulation and investments, putting at the disposal of the economy resources necessary for accumulation, and the choice of investments.

Accumulation was normally based on three sources: profits from socialized enterprises, contributions of the rural population in different ways, and revenue from taxation. The designations of investments and technologies were chosen so as to ensure the maximum obtainable increment in the productive capacity of the national economy.

Now, if we consider the formulation of the Plan from a technical point of view, we note that the planning technique, or what we generally call the planning methodology, was based on two presuppositions: on one side, the reproduction theory elaborated by Marx, and, on the other, the principles of accounting and of the construction of budgets which historically originated within the capitalist enterprise. From the merger of Marx's reproduction theory and practical budget accounting was derived the method of balances which is applied to the National Economy. Balances were calculated in physical terms as the production of coal, electrical power, existing reserves of manpower, and so on; these particular balances were organized into a "flow of products" plan for the national economy which later formed the basis of input–output analysis. National accounting has to consider not only the product mix but also the financial resources. We began therefore to draw up the balances of income and expenditure of the population to ensure the financial equilibrium in the national economy.

Finally, these two kinds of balances, the physical and the financial, are aggregated so as to obtain a general balance for the national economy. This gives a description, in the form of tables, of the sources of national income, of its distribution, and of all the secondary redistributions resulting from the operations of the financial mechanism.

Balances are to ensure the feasibility and internal consistency of the Plan. It is clear that if we decide to increase, for example, the production of steel, it is necessary to increase, at the same time, proportionally the production of iron ore, coal, power, and to train and provide a certain contingent of skilled and other manpower, and so on. These factors must obviously be co-ordinated if we want to avoid making decisions which would result in incompatibility of the factors themselves, and if we want to avoid the disequilibria which would hamper the realization of the plan. For the plan to be effectively feasible it is indispensable that it be drafted in an harmonious way, in other words, that it ensures the compatibility of the particular decisions which form the plan.

The balances system was applied for the first time in the Soviet

Union, and later on was adopted by other countries which derived it partially from the Soviet system and also from their own situation. One can say that what is called in Western Countries "national accounting" corresponds—*mutatis mutandis*— to the balance system of the national economy developed originally in the socialist countries.

An important step toward the theoretical elaboration and practical application of balances is the discovery that, from a mathematical viewpoint, they appear as systems of equations. In a certain way it is not a real discovery, because Marx's reproduction schemes, which constituted balance formulations in macroeconomic terms, also appeared as systems of equations, reaching equilibrium under certain conditions. It is from this that began the studies which later resulted in the elaboration of the input–output analysis, i.e., in the formulation of the mathematical theory of balances, or more accurately as part of the balances, as in the product mix balances. This approach aroused great interest in the scientific world and also had certain repercussions on planning theory. Nevertheless, its importance (in practice also) became effective only with the application of the most up-to-date techniques of calculus, i.e., electronic computers which enable us to solve practically very complex systems of equations. I think that recourse to these techniques will form a very important contribution to planning techniques. Up to now, however, the use of electronic computers in planning on a national scale has not yet been achieved. Scientific research dealing with the above mentioned problem has been carried out, but till now, or at least until recently, all the input–output analyses were based on available statistical data, while if we want to use this method as a valid instrument for internal plan feasibility, it is necessary to impute future data.

In conclusion, the main problem of planning has till now been the elaboration of balances so as to ensure the internal feasibility and consistency of the Plan. Now, a new objective in planning is beginning to emerge, i.e., the optimization of the Plan. We can say that the socialist countries are shifting, or better, are trying to shift, from a phase in which the main problem was the internal feasibility of the Plan to another one in which it will be possible to improve the plan by adjustment coefficients thanks to mathematical calculus.

In a certain sense, the optimization problem always existed. The plan content and the alternatives of a political economy which were for a long time objects of discussions, were carried out with instruments and criteria of a traditional political economy. The plan content was determined on the basis of common sense and intuitive evaluation of the economic situation and the possibility of development, on the grounds of what the English call: "a sound judgement".

It is not my intention to minimize the value of good common sense and intuition in planning, and in economic policy in general; on the contrary, I think that these will always remain fundamental factors. Mathematical calculus is not a substitute for good common sense; it merely furnishes new, more precise, and more reliable tools for the drafting and solution of problems. Furthermore, in this sense, optimization, when based on mathematical calculus, acquires practical importance with the development of new technical aids such as electronic computers. In the majority of cases, and especially when we want to apply the optimization calculus to the economy as a whole, the calculus operations would become too complex and would require too much time without the help of computers. It is interesting to observe at this point how the development of technology creates the possibility of a revolution in planning methodology as such.

Considering the optimization problem and its application to the national economy, it is necessary to ask what has to be optimized. To optimize means to maximize or minimize certain factors. We arrive at a problem dealing less with planning technique than with economic theory. The classical socialist literature repeatedly indicates that the goal of the socialist economy is the satisfaction of men's needs as opposed to the capitalist economy whose goal is the maximization of enterprises' profits. At the beginning of socialist planning, during the period of industrialization, we did not renounce this formulation of goals, but in reality we were concerned with a closer objective: the development of the productive capacities of the economy. Without making mathematical calculations, those investments were chosen and techniques selected which would yield the maximum increment in productive capacities. We tried a certain maximization of the growth rate of the national economy without resorting to mathematical calculus.

But now that the socialist economy has entered a more mature stage, the development problem is no longer considered separately. Now, we must ask "Growth" for what purpose and in which direction? Reconsidering the old socialist formula, we can answer today: "Growth" for the maximum satisfaction of needs. But is it really possible to measure human needs and, more precisely, is it possible to measure the maximum satisfaction of social needs by a single numerical index? Or, there being a multiplicity of needs, should we rather use a multiplicity of indices not comparable with each other?

In mathematical language the question could be put in the following way: Can the goal of a socialist economy, that is, the value we have maximized, be expressed as a quantity or as a vector with some incommensurable components?

It is not my intention to examine thoroughly this problem of Socialist economic theory, but personally I think that it is possible to choose the objectives of the socialist economy and to express them by a single scalar magnitude, i.e., National Income. The objective could be formulated in terms of the maximization of national income in a given period of time, which is tantamount to the maximization of the increase in national income in a given period. This means that the various products which comprise national income are in some way weighted and that the weighted sum equals the national income. It is also possible to proceed in the way indicated by Barone and thus arrive at very interesting results i.e., one could choose what is called the "Paretian maximum", which is a condition in which it is impossible to increase the production of a good without diminishing the production of other goods. Now, the most interesting fact is that Barone shows that this condition can be expressed as a maximization of a weighted sum, which is again the national income. Thus, if the national income is chosen as the objective to be maximized, then all the problems of planning, from the mathematical point of view, become a problem of programming.

As far as the third problem is concerned, i.e., that of plan implementation, I shall only make some short observations concerning the socialist economy. Implementation of the plan is linked to two problems. The first problem arises from the more or less analytical nature of national economic planning and from the possibility of introducing partial plans at territorial or sectorial levels, or at the level of single enterprises or industries. Thus, by the maximization of partial plans it is possible to obtain the maximization of the national objective. In other words, it has to be seen up to what point the national plan can be disaggregated and up to what point it is possible to formulate independent partial plans directed at the solution of those problems which are usually called problems of "underoptimization" at different levels of the national economy. It still involves a problem of planning or, more precisely, of programming theory.

The second problem connected with the implementation of the plan is of importance not only because of its theoretical interest, but also because it is of fundamental economic and sociological concern: I refer to incentives which are necessary for the fulfilment of the plan. In this case it is no more a problem of planning, but a problem which is usually called management of the national economy. The plan is a logical elaboration which cannot be said for its management. The plan has to be applied by men, by millions of men who have to be interested in the execution of the Plan. It is thus necessary to introduce into the national economy a system of incentives which will induce individuals and various organizations (industrial enterprises and various institutions) to act in the directions outlined in the plan. A bad incentives system can lead to results different from those laid down in the Plan as targets. I am, of course, always considering the socialist economy where at least in theory neither private property nor private interests exist and it is possible to introduce incentive systems with a wide range of freedom.

The problem of incentives is linked with the problem of the organization of management of the national economy, which, in a socialist system, coincides with the management of Plan implementation. Abstracting from the problem of incentives, it arose from the problem of optimal organization. From the press we know that in socialist countries, from time to time, management of the national economy is reorganized according to economic growth and as new tasks arise. In this field, too, decisions have been made on the basis of common sense and of a certain political and organizational intuition, the importance of which cannot be underestimated. But the new science, i.e., cybernetics, at present gives us the possibility of scientifically studying these problems, especially in the sphere of the socialist economy. Cybernetics, as known, studies problems dealing with the control and direction of systems of interrelated elements; it has a very wide field of application, extending from automatic machinery to biological and social organisms.

If one wants to apply cybernetics to the study of the socialist economy, two kinds of problems must be faced; on the one side, the flow and the rate of flow of the existing information in the national economy, and, on the other side, the capacity of the decision centres to make a certain number of decisions in a given period of time, say a day. For example:

let us assume that in Italy the firemen are organized in such a way that when a fire breaks out, say, in Naples, it is necessary to call Rome and ask which decision has to be taken and what the orders are. It is easy to imagine what the results would be: the orders would arrive too late and the damage would be inevitable and irreparable. Thus, the problem of information flow and its speed—in fact it is clear that such a system, where the relays can today be handled by telephone—would have appeared absurd a hundred years ago when it would have been necessary to send the messages via horse couriers.

The second problem concerns the decision centres. Suppose that several hundred calls arrive at the same time; it is clear that the related decisions could not be all taken at the same time; the phonograms would accumulate which would cause a certain delay in the decision taking so that orders would arrive too late. This problem presents some analogies with the problem which arises from some automatic machines: a telephone switchboard can be overloaded; this means that it could not satisfy the number of required connections at a given time. How to deal with this problem? It is necessary to create auxiliary sets and sub-stations, i.e. to devise a system of decentralizing decisions.

Economic cybernetics, i.e., cybernetics applied to the optimal organization of management of the national economy (considered as a problem of plan implementation), constitutes perhaps the newest field of studies for economists. In Poland, for instance, Professor Greniewski has started to prepare tables similar to the input–output analysis tables, in which not only does the flow of products appear but also the flow of signals and requirements. In this way, economists can study the functioning of the management mechanism, the points in which difficulties arise, and so on.

Summarizing, the three most important scientific instruments for economic planning and its implementation are at present: the formation of balances in mathematical form with the help of electronic computers, the optimization calculus linked to fundamental problems of economic theory, and last but not least economic cybernetics, considered as a science of the optimal organization of management of the socialist economy.

I have now concluded the observations which I wanted to make. Thank you very much for your attention.

Discussion

Dr. FRANCO PILLOTON:

I should like to ask for some explanations on the temporal aspects of the main objectives of Planning. Prof. Lange has said, and, I think, on this point all of us will agree with him, that planning is intended to maximize the satisfaction of the needs of mankind. He has added that this objective can be obtained by the maximization of the rate of growth of national income in a certain period of time. I am not very convinced on the second point because one ought to define more precisely the time interval with which we are dealing. It is clear that in the medium-term plan, covering 4–5 years, maximizing the increase in income is an antithesis to increasing consumption. For longer periods of time, this antithesis can be eliminated, and I think that the choice of the period of time in which the maximization of consumption increase can be obtained by the maximization of income expansion is a problem of very great interest. I should like Prof. Lange to say a few more words on this problem if possible.

Professor LANGE

There are some economists who deal directly with the problem of consumption maximization in a given period of time. There are several theoretical solutions: in fact, if we maximize only consumption over a short period instead of investments negative investments would appear; on the other hand, keeping the objectives of consumption maximization in mind, it is possible, to provide, among the conditions to be met, for a minimum volume of investment; or it is also possible to proceed in the way which I previously indicated in an article printed in *Econometrica*. In that article I was dealing with the maximization of growth of the national income and one of the conditions which I introduced was that every year a minimum level of consumption had to be kept under as a floor; this minimum can increase from year to year. In the same way, it is possible to maximize consumption for a given number of years, adding as a condition that investment ought not to fall below a certain level which increases from year to year.

In a recent article Strumilin was dealing with the problem of an optimal allocation of the national income between consumption and investment. The author pointed out two possible alternatives: the first one is that each increase in national income is invested so that consumption remains constant and only investment increases. The author stressed that if such a choice could be justified in the first years of the socialist system, in a situation of underdevelopment, it is no longer possible today when the Soviet economy has reached a certain degree of maturity. The other alternative is that every increase in national income is consumed. This is clearly impossible because without investments there is no possibility of increasing the national income apart from that increase which is obtained from technological progress. This means that no new investment would appear, only replacement by more efficient technology taking place, which is tantamount to saying that the consumption increase depends on future technological progress.

It is, therefore, necessary to calculate the possible maximization and to choose an intermediate point between the two extremes. Strumilin maintained that it was necessary to maximize consumption in a given period of time. If I remember well, he determines the length of the period on a demographic base, say, the lifetime of one or two generations. We are interested chiefly in ourselves and in our children and, therefore, we refer to this period of time and we formulate a plan which involves the investments necessary for consumption in this period of time to be maximized. At this point, Prof. Strumilin assumes that the marginal utility of consumption decreases and also applies Bermulli's formula, that the richer a given society becomes the less it is interested in increasing consumption, and therefore also in adjunctive investments. Consequently, he assumes that the share of the national income which is invested decreases over time. The author also considers demographic problems, but I would say that his calculations are only an academic exercise and I do not think that up to now they have had any practical influence on planning.

Let us rather consider the adopted concrete solutions. In Poland the choice is, I would say, easier and at the same time limited by the fact that it is an underdeveloped country. The objective is to reach and overtake the level of consumption in Western Europe, which means to reach a higher rate of increase than that obtained in those countries. One could ask how many years would be necessary to reach the level of Western Germany or say France in *per capita* energy generation or in *per capita* consumption of meat or television sets, comparing the levels of consumption and the rate of increase in Poland with those of these countries. These kinds of comparison which do not involve complicated calculations, have a high place in drafting the plan. Thanks to them, it is possible in Poland to plan consumption—which would not be possible in Western countries—on the assumption that, given a certain increase in national income, the structure of consumption would roughly follow the pattern of Western Europe.

Let us take a very simple example: consider the regularity which takes place in the mechanization of personal means of transport (in time). We have first the bicycle, then motorcycle and then the car. One could say that in Poland the peasants have already entered the bicycle stage, reducing the use of horses as a means of transport; skilled workers have entered the motorcycle stage, and engineers the car stage. Within ten years, it is foreseeable that workers will ask for cars and peasants for motorcycles; thus, in the plan formulation such an hypothesis is assumed:

Dr. Massimo Finola

I should like to know what is the role of the market in a socialist economy and which marketing systems are utilized by the planners in drafting plans?

A second question: How is the problem of income maximization in a given country reconciled with the fact that in the socialist countries an unified plan of several national economic plans with a related labour division must be considered?

Professor Lange

The first question concerns a very complex and debatable problem which would require a very thorough analysis. Considering that we do not have available a great deal of time, I shall answer briefly. In the present stage of the socialist economy notwithstanding the existing differences among countries, the main role of the market is to act as a means of allocating consumption goods. Poland has accepted the principle that the market should act also as a means of distribution for capital goods. In practice, there are so many exceptions that one is induced to think that this principle does not have any concrete application. One such exception is given by the controlled distribution of raw materials; such a control is introduced whenever a difficult situation arises in foreign trade and in the balance of payments.

As far as the second question is concerned, namely, of the relations between different socialist economies, in my opinion, up to now the problem of common optimization has not arisen. In other words, a common socialist economy does not exist; one finds rather co-operation among the various national economies. It could be possible to study in which ways this co-operation helps to increase the national income of each country; up to now, this problem has not been studied mathematically, but it has been analysed practically as a problem of organization and exchange planning. Until recently, perhaps 4 or 5 years ago, the problem of plan co-ordination existed only for foreign trade. If, for instance, Poland and Czechoslovakia signed a commercial trade agreement for trading certain products, exported and imported quantities were balanced and taken into account in planning production. Five-year commercial agreements are now used, usually covering the period of a plan.

At present, further progress has been made in investments co-ordination from the point of view of division of labour in order to avoid duplications and to draw up plans on a larger scale. This would allow a reduction in the costs of production. Today, in all socialist countries twenty-year plans are drafted and commissions from various branches of industry are entrusted with the task of studying the allocation of investments; moreover, the possibility of common investments and the drafting of common plans is already being studied. I should say that this is the newest and the most interesting aspect because mixed investment plans in the past, say, in international pipelines, actually consisted of investments made by each country in his own territory and in fact were no more than simple investment co-ordination. Nowadays, on the contrary, Poland and Czechoslovakia have started to utilize real common investments and the European socialist countries are on the verge of creating a special financial link.

The problem of plan co-ordination is above all now a budgetary problem, for the European socialist countries rely in large measure on the Soviet Union for the supply of raw materials, especially for mineral ores. Poland and Hungary, for example, cannot draft autonomous plans of industrial development; they must first be sure of the proper supply of needed raw materials. Therefore, the co-ordination problem becomes a problem of international balances which, up to now, have been considered for individual sectors only, particularly the raw materials sector, and not for the whole economy.

Dr. FRANCO FIORELLI

It seems to me that the preceding questions have contributed to the conclusion that income maximization cannot be achieved in the abstract but is a function of predetermined choices of a political nature. I should like now to ask if, in a socialist country which has already achieved the transrfomation of production relations, there still remain problems of income distribution; I refer particularly to the expansion and moreover the modification of the consumption structure related to the different levels of productivity of industrial and agricultural activity. These are problems, I think, the solution of which involves value choices, i.e., political choices related to the democratic nature of planning.

Professor LANGE

As you have already mentioned, it is a very complex problem, particularly for long-term planning. It is impossible to separate the problem of the increase in national income from that of the consumption structure. For the latter, in turn, is linked with the distribution of national income and the socio-economic structure of the population.

In fact, taking Poland as an example (bearing in mind that it is a general phenomenon existing also in Italy), within the last ten years, roughly 10% of the gainfully employed population has shifted from the agricultural sector to industry. This shift has caused a revolution not only in the distribution of the monetary income but also in the structure of needs. In fact, peasants who are settling in towns do not conform immediately to a completely different pattern of needs than that which they had been accustomed to. In the majority of cases, they shift from a semi-natural economy to an intensely monetary one. Consequently, it is necessary to forecast the transformations in the social structure caused by investment plans. It is exactly what we do in practice, assuming that within a few years of residence in towns, peasants usually will adopt the needs pattern of the urban population. This assumption is perhaps not very exact; however, it is normally assumed as a starting point in planning.

Shifting to the second part of the question, i.e., the differences in productivity, we must note that in Poland the situation differs from the majority of the other socialist countries. In fact, there is a relative uniformity in the distribution of national income. From an economic point of view, we can say that differences in income are less than differences in productivity and, therefore, the income distribution ought to become less uniform and income differentials should increase (for instance differentials between incomes of unskilled and skilled workers, engineers and industrial managers). On the other hand, we cannot undervalue the sociological aspect of the problem. A uniform distribution of national income offers political, social, and moral advantages, and in this respect we would support this solution. In other words, in one respect income differentials are too weak an incentive to higher productivity, and in another respect we must consider the pressure of the democratization process tending to eliminate wage differentials.

Dr. MARSAN

Turning back to the organization of plan implementation, I should like to ask what role can we attribute to the enterprise's profit in the fulfilment of the plan, both from the theoretical and practical point of view. For instance, in Poland, enterprises are managed on the principle of profitability; how does this influence the organization of the economy in the implementation of the plan?

Dr. CAMPA

I refer to what you said about the role of economic cybernetics. The management problem in drafting a plan is, as you pointed out, essentially a problem of persons, a problem in which all the subjects of the economic system take part. Now, I shall ask if it is possible to compare a complex of men to an electronic complex; besides the possibility of comparing a human being with an electronic device, it seems to me that in an electronic device, mistakes are, at least theoretically, inconceivable, especially if we consider the possibility of controls. On the contrary, in a system whose centres are composed of human beings, mistakes are, theoretically again, highly probable. If we applied cybernetic laws to this "human" system, we could not exclude the eventuality of mistakes, assuming that it is unworkable to put a human centre and an electronic one side by side, provided that the mechanical device could solve all the problems which might arise in connection with planning.

It seems to me that the central problem is to optimize the management of drafting plans. In my opinion this is possible without recourse to the laws of cybernetics, but rather via a solution similar to Prof. Frish's. The main point is the improvement of individual performance of those participating in management. In other words, it is a problem of civility, to which I guess neither cybernetic laws nor any other laws can be applied.

Dr. D'Antonio

Proceeding to another argument, which perhaps was not dealt with in today's lecture, I should like to know if the problem of balanced development in a planned economy arises only when this economy reaches a certain degree of maturity, or whether it is possible also at an earlier stage of economic growth. I should appreciate if, on this point, you could touch upon the discussions in the U.S.S.R. between 1923 and 1926, led by the economists of the Bakunin group and the Trotskyists, particularly by Prof. Preobrazhenski.

Professor Lange

In reply to the first question concerning the role of industrial profits, I can shortly answer that some differences exist among the various socialist countries. In Poland, we accepted the principle that profit must be the only maximization criterion for the socialist enterprise. This principle was not fully enforced in practice because many other objectives of planning have been added, for example, a differentiation of production or the employment of a certain quota of manpower.

The cause of such a dichotomy has to be found in the fact that, at the beginning in 1957, when we decided to adopt profit as the only criterion, a reform of the price system was planned which subsequently was not applied. A contrast between the profit criterion and the plan content thus developed. Enterprises were continuously criticized because they produced highly profitable (for them) commodities, and not those required by the Plan. This demonstrated that the price system was incorrect. The problem of maximization criteria for enterprises is again being debated also in the U.S.S.R.

In my view, if the maximization of national income is the main goal, the guiding criterion for the socialist enterprise has to be the maximization of the net product and not only of profit. Only in cases where the plan contains provisions for cost of production factors, for example, the wages bill, would we be entitled to accept the profit maximization criterion. But in Poland, as I said, we are facing a mixed situation in which incentives systems are also mixed. On the one side, workers participate in the enterprise's profits, and on the other side, we have a system of bonuses related to other fulfilments of the plan, calculated in physical terms.

Turning to the first question of Dr. Campa, I should like to say that I agree with him only on the impossibility of solving management problems in a planned economy (and also in other types of economies), on the basis of cybernetic laws only. These problems in fact have many other aspects, the most important among them being the conscious participation of workers in the management of the national economy. However, I think that a good theory of management could utilize cybernetic methods, without relying solely on them, bearing in mind that the problem has also a fundamental sociological aspect. I spoke today of cybernetics as a scientific tool in economic planning, that is, we may say, a tool of a mathematical nature, and I have, therefore, discussed only that aspect of the problem.

Let us now proceed to the last question on balanced economic growth. In theory, one can think that plans drafted by the method of balances are plans for balanced growth. In fact, however, the growth of socialist economies, particularly during the stage of massive industrialization, did not proceed in a balanced fashion. At this point we ought to specify what we mean by "balanced" and "unbalanced" growth. Without enquiring very thoroughly into the problem, I think that we can accept the definition by which balanced growth is that which provides internal consistency.

Now, at the stage of extensive industrialization in Poland, some very strong disequilibria arose, in the sense that balances were not observed and difficulties in the implementation of the plan made it necessary to modify the plan. The causes of such disequilibria are many, but the most important in my view was the "indivisibility" of certain types of investment. During the realization of the Plan, we discovered that planned investments, particularly in heavy industry, had to be made on a larger scale. Another important cause was to be found in technical obsolescence originating during the investment process. Within three or four years after the plan has been drawn up the project was often already obsolete. All the adjunctive investments which were not foreseen in the plan, but which became necessary because of continuous modifications in implementation (technical progress was only one of the factors in such modifications) also led to disequilibria.

Another great problem were imports for the domestic market. The first development plans, during the stage of sustained industrialization in Poland, and also, I guess, in other countries, had the goal of attaining the highest possible rate of development. According to such instructions, balances were drafted without adequately considering reserves. Let us assume, for example, that all the available coal was allocated for certain defined targets. If suddenly production decreased for technical reasons, or demand increased because of, let us say, a particularly severe winter, immediately a gap in balances arose, creating the necessity for some adjustments. I hope that such experiences will be useful and that we can obtain a systematic forecast of reserves within balances.

It is also necessary to remember that, as far as the criterion of profit and those of the management of enterprises are concerned, the fact that socialist countries utilize 100% of available capacities makes the building up of reserves and changes extremely difficult.

As to the question of the market considered as a mechanism for the distribution of capital goods, according to the accepted principle in Poland, we have to remember that it is only partially operative. Enterprises can choose their supplier and stipulate contracts, but if, for example, they wish to buy machinery and no firms can furnish it, having already received orders for the next four or five years, they face an obstacle that the market mechanism can not eliminate.

We therefore have a system that operates without reserve capacity, under continuous pressure of obtaining the maximum possible growth rate. Under such conditions, it is enough for a single enterprise not to fulfil its production plan and a series of chain reactions are set in motion in other enterprises, causing disequilibria and shortcomings.

A new theoretical problem arises which can apparently be solved without difficulties by planning for a certain reserve of raw materials and equipment to be kept in stock. It will then be necessary to ask, from the optimization view point, how large should such reserves be to ensure that their costs are less than the cost of disequilibria we intend to avoid by creating such reserves.

CURRENT PROBLEMS
OF THE SOCIALIST ECONOMY

This is the third time that I have had the opportunity to speak at the Gramsci Institute. In fact, I feel close to this Institute because of my preceding visits and, above all, because of the ideal the Institute represents. I am therefore very glad to be able to talk this evening to a group of people belonging to this Institute.

I shall speak about the current problems of the socialist economy. This is a very large topic, too large to be discussed fully. I shall, therefore, concentrate on the new problems actually confronting the economies of socialist countries.

The number of socialist countries is today very large and embraces countries at very different stages in their socio-economic development and with varying historical backgrounds. Therefore, it will not be feasible to speak about current problems of the socialist economy as a whole. Consequently, I shall now talk only about the problems facing the Soviet Union and the European People's Democracies. The economic problems of People's China, Korea and North Vietnam present special cases; for this reason it will be difficult to deal with all these problems in one lecture.

But even having defined the topic, a great variety of problems and situations remain still untouched. Even if, as in my opinion, the basic problems of the European socialist countries are at least theoretically the same, the particular forms and aspects which they present differ. For this reason, I shall speak in a very general way about the problems facing European socialist countries; for the sake of precision and concreteness, I shall deal with the particular case of Poland. It is evident that many of these problems are not only Polish problems; they are of a very general character, but the way in which they arise and the solutions they lead to may be very different.

The main problem of the socialist economy nowadays consists in the historical fact that the socialist economy is entering into a new stage of economic growth. The socialist economy was first of all developed by countries which were economically relatively backward, i.e., the U.S.S.R. and the Eastern European countries. This fact has given, right from the beginning, a particular character to the development of the socialist economy in these countries. The main problem was the development of productive forces, particularly the industrialization of the country and the modernization of agriculture. The development of the socialist economy has been dominated by this fundamental problem: to ensure a sustained rate of economic growth which could be achieved mostly by means of accumulation in order to narrow the gap separating it from the developed capitalist countries. Accumulation has been, therefore, the main task of the economy in this period, and the techniques of planning and rational management of the national economy had to be adapted to it. But in the group of countries, mentioned above, economic development has recently entered a new phase. These countries, formerly backward, have been industrialized to a great extent (the Soviet Union now ranks second among the world's industrial powers), and the general standard of living has risen.

We can say that the economies of the socialist countries have matured; they are no longer underdeveloped economies, but rather already modern and industrialized. This fact creates new problems of economic policy and of methods of directing economic growth. The development of productive forces which has taken place in socialist countries, has, first of all, resulted in an improvement in the standard of living and, at the same time, has increased the diversity and complexity of the socialist economies. This ever-growing complexity poses new problems for the direction of the economy.

In parallel with the growing complexity of economic life, another phenomenon arose, i.e., the transition to new conditions of economic growth. Economic development in the first period has been obtained by what I shall call extensive methods. In all these countries there were large reserves of manpower and natural wealth. The manpower reserves were mainly the result of agricultural overpopulation and, partially also, of the unemployed urban population. How to mobilize these reserves in manpower and natural wealth but by investment? Accumulation and investment have, therefore, been the means which have ensured economic growth. Factories have been built, mines have been opened, employment has increased and the results have been indisputable: increased production.

Now the economies of the socialist countries, and particularly of the People's Democracies in Europe, have reached a stage in which reserves are diminishing more and more. In order to maintain stable economic growth it is necessary to shift from extensive to intensive production. Intensive systems mean increased labour productivity, increased efficiency of management, and increased technical progress. It is no longer sufficient to say that accumulation, provides the means for investment or that by utilizing manpower and national wealth, production will increase automatically. The problem is quite different; we must now increase the productivity and efficiency of the means we have at our disposal. These two factors, viz. the growing complexity of the economy and the shift from the extensive to the intensive stage poses new problems. They pose problems concerning:

(1) Planning methodology.

(2) Organization and management of the national economy.

(3) Means to be utilized to increase productivity and efficiency in the economy.

Since 1956 approximately, we note in all these countries a process of change in planning methods, and in the organization and management of the national economy. To these changes are linked the scientific debates I am going to mention.

The question which is raised in the different socialist countries is in principle the same. It is primarily the methodology of planning, the problem of ensuring the highest possible efficiency, particularly better internal consistency of plans. Planning is currently passing from concern over the internal consistency of plans (by the method of balances) to the next stage in which more and more consideration is being given to optimization tests.

To this development are linked the well known debates dealing with the methodology of planning, and specifically with the possibility of applying mathematical aids in the optimization of plans. Electronic computers have already proved to be useful instruments for more precise planning, which, at the same time, gives better results from the point of view of optimization than was possible to obtain by traditional methods.

The second problem, namely of the organization and management of the national economy, also faces all these countries. The main point is to determine the degree of centralization and decentralization in the management of the socialist economy.

In the former period, planning was very detailed and consequently economic management, which is no more than the implementation of the plan, was highly centralized. This centralization was possible because the economy was very simple, even primitive in a certain sense. It was possible to direct the whole economy from a central body to the smallest details. On the other hand, this centralization appeared necessary because the main decisions of industrializing the country and modernizing the agriculture were at the same time decisions involving revolutionary changes in the socio-economic structure. In other words, these were decisions which could only be adopted in a centralized way, and the implementation of which also had to be in all details directed and guided from the centre. It was not possible otherwise to mobilize for and concentrate all the available resources on changing the economic and social structure, to industrialize the country, and to modernize the agriculture. One could not run the risk of seeing all efforts lost because of lack of co-ordination or dispersion in various directions.

Now that the economy is larger and more complex, the problems we have to face are different. In the Soviet Union several years ago, there were 200,000 industrial enterprises and 100,000 building enterprises, which means 300,000 units. Today, this number is much higher. It is very clear that it is impossible to manage an organism of this kind in the same way it was done twenty years ago when the number of units was, let us say, one-tenth or one-twentieth of what it is now. Therefore, I conclude that the decentralization problem in management has become a crucial one in all the socialist countries.

In the Soviet Union, the solution has taken the form of a territorial organization, a very well-known form, to which attention was drawn by the world press. In the U.S.S.R. different solutions have been tested and very advanced decentralization has been introduced in hundreds of territorial units, the so-called National Economic Councils. Recently, there has been a certain move towards concentration which brought about a reduction in the number of these units to a quarter of their former size, while maintaining the idea of territorial organization in the management of the national economy. The principal idea is still that of central planning, but managed (that is to say implemented) in a more or less decentralized way.

In Poland, in principle, we proceeded in a similar manner with the difference that the new organization is not based on territorial units. I think that the territorial character of decentralization in the Soviet Union was dictated by the geographical size of the country. In Poland, the problem was not the same; the country is not large. A certain decentralization was, therefore, introduced, ensuring greater autonomy for enterprises and industrial concerns. This was for example, the case of the coal industry, the chemical and other industries. In Czechoslovakia, a system similar in principle to the Polish one has been introduced; it is based on a certain degree of decentralization of industrial enterprises and not on a territorial basis, with the difference that it was not the individual enterprise which was the basis of decentralization but a whole group of enterprises belonging to the same industry. In other countries, methods differing in details have been applied, but the principal idea is the same.

As far as Poland is concerned, to give a concrete example, we have increased the autonomy of enterprises, leaving to them the right to make decisions about the choice of production and, even more, permitting them to make certain autonomous investments. Continuing with the Polish case, the principal investments of the enterprise are determined by the central plan and assume the form of an allowance from the Treasury to the enterprise. The enterprise has its own fund which it can utilize for supplementary investments without authorization; it is also entitled to make new investments with funds borrowed from the bank. The fundamental idea is to have the principal investments, say 70–80% of the total, determined centrally by the Plan authorities, i.e., enough to effectively control the path of national development. On the other hand, we leave it to the individual enterprises to allocate other autonomous investments so as to ensure a certain degree of flexibility in the economic system. In practice, we have run into some difficulties; it is not always exactly as I have described it to you, but in all cases this principle was adopted.

Another problem, which is raised in the transition from one stage of growth to another, is the question of the means of implementing the plans. We can distinguish, generally, between two kinds of means: administrative measures, and economic measures. Administrative measures mean the direct allocation, in physical terms, of investments, raw materials, and production targets. By economic measures we mean the utilization of economic incentives to ensure that enterprises or other units of the national economy act in the direction indicated by the Plan.

We have often discussed in Poland and in the other socialist countries what priority to give to the economic and administrative measures. The former period was characterized by the almost exclusive use of administrative measures; afterwards, on the contrary, we thought of entirely abandonning administrative measures in the management of the national economy.

In the end, we reached an agreement, deciding that priority of means depends upon objective conditions and that one or the other will be adopted depending upon the necessities we face. The real problem in managing the socialist economy now consists in harmonizing the administrative and the economic measures, so as to avoid a situation (which sometimes does arise) in which the economic means, the economic incentives, force enterprises or other economic units to act in a way completely different from the one sought by the administrative orders issued by the central organs. The problem of combining the economic and administrative measures with the tasks required by the Plan, in other words, the problem of economic incentives, still remains the main problem of management in the socialist economy.

One of the aspects of this problem is the determination of prices in the socialist economy. This problem as already mentioned faces almost all socialist countries; it is at the centre of all economic discussions. What are the principles governing prices in a socialist economy? How can we determine prices so that they act as incentives of economic growth? I do not want to enter here into this discussion; it is, I believe, one of the most well-known and controversial aspects in the debate.

Another aspect of the problem is the choice of criteria for the activity of the socialist enterprise, specially the question of knowing if it is possible to establish a single criterion of efficiency, for a socialist enterprise, viz. if, besides the profit criterion, it is necessary to add others, as for instance different criteria of a physical nature (such as production assortments, number of employees, etc.). Even now, we have not yet reached general agreement about these aspects. This problem is directly linked with that of the price structure. The opponents of the profit criterion, as the sole indicator of efficiency of socialist enterprises, affirm that this criterion leads the enterprises to produce an assortment of goods different from that required by the plan. Well, let us see what happens. Assuming an efficient price system is established, we could be sure that the goods which have been given a greater priority by the plan are exactly the ones most profitable for the enterprises. Consequently, we can see how the profit criterion, as a measure of the efficiency of enterprises, is directly connected with the price system.

In speaking about the changes in planning methods and in the management of a socialist economy, it is necessary to remember that the socialist countries not only passed through a stage of transformations in their economic structure, but they also achieved an important change in their social structure. At the beginning, these countries had a large majority of their population employed in agriculture. Industrialization increased the working class but did not rid them of the many sociological, psychological and even political attributes of the peasantry. This working class matures, crystallizes and is incorporated more and more into the life of an industrial society. This poses new sociological problems in the management of the socialist economy—the fundamental one being the problem of workers' participation in the management of the enterprise, and the problem of workers' self-management in industry.

In countries like Poland this problem was already actual in 1956; recently the Soviet Union has done much towards its solution. I believe that this is only the beginning of a development, because the maturing, the crystallizing of the working class, its achieving self-consciousness, is going to exert a deep influence on the development of the management of socialist economies.

Another factor which, at this stage, takes on particular importance is the development of a new socialist intelligentsia—engineers, directors, as well as teachers and specialists in scientific research. This fact, too, influences the development of the methods of management. We can say, summing up, that, as the working class gradually becomes more conscious of itself and of its role, it can lead to the democratization of management by increasing its own participation in management. The intelligentsia, on the other hand, become the champions of efficiency in the socialist economy, of the use of methods based on new scientific developments, of tendencies such as the use of mathematical procedures in planning, and of the use of cybernetic methods in the organization of management.

It is still too early now to say how these two factors of a sociological nature, which I have presented here in a very simplified form, are going to influence the future development of the socialist economy.

Moreover, I want to stress that the growth of a socialist economy poses more and more the problem of economic co-operation among socialist countries. Industrialization raises more and more, for most socialist countries, the problem of foreign trade, of imports and exports. In this field there is a certain difference between the Soviet Union and the People's Democracies in Europe. The Soviet Union is geographically such a vast territory, and has such wealths of natural resources of every kind, that for her the problem of foreign trade does not play so essential a role as for the other countries. The latter, territorially much smaller, do not have such natural resources and thus depend much more on imports. I believe that in Poland nearly 20% of the national income is spent on imports; in Czechoslovakia and in Hungary the share is even larger. This poses two problems: the problem of economic relations among socialist countries and the problem of the relations of these countries with the capitalist world. I shall confine my considerations to the first problem only. The problem of co-operation among socialist countries consists in the co-ordination of their development plans. About five years ago, the co-ordination of national plans of the different socialist countries was still pursued in an indirect way, by long-term commercial agreements. As a matter of principle, five-year agreements were signed. These agreements served as the basis for planning because they had to be considered as part of the plans for the production of commodities for exports and imports by the countries entering into these agreements. But such methods of indirect co-ordination are no longer sufficient today, as they are inadequate at the stage of development the socialist economies have reached.

Now, we must proceed to a system of direct co-ordination of plans; this practically means working out, in the first place, a system for the co-ordination of investments. Must Poland produce automobiles if Czechoslovakia does? In the affirmative, which types have to be reserved for Czechoslovakia? Recently, the socialist countries have decided, in the framework of the Mutual Economic Assistance Council—Comecon, as it is called in the West—to formulate twenty-year development plans until 1980. It has been decided to co-ordinate these plans, by mutual agreement, in the form of mixed commissions dealing with the different lines of development such as the fuel industry, the machine industry, the chemical industry, etc., in addition to certain general problems. Their purpose is to ensure an adequate division of labour among the socialist countries participating in the Mutual Economic Assistance Council. Besides the general co-operation agreements between the member countries of the Council, special co-operation agreements between two or more countries are also envisaged. In particular, for the development of the machine industry, and later also of the chemical industry, a proposal has been put forward for the initiation of similar co-operation between Poland, Czechoslovakia and the German Democratic Republic. Other special agreements may also be signed in other fields, between two, three, or four countries, depending on the circumstances.

The purpose of this process of specialization is, in the first place, to increase productivity and to lower the cost of production. It is even possible to note a certain tendency to build common enterprises by two or more socialist countries. For the moment, this process towards the formation of common enterprises is only at an embryonic stage. One example are the pipelines laid from the Soviet Union across to Poland, Hungary, Czechoslovakia and the German Democratic Republic. But this does not yet represent a really common enterprise in the full meaning of the term, because the investments are carried out in every country by the country concerned; it represents therefore only a co-ordination of investments according to a common programme. But the International Bank which is going to be established will enable to create really common enterprises, by financing such ventures between different socialist countries.

On the other hand, this growing co-operation among socialist countries does not aim at a policy of political autarchy, within the socialist camp. I believe that here it is worth while describing two points in detail. The Bank, I have mentioned above, will also have the task of giving credits to member countries in order to enable them to develop trade relations with non-socialist countries. This will be possible because a fund of hard currencies will be established. A project of co-operation exists in the field of the machine industry between Poland, Czechoslovakia and the German Democratic Republic. The principal task of this co-operation is to reduce the cost of production, for every country will have the possibility to switch from the production of a large number of different types of machines to a more specialized production on a larger scale. A reduction in costs is the immediate aim, but there is also the advantage of making it easier to export machines to countries outside the socialist camp.

The two points, I have mentioned above, demonstrate that co-operation among developing socialist countries does not have the purpose of creating an autarchy inside the socialist camp. It has as its principal task to increase production, national income and the well-being of socialist peoples. And the economic relations with non-socialist countries form an important part in this task. International co-operation with the whole world is and always will be an essential and decisive factor in the development of the socialist economy.

Development of Economic Planning

It is with great hesitation that I am going to speak to you, because I am afraid that my speech will not correspond, as much as I would like, to what you expect from me. I am going to speak to you about planning, but I do not at all intend to give a summary of planning theory. Economic planning is a very practical thing, which is not suited very much to summation, and even less to a dogmatic doctrinary summation like a "Summa Theologica". That is why I am going to present the problem of economic planning from a historical viewpoint and I shall deal therefore with the historical development of the methods of planning.

Economic planning is, in a sense, a new development. It has been developing since a socialist system of production has been introduced in a number of countries; today, on the other hand, the idea of planning has found a broad acceptance even outside the socialist bloc. Nearly all the countries which are considered as underdeveloped—Asia, Africa, and Latin America—prepare plans of economic development, and the idea of planning has penetrated even old capitalist countries such as France, and others. It is possible to say that economic planning has become a new branch of economics, and, at the same time, a new method of promoting economic development.

Today I would like to present to you a historical outline of the methods of planning in the socialist countries, namely, in the countries where economic development and the management of the national economy are based on planning. The history of planning follows in broad outline the history of the development of the socialist countries. As a matter of fact, the needs which planning must meet, the tasks which planning has to fulfil, undergo changes related to the historical changes of the economic background. But, at the same time, the history of planning is not only determined by economic development, but also by the domestic evolution of economic sciences and in particular of the science of planning. And it is just this mutual, dialectical interaction between the development of the national economies and the evolution of scientific ideas within the economy which determines the historical course of socialist economic planning.

In economic planning the following basic elements must be considered:

(1) the object of planning;

(2) the means for its implementation.

These two elements determine the methodology of planning.

The first problem which came to the fore in the development of plan implementation, as well as in the theory of planning, was to ensure the inner coherence of the plan. Just as the national economy is an integrated entity whose constituent parts are interdependent, a plan of development of the national economy must also be an integrated whole, co-ordinated in its different constituent parts.

If we plan, for instance, to increase the production of steel, we must, at the same time, plan to increase the production of coal, iron ore, the necessary electrical power; and, moreover, we must provide for the manpower involved in such development. These are the needs of co-ordination related to economic planning. The first logical task of planning consists therefore in the internal co-ordination of the plan. If this co-ordination fails, the plan is not feasible.

In the framework of the given example, it is plain that we cannot increase the production of steel if we do not at the same time increase the production of coal, iron ore, etc. The inner co-ordination of the plan is the condition *sine qua non* of its practical implementation. This logical task has also been faced historically as the primary problem in planning implementation. With the development of the first socialist economies, planning has become a new historical enterprise, practically without precedent.

But, were there any methods utilized by the old capitalist economies which could be utilized in socialist planning? There was one, namely, the accounting practice as established first in the area of trade, and afterwards in industry, within the framework of the capitalist enterprise, especially the method of constructing the balances. But, in order to fulfil the tasks carried out in socialist planning, these balances had to be generalized and increased because the balances had to be prepared, not for the individual enterprise, but for the whole national economy. The balances of the national economy were the first technical and methodological instrument of economic planning. It was necessary to prepare different balances for the production and utilization of different products, say, coal, electric power, manpower, etc.; by compiling all these balances into a single whole, we arrived at a balance of the national economy, showing all the processes of production and of distribution at work in the national economy.

In the beginning, these balances were made in a primitive manner, using the traditional arithmetical means in capitalist enterprises accounting. Later on, the mathematical character of balances was discovered, i.e., that balances are in fact, from a mathematical point of view, a system of equations. In a system of equations there are given quantities, namely, the resources which are at the disposal of the national economy and the aims of the plan stated by the economic policy. There is also a third category of quantities, i.e., the unknowns of the equations, whose determination is the task of planning. For example, the balances of the plan incorporate the productive capacity of the different industries, the production of raw materials and the coefficients of production establishing technical relationships between produced quantities, raw materials, and utilized capacities. On the other hand, there are the aims of the plan set by economic policy and represented by the production of different products in demand. There are also, as unknowns of the problem, the allocation of raw materials to industries, the degree of utilization of different capacities in different industries, and the allocation of manpower, etc. These unknowns are to be determined in order to attain the ends, the objectives of economic policy under the given objective conditions. Consequently, the question of balances, which are the basis of the internal co-ordination of the plans, becomes more and more a problem of study of mathematical economics. Such is the most important task and, at the same time, the first historical stage in planning.

There is another task which has only recently been formulated in a precise manner: the optimization of the plan. Many different plans, internally co-ordinated and consequently feasible, can be drawn up but they may differ in the extent to which the aims of economic policy are fulfilled. Thus, we have to face the problem of choosing among these alternative plans the optimal one. But how can the optimal plan be determined? We now come to the issue of the goals of a socialist economy.

In the first period of planning, this problem was not formulated with very great precision; it was considered in a vague, intuitive way, which was clear enough for the given conditions. Where the economy was destroyed by war and occupation, the aim was simple; what had been destroyed had to be rebuilt though perhaps in some new form. Later, in the period of large-scale industrialization which the socialist countries embarked upon or are still pursuing, the objective was and still is viewed in a simple way, in terms, I would say, of good common sense. It was known that the basic industries which were to produce the means of production would have to be given priority over the industries assigned to producing consumer goods and even over agriculture. On the basis of such an approach, it was also possible to say that at a certain stage, the proportions of investments assigned to different activities would have to be changed.

But, as the socialist economy grows more mature, it becomes larger and also more complex. The number of enterprises which have to be considered by the plan increases; the variety of products to be planned increases too; the diversity of the possible variants of investment methods is greater, and even technical progress imposes new choices, etc. This is so as in other fields, say, in navigation: other instruments are needed to steer a big modern ship than the old caravels of Columbus; very different methods are used for flying a jet from those which were used for the airplane invented by the Wright brothers. It is in this way that the question of the formulation of the objective of the socialist economy, in which planning is utilized as an instrument, must be answered more distinctly and more precisely.

In the traditional socialist literature the purpose of a socialist economy has always been the satisfaction of the needs of men in opposition to the purpose of the capitalist economy which is the maximization of capitalists profits. As a matter of principle it is accurate. But in the capitalist economy there is not only one dominant aim, there are a multiplicity of aims, including profits of every enterprise or a group of enterprises. The development of the capitalist economy is the outcome of the striving towards different particular objectives, represented by the profits of different enterprises. But the socialist economy is an integrated whole, in which all enterprises aim at the realization of a plan of economic development. Because of this, the problem of formulating in a precise way its objectives is of particular importance. On this point it is necessary to say that the opinions are still divergent.

The problem is the following; can the aims of a socialist economy be given by a single numerical index whose maximization will be the aim of the plan, or, on the other hand, is there a set of objectives, a series of non-comparable indexes which must be stated?

I do not want to enter now deeply into this problem and the arguments advanced by both sides. I shall only say that, personally, I believe that the aim of the socialist economy can be formulated in a single synthetic index and that this index must be the national income. In this case, the objective of planning can be formulated as being the maximization of national income, or, what is the equivalent—the maximization of the growth of national income over a chosen period of time. Given the national income of the present year, if I now strive to maximize the increase, say in the next year, it is then just the same as if I had striven to maximize the national income in the next year.

If we are to consider the problem from this point of view, we can see how the different tasks of planning are comparable and how this is derived from a general unique objective. On the other hand, if there are different partial objectives, then it would be impossible to compare the different parts of the plan. The task of planning becomes an application of the mathematical theory of programming. Such a theory provides us with the mathematical methods for finding the maximum of a certain end restrained by a number of given conditions.

If we are to accept the above hypothesis, we can determine the partial aims of the different enterprises, of the different parts of the national economy as integral parts of this general objective of which I am speaking; in particular, it is possible to determine the objective of the activity of the socialist enterprise. If the general objective of the plan is maximizing national income, it follows that the goal of every enterprise must be to make the greatest contribution to the national income. And what is contribution of an enterprise to national income? It is its net product. Then, under this criterion of optimization, the optimum behaviour of the enterprise becomes the maximization of its net product. Under general conditions—but only under well defined conditions which I do not want to discuss now—this criterion is equivalent to the maximization of profit. But this is not a general rule. Starting from our hypothesis, we can moreover determine the criterion of effectiveness of investments. In socialist countries, the criteria of economic effectiveness of investments have been widely discussed; but these discussions did not achieve any positive results because they have been conducted without clearly defining the objective of the socialist economy.

If we are to accept as a criterion of optimization of the plan the maximization of national income, then it is clear that the economic effectiveness of investments can be measured by their contribution to increasing the national income. If we accept, on the other hand, other criteria of optimization of the plan, then there must be other criteria for determining the effectiveness of investments.

The problem of optimization of the plan is therefore the second issue posed by planning, the first one being the need of ensuring its inner co-ordination. But in order to be able to truly establish, in a precise and efficient way, the internal co-ordination of the plan and, even more, the optimization of the plan, we need special technical tools, particularly in an economy as ours which is growing in size and in complexity. Such tools have been furnished to us by the development of electronic computers.

The idea that a balance of the national economy or of its different parts can be theoretically understood as a system of mathematical equations is not new. But it is only with the introduction of electronic computers that this idea has acquired a practical value. Quesnay and Marx and—in a different framework of ideas, but under an explicit mathematical form—the Italian economists Pareto and Barone had already conceived the idea that the balance of the national economy is just a system of equations. But what was understood in practice by the idea that such a balance is a system of equations? It was said: well, we cannot solve these equations—there are thousands, may be millions of them to be solved. There is only one means that can solve them in a spontaneous way, and this is the market. And even the first discussions on economic accounting in the socialist economy had to take into consideration the possibility of solving the complex system of the inter-action of the different parts of the national economy through the market mechanism. The role of the market was conceived in these discussions as that of a computer, of a machine able to solve a huge number of simultaneous equations.

I do not want to speak here about the role of the market in the socialist economy. It is an interesting subject that deserves, by itself, to be the subject of discussion. But what I would like to stress is that today we do have electronic computers. We have practical possibility of putting the balances of the national economy in the form of equations and of solving them effectively in a quantitative way—without the help of the market as a substitute computer. The important fact is that the solution may be very quick. In order to utilize the mathematical methods in constructing the balances of the national economy, it is necessary to be able to make the calculations quickly, even very quickly, because if the calculations are done with much delay, they will be of no practical value.

It is necessary to say that presently in the socialist countries only preparatory theoretical works have been carried out; we do not use as yet computers on a national scale in preparing the balances of the national economy. The question is not to make balances from statistical data of the previous years; this is made at present as a preliminary exercise. The problem is to prepare and to calculate the balances from data planned for the future and to ensure both harmonization and inner co-ordination of the plans. Only the first steps toward such a practical optimization of plans have been made.

In this field great prospects appear. Until now we have not had the possibility of drawing up alternative plans and choosing the best one. The preparation of the plan takes quite a lot of time and work not only in the planning commission but also in the ministries, in enterprises, and at other echelons where the plans are discussed and prepared. Once the plan has been drawn up, once it has been to a greater or lesser extent internally co-ordinated, based on balances laboriously prepared, then the plan acquires a life of its own and has nothing to do any more with the planners. It becomes very difficult indeed to change it. Obviously, if it is going to be modified, it will have to be discussed by parliament, in the commissions, in the enterprises, in the trade unions, in the press, and in public meetings, etc., though the adjustments which can be made are of marginal importance only. Nobody is going to propose to remake the plan radically, from beginning to end, because it would be practically impossible. It would take, say, half a year or even more to do it, and consequently the new plan would arrive much too late. In fact, after those scrutinies, the plans are implemented; they will be changed only if important objective conditions change and major difficulties oppose their implementation. It is the implementation that often requires adjustments in the plans, at times even radical ones.

The perspective before us is very broad, indeed; the ideal would consist in having a number of alternative plans, to calculate first—as I have proposed—the growth of national income and, after such a comparative calculus, to choose the best plan.

My purpose brings me to a third factor influencing the method of planning. I have already spoken of two factors: of the development of the socialist economy and of the development of the science of economics and of their dialectical interaction. Now a third factor has come to the fore: the technical—the availability of electronic computers. This technical revolution makes possible new methods of planning. As I have already said, now we are still in the preparatory scientific stage; making an analogy, we can say, that we are still at the stage where the first sources of propelling energy have been found, but we have not yet launched the first satellites. This will take a certain time. But we can say that in most of the socialist countries, particularly in the Soviet Union, in Poland and in Hungary, we are doing very important and intensive scientific work in this field.

In the context of this brief outline of the historical development of planning and of the perspectives planning offers, I have to stress that such a development is not only the result of the evolution of the science of planning and of the means that technology puts at our disposal, but, as I have already pointed out, it is also the result of the historical development of the socialist economy. Summing up, we can say generally speaking, that until now the economy of the socialist countries, for historical reasons which I am not going to discuss here, has developed in an extensive way. There were large reserves: unemployed manual workers, particularly in agriculture, and unexploited natural resources. The historical situation was one of economic underdevelopment. What had to be done was just to make investments, to employ the idle manpower, and to exploit the natural resources. It is the planned investment which has mobilized the working forces and at the same time utilized the natural resources. And it is just on this basis that the growth of the production, so remarkable in socialist countries, has been achieved.

Under these historical conditions, the problems of planning were simple and the methods of planning were primitive. If a factory was built, people who were not needed in the rural areas had to be hired, work had to be given to them in the factory, while the necessary raw materials had to be prepared; the economic result was always production, and therefore economic progress. The problem of efficiency of this production is not, in the conditions we have indicated, the principal problem; the alternative is to have the resources for work from nature otherwise dormant and inactive, or to activate them by means of investment. Whatever the manner of putting these resources to use, the results will always be positive.

But we can now say that in many socialist countries—and this is the case of Poland—economic development has attained a stage where the old extensive method is no longer adequate. There are no longer— at least not to the same extent—unutilized resources, sleeping reserves waiting at the threshold of economic development. Consequently, economic development has to be sustained more and more by intensive methods, which means increasing the efficiency of investments and of the organization and the management of the economy, furthering technical progress, and establishing a system of economic incentives in order to mobilize these forces. It seems to me that in Poland and in many, even if not in all, socialist countries we are now in a transition period, from the first stage of economic development, characterized by the use of extensive methods, to a new stage in which different methods must be used.

This situation poses new methodological problems for the technique of planning. Balances must be more precise now that the problem of optimization of plans and of the activity of every part of the national economy is of prime consideration. The new ideas arising in the field of economic planning have their roots in the transition of the socialist economies to a new stage of development. They correspond to the practical needs of the new stage, they are an attempt to find a solution to the new problems that the new stage poses both to the theory and to the practice of planning.

This is the essence of the brief report I outlined to you on the evolution of planning. I have spoken of an evolution that is going to be accomplished. I have spoken, too, about the perspectives of this evolution. It must be well understood that the socialist economy being a growing one, the methods of planning cannot be static. They undergo changes, and they always will change adapting themselves to the needs, to the dynamism of the life of a socialist society. And that is why, in concluding my speech I would like now to repeat what I have already said at the beginning: in the field of planning there is no summit, certainly no "Summa Theologica". But there is indeed a sum of practical experiences which we utilize, a sum of scientific knowledge, based on this experience, a sum of technical means for solving the problems connected with the practice of planning. This total of experiences, of knowledge and of techniques, we are trying to improve in order to make it a more and more efficient instrument for the conscious direction of the socialist economy.

BIBLIOGRAPHY OF WORKS 1925-1963

1925

1. Lokalizacja miast Wielkopolski właściwej na prawie niemieckim w wiekach średnich (Settlement of Cities of Polonia Maior Proper on German Law in the Middle Ages), *Pamiętnik Historyczno-prawny*, Vol. I, No. 5, Lwów, 1925.

1928

2. Koniunktura w życiu gospodarczym Polski 1923–1927 (Business Cycle in the Polish Economic Life in 1923–1927) in collection: *Przewroty gospodarcze i walutowe po wielkiej wojnie* (Economic and Monetary Upheavals after the Great War), PAU, Cracow, 1928.
3. Socjologia i idee społeczne Edwarda Abramowskiego (Edward Abramowski's Sociology and Social Ideas), a reprint from *Przegląd Współczesny*, Cracow, 1928.

1929

4. Wrastanie w socjalizm czy nowa faza kapitalizmu (The Growing into Socialism or a New Stage of Capitalism), *Robotniczy Przegląd Gospodarczy*, No. 3, pp. 69–74, Warsaw, 1929.

1931

5. Rola państwa w kapitalizmie monopolistycznym (The Role of State in Monopolistic Capitalism), *Kwartalnik Socjalistyczny*, No. 1, pp. 18–27, Warsaw, 1931.
6. Statystyczne badanie koniunktury gospodarczej (Statistical Investigations of Business Cycle), a reprint from *Czasopismo Prawnicze i Ekonomiczne*, Cracow, 1931.

1932

7. *Die Preisdispersion als Mittel zur statistischen Messung wirtschaftlicher Gleichgewichtsstörungen*, Leipzig, 1932.
8. Die allgemeine Interdependenz der Wirtschaftsgrössen und die Isolierungsmethode, *Zeitschrift für Nationalökonomie*, Bd. 4, Heft 1, SS. 52–78, Vienna, 1932.

1933

9. *O pracy Engelsa*: *Rozwój socjalizmu od utopii do nauki* (On Engels' Work: Socialism Utopian and Scientific), Introduction to F. Engels's book: *Socialism Utopian and Scientific*, Warsaw, 1933, Reprinted: Wiedza, Warsaw, 1948.

1934

10. The Determinateness of the Utility Function, *The Review of Economic Studies*, Vol. 1, No. 3, pp. 218–225, London, 1934.
11. Notes on the Determinateness of the Utility Function, *The Review of Economic Studies*, Vol. 2, No. 1, London, 1934.
12. Droga do socjalistycznej gospodarki planowej (The Road to Socialist Planned Economy), in collective work: *Gospodarka—polityka—taktyka—organizacja socjalizmu* (Economics—Politics—Tactics—Organization of Socialism), Płomienie, Warsaw, 1934.

1935

13. Marxian Economics and Modern Economic Theory, *The Review of Economic Studies*, Vol. 2, No. 3, pp. 189–201, London, 1935.
14. Formen der Angebotsanpassung und wirtschaftliches Gleichgewicht, *Zeitschrift für Nationalökonomie*, Bd. 5, Heft 4, SS. 358–365, Vienna, 1935.
15. Czy ekonomia jest nauką społeczną? (Is Political Economy a Social Science?), *Czasopismo Prawnicze i Ekonomiczne*, Vol. 30, pp. 244–251, Cracow, 1935.

1936

16. On the Economic Theory of Socialism, *The Review of Economic Studies*, London, 1936, Vol. 4, No. 1, pp. 53–71, Polish translation (Part I) in *Ekonomista*, No. 4, pp. 53–75, under the title "Zagadnienia rachunku gospodarczego w ustroju socjalistycznym", Warsaw, 1936.
17. The Place of Interest in the Theory of Production, *The Review of Economic Studies*, Vol. 3, No. 3, pp. 159–192, London, 1936.
18. Cena wolnokonkurencyjna (Free-competition Price), *Encyklopedia Nauk Politycznych*, Vol. I, pp. 606–614, Warsaw, 1936.

1937

19. On the Economic Theory of Socialism, *The Review of Economic Studies*, (Part II) Vol. 4, No. 2, pp. 123–144, London, 1937.
20. Straty kapitałowe jako korzyść społeczna (Capital Losses as a Social Gain), *Ruch Prawniczy, Ekonomiczny i Socjologiczny*, No. 1, pp. 307–314, Poznań, 1937.

1938

21. *On the Economic Theory of Socialism*, Minneapolis, 1938. A revised publication in a book form of the articles from *The Review of Economic Studies*, see 1936 and 1937, Nos. 16 and 19.
Reprinted: Minneapolis, 1948.
Arabic translation: Cairo, 1958.

22. Ludwik Krzywicki jako teoretyk materializmu historycznego (Ludwik Krzywicki as a Theoretician of Historical Materialism), from the book—*Ludwik Krzywicki Praca zbiorowa poświęcona jego życiu i twórczości* (Ludwik Krzywicki: The Collective Work on His Life and Work, pp. 89–113), Warsaw, 1938.
The reprint published by Instytut Gospodarstwa Społecznego, Warsaw, 1938.
Reprinted: Wiedza, Warsaw, 1947.

23. The Rate of Interest and the Optimum Propensity to Consume, *Economica*, London, 1938. The revised reprint in collection: *Readings in Business Cycle Theory*, Philadelphia, 1944; in collection under the same title, pp. 169–192 London, 1954.

1939

24. Saving in Process Analysis, *Quarterly Journal of Economics*, pp. 620–622, Cambridge, Mass., 1939.

25. Is the American Economy Contracting? *American Economic Review*, Vol. 29, No. 3, pp. 503–513, Evanston, Ill., 1939.

26. The Economic Structure of a Socialist Society, *Controversy*, Vol. 1, No. 7, pp. 18–20, London, 1939.

27. Neoklasyczna szkoła w ekonomice (Neo-classical School in Economics), *Encyklopedia Nauk Politycznych*, Vol. 4, No. 1, pp. 23–35, Warsaw, 1939.

1940

28. Complementarity and Inter-relations of Shifts in Demand, *The Review of Economic Studies*, Vol. 8, No. 1, pp. 58–63, London, 1940.

1942

29. *Say's Law: A Criticism and Restatement*, in collection under the title *Studies in Mathematical Economics and Econometrics*, pp. 49–68, Chicago, 1942.

30. Theoretical Derivation of Elasticities of Demand and Supply—The Direct Method, *Econometrica*, Vol. 10, No. 3/4, Chicago, 1942.

1943

31. A Note on Innovations, *The Review of Economic Statistics*, Vol. 25, No. 1, pp. 19–25, Cambridge, Mass., 1943.

Reprinted in *Readings in the Theory of Distribution*, Philadelphia, 1946; London, 1954.

32. On the Theory of the Multiplier, *Econometrica*, Vol. 11, No. 3/4, pp. 227–245, Chicago, 1943.

33. *We Will Join Hands with Russia.* On Polish-Soviet Relations. National Council of American-Soviet Friendship, pp. 38, New York, 1943.

1944

34. Price Flexibility and Employment, *The Principia Press*, p. IX, Cowles Commission Monographs, No. 8, Bloomington, Ind., 1944.

35. What Peace for Germany? *The Nation*, Vol. 159, No. 27, pp. 793–795, New York, 1944.

36. *The Stability of Economic Equilibrium*, Cowles Commission Papers, No. 8, Chicago, 1944.

37. *The Working Principles of the Soviet Economy*, Research Bureau for Post-war Economics, 2nd ed., New York, 1944.
    Reprinted in *U.S.S.R. Economy and the War*.
    Translation into Spanish: Los Principios de la Economía Sovietica in *El Trimestre Economico*, Vol. 11, No. 2, pp. 284–313, Mexico, 1944.

38. *Poland and the United Nations*, The Kościuszko League, Detroit, 1944.
    Covers: Letter published in *Gwiazda Polarna*, p. 5.
    To blame for Polish Break, pp. 6–8.
    The Outlook for Poland, pp. 9–12.
    Poland's Place in Post-war World, pp. 13–15.
    For the Unity of Polish Democracy, pp. 16–18.
    Speech delivered at Meeting in Town Hall, pp. 19–24.
    Outlines of a Constructive Policy, pp. 25–30.

1945

39. Marxian Economics in the Soviet Union, *American Economic Review*, Vol. 35, No. 1, pp. 128–133, Evanston, Ill., 1945.

40. Economic Controls after the War, *Political Science Quarterly*, Vol. 60, No. 1, pp. 1–3, New York, 1945.

41. The Scope and Methods of Economics, *The Review of Economic Studies*, Vol. 13, No. 33, pp. 19–32, London, 1945.
    Polish translation in *Ekonomista*, pp. 5–30, Warsaw, 1947.
    Spanish translation in *El Trimestre Económico*, Mexico, 1947.

42. Forming of New Lublin Government Will Speed Reconstruction of Poland, *PM Daily*, Vol. 5, No. 169, p. 8, Detroit, 1945.

1948

43. PPS wobec sytuacji międzynarodowej (Polish Socialist Party in Face of International Situation), Report on XXVII Congress of Polish Socialist Party, *Przegląd Socjalistyczny*, No. 1/2, pp. 9–11, Warsaw, 1948.

Abbreviated version under the title "Od lewicy socjalistycznej do marksizmu-leninizmu" (From Left-Wing Socialism to Marxism-Leninism), *Robotnik*, 29 September, 1948.

44. Przez Demokrację Ludową do Socjalizmu (Through People's Democracy to Socialism), *Przegląd Socjalistyczny*, No. 6, pp. 5–9, Warsaw, 1948.
45. Wspólna Partia—wspólna ideologia, (Common Party—Common Ideology), *Nowe Drogi*, No. 9, pp. 16–20, Warsaw, 1948.
46. La coopération économique entre l'Est et l'Ouest de l'Europe, *Politique Etrangère*, No. 5–6, pp. 395–402, Paris, 1948.

1949

47. The Practice of Economic Planning and the Optimum Allocation of Resources, *Econometrica*, Vol. 17, pp. 166–178, Chicago, Ill., 1949.
48. L'Économie polonaise, *Cahiers Internationaux*, No. 12, pp. 17–28, Paris, 1949.
49. Dwie drogi rozwojowe w gospodarce światowej (Two Roads of Development in World Economy), *Ekonomista*, No. 3, p. 22, Warsaw, 1950.
    Reprint—Polgos, Warsaw, 1950.
    French translation: *Cahiers Internationaux*, No. 12, pp. 9–20, Paris, 1949.
50. Spółdzielczość narzędziem budownictwa ustroju socjalistycznego, (Co-operatives as a Tool of Building Socialism), *Społem*, No. 11, pp. 2–3, Warsaw, 1949.

1950

51. Zagadnienie kadr w spółdzielczości (Problem of Cadres in Co-operatives), *Przegląd Spółdzielczy*, No. 7/8, pp. 355–366, Warsaw, 1950.
52. Zagadnienia spółdzielczości w realizacji Planu 6-letniego (Problems of Co-operatives in the Realization of the Six-Year Plan), *Przegląd Spółdzielczy*, No. 9–10, pp. 439–443, Warsaw, 1950.

1951

53. Zagadnienie I-szego Ogólnopolskiego Naukowego Zjazdu Ekonomistów w Warszawie w dn. 8–10 grudnia 1950 (Introductory Speech at the First National Scientific Congress of Economists in Warsaw, 8–10 December, 1950), *Ekonomista*, No. 1, pp. 3–7, Warsaw, 1951.
54. Współistnienie dwóch systemów gospodarczo-społecznych w ekonomice i polityce światowej (Coexistence of the Two Economic and Social Systems in World Economy and Politics), *W Obronie Pokoju*, No. 4, pp. 9–20, Warsaw, 1951. Appeared simultaneously in English, Chinese, French, Spanish, German and Russian in *Défense de la Paix* and in respective versions of this paper in 1951.
55. Polska gospodarka narodowa w drugim roku Planu 6-letniego (Polish National Economy in the Second Year of the Six-Year Plan), *Ekonomista*, No. 2, pp. 3–21, Warsaw, 1951.
    Reprint, Książka i Wiedza, pp. 31, Warsaw, 1951.

56. O twórczości rozwoju teorii marksistowskiej (On Active Development of Marxist Theory), *Życie Nauki*, Vol. 6, No. 1/2, pp. 25–34, Warsaw, 1951.

1952

57. *Teoria Statystyki* (The Theory of Statistics), Polgos, Warsaw, 1952.
Japanese translation: Tokio, 1955.
58. Podstawowe prawo ekonomiczne współczesnego kapitalizmu (The Basic Economic Law of Contemporary Capitalism), *Nowe Drogi*, No. 12, pp. 22–41, Warsaw, 1952.
59. Międzynarodowa Konferencja Gospodarcza w Moskwie (International Economic Conference in Moscow), *Trybuna Ludu*, No. 71, Warsaw, 1952.
60. Sukces Międzynarodowej Konferencji w Moskwie (The Success of the International Conference in Moscow), *Trybuna Ludu*, No. 117, Warsaw, 1952: *Świat* No. 18, p. 10, Warsaw, 1952.

1953

61. *Zagadnienia ekonomii politycznej w świetle pracy J. Stalina "Ekonomiczne problemy socjalizmu w ZSRR"* (Problems of Political Economy in the Light of J. Stalin's Work "Economic Problems of Socialism in USSR"), Warsaw, 1953.
Covers:
(a) Economic Laws of Socialism, p. 3.
(b) The Basic Economic Law of Contemporary Capitalism, p. 75 (see No. 58, 1952).
(c) Split of the Uniform World Market and Formation of Two Parallel Markets in World Economy, p. 15.
62. Rozkład jednolitego rynku światowego i ukształtowanie się dwóch równoległych rynków w gospodarce światowej (Split of the Uniform World Market and Formation of Two Parallel Markets in World Economy), *Ekonomista*, No. 1, pp. 137–158 (see No. 61c, 1953, Warsaw, 1953).
63. Prawa ekonomiczne socjalizmu w świetle ostatniej pracy J. Stalina (The Economic Laws of Socialism in the Light of J. Stalin's Last Work), *Nauka Polska*, No. 1, pp. 9–54, (see No. 61a, 1953), Warsaw, 1953.
English translation: *International Economic Papers*, Vol. 4, London, 1954.
64. Ostatni wkład J. Stalina do ekonomii politycznej (J. Stalin's Last Contribution to Political Economy), *Nauka Polska*, No. 2, pp. 26–49, Warsaw, 1953.
65. Rewolucyjna treść nauki Marksa (Revolutionary Content of Marx's Teaching), *Ekonomista*, No. 3, pp. 24–32, Warsaw, 1953.

1954

66. Rozwój Gospodarczy Polski Ludowej w latach 1945–1954 (The Economic Development of People's Poland in 1945–1954), *Ekonomista*, No. 3, pp. 3–23, Warsaw, 1954.

Czech translation: *Planove Hospodarstvi*, pp. 587–591, Prague, 1954; Bulgarian translation: *Izviestia na Ekonomicheskija Institut*, Sofia, 1955.

67. Walka o marksistowską naukę ekonomiczną w Polsce Ludowej (The Fight for Marxist Economic Science in People's Poland), *Nauka Polska*, No. 2, pp. 28–79 Warsaw, 1954.

New revised edition under the title *Nauki ekonomiczne* (Economic Science) in publication: *10 lat rozwoju nauki w Polsce Ludowej* (10 Years of Development of Science in People's Poland), pp. 265–300, Warsaw, 1956.

68. Nouvelle orientation économique des pays de l'Est et ses repercussions sur le marché mondiale, *Défense de la Paix*, No. 34, pp. 46–57, Paris, 1954.

It appeared simultaneously in English, Chinese, French, Spanish, German Polish and Russian in the respective editions of the periodical in 1954.

1955

69. Statistical Estimation of Parameters in Markov Process, *Colloquium Mathematicum*, Vol. 3, fasc. 2, pp. 149–160, Wrocław, 1955.

70. O konsekwentne stosowanie analizy marksistowskiej (On the Need of Consistent Applying of Marxist Analysis), *Przegląd Kulturalny*, No. 49, Warsaw, 1955 Reprint: Książka i Wiedza, Warsaw, 1955.

Italian translation in *Critica Economica*, No. 1, pp. 52–65, Rome, 1956.

French translation in *Cahiers Internationaux*, No. 76, pp. 41–50, Paris, 1956

1956

71. *Fundamentals of Economic Planning*.

Report written in May 1955 in Indian Statistical Institute. First published in English and in Arabic by the Planning Commission of the President of the Republic, Cairo, 1956.

Italian translation in *Critica Economica*, Rome, 1957.

French translation in *Cahiers de l'Institut de Science Économique Appliquée* No. 49, pp. 1–28, Paris, 1957.

Spanish translation: Tres ensayos sobre planeación económica, in *El Trimestre Económico*, Mexico, 1959.

72. Na drodze do industrializacji (On the Road to Industrialization), *Przegląd Kulturalny*, No. 21 (on India), Warsaw, 1956.

73. Il problema dei Paesi Sottosviluppati, *La Comunita Internationale*, Vol. 11, fasc. 2 (Lecture delivered in Società Italiana per l'Organizatione Internazionale in Rome), Rome, 1956.

74. Aktualne problemy nauk ekonomicznych—II Zjazd Ekonomistów 7–10 czerwca 1956 r. (Current Problems of Economic Sciences—II Congress of Economists 7–10, June, 1956), *Ekonomista*, No. 5, pp. 3–5; *Nowe Drogi*, No. 6, pp. 24–35. Italian translation in collection: *Cecchia e nuova pianificazione economica in Polonia*, pp. 11–28, Milan, 1960.

75. Końcowe przemówienie na II Zjeździe Ekonomistów Polskich w Warszawie (Closing Speech at the II Congress of Polish Economists in Warsaw), _Ekonomista_, No. 5, pp. 145–149; _Gospodarka Planowa_, No. 7, pp. 1–3, Warsaw, 1956.

76. W sprawie doraźnego programu (On Immediate Programme), _Życie Gospodarcze_, No. 14, _Życie Warszawy_, No. 170, _Przegląd Kulturalny_, No. 29 under the title "Najbliższe zadania" (The Most Immediate Tasks), Warsaw, 1956.
   French translation: _Cahiers Internationaux_, No. 79, pp. 72–80, Paris, 1956.
   English translation: _International Economic Papers_, pp. 145–155, London, New York, 1957.

77. _Najważniejsze zadania w dziedzinie polityki gospodarczej_ (The Most Important Tasks in the Sphere of Economic Policy), published by Stołeczna Komisja Porozumiewawcza Stronnictw Politycznych i Organizacji Społecznych (pamphlet), Warsaw, 1956.

78. Socjalistyczna demokratyzacja (Socialist Democratization), _Trybuna Ludu_, December 5, Warsaw, 1956.
   French translation: _Cahiers Internationaux_, No. 82, p. 91, Paris, 1957.

79. Jak sobie wyobrażam polski model gospodarczy (Polish Economic Model—as I See it), _Trybuna Ludu_, No. 363, December 31, 1956 and January 1, 1957.

80. Budowa nowego modelu gospodarczego musi się oprzeć na dynamice klasy robotniczej i socjalistycznej inteligencji (New Economic Model Must Be Based on the Dynamics of the Working Class and of the Socialist Intelligentsia), _Nowe Drogi_, No. 11–12, pp. 25–30, Warsaw, 1956; Reprint in collection: _Dyskusja o polskim modelu gospodarczym_ (Discussion on Polish Economic Model), pp. 7–16, Warsaw, 1957.
   Italian translation in collection under the title; _Vecchia e nuova pianificazione economica in Polonia_, pp. 138–144, Milan, 1960.

81. Zjazd wielkiej partii. O VIII Zjeździe Komunistycznej Partii Chin (Congress of the Great Party. On VIII Congress of the Communist Party of China), _Życie Partii_, No. 10 (18), pp. 9–17, Warsaw, 1956.

82. John Strachey o współczesnym kapitalizmie (John Strachey on Contemporary Capitalism), _Życie Warszawy_, No. 270, September 9, Warsaw.
   French translation: _Cahiers Internationaux_, No. 81, Paris, 1956.
   Reprint in the book under the title _O współczesnym kapitalizmie_ (On Contemporary Capitalism), pp. 1–14, Warsaw, 1960.
   Italian translation in the book: _Dibatitto sul capitalismo contemporaneo_, Milan, 1958.

1957

83. Planung und Statistic, _Statistische Praxis_, No. 12/5, pp. 83–86, Berlin, 1957.

84. He Polonike Oikonomia (speech in English delivered at the session of the European Economic Commission of the UN in Geneva in 1957). Greek translation in _Nea Oikonomia_, No. 6, pp. 349–354, Athens, 1957.

85. Niektóre zagadnienia polskiej drogi do socjalizmu (Some Problems of the Polish Road to Socialism), in a collection under the title _Aktualne zagadnienia polityki_

Partii i Rządu (The Current Problems of the Party and Government Policy), Książka i Wiedza, pp. 39–66, Warsaw, 1957.
Reprint Książka i Wiedza, Popularna Biblioteczka Wiedzy Politycznej, 1957.
English, French, Spanish, German and Russian translations, *Polonia*, Warsaw, 1958.
Telegu translation, *Vijayawada*, India, 1957.

86. *Dlaczego kapitalizm nie potrafi rozwiązać problemu krajów gospodarczo zaco-fanych* (Why Capitalism Cannot Solve the Problem of Underdeveloped Countries), Książka i Wiedza, Popularna Biblioteczka Wiedzy Politycznej, Warsaw, 1957.

87. Problem krajów gospodarczo słabo rozwiniętych—ich programy rozwojowe (The Problem of Underdeveloped Countries—Their Development Programmes) in the collection under the title *Niektóre zagadnienia współczesnego kapitalizmu* (Some Problems of Contemporary Capitalism), Książka i Wiedza, pp. 155–177, Warsaw, 1957.
Reprint in the collection under the title *Zagadnienia współczesnego kapitalizmu* (Problems of Contemporary Capitalism), Książka i Wiedza, pp. 355–377, Warsaw, 1960.

88. Po VIII Zjeździe Komunistycznej Partii Włoch (After the VIII Congress of the Communist Party of Italy), *Nowe Drogi*, No. 2/92, p. 93, Warsaw, 1957.

89. *Some Problems Concerning Economic Planning in Underdeveloped Countries*—report written in May 1955 in Indian Statistical Institute.
Italian translation in *Critica Economica*, Rome, 1957.
French translation in *Cahiers de l'Institut de Science Économique Appliquée*, No. 49, pp. 29–31, Paris, 1957.
Polish translation in collective works under the title *Problemy wzrostu ekonomicz-nego krajów słabo rozwiniętych* (Problems of Economic Growth of the Underdeveloped Countries), Polgos, pp. 491–504, Warsaw, 1958.
Spanish translation: Tres ensayos sobre Planeación Economica in *El Trimestre Económico*, Mexico, 1959.

90. Some Observations on Input–Output Analysis—report written in May 1955 in Indian Statistical Institute. First published in *Sankhya—The Indian Journal of Statistics*, Vol. 17, No. 4, pp. 305–336, Calcutta, February 1957; French translation in *Cahiers de l'Institut de Science Économique Appliquée*, No. 49, p. 33, Paris 1957.
Spanish translation: *Tres Ensayos sobre Planeación Económica*, Mexico, 1959.
Polish translation in *Przegląd Statystyczny*, No. 2, pp. 172–208, Warsaw, 1958.
Russian translation in collection: *Primienienya matiematiki v ekonomicheskikh issledovanyakh*, ed. V. S. Nemchinov, pp. 214–250, Moscow, 1959.
Japanese translation: Tokio, 1959.

1958

91. *Wstęp do ekonometrii* (Introduction to Econometrics), Państwowe Wydawnictwo Naukowe, Warsaw, 1958.

2nd ed. revised and enlarged, Państwowe Wydawnictwo Naukowe, Warsaw, 1961, English translation: Pergamon Press, London, 1959.

2nd ed., revised and enlarged reprinted, Pergamon Press, London, 1962.

92. *Socjalizm a kapitalizm* (Socialism and Capitalism), the lecture delivered in Stołeczny Ośrodek Propagandy Partyjnej, Biblioteczka Zagadnień Marksizmu i Leninizmu, Książka i Wiedza, Warsaw, 1958.

Reprint supplemented in a collection under the title *Węzłowe zagadnienia budownictwa socjalizmu w Polsce* (The Crucial Problems of Building Socialism in Poland), Książka i Wiedza, pp. 7–39, Warsaw, 1960, and O. Lange, J. Danecki, M. Rakowski, *Materiały do szkolenia politycznego* (Materials for Political Training), Książka i Wiedza, pp. 9–37, Warsaw, 1960.

93. Marksizm a ekonomia burżuazyjna (Marxism and Bourgeois Economy) *Polityka*, No. 9/10, Warsaw, 1958.

Reprinted in *Przegląd Polski i Obcy*, Vol. 2, No. 3, pp. 3–19, Warsaw, 1958; *Życie Szkoły Wyższej*, No. 3 and 4, Warsaw, 1958.

Italian translation in *Polityka ed Economia*, No. 3, pp. 21–29, Rome, 1958.

French translation in *Cahiers Internationaux*, p. 79, Paris, 1958.

Japanese translation in *The Keizai Seminar*, pp. 55–64, Tokio, 1959.

English translation in *Enquiry*, No. 1, New Delhi, 1959.

Serbo-Croatian translation in collection: *Poljski Ekonomisti o Problemima Socijalisticke Privrede*, pp. 9–32, Belgrade, 1960.

94. Podstawowe zagadnienia okresu budowy socjalizmu (Basic Problems of the Period of Building Socialism), in a collective work, O. Lange editor: *Zagadnienia ekonomii politycznej socjalizmu* (Problems of Political Economy of Socialism), Książka i Wiedza, Warsaw, 1958.

Second edition, revised and enlarged, Książka i Wiedza, Warsaw, 1959.

3rd ed., Książka i Wiedza, Warsaw, 1960.

95. *Essays on Economic Planning*, Calcutta, 1958.

2nd ed., Bombay, 1959.

Consists of articles:

(a) Fundamentals of Economic Planning,

(b) Some Problems Concerning Economic Planning in Underdeveloped Countries,

(c) Some Observations on Input–Output Analysis (see 1956, No. 71, and 1957, Nos. 81 and 90).

96. Charakter i działanie praw ekonomicznych (Character and Functioning of Economic Laws), *Ekonomista*, No. 6, pp. 1319–1345, Warsaw, 1958.

97. Rola spółdzielczości w budowie socjalizmu (The Role of Cooperatives in Building Socialism). In the collection under the title *Wpływ Rewolucji Październikowej na ruch spółdzielczy* (The Impact of the October Revolution on the Co-operative Movement), Spółdzielczy Instytut Badawczy, pp. 86–99, Warsaw, 1958.

98. *The Political Economy of Socialism*, the lecture in English delivered in the Institute of International Politics and Economics in Belgrade on November 18, 1957.

Published for the first time in Polish in *Sprawy Międzynarodowe*, No. 1, pp. 17–36, Warsaw, 1958, then in abridged form in the collective, work, O. Lange editor: *Zagadnienia ekonomii politycznej socjalizmu* (Problems of the Political Economy of Socialism), Książka i Wiedza, Warsaw, 1958; 2nd ed., Książka i Wiedza, 1959; 3rd ed., Książka i Wiedza, 1960.

Serbo-Croatian translation in *Mezdunarodni Probleme*, No. 1, pp. 3–17, Belgrade, 1958, and in the book *Savremeni problemi privrednojrazvoja u socjalizma*, pp. 81–94, Belgrade, 1960.

Published in English in a book of the series: Publications on Social Change, Institute of Social Studies, No. 16, pp. 1–15, The Hague, 1958.

Further reprints in English in *The Economic Weekly*, Vol. 10, No. 15, p. 509, Bombay, 1958; *Science and Society*, Vol. 23, No. 1, pp. 1–15, New York, 1959.

Spanish translation: Las Conferencias Ineditas, in *El Trimestre Económico*, Mexico, 1959.

99. *The Role of Planning in Socialist Economy*, the lecture in English delivered in the Institute of International Politics and Economics in Belgrade on 19 November, 1957.

Published for the first time in Polish in *Sprawy Międzynarodowe*, No. 2, pp. 17–47, Warsaw, 1958.

Published in English in the book: O. Lange, *The Political Economy of Socialism* as one of the series: Publications on Social Change, Institute of Social Studies, No. 16, pp. 16–28, The Hague, 1598.

Further reprints in English in *Economic Review*, Vol. IV, pp. 11–21, Sydney, 1958; *The Indian Economic Review*, Vol. IV, No. 2, pp. 1–15, New Delhi.

Spanish translation: Las Conferencias Ineditas, pp. 235–248.

Italian translation in the collection under the title *Vecchia e nuova pianificazione economica in Polonia*, Feltrinelli, pp. 110–124, Milan, 1960.

Serbo-Croatian translation in *Mezdunarodni Probleme*, No. 1, pp. 18–32, Belgrade, 1958.

1959

100. *Ekonomia Polityczna* (Political Economy), Vol. I, Państwowe Wydawnictwo Naukowe, Warsaw, 1959.
2nd ed. enlarged, Państwowe Wydawnictwo Naukowe, Warsaw, 1961.
3rd ed., Warsaw, 1963.
4th ed., Warsaw, 1966.
French translation: Presses Universitaires de France, Paris, 1962.
Italian translation: Editori Riuniti, Rome, 1962.
English translation: Pergamon Press, London, 1963.

101. Model wzrostu gospodarczego (The Model of Economic Growth), *Ekonomista*, No. 3, pp. 523–552, Warsaw, 1959.

102. Produkcyjno-techniczne podstawy efektywności inwestycji (The Economic and Technological Foundations of the Efficiency of Investment), *Ekonomista*, No. 6, pp. 1159–1189, Warsaw, 1959; reprinted, revised and enlarged in: O. Lange, *Introduction to Econometrics*, Pergamon Press, 2nd ed. (reprinted), Oxford, 1966.

103. Polish Economy: Achievements and Prospects, *Link*, New Delhi, August 15, 1959.

104. Rola Nauk Ekonomicznych (The Role of Economic Sciences), a conversation with the delegates to III Party Congress, *Życie Gospodarcze*, No. 12, Warsaw, 1959.

105. Zasada racjonalnego gospodarowania (The Principle of Economic Rationality), *Życie Gospodarcze*, No. 17 and No. 19 (Parts I and III), Warsaw, 1959.

106. Przedmiot ekonomii politycznej w ujęciu niemarksistowskim (The Subject of Political Economy in a Non-marxist Approach), *Życie Gospodarcze*, No. 20, Warsaw, 1959.

107. *The Tasks of Economic Planning in Ceylon.* Memorial prepared on request of Ceylon Government in 1959. First published in *National Planning Council Papers by Visiting Economists*, pp. 73–91, Colombo, 1959.
Polish translation: *Sprawy Międzynarodowe*, No. 2, Warsaw, 1960.

1960

108. Problèmes de la Planification. Lecture in Institut d'Étude du Développement Économique et Social auprès de l'Université de Paris, *Cahiers Internationaux*, No. 109, p. 43, Paris, December 1959–January, 1960.

109. The Output–Investment Ratio and Input–Output Analysis, *Econometrica*, Vol. 28, pp. 310–324, New York, 1960.

110. Leninowska teoria rewolucji a kraje gospodarczo słabo rozwinięte (Lenin's Theory of Revolution and the Underdeveloped Countries), *Nowe Drogi*, No. 4, pp. 19–28, Warsaw, 1960.
Hebrew translation in *Baszaar*, No. 5, pp. 32–38, Tel-Aviv, 1960.

111. Człowiek i technika w procesie produkcji (Man and Technique in the Process of Production), *Polityka*, No. 21, Warsaw, 1960.
French translation in *Cahiers Internationaux*, No. 113, p. 29, Paris, 1960.

112. Disarmament and the World Economy, report in English delivered at XV Plenary Assembly WFUNA, 6 September, 1960.
Published in English and French in *Polish Perspectives*, Vol. III, No. 10, Warsaw, 1960.
Polish translation in *Nowa Kultura*, No. 39, Warsaw, 1960.

113. O stosowaniu metod matematyczno-ekonomicznych w ZSRR (On Using Mathematic-Economic Techniques in USSR), *Życie Gospodarcze*, No. 46, Warsaw, 1960.

1961

114. Nauka na zakręcie: Ekonomia (Science at the Turning Point: Political Economy), *Przegląd Kulturalny*, No. 15, Warsaw, 1961.

115. *Teoria reprodukcji i akumulacji* (The Theory of Reproduction and Accumulation), Państwowe Wydawnictwo Naukowe, Warsaw, 1961.

116. Economic Development, Planning and International Co-operation. Three lectures delivered at The Central Bank of Egypt in 1960: